# THE MAKING OF VIRGINIA ARCHITECTURE

Virginia Museum of Fine Arts, Richmond

# The Making of VIRGINIA ARCHITECTURE

by
Charles E. Brownell
Calder Loth
William M. S. Rasmussen
Richard Guy Wilson

Virginia Museum of Fine Arts
Richmond

Distributed by the
University Press of Virginia
Charlottesville and London

This book was first published as a companion to
THE MAKING OF VIRGINIA ARCHITECTURE:
DRAWINGS AND MODELS, 1719–1990,
an exhibition organized by the Virginia Museum of Fine Arts, Richmond,
November 10, 1992, through January 3, 1993.

This book and the exhibition were made possible by grants from:
*The Council of the Virginia Museum of Fine Arts*
*The National Endowment for the Arts, a federal agency*
*The Camp Younts Foundation*
*The Windsor Foundation*
*The Richard and Caroline T. Gwathmey Memorial Trust*
*Pella Virginia, Inc.*
*The T. David Fitz-Gibbon Charitable Trust*
*The Leslie Cheek, Jr. Publications Endowment*

Library of Congress Cataloguing-in-Publication Data:
The Making of Virginia architecture
   by Charles E. Brownell . . . [et al.].
     p.  cm.
   Companion to an exhibition held at the Virginia Museum
of Fine Arts, November 10, 1992 to January 10, 1993.
   Includes bibliographical references and index.
   ISBN 0-917046-34-X (hardcover); ISBN 0-917046-33-1 (paper)
   1. Architecture—Virginia.   I. Brownell, Charles E.
    II. Virginia Museum of Fine Arts.
NA730.V8M35   1992
720′ .9755—dc20                    92-16363
                                  CIP

Virginia Museum of Fine Arts / Office of Publications
2800 Grove Avenue / Richmond, Virginia 23221-2466 USA

Edited by Monica Scanlon Rumsey
with editorial assistance from Rosalie A. West
Photographic research coordination by Caryl Burtner

Book Design by Sarah Lavicka
with production assistance from Rosemarie Kaspersen
Type is Sabon and Univers 57 Condensed,
set by Coghill Composition Company, Inc., Richmond.
Printed on acid-free Warren Lustro Dull paper by Carter Printing, Richmond.

Photo Credits: Except as noted otherwise in captions,
all photographs were taken by Virginia Museum staff photographers
Ronald Jennings, Ann Hutchison, and Grace Wen Hwa T'sao

COVER: *Architectural process and product combine in a photograph of one of
America's most beloved homes—***Thomas Jefferson's Monticello***—and a finely rendered
elevation of the building, drawn for Jefferson by the young draftsman Robert Mills,
later a noted architect in his own right. Photograph of Monticello hand-colored
by Marsha Polier Grossman. Cover images combined with kind permission of
the Thomas Jefferson Memorial Foundation, which owns and operates Monticello,
and the Massachusetts Historical Society, which owns the Mills drawing.
(See survey number 12, Monticello, Second House, page 220.)*

TITLE PAGE: **An initial sketch for Dulles Airport by Eero Saarinen** *brings the
architect's first ideas for a new, modern airport to life; the completed building turns
idea into reality. (See survey number 107, page 410.)*

# CONTENTS

# FOREWORD

This book is not merely a compilation of facts and images, it is in a sense a parcel of history. It represents not only the combined efforts of many years' careful research and thoughtful writing on the part of its authors, and the diligent and creative efforts of those who gave it shape and form; it also stands as a monument to those thousands of men and women who have lived, dreamed, and labored to create architecture in the Commonwealth during the past three centuries. Their buildings, plans, and projects have tapped into the widest span of architectural tradition, from the enduring structures of Western classical civilization to the practical wooden-frame shelters that had long served the needs of Native Americans when the first Europeans stepped onto Virginia's shores. Working as self-taught builders and as highly trained architects, they combined their knowledge and their inspiration into new forms in which to live, work, study, govern, and worship.

It is with great pleasure and pride that we invite you to explore the ideas and images that await your discovery in the following pages. In the end, we hope you will find in this volume a new and deeper appreciation for the range and variety of architecture in Virginia.

KATHARINE C. LEE
Director, Virginia Museum of Fine Arts

# PREFACE

This publication began with a luncheon conversation several years ago about Virginia's principal artistic accomplishments. The question posed was in what field has the Commonwealth made the greatest contribution to the arts? Virginia has seen significant achievements in painting, sculpture, literature, music, and other art forms, but the conclusion was that we are best known for our architecture. Our stately colonial mansions and the works of Thomas Jefferson are world renowned. In fact, the making of Virginia's architecture is one of many accounts in the building of an American tradition. And while the earliest buildings were designed and built by immigrant professionals or native-born amateurs, the seeds of the professional practice of architecture in America were planted in Virginia in 1799, with the arrival from England of B. Henry Latrobe. In addition to many buildings by native talent, Virginia also boasts representative works by nearly every major American architect: William Buckland, Ralph Adams Cram, Alexander J. Davis, Bertram Grosvenor Goodhue, Richard Morris Hunt, Minard Lefever, Robert Mills, Richard Neutra, John Russell Pope, James Renwick, William Strickland, Thomas U. Walter, Stanford White, and Frank Lloyd Wright among them. The Colonial Williamsburg restorations, begun in the 1930s, have influenced residential and commercial architecture throughout the country and made the Colonial Revival an essential part of our national image. And Eero Saarinen's Dulles Airport in northern Virginia remains probably the most admired American building of the second half of the twentieth century. In short, Virginia possesses a remarkable legacy of artistic achievement in the form of architecture—as rich and varied as any other state, perhaps more so.

Unfortunately, of all the art forms, architecture is probably subject to the greatest pressures. Widespread destruction of paintings or sculpture nowadays is highly unusual. Literary works can be preserved indefinitely with minimal effort. But the very nature of buildings results in constant threats to their existence. They are regularly exposed to the destructive forces of weather and the danger of fire. Maintenance can be costly and few buildings are kept standing if they are not economically viable. Moreover, architecture rarely receives the same degree of curatorial attention as other forms of art. All of this is regrettable, for few art forms are so immediately accessible to so many people as architecture. Most any large or medium-sized American city has a pageant of architecture sprinkled through its principal streets: mansions, churches, schools, civic buildings, commercial works, and monuments. This architecture can be seen and enjoyed by anyone at any time simply by driving or walking the streets and taking it in.

Virginia, like everywhere else, has suffered significant losses to its architectural heritage. Economic forces and demographic changes have drastically altered the appearance of many of our historic cities. Fires and other natural disasters have deprived us of numerous landmarks, especially early farmhouses and village cores. Highly significant properties have been destroyed in the course of three wars—the Revolutionary War, the War of 1812, and the Civil War. Changes in the social order have resulted in much of our plantation architecture being lost through abandonment and neglect. Finally, changes in fashion have meant loss of architectural integrity through insensitive alterations in many noteworthy buildings.

Preserving works of architecture is an ongoing effort. And although some losses are inevitable, Virginia's progress in preserving its many architectural treasures, particularly in recent years, has been exceptional. Recognition of the importance of architectural resources to our cultural identity and economy is ever-increasing. Visitors from around the world come to see our many well-preserved landmark buildings and historic districts. Adaptive re-use of older buildings has become an important industry and has breathed new life into many historic structures. In fact, some of the country's most scholarly and scientific restoration projects are currently being carried out in Virginia, setting new standards in the quality of how we treat our national landmarks.

Running parallel to Virginia's efforts in historic preservation is the ever-deepening scholarship of its architecture. Virginia's buildings, particularly its historic houses, have long been subjects for scholarly research. In recent years especially, architectural historians and other scholars are turning their attention to more thorough examinations of other forms of Virginia architecture. Particularly significant has been the attention devoted to our vernacular architecture. Virginia has extraordinary diversity in non-architect-designed building types. These studies of the heritage we have received from our folk culture has helped us understand and appreciate the richness and complexity of the everyday world and the people who built it.

While much time and effort has been expended in studying and preserving our architecture, there has been little effort on behalf of the Commonwealth itself to recognize the craft of the architect as a significant art form. When one speaks of Virginia artists, the implication is painters, sculptors, or craftsmen, not architects. Exhibitions or events dealing with the arts in the Virginia rarely mention architecture. Indeed, few of the Commonwealth's art or history museums devote much attention to our architectural legacy. Most of our historic house museums stress social history and decorative arts in their interpretation rather than the quality or complexity of the design of the very buildings that they exhibit. And sadly, art education in our schools, particularly our public schools, has little to say about architecture.

Recognizing that the Virginia Museum of Fine Arts has a responsibility to give a balanced emphasis to all arts in the Commonwealth, it was duly noted that it had been nearly a quarter-century since the Museum had turned its attention to the subject of Virginia architecture. In 1968 the Virginia Museum sponsored and published William B. O'Neal's excellent guidebook *Architecture in Virginia*, now long since out of print, and shortly thereafter organized its single major loan exhibition dealing specifically with architecture, *Architectural Drawing in Virginia 1819–1969*. That exhibition, also assembled by William B. O'Neal, was a pioneering but limited effort to acknowledge the broad range of the state's architectural achievements.

Considering this lack of emphasis on architecture, the suggestion was made to Paul Perrot, former director of the Virginia Museum, that the state should make up for its past oversight of the subject. Thus Mr. Perrot agreed that the Virginia Museum should appropriately celebrate Virginia's architectural heritage by sponsoring a major exhibition. To expand on the theme of the exhibition, and to lend permanence to this celebration, it was also decided that the Museum might publish a scholarly survey of the history of Virginia architecture. Unlike earlier efforts, this exhibition and its accompanying book would stress both the process and the artistry of Virginia architectural design, using examples from the earliest colonial settlements to the present.

Surveys of architecture are challenging, to say the least, especially in a state where so much as has been published about its historic buildings. How can one give appropriate coverage to the key works of this legacy without simply repeating so many of the books already produced? Hence the concept evolved that an effective way to show both the artistic qualities of our architecture and the creative process by which ideas for buildings become reality, was to do so through the architects' own medium of communication, their drawings. Like the sculptor's clay model, or the composer's manuscript, the architectural drawing is not the final product but a set of instructions, a means of communicating how the work of art is to be.

As it happens, many architectural drawings are works of art in themselves, a fact well demonstrated in the drawings of B. Henry Latrobe and Alexander J. Davis. Others—such as the almost crude drawings of Thomas Jefferson, with their notes and erasures—fall into the category of rare documents, showing the thought-process of a highly original designer, albeit an unskilled draftsman. But regardless of its quality the architectural drawing, coming directly from the hand of the architect, has a special immediacy. The drawing establishes an intimate connection between designer and design, one that in many ways is more profound than the connection between the architect and the building itself, especially when the design has been modified during construction or if the building has been altered over time. The architectural drawing thus becomes a particularly perspicacious vehicle for illustrating the art of architecture.

Using drawings instead of photographs for an architectural survey also provides a unique opportunity to show important but unrealized designs, works that might have been. Seeing the drawing for Newmarket ( SURVEY NO. 14 )—which if it had been built, could well have been the largest Neoclassical house in America in its day—adds a new dimension to the study of Virginia architecture. One cannot fully appreciate the significance of Morven Park ( SURVEY NO. 49 ) as a Romantic fantasy until one is confronted with the original rendering and sees the extravaganza its architect had in mind. And, because so many historic buildings have been altered over the years, an architectural drawing lets us see what its designer originally intended. A photograph of Belmead in its current state ( SURVEY NO. 38 ), stripped of all its finials, offers no hint of the Gothic grandeur originally bestowed on it by A. J. Davis. But in viewing Davis's elevation, seeing all the ornaments the house once had, the original pageantry of one of America's greatest Gothic Revival works becomes at once apparent.

Assembling a broad range of Virginia architectural drawings would have been difficult to do before now. Until the past few decades it was assumed that other than the Jefferson and Latrobe collections, there simply was no significant body of architectural drawings relating to Virginia. O'Neal's 1969 exhibition opened our eyes to the fact that much important material did indeed exist, but his effort gave little hint of the staggering quantity that would later be found. Over the past twenty years, however, through ever-increasing scholarship in American architectural history and with continuing research in the cause of historic preservation, archives and private collections gradually began to reveal their treasures. It might be a single work such as the charming drawing of Sweet Briar House ( SURVEY NO. 44 ), hidden away for many years in the college archives. Or it might be a whole body of previously unknown material, such as the archives of Thomas U. Walter acquired by the Athenaeum of Philadelphia from Walter's descendants in 1982, material that established Walter's authorship of several important Virginia buildings. One small but very significant exhibition, *Architectural Drawing in Lexington, 1779–1926*, held in Lexington, Virginia, in 1978, demonstrated most effectively the variety of riches that could exist in just one small community. Through its research for the registration of historic landmarks, the Virginia Department of Historic Resources has found an impressive number of Virginia-related architectural drawings. And more recently, many architectural drawings of pre-Civil War Virginia buildings were located and published for the first time in 1987 by Mills Lane in his excellent volume *Architecture of the Old South: Virginia*. But for the present project, the aim was to document as broad a sweep as possible—going back much earlier than O'Neal's seminal study, and continuing on further than Mills.

In order to illustrate as many facets of the art of Virginia architecture as possible, the selection process for this book considered many factors: the scope of Virginia history; the aesthetic quality of any given drawing; a variety of drawing types, building types, and architectural styles; the historic and architectural significance of the subjects; a broad representation of architects, both native-born and out-of-state; and wide geographic distribution. The authors also wanted to show architectural drawings never before published, such as the elevation for the Virginia School for the Deaf and the Blind ( SURVEY NO. 33 ) by Robert Cary Long, Jr., and J. Danforth's drawing for the fanciful Carpenter Gothic-style Chapel for Waddell Memorial Church ( SURVEY NO. 51 ).

With so much material from which to work, making the selections can be a frustrating process. The number of surviving drawings from Thomas Jefferson's hand alone is many times the total number illustrated in this publication; which two or three does one choose as examples? Achieving an acceptable balance with such a range of selection criteria is no simple task. Naturally, each of the contributors had favorites, and in some instances the selection process came dangerously close to bargaining.

Publication deadlines and the need to keep this book to manageable proportions prevented many interesting drawings from being included. Nevertheless the final selection, presented in the Survey (Chapter 6), illustrates a number of interesting trends in the making of Virginia architecture. Foremost is the strong influence of history on the state's architectural design. Beginning with the design of Bremo Recess in the 1830s ( SURVEY NO. 31 ) Virginians have reflected on their history in many buildings. Our continuing infatuation with colonial architecture has helped shape the national image, particularly in the twentieth century. Yet despite our love of the aura of history, Virginia has also excelled in forward-looking designs. Jefferson gave the nation its first essay in the Classical Revival with his design for the State Capitol ( SURVEY NOS. 9, 10 ) while the State Penitentiary ( SURVEY NOS. 16, 17 ) by Latrobe, was a precursor of modern functional architecture. And Eero Saarinen provided a foremost landmark of modern Expressionist architecture with his design for the Dulles Airport Terminal ( SURVEY NO. 107 ).

Another trend brought into focus by this project is the tendency by Virginians to call in outside talent for many of their most important commissions. We have not supported home-grown talent as much as we might. Interesting also is the fact that, except for Jefferson, few Virginia-born architects have sought or enjoyed significant influence outside the state. Our designers have generally been comfortable sharing their talents among other Virginians.

Though readers will inevitably think of other examples that might have been included to make whatever point, I trust this book nonetheless proves that it is surely in architecture that Virginia has made its main contribution to the arts. Finally, because the drawings discussed here are but a sampling of the materials to be tapped, it is hoped that this work will inspire further and more detailed scholarship of Virginia architecture through the very drawings that brought it into being.

CALDER LOTH
Senior Architectural Historian
Virginia Department of Historic Resources

# ACKNOWLEDGMENTS

The authors and editor wish to thank all those who so generously gave of their time and expertise, shared information from their archives, and granted permission to reproduce herein images from their collections. Additional thanks is due as well to the following:

American Institute of Architects Foundation, especially Tony Wrenn, Archivist, and Sherry Birk

Athenaeum of Philadelphia staff, especially Dr. Roger W. Moss, Librarian

Avery Architectural and Fine Arts Library at Columbia University, New York City, especially Janet Parks, Curator of Architectural Drawing, and Herbert Mitchell

Dr. Thomas C. Battle, Howard University, Washington, D.C.

Mrs. Robert Blount, Norfolk, Virginia

The Honorable Sir Clive Bossom III, Eaton Mansions, London, England

Martha B. Boxley, Roanoke, Virginia

Deneen D. Brannock, Historic Staunton Foundation, Staunton, Virginia

Bess T. Brownell, Midlothian, Virginia

Louise T. Brownell, Chicago Historical Society, Chicago, Illinois

Marshall Bullock, Adult Services Librarian, Petersburg Public Library, Petersburg, Virginia

Joe Bunton, Project Engineer's Office, Arlington National Cemetery, Arlington, Virginia

S. Allen Chambers, Jr., Washington, D.C.

Mr. and Mrs. Leslie Cheek, Jr., Richmond, Virginia

Richard Cheek, Belmont, Massachusetts

The Colonial Williamsburg Foundation, especially Cary Carson, Edward A. Chappell, Mary O. Keeling, Carl R. Lounsbury, Mark R. Wenger

Julia Moore Converse, Architectural Drawings Collection, University of Pennsylvania, Philadelphia

W. Kent Cooper, Cooper Lecky Architects, Washington, D.C.

Mrs. Robert R. Cosby, Powhatan, Virginia

Carlos H. Costas, Carneal & Johnston, Richmond, Virginia

Frederic Cox, Marcellus Wright, Cox & Smith, Richmond, Virginia

Warren Cox, F.A.I.A., Hartman-Cox, Washington, D.C.

Randolph L. Darnell, University of Richmond, Virginia

Martin A. Davis, College of Architecture, Clemson University, Clemson, South Carolina

Robert C. Dean, Perry, Dean, Rogers and Partners, Boston, Massachusetts

Arthur Channing Downs, Newtown Square, Pennsylvania

Richard K. Dozier, Morgan State University, Baltimore

Mr. and Mrs. Dan Duhl, Virginia Beach, Virginia

Jackie Duresky and staff, Best Secretarial, Richmond, Virginia

Rebecca A. Ebert, Archives Librarian, The Handley Library, Winchester, Virginia

Lucious Edwards, Archivist, Virginia State University, Petersburg

John Page Elliott, Charlottesville, Virginia

Rae Ely, Hawkwood, Louisa County, Virginia

Amy E. Facca, Mesick, Cohen, Waite, Architects, Albany, New York

Betsy Fahlman, School of Art, Arizona State University, Tempe

Andrew and Kim Fink, Norfolk, Virginia

Selmon T. Franklin and Associates, Chattanooga, Tennessee

W. Douglas Gilpin, Jr., Browne, Eichman, Dalgliesh & Gilpin, Charlottesville, Virginia

Rebecca C. Glasser, Jones Memorial Library, Lynchburg, Virginia

Grady Gregory, Gregory & Associates, Roanoke, Virginia

Robert Harper, Centerbrook Architects, Essex, Connecticut

Geoffrey Henry, Charlottesville, Virginia

Mr. and Mrs. William Hershey, Fairview Village, Pennsylvania

Sinclair Hitchings, Boston Public Library, Boston, Massachusetts

Peter Hodson, Portsmouth University, Portsmouth, England

Davyd Foard Hood, Vale, North Carolina

Dr. Lou Ross Hopewell, Blessed Sacrament High School at Belmead, Powhatan, Virginia

Greg Hunt, Alexandria, Virginia

Stephen Jerome, Curator, Devotion House, Brookline, Massachusetts

Mr. Floyd Johnson, F.A.I.A., Charlottesville, Virginia

Harvey Johnson, Jr., Portsmouth, Virginia

Joseph Johnson, T. J. Collins & Son, Staunton, Virginia

Maral S. Kalbian, Boyce, Virginia

Elizabeth Kostelny, Association for the Preservation of Virginia Antiquities, Richmond

Mills Lane, The Beehive Press, Savannah, Georgia

Rebecca Massie Lane, Sweet Briar College, Sweet Briar, Virginia

Robert Larus, Richmond, Virginia

William A. Lundquist, Hampton, Virginia

Gayle D. Lynch, Archivist, Brown University, Providence, Rhode Island

Massachusetts Historical Society, Boston, especially Mr. Lewis L. Tucker, Director, and Peter Drummey, Librarian

Bonnie McCormick, Baskervill & Son, Richmond, Virginia

Travis McDonald, Poplar Forest, Virginia

Carden McGhee, Washington, D.C.

Edmund P. Meade, Robert Silman Associates, P.C., New York City

The late Robert Bruce Miller, Los Angeles, California

Mrs. William H. Moses, Jr., Hampton, Virginia

Mount Vernon Ladies' Association, especially Barbara A. McMillan, Librarian; Dennis J. Pogue, Chief Archaeologist; and John P. Riley, Archivist

Kevin Murphy, National Building Museum, Washington, D.C.

National Park Service, Yorktown, especially James N. Haskett, and Jane N. Sundberg

Dottie Nielsen, Secretary for Leslie Cheek, Jr., Richmond, Virginia

Philip T. Noblitt, Blue Ridge Parkway Commission, Asheville, North Carolina

Osmund Overby, University of Missouri, Columbia

John Owen, Lynchburg, Virginia

Ford Peatross, Architectural Drawings, Prints and Photography, Library of Congress, Washington, D.C.

Loren B. Pope, Alexandria, Virginia

Durward Potter, Charlottesville, Virginia

Allen W. Prusis, Michael Graves Architect, Princeton, New Jersey

John Richardson, Richmond, Virginia

David Riggs, National Park Service, Jamestown

James V. Righter, Architect, Boston, Massachusetts

Teresa Roane, Assistant Supervisor of Research Services and Registration, The Valentine Museum, Richmond, Virginia

Mari Anne Ronus, Librarian, Handley Library, Winchester, Virginia

Dr. and Mrs. Herbert McKelden Smith, Staunton, Virginia

John Spencer, Chair, Architecture Department, Hampton Institute, Hampton, Virginia

Elizabeth Stone, Roanoke, Virginia

Donald W. Tate, Central Fidelity Bank, Richmond, Virginia

Thomas Jefferson Memorial Foundation staff, especially Dr. Daniel P. Jordan, Executive Director; William L. Beiswanger, Director of Restoration; Susan R. Stein, Curator; Libby Fosso, Communications Officer

Gavin Townsend, Art Department, University of Tennessee, Chattanooga

University of Virginia Libraries, especially Jack Robertson, Librarian, Fiske Kimball Fine Arts Library, and staff; and the staff of the Special Collections Department

University of Virginia, School of Architecture, especially K. Edward Lay; Betty S. Leake, Lori Laqua; and graduate and undergraduate students in the Department of Architectural History, especially research assistants Bryan Clark Green, Joseph Michael Lasala, Donald W. Matheson, and Martin C. Perdue

Dell T. Upton, University of California, Berkeley

Virginia Department of Historic Resources, Richmond, especially Hugh C. Miller, F.A.I.A., Director; John S. White III, Archivist; John Wells, and Mary Harding Sadler

Virginia Historical Society, especially Charles F. Bryan, Jr., Director, and the Society staff, especially Frances Pollard, Librarian; Lee Shepard, AnnMarie Price, Joe Robertson, and Linda Leazer

Virginia Museum of Fine Arts Trustees, Director, and staff, especially Dr. David Park Curry, Margaret Burcham, Catherine Ritter, Evelyn Oosterhuis, Betty Stacy, Carla Welsh, Michelle Wilson, Marian Winer, Richard Woodward, Elizabeth Yevich, and the Departments of Development, Finance, Purchasing, and Public Affairs

Virginia Society of American Institute of Architects, especially John Braymer and Vernon Mays

Virginia State Library and Archives, Carolyn S. Parsons, Picture Collection, and the Periodicals Archivists

Norman R. Weiss, New York, New York

W. L. Whitwell, Art Department, Hollins College, Hollins, Virginia

Christopher L. Wigren, Connecticut Trust for Historic Preservation, Hamden, Connecticut

John G. Zehmer, Historic Richmond Foundation, Richmond, Virginia

# 1

# DRAFTING THE PLANS

*Pride and Practicality in Virginia's Colonial Architecture*
*1643–1770*

by WILLIAM M. S. RASMUSSEN

*"They live in the same neat manner, dress after the same modes, and behave themselves exactly as the gentry in London. . . . The habits, life, customs, computations &c of the Virginians are much the same as about London, which they esteem their home."* [1]

HUGH JONES, *THE PRESENT STATE OF VIRGINIA* (LONDON, 1724)

*"Things that are not so dear seems [sic] much better to fit the circumstances of our country."* [2]

ROBERT "KING" CARTER TO THE WIFE OF AN ENGLISH MERCHANT, CIRCA 1700–1720s

When prosperous planters in the Virginia Colony attempted to duplicate the way of life and accommodations of the English gentleman, they established in the region a tradition of fine architecture. Predictably, the process was one of conflict between Old World ideals and the very different physical and social conditions in the New World that governed their settlements. Early Virginians were quick to adapt new materials and resources for their buildings and to alter traditional forms to fit local "circumstances." At the same time, however, they repeatedly looked to English art and architecture as means to overcome their provincial status. By the late Colonial period, as Hugh Jones noted, many Virginians with wealth even perceived themselves as Londoners and tried to match on the frontier an extravagant architectural tradition. Instead they developed a vigorous regional variation that has long been recognized as a significant contribution to American culture. Primarily a body of design devised for country and domestic applications, Virginia's Colonial architecture has nonetheless shaped the aesthetic ideals of generations of American architects.

For more than half of the seventeenth century, architecture was a low priority in the colony, as settlers directed their resources almost entirely to the interrelated goals of acquiring land and producing the sometimes-profitable crop of tobacco. Those who settled in Virginia sought what we now call "upward

FIGURE 1.1. **Detail, sketch of Green Spring.** *built in James City County in southeast Virginia between 1643 and 1676. See figure 1.3.*

mobility," no easy task in a hardy society as materialistic and competitive as the one they had left behind. But few could garner the wealth needed to build fine architecture. Even fewer had the will to build permanent structures, for in the colony the population was not only on the move but predominantly male and young, with a high mortality rate and loose ties in family and community social structures. Some of the wealthier residents soon longed to return to England.[3]

## The Earliest Architecture: Shelter in the Wilderness

FIGURE 1.2. **Scale Model**, *at Stratford Hall, of the lost* **Manner House** *of Clifts Plantation (Westmoreland County, circa 1670, 18.5 by 41 feet). This was a post-hole house, long since lost to decay. Model and archaeological excavation of the early site are the work of Fraser D. Neiman. Clifts Plantation was purchased in the early eighteenth century by Thomas Lee, who built Stratford Hall on the same property around 1738.*

What houses the earliest Virginians built—none of which survive today—tested a multitude of English styles and local materials. These buildings were scattered across the countryside of Tidewater Virginia, but their variety was evident at Jamestown as well. There, archaeologists in the first half of the twentieth century uncovered foundations that suggest the early capital was a sprawling village, hastily and inconsistently built. Its small frame houses were constructed in every conceivable manner—on wooden earthfast posts, on wooden blocks and sills, and on brick foundations, sometimes in combination with brick flooring and with or without brick chimneys. A few small houses entirely of brick also appeared before the mid-seventeenth century. For the most part, probably, these buildings were one-and-a-half stories high and simple in elevation, as they appear occasionally sketched on Jamestown land deeds from the late seventeenth century. Of the various forms found in the capital and throughout Colonial Virginia the most popular was unquestionably the post-hole house built of wood ( FIGURE 1.2 ), which was well suited to the local "circumstances."[4]

In earthfast construction, as it developed on Virginia plantation sites, fifteen-foot posts were set in holes dug four feet into the earth to form the wall structure of a one-and-a-half story riven clapboard house. Earthfast buildings have not survived, of course, for their posts rotted in a matter of decades. In Virginia there were several advantages to post-hole construction, which was not unknown in England and may have been used there with more frequency than has thus far been suspected. Wood for use in construction was easily available on the plantations, while brick was not. And hole-set houses could be built more simply, thus more quickly and for less expense, than massive frame houses of the type built in the New England colonies. The economy of building a post-hole home allowed a planter to channel his funds into the purchase of essential servants and land, to produce labor-intensive and soil-exhaustive tobacco.[5]

At first the plan of the Virginia post-hole house followed that of the timber-frame farmhouse of southwest England, but eventually—by the second half of the seventeenth century—the central chimney was eliminated in most new buildings, and the cross-passage/service end of the English type was moved to outbuildings, leaving two rooms for hall and chamber or parlor. Memories of a similar two-unit medieval cottage, with gable-end chimneys—once common in the West Country and Highland areas of England—must have influenced those modifications. The interiors of the best Virginia houses were eventually developed into imposing spaces, apparently more lavish than their English prototypes, to provide a setting more suited to their way of life. This was a maturing society that was becoming increasingly attentive to its architecture. Rooms in Virginia could be handsomely finished with wood floors and white-limed walls. This hall-parlor earthfast type was so prevalent in the colony in the seventeenth century that it was then known simply as the "Virginia house" form and was frequently mentioned in documents without further explanation.[6]

### Improvements on the Post-Hole House of Virginia

One Virginian determined to live in more than a post-hole house was Sir William Berkeley, the governor of the colony in the mid 1600s. His mansion, Green Spring, near Jamestown, was a huge structure, 68 by 70 feet, two-and-a-half stories tall, with brick foundations and timber framing ( FIGURE 1.3 ; right portion). It was built, however, with sadly insufficient attention to design and planning: rooms were massed three-deep and covered by parallel gable roofs. Such impractical roofing (with poor drainage) had been common in contemporary England for double-pile houses. A later addition of around 1670 (to the left in FIGURE 1.3 ) was a more imposing structure that represents a further stage in the evolution of Virginia Colonial architecture. A single-pile house, 25 by 97 feet, later extended into an L-plan, the newer mansion featured an arcaded porch and a raised main floor (the *piano nobile*). Easily roofed, well-ventilated and well-lit, this new, regional type better suited local conditions. To Berkeley's thinking, one purpose of Green Spring was to set a cultural example in Virginia. After mid century, a number of colonists were ready to follow his lead.[7]

FIGURE 1.3. **Sketch of Green Spring** *(James City County, circa 1643–76) from a land survey of 1683 in the William Salt Library, Stafford, England. The portion to the right was the original 68-by-70-foot structure; the one to the left was a 1670 addition. (Photograph © Peter Rogers [Photographic] Ltd., Stafford, England.)*

FIGURE 1.4. *A self-made man who was the owner of an early gentry house was the English-born* **William Fitzhugh** *of Stafford County. Portrait copied by John Hesselius in 1751 from a now-lost original by an unknown artist, 1690–95. Oil on canvas, 30 by 25 inches. Collection of the Virginia Historical Society, bequest of Alice-Lee (Thomas) Stevenson. (Photograph courtesy of the Virginia Historical Society.)*

FIGURE 1.5. **Arthur Allen House** *or* **Bacon's Castle** *(Surry County, circa 1665), now owned and operated by the Association for the Preservation of Virginia Antiquities. This view from the side shows curvilinear gables fashionable in fine English architecture of the sixteenth-century, and chimney-stacks set on a diagonal to the house.*

As early as the 1660s, Virginia society had matured sufficiently for a proto-aristocracy to begin to emerge. By then many colonists were native-born and well rooted in the region. Power was already accumulating in the hands of a few. By the end of the century ten percent of the population would hold one-half to two-thirds of the land, and two to five percent would corner fifty percent of the wealth. Not completely comfortable with their newly earned status yet full of new-found regional pride—and troubled by the colony's disreputable image in London brought about by their self-described "wild and Rambling way of living"—the wealthier Virginians began to sit for painters, increasingly imported silver, porcelain, and other fine household items, and began to replace their post-hole structures with permanent architecture. They tested a variety of building types, as the sifting continued for a more suitable style of architecture for Virginia.[8]

Of the owners of the early gentry houses, we know perhaps the most about English-born William Fitzhugh (1651–1701) of Stafford County, a prolific letter-writer who sat for his portrait around 1690. Both his letters and the portrait (which survives in an early copy; FIGURE 1.4) reveal a self-made man not yet truly comfortable with his new social prominence. In his own words he chose to live "comfortably & handsomely" in neither "poverty nor pomp"; he never overindulged at "Bacchus Orgyes," at "Ceres shrine," or as "one of Venus Votarys." Fitzhugh did assemble a staggering 122 pieces of English silver that signaled his position in society, but he selected "strong & plain" examples he might convert to hard cash if needed. Instead of a common earthfast house, Fitzhugh built in about 1680 a "very good" English wood-framed residence on masonry foundations. Unfortunately, it does not survive. Few like it, probably, were ever built in Virginia. According to Fitzhugh, construction took three times longer than it would have in London and cost a third more: the process was plausible only if a bricklayer and a carpenter were engaged in England for the task as indentured servants. When exerting such effort and expense, most Virginians opted for brick buildings. Fitzhugh's house was large enough to have thirteen rooms, the best of which were furnished with "accommodations for a comfortable and gentile living," including hung tapestries, family portraits, and the silver collection.[9]

An earlier gentry building (circa 1665; FIGURE 1.5), the Surry County residence of Arthur Allen (died 1669), was an even more surprising accomplishment for its time and place. It is today probably the finest surviving seventeenth-century house in America. Known as "Bacon's Castle" after it was occupied by the rebellious followers of Nathaniel Bacon in 1676, the house has a size and grandeur that made it as unusual in the Virginia landscape as its popular name suggests. No less impressive than its tall elevation of two floors and a garret raised above a full basement is the distinctive detailing of curvilinear Jacobean gables and diagonally set clustered chimney stacks. This cross-plan type with shaped brickwork, which was influenced by Dutch traditions, was developed in southeastern regions of England like Kent, from whence Allen's talented craftsmen may well have emigrated.[10]

FIGURE 1.6. **Adam Thoroughgood House** *(Virginia Beach, circa 1685–1720), the best-known example of a brick version of the post-hole "Virginia house," with a hall-parlor plan, steep roof, and less than symmetrical pattern of windows and doors.*

FIGURE 1.7. **Pear Valley** *(Northampton County, first half of the eighteenth century). The modern metal roof and wooden siding are recent external repairs that preserve a finely crafted eighteenth-century structure. (Photograph by Dale L. Kostelny, courtesy of the Association for the Preservation of Virginia Antiquities.)*

One early builder who must have been influenced by Green Spring was John Custis II, whose Eastern Shore mansion of Arlington (Northampton County, circa 1676) was constructed at considerable expense (Custis said it cost 6000 pounds) and was of comparable size: he described it as "upwards" of 60 by 80 feet and three stories in height. Nothing survives of Arlington, which typified only the changing mood amidst the gentry and must have been even more of an anomaly in the Virginia landscape than Bacon's Castle.[11]

### The Hall-Parlor Type of the Pre-Georgian Period

Predictably, a brick variation of the post-hole "Virginia house" was developed by the new gentry, though the decade it appeared is uncertain. The best-known example is the Thoroughgood house (Virginia Beach, possibly as early as circa 1685, or as late as around 1720, the date of its interior; FIGURE 1.6 ). It shares the hall-parlor plan, steep gable roof, and asymmetrical arrangement of openings believed to be characteristic of the post-hole buildings. It also resembles the masonry cottages with gable-end chimneys of western and upland England that must have been a direct influence for some Virginia builders. Unlike the other types tried after mid-century, this form remained popular both on the plantation and in the city through the end of the Colonial era. It was refined in the eighteenth century with more careful proportioning (visible in the size and spacing of windows) and with rich, classical detailing, particularly its modillioned cornices and sash windows.[12]

Just as carefully constructed as the finest hall-parlor houses and built at the same time or earlier were smaller, single-room structures with lofts. Pear Valley on the Eastern Shore is the only early Virginia survivor of a type once widespread in the Tidewater region (Northampton County, first half of the eighteenth century, 16 by 20 feet exclusive of chimney; FIGURE 1.7 ). The house displays handsome craftsmanship throughout its small fabric: the ceiling joists and other exposed structural posts are neatly chamfered, tilted "false plates" that support the rafters are visibly pegged through round-ended ceiling joists, and glazed headers in the brick end-wall form decorative patterns—popular on the Eastern Shore—that accent the line of the roof ridge.[13]

To judge from the foundations uncovered by archaeologists and from documentary references to buildings in Jamestown, the Thoroughgood hall-parlor type and the Pear Valley one-room type were known in the Colonial capital. But of the roughly two-dozen brick houses built there in the second half of the seventeenth century, other types were just as prevalent. Surprisingly little can be stated about the entire group with certainty. Some of the buildings were no doubt a peculiar mix of local ideas with strong English traditions that persisted in the fledgling city. At least one house, a large U-shaped structure, was lavishly decorated with ornamental plaster modeled in the English pargetry tradition ( FIGURE 1.8 )—evidence, like portraiture or silver, of the new interest in the accoutrements of gentrification. And odd but probably impressive townhouse rows replaced earlier, less substantial buildings. Though the idea made

FIGURE 1.8. **Fragment of ornamental plaster** *(pargetry), part of a ceiling or chimney-piece excavated from the foundation of the William Sherwood house, one of the larger Jamestown dwellings of the second half of the seventeenth century. This fragment measures about five inches across.*

little sense in the expanse of early Virginia, to English thinking a town should have row houses. Thus a fashionable London town-house plan, which creates a narrow 40- by 20-foot house two rooms deep with connecting side passage and center fireplaces, was tried as a row of three units ( FIGURES 1.9, 1.10 ). Two longer rows, of four and five buildings ( FIGURE 1.11 ), were a different blend of English tradition with Virginia experience: in these the 20- by 40-foot plan was turned laterally to produce an easily roofed structure—like the Green Spring addition—that was well-lit and well-ventilated.[14]

FIGURE 1.9. **Jamestown, "Structure 17,"** *a row of three early Colonial town-house plans, as excavated in 1934. (Photograph courtesy of the National Park Service, Jamestown.)*

FIGURE 1.11. **Jamestown, "Structure 115,"** *a row of four single-pile houses, as shown during excavation in 1954–56. (Photograph courtesy of National Park Service, Jamestown.)*

FIGURE 1.10. *In his book* Mechanick Exercises *(London, 1703, plate 5), Joseph Moxon provided this elevation of a* **typical London house,** *similar in floor-plan to the town houses excavated at Jamestown as illustrated in figure 1.9. But because the foundations of the Jamestown houses were narrow, they were probably not capable of carrying the weight of three stories. The actual elevations and roof forms of all the early Jamestown buildings are unknown. (Photograph courtesy of the Virginia Historical Society.)*

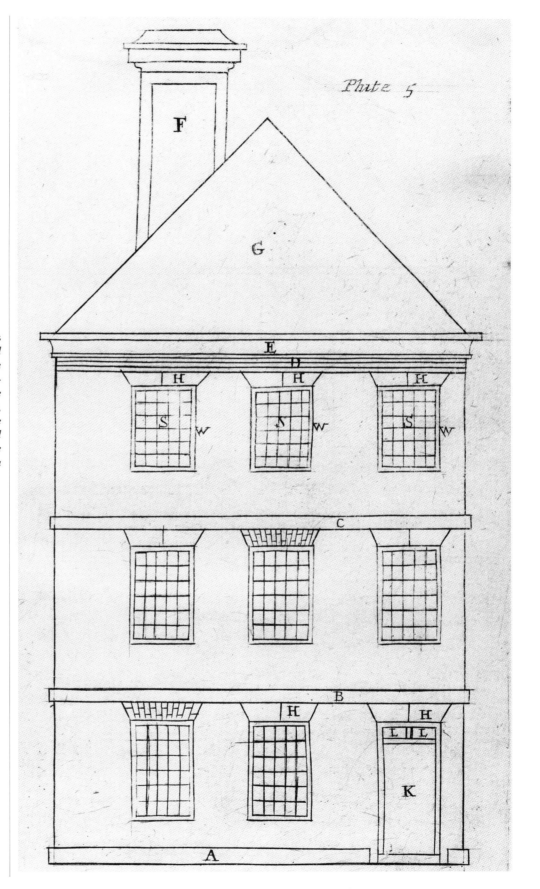

The long building was a logical choice for the few transitional mansions built on the eve of the colony's Georgian era. At Green Spring it had made a powerful statement of greater social status, repeated at Fairfield ( FIGURE 1.12 ), a similar structure (20 by 80 feet) developed into an L-plan and built around 1692 by wealthy Lewis Burwell of Gloucester County. With a combination of clustered Jacobean chimneys, a Classical cornice, and the horizontal mass of a Classical building, Fairfield adapted two styles of architecture—the old and the new—to a regional plan.[15]

Probably similar in elevation, both to the second Green Spring and to Fairfield, was Corotoman ( FIGURE 1.13 ), the early eighteenth-century Lancaster County house of an even wealthier Virginian, Robert "King" Carter (1663–1732), owner of a thousand slaves and forty-four tobacco plantations. In his love of wealth but his disapproval of extravagance as inappropriate to the "circumstances" of the colony, Carter typified Virginia's proto-aristocracy. As with the Burwell mansion, the local definition of moderation was stretched by his 90-by 40-foot house. It featured a gallery running the length of a single-pile plan of three major rooms, with large English "closets" circling the end chimneys and a center entry hall paved with polished white marble imported from England. Matching marble and delft tiles decorated two hearths. We can only speculate about the elevation of Corotoman, lost to fire in 1729; but, like Fairfield, it was a solid house, at least two stories tall. The foundations on the river facade indicate end pavilions, a central porch pavilion, and a long arcade below the gallery; fragments found there suggest a facade that was enriched with applied pilasters and door pediments of stone and brick. Long and tall yet narrow in depth beyond the gallery, simple in plan yet richly ornamented, Corotoman was a curious regional product built by an extremely competent self-made man, an emerging aristocrat like William Fitzhugh, who was comfortable with plainness if it was mixed with as much finery as local conditions would permit. With the next generation would come even greater ambition—the drive to equal the London fashion.[16]

### Setting the Style: Churches in the Colony

Predictably, the proto-aristocrats also constructed the colony's first permanent church buildings. From the start, the Anglican church had been important in Virginia, where it was the state religion, supported by public taxation. Thus in the seventeenth century alone, colonists in fifty parishes erected churches, most of which were earthfast buildings. As with the post-hole "Virginia house," the later ones could be tarred on the outside yet handsomely furnished within: the 1677 Poplar Spring Church of Petsworth Parish in Gloucester County, probably the best of the group, had paneled pews, a chancel screen built with turned balusters, a massive triple-decker pulpit "made with 6 sides," a compass ceiling arched to suggest the sky, and even "Cherubin"[sic] painted on its ceiling or chancel wall.[17]

Even more ambitious than the Petsworth parishioners were the few vestries that at the same time erected large brick buildings with fashionable pre-Georgian features like Gothic buttresses and tracery and Dutch-inspired shaped gables. One famous example is the last (and lost) Jamestown church; the best survivor is St. Luke's Church (originally Newport Parish Church, Isle of Wight County, circa 1680; FIGURE 1.14). Its Gothic details perpetuated on Colonial soil medieval features of the English rural church built of local stone or brick. With little stone to quarry in Tidewater Virginia, brick was the easy choice of material. Its progressive plan is the rectangle of the "room" or "auditory" church, a type that had emerged in England in the beginning of the century as an alternative to the medieval preference of a separate wing for the chancel. This group of churches—like Bacon's Castle—was transitional in style: the buildings were soon outmoded in Georgian Virginia. Even their plan would be refined, as the chancel was increasingly diminished in prominence and definition.[18]

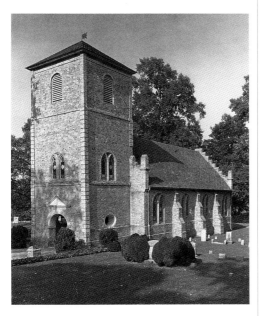

FIGURE 1.14. **St. Luke's Church** *(initially Newport Parish Church, Isle of Wight County, 1680), retains Gothic details in its stone-masonry and brickwork.*

### Williamsburg Builds for Publick and Private

In the 1690s, with what must have seemed dramatic suddenness, an entirely new standard of architectural quality was established in the region. A college building of fashionable London design and enormous size—much larger than any other structure in the American colonies—was erected in Williamsburg. An equally impressive statehouse and a seemingly palatial governor's residence soon followed. Virginian Robert Beverley was both proud and accurate in 1705 when he described the College of William and Mary and the Capitol ( FIGURE 1.15 ) as the "most Magnificent" buildings in America. To Reverend Hugh Jones they were "exceeded by few of their kind," even in his native England.

These prominent structures initiated a flowering in Virginia of Classical architecture. Their importance cannot be overstressed.[19]

Only a combination of efforts made both locally and in London account for the College's creation. As early as 1660 the emerging aristocracy, interested in the welfare of its heirs, had attempted through legislation to found a college. A generation later in England, the Glorious Revolution of 1688 that brought William and Mary to the throne renewed government interest in the Crown's oldest colony, and the Anglican church became involved in the new enthusiasm to better Virginia. A position of Commissary of the Bishop of London, with jurisdiction over the colony, was created and bestowed upon the Reverend James Blair, who would be instrumental in establishing a college in Virginia that could produce Anglican ministers. He would become its first president.[20]

To obtain a design for the College, the energetic Blair may have turned in London to the Surveyor General of buildings for the Crown, Sir Christopher Wren. As a royal project, the College was the responsibility of Wren's Office of Works. But because the original building burned in 1705 and was rebuilt with

FIGURE 1.15. *The "Bodleian Plate," a copperplate engraving, circa 1732–47, formerly owned by the Bodleian Library, Oxford. On the top row, center, this perspective shows the* **College of William and Mary** *in its second form, after the fire of 1705, flanked to the left by the* **Brafferton Indian School** *(1723) and to the right by the* **College President's House** *(1732–33). On the middle row, left, is the* **Capitol** *(1699–1705) and to the far right is the* **Governor's Palace** *(1706–21). On the bottom row are sketches of Virginia Indians, native plants, insects, and a seahorse. (Photograph courtesy of Colonial Williamsburg Foundation.)*

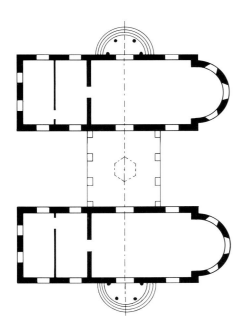

FIGURE 1.16. **Williamsburg Capitol,** *H-plan as built circa 1701–05. (Courtesy of Carl R. Lounsbury.)*

FIGURE 1.17. *Reconstructed drawing of* **west elevation, the Williamsburg Capitol,** *based on archaeological and documentary evidence. (Drawn by and courtesy of Carl R. Lounsbury.)*

major changes—one full story less on the front and apparently a wider pavilion, to which a pediment was added—essentially what we see today—a solid attribution of that first design is impossible. As best we can reconstruct the original building, its geometrical plan of three lateral squares (probably extended into three cubes) and its peculiar classicism—which blended the astylar facade and verticality of the northern Anglo-Dutch tradition with a modest sculptural quality derived ultimately from the Italian Baroque—in no way deny the hand of Wren or his office. The important point is that the most fashionable architecture in the realm was competently exported to Virginia in 1695. At that time the English "surveyor" Thomas Hadley, three English bricklayers, and other "workmen [from] England" began to raise the walls of a 138-foot, three-and-a-half story building with basement, balconies, a grand cupola, and a rear arcade or so-called piazza.[21]

At the opposite end of the emerging town of Williamsburg, a statehouse was soon under construction. Whether Governor Francis Nicholson or others conceived its design, the process seems to have been local, for regional features were incorporated to produce a unique design. The ubiquitous two-room "Virginia house" plan, possibly used at the last Jamestown statehouse (the identity of which is uncertain), was repeated in matching wings—for Court and Assembly—joined to form an H-plan ( FIGURE 1.16 ). The "house fronts" of each wing became the principal facades. And as initially planned, the connecting arcade or "piazza" was even to have resembled the seventeenth-century cross-plan type. Just as provincial and more surprising because actually built—and only recently recognized because the burned building was incorrectly reconstructed in the 1930s—was the placement of entrance porches on the major (west and east) facades on center with the total width of the wings, but out of balance with the surrounding windows ( FIGURE 1.17 ). So blatant a violation of Classical symmetry—of course poorly known in the colony at so early a date—was a by-product of the design of the south ends of the wings as semicircular apses, which eliminated a potential south bay. Not only graceful, the apses suggested the ancient basilica form—used by the Romans as a court of justice and assembly hall—and served as an appropriate link to its namesake, the Capitoline Hill of ancient Rome.[22]

From the start, the Capitol was intended to be an impressive building. As defined in the Act of Assembly that commissioned it, the two-and-a-half story, five-bay structure was to have generous ceiling heights of 15 and 10 feet, unusually thick walls and foundations, and sash windows—a recent innovation even in England. Fashionable elements from the College—the cupola, balconies, and the arcade—were to be repeated: these were well-known, traditional features of the town halls, guildhalls, and markethouses of England.[23]

Though the Capitol burned and its appearance is known only from a contemporary print, the so-called Bodleian plate ( FIGURE 1.15 ), the building apparently shared with the College a sense of style. Its extreme verticality and flat facades, conceived in the Anglo-Dutch tradition, and the dynamic treatment of space around and through the structure, suggest a developing sophistication

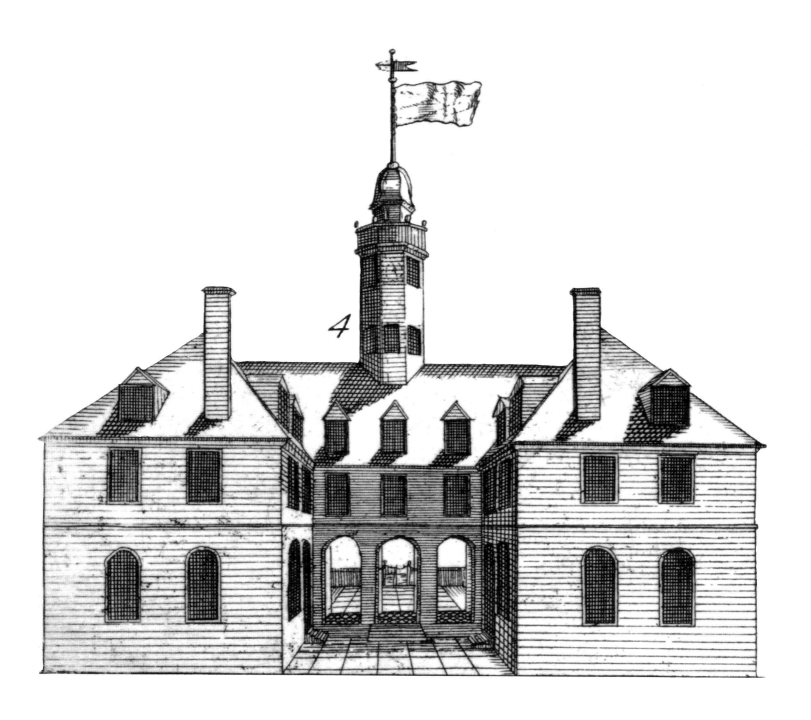

FIGURE 1.15A. *Detail of the Bodleian Plate, showing the Capitol building at Williamsburg, with its central arcade and piazza.*

and aesthetic awareness in the colony. That growth can even be documented. In 1701, overseer Henry Cary had accumulated sufficient quantities of building materials, had six English bricklayers and carpenters under his supervision, and was finally ready to build. A second Act of Assembly then refined the provincial elements of the original design: the "piazza" was simplified to the square form known today, the first floor was raised two feet above ground, and the lower-floor windows and doors were given compass-heads to make the building appear less domestic and to bring it closer to the architecture of English town halls and markethouses.[24]

FIGURE 1.18. **Hanover County Courthouse,** *circa 1735, like many Virginia county courthouses, repeats the arcade design of the Capitol building at Williamsburg (compare figure 1.15A).*

The arcade of the Capitol ( FIGURE 1.15A ), its most distinctive feature, was copied in the best of the Virginia county courthouses, of which a half-dozen of this type survive ( FIGURE 1.18 ). As at Williamsburg, the courthouse "piazza" furnished both a useful gathering-place in inclement weather and a pre-trial conference spot. It further provided an understated dignity befitting the building's function and did little to overspend the ever-limited public funds. Courthouses in eighteenth-century Virginia were generally of two types—many were long, rectangular buildings with a jury room opposite the justice's bench; others, like the Hanover example, were T-shaped structures with flanking jury rooms in the wings. With all rooms below, this plan better suited the region's warm climate than did the seventeenth-century Virginia courthouse that invariably placed the jury room or clerk's office in a loft above the first floor. Though ultimately derived from European town halls and marketplaces, Virginia courthouses—like the Williamsburg Capitol—were unique to the region because of their adaptations to local conditions. They constitute a distinct contribution to Georgian design.[25]

Like the College, the Governor's Palace ( FIGURE 1.15 ; middle right) resulted as much from London directives as from local efforts. In the 1680s and until 1705 the London Board of Trade clamored for construction of a governor's residence. Proud of the newly completed College and Capitol, the Assembly finally appropriated funds, and in an Act of 1706 defined the essential features of the house: it would be a brick, two-story, double-pile structure, 48 by 54 feet, with cellars, sash windows, a slate roof, and support buildings for a kitchen and stables. It had a balcony, dormers, and cupola to match the ones at the Capitol and the College, the focal points at the ends of the new city's major axes.[26]

Unlike the Capitol, so provincial in its asymmetrical facade, the new building—which also burned and is now reconstructed—was a more proper mix of Georgian elements. The unusual (and totally symmetrical) spacing of windows at the Palace, known from the same contemporary print, suggests the influence of a sixteenth-century Italian design book, Sebastiano Serlio's *Architettura* (republished in London in 1611). Still other features of the building characterize the architecture of contemporary country houses built in the Anglo-Dutch style in both England and Holland. Those brick buildings share with the Palace a vertical and cubical form and a Classical yet fashionably flat facade. Such houses must have been known in Virginia through prints or books, for the sure, sophisticated design of the Williamsburg Palace is a clear derivation. The flat brick facade of the Anglo-Dutch style, which so appealed to the practical temperament in Holland, was well-received throughout conservative Virginia.[27]

Because it was not a port city, the town of Williamsburg developed slowly though steadily until mid century, when a decision to reconstruct the Capitol after a fire in 1747 produced a minor building boom. The town followed a highly successful plan, probably devised by Governor Nicholson, who earlier had moved the Maryland capital to Annapolis and initiated the Virginia relocation in 1699. The major axis, the Duke of Gloucester Street, was made six poles wide (99 feet), following the precedent of John Evelyn's proposals for rebuilding

FIGURE 1.19. **Nelson-Galt House** *(Williamsburg, 1707–09) is a good—and early—example of the subtleties of the new Classical style adapted for home design. (Photograph courtesy of Colonial Williamsburg Foundation).*

FIGURE 1.19 A. **East Room paneling, Nelson-Galt House,** *demonstrates that attention to fine detailing underlies Classical design. (Photograph courtesy of Colonial Williamsburg Foundation.)*

FIGURE 1.20. **Lower Chapel, Christ Church Parish** *(Middlesex County, 1714–17), an early example of a newer, simplified church design.*

the principal streets of London after the Great Fire. London streets were then given focal points, after the manner of French Baroque ideals, an idea—mentioned above with regard to the College, the Capitol, and the governor's residence—that became the most significant feature of the Williamsburg plat. The city's plan of development, which borrowed rules from earlier Virginia town-planning efforts, was equally successful. Lots, a half-acre in size, had to be built upon within two years of purchase to be retained; construction of larger houses on adjoining lots was encouraged; houses on principal streets had to "front alike" and be no smaller than a minimum size (20 by 30 feet) and height (10 feet to the eaves). Prudently, no provision banned construction with wood.[28]

Nowhere were the subtleties of the new Classical style better developed for small domestic buildings than in the new capital. A good, early example is the Nelson-Galt house (before 1718, later lengthened a bay at each end, FIGURE 1.19 ). While the dimensions of its plan (20 by 48 feet) were governed by the town's building requirement for a two-lot purchase (20 by 40 foot minimum), elevation proportions were determined by the simplest of geometric formulas: the distance from the ground to the eaves (14 feet) equals the distance from the eaves to the roof ridge. A number of Williamsburg builders used the same logical means to select proportions and were equally generous with sash and Classical detailing ( FIGURE 1.19A ). From the bold profiles of chair-boards (today called chair-rails), cornices, muntins, and door panels, to the beading of corner-boards, the upward tapering of a gable rake-board, or the reduced proportions and graceful roof slope of tall dormers, these houses were thoughtfully conceived and carefully constructed.[29]

With its unusually harmonious balance of public and private architecture, Williamsburg became a special place, and remains an unsurpassed example of environmental design—of town planning with a sensitivity to configuration, building size, proportion, and materials.

## Colonial Churches Gain in Grace

Probably because the College was an ecclesiastical project, church builders were among the first in the colony to borrow its lessons of Classical design. The Lower Chapel (1714–17; FIGURE 1.20 ) for Christ Church Parish of Middlesex County is an early example of a new, distinctive type they devised: simple in form but sensitively proportioned, with a subtle roof line, and compass-head windows set against plain brick facades. Though the chancel of the Lower Chapel originally retained its medieval screen, the open-plan eighteenth-century Virginia church type, with emphasis on the pulpit and the spoken word, was nearly evolved.[30]

Larger in size and prominently located in Williamsburg is the colony's earliest cruciform church, a second type that would proliferate in Virginia. Bruton Parish Church (1711–15; FIGURE 1.21 ) offered a practical solution: an interior that was spacious, yet easily spanned and within hearing of the pulpit. The church was designed by Alexander Spotswood, the multi-talented governor

FIGURE 1.21. **Bruton Parish Church,** *designed by Governor Alexander Spotswood, provided ample seating for the colony's one large congregation. (Williamsburg, 1711–15, chancel enlarged 1751–55, steeple added 1769–71; photograph courtesy of Colonial Williamsburg Foundation.)*

FIGURE 1.22. **Christ Church** *(Lancaster County, 1732–35) has long been recognized as one of the great buildings of colonial America. (Photograph courtesy Trustees, Christ Church Foundation.)*

FIGURE 1.22 A. **Triple-decker pulpit at Christ Church** *shows the skilled eye and hand of an anonymous master craftsman.*

who led the colony from 1710 to 1722, as an exercise in geometry that the vestry applauded for its "commodiousness and conveniency."[31]

Closely related is Christ Church, Lancaster County (1732–35; FIGURE 1.22), long valued as one of the great buildings of colonial America. With tall, flat brick walls, a steep double-pitched roof, and a nearly centralized cross plan, the church is vertical and cubical in its massing and boldly geometrical in form. It is an imposing and entirely original creation in the Anglo-Dutch style, within the limits of which it presents brick and stone detailing unsurpassed in the colonies. The window and door treatments and the bold entablature suggest a professional hand of no small talent, a designer whose name—like the details of the commission—is lost to us. Equally striking is the interior finish that features a triple-decker pulpit ( FIGURE 1.22A ), a massive Classical altarpiece, and tall paneled pews set on stone pavers.[32]

The church was lavishly detailed because its construction was financed by wealthy Robert "King" Carter, who believed that "the more [God] lends us, the larger accounts he expects from us." Carter's sizable "accounts" were paid at the very end of his life by the finest regional architecture that the "circumstances" in the colony in 1732 would allow.[33]

### The "Manner House" Grows Stately Tall

A decade earlier, in the 1720s, Virginia had markedly "improved in wealth and polite living," to cite Hugh Jones's assessment of 1724. Second and third generations of native-born Virginians—"creoles"—were then inheriting, intermarrying, and generating new income through increased slave labor. A full-blown

FIGURE 1.23. **Rosewell** *(Gloucester County, 1721–41) in ruins after being destroyed by fire in 1916. (Photograph courtesy of Virginia State Library.) Compare with reconstructed drawing by Thomas T. Waterman, illustrated in Chapter 3, figure 3.43, and photograph of woodwork in Chapter 4, figure 4.5.*

FIGURE 1.24. *Frederic Edwin Church,* **Shirley,** *1851, pencil on paper, 8 by 10½ inches, courtesy of Shirley Plantation. The mansion and dependencies were built in the late 1730s, and the three-story dependency to the right of the main house was demolished in 1868. Church, a noted American landscapist, visited the Carters in 1851 and in a letter of June 12 from Natural Bridge (now in the archives at the Colonial Williamsburg Foundation) he thanked the family for their hospitality at Shirley, citing this "slight sketch" as an expression of his appreciation.*

aristocracy was entrenched with the means and the inclination to pursue the way of life of the London gentry. Its members would enjoy increasing prosperity as the economy expanded and tobacco exports increased a phenomenal 250 percent. Their portraits ( FIGURE 1.33 ) now show sitters comfortable with the full trappings of wealth. Conscious of status, they defined it by ownership of land, slaves, objects, and architecture—the appearance of which mattered very much to them. So changed were they from their fathers' philosophy that in the 1730s a Londoner felt compelled to warn a traveling Philadelphian that "well-dressed" Virginians "look perhaps more at a man's outside than his inside." Other late Colonial societies at that time increasingly adopted more English manners, but none carried the imitation so far as did Virginians, nor built as many houses so grand as the Georgian mansions of Virginia.[34]

One of the first was Rosewell ( FIGURE 1.23 ), the Gloucester County mansion begun by Mann Page I after the loss of an earlier house to fire in 1721. Perhaps the grandest Georgian structure ever built in America and a house beautifully crafted by English masons and joiners, its appearance in a rural landscape then dominated by earthfast structures must have been startling. A son-in-law of "King" Carter, Page dared to better the Palace, which was his influence: he made Rosewell one story taller, ten feet longer (71 feet), and gave the house two cupolas instead of one.

In type, Rosewell—surprisingly—was an English town house, though flanked by support buildings and considerably larger than the variety tried earlier at Jamestown. Its masonry keystones, apron window panels, compass-head stair windows, and crowning brick parapet are features of a specific Georgian house design developed in London when fire-prevention ordinances of 1707 and 1709 abolished wooden cornices. The Rosewell interior, which had

FIGURE 1.24 A. **Shirley Plantation,** *as it looks today, still reflects its Anglo-Dutch roots that echo those of the Governor's Palace at Williamsburg (compare figure 1.15).*

one of the best carved staircases of the period, just as closely resembled its English models (see FIGURE 4.5). How better could Page pursue the lifestyle of the London gentry than to live in a fashionable London town house?[35]

Rosewell was too expensive and too difficult an undertaking in Virginia: Mann Page II was still paying building debts in 1741, a decade after his father's death. Nonetheless in the late 1730s, John Carter III, the eldest son and principal heir of "King" Carter, erected an equally extraordinary and certainly unique group of buildings at Shirley (Charles City County; FIGURES 1.24, 1.24A), his wife's estate, which he also inherited. At the center of a strict geometrical layout of house and dependencies is a three-story mansion, 48 feet square and nearly a cube, an original design in the Anglo-Dutch style so prominently introduced at the Williamsburg Palace. Its double porticoes, added by Carter's son after 1771, replaced original stone steps and the gauged brick surrounds of a once-flat facade. Flanking the house at distances of 36 feet were equally tall three-story, single-pile long houses, destroyed in the nineteenth century and only recently excavated. Their dimensions of 24 by 60 feet are further multiples of the number 12, the mathematical key to the mansion complex, all of which was probably designed by a creative amateur. Four smaller dependencies that may also date to John Carter's tenure extend the courtyard. The social statement made by these impressive buildings must have been unsurpassed in all the English colonies.[36]

Both Rosewell and Shirley demonstrate eighteenth-century Virginians' audacity to attempt to simulate the grand lifestyle of the London gentry, thereby to prove their cultural sophistication. Their efforts reveal the unique position of Virginia's frontier society as close to England yet far from identical to it.

Other mansions indicate just as clearly how Virginians' social needs and the colony's warm climate shaped the development of Georgian architecture in the region. For the very wealthy, isolated on their plantations, entertaining had become a significant activity as early as the 1680s, when Virginians were said never to have "anything to do except make visits to their neighbors." A few in those early years even built "banqueting houses" for the sole purpose of neighborly entertainment at a convenient location. In the 1690s some Virginians even dared to criticize Governor Nicholson for serving only one dish of meat at his table. As early as 1705, according to Robert Beverley, they dined "as at the best Tables in London" and offered hospitality unmatched in the world. Over the next two decades, as they "improved in . . . polite living," their drinking and dining vessels—of costly silver, ceramics, and glass, as listed in their inventories—multiplied in number and the ceremony of dining became a formal domestic ritual. Until the last quarter of the eighteenth century, when a separate dining room and a separate parlor came into vogue, a single room, the best in the house—large, well-appointed, and prominently positioned—was given to that ritual. It was an outgrowth of the old multi-purpose hall, variously and confusingly called the "hall," "parlor," or "dining room." At Nomini Hall in Westmoreland County, that space was instructively described as the "dining room where we usually sit."[37]

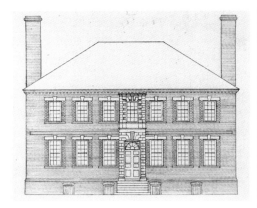

FIGURE 1.25. **Sabine Hall** *(Richmond County, circa 1733–42), reconstruction of the original facade by the author.*

FIGURE 1.26. **Lower Hall interior, Sabine Hall,** *has the generous proportions and gracious setting needed by its owners, the Landon Carters, to accommodate their custom of lavish entertainment.*

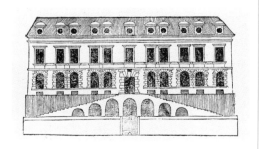

FIGURE 1.27. **Illustration from Book 7 of** Sebastiano Serlio's *Architettura, (Venice, 1600) probably the design inspiration for Sabine Hall.*

FIGURE 1.25A. **Sabine Hall** *as it looked when it was photographed in the nineteenth century. The original roof was lowered, and a portico and wing were added in the 1820s. (Photograph courtesy of the Virginia State Library.)*

But if a planter intended to entertain lavishly, he needed more than one room for his guests. Such was Landon Carter's solution at Sabine Hall ( FIG-URES 1.25, 1.25A ), built about 1733–42 in Richmond County. Each New Year's, and for the next three days according to his diary, this younger son of "King" Carter entertained some five dozen of the local gentry. The inventory taken at his death tells us that guests were served in the lower parlor—the closet of which held dozens of wine glasses and spoons—and in the large upstairs central hall—treated as a *piano nobile,* with a full entablature and holding in its closet a staggering ten dozen plates, along with a full complement of cups, bowls, and glasses. Visitors could also congregate in the lower hall ( FIGURE 1.26 ).

For the design of Sabine Hall, Carter probably turned to an early architectural book, *Architettura,* the Venetian publication of 1600 by Sebastiano Serlio that may have been used previously at the Governor's Palace. We have no proof that Carter owned a copy of Serlio, but in that book we can see the essential elements for both his plan and his elevation of a rusticated door with embellished windows ( FIGURE 1.27 ). A narrow pavilion, not in the Serlio illustration, must have been the owner's invention, perhaps an adaptation of a feature he knew from the College of William and Mary. To meet his entertainment needs, Carter widened Serlio's narrow passage to 17 feet on both floors. In so doing he adapted the plan to a warmer climate, creating two major spaces with cross-ventilation. For the same reason, two of the corner rooms on the ground floor were put to use as cool bedchambers. Landon Carter's house is a unique Virginia blend of European influences adapted to a region's peculiar conditions.[38]

FIGURE 1.28. **Garden Front, Stratford Hall** *(Westmoreland County, begun around 1738). All exterior stairs of the house are incorrect restorations dating from the early twentieth century. The original stair design is not known (Photograph © Richard Cheek.)*

FIGURE 1.28 A. **Long Front, Stratford Hall.** *The design of this house blends European elements with features that allow for cross-ventilation, a necessary adaptation of form to site. (Photograph by Richard Cheek for the Robert E. Lee Memorial Foundation).*

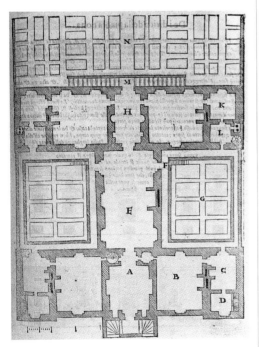

FIGURE 1.29. *The popular* **H-Plan,** *as illustrated in Serlio's* Architettura. *(Photograph courtesy of the Virginia Historical Society.)*

So is Stratford Hall ( FIGURE 1.28 ), the massive (63 by 93 feet) Westmoreland County mansion built by Thomas Lee around 1738. The design adapts the Baroque monumentality of the English school of Sir John Vanbrugh and Nicholas Hawksmoor to the region's climate, building, materials, and social needs. It uses an H-plan, a Jacobean type that had been recently revived in English Georgian houses like Belton (Lincolnshire). But local Colonial architecture was just as likely an influence: at the Capitol, Lee had experienced the comfortable lighting and ventilation of a large H-plan building, and at Green Spring, which his wife Hannah Ludwell inherited, he knew the pleasant disposition of a raised main floor or *piano nobile* reached by tall outside stairs. Like Landon Carter, Lee may also have looked in Serlio's *Architettura*, which offers an H-plan with the same unusual long passage running the length of the house ( FIGURE 1.29 ). As at the Capitol and in Serlio's design, one facade at Stratford is its narrow east facade, where the garden is planted and the earliest roads led. The longer south facade, which faces inland and is framed by four dependencies, is its most visible front ( FIGURE 1.28A ).[39]

Lee's large H-plan provided in two wings abundant space for the activities important to his generation of Virginians. In the garden wing, as best we can judge from inventories that do not specify room location, the two largest rooms on the upper floor seem to have been given to dining and sitting. At the center of the house and also on the *piano nobile* is the great hall, 29½ feet square, ornately decorated with Corinthian pilasters beneath a 16½-foot coved ceiling—one of the most handsome rooms created in colonial America. It is a space well-ventilated from four directions. Also appropriate in Virginia's warm climate were Lee's four cool bedchambers on the ground floor of the more private back wing. Stratford, an original creation, clearly defined the high status of its owner, the extent of his hospitality and, to our modern eyes, demonstrates his vigorous, provincial spirit.[40]

## The Practical with the Proud: The Cross-Passage Plan

FIGURE 1.30. **Ambler House** *(Jamestown, mid seventeenth century; destroyed by fire in 1895), which had the ample dimensions of the Governor's Palace, adapted an English floor plan to make better use of cross-ventilation.*

The need in Virginia for cross-ventilation in a double-pile structure found its simplest solution in the cross-passage house, the most common double-pile type in the colony. The passage had been introduced in Virginia in single-pile houses as a means of privacy: by the first quarter of the eighteenth century, to judge from inventories, its use was established. But the region's heat, which seemed to Englishmen "beyond . . . conception," caused its development in large houses beyond privacy and circulation into what Hugh Jones described as "an air-draught in summer."[41]

The Ambler house (Jamestown, mid eighteenth century; FIGURE 1.30) was a cross-passage building that resembled the Governor's Palace in size (38 by 54 feet). Earlier in the century in southeastern England, a brick Georgian house remarkably close to this Virginia type had been developed. But the passage in those English houses is broken at the center, narrow, and totally undeveloped as an air-draught. What is significant is that a similar but different house-type developed on a parallel course in Virginia, as a regional solution. The 13-foot wide passage at the Jamestown house (defined by two-story interior brick walls) was designed not only to provide easy circulation but also to draw the summer breezes more effectively.[42]

It has long been long thought that the Ambler house was built early in the century by Edward Jaquelin (1668–1730; his daughter married Richard Ambler) and was "the mansion house of the said Edward Jaquelin" mentioned in a land deed of 1721. But the archaeological evidence from an earlier building on the same site (presumably one that Jaquelin built or inherited through marriage) proves its existence beyond 1721. An emigrant from France via England, Jaquelin certainly aspired to a cultured lifestyle, for in the early 1720s he commissioned seven family portraits that derive a decidedly aristocratic bearing from fashionable London prints of the royal circle (FIGURE 1.31). To our twentieth-century conceptions it may seem surprising that the ambitious figure whose image we know through his portrait was content to live in what must have been a less sophisticated building than the Ambler house that replaced it. The explanation is that the pursuit of both art and architecture was particularly difficult in the colony before the mid eighteenth century. The Jaquelin portraits are markedly provincial in execution, and brick Georgian mansions were no easy undertaking on a frontier. We need only remember the difficulties at Rosewell, the magnitude of Carter Burwell's efforts to construct Carter's Grove (to be discussed further on), or the problems John Carlyle reported to his brother when he built his large house in Alexandria at mid century. Carlyle lay the blame on the scarcity of craftsmen and the use of slave labor.[43]

FIGURE 1.31. **Edward Jaquelin** *was a Frenchman who came to the colony by way of England and brought with him both sophistication and ambition. Portrait from a series of seven attributed to Nehemiah Partridge, circa 1722. Oil on canvas, 31½ by 26 inches, Virginia Museum of Fine Arts, on long-term loan from the Ambler Family.*

Even William Byrd II, who spent much of his life in London, never attempted to transplant a purely English design to Virginia. He built a distinctly Virginia structure if it was he who constructed Westover (Charles City County, late 1730s or 1750s; FIGURE 1.32). It was just as possibly the creation of his son William Byrd III—we have no proof. At more than sixty years of age, Byrd (like

FIGURE 1.32. **Westover** (*Charles City County, late 1730s or 1750s*), *is perhaps the grandest of the colony's cross-passage mansions. The flanking dependencies were unconnected to the house until the twentieth century, when the one to the right in the photograph was rebuilt. (Photograph courtesy The Valentine Museum, Richmond.)*

Edward Jaquelin) may have made do with what was probably one of the better pre-Georgian dwellings in the colony. That earlier house—flanked by a series of dependencies, at least two of which had elegant Flemish-shaped gables—was entered through an English wrought-iron gate that survives with its stone finials, and was surrounded by extensive gardens: the entire architectural complex was impressive. The house that replaced it is the grandest of the colony's cross-passage mansions and arguably the epitome of domestic Georgian architecture

FIGURE 1.33. **William Byrd II,** *attributed to the English artist Hans Hyssing, circa 1724. (Oil on canvas, 50 by 41 inches, Virginia Historical Society, presented by William Byrd of Princeton, New Jersey.) Byrd's adventures and enterprise spanned the Atlantic, and his published diaries have brought him twentieth-century renown.*

in America. It is a large structure—seven bays wide with a 13-foot passage placed off-center and lit by a major window. The asymmetrical alignment of its passage, which allows variety in the size of adjacent rooms, was not a Virginia invention, but the development of the passage as a lit and well-ventilated summer living space was.[44]

A curious figure, William Byrd (1674–1744; FIGURE 1.33) was born in Virginia but enjoyed the company of well-placed London acquaintances, including the poet Alexander Pope and the satirist Jonathan Swift. Byrd gained membership in the Royal Society and, according to traditional accounts, was even received by Louis XIV at Versailles. Byrd was a complex character: he read the classics in several languages yet was known to have caroused with bawdy street-women in London. When Byrd returned to Virginia for good, at age fifty-five, he brought London culture to the colony in his impressive holdings of English silver, valued at his death at 662 pounds, and portraiture, a collection of some thirty paintings. He also brought to Virginia the same number of architectural books. He had once toured the countryside of England noting its architecture and had experienced the Palladian revival in London, even going so far as to purchase a copy of Colen Campbell's important tome, *Vitruvius Britannicus.*[45]

That so sophisticated a patron of the arts either built no new house or—if he constructed Westover—settled for one only moderately English in its plan

FIGURE 1.34. **Indian Banks** *(Richmond County, circa 1728) combines the grandeur of the colonial mansion with the practicality of a house built for economy and comfort. (Photograph courtesy of the Virginia State Library.)*

FIGURE 1.35. **Tuckahoe** *(Goochland County, circa 1720s–30s, bears a plain facade that belies the embellishment of its interior woodwork. (Photograph © Richard Cheek, Belmont, Massachusetts.)*

FIGURE 1.36. **Wilton** *(Middlesex County, mid eighteenth century. incorporates a gambrel roof form that, though ill-suited to the colony's warm climate, did enjoy some popularity in Virginia. (Photograph courtesy of the Virginia State Library.)*

and features, underscores the significance of local conditions in determining the development of Colonial architecture in Virginia. The Byrd family house could not be a stone Palladian mansion of Lord Burlington's London circle. It was to be built with Virginia materials, exquisitely proportioned and finely crafted with the restraint of the Anglo-Dutch tradition, and was to have a Virginia plan, to suit the climate. Only two prominent London features were incorporated— segmentally arched windows and massive Portland stone doorways, the latter imported from England. These types of doorways were so much the vogue there that they are pictured in the contemporary design book, *Palladio Londinensis*.[46]

Virginians devised a surprising variety of early Georgian house forms. Some planters, including those wealthy enough to afford the double-pile mansion, rejected that large type as impractical for their needs. Certainly three rooms were convenient for the purposes of entertaining, sleeping, and informal dining (for lesser members of the household, such as children and tutors), but the fourth corner room served no pressing social need. Accordingly, they devised a group of handsome, two-story, single-pile Georgian houses, with an L-plan or T-plan that provided only the desired third room on each floor. Indian Banks (Richmond County, circa 1728, FIGURE 1.34) is a good example that combines the merits of both Classical and vernacular traditions: the stately grandeur of a mansion and the cross-ventilation and comfortable lighting of a single-pile structure, easily roofed. Thus the type persisted in Virginia in farmhouse designs into the modern era.[47]

## Fine Joinery Embellishes Hall and Wall

Brick, of course, was too lavish a material to fit all "circumstances" of the country. Accustomed to simplicity, many Virginians in the Georgian era continued to build plain elevations in wood, to which they could add elaborate interiors. Examples abound in Williamsburg. The farmhouse exteriors of Tuckahoe (Goochland County, circa 1720s–30s; FIGURES 1.35, 1.35A) or Marmion (King George County, second quarter of eighteenth century) inadequately prepare us for the ornate joinery within. Tuckahoe has staircase carving that could comfortably grace a fine London house, while Marmion's paneled and painted drawing-room is one of the more ambitious American interiors of the period. In such peculiar, handsome buildings as these—and in comparable brick examples such as Gunston Hall—the region's tradition of conservative architecture once again collided with the ambitions of colonists to follow the opulent tastes of their London contemporaries.[48]

In an effort to give a more stately appearance to the hall-parlor house, and to provide—at least on the inside—the illusion of a full second story, some builders developed the gambrel-roof type, a poorly ventilated house surprisingly popular in Virginia's warm climate. Wilton (Middlesex County, enlarged in 1763; FIGURE 1.36) was a brick story-and-a-half hall-parlor structure transformed at an early date with a new roof line into a building of increased status. The gambrel-roof house form was also built in wood.[49]

At mid century, some wealthy Virginians ready to erect mansions turned to contemporary English designs with central halls and saloons that could draw cross-ventilation, meet the local need to entertain, and at the same time represent the latest London fashion. As we have learned to expect, when these plans were adapted locally, at houses like Carter's Grove and Mount Airy, they were so changed in size and materials that the results were uniquely and unquestionably Virginian.

The paneled hall at Carter's Grove (James City County, circa 1745–55; FIGURE 1.37 )—long considered one of the handsomest Georgian rooms in America—is richly embellished with a Classical entablature and Ionic pilasters that are both carefully carved and impeccably proportioned. The staircase, with elegantly turned balusters and exquisitely crafted stair-brackets and landing panel, was unsurpassed in the colonies. In appearance and quality, the Carter's Grove interior is surprisingly close to those of considerably grander English country houses like Frampton Court (1731–33, Gloucestershire), a stone Palladian building with an imposing temple-pediment exterior that found no imitation in detail or material in any of the American colonies. Carter Burwell, a wealthy grandson of "King" Carter, had paid the passage to Virginia of a highly talented joiner, Richard Bayliss, presumably an Englishman, who had worked in Charleston as early as the 1730s. For the exterior ( FIGURE 1.37A ), a provincial creation, Burwell was content for local brickmason David Minetree to work in the conservative Virginia tradition of Anglo-Dutch design.[50]

THE Subscriber being in want of Bricklayers, will give at the Rate of Four Pounds per Month, for good Workmen.

*Carter Burwell.*

ADVERTISEMENTS.

THE Subscriber being in Want of Oyster Shells, will give at the Rate of Three Shillings per Hogshead, for any Quantity that can be delivered at his Landing by the last of March,

*Carter Burwell.*

The "circumstances" of Colonial living made an ornate Palladian exterior like Frampton Court impractical in Virginia. At Carter's Grove, where Burwell served as his own overseer of construction, the process was difficult, lengthy, and involved some three dozen craftsmen. His account-books show he bought and had made hundreds of thousands of bricks; he purchased whole trees and quantities of plank for framing the house; and he advertised in the *Virginia Gazette* to engage brickmasons and to buy oyster shells for mortar ( FIGURE 1.38 ). The magnitude of the undertaking is apparent from the accounts. Nothing grander would have been feasible in the colony.[51]

FIGURE 1.39. *The landward facade at* **Mount Airy** *(Richmond County, circa 1754–64), one of the finest still standing of Virginia's mid-Georgian mansions.*

On the exterior, Carter's Grove is one of the last and handsomest of Virginia's early Georgian mansions. Nearly contemporary is Mount Airy (Richmond County, circa 1754–64; FIGURE 1.39 ), an impressive five-part Palladian country house with pavilion and pediment characteristic of the Colonial mid-Georgian style. The design, adapted from James Gibbs's popular *Book of Architecture* (London, 1728; FIGURE 1.40 ), was reduced to a scale attainable in Virginia (seven bays instead of nine), and built with local materials (Aquia sandstone from northern Virginia and a peculiar dark sandstone quarried on the site). With its original interiors—later lost to fire—and extensive gardens, the house once had a grandeur unsurpassed in the colonies.[52]

Like Carter Burwell at Carter's Grove, John Tayloe II, the owner of Mount Airy, was not content with an existing plantation house to convey the exalted social position of the English gentry, to which his inherited wealth entitled him. In 1754 he sought advice from an accomplished builder and friend of the family, Edmund Jenings, whose house in Annapolis was renowned in its day and whose father had participated as a committee member in planning the large public buildings of Williamsburg. Jenings's response confirms that "Country & Climate," as he phrased it, remained the determinants in adapting English architecture to a new environment. Jenings recommended the fashionable and expansive country villa plan as appropriate for Virginia's "Cold . . . & Large Familys & frequently much Compan[y]."[53]

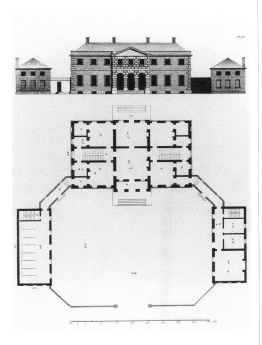

FIGURE 1.40. **"A Design made for a Gentleman in Dorsetshire,"** *plate 58 from James Gibbs,* Book of Architecture *(London: 1728), the source for the river facade at Mount Airy. (Photograph courtesy of the Virginia Historical Society.)*

FIGURE 1.41. **Blandfield** (*Essex County, circa 1769–74), was built by wealthy planter Robert Beverley after he returned from thirteen years of study and travel in England. The new house was to replace what he called his father's "old cabin" across the river.*

FIGURE 1.42. **Plate 63 from James Gibbs's *Book of Architecture*** (*London: 1728), one of several plates in Gibbs believed to be the design source for Blandfield.*

Across the Rappahannock River, Robert Beverley, after spending thirteen years studying and traveling in England, replaced his father's comfortable house, which he termed an "old Cabin," with a mansion more suited to the London manners to which he had become accustomed. Like Tayloe, he turned to Gibbs's *Book of Architecture,* finding there a plan and elevation for Blandfield (Essex County, circa 1769–74; FIGURES 1.41, 1.42 ), a five-part Palladian mansion built in brick. In ordering fashionable wallpapers for the house from a London merchant, he re-stated the Virginian's recurring dilemma: though he was conservatively "fitting [Blandfield] up in a plain neat Manner, . . . foolish Passion had made its way, Even into this remote Region," so that Beverley wanted the same "pretty" blue paper bordered with gilt leather that the Governor, Lord Botetourt, had installed at the Williamsburg Palace.[54]

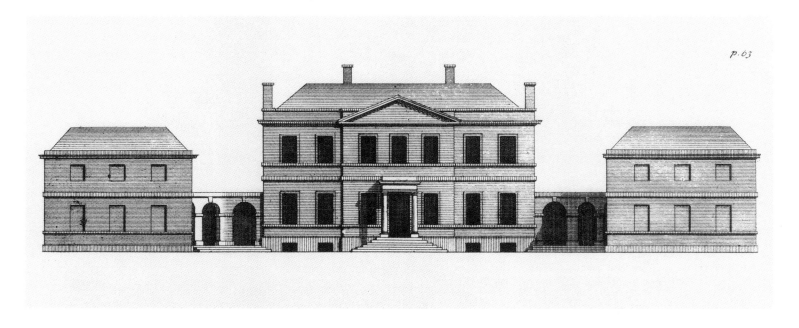

FIGURE 1.43. **Aquia Church** *(Stafford County, 1754–57), was influenced both by the Classical tradition that developed in Virginia and by models of church design from the colonies to the north.*

FIGURE 1.44. **Falls Church** *(City of Falls Church, 1767–70) expands on the rectangular church form.*

FIGURE 1.45. **Interior, Christ Church** *(Alexandria, 1767–73), shows an unusual arrangement also based on Northern church design: the pulpit is centered above the communion table. (Photograph taken in 1936 for the Historic American Buildings Survey; courtesy of the Library of Congress.)*

Particularly appropriate for the region's climate and the means of its builders was a single-pile, relatively small five-part Palladian villa published in Robert Morris's *Select Architecture* (London, 1755). Morris's type was adapted at Virginia houses like Battersea (Petersburg, circa 1765–75), which fully utilized the effects of light and ventilation that had made single-pile houses popular in the colony since the seventeenth century.[55]

## Classicism and Church Architecture at Mid-Century

While mansion-builders turned more often to English architectural books for new ideas, church-builders in the colony did the same, finding Classical designs they could incorporate as doors, altarpieces, and pulpits. And some northern Virginia builders devised taller elevations with two tiers of windows, following precedents in the architectural books but influenced more, it would seem, by church architecture in colonies to the immediate north. An early example that shows both changes is Aquia Church (Stafford County, 1754–57; FIGURE 1.43), built on the familiar Virginia cross plan.[56]

In Fairfax County, at Falls Church (1767–70; FIGURE 1.44) and Pohick Church (1769–73), the other popular Virginia church form, the rectangular type, was expanded in both plan and elevation. So that the sermon could be heard throughout the building, the pulpit was moved to the center of the north wall and the south door was shifted on center to match it. The chancel remained at the east end. The ceiling was raised to two stories. Underlying these major changes was an appreciation of the tall, symmetrical meeting-house with center-wall pulpit, which had been used by dissenting congregations in the neighboring colonies of Maryland and Delaware. Christ Church, Alexandria (1767–73; FIGURE 1.45) was influenced by a different northern type, one popular in urban settings: before an elaborate Palladian window at the chancel, the pulpit is centered above the communion table, an arrangement found nowhere else in Virginia.[57]

The northern Virginia churches were given finely crafted brickwork in the Anglo-Dutch tradition, with increasingly rich Classical detailing, both inside and out. For example, the sandstone doorways at Christ Church, cut in the Tuscan order, are boldly rusticated. For the interior, the vestry commissioned an equally elaborate pulpit, canopy, and altarpiece "in the Ionic Order." The same were ordered and built at Falls Church and the church at Pohick.[58]

## Valley Builders Borrow Continental Traditions

Just as religious architecture in Virginia added to its mix of ingredients the influence of northern churches, so the settlers of the Valley of Virginia melded German traditions—brought from their homeland via Pennsylvania—with the English Georgian style they carried westward. German and Scots-Irish settlers who migrated down the Valley left not only a tradition of log houses but also built as early as the mid eighteenth century imposing residences, churches, and

FIGURE 1.46. **"Fort" Stover** (*Page County, late eighteenth century*), *a stone house in the Valley of Virginia that has the traditional German three-room floor plan.*

FIGURE 1.47. **Mount Zion** (*Warren County, circa 1771*), *a massive stone house that exhibits both Georgian and vernacular influences.*

FIGURE 1.47 A. **Parlor Chimney Piece at Mount Zion** *shows a curious mix of Classical and folk motifs.*

Quaker meeting-houses in sturdy, local limestone—a favorite building material among the Pennsylvania Germans, perhaps recalling the Bavarian limestone of their fatherland. They brought along, as well, a Continental and Pennsylvania-German system of heavy roof-framing and a tradition of carved woodwork for the parlor. Some stone houses, like the misnamed Fort Stover (Page County, late eighteenth century; FIGURE 1.46) retain the traditional German vaulted cellar for storing food and drink and the three-room floor plan (the "Flurku-chenhaus" type), in which the kitchen is the third room. Yet the symmetrical, geometric form of these houses, with chimneys placed on exterior walls, is a direct influence of Virginia's continuing Georgian tradition.

The melding of Georgian and vernacular influences is particularly apparent at Mount Zion (Warren County, circa 1771; FIGURE 1.47), a massive and symmetrical Georgian mansion, with a compass-head window centered on one elevation (a Palladian window on the other front), yet little of the refined proportions so integral to the best buildings of the Tidewater region. Within is a vernacular style of carved woodwork. A folk-motif—the pinwheel—was chosen for one parlor, while the spectacular chimney piece in another ( FIGURE 1.47A ) is ultimately Classical and English in its inspiration, and surely unique.

This curious yet vigorous mix of disparate influences is found as well in the Valley's furniture production, which combines the painted folk tradition of Germany with English federal designs carried out of Baltimore. Although the blending is unique, the mixing of influences is entirely characteristic of architecture as it developed in the colony.[59]

### *The Lasting Legacy of Georgian Styles*

So strongly established and so widespread was Georgian architecture in colonial Virginia that it has never been forgotten in the state. Thomas Jefferson may have condemned its provinciality but he developed his architecture from within its tradition. For the planters of the early nineteenth century, English models provided a standard of architectural success. And as the Old Dominion lost its position of national leadership after 1830, its Georgian architecture came to stand as a strong symbol of the region's superior cultural heritage. Inevitably restored and endlessly revived, that same Colonial legacy has remained in the minds of architects who were active in Virginia. When the medievalist Ralph Adams Cram explained his Neo-Georgian design for Sweet Briar College (1901–06) as "pre-determined" by "history, tradition, and architectural style," he predicted the persistence of that tradition throughout the twentieth century.[60]

ACKNOWLEDGMENT

I am indebted to Charles Brownell, Cary Carson, Edward Chappell, Calder Loth, Carl Lounsbury, and Mark R. Wenger for suggestions and corrections that have been incorporated in this essay.

— W M S R

1. Hugh Jones, *The Present State of Virginia*, ed. Richard L. Morton (Chapel Hill: University of North Carolina Press, 1956), 71, 80 (Jones stresses the orientation of Virginians to London as opposed to provincial regions of England). The cultural and psychological bond between Tidewater Virginia and London was perpetuated by a reliance on material goods (Rhys Isaac, *The Transformation of Virginia, 1740–1790* [Chapel Hill: University of North Carolina Press, 1982], 15).

2. Clifford Dowdey, *The Virginia Dynasties: The Emergence of "King" Carter and the Golden Age* (Boston and Toronto: Little, Brown and Company, 1969), 352. Carter's statement was made in reference to a daughter's clothing.

3. Virginia settlers for the most part emigrated from the cities and surrounding countryside of London, Bristol, and Liverpool. English migration to all the New World colonies was slight in the early years of the seventeenth century compared to ten times that number who emigrated between 1630 and 1660. Immigration to Virginia was particularly heavy between 1660 and 1700. Tobacco production encouraged migration there and dictated a spread-out rural settlement along the region's many tidewater rivers that provided convenient avenues for shipping the crop and receiving English goods. Unlike the New England settlements, no social reform was attempted in Virginia. A thorough overview of the period is provided in Jack P. Greene, *Pursuits of Happiness: The Social Development of Early Modern British Colonies and the Formation of American Culture* (Chapel Hill and London: The University of North Carolina Press, 1988); see especially 5, 8–10, 13, 15, 18, 21, 26–29, 31, 34. See also Philip Alexander Bruce, *Economic History of Virginia in the Seventeenth Century* (New York: The Macmillan Company, 1907), 1: 104, 254, 320, 347, 401, 459; 2: 170, 244, 247; and Isaac, *Transformation of Virginia*, 71.

4. Anxious for raw materials like timber and metals, as well as products to be sold in European markets and secure harbors for the English fleet, and convinced that colonization was impossible without towns, London officials repeatedly encouraged the development of Jamestown from a swamp-surrounded, ever-decaying wooden village into a permanent metropolis built of masonry and with distinction. They never succeeded, for their goals stood in direct opposition to those of the colonists—whose opportunities lay far outside of Jamestown. The city was burned in Bacon's Rebellion of 1676 and never recovered its former prominence. By 1900 a good part of it was lost under the encroaching James River. See Bruce, *Economic History of Virginia*, 1: 10, 189; 2: 522–25; and John W. Reps, *Tidewater Towns, City Planning in Colonial Virginia and Maryland* (Williamsburg: Colonial Williamsburg, 1972), 22, 46.

The impermanent buildings were crudely constructed in multiple sizes: most were 16 or 20 feet deep and 24, 30, or 40 feet long. At least one was 52 feet long. The few early brick houses at Jamestown were as compact as 16 by 22 feet. Because the documentary evidence is frequently inconclusive, our knowledge of Jamestown architecture is based largely on archaeology, some of which was early and not adept: see, however, John L. Cotter's thorough study *Archaeological Excavations at Jamestown Colonial National Historic Park and Jamestown National Historic Site, Virginia* (Washington: National Park Service, 1958), 33–35, 40, 57, 60–66, 94–96, 102–09, 112–20, 129–31, 162–64; Reps, *Tidewater Towns*, 46–48, 50–51, 303; Bruce, *Economic History of Virginia*, 2: 148, 526–30, 534–35; and Forman, *Jamestown and St. Mary's*, 54–55, 102. For land deeds

with simple sketches of small houses, see the three volumes of the Ambler Family Papers in the Library of Congress. I would like to thank David Riggs, curator at the National Park Service, Jamestown, for sharing his knowledge of Jamestown architecture.

5. The significant feature of the Virginia post-hole house is the "false plate," a long horizontal beam—laid across the joists—to which the common rafters are easily attached, with their thrust contained, and with less of the complex joinery necessary in contemporary New England frame houses. See Cary Carson, Norman F. Barka, William M. Kelso, Gary Wheeler Stone, and Dell Upton, "Impermanent Architecture in the Southern American Colonies," *Winterthur Portfolio* 16 (Summer/Autumn, 1981): 135–78; Fraser D. Neiman, "Domestic Architecture at the Clifts Plantation: The Social Context of Early Virginia Building," in *Common Places, Headings in American Vernacular Architecture* (Athens and London: The University of Georgia Press, 1986), 292–314; and Bruce, *Economic History of Virginia*, 2: 145. Three earthfast buildings from the colonial period survive in tidewater Maryland: these are Cedar Park (Anne Arundel County, circa 1702), Sotterley (St. Mary's County, circa 1710), and an earthfast barn outside of Annapolis ("Impermanent Architecture," 174). A post-colonial earthfast barn has been located in southside Virginia (information courtesy of Cary Carson and Mark R. Wenger).

6. See Neiman, "Clifts Plantation," 307–11; Carson, Barka, Kelso, Stone, and Upton, "Impermanent Architecture," 143–44, 158–59, 163; Bruce, *Economic History of Virginia*, 2: 151–53; and Durand de Dauphine, *A Frenchman in Virginia, Being the Memoirs of a Huguenot Refugee in 1686*, copyright by Fairfax Harrison (privately printed, 1923), 111–13.

7. Berkeley's widow called Green Spring "the only tolerable place for a Governour" in Virginia. See Edward A. Chappell, "National Register of Historic Places Nomination for 'Governor's Land Archaeological District' " (Virginia Department of Historic Resources: July 1973); Louis R. Caywood, "Green Spring Plantation," *Virginia Magazine of History and Biography*, 65 (January 1957): 67–83; and Caywood, *Excavations at Green Spring Plantation* (Yorktown: Colonial National Historic Park, 1955). The L-plan was indicated by archaeology and sketched by B. H. Latrobe in 1796 (illustrated in Edward C. Carter, John C. Van Horne, and Charles E. Brownell, eds., *Latrobe's View of America, 1795–1820, Selections from the Watercolors and Sketches* [New Haven and London: Yale Univ. Press for the Maryland Hist. Soc., 1985], 101.)

8. Letter from Colonel Nicholas Spencer, 9 July 1680, "Virginia in 1680," *Virginia Magazine of History and Biography* 25 (1917), 144, cited in Reps, *Tidewater Towns*, 67. Virginia society matured at precisely the time New England's population began to decline. Slavery was not yet a dominant characteristic of Virginia society: slaves would increase from 10 percent of the population in 1700 to 40 percent by 1760. (See Greene, *Pursuits of Happiness,* 55, 81–84, 92.) There was no need to establish a heraldry office in Jamestown, as a contemporary English historian joked in 1708 (Oldmixion, *British Empire in America*, 2: 289, cited in Jones, *Present State of Virginia*, ed. Morton, 181), but wealthy Virginians behaved as if there were. Class distinction in late-seventeenth-century Virginia was readily apparent to visitors (see Durand, *A Frenchman in Virginia*, 21, 77, 95–96). However, social inequality in contemporary England was greater (see Greene, *Pursuits of Happiness*, 100.)

9. Richard Beale Davis, ed., *William Fitzhugh and His Chesapeake World, 1676–1701: The Fitzhugh Letters and Other Documents* (Chapel Hill: The University of North Carolina Press, 1963), 92, 142, 171, 173, 175, 202–03, 205, 215, 246, 366, 378–79, 382.

10. Daniel D. Reiff, *Small Georgian Houses in England and Virginia* (London and Toronto: University of Delaware Press, 1986), 131, 200.

11. "The Schedule of real and personal estate of Daniel Parke in Virginia . . . ," Emmet Collection 6077, Manuscripts and Archives Division, New York Public Library, cited in Jo Zuppan, "Father to Son, Letters from John Custis IV to Daniel Parke Custis," *Virginia Magazine of History and Biography* 98 (January 1990), 84.

12. The second-floor interior wood finishing of the Thoroughgood house has been tested by dendrochronology and dated to circa 1720. No study has been made of the first-floor joists because they are of pine, a more difficult wood for dendrochronology than oak. The nearby and similar Lynnhaven house, built with first-floor oak joists, has been dated by dendrochronology to 1723. (Information courtesy of Patrick Brennan of the Chrysler Museum, Norfolk, and Cary Carson.)

Tasteful one-and-a-half story hall-parlor houses of wood and brick were scattered throughout the Virginia colony and survive in considerable numbers. For several dozen examples, see Calder Loth, ed., *The Virginia Landmarks Register* (Charlottesville: The University Press of Virginia, 1986).

13. The chimney of Pear Valley was built as part of an earlier structure that pre-dated the present brick-end building. At some early date the house was covered with shingles that were pegged into place. Its clasped-purlin roof structure (horizontal, stabilizing purlins rest at the juncture of the rafters and collar beams) was rarely seen in early Virginia but is a known English type. See the following typescripts at the Association for the Preservation of Virginia Antiquities: Dell Upton, report of 10–25–76; Willie Graham, Orlando Ridout V, and Mark R. Wenger, "Pear Valley, Northampton County, Virginia," 7–21–86; William M. Kelso, "Archaeological Testing at Pear Valley, Virginia, 1987–88," 9–15–88; Edward Chappell, 4–30–91. I would like to thank Elizabeth Kostelny of the A.P.V.A. for providing me with those reports. See also H. Chandlee Forman, *The Virginia Eastern Shore and Its British Origins, Histories, Gardens & Antiquities* (Easton, Maryland: Eastern Shore Publishers' Associates, 1975), 48–54. The studies of Pear Valley point to its importance both as a rare survivor and as evidence of the sophistication of Virginia craftsmanship.

14. I am indebted to Cary Carson for telling me that the fragments of seventeenth-century plasterwork figures were part of the debris from the U-shaped building (Cotter's S–44–53–138) located on the site where the large Ambler house would be built in the next century, and were not original to the small, hall-parlor structure (S–31), where they were dumped and where Cotter states they were found. Cotter, *Excavations at Jamestown*, 25, 36–39, 45–51, 75–78, 121–29, 164. The long town-house rows measured 240 and 160 feet.

The archaeological and documentary evidence from Jamestown after mid century suggests a continued searching for an appropriate architecture. Central chimney placement was tried and rejected. Entry porches were introduced as a means to expand the hall-parlor plan. In response to the distress in London that so few masonry buildings existed in Jamestown, an act of the Virginia Assembly in 1662 called for the construction there of 32 brick houses, each at least 20 by 40 feet in size, with an 18-foot elevation beneath a 15-foot-tall roof (William Walter Hening, ed., *The Statutes at Large of Virginia* [Richmond: Samuel Pleasants, 1809–23], 2: 172). At best, only a few of the 32 houses were built. Perhaps the 18-foot elevation was derived from the standard 9-foot plus 9-foot floor heights of the two-and-a-half story London town house, a type without a raised cellar, described in 1700 as the "least sort of Building" in that city (J. Moxon, *Mechanick Exercises; or the Doctrine of Handy-Works. Applied to the Art of Bricklayers-Works* [London, 1700], 24). The call for walls "eighteen foote high above the ground" did not take hold in the colony, where the hot climate made taller ceilings much more comfortable. In 1705 Robert Beverley would boast in his history of the colony that Virginians were then making "their Stories much higher than formerly" (*The History and Present State of Virginia*, ed. Louis B. Wright [Chapel Hill: University of North Carolina Press, 1947], 289).

15. See Thomas Tileston Waterman and John A. Barrows, *Domestic Colonial Architecture of Tidewater Virginia* (New York: Charles Scribner's Sons, 1932), 30–35.

16. The foundation walls at Corotoman are a thick 30 inches. Carter L. Hudgins, "Archaeology in the King's Realm: Excavations at Robert Carter's Corotoman," *Notes on Virginia* 19 (Summer 1979), 28–31; Hudgins, "The 'King's' Realm: An Archaeological and Historical Study of Plantation Life at Robert Carter's Corotoman" (M.A. Thesis, Wake Forest University, 1981); Hudgins, "Patrician Culture, Public Ritual and Political Authority in Virginia, 1680–1740" (Ph.D. diss., College of William and Mary, 1984). Carter wrote to a London merchant regarding "a fine gay cloak" sent him: "It's fitter for an Alderman in London than a planter in Virginia, I love plainness and value my clothes more for their use than their finery" (Dowdey, *Virginia Dynasties*, 352).

17. Dell Upton, *Holy Things and Profane: Anglican Parish Churches in Colonial Virginia* (New York and Cambridge: Architectural History Foundation/MIT Press, 1986), xiv, 4–6, 35, 47, 57, 74, 103, 114, 119–20, 133, 139. Upton's book is a thorough study of Virginia's colonial Anglican churches. Even though gifts of church silver, almost invariably commissioned from London silversmiths, were received from parishioners since early in the century, church architecture of merit was as slow to appear as its domestic counterpart. See Helen Scott Townsend Reed, *Church Silver of Colonial Virginia* (Richmond: Virginia Museum of Fine Arts, 1970).

18. Upton, *Holy Things and Profane*, 38–39, 56–65, 72, 203–04; Cotter, *Excavations at Jamestown*, 17–22. A comparable structure, though one heavily restored, is St. Peter's Parish Church (New Kent County, 1701–03); also similar was the lost second Bruton Parish Church (Middle Plantation [Williamsburg], 1681–83). St. Luke's Church and Bacon's Castle are related in materials and style.

19. Beverley, *History of Virginia*, ed. Wright, 289; Jones, *Present State of Virginia*, ed. Morton, 70.

20. Blair was ably aided in establishing the College by the philosopher John Locke, a member of the English Board of Trade who took an interest in Virginia's development, and by Queen Mary herself, who saw the institution as a means of improving her people. A royal charter was granted in 1693. See James D. Kornwolf, *"So Good A Design," The Colonial Campus of the College of William and Mary: Its History, Background, and Legacy* (Williamsburg: Joseph and Margaret Muscarelle Museum of Art, College of William and Mary, 1989), 13–22; Marcus Whiffen, *The Public Buildings of Williamsburg, Colonial Capital of Virginia: An Architectural History* (Williamsburg: Colonial Williamsburg, 1958), 4–6. Beverley called the College a "Nursery of Religion" (*History of Virginia*, ed. Wright, 99).

21. Kornwolf, *"So Good A Design,"* 14, 33–56, 75–78, 109–11; Whiffen, *Public Buildings of Williamsburg*, 18–32, 96–103.

Hadley answered to a building committee, which reported to him the site already selected and the requirements for the building but apparently was not involved with design or details of construction. As a surveyor, Hadley would have been capable of design (Moxon [*Mechanick Exercises*, 116] writes: "The drawing of Draughts is most commonly the work of a Surveyor").

22. See Carl L. Lounsbury, "Beaux-Arts Ideals and Colonial Reality: The Reconstruction of Williamsburg's Capitol, 1928–1934," *Journal of the Society of Architectural Historians* 49 (December, 1990), 373–89; Whiffen, *Public Buildings of Williamsburg*, 34–39, 50; Reps, *Tidewater Towns*, 146; Kornwolf, *"So Good A Design,"* 126–29. As at the College, simple geometry determined the dimensions of the Capitol: the wings were each 25 by 75 feet, the arcade 15 by 30 feet (changed in 1701 to 30 by 30 feet).

23. Whiffen, *Public Buildings of Williamsburg* 35, 42, 227–28; Carl Lounsbury, "The Structure of Justice: The Courthouses of Colonial Virginia," in *Perspectives in Vernacular Architecture* vol. 3 (Columbia: University of Missouri Press, 1989), 219–21. The first-floor walls of the Capitol were to be three brick-lengths thick, beyond even London requirements (two-and-a-half bricks thick) for four-story townhouses of distinction (Moxon, *Mechanick Exercises*, 25).

24. Whiffen, *Publick Buildings of Williamsburg*, 40–42, 228. Henry Cary, Sr., was a local builder who only four years earlier (in 1697) had undertaken an unpretentious courthouse at Yorktown (Edward M. Riley, "The Colonial Courthouses of York County, Virginia," *William and Mary Quarterly*, 2d. ser., 22 [October 1952]: 399–402). In 1702 room use of the Capitol was settled: the General Court would assemble in one wing, the House of Burgesses in the other, with the governor and his Council sitting in state on the *"piano nobile"* or second floor of one wing (Whiffen, *Public Buildings of Williamsburg*, 43–45). Jones called the Capitol "the best and most commodious pile of its kind that I have ever seen or heard of" (*Present State of Virginia*, ed. Morton, 69).

25. This subject is discussed at some length in Lounsbury, "The Courthouses of Colonial Virginia," 214–26.

26. As early as 1618 instructions from London urged that successive governors should reside in the same house (Forman, *Jamestown and St. Mary's*, 52). See Whiffen, *Public Buildings of Williamsburg*, 53–58; Kornwolf, *"So Good A Design,"* 134–35. If we can believe the excavated foundations of the burned Palace, its original off-center plan—if it was a double-pile variation of the hall-parlor house—was peculiar and a product of local influences. See Whiffen, *Public Buildings of Williamsburg*, 63–65.

27.   Dutch Palladian architecture of the seventeenth century had brought Classical balance and order into mix with a northern, Gothic-inspired, steep-roofed house form. The style was widely disseminated and reached England through travel and through publications by the Dutch architect Philips Vingbooms (1607/8–1678). English ties with Holland and her architecture were only strengthened by the Glorious Revolution and the accession in England in 1688 of Dutch monarchs. Thus in 1700 the Anglo-Dutch style was the most fashionable type the colonial gentry could emulate. See Kornwolf, "So Good A Design," 86–94, 111–12, 135–37; Whiffen, *Public Buildings of Williamsburg*, 61; Nancy Halverson Schless, "Dutch Influences on the Governor's Palace, Williamsburg," *Journal of the Society of Architectural Historians*, 28 (December 1969), 254–70.

Alexander Spotswood arrived as governor in 1710, in time to provide for the governor's house what a contemporary described as "considerable Improvements" (Sir William Keith, *History of the British Plantations in America* [1738], cited in Whiffen, *Public Buildings of Williamsburg*, 68). He devised "gates, fine gardens, offices, walks, a fine canal, orchards, etc." (Jones, *Present State of Virginia*, ed. Morton, 70). He filled the house with handsome furnishings like the "gilt Leather hangings, 16 Chairs of the same, two large looking glasses," and marble-top tables that he proposed for the second-story state room. Because these expenditures seemed lavish to conservative Virginians more accustomed to earthfast buildings, the house by 1714 was termed a "Palace." It was not completed until 1721. See Whiffen, *Public Buildings of Williamsburg*, 65, 88–93.

28.   The slow development of Williamsburg was noted by Jones, who in 1724 expressed "hope" that it would thrive (*Present State of Virginia*, ed. Morton, 71). By mid century the streets were still not paved. See Reps, *Tidewater Towns*, 141–85; Whiffen, *Public Buildings of Williamsburg*, 9–14; Kornwolf, "So Good A Design," 125–26. Earlier efforts in Virginia at town planning provided useful precedents for the Williamsburg planners (Reps, *Tidewater Towns*, 1–21, 65–91, 116). I am indebted to Mark R. Wenger for pointing out to me the mid-century building boom, first recognized by Pat Gibbs. At that time a number of projects were initiated in Williamsburg, many of them involving the construction of public assembly rooms.

29.   Marcus Whiffen, *The Eighteenth-Century Houses of Williamsburg: A Study of Architecture and Building in the Colonial Capital of Virginia* (Williamsburg: Colonial Williamsburg Foundation, 1960), 44–86.

30.   Upton, *Holy Things and Profane*, 31, 35, 69–70, 74–77, 95, 104–05. The south chancel door of the seventeenth-century English screened-chancel church was moved to the nave at the Christ Church Lower Chapel to diminish the traditional emphasis on communion. An earlier transitional building is Yeocomico Church (Westmoreland County, 1703–06), where only the traditional south (side) entry porch of the English parish church survives (*Holy Things and Profane*, 65, 71). Reverend Hugh Jones succinctly described the new Virginian Georgian church as "very strong and handsome, and neatly adorned" (*Present State of Virginia*, ed. Morton, 97).

Some of the earliest Georgian brick domestic buildings were the glebe houses of the church parishes: for example, for St. Anne's Parish (Essex County, circa 1719), Abingdon Parish (Gloucester County, circa 1724), Southwark Parish (Surry County, circa 1725). All are pictured in Loth, *Virginia Landmarks Register*.

31.   It can be argued that T-plan additions to earlier and simpler Virginia churches and houses influenced the Bruton Parish Church plan and that precedent existed in post-Reformation Scottish church design (see Upton, *Holy Things and Profane*, 78–82; Whiffen, *Public Buildings of Williamsburg*, 83–84). Starting with the 66–foot length of the surveyor's chain, Spotswood drew for Bruton Parish "a platt or draught" based on the relationships of equilateral triangles and simple proportioning (Whiffen, *Public Buildings of Williamsburg*, 77–82). The church was copied in Hampton, Norfolk, and King and Queen County (Upton, *Holy Things and Profane*, 82, 84).

32.   The plan of Christ Church is a Latin cross, but because the sizable transept of the building equals its length, the whole structure has more of the centralized appearance of a Greek-cross church. A true Greek-cross plan would have given more cubical elevations, but it would have overemphasized the chancel, contrary to the interests of Virginia Anglicans. A carved stone font and elaborate carved tombs complete an ensemble of furnishings at Christ Church that established a standard of excellence for rural ecclesiastical architecture. Even the construction techniques used for the building were exceptional for their time and place. To span the 30-foot widths of the church a principal rafter roof was inadequate: a more sophisticated king-post truss system was employed. Christ Church inspired similar buildings in neighboring parishes of Lancaster County, Northumberland County, and Richmond County.

33.   Letter dated 23 February 1720/21, in the Fairfax Papers, Huntington Library, San Marino, California, quoted in Wayne Craven, *Colonial American Portraiture: The Economic, Religious, Social, Cultural, Philosophical, Scientific, and Aesthetic Foundations* (Cambridge: Cambridge University Press, 1986), 215.

34.   Jones, *Present State of Virginia*, ed. Morton, 87; Greene, *Pursuits of Happiness*, 85, 87, 93–94; Isaac, *Transformation of Virginia*, 34–43, 98, 131, 137; letter of 17 February 1737 from Peter Collinson to John Bartram, quoted in Craven, *Colonial American Portraiture*, 230. In England at the same time, circa 1715–45, an enormous amount of building took place (Reiff, *Small Georgian Houses*, 174).

35.   See Reiff, *Small Georgian Houses*, 166–73, 288–94; Betty Crowe Leviner, "The Pages and Rosewell," *Journal of Early Southern Decorative Arts* vol. 13, no. 1 (May 1987), 1–51. Page undoubtedly indentured highly skilled and experienced English craftsmen, who must have arrived with adequate memories and probably better sketches of houses they had built in or near London. The similarity of their work at Rosewell with the detailing at Christ Church, Lancaster County, suggests the probability of the exchange of ideas and craftsmen in colonial Virginia.

36.   Theodore R. Rhinehart, ed., *The Archaeology of Shirley Plantation* (Charlottesville: University Press of Virginia, 1984), 62, 67–69, 74–75, 81, 86, 95, 97, 117, 124, 149. See also Catherine M. Lynn, "Shirley Plantation, A History" (M.A. thesis, University of Delaware, 1967). Shirley is related in plan to the Williamsburg Palace and to Rosewell: apparently all are adaptations of the traditional hall-parlor layout to the double-pile house. At Shirley two of those plans are combined, one reversed, in what would seem to be an imaginative local solution.

37.   Durand, *A Frenchman in Virginia*, 98; Upton, *Holy Things and Profane*, 165–66; Beverley, *History of Virginia*, ed. Wright, 291; Mark R. Wenger, "The Dining Room in Early Virginia," in *Perspectives in Vernacular Architecture* vol. 3 (Columbia: University of Missouri Press, 1989), 149–57; Hunter Dickinson Farish, ed., *Journal and Letters of Philip Vickers Fithian, 1773–1774: A Plantation Tutor of the Old Dominion* (Williamsburg: Colonial Williamsburg, 1957), 80. See also Edward Chappell, "Williamsburg Architecture and Social Space," *Fresh Advices* (Colonial Williamsburg, November 1981): i-iv.

38.   William M. S. Rasmussen, "Sabine Hall, a Classical Villa in Virginia," *Journal of the Society of Architectural Historians*, 39 (December 1980): 286–96. The present facades and the major rooms are illustrated in this article.

39.   The date for Stratford has been established by dendrochronological study of beams in the house; Marcus Whiffen, "Some Virginia House Plans Reconsidered," *Journal of the Society of Architectural Historians* 16 (May 1957), 17–19. I would like to thank Carl Lounsbury for alerting me to the precedent of Georgian H-plan houses like Belton.

40.   From their architectural evidence, the lower rooms in the garden wing at Stratford seem to have been designed as work areas for servants. See inventories of 1758 and 1776, cited in William M. S. Rasmussen, "Stratford Hall" (unpublished research paper, Stratford Hall Library, 1982).

41.   Letter of 26 March 1765 from Stephen Hawtrey to Edward Hawtrey, in the Faculty/Alumni file, Swem Library, Archives, College of William and Mary, cited in Mark R. Wenger, "The Central Passage in Virginia: Evolution of an Eighteenth-Century Living Space," in *Perspectives in Vernacular Architecture* vol. 2 (Columbia: University of Missouri Press, 1986), 140; Jones, *Present State of Virginia*, ed. Morton, 71. For a discussion of the Virginia passage, see Wenger, 137–49; Dell Upton, "Vernacular Domestic Architecture in Eighteenth-Century Virginia," *Winterthur Portfolio*, 17 (Summer/Autumn 1982): 103–06; and Reiff, *Small Georgian Houses*, 130–40. An unusually early reference to a Virginia passage was found by Bruce (*Economic History of Virginia* 2: 182) in the inventory of the house of Mrs. Elizabeth Digges (records of York County, 1690–94, 213).

42.   I am indebted to Cary Carson and Edward Chappell for providing me information about dating the Ambler house. In examining the archaeological evidence from the site, they have found that demolition debris that filled the cellar of the earlier structure contained eighteenth-century materials that could not have found their way into such a context if the Ambler house was already standing. Reiff, *Small Georgian Houses*, 123–24, 141–61, 234–35; Cotter, *Excavations at Jamestown*, 28.

43.   Carlyle wrote on November 12, 1752: "I have had a very troublesome year. I am now out of hopes of getting into my house this winter. The violent rains we have had this fall has hurt the stone walls. We was obliged to take [them] down after it was nigh its height. It's a pleasure to build in England but here, where we are

obliged to do everything with one's own servants and thise Negros make it require constant attendance & care, so much trouble that if I had suspected it woud [have] been what I have met with I believe I shoud [have] made shift with a very small house!" (Carlyle Family Papers, Virginia Historical Society; cited in Mills Lane, *Architecture of the Old South: Virginia* [Savannah: The Beehive Press, 1987], 62).

44.   See Mark R. Wenger, "Westover: William Byrd's Mansion Reconsidered" (M.A. thesis, University of Virginia, 1981)(the dependencies with Flemish gables are shown in Wenger's fig. 65 [a sketch from the journal of Robert S. Glennie, 1811, Firestone Library, Princeton]); Edward Chappell, "Looking at Buildings," *Fresh Advices* (Colonial Williamsburg) (November 1984): v-vi. In 1735 Byrd had "got a person to make a draught of [his house]" (pp. 98–100), but was this the old house or a new one? See Upton, *Holy Things and Profane*, 239, n. 7, regarding the possibility of a later date. Wenger has shown that the interiors of Westover post-date the 1749 fire that may have gutted the building (see pp. 42–60). The Westover gardens in 1736 impressed visiting Philadelphia botanist John Bartram (p. 96).

45.   Wenger, "Westover," 86–101; Craven, *American Portraiture,* 203–13; David Meschutt, "William Byrd and His Portrait Collection," *Journal of Early Southern Decorative Arts* vol. 12, no. 1 (May 1988): 19–46. See also Mark R. Wenger, ed., *The English Travels of Sir John Percival and William Byrd II: The Percival Diary of 1701* (Columbia: University of Missouri Press, 1989).

46.   Just as Byrd's house had to be a local type, so his young children could be painted in Virginia only by the lesser hand of Charles Bridges, practically the only artist then active in the colony (Meschutt, "Byrd and His Portrait Collection," 36–38).
     Beyond the Classical doorcases, the Westover facades present an elegance and simplicity that is characteristic of the best Colonial American architecture. The elegance is achieved in part by a geometric proportioning of elements: the height of the house to the eaves, for instance, is half its length. The same effective proportioning, fine detailing, and restrained, tasteful use of brick-work characterize as well a number of smaller, superbly designed Virginia mansions, of which Salubria (Culpeper County, 1760s) is a representative example (pictured in Loth, ed., *Virginia Landmarks Register*, 114). Those buildings prove the point that the essence of Virginia Georgian design lies not in size or opulence but in the relation of parts to the whole and in craftsmanship.

47.   Indian Banks, an L-plan house, and Lansdowne (Urbanna, mid century), a T-plan house, are two of the most handsome and functional Georgian structures built in the colony. (Lansdowne is pictured in Loth, ed., *Virginia Landmarks Register*, 274). For a discussion of room usage, see Upton, "Vernacular Domestic Architecture," 106–14.

48.   From the start, colonists had been denied opulence as they secured the necessities of life. Early settlers told not to wear silk or weave gold in their clothing had become accustomed to simplicity (Bruce, *Economic History of Virginia*, 2: 187). Throughout the seventeenth century most Virginians were in no way troubled by the undistinguished appearance of the post-hole houses that dominated the landscape. Marmion is illustrated in Lane, *Virginia*, 36–37.

49.   Gambrel-roof houses in Williamsburg, like the Lightfoot and Tayloe residences, are pictured in Whiffen, *Houses of Williamsburg*, 131, 134, 150, 152, 186–87. Another alternative for the Virginia planter of some means was to adapt the hipped roof of the Georgian mansion to the small hall-parlor house, producing a variation called a clipped gable, as seen, for example, at Mayfield (Dinwiddie County, mid century, pictured in Loth, ed., *Virginia Landmarks Register*, 124).

50.   Daniel Reiff has pointed out the similarity of the Frampton Court interiors, which he illustrates, to those at Carter's Grove (see *Small Georgian Houses*, 312–14). Burwell had purchased a copy of William Salmon's book *Palladio Londinensis*, perhaps to acquaint himself with architecture in general and its costs. Interestingly, it furnished at Carter's Grove only the impost detail of the arch in the entry hall. I am indebted to Mark R. Wenger, who has studied the house, for information about Bayliss's Charleston experience (discovered by Wallace Gusler) and for pointing out Bayliss's deviation from Salmon. See also Mary A. Stephenson, *Carter's Grove Plantation: A History* (Williamsburg: Colonial Williamsburg for Sealantic Fund, 1964).

51.   Stephenson, *Carter's Grove*, 25–56.

52.   The lost Mount Airy interiors, crafted by William Buckland, can at least be imagined when viewing the spectacular rooms by him that survive at Gunston Hall and at the Hammond-Harwood and Chase-Lloyd houses in Annapolis. According to a contemporary, the "large well formed, beautiful Garden" at Mount Airy even contained "beautiful Marble Statues" (William M. S. Rasmussen, "Palladio in Tidewater Virginia: Mount Airy and Blandfield," in *Building by the Book* 1 [Charlottesville: University Press of Virginia for the Center for Palladian Studies in America, 1984], 75–85).

53.   Rasmussen, "Palladio," 77–78. See also Maurer Maurer, "Edmund Jennings and Robert Carter," *Virginia Magazine of History and Biography* 55 (1947): 20–30.

54.   Rasmussen, "Palladio," 85–93.

55.   See the Skipwith family drawing (survey no. 2) of a similar house. Battersea is illustrated with that entry.

56.   Upton, *Holy Things and Profane*, 88–89, 107–08, 127, 133–34, 230.

57.   For a full explanation of these changes and influences, see Upton, *Holy Things*, 89–95. The central-entrance meeting-house form collided with the Virginia rural church tradition in buildings like Lamb's Creek Church (King George County, 1770), a simple rectangular type expanded to an 80-foot length to seat a large congregation. With the pulpit at the center of the north wall, no pew was too far distant. Lamb's Creek Church is pictured in Upton, 91.

58.   See Upton, *Holy Things*, 133, 137. The churches of northern Virginia proclaim with vigor the traditional prominence in the colony of Anglican authority at a time when it was newly threatened by movements of religious dissenters (Greene, *Pursuits of Happiness*, 97–98).

59.   A surviving but post-colonial example of Valley log construction is the Baxter house in Rockingham County (pictured in Loth, ed., *Virginia Landmarks Register*, 411). One half of the cabin is constructed with dovetail corner notching and tightly fitted logs, in the German tradition; the other half follows the Scots-Irish method of filling the gaps between rough-cut logs with a "chinking" compound. See Edward A. Chappell, "Architecture in the Shenandoah Valley: Rhenish Houses of the Massanutten Settlement," in *Common Places, Readings in American Vernacular Architecture* (Athens and London: The University of Georgia Press, 1986), 27–57; K. Edward Lay, "European Antecedents of Seventeenth and Eighteenth Century Germanic and Scots-Irish Architecture in America," *Pennsylvania Folklife* 32 (Autumn 1982): 2–43. The carved interiors of Mount Zion may postdate the Revolution.

60.   Ralph Adams Cram, *My Life in Architecture* (Boston, 1936), cited in S. Allen Chambers, Jr., *Lynchburg, An Architectural History* (Charlottesville: University Press of Virginia, 1981), 369.

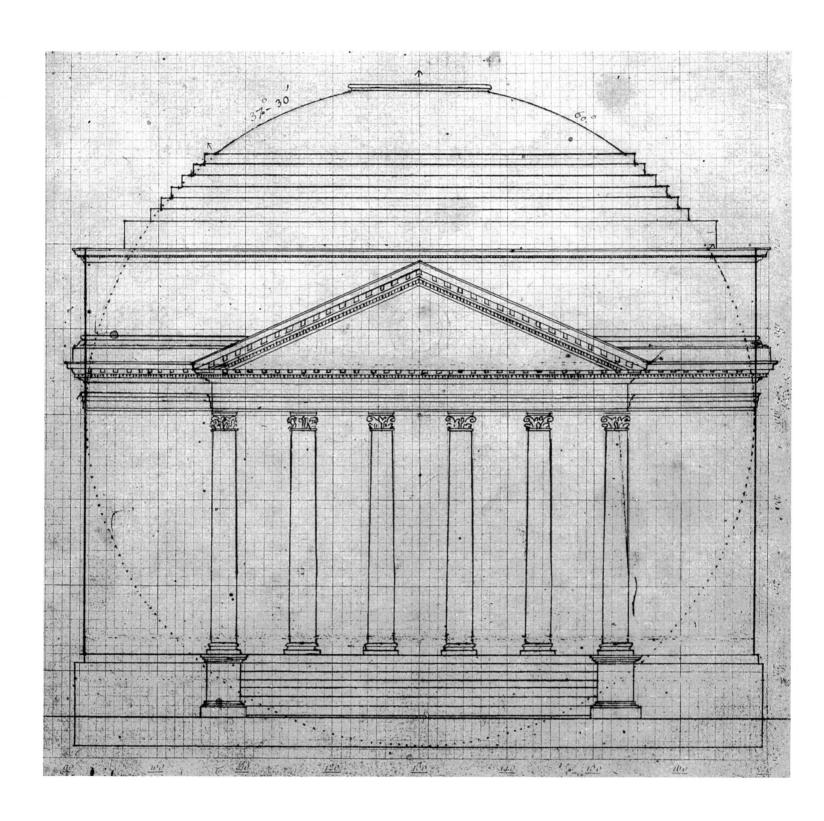

# 2

# LAYING THE GROUNDWORK

*The Classical Tradition and Virginia Architecture, 1770–1870*

by CHARLES E. BROWNELL

When studying the development of architecture in Virginia from the early seventeenth century to the late nineteenth century, one sees the coming of elements from northern Europe, the coming of elements from the Classical tradition of southern Europe, and the emergence of buildings that cannot be mistaken for European architecture. The story is rich and complex, and does not follow a simple sequence. This chapter offers a preliminary sketch of the second theme, the relations between Virginia architecture and the tradition that dominated Western European architecture from the Renaissance to the age of Neoclassicism. These observations radiate from one central thesis: that, beginning with a sprinkling of ornamental details in the seventeenth century, and proceeding to more fundamental debts, stylish American architecture, down to the mid nineteenth century, normally reflected the authority that the Classical tradition wielded in European architecture of the same period. More precisely, this thesis deals with the deliberately stylish architecture—sometimes called academic architecture—built in North America by those inhabitants whose cultural roots lay in Great Britain or on the Continent.

The chronological limits for this essay—the century between the beginning of Thomas Jefferson's work as an architect and the crystallization of so-called High Victorian taste in Virginia—were set as a matter of expedience in distributing the work for a publishing project of this scope; to tell the full story of the Classical tradition in Virginia would require going back farther. But the present limits permit one to sketch out how the tradition passed through two key phases. It reached its peak not only in Virginia, but also in the United States at large (due to the primary influence of Thomas Jefferson, with B. Henry Latrobe just behind him). Later, the authority of that tradition dissolved in North America, as abroad, marking the end of an epoch.[1]

*Thomas Jefferson's **Elevation for the Rotunda** at the University of Virginia, circa 1817–21 (see survey no. 27), brings together two of the most noble elements from the Classical tradition, the pure geometry of the sphere and a lofty Corinthian order.*

A matter of continuity, then, underlies this chapter, as well as the essay on architectural graphics in Chapter 4, and the commentaries on architectural drawings in the survey. Art historians have assembled a vast assortment of labels that can distract one's attention from this continuity. Some of these labels refer to broad phenomena, as in the case of *Mannerism* or *Palladianism*; others designate subordinate categories, as in the case of *Anglo-Netherlandish Mannerism* or *British Palladianism*. Such terms can work well as long as one sees the phenomena to which they refer as different members of the same family. But some historians see these developments as a succession of discrete styles, a misconception to which American specialists seem prone. However much anyone chooses to debate the soundness of European stylistic labels (such as *Mannerist*) or the legitimacy of such labeling altogether, one must admit that many of the terms used for North American buildings do nothing to acknowledge the continuity of Classical influence in Western culture. To eliminate this and other factors that can cause confusion, this author avoids many familiar stylistic terms, such as *Georgian* and *Federal*. (How often have American specialists declared that the "Federal style" represents a turn toward Classical influence *in place of* "Georgian influence" [sic]?) This chapter offers, instead, what the writer believes to be the least misleading stylistic labels, along with labels referring to *building type* or *typology* (such as the *Temple Revival*, discussed below).

To help trace the history most readily, this chapter follows chronological order. It begins not with the appearance of ambitious Classical buildings in Virginia during the later eighteenth century, but with the British developments that underlie those Virginia structures. It closes in the 1870s, when an architect faced a choice of alternatives to the tradition of Ictinus, Vitruvius, Palladio, and Lord Burlington.[2]

## A Bird's-Eye View of the Movements

The reader will grasp the ideas presented in this chapter more quickly by glancing first at the largest patterns. Let us begin by considering a mighty surge of classicizing influence, the *British Palladian Movement*, and two accompanying phenomena, the impact of James Gibbs and the burgeoning British receptivity to natural scenery. The development of British Palladianism in what later became the United States tended to break into two parts, a wave of activity from the middle of the eighteenth century to the Revolutionary War, and a second wave at the end of the century. In Jefferson's work, British Palladianism and its concomitants underwent such a metamorphosis that the results need their own label: *Jeffersonian Palladianism*.

The second Palladian wave coincided with the coming of the *Neoclassical Movement*. Neoclassicism resembled British Palladianism in being a reform movement, but differed in being international rather than merely British; in affecting many arts rather than just architecture and the allied arts; in drawing upon a far greater range of architectural sources; and in inaugurating the Modern Era of architecture, if one accepts the mid eighteenth century as the border

FIGURE 2.1. *Portrait of* **B. Henry Latrobe** *(1764–1820), by the great American portraitist Charles Willson Peale, circa 1804. (Photograph courtesy of the White House archives.)*

FIGURE 2.2. *Portrait of* **Thomas Jefferson** *by the prolific American portraitist Gilbert Stuart, circa 1805–07. (Photograph courtesy of the Bowdoin College Museum of Art, Brunswick, Maine.)*

across which our epoch lay. The expressions of Neoclassicism, from the mid eighteenth to the mid nineteenth century, belong simultaneously to the tradition established in the Renaissance and to a Modern world that, during this same hundred years, replaced much of the Classical tradition. Traits of the Modern Era include the multiplication of building types and the emergence of architecture as a profession, comparable to law or medicine.

In the British Isles, the *First Phase of Neoclassicism* became a force to reckon with in the 1760s when Robert Adam, William Chambers, and James Stuart offered their quite diverse approaches to architecture.[3] The brief *Second Phase* belonged especially to the 1790s and to such leaders as George Dance the Younger and John Soane. Both phases began to exert a major influence on North America only in the 1790s—at the very time that British-American Palladianism enjoyed a peculiar "Indian Summer." The American giant of the first phase of Neoclassicism was Charles Bulfinch, and that of the second was B. Henry Latrobe (1764–1820; FIGURE 2.1). Palladianism largely faded away at the start of the next century. But it persisted in the work of Thomas Jefferson (1743–1826; FIGURE 2.2), who gave his individual transformation of British Palladianism its finest expressions in the first quarter of the nineteenth century, some hundred years after the movement, long-dead in Britain, had arisen there.[4] Despite Continental and particularly French elements in these developments, and despite the persistence of Continental traits in various ethnic enclaves, the United States remained, architecturally speaking, a set of provinces of Great Britain.

An Hellenic element, important in the First Phase of Neoclassicism and much more important in the second, continued to grow stronger. Because it is probably too late to eliminate the dubious label *Greek Revival*, it is probably best to feel satisfied with restricting its use to a set of Neoclassical possibilities that flourished from the later 1820s. The 1840s saw the United States embrace two other late manifestations of Neoclassicism, the *Palazzo Revival* or *Renaissance Revival*, and the *Italianate Villa*, both of which would evolve into "Victorian" forms at various degrees of distance from Neoclassicism.[5]

At mid century, however, the central authority of the Classical tradition had begun to crumble, even in conservative North America. It faced successful challenges from possibilities that had developed for decades, including possibilities that had once worked in harmony with Classical architectural styles. The rediscovery of medieval architecture, a renewal of Northern European traditions, became impassioned. In some American quarters, as in some European ones, the *Gothic Revival* actually became intense enough to discredit architecture from the Renaissance through Neoclassicism. Like the adulation of Greece, this attitude is a fundamental one of the Modern Era, but its representatives have often failed to recognize that they had read ideas from the Classical tradition into medieval buildings. For although the Classical tradition had lost its central authority, it has continued to contribute to the evolution of architecture down to the present. It has had its part to play in one of the most important Modern architectural phenomena, the willingness to unite elements from the Classical legacy, the medieval past, vernacular and folk architecture, non-Western sources, and the unique circumstances of modern life. In the array of possibilities available around the time of the Civil War, one begins to detect an all-important option for the future: the use of Continental ideas—above all, French ideas—to pry American architecture away from its British provincial status.

## British Palladianism and Its Accompaniments

By the early 1740s, three related sets of design possibilities had begun to show up in the colonies. Foremost came a Classical movement—already past its prime in Britain—best called *British Palladianism*.[6] This phenomenon incorporated much of what made the Classical tradition compelling to Western designers from the Renaissance to Neoclassicism. Therefore, we shall give it a somewhat more detailed look than its successors, in order to understand issues that, operating throughout that tradition, showed up in those later movements as well as in the Palladian one. At the same time, we shall gain a sounder understanding of Virginia's greatest architect, one of the supreme representatives of the Palladian tradition, Thomas Jefferson.

In a variation of a theory that the Renaissance Italians had established, the British Palladians believed that the "ancients" in the Mediterranean world had extracted the eternal, reasonable laws of architecture (and of all the other arts) from Nature. The Italian architect Andrea Palladio (1508–1580) had supposedly surpassed all the other Continental "moderns" (the other architects since the beginning of the Renaissance) in recovering those laws. And, said this theory, Inigo Jones (1573–1652) had brought these changeless principles to Britain. It is this doctrine—that true architecture rested on the threefold authority of Nature, Reason, and Antiquity—that had made the Renaissance tradition almost irresistible in Western architecture. Scholars have argued for the humanistic doctrine's affinities with the Enlightenment and British liberalism in the Augustan Age of the early eighteenth century.[7] Alexander Pope, the great poetic interpreter of that age, cast the doctrine in eminently quotable lines, such as those from his "Essay on Criticism," which Robert Morris (circa 1702–1754), chief theorist of British Palladianism, placed on the title page of his *Essay in Defence of Ancient Architecture* (London, 1728):

> Learn hence for Ancient *Rules* a just Esteem;
> To copy Nature is to copy Them.[8]

These lines can stand for something much larger than any British Palladian issue. An architectural theory that convincingly claims the authority of Nature's laws has enormous force. Pope's lines suggest why the development that began with Filippo Brunelleschi (1377–1446) in fifteenth-century Florence took over the central place in Western architecture, in metamorphosis after metamorphosis, until the mid nineteenth century. It had the momentum to outlast the decline of the Humanism that originally propelled it and, even more impressively, to resist devastating assaults during the first century of the Modern Era. With most of the American architects who accepted the tradition—such as Thomas Jefferson, B. Henry Latrobe, and Alexander J. Davis—one has at best a fragmentary understanding of why they did so. An inability to name the specific reasons for their acceptance makes it all the more important to recognize the general potency of the tradition.

For the phase of that tradition under review here, the name *British Palladianism* seems the one to use, rather than any of the current alternatives. The term *Anglo-Palladianism*, for instance, acknowledges only the English element in a movement that had many important results elsewhere in the British Empire; while the label *Palladianism* should rightly embrace all of the developments that paid allegiance to Palladio's work, not just those that took place in the English-speaking world.

But none of the possible labels expresses a fundamental truth: "Palladianism" in the British Empire does not mean simply the influence of the great North Italian master, but rather his influence as reshaped extensively first by his disciples on the Continent and then by those in the English-speaking world. The history of Virginia architecture would look very different but for such reinterpreters of Palladio as Vincenzo Scamozzi (1552–1616); Roland Fréart, Sieur de Chambray (1606–1676); Inigo Jones (1573–1652); John Webb (1611–1672); Giacomo Leoni (1686?–1746); Colen Campbell (1676–1729); Richard Boyle, third Earl of Burlington (1694–1753); William Kent (1685–1748); Robert Morris (circa 1702–1754); and Isaac Ware (died 1766). Their literary activities—writing, editing, and translating—gave wings to their influence. To their publications one must add the torrent of inexpensive builders' guides by men who were anything but Palladian purists, chiefly Batty Langley (1696–1751) and William (died 1755) and John Halfpenny. This unique phenomenon of the popularizations (in historian Rudolf Wittkower's view) swiftly turned an imported manner for the few "into a truly national style."[9]

The Classical tradition fertilized European architecture from the fifteenth to the nineteenth centuries because it claimed to provide objectively valid standards of beauty, above all else in the area of proportion. The Roman architect and engineer Vitruvius (circa 90–circa 20 B.C.), author of the only known comprehensive architectural treatise in antiquity, bequeathed to history a body of proportional lore. For example, in a famous passage (3.1.3–4.), he asserted that Nature had set out the proportions of the parts of the human body to the whole in accordance with the geometry of both a circle and a square ( FIGURE 2.3 ), and that architects should apply the same principle to buildings. Some applications of ideal proportions commanded great interest. In the family of proportional systems derived from the square, Jones and his followers explored possibilities based on single or multiple cubes, as in Jones's single-cube entry hall at the Queen's House at Greenwich (1616–19; 1630–35), his double-cube Banqueting House in Whitehall (1619–22), and John Webb's Cube and Double-Cube Rooms at Wilton House, Wiltshire (1648–50; FIGURE 2.4 ). Some of the most important eighteenth-century designs in Britain and America descended from these schemes.

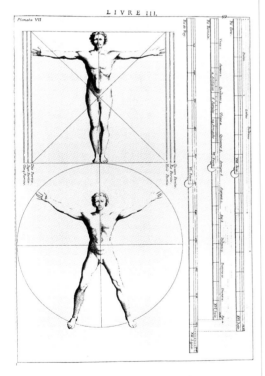

FIGURE 2.3. *These* **Diagrams of Human Proportions** *were meant to illustrate the harmonious relations between the parts and the whole. The Roman architect Vitruvius urged that architects use such proportions in buildings. This illustration comes from the French edition of Vitruvius that Thomas Jefferson supposedly owned before 1775. (Plate 7 from Book 3 of Vitruvius as illustrated in* **Dix Livres,** *translated from the Latin by Claude Perrault [2nd ed., 1684].)*

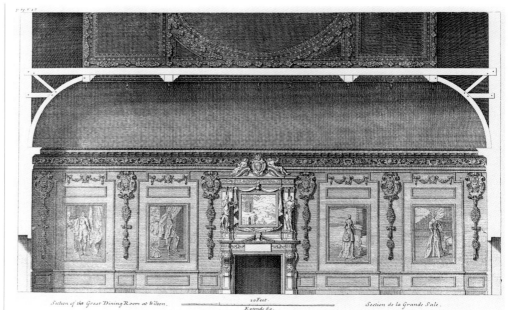

*p. 23. v. 2*

Section of the Great Dining Room at Wilton.     10 Feet. Extends 60.     Section de la Grande Sale.

FIGURE 2.4. *This* **Section of the Great Dining Room at Wilton** *shows a room created according to the proportions of a double cube by John Webb at Wilton House in Wiltshire, England, 1648–50. In the Vitruvian tradition, Webb's teacher Inigo Jones had introduced "cubic" proportional systems to the English-speaking world, but such proportions became popular only later, in the eighteenth-century. (Plate 63 from Colen Campbell, et al.,* **Vitruvius Britannicus,** *vol. 2 [1717].)*

The consummate embodiment of supposedly ideal proportions, and the nearly ubiquitous one, however, is the Orders ( FIGURE 2.5 ). From the Renaissance through Neoclassicism, the Orders normally served as the main form of architectural adornment. An order might appear full-fledged, as freestanding columns carrying a complete entablature (a beam made up of architrave, frieze, and cornice), perhaps with the ancillary "ornaments" of pedestal and pediment. An order might appear in a relief variant with engaged columns or pilasters. It might show up as an *aedicule* (literally a "little building") or *tabernacle frame*, a combination of uprights and beam, often with a gable, used,

The Five Orders of **ARCHITECTURE** with their **PEDESTALS**.

FIGURE 2.5. **The Five Orders of Architecture** *illustrates an ideal set of columns, entablatures, and pedestals as devised by Andrea Palladio. The Orders served as the chief kind of architectural decoration from the Renaissance through Neoclassicism. (Plate 2 from Isaac Ware,* **Complete Body of Architecture** *[1755–1757].)*

FIGURE 2.5A. *These three* Designs for Rustick Doors *show variations on a framing element called an aedicule, one of the most widely used decorative applications of the Orders. (Plate 57 from William Kent's* Designs of Inigo Jones, *1727.)*

with widely varying degrees of freedom, for door- and window-cases ( FIGURE 2.5A ) and, often in double-decker form, for chimney pieces (see Chapter 4, FIGURE 4.9A ). Or it might put in a fragmentary appearance as an architrave wrapped around an opening, or a cornice carried along the top of a wall, sometimes with a continuous pedestal beneath.

As the essential form of ornamentation, the Orders claimed deep and explicit respect. Such tribute was in no sense peculiarly "Palladian." One of the most important statements of it available to the British Palladians—"The principal ornament in all Architecture certainly lies in Columns"—came from Giacomo Leoni's translation of the fifteenth-century treatise on architecture by Leon Battista Alberti (1404–1472).[10] Another—"In all Compositions of Architecture, the Column, being the principal Figure, should be perfect in its Proportions, as they are taught us by the Antients"—came from British architect James Gibbs.[11] And a more fitting characterization of the established role of the Orders (more fitting in that it did not limit itself to freestanding columns) came from the Neoclassical camp. Sir William Chambers (1723–1796) declared that "The Orders of Architecture . . . are the basis upon which the whole decorative part of the art is chiefly built. . . . In them originate most of the forms used in decoration; they regulate most of the proportions; and to their combination . . . arranged in a thousand different ways, architecture is indebted, for its most splendid productions."[12] The American builder-architect and architectural writer Asher Benjamin (1773–1845), lifting whole chunks out of Chambers, repeated this passage verbatim in the second (1811) through sixth (1827) editions of *The American Builder's Companion*, one of the sourcebooks most responsible for popularizing Neoclassicism in the United States.[13]

Thus swiftly it has become impossible to discuss British Palladianism without veering into the second set of design possibilities alluded to in the opening paragraph—the avenues paved by the versatile, individualistic James Gibbs (1682–1754).[14] The great eighteenth-century master of steeple design, and the man who united the Southern temple portico with the Northern spire at St. Martin-in-the-Fields (London, 1722–26; FIGURE 2.6 ), Gibbs as a church designer drew upon the legacy of Sir Christopher Wren and on the Late Roman

FIGURE 2.6. **A Perspective View of St. Martin's Church,** *plate 1 from James Gibbs's* Book of Architecture *(1728), reveals how, in this London church of 1722–26, Gibbs successfully combined the ancient Mediterranean temple portico with the Northern European steeple.*

Baroque rather than on the sources admired by British Palladians. Most churches in eighteenth-century Virginia did not have towers and none had temple porticoes. Unlike other regions, the full-blooded sequels to Gibbs's ecclesiastical achievement took place in Virginia only in the nineteenth and twentieth centuries ( SURVEY NO. 34 ).[15] (Virginia's unexecuted designs for freestanding Gibbsian towers [ SURVEY NOS. 7, 43 ] stand in a class by themselves.)

By contrast, the designs for houses in Gibbs's *Book of Architecture* (London, 1728) belonged to his own brand of Palladianism, and they played a major part in spreading the movement. Mount Airy (Richmond County, circa 1754–64; FIGURE 1.39 ), one of the pinnacles of British Palladianism in the colonies, depends for its most successful features not on a publication by one of the orthodox Palladians in Lord Burlington's circle, but on the plates published by Gibbs ( FIGURE 1.40 ). The interweaving of British Palladianism and Gibbs's designs is a crucial pattern, and one on which, to no small extent, the idea of a "Georgian style" rests. Thus the builders' guides often contain a mixture of designs taken from Jones and from Burlington's circle, with designs taken from Gibbs. The six editions of a book important for Virginia, Batty Langley's *City and Country Builder's and Workman's Treasury of Designs* (London, 1740) strikingly exemplify this mix.[16]

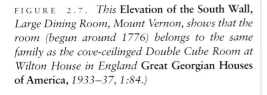

FIGURE 2.7. *This* **Elevation of the South Wall,** *Large Dining Room, Mount Vernon, shows that the room (begun around 1776) belongs to the same family as the cove-ceilinged Double Cube Room at Wilton House in England* **Great Georgian Houses of America,** *1933–37, 1:84.)*

FIGURE 2.7A. *This* **Portrait of the Young George Washington,** *painted by Charles Willson Peale in 1772, is the earliest portrait of Washington painted from life. (Photograph courtesy of the Washington/Custis/Lee Collection, Washington and Lee University, Lexington, Virginia.)*

What did British Palladianism (or rather, British Palladianism plus Gibbs) offer to Virginians? It offered standards. First, it offered proportional systems. Scholarship has not yet tracked Anglo-Palladian proportional systems very far in the New World. To Jefferson, the most important recipient, we shall come in a moment. Another important case regards the Large Dining Room at Mount Vernon (1774; FIGURE 2.7 ), a room that often passes simply as Neoclassical because of the decoration applied to it. But the form of this room assuredly belongs to the same British Palladian family as Wilton's cove-ceilinged, Double-Cube Room ( FIGURE 2.4 ), which had become a dining room by the early eighteenth century. George Washington (1732–1799; FIGURE 2.7A ), the statesman and gentleman-architect who gave shape to Mount Vernon, very likely meant his room to follow the arithmetic progression 2, 3, 4.[17]

FIGURE 2.8. **Gunston Hall,** *Fairfax County, 1755–and later.*

FIGURE 2.9. *For the woodwork in the* **Little Parlor at Gunston Hall,** *the accomplished architect and craftsman William Buckland used Ionic moldings and other elements suited to the Ionic order.*

FIGURE 2.10. *The* **Ionic Order of the Temple of Portunus,** *formerly called the Temple of Fortuna Virilis (from Chapter 14 of Fréart de Chambray's* **Parallel of the Antient Architecture,** *1722 edition), is the basis for the main cornice and the chimney-piece cornice in the Little Parlor at Gunston Hall.*

The British Palladian/Gibbsian publications furthermore offered proportions as embodied in that basis of architectural ornament, the Orders. The Orders came across in many guises, including aedicules, architraves bent around openings, and cornices alone or over continuous pedestals, with pilasters and other moldings omitted. How far North Americans respected proportional principles remains a question, but the doctrine of *decor* or propriety, rooted in Vitruvius, clearly had an impact here.[18] Following this tenet of propriety at Gunston Hall (Fairfax County, 1755 and later;  FIGURE  2.8 ), William Buckland (1734–1774) basically graded the Orders from the Doric for the most public and formal areas, through the Ionic, to the Corinthian for the most festive apartment, the so-called Palladian Room.[19] In this sequence, as a molding-by-molding comparison has revealed, the Little Parlor ( FIGURE  2.9 ), took its key from the entablature of the Ionic Temple of Portunus, formerly called the Temple of Fortuna Virilis (Rome, late second century B.C.;  FIGURE  2.10 ).

As Gunston Hall aptly illustrates, *decor* likewise legislated for an issue of correctness: in the most formal places, one must employ an orthodox handling of the Orders and their appendages; in other locations, one might break the rules. Though a British Palladian would not normally tamper with a pediment on a formal facade, he could break it—and its accompaniments, such as its entablature—into elaborated shapes for richer internal decoration. This distinction between the closed pediment on the exterior and the open one on the interior, and, more broadly, between the simple, orthodox use of a motif outside and the complex, licentious use of the same motif inside—shows up not just amid the splendors of Gunston Hall, but at countless more modest North American buildings as well. (One suspects that the distinction spread mainly because models in British pattern-books conformed with it.) Another widely disseminated treatment shows up on the exterior of Gunston Hall: Palladio's Ionic cornice ( FIGURE  2.13 ). Future research will almost surely establish that this cornice, satisfying in the lucid play of its concave and convex moldings, enjoyed phenomenally widespread use in North America and that, as the chief exterior ornament on numerous simple buildings, it brought them into the domain of the Orders.[20]

British Palladianism and Gibbs offered ideas on materials and planning. To Virginians, who customarily built in wood, they offered an ideal of durable masonry wall-construction. (The great days for masonry vaulting in the English-speaking world came later, with the second phase of Neoclassicism.) The books offered some planning ideas that bloomed late. A line of unforgettable re-creations of the Roman house—above all, Palladio's Villa Rotonda (Vicenza, 1565/66 and later; FIGURE 2.11), Scamozzi's Rocca Pisani (Lonigo,

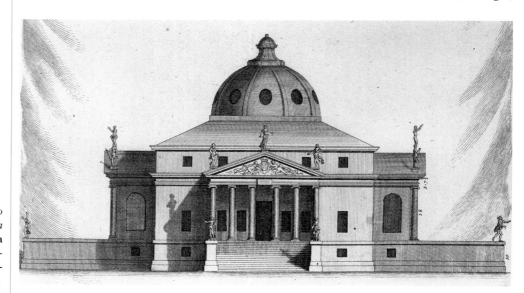

FIGURE 2.11. *Andrea Palladio's attempts to recreate the ancient Roman house reached a uniquely compelling form in the* **Villa Rotonda** *(Vicenza, 1565/66 and later), here altered in an illustration published by Giacomo Leoni in* **The Architecture of A. Palladio; in Four Books,** *2nd ed., 1721.*

1575–78), and Burlington's Chiswick House (London, circa 1730)—brought to the English-speaking world the rotunda-house. The numerous Virginia succession includes a whole aggregation of Jefferson designs for official residences, such as his "Building suited to a Public Officer" (1803; FIGURE 4.29) and Samuel Dobie's project for the U.S. Capitol (1792; FIGURE 4.28). Others include at least three Latrobe designs made in or for Virginia, such as the proposal for Clifton (Richmond, circa 1807; SURVEY NO. 20); Alexander Parris's Wickham House (Richmond, 1811–13; SURVEY NO. 24) and a series of Alexander J. Davis's designs, not least of all (by virtue of its circular upstairs hall) Belmead (Powhatan County, 1845–48; SURVEY NO. 38). Certain Palladians, chiefly Robert Morris, accepted and promoted the bow window, firmly authorized as a feature of the Roman house by a letter of Pliny the Younger (A.D. 62[?]–circa 113), specifically as interpreted by Robert Castell (died 1728).[21] Bow windows developed in Virginia from the 1770s; their popularity in the nineteenth century divorced them from any Classical association. Something of the sort also holds true for the general use of contrasting room-shapes within a house, a possibility that Burlington had explored as a supposed ancient treatment, but that came into its own only when the Neoclassicists picked it up and passed it on to the nineteenth century.

The British books offered another set of planning ideas. They illustrated countless variations by Palladio and his disciples on the theme of the bilaterally symmetrical country-house composition with a center joined to service dependencies, especially via colonnaded or arcaded walks (see FIGURE 1.42, Gibbs plate 63). Typically the walks have one closed wall, to conceal what were often utilitarian areas behind. On occasion—apparently rarely—a Palladian tried out the effect of a "transparent" wing with two open sides. At Mount Vernon, George Washington used this handling with enormous distinction when he treated the arcaded wings (1778–83; SURVEY NO. 5) as screens through which to view the Potomac scenery that he loved.[22]

With wings that were meant to frame the scene (and with bay windows, which are intimately associated with enjoying views) we come upon the third set of possibilities affecting design, those revolving around the British response to natural scenery, which is very likely the greatest contribution that Britain has made to the aesthetic life of Westerners. British Palladianism overlapped with the evolution of the love of scenery in eighteenth-century Britain. *Overlap*, of course, means that part of the evolution has an intimate connection with British Palladianism and part of it does not.

The intimate connection occurred with the emergence of the Picturesque movement.[23] This development depended on the principle that one could apply compositional standards from landscape painting to other arts, even to the works of Nature herself. The Picturesque fused with the irregular plans of the "English garden," the kind of gardening favored by the British Palladians, who veered away from the predominantly formal layouts of Continental practice. Britons learned to judge the open countryside as if it formed a series of pictorial compositions through which they could walk. This new sensitivity to "landskip" affected not just the settings of buildings but also architecture itself within the Palladian movement. Theoretically, Picturesque connoisseurship rested on paintings by Claude Lorrain (1600–1682; see FIGURE 2.12) and other Continental masters. But to the standards that Britons gathered from this static material, they added standards garnered from the shifting "pictures" that they found by walking through natural scenery.

The coexistence of the taste for geometrically ordered Palladian architecture and the taste for irregular settings has long piqued scholars' interest. The remainder of this chapter depends on the following line of thought: it seems unlikely that any two movements, however complementary, run truly parallel with each other. But from British Palladianism to the middle of the nineteenth century, Classical movements in British architecture were, if not precisely parallel with the Picturesque movement, inseparable from it. The Picturesque in fact has roots in the Classical tradition, and perhaps one should see it in origin as simply an outgrowth of that tradition. This author endorses the argument that the love of Classical architecture and the love of Picturesque landscape originally complemented each other because both appeared to conform with Nature, Reason, and Antiquity. But during the first half of the nineteenth century in Britain, affinities grew between the Picturesque and non-Classical developments. In this

half-century, the alliance between the Picturesque and the unclassical (most of all the rediscovery of Medieval architecture) played a role second to none in dethroning the Classical tradition. In North America, the discovery of Picturesque values proceeded more slowly than the acceptance of Classical architectural styles. But although belatedly, Americans reunited Palladianism and the Picturesque at sites as important as Mount Vernon ( SURVEY NO. 5 ) and Monticello ( SURVEY NOS. 7, 8, 12 ).

Another side of this landscape movement had little if any connection with Palladianism: the love of the Sublime. The devotees of the Sublime sought in Nature (as well as in the arts) for what would fill them with an elevating, soul-expanding awe. Such a response might be intense or serene and stilled. Like the Picturesque, the Sublime became the object of a mania in Britain in the later eighteenth century, and at that point the interest in both tastes surfaced in North America. The cult of the Sublime had important ties to the Classical tradition, but its greatest architectural importance lies in a split from Classical authority. The late eighteenth century bequeathed to the nineteenth the idea that the Gothic far exceeded Classical architecture in Sublime qualities, and that the Gothic therefore suited sacred purposes far better.[24]

### *The Architectural Achievement of Thomas Jefferson*

We do not often get to see what eighteenth-century Virginians thought of the European architectural repertory. With Jefferson, however, we have writings, drawings, and buildings that have much to tell us, though it may take years before that evidence speaks clearly.

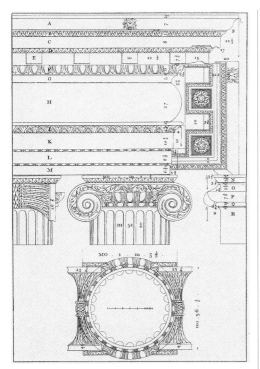

FIGURE 2.13. **Ionic Capital and Entablature,** *plate 20 from Book 1 of Palladio's* **Quattro Libri,** *1570 edition. Compare this with figure 2.14 to see how Jefferson's understanding of Palladio was distorted by his reliance on Giacomo Leoni's editions of Palladio's treatise.*

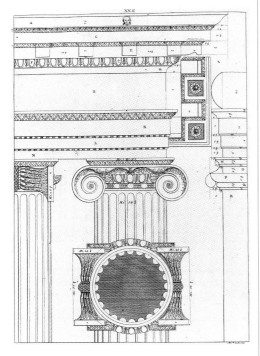

FIGURE 2.14. **Ionic Capital and Entablature,** *plate 22 from Book 1,* **Architecture of A. Palladio,** *as edited by G. Leoni, (2nd edition, 1721). Leoni boasted of having altered Palladio's designs.*

Jefferson's life (1743–1826) ties many strands together. To begin with, Jefferson belonged to America's first great artistic generation, a group of people born around 1740. Among his contemporaries were John Singleton Copley (1738–1815), Benjamin West (1738–1820), and Charles Willson Peale (1741–1827), the most important of the other practitioners of the visual arts.

It is the architectural strands, though, that concern us here. We can begin with the issue of architectural authority, which means the claims of the "ancients" versus the "moderns." Just what Jefferson believed about ancient architecture still needs much clarification, but his conception of it set his standards, and he preferred to model the most important public buildings on great ancient edifices. In 1786, apropos of the design for the Virginia Capitol (Richmond, 1786 and later; SURVEY NOS. 9, 10), he explained why: "two methods of proceeding presented themselves to my mind. The one was to leave to some architect to draw an external according to his fancy, in which way experience shews that about once in a thousand times a pleasing form is hit upon; the other was to take some model already devised and approved by the general suffrage of the world."[25] One must note that only a restricted portion of Jefferson's thinking about ancient architecture actually came from ancient sources. What he believed came largely from the "moderns," and not a very diversified group of "moderns" at that. Among the "modern" interpreters of antiquity, Palladio held first place in Jefferson's esteem. We have much other evidence that tallies with the report about a consultation with Jefferson, by Colonel Isaac A. Coles to General John Hartwell Cocke in 1816: "Palladio he said 'was the Bible.' "[26] As Frank H. Sommer has written, however, "between Palladio and Jefferson stood a barrier of neo-Palladianism," that is, the barrier created by the Palladio followers who reworked the Palladio legacy.[27] Thus, all his life Jefferson accepted as Palladio's *Quattro Libri* the corrupt editions of Giacomo Leoni, with plates that Leoni had boasted of altering for the better ( FIGURES 2.13, 2.14 ), and with impure texts.[28]

Roland Fréart, Sieur de Chambray, a French lover of both antiquity and Palladio who posthumously became one of the basic authorities for British Palladianism, left his mark on Jefferson, too. This began indirectly, for instance via Leoni's Palladio, which openly acknowledges some of Leoni's extensive debts to Fréart's edition of the *Quattro Libri* (Paris, 1650), and via Robert Morris's *Select Architecture* (London, 1755). Later the influence became direct, above all by way of Fréart's *Parallèle de l'architecture antique et de la moderne* (Paris, 1650), which Jefferson reputedly bought after 1789.[29]

William Kent's *Designs of Inigo Jones* (London, 1727)—which contained designs by architects other than Jones, such as Burlington—exerted a formative influence on Jefferson, as did Morris's *Select Architecture*.[30] Jefferson made great use of Gibbs's books. In his simultaneous purchase of copies of Kent's *Designs of Inigo Jones* and Gibbs's *Book of Architecture* in 1778 (as also in his architectural career more widely), one sees the characteristic confluence of the British Palladians and Gibbs.[31] (One also sees a characteristic American backwardness in the dependence on fifty-year-old publications.) Jefferson's architec-

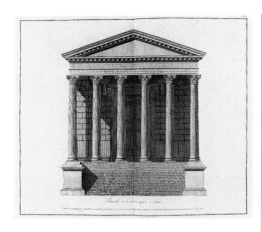

FIGURE 2.15. **Facade de la maison quarrée a Nismes,** *plate 2 from Charles-Louis Clérisseau's* **Antiquités de la France** *(1778). Jefferson came to see this temple as a great example of "cubic" architecture and used it as one of his principal models for the Virginia State Capitol at Richmond. (Compare survey no. 9, figure 1.)*

ture grew out of the books of a bookish movement. Latrobe, the professional who emphatically did not depend on a library when he designed, paid him a telling, qualified compliment in calling him an "excellent architect out of books."[32]

Jefferson left extensive but puzzling evidence regarding his sets of standards for proportions and for the orders. One can take it as a working hypothesis that he found ancient architecture authoritative because he saw it as the embodiment of proportional systems. He wrote that "the Capitol in the city of Richmond . . . is the model of the Temples of Erectheus at Athens, of Balbec, and of the Maison quarrée of Nismes [ FIGURE 2.15 ]. All of which are nearly of the same form and proportions, and are considered as the most perfect examples of cubic architecture, as the Pantheon of Rome is of the spherical."[33]

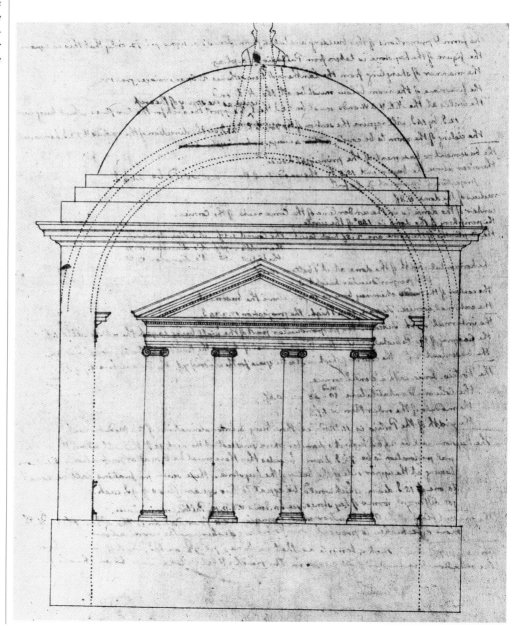

FIGURE 2.16. **Elevation of a Project for Remodeling the South Pavilion, Monticello,** *circa 1778 (Courtesy of the Massachusetts Historical Society). Jefferson must have taken a step toward his mature notions about "cubic" and "spherical" architecture when he made this unexecuted design for remodeling a square outbuilding of 1770 on the model of a miniature round temple (see figure 2.17).*

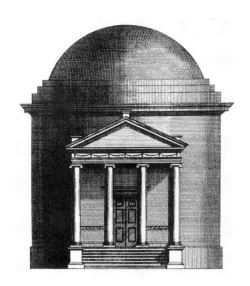

FIGURE 2.17. **Elevation of the Rotunda, Chiswick.** *Jefferson based the remodeling scheme for his South Pavilion on this miniature Pantheon, which Lord Burlington had designed for his garden at Chiswick by 1727. (Detail, plate 73, from volume 1 of William Kent's* **Designs of Inigo Jones,** *1727).*

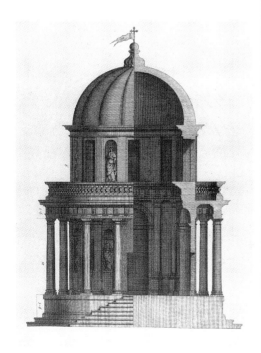

FIGURE 2.18. **Elevation of the Tempietto, Rome.** *For certain details of his South Pavilion project, Jefferson imitated examples of ideal geometry other than Burlington's Rotunda. Jefferson modeled the pavilion chimney on the finial of Donato Bramante's Tempietto (1502 [?]), as illustrated in plate 49 from Book 4 of* **Architecture of A. Palladio,** *ed. Giacomo Leoni, 2nd edition, 1721.*

With his Virginia Capitol ( SURVEY NOS. 9, 10 ) he had, in the 1780s, succeeded in building a monumental cubic temple. In the 1790s he hoped to see a giant spherical temple house the national legislature ( SURVEY NO. 11 ), but it took another thirty years (and prompting from Latrobe) before he brought the spherical scheme to realization at the University of Virginia (Charlottesville, 1817 and later) as the Rotunda ( SURVEY NO. 27 ).

No scholar has unriddled what Jefferson meant by "cubic" or "spherical" architecture, but the conception obviously fits into the line of descent from Vitruvius 3.1.3–4 ( FIGURE 2.3 ).[34] (Indeed, Jefferson may have acquired the second edition of Claude Perrault's translation of Vitruvius [Paris, 1684] early, before 1775.)[35] But Vitruvius seems to have had little to do with Jefferson's buildings overall, and one suspects that Jefferson formed his proportional ideas chiefly from books by "moderns." Assuredly his cube rooms, such as the dining rooms that he devised for his houses at Monticello and Poplar Forest (Bedford County, 1806 and later) grew, via eighteenth-century publications, from the tradition that Jones and his circle had founded in Britain ( FIGURE 2.4 ).[36] A significant place in the evolution of his ideas about proportion and about the imitation of temples must belong to Jefferson's project (circa 1778; FIGURE 2.16 ) for remodeling Monticello's square south pavilion (1770) into a rectangular version of the Rotunda, a miniature Pantheon that Burlington had designed by 1727 for his garden at Chiswick ( FIGURE 2.17 ). In other words, Jefferson proposed to revise a square building on the model of a round miniature temple that imitates the great example of spherical proportions, the Pantheon. His notes on the back of the drawing underscore the design's relation to ideal proportions. As models for details, he considered four "ancient" and "modern" buildings, such as Bramante's Tempietto (Rome, 1502[?]; FIGURE 2.18 ), the one "modern" edifice that Palladio had ranked with the temples of ancient Rome.[37]

For Jefferson, architecture revolved around the use of the Orders.[38] From near the beginning of his architectural activity to the culmination of that activity at the end of his life, he treated buildings as opportunities to display examples of the best Orders. The current study of his Orders continues to produce so many surprises—even shocks—that one can generalize only cautiously.[39] One hypothesizes that his last word on the subject, the Lawn of the University of Virginia ( SURVEY NOS. 26-28 ), depends on the idea of opposing the Doric, the Ionic, and the Corinthian of the greatest "modern," Palladio, on the west, to a great "ancient" Doric, Ionic, and Corinthian on the east. (The growth of the building program enabled him to add the group of especially rich orders at the head of the Lawn and the group of less desirable "ancient" and "modern" orders at Pavilions IX and X.)[40]

With the Orders, as with other architectural elements, Jefferson achieved a more-than-Burlingtonian purity. His use of the liberties permitted by the *decor* tradition seems remarkably spare. In 1822 he wrote of a favorite Order of his, the Doric of the Baths of Diocletian ( FIGURE 2.19 ), that the metopes "are all human faces, and so are to be those of our Doric pavilion [Pavilion I]. But in

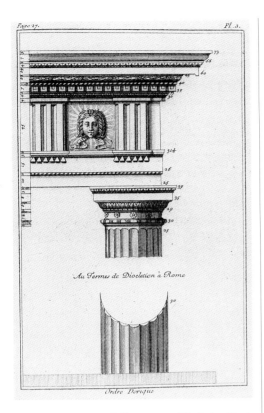

FIGURE 2.19. *Jefferson modified the* **Doric Order of the Baths of Diocletian** *for entablatures at Monticello and Poplar Forest. But he had the order copied more closely for the exterior of Pavilion I at the University of Virginia (figure 2.22) because he believed in following authoritative precedent more strictly in a public building. (Plate 3 from Fréart de Chambray's* **Parallèle de l'architecture,** *1766 edition).*

my middle room at Poplar Forest, I mean to mix the faces and ox-sculls, a fancy which I can indulge in my own case, altho in a public work I feel bound to follow authority strictly."[41] Without having combed the evidence, one suspects that he eschewed so conventional a breach of purity as the interior broken pediment.

Jefferson embraced the important ideas on materials and planning already enumerated here as offerings in the British Palladian/Gibbsian books. He inveighed against wooden buildings in his *Notes on the State of Virginia* (English edition, London, 1787) and promoted the masonry wall.[42] Apparently taking the Villa Rotonda ( FIGURE 2.11 ) as the ideal model for a civil official's house ( FIGURE 4.29 ), he rang changes on the rotunda-house theme. He became a devotee of the bow window ("they were charming—they gave you a semicircle of air & light") and arrived at—perhaps invented—a distinctive form, the bow window "caged" inside a temple portico ( SURVEY NO. 12, FIGURE 1 ).[43] He spent a lifetime exploring the Palladian wing, and from Monticello I through the University he developed a pattern in which two-story pavilions interrupt a walk that runs in front of a single-pile string of rooms.[44]

Lastly he responded to, and influenced, the novel, imported love of natural scenery. In his *Notes*, his comments on the Natural Bridge and on the passage of the Potomac and the Shenandoah rivers through the Blue Ridge Mountains not only recorded his appreciation of the Sublime and the Picturesque; they also established those sites in the developing canon of American scenery.[45] To take advantage of wondrous views, Jefferson built his main house in the sky and, in time, dissolved its walls with windows. He even contemplated building an observation tower ( SURVEY NO. 7 ) that would have served both as a Picturesque "eye-catcher" from the house and as a height for taking still more awe-inspiring views.[46]

Jefferson lived abroad in 1784–89, mainly in France. Having made up his mind about the true principles of architecture, he did not let the experience of a metropolis confuse him. With a connoisseurship cultivated on the fringe of the civilized world by reading outdated British architectural books, he wrote of Paris in 1785 that "the style of architecture in this capital [is] far from chaste."[47] He made this statement in explaining the difficulty that he had had in finding a collaborator for the Virginia Capitol scheme; he selected no member of the architectural avant-garde but rather an elderly draftsman, antiquary, and decorator, Charles-Louis Clérisseau (1721–1820).[48] In England, where most of the major Palladians had been dead for more than a generation, he found still worse architecture, "in the most wretched stile I ever saw."[49] He surely referred to the iconoclastic Neoclassicism of Robert and James Adam.[50] He knew the style from examples of the supreme caliber of Syon House (near London, remodeled 1762–69), where his dearest principles came under fire from the moment he sighted the lion's-paw pilaster bases and the rest of the two lawless orders at the gateway (1773; FIGURES 2.25, 2.26 ).[51] (He probably referred to the Adamesque again thirty years later when he spoke to Isaac Coles of "false architecture, so much the rage at present.")[52]

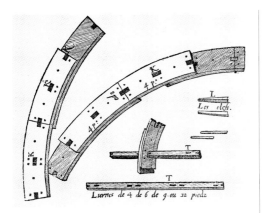

FIGURE 2.20. *In Paris, Jefferson eagerly accepted the* **Delorme Laminated Rib,** *a way of making the framework for domes and other coverings by layering short planks. Philibert Delorme had devoted his* **Nouvelles Inventions** *(1561) to this light, quick, easy, and cheap technique (here illustrated from page 14 of the 1576 edition, which Jefferson owned).*

This does not mean that Jefferson failed to make architectural discoveries with which to pursue the reform of Virginia architecture. Aesthetically neutral discoveries he probably accepted readily, such as the light, quick, easy, and inexpensive method of laminated plank construction ( FIGURE 2.20 ) that Philibert Delorme (1514–1570) had published in the sixteenth century.[53] As to style, he approved what his self-education had prepared him to approve. Leoni's Palladio had led him to accept the non-Classical effect of a dome perforated along the sides. He became enamored of the perforated dome (1782–83) that Jacques-Guillaume Legrand, Clérisseau's son-in-law, and Jacques Molinos, using Delorme ribs, had raised over the Paris grain market, or Halle au Blé (demolished).[54] (He probably considered using such a "modern" dome only on buildings taken from "modern" models.) Jefferson's forty-year promotion of the Delorme rib and the Halle au Blé model for domes profoundly altered the course of American architecture.

A similar case of finding what he was prepared to accept concerns Fréart's *Parallèle,* for which Jefferson's British Palladian readings readied him in various ways long before he saw the book. For instance, Morris's *Select Architecture* and perhaps other British Palladian material had weaned Jefferson from the Composite order (see his Observation Tower for Monticello; SURVEY NO. 7 ) with a derivative of Fréart's argument that one should use only the Doric, Ionic, and Corinthian. (Fréart's and Morris's arguments against the Composite

FIGURE 2.21. *Despite theorists' censure of the coarse Tuscan order, some architects, including Jefferson, used the Tuscan partly because it was inexpensive and practical. But this order also had the authority of Inigo Jones's* **St. Paul's, Covent Garden, London** *(1631–33), which enjoyed enormous esteem in the eighteenth and nineteenth centuries because of the purity of its temple form. (Plates 21/ 22 of Book 2, Colen Campbell's* **Vitruvius Britannicus,** *1717.)*

brought results in Britain and America, but the two theorists combined could not eliminate the serviceable, inexpensive Tuscan. To the Tuscan, moreover, Inigo Jones had given his imprimatur [ FIGURE 2.21 ].)

Jefferson apparently caught up with Fréart by degrees. First, it is supposedly in Paris that he bought Fréart's edition of Palladio, which he had known of all along from explicit references in his Leoni editions of Palladio. Later, he equipped himself with the Fréart publication that really affected his designs, Fréart's *Parallèle.* Presumably it was his French stay that led him to acquire a French edition rather than one of the four English ones.[55] When he built his great

FIGURE 2.22. **Detail, Entablature of Pavilion I at the University of Virginia.** *When Jefferson selected the Orders to display as models at his University, he largely accepted Fréart de Chambray as his guide in picking the "ancient" examples—that is, those from ancient Rome (compare figure 2.19).*

FIGURE 2.23. **Detail, Entablature of Pavilion V at the University of Virginia.** *When Jefferson chose the Orders to exhibit as models at his University, he chiefly used Leoni's modifications of Palladio's orders for his "modern" examples—that is, the examples from the period beginning with the Italian Renaissance (compare figure 2.14). The flat frieze here is the giveaway that Jefferson used Leoni's version of Palladio's Ionic.*

outdoor museum of the Orders along the Lawn, he largely used the *Parallèle* as his guide to choosing the "ancient" examples ( FIGURES 2.19, 2.22 ), while he mainly took the "modern" ones from Leoni's modifications of Palladio's orders ( FIGURES 2.14, 2.23 ).

Jefferson's architectural masterpiece, his university, gives the closing testimony that Jefferson was a unique outgrowth of British Palladianism. A popular notion declares that these buildings exemplify Jefferson's supposed liberation from "Georgian" architecture and his unanimity with such French Neoclassicists as Claude-Nicolas Ledoux (1736–1806) and Etienne-Louis Boullée (1728–1799). This claim rests on ill-assorted misrepresentations, such as the strange assertion that Jefferson designed the niche of Pavilion IX ( FIGURE 2.24 ) as a heartfelt tribute to Ledoux.[56] Given that Jefferson wished his tombstone to record only three accomplishments, the third being "Father of the University of Virginia," then the list of architectural books that he drew up for the University must count as important evidence of his architectural allegiances.[57] This list, an edited version of the holdings in his "Great" library, simply will not pass as the doing of an architectural Francophile, much less a soul-mate of the radicals of the 1780s. Jefferson did not order for the University (nor acquire for himself) so much as a book by Jacques-François Blondel, Marie-Joseph Peyre, Jean-François de Neufforge, Jean-Charles Delafosse, Antoine-Chrysostome Quatremère de Quincy, Charles Normand, or Ledoux himself. He likewise did not order (nor own) the *Précis des leçons* (Paris, 1802–05) by Boullée's pupil J.-N.-L. Durand, nor any of the volumes illustrating the winning entries for the Grand Prix de Rome, nor—in the case of a theorist sometimes invoked as a key to Jefferson's thought—either Marc-Antoine Laugier's *Essai sur l'architecture* (Paris, 1753) or Laugier's *Observations sur l'architecture* (The Hague, 1765). Instead, Jefferson ordered those century-old tomes, Kent's *Designs of Inigo Jones* and Gibbs's *Book of Architecture*, to say nothing of Leoni's Palladio, which, although supplanted in 1738 by the Isaac Ware/Burlington edition, evidently persisted as his architectural bible to the end.

Does the foregoing "explain" Jefferson's architecture? Hardly. A longer essay could fill in blanks. One can probably identify as a great force in Jefferson's aesthetic life a love of the light and the airy—light and airy both literally and figuratively, in cases as diverse as bay windows, intercolumniations, the Natural Bridge, and perforated domes. It takes this taste to help explain how Jefferson transformed Monticello from an assemblage of box-like units with holes cut through the walls ( SURVEY NO. 8 ) into a radiant if idiosyncratic composition of spaces and light. For assuredly it takes explaining to understand how, even with British Palladian bays and polygons to study, the Master of Monticello came this far in breaking out of the box.[58]

Such a performance, like much of what is choicest in Jefferson, resisted imitation if it did not outright defy it. His architectural ideas did wield influence, to be sure. Far more than any other individual, he deserves credit for establishing monumental Classicism in the civic architecture of an artistically provincial young nation. This result owed at least as much to his activities as a propagandist

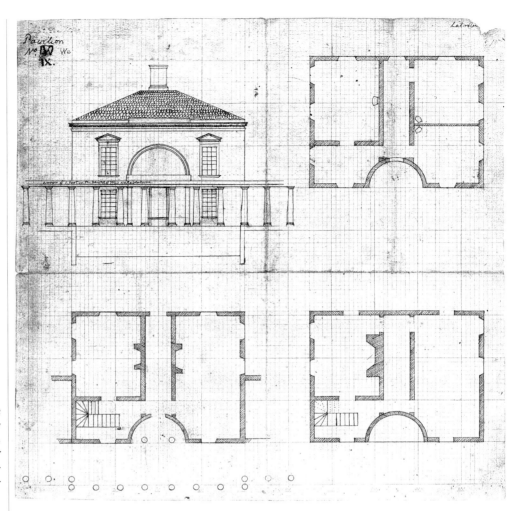

FIGURE 2.24. *At least three times, Jefferson identified the facade for* **Pavilion IX at the University of Virginia** *as the conception of B. Henry Latrobe. Thus Jefferson wrote Latrobe's name in the upper right-hand corner of Jefferson's own sheet of drawings for the pavilion. (Photograph courtesy of Alderman Library, University of Virginia, N-357).*

and a patron as it did to any of his architectural designs, and American Classicism swiftly departed from his stylistic preferences. With that said, we can return to his architectural artistry.

Jefferson the architect persistently eludes interpretive formulations. The man who lined the Lawn with models of the Orders and crowned the terraces with a spherical temple sought universal standards in architecture, or so it would seem. Yet the man who animated the Lawn with a subtle, even magical, variety by making no two pavilions alike, also incomprehensibly abandoned one of the most fundamental principles of his architectural tradition, the rule of axial symmetry.[59] Still, although Jefferson slips through the nets, one has good grounds for offering a working characterization. Out of British Palladianism, its concomitants, and congenial material that Jefferson found in other quarters, particularly France, the action of his mighty, wide-ranging mind fashioned an individual—indeed, unique—species of Classicism. Clumsy and amateurish though the buildings are in places, still the best specimens of this Jeffersonian Palladianism are some of the most refreshing and invigorating architecture in the country. Yet we must take care to admire these buildings, not for what we might read into them, but rather for what Jefferson genuinely achieved in them.

Elevation of the Gateway to Sion House and Porters Lodges, Fronting the great East Road, Eight Miles from London.

FIGURE 2.25. *Robert Adam spotlighted his* **Gateway to Syon House** *(near London, 1773) by making it the subject of the first illustrations in his and James Adam's* **Works in Architecture.** *(Plate 1 from vol. 1, no. 1, 1773.)*

FIGURE 2.26. *Robert Adam's* **Detail, Gateway to Syon House** *exhibits such liberties as mixing the Doric and Corinthian orders (Plate 2 from Adam's* **Works in Architecture,** *vol. 1, no. 1, 1773.)*

## Neoclassicism and Its Alternatives

Jefferson erected his models for the Orders along the Lawn far too late. His workmen, it is true, did carry away to commissions of their own certain of his architectural preferences, including preferences regarding the Orders.[60] But Jefferson's brand of Palladianism did not long survive him. Other and powerful architectural forces had taken shape internationally at the middle of the eighteenth century, even as Jefferson entered his teens.

To study those forces, we can take our first step by looking at three early Modern approaches to the Classical tradition; we shall look at how three British books (written by five authors) enunciated these approaches, and then we shall look at what happened to these approaches in one American book and one American house. Our second step acknowledges the multiplication of building types as one of the essential features of the Modern Era: we shall look at one function, the national monument; one way of wrapping the contents of a building, the Temple Revival; and one theoretical issue, the desirability of making a building express its nature.

In our first step, we sample the lore of the Orders provided by five men who, as of the 1760s, had begun to publish or would shortly publish books stating their widely different positions.[61] Robert Adam (1728–1792) and his brother, James Adam (1732–1794), who conquered the fashionable world in the 1760s, put their views into print later in their *Works in Architecture* (London, 1773–79).[62] Recognizing the chasm between actual Roman architecture and the species of Classicism practiced since the Renaissance, the Adams claimed to have been able to seize "the beautiful spirit of antiquity, and to transfuse it, with novelty

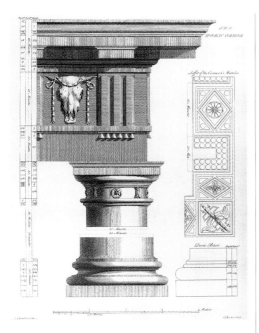

FIGURE 2.27. *Sir William Chambers's* **Doric Order** *mediates between the Doric orders of ancient Rome and those of "modern" architecture. (From Chambers's* **Treatise**, *between pages 46 and 47, 3rd ed., 1791.)*

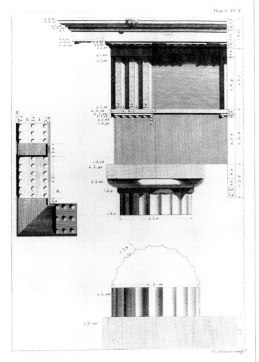

FIGURE 2.28. *By publishing such Greek buildings as* **A Doric Portico at Athens**, *James Stuart and Nicholas Revett offered alternative models to the ones presented by the Adam brothers and Chambers. (Plate 5 from from Stuart and Revett,* **Antiquities of Athens**, *vol. 1, chap. 1, probably 1763.)*

and variety, through all our numerous works." They boasted of vanquishing what the British Palladians had considered the true interior domestic manner of the ancients, with its highly plastic use of the Orders for decoration (compare the Little Parlor at Gunston Hall and the Parlor at Monticello I; FIGURE 2.9 and SURVEY NO. 8, FIGURE 1), and of replacing that with their revival of the ancient spirit, entailing a delicate use of elements from the Orders, grotesques, and other light motifs. Asserting that, as in antiquity, only students, not masters, obeyed rules, they illustrated such orders as the two for the Duke of Northumberland's gateway at Syon House (FIGURES 2.25, 2.26). The gateway orders typify the Adam brothers' rejection of orthodox systems of proportion, their iconoclastic mixing of orders (here, combining Doric features with Corinthian ones), and their arbitrary handling of elements (such as two allusions to the crest of the patron: a little lion-mask in place of the rosette that usually occupies the center of the Corinthian abacus, and the lion-paw pilaster base). (The Adams' work elsewhere exhibits a mixture of Roman material with elements from the newly knowable remains of Greek antiquity.) Putting fanciful elements outdoors on the main entry to a great nobleman's mansion had, at the least, a questionable relation to *decor*; nonetheless, traditional propriety manifested itself indoors, insofar as the rooms run from a reserved Doric hall through an intermediate Ionic antechamber to festive Corinthian rooms for company. The delicate domestic Adam style, reviving the fanciful side of Roman antiquity and expressly aimed at giving pleasure, brought with it an elegant development of the Picturesque; the Syon gateway, which the Adams had exquisitely engraved to emphasize how the landscaped park peeped through this airy screen, may, like many Adam features, represent an inspired development of British Palladian precedent. In any case, the conspicuous publication of the design surely helps explain such Picturesque Neoclassical screens as the colonnades proposed for Newmarket in Caroline County (SURVEY NO. 14). (The treatment of exterior architecture as "scenery" [in the language of the period] had a counterpart inside. Syon House brilliantly exemplifies scenic variation in the shape and decoration of rooms.) The architecture of the brothers Adam was captivating, but its principle was explosive: their modern view that antiquity could not provide architectural rules forecast the collapse of the very tradition within which they practiced.

As the appeal of the Adam brothers declined, that of their archrival, Sir William Chambers (1723–1796), grew. His chief book, first published in 1759, went into its third edition as *A Treatise on the Decorative Part of Civil Architecture* (London, 1791).[63] Chambers's orders represent a sophisticated, empirical culling from the "ancients" and the "moderns" (FIGURE 2.27) with a strong coloration from French preferences. His criteria, in which he did not have recourse to supposed laws of nature, mark him, too, as a denizen of the Modern Era. For all its elegance, Chambers's style lacked the seductive quality of the Adamesque. But Chambers's standards—for instance his valuable remarks on propriety give the book one of its major themes—contained so much of substance that they remained authoritative in Britain for most of the nineteenth century. Chambers's resistance to one discovery fundamental to the Modern period has become notorious: his detestation of Greek architecture, above all the Greek Doric order ( FIGURE 2.28 ). This reaction, on the part of one of the most cosmopolitan architects in the Western world, speaks volumes about the unsettling nature of the Greek discoveries.[64]

Volume I of the *Antiquities of Athens*, the book begun by James Stuart (1713–1788) and Nicholas Revett (1720–1804), probably reached publication in 1763 with two more volumes following (London, 1790, 1795). These volumes published the first accurate illustrations of Athenian architecture. In the second volume, Stuart referred to the first as a book of the Orders—five orders, the usual number in canons.[65] From the first volume we learn his opinion that while liberty, prosperity, and love of glory flourished, Athens presided as uniquely "the great Mistress of the Arts, and Rome [was] no more than her disciple." His book "might contribute to the improvement of the Art [i.e., architecture] itself." Despite the "second birth" of architecture in the Renaissance, "it has not yet by any means recovered all its former Perfection." The best books on the ancient architecture of Italy (such as Palladio) "cannot . . . afford a sufficient variety of Examples for restoring even the three Orders," for lack of Doric and Ionic models.[66] Whatever Stuart's and Revett's views of the relation between their researches and current practice, the Greek orders made their way into architecture. They put in a scattered appearance during the first phase of British Neoclassicism; they became important to such masters of the brief second phase as Latrobe who, with his pupils, protracted the life of that style in North America; and they multiplied phenomenally in the British and American "Greek Revivals" of the nineteenth century.

We have just sampled three major alternatives that had come into existence (and gone into practice, though with far different degrees of popularity) among British Classicists as of the 1760s. One must also observe that, new elements aside, British Neoclassicists habitually owed great debts to British Palladianism. This evidence should already have begun to suggest that it is timely to take a fresh look at the consequences in North America, without depending on customary characterizations of "the Federal style" or of a sequence in which a "Roman Revival" gave way to a "Greek Revival." The members of a generation of architects born right around 1760 each pursued one or more of these possibilities in the United States. The most important among them are an amateur architect, Dr. William Thornton (1759–1828; SURVEY NO. 26 ); an amateur who became a professional, Charles Bulfinch (1763–1844); and a professional, B. Henry Latrobe (1764–1820; SURVEY NOS. 15–21 ). Their careers would illustrate the disorderly transmission of the possibilities to the new nation where, in the 1790s, British Palladianism, and the first and second phases of Neoclassicisms all achieved remarkable American manifestations.

We will gain fresher insights, though, by looking to a slightly later generation, the artisan-authors of the first builder's guides written in the United States. Among these men, perhaps all born in the 1770s, the Philadelphian Owen Biddle (1774–1806) repays examination for present purposes less than do his Boston-

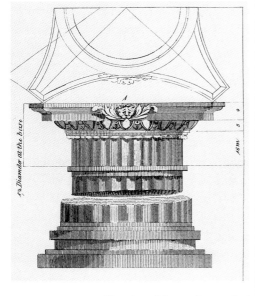

FIGURE 2.29. *The six editions of a seminal American handbook, Asher Benjamin and Daniel Raynerd's* American Builder's Companion, *belatedly retraced much of the course of British Neoclassicism. The Adamesque first edition (1806) introduced Raynerd's* Base and Capital, Which Will Be Proper for the Doric Order, *but which in fact mixed Doric and Corinthian elements. (Compare figure 2.26. Detail, plate 22 from 6th ed., 1827.)*

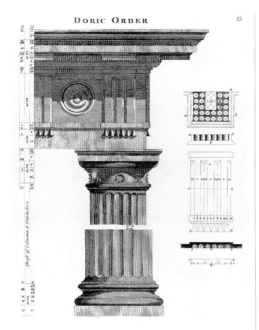

FIGURE 2.30. *In the second edition of the* **American Builder's Companion** *(1811), influence from Chambers displaced part of the original Adamesque material. Benjamin now illustrated a set of orders à la Chambers, such as a* **Doric Order.** *(Compare figure 2.27. Plate 13 from 6th ed., 1827.)*

FIGURE 2.31. *In the sixth and last edition of the* **American Builder's Companion** *(1827), Greek influence at last entered with such illustrations as plate D-E,* **Grecian Doric. Roman Doric. Grecian Ionic** *(compare figure 2.28). Incongruously, this edition recommended the Greek orders as the best but mainly republished material from earlier editions, including the orders shown in figures 2.29 and 2.30.*

ian rivals, two members of the Bulfinch orbit, Asher Benjamin (1773–1845) and Daniel Raynerd (died 1815). Their collaboration, *The American Builder's Companion* (Boston, 1806), approximately recapitulated the pattern just sketched out in England.[67]

As the *Companion* went from one edition to another, it accumulated conflicting Neoclassical stylistic possibilities. Like an archaeological dig, the book shows contrasting strata. The Orders tell the story:

*Bottom Layer: First Edition, 1806.* Benjamin and Raynerd published a belated popularization of the subjective, iconoclastic kind of Neoclassicism adopted by Robert Adam, with significant vestiges of British Palladianism. In *The Country Builder's Assistant* (Greenfield, Massachusetts, 1797), Benjamin's first book and the first original American book on architecture, Benjamin had published a set of the Orders. He based that set on the British Palladian past, but gave it some Neoclassical traits, chiefly Adamesque attenuation. In the new book he made this set of orders more Adamesque, and the volume included a plate of five Adamesque capitals signed by Raynerd ( FIGURE 2.29 ). Raynerd's figure 1 crosses Doric and Corinthian elements and has a lion mask in place of a Corinthian rosette on the abacus. The accompanying text calls the design "proper for the Doric order."

*Middle Layer: Second Edition, 1811.* After buying Raynerd out, Benjamin revised the book extensively under the influence of Chambers's *Treatise*. He modified his set of Orders under the influence of Chambers's plates ( FIGURE 2.30 ), and added comments on the Orders plagiarized from Chambers's text. But he would not give up many British Palladian and Adamesque elements, including Raynerd's plate of five capitals. The text no longer associates Raynerd's figure 1 with a canonical Order.

*Top Layer: Sixth and Last Edition, 1827.* By 1826, "Greekomania" had made such headway in Britain that the publishers of the fourth edition of Chambers's *Treatise* added plates of Greek Orders. In the United States, where the Greek taste was likewise mounting, the last edition of the *Companion* admitted four pages illustrating Greek Orders in the following year ( FIGURE 2.31 ). The same binding held Raynerd's Adamesque capitals, the Chambersian state of the Adamized British-Palladian Orders, and examples of the Greek Doric and Ionic.

Thus the *Companion* sketches the fortunes of three opposed varieties of Classicism that arose in Britain shortly after the mid eighteenth century, and also suggests a good deal about the afterlife of British Palladianism. The Adam vogue flourished first; the Adamesque declined to the advantage of Chambers's approach; and the Greek taste came into its own the last of the three. (A more detailed look would isolate the roles of British intermediaries, such as William Pain [circa 1730–1794(?)], the main Adam popularizer, but we shall stick with the larger contours.) In the provinces, where the distinction in principles was neither clear nor urgent, the historic pattern took on far less regular outlines.

A great Virginia house amplifies the evidence just brought forth. Migrating from the economic woes in New England that followed on the Embargo Act of

1807, Yankee architectural artisans tried their luck in Central Virginia. The most important figure, Alexander Parris (1780–1852), began as a housewright but eventually rose to professional status. In fact, like Robert Mills (1781–1855), William Strickland (1788–1854), and Ithiel Town (1784–1844), he represents the first full generation of American-born professional architects, the men of the 1780s. In Richmond, Parris secured the commission for John Wickham's lavish town mansion (1811–13; SURVEY NO. 24).[68]

Parris originally followed the first phase of Neoclassicism, specifically as practiced in the Bulfinch sphere of influence. He fell under the influence of Latrobe partly, it seems, because Wickham admired the Harvie-Gamble house (Richmond, 1798–99; demolished), the denatured adaptation of a Latrobe design (SURVEY NO. 24, FIGURE 1). The broad surfaces, crisp geometry, and Greek Doric order of Latrobe's Harvie-Gamble project embody the second phase of Neoclassicism. By degrees, the Wickham House acquired many

FIGURE 2.32. *Alexander Parris's* Front Porch Capitals, Restored, at the Wickham House *(Richmond, 1811–13) closely follow Daniel Raynerd's* Adamesque Capital, Which Will Be Proper for the Doric Order *in* The American Builder's Companion *(compare figure 2.29).*

of the features of the Harvie design. But the three-dimensional ornament, much of it corresponding with patterns in the *American Builder's Companion*, remained true to earlier Neoclassicism. Thus the columns on the Wickham entry front follow the Adamite capital that Raynerd called "proper for the Doric order," evidently without the lion-mask but with the same eccentric base (FIGURE 2.32). The Doric stair-hall, by contrast, adapts Benjamin's more normal, Chambers-like Doric order (FIGURE 2.33). The other two-dimensional and three-dimensional decoration of the house conforms to the same pattern: as in the *Companion*, three kinds of Neoclassicism wash up on the same shore. Reestablishing himself in Boston, Parris would lead a Latrobean transformation of New England Neoclassicism (and would emerge as a professional architect) even while the Bulfinch-Benjamin-Raynerd strain of early Neoclassicism that he had helped carry to Virginia spread there. In Boston his work shook off the old decoration, as in the case of his domestic masterpiece, an opulent dwelling closely related to Wickham's, the David Sears Mansion (Boston, 1819–21). Simultaneously, the manner that he had left behind (Raynerd capital and all) spread in Central Virginia, as witness such fine houses as the Hayes-McCance House (Richmond, circa 1816; demolished) and Hampstead (New Kent County, circa 1825).[69]

FIGURE 2.33. *The* Stairhall Capitals at the Wickham House *imitate Asher Benjamin's Chambers-style* Doric Order *in* The American Builder's Companion *(compare figure 2.30).*

Although the Wickham House violates traditional standards of propriety by putting fanciful ornament in public rather than reserving it for more private areas, it observes *decor* in a familiar fashion. The luxurious ornament follows a progression from Doric in the most public areas to the more adorned and festive orders in the rooms for entertaining. This pattern joins hands with another that perhaps came to international prominence only with Neoclassicism and that remained in force throughout the periods that concern us: the use of ornament to refer to the purpose of a room. Raynerd, after writing of ceilings that "regard ought to be paid to the use of a room, as it is as easy to introduce emblematical subjects as those void of meaning," had given two paragraphs of detail.[70] The Wickham relief decorations on the ceilings and walls follow not only his advice—for the hall, the strong, solid Doric order; for the drawing room, "foliage, wreaths, festoons, or baskets of flowers"; for the dining room, "grapevines, wheat, . . . or any thing that denotes eating or drinking"—but also some of his very patterns, perhaps executed by his own hand. (The nineteenth century would persist in this course: a Renaissance Revival sideboard of the 1870s, with carved trophies of game and other foodstuffs, represents the same principle.) The Wickhams' painted decorations observe propriety in a similar fashion. Probably executed by George Bridport (died 1819), a favorite of Latrobe's, the paintings largely square with the second phase of Neoclassicism and some of the Hellenic preferences that led beyond. But they may also hint at a major change ahead for the practice of differentiating the decoration of rooms: the use not just of different motifs but of different styles.[71]

Of course, the challenges that Modern life posed to the idea of one true Classical style mounted, presenting the designers of buildings with great problems of choice. These men—many of whom were the new kind of practitioner, the professional—faced another demanding set of problems in the overlapping area of architectural typology.[72] The Modern Era has as one of its pronounced traits the multiplication of building types. We shall have a look at three facets of this matter by examining, first, the national monument, a new kind of building. (We shall treat this as a typological study *by function*.) Second, we shall consider the temple-shaped public building, a revived exterior treatment. (We shall treat this as a typological study *by form*, looking at an inseparable matter of taste, the vicissitudes of the monumental versus the tiered facade.) And third, we shall examine the problem of how to express the nature of building types, both new and old.

In the Modern era, buildings have had to satisfy new functions and greatly modified older functions. Thus the monument to an hereditary ruler has given way to the national monument. In the United States during the period covered in this chapter, the story centers on one of the supremely important developments in the history of American art between the Revolution and the Civil War, the evolution of ideas for honoring the memory of George Washington.[73] The record is enormously intricate, but three ideas stand out: erecting a bronze equestrian statue of Washington in the nation's capital city; creating a rotunda in the national Capitol building to hold Washington's tomb and a white marble monument to him; and constructing a free-standing building to his memory. The equestrian figure, the white marble memorial in a statehouse, the official sepulcher, and the free-standing building also belong to major episodes in the history of the arts in Virginia.

As to the equestrian conception, in 1783 the Continental Congress voted to commission from the best sculptor in Europe a bronze equestrian statue of Washington—the great general, not yet president—and to erect this statue at a yet-to-be established permanent seat of government. (The completion of Etienne-Maurice Falconet's colossal Peter the Great monument in St. Petersburg in 1782 surely influenced the American conception.) This national pledge resounded for decades: thus, Jean-Antoine Houdon saw the commission for his standing figure of Washington (Virginia State Capitol, 1785 and later; FIGURE 2.34) as the first step to securing the vastly more important equestrian commission. The second central idea, the Capitol rotunda, surfaced in 1793, in the design for the national Capitol that the federal government accepted from Dr. William Thornton. The hero died in December 1799; the third idea, of a free-standing building in his honor, entered the picture in 1800. The most important example was Latrobe's project for a 100-foot-tall pyramidal tomb ( FIGURE 2.35 ).

Between 1799 and 1801, Congress debated but did nothing. In the long run, all three ideas bore fruit in Washington, D.C. Bulfinch largely built the rotunda over a tomb for Washington (1818 and later). But the primary purpose of the rotunda changed from a secular temple and tomb for Washington—whose

FIGURE 2.34. *When Jean-Antoine Houdon accepted the commission from the Commonwealth of Virginia for his standing figure of* **George Washington** *(1785 and later), he hoped that this project would bring him the greater commission for a national equestrian monument to Washington.*

FIGURE 2.35. *B. Henry Latrobe proposed his* **Project for Washington's Mausoleum** *(1800) as an alternative to a national equestrian monument to Washington. In 1812 Latrobe reworked this conception when he drew survey no. 21,* **Sketch, Elevation, Richmond Monument and Church.** *(Photograph courtesy of the Library of Congress.)*

remains have never left Mount Vernon to occupy the crypt built for them at the Capitol—into a hall for patriotic paintings in the grand manner, landmarks in the breakaway from the tyranny of the portrait over American painting. The rotunda did—briefly—get the white marble sculptural centerpiece in honor of Washington, Horatio Greenough's seated statue of him on the model of the Olympian Zeus (1832 and later, Smithsonian Institution), the first major federal commission to go to an American sculptor. The free-standing building reached execution as Robert Mills's Washington Monument (1848–84), seemingly the tallest building in the world until Gustave Eiffel's tower in Paris five years later reached nearly double the monument's height. And, in 1853, only seventy years late, Congress commissioned an equestrian Washington (Washington Circle, 1853–60) from Clarke Mills, in response to the success of that sculptor's equestrian statue of Andrew Jackson (Lafayette Square, 1848–53), supposedly the first bronze equestrian statue ever cast in the United States.

The Virginia sequels to the Washington, D.C., story hold little less interest. The architectural monument rose to national dominance in the 1810s. In 1812, for a Richmond Theatre Fire Monument ( SURVEY NO. 21 ), Latrobe reshaped his Washington pyramid, ultimately almost past recognition, and he almost certainly revised the pyramid again in 1813 for the Baltimore Washington Monument competition. In both cases he lost the commission to his pupil Robert Mills. Mills, who created the ingenious Monumental Church for the Richmond commission (1812–17; SURVEY NO. 21, FIGURE 1 ), emerged as an intensely (even overpoweringly) inventive specialist in the design of monuments.

FIGURE 2.36. *Robert Mills, the first American specialist in designing monuments, entered this* **Project for the Virginia Washington Monument** *in the 1849–50 competition for the commission. Figure 2.36 shows only the lower part of Mills's design for a lofty column. (Photograph courtesy of the Virginia Historical Society.)*

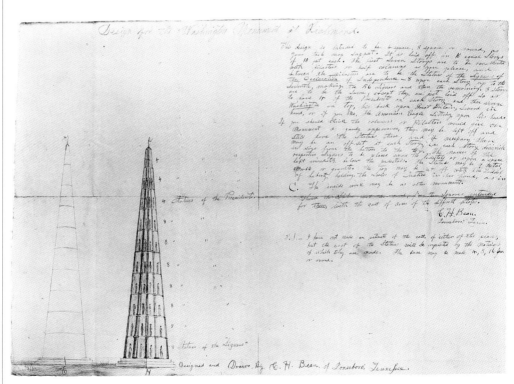

FIGURE 2.37. *In describing his* **Project for the Virginia Washington Monument,** *circa 1849–50, C. H. Bean of Jonesboro, Tennessee, would put "the statue of George Washington on top, his back upon Great Britain, sword in hand, or if you like, the American Eagle sitting upon his head." (Photograph courtesy of the Virginia State Library.)*

Maximilian Godefroy (1765–1840[?]) likewise lost to Mills in the Baltimore competition. (Godefroy did secure a by-product of that competition, the commission for the Baltimore Battle Monument [1815–25]. It testifies to the rarity of monuments in the period that this shaft and Mills's won Baltimore the epithet "Monumental City.") Godefroy sought to transplant his rejected proposal ( SURVEY NO. 22 ) to Capitol Square in Richmond in 1816, but failed. The commissioners for the Virginia monument advertised an unproductive and now-

FIGURE 2.38. **Washington Monument, Richmond,** *1850–69, by Thomas Crawford and Randolph Rogers, marks a turning-point in the preference for the representational equestrian monument over the architectural monument. Crawford's conception grew out of his unsuccessful attempt to get the same national commission that had eluded Houdon (see figure 2.34).*

mysterious competition in 1818. In their competition of 1849–50 (their second and apparently Virginia's second national architecture-related competition), an array of architects entered, from Robert Mills himself ( FIGURE 2.36 ), to one C. H. Bean of Tennessee ( FIGURE 2.37 ), who wrote on his drawing that the figure of Washington atop Bean's obelisk could have an eagle on its head (see SURVEY NOS. 42–43 ). The giant column competed against the arch, the tower, the temple, and less orthodox forms; non-classical styles contended against classical ones—and a sculptor won. Thomas Crawford's Washington Monument in Richmond (Capitol Square, 1850–69; completed by Randolph Rogers; FIGURE 2.38 ) has a lineage back to the resolution of 1783, for it must, to no small extent, have grown out of Crawford's attempts to get that national commission. As only the second in a wave of American commissions for equestrian monuments, Crawford's victory comes at the turning point in the national ascendancy of the representational equestrian monument over the architectural monument. And yet the architectural monument would take on a new guise within the decade, when Ann Pamela Cunningham's Mount Vernon Ladies' Association of the Union began the purchase (1858) and the restoration (1859) of Washington's home (see SURVEY NO. 53 ). Here a possibility voiced as early as the 1820s branched off to become the first national triumph of a distinct development, the preservation movement.[74]

We can conclude this review of the early years of the national monument in the United States with six summary points. First, the account has revolved not around the enterprises of carvers, limners, and house joiners, nor around the activities of gentlemen architects and foreign-born artists, but rather around the painful ascent of American-born sculptors, painters, and professional architects. This ascent means likewise the establishment of monumentality in architecture and of the grand manner in painting and sculpture. Second, among monuments, we have dealt with the rivalry among the arts for patronage and with the successive popularizations of the architectural shaft and the equestrian figure. Third, we have beheld how, in the small world of early nineteenth-century America, any major public commission normally had some connection with every other major public commission. We have seen, fourth, manifestations of a Modern pattern whereby what once belonged to princes passed into the public realm, and fifth, manifestations of another pattern—not unique to Modernity but essential within the period—whereby formerly sacred elements became secularized. Lastly, we have recognized the phenomenally fruitful effects on the arts of the so-called cult of Washington.

We have just performed an exercise in typology *by function*, which has enabled us to learn something about a consummate development in nineteenth-century American architecture. We can learn about another supremely consequential development if we look at the vogue for temple-shaped buildings and thus undertake an exercise in typology *by form*. Buildings meant to look like rectangular temples appeared in such quantities during the nineteenth century that the phenomenon needs a name, and the name here offered is the *American Temple Revival*.[75]

Jefferson, of course, set the development in motion. Ever since the Renaissance, European architects had experimented with re-creating the outlines of a Classical temple, but they did so only on occasion. We have seen that Jefferson learned of some of the possibilities from Palladio (Tempietto, FIGURE 2.18); and his disciples (Chiswick Temple, FIGURE 2.17); that he succeeded in giving Richmond a "cubic" temple on a mighty scale (SURVEY NOS. 9, 10); and that he hoped to give the "foederal city" a "spherical" temple of colossal dimensions with his plan for the U.S. capitol (SURVEY NO. 11). When the latter idea failed, he continued to hold out hope that Etienne-Sulpice Hallet (circa 1760–1825) could provide a cubic temple/statehouse. Even after this scheme faded, the "spherical" temple lived on as the Capitol Rotunda, that secular temple meant for the remains of Washington.[76]

More fruitfully, in Philadelphia — the temporary national capital from 1790 to 1800 — Secretary of State Jefferson's temple notions made the rounds. During 1799 to 1801 Latrobe, at the behest of an ambitious patron, created the second major monument of the Temple Revival movement with the Bank of Pennsylvania (FIGURE 2.39; demolished). Not long after coming from London, Latrobe recast the temple idea in accord with the ideas of the Neoclassical avant-garde there. The first American champion of true vaulting (the opposite of Jefferson, protagonist of the Delorme method), Latrobe built his banker's temple of masonry and cased it in white marble. And he gave two Greek porticoes — only a dozen columns — to the chaste, crisply defined body, inspired by Roman architecture. For this performance Philadelphia, the American metropolis, had seen only crude precedents, such as certain attempts at classical porticoes in various materials in the years around 1790. The bank, which would have created excitement even in London, instantly became a national wonder. It occasioned little imitation, however, until Latrobe's pupil, William Strickland, created a derivative on much the same terms, the second Bank of the United States (Philadelphia, 1818–24). We have thus far no more reason to speak of a "Greek Revival" than we would in examining the work of Sir John Soane or Claude-Nicolas Ledoux. We shall see the circumstances change, but first we must examine the conceptual and architectural significance of putting a legislature or a bank inside a temple-like box.

The adoption of the temple form by Jefferson and Latrobe illustrates one of the basic traits of the early Modern period internationally. Faced with housing new or deeply altered functions, architects turned to the accumulated building types of the past, when architects had needed to design for far fewer functions. Again and again, the early Moderns shaped a container for the purpose at hand out of either a domestic precedent or a sacred one. In the domestic class, for instance, Chambers gave the first great British governmental office building, Somerset House (London, 1776–96 and later), the form of a palace; George Dance the Younger evolved Newgate Prison (London, 1770–80 and later, demolished; FIGURE 2.49) from other palace prototypes; and, on a less sophisticated level, Samuel Dobie proposed a big Villa Rotonda for the United States Capitol (FIGURE 4.28).

FIGURE 2.39. *Following Jefferson's use of the cubic temple form for the Capitol at Richmond, the second major monument in the American Temple Revival style was* **The Bank of Pennsylvania, Philadelphia, 1799–1801, by B. Henry Latrobe.** *(Reproduced from plate 21 of William Birch's* **The City of Philadelphia . . . as it appeared in the year 1800,** *1804; courtesy of the Winterthur Library, Printed Book and Periodical Collection.)*

FIGURE 2.40. **Powhatan Courthouse, 1848–49, Alexander J. Davis.** *In this Temple Revival building, a great stylist gave his distinctive touch to the temple-form public building that Jefferson had popularized. The courthouse facade belongs to the pattern called* **distyle-in-muris.**

Like domestic prototypes, sacred models make a major showing in this book on Virginia architecture, chiefly in the form of pseudo-classical temples. When it becomes fully understood why Jefferson, and later Latrobe, accepted antique temples as models for the exteriors of American public buildings, the reasons will take an essay as long as the present one. What matters now is that first, by accepting the temple, these men participated in a fundamental, Modern pattern. The pattern shows up likewise—to give an international example—in the extension of the Gothic Revival, based primarily on Medieval ecclesiastical architecture, to secular uses at large.[77] The second issue is that Jefferson used the temple model only for important civic buildings, and Latrobe resorted to such prototypes even more sparingly.

In the 1820s, temple-form buildings became a national craze. Although these structures normally do no more than approximate the exterior outlines of the genuine article, one can apply the classifications of temple recorded by Vitruvius (3.2). Particularly useful are the terms *prostyle* (from *pro-*, in front, and *style*, column), that is, with a portico across only the main front (for instance, Walter's Second Baptist Church, Richmond; SURVEY NO. 35 ); and *amphiprostyle*, the rarer, more ambitious type with a portico across both (*amphi-*) ends (as in Latrobe's Bank of Pennsylvania). In an indiscriminate fashion that would have displeased Jefferson and appalled Latrobe, Americans tried packing almost every conceivable function inside oblong buildings with some version of a temple portal on at least one end. As in the Courthouse at Powhatan, Virginians proved partial to the temple-form courthouse ( FIGURE 2.40 )—as derivatives of Jefferson's Capitol, these had begun to appear by the 1810s—and to the temple-form church ( SURVEY NOS. 34, 35 ).[78] They also indulged in the temple form for the bank, the academic building, and the dwelling, but only on occasion, unlike the denizens of other regions. Thanks in part to Jefferson's residual influence, many Virginia temple-shaped buildings persisted in the Roman orders and entirely non-Hellenic detail, a circumstance that has not kept observers from calling them "Greek Revival." Clearly, though, a new taste operated in the proliferation of temple-like structures.

FIGURE 2.41. *When the American Greek Revival crystallized in the 1830s, it embraced the older Temple Revival and a newer vogue for the Greek Orders. Alexander J. Davis designed the* **United States Custom House, New York City,** *1833–42, as a Greek Revival "super-temple," meant to outdo such earlier buildings as Latrobe's Bank of Pennsylvania (see figure 2.39). Lithograph with watercolor by Alexander J. Davis. (Photograph courtesy of the New-York Historical Society, A. J. Davis Collection.)*

CUSTOM HOUSE, NEW YORK.
DESIGNED BY ITHIEL TOWN AND ALEXANDER JACKSON DAVIS, ARCHITECTS.

CUSTOM-HOUSE, N.Y. PLAN OF THE PRINCIPAL FLOOR.

FIGURE 2.42. **Ancient Tomb on the Appian Way,** *from Pietro Santi Bartoli,* **Gli Antichi Sepolcri overo Mausolei Romani et Etruschi,** *1697. (Reprint. Bologna: A. Forni, 1979.)*

FIGURE 2.43. *The* **distyle-in-muris** *facade blended elements from Roman tombs (compare figure 2.42) and from temple formulas (figure 2.21). Peter Nicholson, a British writer popular in the United States during the 19th century, repeatedly published his* **Design for a Chapel.** *(Plate 23 from Nicholson,* **New Practical Builder,** *1823–[25?], 3rd series.)*

By the 1830s a new taste also operated in the proliferation of Greek and Greek-looking Orders. Older architects, such as Robert Mills, and members of the newer generation born around 1800—particularly Alexander J. Davis (1803–1892) and Thomas U. Walter (1804–1887)—created stellar examples. The vogue for the temple casing united with the vogue for the Orders, though rarely with results as extraordinary as in the United States Custom House in New York (1833–42 by Town and Davis and others; FIGURE 2.41). One of a cycle of "super-temples" that arose to outdo Philadelphia's marble banks on their own terms, this building presents a parade of the Greek Orders. Just as interestingly, Davis adorned the flanks with chunky engaged pillars, a cross between Greek and Roman precedent, that create the effect of an expensive, impractical colonnade while enlivening the wall with bold, vibrant, Picturesque shadow patterns. This treatment differs altogether from those of the old Latrobe manner, as seen in the Bank of Pennsylvania, with its few columns and smooth, jointed planes.[79]

The passion for the temple-body and for Greek and Greek-looking Orders needs a name to set it off from the style that Latrobe popularized. The existing expression *Greek Revival* and the buildings themselves seem to make a workable match.

One representative of the temple craze merits special attention. The kind of temple here named *distyle-in-muris* (as seen in St. Paul's Church, Petersburg; SURVEY NO. 34), became a staple both nationally and in Virginia. With these buildings, the main front follows the general outline of a temple portico. But instead of having a full, free-standing colonnade, the facade has only two free-standing columns positioned in the center, in front of the principal entry. Usually in American practice the wall pushes forward on either side of them, to hold two staircases. The blocky form of angle pilaster called an *anta* may or may not frame the projecting sections of wall. The projecting wall not only provides a place for stairs but also reduces the cost by eliminating columns.

It has become customary to refer to this formula by the misnomer *distyle-in-antis*. That label, based on Vitruvius (3.2.1–2), names a genuine antique temple type that has *two columns between antae* (compare St. Paul's Church, London, FIGURE 2.21). Our pattern, a pseudo-antique one, has two columns inserted *within the walls* instead. It represents a cross between the true temple *in antis* and a temple-fronted Roman-tomb type that became well published no later than the early eighteenth century (FIGURE 2.42).[80] This cross-bred type caught on with Neoclassicists. It evidently found its way to the United States with British books, particularly several titles by Peter Nicholson that published the same design (FIGURE 2.43) and with one English-born architect, John Haviland, who illustrated the type in his *Builder's Assistant* (Philadelphia, 1818–21). The *distyle-in-muris* pattern ostensibly made its debut in American building practice in New England in the early 1820s with Alexander Parris, who grafted it onto his version of the temple manner that he had learned from the Bank of Pennsylvania.[81] Thereafter it traveled by increasingly numerous routes, but Ithiel Town very likely picked it up from Parris's work

FIGURE 2.44. **Distyle-in-muris** *Temple Revival buildings became popular in Virginia (compare figure 2.40 and survey no. 34). Thomas U. Walter established a tradition for Baptist church design in Richmond with his* **Old First Baptist Church,** *1839–41. (Photograph taken 1914, before the loss of the cupola. Courtesy of the Valentine Museum, Richmond, Cook Collection.)*

and communicated it to his partner, Alexander J. Davis.[82] Davis perfected the firm's version, with Greek columns, regular intercolumniations across the front, and anta-like pilasters along the flanks. He at last gave Virginia an example with the Courthouse in Powhatan (1848–49; FIGURE 2.40), one of the choicest examples of the type to survive in this country.[83] Similar buildings by Thomas U. Walter suggest that Walter simply adapted the Town and Davis type in such commissions as Old First Baptist Church (Richmond, 1839–41; FIGURE 2.44).[84] That building sired an extraordinary family line of Richmond Baptist churches into the late twentieth century, including Old First African Baptist (1876), Fourth Baptist (1884), and First Baptist (1927), the Monument Avenue replacement for Walter's building. The distyle family tree has quite a few other branches in Virginia, but despite the old misconception that Jefferson popularized the type, he did not even use it.[85]

One suspects that both the *in antis* and the *in muris* types had connections with speculation about the beginnings of architecture, and sometimes with speculation about the Egyptians as the inventors of architecture. Such thinking probably underlies the resemblance between *in muris* fronts and designs adapted from Egyptian models, such as Thomas S. Stewart's Egyptian Building (Richmond, 1844–45; SURVEY NO. 37).

The victory of the temple in Virginia partook of an international tide in taste. Knowing this tide leads us to recognize a very large pattern in nineteenth-century architecture. One finds, as the century dawned, an international group of architectural leaders successfully promoting what one can call an "aesthetic of the temple." That is, they favored facades that had the unity and grandeur of a great antique temple portico, and they despised facades that broke emphatically into tiers of small-scale elements. In the facades that most nearly approached their ideal, the elements corresponded to a temple platform, a column, and an entablature (as in Latrobe's Bank of Pennsylvania), and the higher the building's function, the more the handling mattered. These spokesmen commonly stated their case as connoisseurs of the Picturesque who admired the compositional effect of the resultant large-scale shadow patterns. In the reaction that set in abroad during the 1830s, and in the next turn of the wheel in the late nineteenth century, one sees the outlines of nineteenth-century architecture drawn at large.[86]

For a firm footing, we start around 1800 with Latrobe. (Early on, Jefferson apparently accepted both alternatives—the giant order of his "cubic" and "spherical" temples, and the tiered front that, from Monticello to the University, he used in the form of one-story wings interrupted by two-story pavilions. The meaning of his shift from the facades of Monticello I to those of Monticello II [SURVEY NOS. 8, 12] is not completely clear.) Latrobe in 1804 slammed the tiered and varied masses of New York City Hall (FIGURE 2.45) by Joseph François Mangin and John McComb, Jr. (1802–12) as a "vile heterogenous [sic] composition in the style of Charles IX of France, or Queen Elisabeth of England."[87] Jefferson's design for one-story White House wings interrupted by two-story pavilions (1805–11, largely replaced) prompted

FIGURE 2.45. **A View of the City Hall, New York,** *as it appeared in a lottery poster of 1832. The poster's caption notes that "the first story, including the portico, is of the Ionic, the second of the Corinthian, the attic of the Fancy, and the Cupola of the Composite orders." Latrobe jeered at it as "a vile heterogenous composition." By the 1830s this tiered facade had fallen under public attack by those who admired the more unified temple form (compare figures 2.41, 2.46). (Reproduced from Clarence Hornung,* Handbook of Early Advertising Art, *3rd ed., New York: Dover, 1956.)*

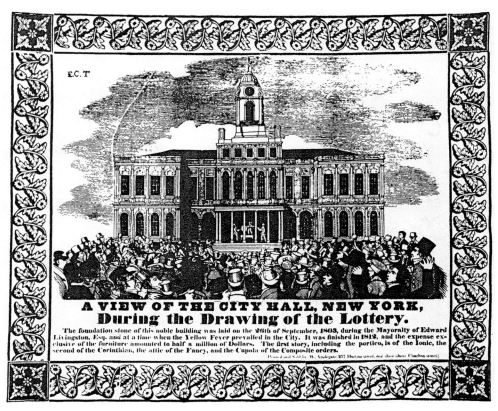

E.C.T

**A VIEW OF THE CITY HALL, NEW YORK, During the Drawing of the Lottery.**

The foundation stone of this noble building was laid on the 26th of September, 1803, during the Mayoralty of Edward Livingston, Esq. and at a time when the Yellow Fever prevailed in the City. It was finished in 1812, and the expense exclusive of the furniture amounted to half a million of Dollars. The first story, including the portico, is of the Ionic, the second of the Corinthian, the attic of the Fancy, and the Cupola of the Composite orders.

Printed and Sold by W. Applegate, 257 Hudson street, one door above Charlton street.

FIGURE 2.46. *For* **St. Paul's Episcopal Church, Richmond,** *1843–45, Thomas S. Stewart used panels to minimize the tiered effect of the windows and to intensify the grandeur of the giant Order. (Photograph, courtesy of The Valentine Museum, shows the church before replacing the steeple with a cupola in 1904–05.)*

Latrobe to the statement (partly quoted already) that their author was an "excellent architect out of books . . . , but loves the taste of Queen Elisabeth best."[88] He shared his distaste for subdivided compositions with an international group of illuminati, such as Soane, who fostered the temple aesthetic more tactfully in his Royal Academy lectures from 1809 onward.[89] In 1817, when Jefferson sent Latrobe his thoughts for the University, he sent a conception very close indeed to the White House wings. Latrobe, in making his all-important proposal of giant Orders, was reforming what he unquestionably saw as an essay in the "taste of Queen Elisabeth" (see discussion in SURVEY NO. 27).

As the taste for ancient simplicity and grandeur grew, other writers compared the City Hall unfavorably with various specimens of the Temple Revival.[90] Thus, in 1834, as the Temple Revival hit its peak, New York's weekly journal of the arts contrasted Town and Davis's project for the New York Custom House (FIGURE 2.41) with the City Hall facade, "deformed with a mass of ginger-bread work."[91] The preference for the effect of a giant Order accounts for a treatment that is well represented in Virginia, the use of a sunk panel between upper and lower windows to create or reinforce the effect of a giant Order. This pervasive treatment affected not only Greek buildings, such as Thomas S. Stewart's St. Paul's Church, Richmond (FIGURE 2.46), but also Stewart's Egyptian Building (SURVEY NO. 37) and even Davis's castellated Barracks at the Virginia Military Institute (Lexington, 1850 and later; SURVEY NO. 39), a conception suffused with late Neoclassical values. (As is well known, Davis called his versions of the idea the "Davisean window.")

As of the 1830s, the reaction against the giant Order had begun to set in abroad with, for instance, the return to Italian Renaissance *palazzi* in London and the revival of the French Renaissance in Paris. These moves eliminated the expense and impracticality of giant porticoes while, by reinstating the tiered facade, they satisfied a developing Picturesque taste for dappled shadow-play. In Virginia, one detects the preferences no later than the 1849–50 Washington monument competition, in the broken forms of certain entries (such as those by John Notman and Napoleon LeBrun, SURVEY NOS. 42, 43), and then in the base of Thomas Crawford's executed monument, which is not a simple Neoclassical plinth but a pyramidal accumulation of pedestals, layer after layer (FIGURE 2.38). At just about the same point, the irregular Picturesque house, which has a different lineage from the layered facade, began to win admirers in Virginia. To the new freedom these houses—chiefly in Gothic Revival or Italianate Villa guises—contributed informal massing and an escape from the tradition that solids must stand over solids and voids over voids (compare Sweet Briar House and King villa, SURVEY NO. 44).

The tiered Italian Palazzo Revival or Renaissance Revival, reaching the United States in the 1840s, developed from a recognizable dependency of Neoclassicism (as seen in the Custom-House by Young, FIGURE 4.38 and SURVEY NO. 45, FIGURE 1, Tefft's preliminary perspective) into a Victorian manifestation (FIGURE 2.47), rich in plasticity and in the resultant chiaroscuro. The other High Victorian styles likewise carried the reaction to an extreme. Davis, having seen his values triumph, could not understand their defeat: in 1872, the French style of the New York Court House and Post Office (1869–80 by Alfred B. Mullett and others; demolished) stirred him to write "Costly, diseased courtesan, broken heap of littleness," and Richard Morris Hunt's Lenox Library (1870–77, demolished; FIGURE 2.48), one of the

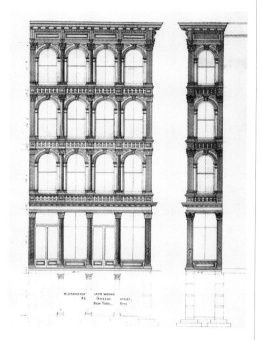

FIGURE 2.47. *Made for an unknown purpose about 1865, the* **Front and Side Elevations of an Ironfront,** *from the M. G. Rosz and Son Ironworks of New York City, embody the reaction against the giant order in favor of the tiered facade. These elevations, resembling ironfronts erected along East Main Street in Richmond, survived among the papers of the architect and engineer Albert L. Rives (compare survey no. 50). (Photograph courtesy of the University of Virginia, Special Collections Department, Manuscripts Division, Rives Family Papers; no. 2313.)*

FIGURE 2.48. *Richard Morris Hunt developed the tiered facade at his* **Lenox Library, New York,** *1870–77. Hunt's building appalled the elderly Alexander J. Davis (compare fig. no. 2.41) but excited the young John R. Thomas, who made it one of his models for Brooks Hall at the University of Virginia (survey no. 54). In time Hunt and Thomas would turn again to the monumental facade. (Photograph courtesy of American Institute of Architects Foundation, Prints and Drawing Collection.)*

models for John R. Thomas's Brooks Hall (Charlottesville, 1876–77; SURVEY NO. 54 ), "indicates," he thought, "a depraved architecture."[92] In Richmond, the juxtaposition of Elijah E. Myers's Old City Hall (1887–93; SURVEY NO. 58 ) with Jefferson's Capitol of just a century earlier ( SURVEY NOS. 9, 10 ), illustrates the pendulum nearing its extreme in the swing away from Classical monumentality toward Picturesque variety. A strong rectilinear organization governs the Capitol: giant pilasters (not intended by Jefferson) unite the stories between the continuous horizontal bands formed by the basement and the entablature. At City Hall, on the other hand, Myers laid stratum upon stratum upon stratum, free of any binding vertical elements. In this Picturesque freedom, below the eaves not one horizontal element runs around the building without a great break. Irregular massing has traveled from the villa into town to the civic building: a great corner tower pries the building away from its essential axial symmetry. Further vivacity comes from the scintillating surfaces of the rock-faced Richmond granite, a gift from the Picturesque movement via H. H. Richardson (1838–1886). But City Hall, an old-fashioned building even when its construction began, misses the point of Richardson's achievement, which belongs to the next cycle of taste. For Richardson and others met the challenge of reestablishing monumentality in American architecture without sacrificing all the advantages that Picturesque experimentation had won since mid-century.

A last matter, one of theory, will take us on to the end. One of the most widespread architectural principles of the early Modern period declares that a building should express its nature. This belief perpetuated the tradition of *decor*, but it embraced new ideas and acquired new names, such as *character*. A passage from one of the older theorists will equip us to understand the early Modern novelties. Writing on "unnatural Productions," Robert Morris gave the examples "as when the Portal to a *Prison* may be of the *Corinthian*, and that of a *Palace* be the *Tuscan Order*. Festoons of Fruit and Flowers have been the Wildness of Fancy in a Seat near the Sea; and a Pavillion [sic] in a Flower-Garden has been group'd with Variety of *Fish*."[93] The idea of distributing the Orders according to a building's purpose goes back to Vitruvius's discussion of *decor* (1.2.5); the rhetorical figure of inverted applications of the Orders was becoming a commonplace; and the notion of relating architectural style to landscape broke new ground. This background prepares us for the testimony of three Virginia buildings by architects bent on disseminating reforms: B. Henry Latrobe, Alexander J. Davis, and John R. Thomas (1848–1901).[94]

Latrobe designed the Virginia State Penitentiary at Richmond (1797–1806, demolished; SURVEY NOS. 16, 17 ) first and foremost as a secure but humane prison. But from the late eighteenth century to at least the late nineteenth, prisons gave architects an unsurpassable opportunity for exploring the expressive power of architecture, and Latrobe made his designs a manifesto of *character*. Four of his choices stand out. First, for the only time that we know of in his architectural drawings, he laid a stormy sky into his perspective, so that the very setting of the penitentiary underscores its somber purpose. Second, he proposed random rubble masonry for the ground-story walls rather than the brick of the upper levels and, when he had to struggle for this material, he pleaded that rough stone for at least the gate would "add to the Solemn character of the building."[95] Third, he wished to ornament the entry with garlands of chains. (Apparently neither the rubble nor the festoons were executed.) Fourth, Latrobe assuredly meant his articulation to express the nature of each part of the building. Thus by means of blind arcades with windows high in the wall, the cells announce their presence as clearly as the gaping portal announces the entry. At the same time, the lunettes assure the onlooker that, in this enlightened place of confinement, the inmates receive light and air.

FIGURE 2.49. *In his design for the Virginia State Penitentiary at Richmond (survey nos. 16, 17), B. Henry Latrobe derived expressive architectural elements from London's Newgate Prison of 1770–80 and later.* **Bird's-Eye View of Newgate Prison, London, by George Dance the Younger.** *(Photograph courtesy of the Trustees, Sir John Soane's Museum, London; reproduced with permission from* **George Dance, Architect, 1741–1825** *by Dorothy Stroud [London: Faber & Faber, 1971]).*

Latrobe derived his expressive or characteristic features from two London buildings by the younger George Dance, Newgate Prison (1770–80 and later, demolished; FIGURE 2.49 ) and St. Luke's Hospital, Old Street (1782–89, demolished).[96] Both buildings betray domestic antecedents (Newgate has ties to the courtyard-plan palace), but both were justly winning international fame as characteristic masterpieces. For Newgate, Dance, mindful of such passages as Robert Morris's on the opposition of palace and prison, at bottom translated the facade of Palladio's Palazzo Thiene (Vicenza, 1542/1546 and later; FIGURE 2.50 ) into the menacing facade appropriate to a prison. In place of Palladio's festive Composite order and floral garlands, Dance used a ponderous Tuscan entablature and, over the two portals, festoons of chains ( FIGURE 2.51 ). He kept the rustication; gave it one of its traditional applications, a prison, and one of its traditional complements, the Tuscan order; and employed it without windows to create man-made rock cliffs for the walls of the prison proper.[97] One reads the openings through the stone—here one enters and leaves, there the Keeper and his family live—more easily than a book.

FIGURE 2.50. *George Dance the Younger based the exterior of Newgate Prison largely on Andrea Palladio's* **Palazzo Thiene** *(Vicenza, Italy, 1542/1546 and later), but Dance "translated" a palace into a prison. (Plate 10 from Book 2 of* **Architecture of A. Palladio**, *ed. Giacomo Leoni. 2nd edition, 1721).*

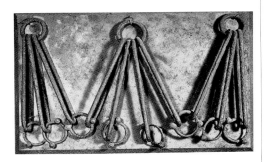

FIGURE 2.51. *In response to the floral garlands that Palladio designed (but did not execute) for the Palazzo Thiene, George Dance devised a* **Festoon of Chains** *for each of the main portals of Newgate Prison. B. Henry Latrobe admiringly took over this expressive or "characteristic" feature in his Virginia State Penitentiary drawings (survey nos. 16, 17). (Photo courtesy of the Museum of London).*

With a nondomestic plan the Virginia penitentiary took a giant step away from the house prototype, and with no expressed order, it took a stride away from *decor*. Latrobe nearly lifted his articulation from Dance's solemn hospital for the insane. This he wished to unite with rock-faced masonry, a counterpart to Dance's rugged rustication, and with grim festoons of chains. Latrobe meant to stamp his building thoroughly with the mark or character of its purpose, and that threatening character, like Newgate's, comes at least into the vicinity of the Sublime. (Assuredly Latrobe had also considered his design as a Picturesque composition.)

Alexander J. Davis's Belmead (Powhatan County, 1845–48; SURVEY NO. 38 ) represents a different combination of principles. Even before consulting Davis, the patron, Philip St. George Cocke, son of the builder of Upper Bremo ( SURVEY NO. 29 ) and Bremo Recess ( SURVEY NO. 31 ), had decided on the Gothic "because I think it much better adapted to Country houses than the more regular & formal Roman & Grecian styles," both as to harmony with the landscape and as to good domestic planning.[98] For Robert Morris a hundred years before, the fitness of a building to its purpose and its landscape depended on the choice of Order, but now that propriety depends on the choice of style. Gone is any idea that the irregular forms of the landscape and the regular forms of Classical architecture obey the same laws of nature. (Still, Cocke would follow his Gothic commission with a "regular & formal" one for the appropriate end, a courthouse for the settlement of Powhatan.)

It seems almost certain that principles of expression guided Davis thoroughly in his designs, so that, for instance, one can "read" the interiors on the exteriors.[99] In 1850 A. J. Downing (1815–1852), Davis's collaborator in popularizing the Picturesque, published in *The Horticulturist* an article on Belmead adapted from a Davis description, and the wording provides insights.[100] After stating that "the details of the architecture are full of character," the article goes into few specifics. We have good reason, though, to think that we are reading the building in a nineteenth-century way when we say that the massing, the multiple chimneys, and the veranda tell us that this is a house, while the size and placement of the openings give us significant information about the spaces behind them. (Downing had explained much of this in his *Cottage Residences* [New York, 1842] when he discussed why "the prominent features conveying expression of purpose in dwelling-houses, are the chimneys, the windows, and the porch, veranda, or piazza.")[101] The *Horticulturist* does give some telling detail on the drawing room: "the bay windows are richly bordered with stained glass of ruby and gold . . . producing a rich and mellow tone of light in the apartment, in admirable keeping with its character; and the several mantelpieces have wheat, maize, and tobacco, the staple productions of the plantation, sculptured upon their marble surfaces." The vegetable motifs (which, with cotton, also adorn the window glass [ FIGURE 2.52 ], and which descend directly from Latrobe's use of maize and tobacco ornamentation at the Capitol in Washington) surely aid in designating the nature of the building. The description goes on to identify the advantages of the highly diversified windows, which

FIGURE 2.52. *The brainchild of Philip St. George Cocke and Alexander J. Davis, Belmead (Powhatan County, 1845–48; survey no. 38) exemplifies "characteristic" architecture. The maize painted on a* **Pane in the Drawing Room Bay Window** *stands for one of the crops that Cocke raised on the Belmead plantation.*

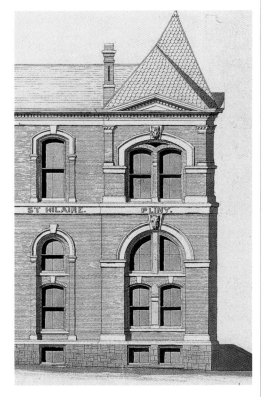

FIGURE 2.53. **Detail, Elevation of Brooks Hall** *at the University of Virginia (1876–77; survey no. 54). John R. Thomas composed this tiered and jointed facade to express the spaces inside the building.*

include convenience internally and Picturesqueness externally, although the text does not spell out a theme voiced elsewhere by Downing (see Sweet Briar House, SURVEY NO. 44), that the variety denotes different uses in various rooms. Practical, Picturesque, and characteristic, this differentiation of the windows weakens the old Classical grid and points toward the free articulation of the 1870s and '80s. (Chambers had spoken for much of the Classical tradition when he had castigated "the common sort of builders" for a "childish hankering after variety" in using many different sorts of window and window ornament on a building, rather than one kind per story.)[102]

The Middle Ages supplied very little of what went into the design of Belmead. In this chapter, for instance, we have identified the pedigree of the rotunda, the bay windows, the maize and tobacco motifs, and a transparent arcade that once led to a service dependency. The Classical doctrine of propriety, too, shaped the house, but like many of the elements just mentioned, it did so in a modified form. Davis and Cocke saw the house as Gothic, and in their world, the principle of fitness supported the coexistence of multiple styles.

With John R. Thomas's Brooks Hall at the University of Virginia (SURVEY NO. 54 and FIGURE 2.53) we see the operation of propriety within quite a different style. A twentieth-century viewer sees Brooks Hall as representing French influence on High Victorian taste. If exceedingly well informed, this viewer recognizes the debts of the design to Henri Labrouste's Bibliothèque Ste.-Geneviève (Paris, 1838–50) and Hunt's Lenox Library (FIGURE 2.48). An important contemporary description, which may well incorporate Thomas's own terminology, states that "this building is of the Italian Renaissance style of architecture, with modern adaptations."[103] Whether Thomas provided the actual words matters much less than that the statement made (and still makes) perfect sense: informed Americans had long grown accustomed to categorize French architecture since the sixteenth century as a subdivision of the Renaissance renewal of antiquity, and this way of classifying gave the High Victorians a means to label their own buildings. (At the same date, for instance, the Washington architect Adolf Cluss characterized the facades of the State, War, and Navy Building [Washington, D.C., 1871–89 by Alfred B. Mullett and others] as "in the rich forms of Italian Renaissance" while acknowledging the "portly mansard roofs.")[104] With Brooks Hall, Thomas did not aim at reviving the extinct style of a lost world. Rather, as the telling phrase "with modern adaptations" accurately reflects, he strove for a new style compounded from various sources, largely resources within the Classical tradition. (Similarly, working in a High Victorian Gothic vein on Lynchburg's First Baptist Church [1884–86 and additions], he sought a new expression for the late nineteenth century, not the restoration of a lost style.) One might suggest in passing that Thomas and his contemporaries also classified Jefferson's University buildings under "Italian Renaissance," specifically under the "Palladian school," and that the notion of a discord between them and Thomas's hall arose only with later points of view.

Thomas used three forms of symbolism to make the exterior of Brooks Hall reveal the building's nature: inscriptions, sculpture, and, less obviously, archi-

FIGURE 2.53A. **Detail showing the Band of Inscriptions and Rhinoceros Head** *from Brooks Hall. The names of natural historians and heads of animals carved on this building express its purpose as a museum of natural history.*

FIGURE 2.54. **Detail, Elevation of the Roman Amphitheater at Nîmes.** *When John R. Thomas developed his design for Brooks Hall, he probably had in mind this tiered and jointed facade with its carved bulls' heads. (Plate 13 of Charles-Louis Clér-isseau's* **Antiquités de la France.***)*

tectural articulation. The names of great natural historians run around the building in a band. (Before execution, someone changed the sequence from what Thomas's extant drawings show and replaced Georges Louis Leclerc, Comte de Buffon, who had denigrated American life-forms, with the University's William Rogers.)[105] A set of sculpted animal heads in the keystones represents zoology. And the singular articulation conveys the disposition of the interior. The two-story arches mean that a two-story space lies within, while the two tiers of windows inside these arches express the existence of two levels (main floor and gallery) within the hall. The break at the inscribed belt-course marks the top story as a separate entity (a result made possible by the escape from the "aesthetic of the temple").

At Brooks Hall, we have ventured some distance into the Modern world. As one major sign of that, its architect practiced more than one style at the same time and assigned absolute authority to no style that had ever existed. The Classical inheritance merely represented one set of options. Contemporaries saw the style of Brooks Hall as "Italian Renaissance," but this style differs profoundly from what Palladio, Lord Burlington, or B. Henry Latrobe had in mind when they thought of the Italian rebirth of antiquity. (Significantly, the pilasters and engaged columns at Brooks Hall are among its least Classical features.)

But if the Classical tradition had ceased to regulate, it had not ceased to fertilize. One recognizes an array of borrowings from the tradition. The several likely inspirations for the use of animal masks to symbolize a building's function include a striking one, *another* Roman building at Nîmes, the Amphitheater ( FIGURE 2.54 ), which seems likewise an impetus behind the tiers and vertical breaks of the museum walls.[106] Recourse to an odd antique model, though, does not matter a tenth as much as the continuity of principle. How much does Thomas's use of both structural and purely decorative elements to express a building's purpose—even to diagramming its internal makeup on its facades—differ from, say, Latrobe's or Dance's? The principle called originally *decor* in its Vitruvian form had passed from hand to hand to hand, acquiring different applications and different names, but the line of transmission had not snapped. Indeed, in the architecture of Virginia as in Western architecture at large, despite misconceptions in recent generations, important chains of continuity with the Classical tradition have not ever broken, even down to the present moment.

1.   This essay belongs to the tradition of scholarship founded in the English-speaking world in 1941 at the Warburg Institute in London by Fritz Saxl and Rudolf Wittkower with their photographic exhibition *British Art and the Mediterranean*. The contents of that exhibition subsequently appeared in book form as *British Art and the Mediterranean* (1948; reprint ed. with corrections, London: Oxford University Press, 1969). I hope that my remarks do credit to my study with Wittkower, one great teacher, and to my work under another brilliant mentor, Frank H. Sommer III, the Head of Library at the Henry Francis duPont Winterthur Museum until his retirement in 1987. Sommer's massive, as-yet unpublished monograph "The Learned Artist" will shed on the arts of the United States the kind of illumination that Saxl and Wittkower provided for Britain.

2.   Many readers may not recognize the pertinence of the Renaissance tradition prior to the flowering of British Palladianism. Three citations can suggest that the Classical tradition by no means always manifested itself in the motifs that a twentieth-century eye most readily connects with the Renaissance legacy. In North America, the tradition became conspicuous first in the decorative arts (including architectural decoration). Sommer, in "The Learned Artist," makes a powerful case for the impact of so-called Mannerism on North American design in the seventeenth century; for another and none-too-successful statement, see Robert F. Trent, "The Concept of Mannerism," in *New England Begins: The Seventeenth Century*, exh. cat., 3 vols. (Boston: Museum of Fine Arts, 1982), 3:368–79. As to the subsequent taste that I would call Late Stuart, Daniel D. Reiff's *Small Georgian Houses in England and Virginia: Origins and Development through the 1750s* (Newark, Delaware: University of Delaware Press, 1986) impressively tracks the mingling of Classical or Southern European influence with Northern European elements (especially vernacular ones) in the creation of the hipped-roof brick house popular in Virginia from the 1720s to the 1750s.

3.   In using the labels *First Phase* and *Second Phase* for Neoclassicism, I am following a simple division proposed by Sir John Summerson in his *Architecture in Britain, 1530–1830*, in the Pelican History of Art. The most recent edition is the 7th, revised and enlarged (n.p.: Penguin Books, 1983). I have adapted these useful labels to fit the somewhat different two-part division of British Neoclassicism laid out in Damie Stillman's *English Neo-classical Architecture*, 2 vols., Studies in Architecture, vol. XXVI (London: A. Zwemmer, 1988), a book that opens fresh vistas of understanding.

4.   For a turning point in recognizing Jefferson's position in relation to British Palladianism, see Frank H. Sommer III, "Thomas Jefferson's First Plan for a Virginia Building," in *Papers on American Art*, ed. by John C. Milley (Maple Shade, New Jersey: Edinburgh Press, for The Friends of Independence National Historical Park, 1976). In arriving at my related interpretation of Jefferson, I have had the advantage of comparing notes with Sommer over the years, most recently when he spoke on "Thomas Jefferson and the Reform of Virginia Architecture" in "Classicism: Visions and Revisions, 1740–1990," Third Annual Symposium, Department of Architectural History, University of Virginia, October 1990. I have also profited greatly from contact with William L. Beiswanger, Director of Restoration, The Thomas Jefferson Memorial Foundation, who has shared his unique expertise on numerous occasions. In reaching my conclusions, I furthermore owe highly pleasant debts to countless University of Virginia students, whom I mention by name

below only when they have produced a publicly accessible work such as a thesis. The responsibility for any imperfections in my conclusions rests, of course, entirely with me.

5.   Henry-Russell Hitchcock judiciously classed the Italianate villa taste and the Central Italian Palazzo Revival à la Sir Charles Barry as originally part of Neoclassicism (or, in his terminology, *Romantic Classicism*) in his *Architecture, Nineteenth and Twentieth Centuries*; see the 4th. ed., 1977; reprinted, with additions to the bibliography, The Pelican History of Art (Harmondsworth, Middlesex: Penguin Books, 1987), 116–17, 138–39, 167. The later, "Victorian" history of the two movements has often overshadowed their Neoclassical origins. See also my essay "The Italianate Villa and the Search for an American Style, 1840–1860," in *The Italian Presence in American Art, 1760–1860*, ed. Irma B. Jaffe, (New York: Fordham University Press, 1989).

6.   A bibliography on Palladianism in the English-speaking world would ideally begin by citing a great synthetic discussion of Palladianism in Western architecture at large, but I know of no such publication. Robert Tavernor's recent survey *Palladio and Palladianism* (London: Thames and Hudson, 1991) essentially restricts its coverage to England and, in North America, to Jefferson. Summerson's *Architecture in Britain* gives the classic history of the movement in the British Isles in his Part Four. His Appendix Two, "English Architecture in America," towers over most American writing on early American architecture but is Summerson's synthesis as of 1954. Rudolf Wittkower's *Palladio and Palladianism* (New York: George Braziller, 1974) collects seminal essays by a scholar who brought a staggering intellectual authority to the field. As to the "ancients" vs. the "moderns," Joseph M. Levine's monograph *The Battle of the Books* will have reached publication via Cornell University Press too late for use here; I have used Levine's enlightening "Ancients and Moderns Reconsidered," *Eighteenth-Century Studies* 15 (Fall 1981): 72–89. John Harris has supplemented Summerson and Wittkower with his anthology of architectural drawings, *The Palladians*, RIBA Drawings Series (New York: Rizzoli, 1982). Four recent works make incalculable contributions to understanding British Palladian and more broadly Palladian books: Eileen Harris, assisted by Nicholas Savage, *British Architectural Books and Writers, 1556–1785* (Cambridge: Cambridge University Press, 1990); John Archer, *The Literature of British Domestic Architecture, 1715–1842* (Cambridge, Massachusetts: MIT Press, 1985); Janice G. Schimmelman, "Architectural Treatises and Building Handbooks Available in American Libraries and Bookstores through 1800," *Proceedings of the American Antiquarian Society*, vol. 95, pt. 2 (October 1985):317–500; and Deborah Howard, "Four Centuries of Literature on Palladio," *Journal of the Society of Architectural Historians* 39 (October 1980):224–41. The volumes of *Building by the Book*, ed. Mario di Valmarana (Charlottesville: University Press of Virginia for the Center for Palladian Studies in America, 1984–) assemble papers given at the Center's conferences; this publication program holds great promise for the neglected field of classicism in North America. Lastly, Melinda Byrd Frierson's fine "Freemasonry and Neo-Palladianism in Early Eighteenth-Century England" (Master of Architectural History thesis, University of Virginia, 1989) offers important correctives to certain voguish notions.

7.   On these affinities see Rudolf Wittkower, "English Neo-Palladianism, the Landscape Garden, China and the Enlightenment,"

chap. 12 in Wittkower's *Palladio and Palladianism*, and Nikolaus Pevsner, "The Genesis of the Picturesque," chap. 4 in Pevsner's *Studies in Art, Architecture and Design*, 2 vols. (London: Thames and Hudson, 1968).

8. For the text of the poem, I have used *The Poems of Alexander Pope*, ed. John Butt, 11 vols. in 12 (London: Methuen & Co., 1951–69), vol. 1, *Pastoral Poetry and "An Essay on Criticism,"* ed. E. Audra and Aubrey Williams, pp. 233–326. Harris, *British Architectural Books*, under "Morris, Robert," characterizes Pope as Morris's "life-long idol." On the significance of Morris's use of Pope on his title page, see Wittkower, "English Neo-Palladianism," pp. 181–82.

9. The quotation comes from p. 105 of Rudolf Wittkower, "English Literature on Architecture," chap. 7 in Wittkower's *Palladio and Palladianism*.

10. *The Architecture of Leon Battista Alberti in Ten Books. Of Painting in Three Books and of Statuary in One Book . . . ,* trans. into Italian by Cosimo Bartoli and into English by James Leoni (London: printed by Thomas Edlin, 1726), Bk. 6, chap. 13. I feel grateful to Dorothea Nyberg, a brilliant teacher at Columbia University, for stressing the importance of this line of thought.

11. *Rules for Drawing the Several Parts of Architecture*, 2nd ed. (London: for the author, 1736), 5.

12. *A Treatise on the Decorative Part of Civil Architecture*, 3rd ed. (1791; reprint; introduction by John Harris, New York: Benjamin Blom, 1968), 32; compare the closely similar statement, p. 17.

13. See Benjamin and Daniel Raynerd, *The American Builder's Companion*, 6th ed., corr. and enl., 1827; reprint with an introduction by William Morgan (New York: Dover Publications, 1969), 30: "The orders of architecture . . . are the basis upon which the whole decorative part of the art is chiefly built. . . . In them, originate most of the forms used in decoration; they regulate most of the proportions; and to their combination . . . arranged, in a thousand different ways, architecture is indebted for its most splendid productions." Compare p. 26. For more on this book, see below.

14. This architect has at last become the subject of a scholarly monograph with Terry Friedman's *James Gibbs*, Studies in British Art (New Haven: published for the Paul Mellon Centre for Studies in British Art by Yale University Press, 1984). See also Harris, *British Architectural Books*, under "Gibbs, James," and Archer, *Literature of British Domestic Architecture*, under "Gibbs, James."

15. On the eighteenth-century churches, see Dell Upton, *Holy Things and Profane: Anglican Parish Churches in Colonial Virginia*, Architectural History Foundation Books, X (Cambridge, Massachusetts: MIT Press, 1986).

16. The point comes from Wittkower, "English Literature," 106. To sample the influence of the *Treasury* in Virginia, see Upton, *Holy Things*, 130–33; 137–38; 145; 229–31; 247–48, notes 37, 41.

17. On this room, see Scott Campbell Owen's trailblazing study, "George Washington's Mount Vernon as British Palladian Architecture," (Master of Architectural History thesis, University of Virginia, 1991), pp. 10–11, 42, 46, 52.

18. Vitruvius's basic discussion occurs in 1.2.1, 5–7. He develops the theme again and again, as in 5.9.3–4, 6.5, 7.4.4–5, 7.5.

19. I am here slightly modifying the conclusions in an excellent study by James Anthony Hall, "William Buckland's Anglo-Palladian Interior Ornamentation at Gunston Hall," (Master of Architectural History thesis, University of Virginia, 1989). The conspicuous order in the Palladian Room is a highly enriched Doric, but Buckland subordinated that to a lavish Corinthian cornice. His decision to frame the openings with aedicules of different sizes in a lesser order, the Doric, and to put only the cornice into the higher Order, the Corinthian, probably reflects his struggle to fit his decorative ideas inside a shell planned before his arrival in Virginia.

20. Maral S. Kalbian and I have together gone much beyond her landmark discussion, "The Ionic Order and the Progression of the Orders in American Palladianism before 1812" (Master of Architectural History thesis, University of Virginia, 1988), but its outline of the story remains sound.

21. Pliny, *Letters*, 2.17.8, describes a form of bow window at his villa at Laurentinum. Castell, in a search for the rules of the ancients, reconstructed Pliny's villas at Laurentinum and Tuscum for his *Villas of the Ancients Illustrated* (1728; reprint ed., with introductory notes by John Dixon Hunt, New York: Garland Publishing, 1982). The reconstruction of Laurentinum holds much interest for the study of buildings with bow-like elements in the eighteenth and early nineteenth centuries. For the indispensable survey of the bow window in Britain (exclusive of the influence of antiquity), see Pierre de la Ruffinière du Prey, "The *Bombé*-Fronted Country House from Talman to Soane," *The Fashioning and Functioning of the British Country House*, Studies in the History of Art, 25 (Washington, D.C.: National Gallery of Art, 1989), 29–49.

22. On Washington, Mount Vernon, and the Picturesque, see Owen, "Mount Vernon," esp. chap. 2.

23. Pevsner, "Genesis of the Picturesque," and Wittkower, "English Neo-Palladianism," have done much to shape the view of the Picturesque offered here. Although some writers on American architecture, such as James D. Kornwolf in "The Picturesque in the American Garden and Landscape before 1800" (*Eighteenth Century Life*, new series, 8 [January 1983]: 93–106) associate the Picturesque garden with British Palladianism, Americans normally neglect the importance of the Picturesque for the United States before the 1830s. The newest examination of the movement known to me is: Sidney K. Robinson, *Inquiry into the Picturesque* (Chicago: University of Chicago Press, 1991). The author, an architect, has based this stimulating volume of speculative essays on the British evidence and has supplied a valuable bibliography. For recent introductions to the Picturesque in Britain and its increasingly voluminous literature, see Malcolm Andrews, *The Search for the Picturesque: Landscape Aesthetics and Tourism in Britain, 1760–1800* (Aldershot, England: Scolar Press, 1989), and Archer, *Literature*, esp. xxv note 18, 28–30, 31, 59–71, 104–11. For the United States, the essays in Edward J. Nygren, et al., *Views and Visions: American Landscape before 1830* (Washington, D.C.: The Corcoran Gallery of Art, 1986) cover a range of topics, and Nygren's comments in his notes, pp. 77–81, provide a rich guide to the literature. So do George B. Tatum's notes to his "Nature's Gardener," in Tatum and Elisabeth Blair MacDougall, eds., *Prophet with Honor: The*

*Career of Andrew Jackson Downing, 1815–1852*, Dumbarton Oaks Colloquium on the History of Landscape Architecture XI (Washington, D.C., 1989), 43–80.

24. Andrews, *Search*, gives a serviceable recent introduction to the Sublime, esp. in relation to the landscape, although the book does not tie the bibliographical strands together. For much of the literature of the last decade, see Edmund Burke, *A Philosophical Enquiry into the Origin of Our Ideas of the Sublime and Beautiful*, 2nd ed. (1759; reprint ed., edited with an introduction by Adam Phillips, Oxford: Oxford University Press, 1990), xxv–xxvi. (For every other purpose, one must instead use Burke's *Enquiry* as edited with an introduction and notes by James T. Boulton, 1958; reprint, Notre Dame: University of Notre Dame, 1968). Nygren's notes in *Views and Visions* discuss literature germane to the United States. For a turn-of-the-century Anglo-American who dealt brilliantly with the problem of Gothic as opposed to Classical sublimity, see the discussion of Latrobe's Roman Catholic cathedral in Baltimore in Charles E. Brownell and Jeffrey A. Cohen, *The Architectural Drawings of Benjamin Henry Latrobe*, 2 vols., *The Papers of Benjamin Henry Latrobe*, 2nd ser. (New Haven: Yale University Press, forthcoming).

25. Jefferson to William Buchanan and James Hay, 26 January 1786, in *The Papers of Thomas Jefferson*, ed. Julian P. Boyd et al., 23 vols. to date (Princeton: Princeton Univ. Press, 1950–  ) 9: 220.

26. Coles to Cocke, 23 February 1816, University of Virginia Library, Special Collections Department, Cocke Papers, No. 640 etc., Box 21.

27. "Jefferson's First Plan," 97.

28. For the boast, see Leoni's "Preface to the Reader" in *The Architecture of A. Palladio; in Four Books*, trans. Nicholas Dubois, ed. Giacomo Leoni, 2nd ed., 2 vols. (London, 1721), 1: no pagination. On Leoni's editions, see Harris, *British Architectural Books*, under "Palladio, Andrea." On Jefferson's ownership, see William Bainter O'Neal, *Jefferson's Fine Arts Library: His Selections for the University of Virginia, together with His Own Architectural Books* (Charlottesville: University Press of Virginia, 1976), under "Palladio, Andrea," nos. 92a–92c.

29. For Jefferson's ownership of the *Parallèle* (in the Paris edition of 1766), see O'Neal, *Jefferson's Library*, under "Fréart de Chambray, Roland." The failure by historians (even Harris under "Fréart, Roland," in *British Architectural Books*) to assess fully Fréart's contribution to the Classical tradition, especially to British Palladianism, remains surprising. I hope that Laurel Costa, a University of Virginia graduate student who has presented an outstanding seminar report on Fréart, will carry this work forward to a still more formal offering.

30. See O'Neal, *Jefferson's Library*, under "Jones, Inigo," and "Morris, Robert," for the ownership and some of the evidence of the influence.

31. On the 1778 purchase, see pp. 175, 176 in William L. Beiswanger, "The Temple in the Garden: Thomas Jefferson's Vision of the Monticello Landscape," *Eighteenth Century Life*, new series 8 (January 1983): 170–88.

32. For this comment see Latrobe to Christian Ignatius Latrobe, 5 June 1805, in *The Papers of Benjamin Henry Latrobe*, microfiche edition, ed. Thomas E. Jeffrey (Clifton, New Jersey: James T. White & Company, for the Maryland Historical Society, 1976), 40/E7. See also Coles to Cocke on Jefferson's inability to draw a design for Bremo because he had sold his books to the nation.

33. I quote from Jefferson, "An Account of the Capitol in Virginia," as most recently edited in Fiske Kimball, "Thomas Jefferson and the First Monument of the Classical Revival in America," 1915; rev. ed., as *The Capitol of Virginia: A Landmark of American Architecture*, edited by Jon Kukla, with Martha C. Vick and Sarah Shields Driggs (Richmond: Virginia State Library and Archives, for the General Assembly of Virginia, 1989), 13. The findings of a University of Virginia Master of Architectural History thesis currently in progress, Brien J. Poffenberger's study "Thomas Jefferson's Design for the Virginia State Capitol," will go substantially beyond the interpretation that I offer here.

34. Susan C. Riddick made the all-important connection between "cubic" and "spherical" proportions and the Vitruvian tradition in "The Influence of B. H. Latrobe on Jefferson's Design for the University of Virginia" (Master of Architectural History thesis, University of Virginia, 1988), 44–45.

One might have expected Jefferson to despise the ellipse as a deformed circle, but, as Beiswanger has kindly stressed to me, he took delight in the shape. For what may have simply been a personal taste he could, at all events, cite high authority, as a student of mine, Maria Lourdes Solera, has detected: the plan of the Colosseum among the "ancients" and Palladio's staircases among the "moderns."

35. O'Neal, *Jefferson's Library*, under "Vitruvius Pollio," no. 125d. Beiswanger, "Temple," 179, points to Jefferson's use of the Perrault Vitruvius in a scheme for temples at Monticello before Jefferson went abroad in 1784.

36. For the Monticello literature, see survey nos. 7, 8, 12. On Poplar Forest, see the important new findings by Amy E. Facca in "Thomas Jefferson's Poplar Forest," Master of Architectural History thesis, University of Virginia, 1988, and C. Allan Brown in "Thomas Jefferson's Poplar Forest: The Mathematics of an Ideal Villa," *Journal of Garden History* 10 (1990):117–39. Numerous books (including Gibbs's *Book of Architecture* and Kent's *Designs of Inigo Jones*) illustrated cubic rooms, but the scant information on Jefferson's first library, which burned with his house at Shadwell in 1770, contributes to the difficulty of understanding Jefferson's formative years in architecture.

37. The basic discussion of the design is now Beiswanger, "Temple," 176. Frederick Doveton Nichols, *Thomas Jefferson's Architectural Drawings . . . with Commentary and a Check List*, 5th ed. (Boston: Massachusetts Historical Society, 1984), catalogues the sheet as no. 91 and reproduces both sides in figs. 5–6. For what Jefferson read on the Tempietto, see Palladio, *Architecture*, Bk. 4, chap. 17. My former student Elizabeth Persichetty has contributed materially to my understanding of this design.

38. See Sommer, "Jefferson's First Plan," 92. See also Sommer's particular source, Jefferson to James Oldham, 24 December 1804, University of Virginia Library, Special Collections Department, Jefferson Papers, Acc. No. 7708; quoted at more length in O'Neal, *Jefferson's Library*, 277.

39. Three works in progress at the University of Virginia while this chapter was being written will dramatically change the state of knowledge on Jefferson and the museum of the Orders: Joseph Michael Lasala's Master of Architectural History thesis, "Thomas Jefferson's Designs for the University of Virginia," draft, 1991; Patricia C. Sherwood's two-semester-long examination of the University drawings for two seminars, 1990–91; and Poffenberger's "Virginia State Capitol."

40. Between 1986 and 1990, more than fifty of my University of Virginia graduate and undergraduate students have written essays wrestling with whether these Orders follow any organization. I thank them warmly for all that they have showed me.

41. Jefferson to William Coffee, 10 July 1822, Massachusetts Historical Society, Coolidge Collection; reproduced in the University of Virginia Library, Special Collections Department, Jefferson Papers, Microfilm, Coolidge Collection, Reel 23. See also Facca, "Poplar Forest," chap. 3, which rewardingly opens up the discussion of Jefferson and *decor*.

42. Ed. with an introduction and notes by William Peden (1955; reprint, New York: W. W. Norton and Company, 1972), pp. 152–54.

43. Quotation from Jefferson in Coles to Cocke, 23 February 1816.

44. Ann M. Lucas's "Ordering His Environment: Thomas Jefferson's Architecture from Monticello to the University of Virginia" (Master of Architectural History thesis, University of Virginia, 1989) isolates the evolution of the Palladian wing as an issue of the greatest consequence in understanding Jefferson's architecture.

45. Pages 19–20, 24–25, 263–64 note 5. Grace Murray, a graduate student in art history at the University of Virginia, has taught me a great deal about how Jefferson's lines established the sites as places to visit and to record for their aesthetic qualities.

46. Helen Scott Townsend Reed has demonstrated the Sublime and the Picturesque traits of the tower projects and has successfully extended this line of thought in "Jefferson's Observatory Tower Projects for Montalto and the University of Virginia" (Master of Architectural History thesis, University of Virginia, 1991).

47. Jefferson to James Buchanan and William Hay, 13 August 1785, in *Papers* 8: 366.

48. To judge from Thomas J. McCormick's monograph, *Charles Louis Clérisseau and the Genesis of Neo-Classicism*, An Architectural History Foundation Book (Cambridge, Massachusetts: MIT Press, 1990), Clérisseau had only a marginal claim on the title of architect. An old belief that he was one of the principal shapers of classicizing movements internationally does not stand up.

49. Jefferson to John Page, 4 May 1786, in *Papers* 9: 445.

50. A number of scholars have suggested that the passage refers to the Adamesque. I owe the point fundamentally to private communication with Sommer, who has the evidence to back it up.

51. He visited Syon House on 20 April 1786. See Edward Dumbauld, "Jefferson and Adams' English Garden Tour," in *Jefferson and the Arts: An Extended View*, ed. William Howard Adams (Washington, D.C.: National Gallery of Art, 1976), 140, 151, 153.

52. Coles to Cocke, 23 February 1816.

53. For extended discussions of the Jefferson-Delorme story, see Douglas James Harnsberger, " 'In Delorme's Manner . . .': A Study of the Applications of Philibert Delorme's Dome Construction Method in Early 19th Century American Architecture" (Master of Architectural History thesis, University of Virginia, 1981), and Brownell and Cohen, *Architectural Drawings*.

54. On Jefferson and the Halle au Blé, see Harnsberger, " 'Delorme's Manner,' " and Brownell and Cohen, *Architectural Drawings*.

55. On Jefferson's acquisition of Fréart's architectural publications, see O'Neal, *Jefferson's Library*, under "Palladio, Andrea," no. 92d, and "Fréart de Chambray, Roland."

56. On a more appropriate occasion I hope to summarize the misrepresentations regarding Jefferson generally and the Lawn particularly in relation to French architecture. Two points will hold the fort. First, Jefferson labeled his elevation for Pavilion IX (figure 2.24) as a Latrobe design, and not just once (in the inscription visible in the upper right-hand corner) but twice, as Lasala has pointed out in the draft of his "University of Virginia." The design probably does reflect admiration for Ledoux, but on Latrobe's part, not Jefferson's. Second, the motif of an exterior screened niche does not "belong to" Ledoux but comes from the Roman baths.

57. For the inscription, see William Peden, "The Jefferson Monument at the University of Missouri," *Missouri Historical Review* 72 (1977): 67–77, a reference that I owe to my student Peter Ciganek. O'Neal, *Jefferson's Library*, notes, entry by entry, what books Jefferson wanted the University to acquire.

58. Vincent Scully has made an essential contribution to understanding Monticello by calling attention to the breaking of the box here. I owe the point to his essay "American Houses: Thomas Jefferson to Frank Lloyd Wright," chap. 4 in Edgar Kaufmann, Jr., ed., *The Rise of an American Architecture* (New York: published in association with the Metropolitan Museum of Art by Praeger Publishers, 1970), esp. p. 164. At the same time, I owe to Susan Stein, curator, the Thomas Jefferson Memorial Foundation, the warning that we see Monticello today, not only with an exterior in an ideal state that Jefferson never saw, but with an interior stripped of a clutter of possessions.

59. The nearly unaccountable axial asymmetry of the Lawn has almost always escaped the notice of writers. In 1977 I called it to the attention of Paul Venable Turner. His discussion of the Lawn in *Campus: An American Planning Tradition*, The Architectural History Foundation/MIT Press Series, VII (1984; paperback ed., New York, 1987), 76–87, takes a giant step forward (83) by connecting the asymmetry with Jefferson's view of the group as an "academical village." At bottom, though, this still leaves one puzzling as to how Jefferson could find his way to using the Orders in an architectural grouping where the right side does not match the left.

60. On the workmen, see two complementary studies: Richard Charles Cote, "The Architectural Workmen of Thomas Jefferson in Virginia," 2 vols. (Ph.D. diss., Boston University, 1986), and K. Edward Lay, "Charlottesville's Architectural Legacy," *Magazine of Albemarle County History* 46 (1988): 28–59.

61. Of the five, it was just three—James Stuart, Sir William Chambers, and Robert Adam—who in practice formulated British Neoclassicism. On the architectural evolution, see the wealth of information in Stillman, *English Neo-Classical Architecture.*

62. My restatements of the Adams' positions summarize passages conveniently contained on pp. 1–2 and 5–6 of a recent reprint of the *Works* (New York: Dover Publications, 1980). Note the key characterizations regarding the internal use of the Orders and their appendages under British Palladianism and after the Adam "revolution" (pp. 1–2): "The massive entablature, the ponderous compartment ceiling, the tabernacle frame . . . are now universally exploded. . . . We have introduced a great diversity of ceilings, freezes [sic], and decorated pilasters," along with elements distinct from the orders, "grotesque stucco, and painted ornaments, together with the flowing rainceau [sic], with its fanciful figures and winding foliage." See also revealing discussion of the book in Harris, *British Architectural Books,* under "Adam, Robert and James."

63. On the *Treatise,* see Harris, *British Architectural Books,* under "Chambers, Sir William."

64. For a detailed review of the rediscovery of the Greek Doric, see Pevsner and S. Lang, "The Doric Revival," in Pevsner, *Studies,* chap. 12.

65. Stuart wrote in his volume 2 of *Antiquities of Athens* that "we selected such Buildings . . . as would exhibit specimens of the several kinds of Columns in use among the ancient Greeks" (reprint, New York: Arno Press, 1980: Advertisement, n. p.). The organization of the volumes had, however, undergone tortuous changes since its conception. On these and the redating of all three volumes, see Harris, *British Architectural Books,* under "Stuart, James, and Revett, Nicholas."

66. My quotations and paraphrases come from Stuart's preface, pages i–v.

67. For the most basic information on this book and on Benjamin, see Henry-Russell Hitchcock, *American Architectural Books: A List of Books, Portfolios, and Pamphlets on Architecture and Related Subjects Published in America before 1895,* new expanded ed., with contributions by divers hands (New York: Da Capo Press, 1976), under "Benjamin, Asher"; "Asher Benjamin and American Architecture," ed. Jack Quinan, *Journal of the Society of Architectural Historians* 38 (October 1979), roughly a special number on Benjamin; and Abbott Lowell Cummings under "Benjamin, Asher," in Adolf K. Placzek, ed., *Macmillan Encyclopedia of Architects,* 4 vols. (New York: Free Press, 1982).

68. The full list of the pertinent literature appears with survey no. 24. In connection with the present remarks, the most fundamental sources are Edward Francis Zimmer, "The Architectural Career of Alexander Parris (1780–1852)," 2 vols. (Ph.D. dissertation, Boston

University, 1984), especially 189–220; and Leslie A. Giles, "Decorative Paintings at the Wickham House, Richmond, Virginia: Their Sources, Their Author, and *Decor*" (Master of Architectural History thesis, University of Virginia, 1990).

69. On the Sears house see Zimmer, "Architectural Career," 400–414. (One does not know how much the craftsmen had to do with selecting the Wickham ornamentation.) On the dissemination of New England Neoclassicism see Mills Lane, *Architecture of the Old South: Virginia,* with editorial assistance by Calder Loth (Savannah: Beehive Press, 1987), 155–58, 163–68, and Sarah Shields Driggs, "Otis Manson and Neoclassicism in Central Virginia" (Master of Architectural History thesis, University of Virginia, 1988).

70. In the sixth edition of the *Companion,* Raynerd's discussion, including all the lines that I quote, appears on pp. 75–76.

71. I have here enlarged upon the indispensable discussion in Giles, "Decorative Paintings."

72. For the standard coverage of the typology of civic and commercial buildings see Nikolaus Pevsner, *A History of Building Types,* The A. W. Mellon Lectures in the Fine Arts, The National Gallery of Art, 1970; Bollingen Series XXXV, 19 (Princeton: Princeton University Press, 1976).

73. Brownell and Cohen deal extensively with the Latrobe episodes in *Architectural Drawings.* For documentation of the later events in the story of Washington monuments see the appropriate survey entries elsewhere in this book.

74. James Fenimore Cooper had suggested that the nation preserve Mount Vernon and the Washington tomb there, in place of erecting a marble monument, in his *Notions of the Americans: Picked up by a Travelling Bachelor,* 2 vols. (Philadelphia: Carey, Lea & Carey, 1828) 2: 197. On the saving of Mount Vernon see Gerald W. Johnson, *Mount Vernon: The Story of a Shrine,* with extracts from the diaries and letters of George Washington selected and annotated by Charles Cecil Wall, revised with an epilogue by Ellen McCallister Clark (Mount Vernon, Virginia: The Mount Vernon Ladies' Association, 1991); and Elswyth Thane, *Mount Vernon Is Ours: The Story of Its Preservation* (New York: Duell, Sloan and Pearce, 1966).

75. For a close consideration of the Temple Revival into the 1820s see Brownell and Cohen, *Architectural Drawings.*

76. For an excellent discussion of the murky developments see Alexandra Cushing Howard, "Stephen Hallet and William Thornton . . . : A Re-evaluation of Their Role in the Original Design of the Federal Capitol, 1791–1797" (Master of Architectural History thesis, University of Virginia, 1974). For a decade, Don Alexander Hawkins of Washington, D.C., has shared with me his research on Thornton's conceptions, and these invaluable findings deserve publication in the near future.

77. Georg Germann takes the secularization of the Gothic as a theme in his stimulating study *Gothic Revival in Europe and Britain: Sources, Influences and Ideas,* trans. Gerald Onn (Cambridge, Massachusetts: MIT Press, 1973).

78. Marcus Whiffen's "The Early County Courthouses of Virginia," *Journal of the Society of Architectural Historians* 18 (March 1959): 2–10 shows the dissemination of forms from Virginia's first and second capitols to county courthouses. Carl R. Lounsbury of Colonial Williamsburg will give the Virginia courthouse a fresh and closer look in a monograph that he has in hand.

79. Jane B. Davies analyzes Davis's development of this anta pilaster in "A. J. Davis' Projects for a Patent Office Building, 1832–34," *Journal of the Society of Architectural Historians* 24 (October 1965): 229–51.

80. An excellent sleuth, Kathleen Froome Howe, reconstructed much of the evolution of the type for a seminar of mine in 1987.

81. On Parris's use see Zimmer, "Architectural Career," 415–22, 439–44.

82. One can follow part of the trail in Jane B. Davies, "Davis, Alexander Jackson" and "Town, Ithiel," in *Macmillan Encyclopedia.*

83. I thank John Richardson of Richmond and Powhatan for assisting me by undertaking important unpublished research on the Courthouse.

84. See Mary Lee Link Allen, "Thomas U. Walter's Greek Revival Church in Richmond, Virginia" (Master of Arts thesis, Virginia Commonwealth University, 1978).

85. In a 1990 seminar report, my student Richard L. Silverman demolished an old attribution to Jefferson of the *distyle-in-muris* facade of the lost church of Christ Church, Charlottesville. Silverman has documented that George W. Spooner added the facade in 1853.

86. The tug-of-war between the cohesive and the diversified facade had actually gone on for centuries. In 1665, for instance, Bernini, proponent of the colossal order, bitingly called the Tuileries Palace in Paris "a colossal trifle, like an enormous troop of tiny children." See Paul Fréart, Sieur de Chantelou, *Diary of the Cavaliere Bernini's Visit to France,* edited and with an introduction by Anthony Blunt, annotated by George C. Bauer, and translated by Margery Corbett (Princeton: Princeton University Press, 1985), xxii, 72.

87. For a slightly different transcription of the full letter from Latrobe to Christian Ignatius Latrobe, 4 November 1804, see Latrobe, *Correspondence,* 1: 563–66.

88. Latrobe to Christian Ignatius Latrobe, 5 June 1805, *Papers,* microfiche edition, 40/E7.

89. See his *Lectures on Architecture, as Delivered to the Students of the Royal Academy from 1809 to 1836 in Two Courses of Six Lectures Each,* ed. Arthur T. Bolton, Publication of Sir John Soane's Museum, no. 14 (London, 1929), especially Lecture 10, pp. 159–60.

90. For another discussion, see Brownell and Cohen, *Architectural Drawings.* James Early's *Romanticism and American Architecture* (New York: A. S. Barnes and Co., 1965) prompted the tack (p. 25).

91. "The New Custom-House," *New-York Mirror*, 23 August 1834.

92. Davis, *Journal*, Metropolitan Museum of Art, Davis Collection, vol. I, entries for 1 September (on Hunt) and 17 October (on Mullett, quoting an unidentified source), 1872.

93. *Select Architecture, Being Regular Designs of Plans and Elevations Well Suited to both Town and Country*, 2nd ed. (1757; reprint ed., with a foreword by Adolf K. Placzek, New York: Da Capo Press, 1973), introduction, no pagination.

94. For a summary of the evolution of the theory of character in Britain, with citations to much of the secondary literature, see Archer, *Literature*, 46–56. I have found Germann, *Gothic Revival* (throughout, but especially 22–23, 37, 52; pt. 2, chap. 1; and 131, 183) indispensable in handling a subject that the architects themselves confused. Brownell and Cohen, *Architectural Drawings*, give a detailed examination of character in respect to Latrobe. At least for most of the period under discussion, it makes no sense to use the non-period label *architecture parlante* which, according to Robin Middleton, was coined by Léon Vaudoyer as late as 1852, and at that, to designate Ledoux's work, of which he disapproved; see Middleton and David Watkin, *Neoclassical and 19th Century Architecture* (New York: Harry N. Abrams, 1980), 237.

95. Latrobe to James Wood and the Council of State of Virginia, 12 July 1797, in Latrobe, *Papers*, microfiche ed., 156/A6.

96. On these two buildings see Stillman, *English Neo-Classical Architecture*, 382, 398, 400–501, with citations to further literature. Harold David Kalman gives the most detailed consideration to the pair in "The Architecture of George Dance the Younger" (Ph.D. diss., Princeton University, 1971), chap. 5.

97. On Tuscan lore see Sir John Summerson, "Inigo Jones," *Proceedings of the British Academy*, 50 (1965): 169–92, and James S. Ackerman, "The Tuscan/Rustic Order: A Study in the Metaphorical Language of Architecture," *Journal of the Society of Architectural Historians* 42 (March 1983): 15–34. On Dance's ownership of the Leoni Palladio, the source for my illustration of the Palazzo Thiene, see Kalman, "Architecture," 79–84.

98. Cocke to William Maxwell, 1 May 1845, University of Virginia Library, Special Collections Department, Cocke Papers, No. 640 etc., Box 189, Letterbook.

99. For this argument, see Patrick Alexander Snadon, "A. J. Davis and the Gothic Revival Castle in America, 1832–1865," 2 vols. (Ph.D. diss., Cornell University, 1988) pp. 57–68 and here and there throughout. Snadon places Belmead before Davis's maturity with this kind of expression.

100. "Belmead," *The Horticulturist* 4 (April 1850): 479–81. On Davis's authorship, see Snadon, "Davis," 57–58 (with a partial transcription of Davis's manuscript) and 200, note 21. Another partial transcription of the manuscript appears in a book that has made spectacular disclosures about Davis's Virginia designs, Lane's *Virginia*, 236.

101. *Cottage Residences: or, A Series of Designs for Rural Cottages and Cottage Villas, and Their . . . Grounds, Adapted to North America. . . .* (New York: Wiley & Putnam, 1842), 10–15.

102. *Treatise*, 118–19. Soane quoted a version of this passage in his *Lectures*, Lecture 4, p. 69.

103. "The Lewis Brooks Museum of Natural Science," *Frank Leslie's Illustrated Newspaper*, 9 March 1878.

104. "Architecture and Architects at the Capital of the United States from Its Foundation until 1875," *American Architect and Building News* 2, supp. (24 February 1877), vi. See also survey no. 54.

105. Jeffrey L. Hantman, "Brooks Hall at the University of Virginia: Unraveling the Mystery," *Magazine of Albemarle County History* 47 (1989): 69–92.

106. The amphitheater appears in Charles Louis Clérisseau's *Antiquités de la France* (Paris: l'Imprimerie de Philippe-Denys Pierres, 1778), pls. X-XIX. One suspects that it began arousing favorable attention as the "aesthetic of the temple" faded. Thus, as a student at the Ecole des Ponts et Chaussées in 1852–53, Alfred L. Rives (see survey no. 50) was assigned the exercise of washing shadows onto an engraved elevation of the amphitheater. This sheet survives in Alfred Landon Rives Drawings, Special Collections Department, University of Virginia Library, Oversize Box N-17, Folder 2313–15 to 2313–20.

# THE JEFFERSON ..

## ▲ EIGHT ROOMS AND TWO BATHS

THE "JEFFERSON" is designed along the same lines as historic Mount Vernon, and is a true example of Southern Colonial architecture—the same type that has endured in many instances for generation after generation. The Southern Colonial type has held its share of popularity from the beginning. Exterior walls of white-painted brick provide a substantial appearance and form a pleasing background for the dark green shutters and roof.

### THE FLOOR PLAN

Dining Room, Kitchen, Living Room and useful, attractive Sun Room all open off the center hall on the first floor. Note the two convenient closets off the vestibule, for outer wraps.

Second floor plan contains hall, four large roomy bedrooms and two baths. This roomy home boasts a total of eleven closets.

Fill out the Information Blank and we will send you complete delivered price, photographic architectural elevations and floor plans, also outline of specifications.

### WHAT OUR PRICE INCLUDES

At the base price quoted, we will furnish all materials needed to build this home, (except brick and masonry) consisting of lumber, lath, roof shingles, building paper, millwork and 6-Panel Doors, Back Band trim, Kitchen Cabinets, Linoleum for Kitchen, Bath and Lavatory, Oak flooring in remainder of rooms, Elgin Manhattan hardware, enamel for interior trim, varnish for doors and floors, sheet metal and outside paint materials.

**MODERN HOME**
**No. 3349**
**NOT ALREADY CUT**

**FIRST FLOOR PLAN**

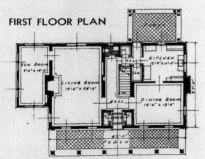

**SECOND FLOOR PLAN**

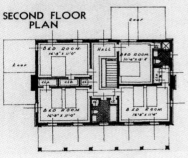

*Sears, Roebuck and Co.*

# 3

# BUILDING ON THE FOUNDATIONS

*The Historic Present in Virginia Architecture, 1870–1990*

by RICHARD GUY WILSON

FIGURE 3.1. *"The Jefferson," a house kit designed by Sears, Roebuck and Company's Architecture Division in the 1930s. In the Sears catalogues for 1932, 1933, and 1937, this design, "along the same lines as historic Mount Vernon," was described as "a true example of Southern Colonial architecture." (Photograph courtesy of The Preservation Press, The National Trust for Historic Preservation in the United States, and Sears, Roebuck and Company.)*

After observing the annual exhibition of the New York Architectural League in 1932, Fiske Kimball, the eminent architectural historian, critic, and museum director, caustically noted: "There is no good architecture south of Washington, D.C."[1] Certainly Kimball did not mean the architecture of the seventeenth through the early nineteenth centuries, about which he had written so eloquently in his many and memorable books nor, one assumes, his own work in Virginia. No, his comments were directed to recent architecture of the South. In a sense Kimball expressed a common Yankee prejudice: the South was a cultural wasteland. "The Sahara of the Bozart" was how H. L. Mencken, using an architectural pun, had summed up the region's culture a few years earlier.[2] This benighted view of the South as artistically barren—especially in the twentieth century—has been revised in so many ways with recognition of literary and educational achievements that it scarcely needs recounting here.

But what about architecture? Yes, the South's architecture, specifically Virginia's, is recognized and hailed. But seldom, if ever, is it the architecture of the past century; rather, lauded and pictured is the earlier Colonial, Georgian, and Jeffersonian. Look in almost any book on American architecture and what do you see that comes from Virginia? There are plenty of seventeenth-, eighteenth-, and early-nineteenth-century buildings, but what is shown that dates since the Civil War? The myth, of course, is that nothing happened for years after The War, and after that, well, it is a purely local affair. The only buildings of national stature that might be pictured are Eero Saarinen's Dulles Airport Terminal ( SURVEY NO. 107 ) and possibly Frank Lloyd Wright's Pope-Leighey House ( SURVEY NO. 96 ), but these could exist almost anywhere in the United States. Also shown would be one other twentieth-century architectural creation, though it will seldom be identified as such: Colonial Williamsburg and the Capitol and Governor's Palace ( SURVEY NOS. 83–86 ).[3]

Ironies abound: Virginia's past is more present than the recent; history exerts a stronger hold and seems more real than the present; and Virginia's best-known recent buildings are by outsiders, non-Virginians.

This chapter explores "recent" Virginia architecture—since the 1870s. It examines the myth of the Old Dominion and the popular picture of a commonwealth of red brick and white trim, of white weatherboards and dentils, of churches modeled after Wren and Gibbs, of Monticellos nestled on hilltops, of large extended-wing James River mansions, of great-columned planters' houses, and the smaller reproductions of the neat and tidy houses of villages and towns like Williamsburg. It also explores some of the causes for these views of Virginia's architecture and the reasons for some of the obscurity of the last century or more, along with other patterns that have emerged from the architectural carpet. But several caveats need to be made. The territory is not completely unmapped; research and commentary on later Virginia architecture has been undertaken, and some of it is of very high quality. However, much of it appears in isolated pockets, the necessary study of individuals, towns, cities, or counties. But the larger picture has not been brought into focus.[4] Hence Virginia's architectural landscape resembles in some ways what the first colonists saw: a vast terrain with the close-at-hand known—a stream, a lake, a large tree, and then, glimpsed off in the distance, a few mountain ranges—but the overall geography is unclear. There is a need to give more contours to this landscape, to understand both its temporal and physical dimensions, to begin to map the surface, to lay down a few trails of observations and suggestions.

History is a mental creation; it is a view of facts arranged in patterns that provide meaning; yet multiple meanings or interpretations do exist, though frequently in contradiction. History is made by those who record it; historians take the actions of individuals, the decisions of patrons, the drawings and designs of architects, the labor of builders, and gives them a pattern. So the one who writes, or creates, or preserves and saves history is important. Architectural history in Virginia has been written by many individuals: the women of the Association for the Preservation of Virginia Antiquities, the architects who measured the colonial remains, the photographers who document what has been built, and the numerous local historical societies. All of these and others have been important in one way or another, but over the years three centers of study have emerged: the University of Virginia since the arrival of Fiske Kimball in 1919, Williamsburg since the beginnings of restoration in the mid 1920s, and the Virginia Historic Landmarks Commission (now more bureaucratically titled the Virginia Department of Historic Resources) in Richmond. Since the mid 1960s this agency has worked to establish a statewide program to identify and preserve significant buildings. Overlaps occur between these three centers, along with changes of emphasis on what is studied; but it is from individuals within these institutions that the shifting views of Virginia's architecture have emerged. The University, being a school of architecture, has tended to emphasize the grand manner, formal design, modernism, and Jefferson and to follow national trends; Colonial Williamsburg, while containing aspects of this formality in its early years, has tended towards the smaller scale and the humble approach; and the Virginia Department of Historic Resources has been far more inclusive, attempting to encompass the entire state. Patterns of interaction have occurred between historians, preservationists, and architects; what interests the one impacts the others at some point. The traffic pattern, though, is not one-way: preservationists have awakened architects and historians to aspects of the past, but equally, there has been another direction, with architects changing our perceptions of what should be studied.

Some aspects of Virginia's recent architecture are fairly clear, for as the examples in the Survey (Chapter 6) illustrate, they follow the broad stylistic contours of the national scene. The architects operating in Virginia, whether native sons or from elsewhere, have created many designs that would not appear out of place in New York, Chicago, or Atlanta. Virginia follows the well-trodden path—High Victorian (and its subtleties Second Empire, Gothic, Romanesque), then Late Victorian and the various eclectic styles (French, Colonial, Tudor Revival or "Tudorbethan"), then Modern and Postmodern. A surprise or two might occur along the road, but the general outline is well known. Architecture, however, is more than the recording of styles; it is more than physical shelter for activities. It also represents a mental shelter, it encompasses values, beliefs, and views about the world, expressions and concepts of status, that need to be explicated.

This chapter investigates what is popularly identified as Virginia architecture and how it came to be. But the state's architecture is too synthetic and too diverse to claim some sort of all-encompassing regional, environmental, functional, or stylistic definition. Wide divergences and little commonality exist among the many buildings constructed within the fictive boundaries of the Commonwealth. Virginia's architecture is quite simply all that which has been built within the state's borders. But out of this apparent chaos, out of these hundreds of thousands of buildings, there are certain patterns that appear to be uniquely Virginian.

One further caveat—architecture both represents and creates social and cultural conditions. In the period from 1870 to 1990, Virginia underwent great changes; the population grew from 1,225,000 to 6,187,358. With it came new cities, buildings, factories, mills, warehouses, roads, highways, commercial strips, settlement patterns, gardens, parks, national forests, and a myriad of other changes. Like other states across the nation, Virginia developed a lively vernacular architecture of the road and the automobile, but these can only be partially inferred from this chapter, for there are many gaps: in this book there are no shopping centers, diners, motels, fast-food outlets, or supermarkets. For this essay does not offer a complete cross-section of the architecture of the state, whatever that may be. The drawings and photographs in this book are of important buildings by significant architects, but they can only show the highlights of what Virginia architecture has meant in the past 120 or so years. And similarly, this essay can only suggest and point to those social and cultural issues that affect architectural design.

Implicit in this selection is the question: What is architecture, and how does it differ from other types of building design? For this book is not a history of the total built environment, although references are made to barns, silos, log cabins, shacks, tract houses, buildings by anonymous builders, and all the other constructed flotsam of American civilization of the past 125 years. This book is above all a study of the sources of inspiration for architecture, the interaction between high and low art, the high art of architecture as practiced by architects and the more popular or common building traditions. Whether they be regional vernacular houses from Louisa County or commercial Colonial Ranch houses at Battlefield Estates is important. There has been interplay in both directions: sometimes architects draw inspiration from the vernacular, as with Floyd Johnson's house ( SURVEY NO. 101 ), and similarly the ubiquitous Builder's Colonial draws upon Virginia's earliest architecture.

The sources for some of Virginia's buildings have also been house pattern-books like Gustav Stickley's *Craftsman Homes* (1909) and house catalogues from Sears, Roebuck and Company ( FIGURE 3.1 ). Equally important have been designs like those shown on a page from a builder's pocket-book dating from the 1860s or 1870s, in which a floor plan and the costs were all that was needed to begin ( FIGURE 3.2 ). The unknown builder of this design had an

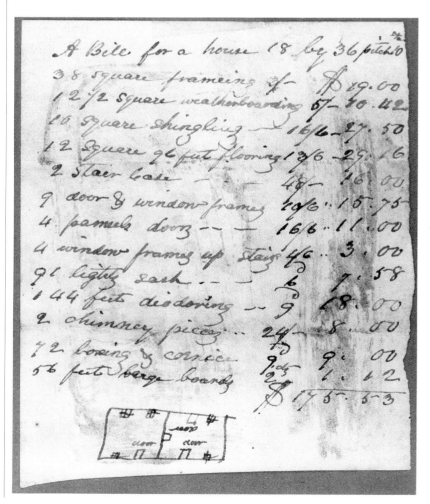

FIGURE 3.2. *On this* page from an unknown builder's pocket-book, *circa 1860, a simple floor plan and a list of the cost estimates were all that was needed to begin construction of a house. Pen on paper, 5 by 6 inches. (Courtesy of Henry J. Browne, Charlottesville.)*

intuitive understanding of what a house plan should be like, and from it the elevations would follow. The Sears "Jefferson" and the unknown builder's sketch are part of the history of recent Virginia architecture, and while they do not bear the imprimatur of a high-art architect, neither can they be ignored. Both illustrate changing views of what might be studied.

One method by which to understand the Commonwealth's architecture from 1870 to the present is to recognize its polymorphous nature: that many patterns are in operation, and that they can be contradictory, exist independently from each other, run parallel, and also overlap. These patterns of contradictions frequently have a bifurcate or dualistic quality. The purpose of history is to sort out the information into usable and understandable patterns but these patterns may still remain contradictory to each other.

## Geography and Art History

One of the most common conditions affecting Virginia's architecture is its geography, which frequently has meant an emphasis on the rural, and a slighting of the urban. Many buildings are identified not by the town where they are located, but by their county. More important architecturally has been the deep and abiding hold that the rural or country mentality exercises upon Virginians. It is the country house, or place, that represents Virginia. The historical survey-books well illustrate this: it is the country house, Monticello and Westover, that appears again and again. The plantation house, or particularly the houses along the James River (Carter's Grove, Westover, Shirley) or the Potomac (Mount Vernon, Gunston Hall) have been appropriated and duplicated throughout the state and across the nation.

Originally, of course, the country house in Virginia was the seat of economic and political power, but in the twentieth century it has become more of a retreat, a stage prop. The "country place" phenomenon began in the late 1890s and grew substantially until the Depression, though in recent years it has expanded again. Country places were large houses that served the wealthy as rural retreats; these properties were not themselves the source of wealth but rather an artifice that imitated the English "squirearchy." Because Virginia was one of the few states that originally had houses on a scale with those of minor English gentry, it became a source for architectural models and a scene of development. In the late nineteenth and early twentieth centuries wealthy Northerners began to move South and to purchase and restore old Virginia estates: members of the duPont family at one time owned Montpelier and Frascati in Orange County, and Ampthill in Cumberland County.[5] This passion for imitating the aristocracy in Virginia soon moved on to constructing entirely new estates resembling the old, as can be seen around Charlottesville in Albemarle County, or the Upperville area in Fauquier County. But there is also a very different aspect of this attraction for the country, the two- or three-acre rural site with a brick ranch and a satellite dish, or the sprawling suburbs around any city. The attraction of the country is strong for citizens of all classes.

But the history of Virginia architecture is not just the house in the country or the suburbs, for an extensive urban architecture has created the state's cities and towns. Virginia's pattern of urbanism and urban architecture has followed the general trend in the United States: urban centers growing in the nineteenth and twentieth century up to about 1940, then a dispersal outwards, and now a decline of the central city. The result has been that the best urban architecture dates from the late nineteenth and early twentieth centuries; buildings after the 1940s tend to be viewed as isolated objects. While Virginia does follow the national pattern, still some of the ethos for this dispersal—and the lack of planning regulation which has led to strip developments—must be laid to Virginia's political heritage: to the Jeffersonian doctrine of a society of small towns and farms, with a minimum of governmental regulation.

Other geographical patterns exist, such as the split between the Tidewater and the Piedmont, or between Virginia east of the Blue Ridge versus the Shenandoah Valley and western Virginia. Historically very different architectural traditions functioned in these areas: the eastern part has operated within the English architectural tradition, and the Valley followed patterns that were brought south from Pennsylvania. Perhaps the most obvious duality is the political one—which has obvious architectural implications—of Northern Virginia (or the Washington suburbs) versus Richmond and the rest of the state. Northern Virginia is architecturally much more of a colony of Washington, D.C., than it is part of the rest of the Commonwealth. Hence some buildings represented in this survey—Arlington Memorial Bridge ( SURVEY NO. 78 ), National Airport ( SURVEY NOS. 97,98 ), the Pentagon ( SURVEY NO. 102 ), and Dulles Airport ( SURVEY NO. 107 )—exist independently from Virginia. They are really national buildings and symbols and only happen to be Virginian because of their geographical location.

Across the state there has been a pattern of strong architects and firms located in the major cities and towns. Architects, even if they are designing country houses, have traditionally operated from urban settings. These architects have exerted their influence both within their city and in their immediate area, and at times had an impact on the state as a whole. Their spread of influence has been directly proportionate to improvements in communication and travel. Geographical politics has also played a role, as can be seen in the commission for the State Capitol expansion of 1904–06 (see SURVEY NO. 67 ). But Northern Virginia notwithstanding, Richmond has long been the first city of the state and from it have come firms with long histories—like Baskervill (originally Noland & Baskervill), Carneal & Johnston, and Marcellus Wright Cox & Smith and others—who have dominated the profession for the past eighty to ninety years. Norfolk, as the leading city of the Tidewater, has been the second city and from there, individuals such as John Kevan Peebles have built a statewide reputation. Beyond are the smaller cities, more regional in their focus—Alexandria, Fredericksburg, Lynchburg, Roanoke, Charlottesville, Staunton, and Lexington—in which local firms have operated, and at times moved on to the larger statewide stage.[6] Stanhope Johnson, for example, dominated architecture in

FIGURE 3.3. *Out-of-state architects often had logical reasons for working in Virginia. In this case, the supervising architect, James G. Hill (1814–1913), was a federal employee for the Treasury Department.* **Front Elevation, U. S. Court House & Post Office, Danville,** *Virginia, 1881. Ink on paper, 37¼ by 25 inches. (Photograph courtesy of the National Archives, Washington, D.C.)*

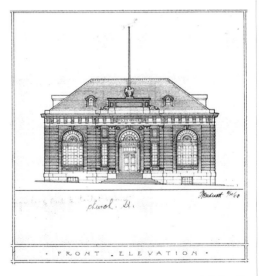

FIGURE 3.4. *Another example of federally sponsored architecture in Virginia:* **Elevation for U. S. Post Office,** *Martinsville, Virginia, 1903, by James Knox Taylor (1857–1929). Ink on paper, 14¾ by 21½ inches. (Photograph courtesy of the National Archives, Washington, D.C.)*

Lynchburg and Charlottesville from the 1920s through the 1940s. Milton Grigg of Charlottesville gained a nationwide reputation for his church designs in the 1940s, and is one of few Virginians to have designed abroad. T. J. Collins & Son dominated Staunton for years and helped to create a particularly cohesive small town there. The growth of Northern Virginia since World War II has attracted large, relatively anonymous firms to set up headquarters in the area, yet they operate on a national scale.

In still another way geography has determined who designs Virginia's notable buildings: in many cases it has been out-of-state architects. However competent Virginia's own architects have been, there had always been a tradition of going to out-of-state architects for many of the state's most important buildings. Early in the nineteenth century one could see the pattern begin to develop, as Robert Mills and Alexander Parris, and later Thomas U. Walter, Alexander Jackson Davis, Samuel Sloan and Ammi B. Young were designing buildings and monuments for Virginia. These were followed in the post-Civil War years by such noted architects as Elijah E. Myers, John R. Thomas, Reuben H. Hunt, Richard Morris Hunt, James O'Rourke, McKim, Mead & White, Wilson Brothers and, after the turn of the century, by Carrère & Hastings, Ralph Adams Cram, Warren & Wetmore, Frank Lloyd Wright, Richard Neutra, Fay Jones, and Charles Moore, to name but a few. In many cases the best work of these architects has not been in Virginia, but the roll-call of eminent American architects who have designed in Virginia is daunting, perhaps unmatched by any other state. It speaks to the aspirations of Virginia patrons for creating first-rank architecture; but then, what does it say about Virginia's own architects?

When the individual commissions for these out-of-state architects are investigated, particular reasons for obtaining them become apparent. James G. Hill, architect of the Federal Courthouse in Danville ( FIGURE 3.3 ); Mifflin E. Bell, who designed the United States Courthouse in Lynchburg; James Knox Taylor, who designed the Post Office in Martinsville ( FIGURE 3.4 ); and James O'Rourke, who designed the Post Office in Roanoke ( SURVEY NO. 61 ) were all on the federal payroll, in the same way that earlier, Ammi B. Young had been the Architect of the Treasury. Federally sponsored architecture, especially of important buildings with a symbolic role, is generally designed by "outsiders." Well-publicized competitions brought in outsiders like Arquitectonica for the Center for Innovative Technology in Herndon ( SURVEY NO. 115 ). Reuben Hunt ( SURVEY NO. 65 ) received his Baptist Church commissions in Newport News through his own association with the church.

Some architects were clearly the leading national, indeed international figures of their time. McKim, Mead & White and Richard Morris Hunt were chosen to work on major projects in Virginia because of their prestige. University campuses, particularly in recent years, have been showplaces of innovative architecture, and consequently the leading stars—Modernists, Postmodernists, and Neo-traditionalists—have been asked to design them. Others were chosen because of their specialties: John Eberson for his colorful theater designs and Alfred Bossom for banks and skyscrapers.

Some patterns are even more determined by geography. To be expected is a large number of New York-based designers, but why so many Philadelphians? Buildings by Watson & Huckel, Yarnall & Goforth, Wilson Eyre, M. Hawley McLanahan, Bissell & Sinkler, Frank Miles Day, Cope & Stewardson, and Kenneth Day can all be found in the state. The Philadelphia presence became established earlier in the nineteenth century with Thomas U. Walter, Samuel Sloan, and others. Railroads created the pattern: Philadelphia was more accessible than New York, which was across the Hudson River. Similarly, Lynchburg had rail connections with Baltimore and numerous Maryland architects, builders, and contractors found their way to the "city of seven hills" and have exercised a presence throughout the state.[7] Given the proximity of Washington, D.C., its architects have a strong presence only in Northern Virginia; elsewhere they are largely absent except for Charlottesville, where Paul Pelz, and the office of Alfred B. Mullett, and later Waddy B. Wood designed buildings at the turn of the century. In other areas, Wood and more recently Hugh Newell Jacobsen have done work in Virginia's hunt country—Middleburg and Warrenton. The connections between these areas and Washington point to the fact that the patrons had stronger ties outside the state than to Virginia.

This reliance on non-Virginia designers indicates a dichotomy in Virginia. On one hand it views itself as part of a national culture; its businessmen and cultural leaders have always had strong ties elsewhere and consequently have turned to architects from those areas. But this stands in direct opposition to the strong sense of identity and pride that many Virginians profess toward their state. Some of this loyalty comes from a reverence for the past, an obsequiousness to the historical Old Dominion. Yet to recreate this history Virginians have often patronized Yankee designers. Might one conclude that Virginians have distrusted "home-grown" architects, especially for the larger, more prestigious commissions?

## Architectural Education and Professionalism

Two historically based patterns have helped to obscure recent Virginia architecture and have contributed to the dominance of out-of-state architects: self-image or promotion, and education. Throughout the nineteenth century the usual path for the training of architects was the apprentice system. Professional, university-based architectural education in the United States did not begin until 1865 when the Institute of Technology (now the Massachusetts Institute of Technology) in Boston established an architectural program based, in part, on the curriculum of the Ecole des Beaux-Arts in Paris. The Beaux-Arts, which many Americans attended until well into the 1920s, served as a model for other American schools of architecture. It was not until the late 1930s that American schools began to reject the Beaux-Arts model and to adopt a new European import, based on the Bauhaus in Germany. By 1900 at least fifteen schools had established departments of architecture: eleven were in the North, two were in Canada, and two were in the South: Tuskegee, founded in 1893, and Tulane, 1894. In the next two decades more schools of architecture were founded in the North, and in the South there was Texas A&M (1905), Auburn (1907), Georgia Tech (1908), the University of Texas (1909), Rice (1912), and Clemson (1917). The first school of architecture in Virginia was at The University of Virginia, Charlottesville, founded in 1919 with Fiske Kimball as the head. The school's first graduating class was in 1923.[8] In 1928 Virginia Polytechnic Institute in Blacksburg established under Clinton Cowgill a program in architectural engineering that became a full degree-granting architecture program in 1957. The third school of architecture in Virginia, established under the direction of William H. Moses at Hampton Institute in 1940, became a full program in 1948.

In spite of its glorious beginnings, the Commonwealth lagged in professional architectural education. Most Virginians, like John Kevan Peebles and Edward Frye, developed their skills through the apprentice system. Lacking any state requirements for licensing, anybody could use the title of architect, and many builders and contractors did so. The builder-architects should not be sneered at, however, for in the nineteenth century they provided much of this country's building stock.[9] But for Virginians who desired well-trained architects with an intellectual basis and the ability to design sophisticated and complex buildings, the state lacked strong academic foundations. Virginians who wanted to be architects went elsewhere for training, and out-of-state architects were invited to design in-state.

Virginia has never lacked for those who call themselves architects, but precisely who qualifies as an architect is a complex question. The professionalization of architects and the exclusion of builder-architects in America is a still an unrecorded history. The professionalization of certain occupations (i.e., doctors, lawyers, teachers) is a recurring theme in the nineteenth century, and architects appear to have lagged. The American Institute of Architects (AIA), founded in 1857, has been the main vehicle for architects. Located in New York until 1899, when it moved to Washington, D.C., the AIA was viewed by most architects outside New York as an exclusive gentlemen's club that did not represent their interests. In the 1880s and 1890s many architects in different cities organized themselves in local "leagues" or "clubs" and held exhibitions of drawings and sponsored guest lectures. In Virginia there was no such organization, although architects from out of state did exhibit their drawings for Virginia buildings elsewhere. Watson & Huckel of Philadelphia, for example, entered their rendering of Christ Church, Norfolk ( SURVEY NO. 72 ), in five different exhibitions. During the late 1880s and 1890s the AIA sought to expand its influence by setting up regional chapters. One was a Southern Chapter, initially based in Atlanta, which only lasted from 1892 to 1896. Of the chapter's thirty-five charter members, three were Virginians: Walter P. Tinsley of Lynchburg served as its secretary and Marion J. Dimmock of Richmond was its second, and final, president.[10] The next attempt to organize professionally came in 1911, when the Richmond Association of Architects was formed, with William C. Noland as president, and other leading local architects, including Henry Baskervill, Marcellus Wright, Charles M. Robinson, and W. Duncan Lee among the eleven founding members.[11] The U.S. Census for 1910 had recorded 163 individuals who called themselves architects in the state.[12] William Noland, along with Frank Baldwin and Phillip Stern of Fredericksburg, and Benjamin Mitchell and Clarence Neff of Norfolk, founded a Virginia chapter of the AIA in 1914. The principal work of this AIA chapter, with its few members, was to lobby for state licensing of architects. The regulation finally passed in 1920.[13] Virginia was the twenty-first state to require licensing of architects, and William Noland received the first license.[14] The Virginia chapter grew very slowly in the 1920s and the 1930s, no doubt because of the Depression. By 1950 the U. S. Census listed 593 Virginians who claimed to be architects; only 344 of them were registered or licensed. The very size of the state meant that many architects had little allegiance to an organization based in Richmond and, over time, regional sections were set up in Northern Virginia, Roanoke, and the Tidewater area, as well as Richmond; all operated from within the Virginia Society of Architects.

Official registration increased professionalism among architects, since it required either university schooling or a lengthy period of apprenticeship and, in time, the passing of a licensing exam. While anyone could design a house, only licensed architects could get designs accepted for large commercial and public buildings. And although architects did not completely give up the single-family house, residential design increasingly meant the high-budget, luxury house, and not middle-class housing, which was left to the developers and builders. The weight of the profession shifted toward large institutional commissions. The educational requirement meant that after the 1940s students were trained as Modernists and would have little sympathy for traditional Virginia architecture, and certainly had little ability to design it.

Virginia architects have generally not promoted themselves or their work in the past 125 years. Articles abound in both professional and popular periodicals on Virginia architecture, but these are largely historical in scope, being more concerned with the glory days of the Colonial and Federal periods. A few Virginia architects have attempted to publish their own work, but their numbers are minuscule, especially when compared to out-of-state architects, like William Lawrence Bottomley, who published their work extensively. Here and there, in *The American Architect and Building News* or *Architectural Record*, appears a design by Peebles, Baskervill, Lee, or Frye, but they are far outnumbered by articles on old Virginia.[15]

Since the late nineteenth century most significant American architectural publishing has originated in New York and Boston, and in that context work by Virginians has not seemed especially distinguished. Even in a regional magazine, such as *The Southern Architect*, based in Atlanta, Virginians are seldom represented.[16] Virginia-based publications have been few and, until recently, limited in appeal.[17] Publication of one's work is admittedly controversial among architects, especially by those who do not publish. And publication certainly does not guarantee quality, but the absence of any attempt to show one's work to the larger world implies that it lacks importance. Such a conclusion might be drawn because it is widely agreed that architectural publication is self-promotion, and Virginia architects by and large have not expended much effort. The architecture created by Virginians fits in most cases within the broad mainstream of America — safe, competent, and mainline — and distinguished only in special cases.

## Race and Gender

The profession of architecture both nationwide and in Virginia has been almost exclusively dominated by white, upper-middle-class males. Certainly there is a history of contributions by blacks, Hispanics, and Native Americans, as well as by women, but such variance still remains to be documented.

Architecture by and for blacks in Virginia is still largely unrecorded.[18] The legacy of slavery and the exclusion of blacks from white middle-class professions continued long after the Civil War. Within their communities black builder-architects have provided houses and other structures, but professionalism for blacks who desired to become architects came slowly. Training for black architects has been split between black colleges and the white-majority schools. Architecture programs were established in the South long ago at black schools such as Tuskegee Institute in Alabama (1893), Howard University in Washington D.C. (1919), and Hampton Institute in Virginia (1940). Commissions for black professionals, largely from other blacks, have been for churches, schools,

FIGURE 3.5. *The first major exhibition structure by a African-American architect was the* **Negro Building, Jamestown Tercentennial Exposition** *(demolished), Norfolk, Virginia, 1906–07, by William Sidney Pittman (1875–1968). (Reproduced from* The Industrial History of the Negro Race of the United States, *by Giles B. Jackson and D. Webster Davis [Richmond: 1908], 176).*

Masonic temples, and similar black institutions and organizations. William Sidney Pittman (1875–1958), a black architect from Washington, D.C., who trained at Tuskegee, designed the Negro Building at the Jamestown Tercentennial in 1907 ( FIGURE 3.5 ). Apparently the first major exhibition structure by a black architect, and one devoted solely to the achievements of black Americans, it was a wood-frame structure with an exterior of pebble dash and a large-columned portico.[19] The Tidewater area has tended to be the most hospitable

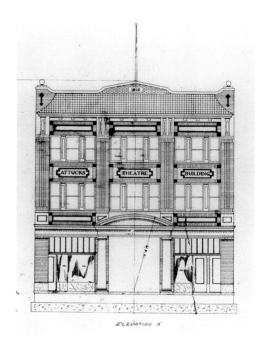

FIGURE 3.6. *African-American architect Harvey Nathaniel Johnson (1892–1973) was active in Norfolk after World War II. Blueprint of front elevation for* **Attucks Theatre and Office Building,** *Norfolk, Virginia, 1919. Collection of Harvey Nathaniel Johnson, Jr., Virginia Beach, Virginia.*

FIGURE 3.7. *William Henry Moses, Jr. (1901–1991), an African-American architect who was on the faculty at Hampton University. (Photograph courtesy of Mrs. William Henry Moses, Jr.)*

region in Virginia for black architects. Among the leaders was Harvey Nathaniel Johnson, the son of a Richmond building contractor, who studied at Virginia Union University and later attended architecture school at the Carnegie Institute of Technology in Pittsburgh. During World War I he was assigned to Washington as an architectural draftsman, but when his race was discovered, he was transferred to Newport News to design warehouses and shipyard facilities. After the war he set up an office in Norfolk with Charles T. Russell, another black architect, and they designed a number of buildings, including the Attucks Theatre building (1919, FIGURE 3.6), a facility named for Crispus Attucks, a half-black, half-Native American, anti-British agitator who was the first colonial to be killed in the American Revolution. Although Johnson entered the ministry in 1924, he continued to design and advise on architecture, especially black churches, for the remainder of his life.[20]

The feeling among many blacks that they were deliberately excluded from the white architectural world can be seen in the controversy surrounding the Virginia exhibit for the 1939 New York World's Fair. In 1938, the Virginia Art Commission sponsored an open competition for the design of the Virginia exhibit, or Virginia Room, at the Fair. Virginia would not have a separate building, but rather would occupy a space in a larger structure. On November 17 of that year, the Art Commission announced that the winner was William Henry Moses, Jr., of Hampton, who would receive a monetary prize of $350. The announcement noted that, according to the rules of the competition, the winning design "could be altered or nullified" by the Virginia subcommittee of the New York World's Fair Commission. Moses' design, estimated to cost $10,000, would feature a scale model of the recently restored Colonial Williamsburg in the middle of the room, with photomurals on the surrounding walls arranged in ten topics—ranging from agriculture to history—that symbolized Virginia. Below would be photographs of the subjects, and a 37-foot-long double-lighted photomontage map of Virginia would cover one wall (FIGURE 3.7).[21]

Although Moses' plan was initially given extensive publicity, it quickly ran into difficulties. In late November 1938, Wilbur C. Hall, Chairman of the State Conservation Commission and secretary of the subcommittee of the Virginia World's Fair Commission, met with executives of Colonial Williamsburg, Inc.; Moses was not informed about the meeting and was not invited to attend. The group criticized his design scheme as being too costly and for placing too much emphasis on Williamsburg. According to a published letter to Virginia's governor James H. Price from Vernon M. Geddy, vice-president of Colonial Williamsburg, Inc., on behalf of the Williamsburg restoration organizations, it was felt that "the exhibit should . . . represent the life of the whole State, and should not feature particularly any one section or place of interest." At the meeting, it was decided to invite Leslie Cheek, Jr., chairman of the Fine Arts Department of the College of William and Mary, to prepare an alternate design. On November 29, 1938, another meeting was held in Williamsburg, at which Cheek accepted the commission.[22]

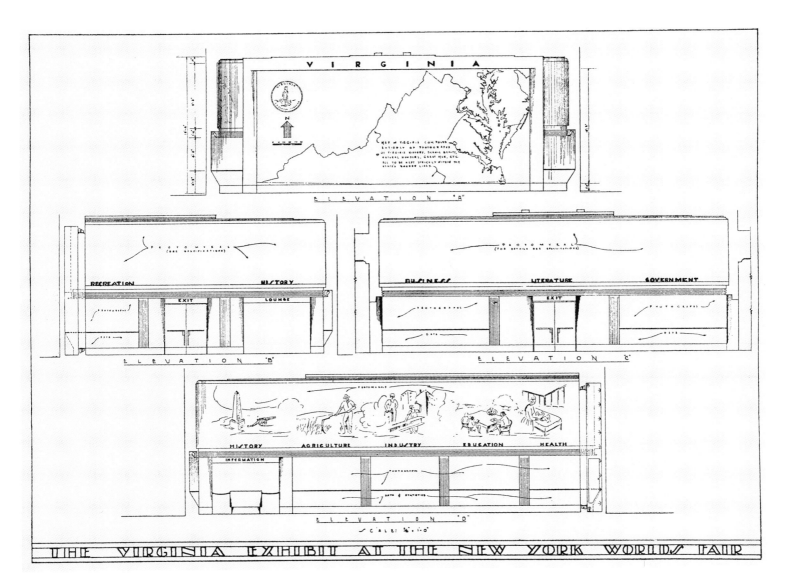

FIGURE 3.7A. *Elevation and plan, 1938* design competition entry for Virginia Exhibit, 1939 New York World's Fair, *by William Henry Moses, Jr. (Reproduced from* Phylon *[1940], opposite page 321).*

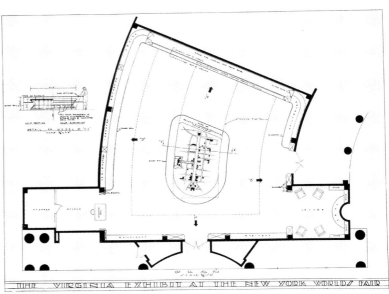

Cheek's design for the Virginia exhibit at the Fair ( FIGURE 3.8 ), which was ultimately carried out, incorporated the work of three associates from the College of William and Mary. In the center of the room was a large fountain with a sculpture of "The Spirit of Virginia's Rivers" by Edwin C. Rust ( FIGURE 3.9 ). Around the walls were twelve niches with murals that symbolized Virginia topics, painted by Leonard V. Haber. Bookcases that lined the walls

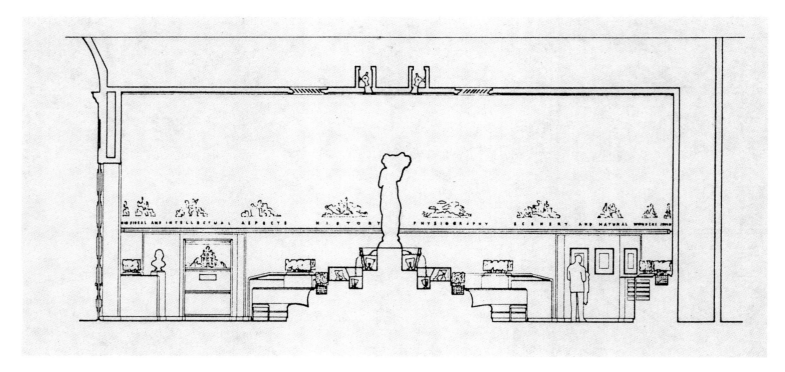

FIGURE 3.8. **Elevation for Virginia Room, New York World's Fair**, *by Leslie Cheek, Jr., 1938. Cheek was chairman of the Fine Arts Department at the College of William and Mary, Williamsburg, and had already established a considerable reputation for his interior designs in New York before his return to Virginia. (Photograph courtesy of the Leslie Cheek archives.)*

held 227 albums with twenty-five photographs each, representing different aspects of the state. Arthur Ross planned the indirect lighting for the room, and sofas and tables provided a comfortable setting, where "a smiling butler distributed glasses of ice water to the tired and thirsty." The cost of the completed installation was just over $30,000. The Virginia Room, as it was called, was in a "simple, modern manner," and received favorable comment in the press.[23]

Moses did not learn that his design would not be followed until he read about Cheek's design in the newspaper on January 6, 1939.[24] Later that month, Wilbur C. Hall, as secretary of the subcommittee of the Virginia New York World's Fair Commission, published his subcommittee's reply to an inquiry from L. R. Reynolds, director of the Virginia Commission on Inter-racial Cooperation. Hall first expressed the subcommittee's regret that "there were only three competitors for the design," and stressed that neither "racial or religious prejudice" had played a role in the decision not to use the Moses design but that the design "called for a photomural plan, with the floor design devoted wholly to Williamsburg . . . which might result in sectional criticism." The subcommittee also stated that, upon investigation, they found that many other states were planning to use photomurals. Also, they had determined that Moses' design with the lighted map would be too expensive to produce.[25]

The cancellation of Moses' design caused outrage among many blacks. A headline in the black-owned Norfolk newspaper, the *Journal and Guide*, proclaimed: "State Spurns Moses' Plan."[26] Another article, by Mentor A. Howe in *Phylon*, a journal edited by W. E. B. Dubois at Atlanta University, observed that "the dilemma created by the winning of an open and anonymous contest by a Negro, however brilliant, is to the 'true Southerner' too embarrassing for comfort."[27]

The history of women in Virginia architecture has been studied even less.[28] For most Virginians the woman's accepted role was extremely traditional, even if the facts proved otherwise. So although women worked in factories and on the farm, higher education for them was confined to circumscribed activities: they might be teachers, homemakers, or active in cultural and civic-minded projects, but architecture, among others, remained a male profession. Within the household, in matters of decor and furniture, and outside, in the garden, women played a major role, but again, little research has been done to document it. As most architects will attest, the woman frequently plays a major role in commissioning the design of a house, and in seeing it get built. Maude Cooke (Mrs. Andrew Cooke) in Virginia Beach kept two sets of account books: one to show her husband, the other containing the real costs, all so she could build her Frank Lloyd Wright house.[29] Carter's Grove became a passion for Molly McCrea, and because of her interest Duncan Lee made substantial alterations, creating a mythical eighteenth-century plantation house.

In the world beyond the home, the female contribution in Virginia has not been so much in design itself as in other areas: Mary Wingfield Scott wrote on historic Richmond architecture, Ann Pamela Cunningham is credited as the savior of Mount Vernon, and Cynthia Beverley Tucker Coleman and Mary Jeffery Galt co-founded the Association for the Preservation of Virginia Antiquities, the first such organization in the United States. The Daughters of the American Revolution and other groups have carried on similar activities with historic houses. The preservation movement in Virginia was not just led by women, they virtually created it. Without so many women's efforts on behalf of preservation, the ruins at Jamestown, Mount Vernon, and many other historic buildings would no longer exist.

The Garden Club of Virginia, which was founded in 1920 and quickly became a leading social force, not only raised public consciousness about architecture and landscaping through its activities, restorations, and tours, but also became an important source of commissions for some architects. For many houses designed by William Lawrence Bottomley, the Garden Club connection was important; many of his clients were members. Virginia W. Christian, who along with her mother, Mrs. Andrew H. Christian, wrote many of the Garden Club's early guidebooks, married Bottomley's favorite Richmond contractor, Herbert A. Claiborne, of Claiborne and Taylor.[30] And Mrs. Herbert McKelden Smith of Staunton was president of the Garden Club in 1928–29 when Bottomley received the commission to design the McKeldens' house, Waverley Hill ( SURVEY NO. 87 ).[31]

FIGURE 3.9. *This vintage photograph shows visitors viewing photo albums of Virginia scenes as they relax in the* **Virginia Room at the 1939 World's Fair.** *Behind them, in the center of the room, is the statue* Spirit of Virginia's Rivers, *created especially for the exhibit by sculptor Edwin C. Rust, another William and Mary faculty member. (Photograph courtesy of the Leslie Cheek archives.)*

Women have also been credited with the creation of Civil War memorials through the United Daughters of the Confederacy and the Confederate Memorial Literary Society. In a related field, the noted photographer Frances Benjamin Johnston (1864–1952), was responsible for an elegant and eloquent survey of Southern and Virginia buildings, which she completed under the auspices of the Carnegie Corporation of New York in the 1930s (see three examples of her work in SURVEY NOS. 3, 29, and 31).

In the design profession women were barred, or at least discouraged, for many years. As for female designers who have earned significant reputations and developed an independent practice, Chloethial Woodard Smith (born 1910) is the best known. With an office in Washington, D.C., Smith was instrumental in introducing modern residential design to Northern Virginia, where she designed parts of Reston, the innovative planned community in Fairfax County.

## The Modern Presence and Postmodernism

FIGURE 3.10. *Colonial and Modern styles combine in apartment architecture:* **Colonial Village**, *Arlington, Virginia, 1935–40, by Harvey H. Warwick (1893–1972). (Photograph courtesy of the Virginia Department of Historic Resources.)*

Although the historical image has dominated Virginia's architecture, still there has been a history of Modernism in the Old Dominion. Modernism can be defined in many ways: for some it is synonymous with contemporary. In this broad sense, nearly every building of the past 250 years was at one time considered "Modern." By a very different definition, Modern is change, a definition in which the present is seen as distinct and different from the past; and this definition involves the development of a historical consciousness. Modernism in this sense only can exist when there is an equally strong concept of tradition or history. Most architects and historians in the twentieth century have defined Modernism as containing elements of this narrower, more precise definition as a self-conscious stylistic movement in which the design of objects, furniture, and buildings should eschew the past and avoid historical precedents. Although it is common to speak of Modernism as a monolithic movement it was not. Instead there were many opinions about what was Modern. High-rise buildings, whether hotels or offices, are primarily Modern structures even though they may be clad in historical garb. Two examples can be seen in Charlottesville's Hotel Monticello and Roanoke's Boxley Building, both dating from the 1920s ( SURVEY NOS. 77, 80 ). Similarly, the style of Harvey Warwick's Colonial Village apartments ( FIGURE 3.10 ) in Arlington, built around 1935–40, is "Colonial" but was in fact an extremely updated concept derived from the Green-Belt ideas developed by Clarence Stein and Henry Wright.

A similar conflict in definition can be seen in a public highway such as the Blue Ridge Parkway, a scenic road linking Virginia's Shenandoah and North Carolina's Great Smoky Mountains national parks. Actually Virginia has three other parkways from the same period: the Skyline Drive in the Shenandoah National Park (1931–39); the Mount Vernon and George Washington memorial parkways (1931–32), which linked Mount Vernon with Washington, D.C.; and the Colonial Parkway (1938–40), which connects Yorktown and Williamsburg.[32] Stanley W. Abbott was the major designer for both the Blue Ridge and the Colonial parkways; his intention was not just to preserve natural beauty, but to enhance it by restoring nature where it had been destroyed.

The Blue Ridge Parkway was a major accomplishment, a design of international stature. Abbott took the idea of a linear park road and elaborated it or, as he described it, "You worked with a ten-league canvas and a brush of a comet's tail," by threading a highway through spectacular scenery. The major features of this park—panoramic views, farm land, old mills, log cabins, tree-lined corridors, sheer rock walls, and quiet ponds—could be appreciated by people riding in that most modern of all twentieth-century machines, the automobile. The roadway, the bridges, and the engineering were all the most up-to-date available, and yet the architectural embellishments, from fences to roadside structures, were consciously designed in a rural vernacular idiom ( FIGURE 3.11 ). In the case of all the parkways, Modern design is put in the service of adapting the use of that machine, the automobile, to historical, or commemorative, or preservation ideas, as well as to the enjoyment of natural beauty. Is this a Modern concept? Yes, it certainly is, but it is not Modern in style.

Self-consciously stylistic Modernism is primarily a twentieth-century phenomenon, but it has roots in the High Victorian and Queen Anne architecture of the later nineteenth century. In buildings such as Elijah Myers's Richmond City Hall ( SURVEY NO. 58 ), or James G. Hill's Danville Federal Courthouse ( FIGURE 3.3 ), the buildings are in fact eclectic assemblages of a variety of motifs—some historical, others newly created, freely adapted and combined in novel ways. The drawing for the Danville Courthouse is a wild concoction of Romanesque, Flemish, English, and American Colonial details. Although orthodox Modernism rejected this wild eclecticism of different sources, the building's freedom of design would be considered a valid and an important feature.

FIGURE 3.11. *Re-creation of a rural vernacular style was consciously followed in every detail in buildings and fence work for the Blue Ridge Parkway. View of* **Blue Ridge Parkway** *showing reconstructed split-rail fence; design by Stanley William Abbott (1908–1975) and others, 1933–69. See also the design for a* Coffee Shop and Gas Station, *figure 3.46. (Photograph courtesy of Blue Ridge Parkway.)*

The earliest example of what would be called Modern architecture in Virginia is probably Frank Lloyd Wright's Larkin Company Pavilion at the Jamestown Tercentennial of 1907 ( FIGURE 3.12 ).[33] Standing amidst other buildings that self-consciously quoted the past, Wright's little pavilion must have seemed like a creature from another planet. Instead of the overall enforced style—red brick, white trim, imitation marble ("staff," a mixture of plaster-of-paris and horsehair), and the columns and pediments on other buildings in the so-called "Colonial city"—Wright's building was predominantly horizontal and asymmetrical. Abstract geometry, not historical images, ruled his design. Wright had essentially reproduced in Virginia one of the Prairie-style houses that he had been designing in the Midwest since the late 1890s. For the Larkin Company, a Buffalo-based concern, he had done a headquarters building and several houses for executives in the Prairie style. Wright had claimed that his Prairie idiom was a response to the midwestern landscape. Interestingly, Wright's pavilion won one of the few gold medals for architecture.[34]

Although Wright is usually identified as a major architect of the Modernist or Progressive movement, especially for later examples such as the Pope-Leighey House ( SURVEY NO. 96 ), the sources of his early work and those of his

FIGURE 3.12. *Most likely the earliest example of Modern architecture in Virginia:* Presentation drawing, **Larkin Company Pavilion, Jamestown Tercentennial Exposition** *(demolished), Norfolk, Virginia, 1906–07, by Frank Lloyd Wright (1867–1959). Pencil on tracing paper, 14 by 20 inches. (Photograph © The Frank Lloyd Wright Foundation, 1987; courtesy of the Frank Lloyd Wright Archives, No. 0706.04.)*

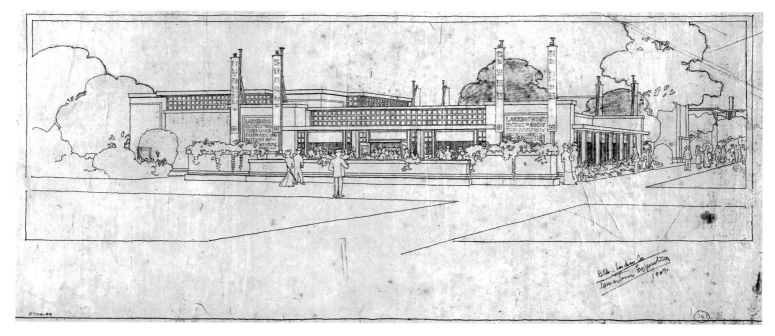

Chicago contemporaries in the Prairie School were in the Arts and Crafts Movement of the turn of the century. This movement originated in England under the artist and designer William Morris and the philosopher and critic John Ruskin, as a corrective measure for an increasingly machine-dominated society. In America, the Arts and Crafts Movement exhibited a variety of attitudes towards the machine. Wright had actually praised it but many others, among them Ralph Adams Cram, despised it. The Arts and Crafts Movement in America encompassed many philosophical and stylistic responses. Cram's, neo-Gothic works at the University of Richmond ( SURVEY NO. 74 ) and Watson & Huckel's

FIGURE 3.13. *The Arts and Crafts Movement in the United States, which saw its fullest flowering under Gustav Stickley's Craftsman Workshops in Syracuse, and Elbert Hubbard's Roycrofters in East Aurora, New York, has yet to be studied thoroughly in the South.* **Arts and Crafts Village, Jamestown Tercentennial Exposition** *(demolished), Norfolk, Virginia, 1906–07. (Photograph courtesy of Sargeant Memorial Room, Norfolk Public Library.)*

FIGURE 3.14. *The Bungalow style, popular in Virginia from the turn of the century to the 1920s, was commonly used for residences but could be applied to public buildings as well.* **Elevation drawing for Oakwood Country Club,** *Lynchburg, Virginia, 1914, by John Minor Botts Lewis (1869–1950). Pen and ink on paper, 34 by 24 inches. (Collection of Jones Memorial Library, Lynchburg).*

FIGURE 3.15. *The influence of Modern architect Louis Sullivan can be seen in this building designed by T. J. Collins & Son of Staunton, Virginia.* **Elevation drawing, Smith Fuel Company Ice Factory Building,** *1910. Ink on linen. (Collection of T. J. Collins & Son, Staunton.)*

Christ Church, Norfolk ( SURVEY NO. 72 ), are examples of a conservative Arts and Crafts approach in contrast to the progressivism of Frank Lloyd Wright and others.[35]

Study of the Arts and Crafts Movement in the South, and in Virginia in particular, is still in its infancy. What encompassed and was identified as Arts and Crafts, except for the most superficial knowledge, is unclear. At the Jamestown Exposition, both Tiffany Studios and Stickley Brothers were represented, and there was an "Arts and Crafts Village" ( FIGURE 3.13 ) populated by "artisans, or really artists," who displayed what were claimed to be seventeenth-century crafts: pottery, copper, silver, wood, rush, textiles, and iron. Although descriptive commentary claimed the seven shingle-covered structures with low-rising roofs to be "old colonial buildings," they were quite clearly new structures, heavily indebted to the New England seacoast and the bungalow.[36] From the early 1900s until well into the 1920s, the bungalow style popularized by Gustav Stickley and others was built throughout Virginia. The Oakwood Country Club in Lynchburg (1914; FIGURE 3.14 ) by John Minor Botts Lewis illustrates the application of the low-rising, essentially a historical bungalow idiom, to other building types. A great sheltering roof engulfs the flat planes of

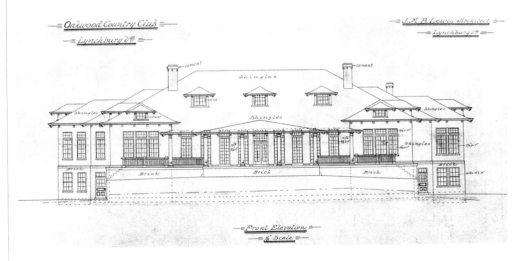

the lower floors.[37] Some of the designs of Staunton's T. J. Collins's sons, Sam and Will ( SURVEY NOS. 60, 68 ), reflect knowledge of the designs of Louis Sullivan. Their Ice Factory Building (1910; FIGURE 3.15 ) for the Smith Fuel Company, is a good example. The Collinses adapted Sullivan's National Farmer's Bank of Owatonna, Minnesota, which they had seen illustrated in *The Architectural Record* magazine. But such designs are rare, and the Collins boys did not follow up on this direction.[38] As can be seen with the Jamestown Village Exposition, the Arts and Crafts Movement has elements of the Colonial Revival, and certainly this guided some of the designers at Colonial Williamsburg in the 1920s, who had been trained by Cram. But this borrowing is still a far cry from citing the Arts and Crafts Movement as a source of Modernism, and indicates the conflicting elements inherent not only within the movement, but also among the many definitions of Modernism.

In the 1920s and 1930s Modernism as a stylistic response becomes much more distinct, though many different approaches ranged from the so-called "stripped Classical" to Art Déco to the streamlined style, and later the International Style. With the Virginia War Memorial Competition, the Commonwealth had a chance to lead the United States with the erection of an early example of stripped or modernized Classicism. Popularized by Paul Cret of Philadelphia, this pared-down version of Classicism was just that: traditional forms and

FIGURE 3.16. *"Stripped Classicism," a conservative Modernism, defines the* **State Highway Commission Building**, *Richmond, Virginia, 1937, by Carneal, Johnston & Wright.*

FIGURE 3.17. **The State Library and Supreme Court Building**, *Richmond, Virginia, 1937–39, by Carneal, Johnston & Wright, and Baskervill & Son, like many government buildings of the 1930s, followed the trend toward a modernized Classical style. (Photograph courtesy of the Virginia State Library.)*

symmetry were retained, but historical ornament and details were eliminated. Cret and Marcellus Wright won the 1925 competition, but the memorial was never built (see drawing, SURVEY NO. 81 ). Stripped Classicism was conservative Modernism. It respected the classical past and became the official government style in the 1930s, seen in numerous public buildings such as the U.S. Post Office and Courthouse in Norfolk (1934) by Benjamin F. Mitchell, and at National Airport in Arlington. The Commonwealth also applied this style in the Department of Highways Building (1937; FIGURE 3.16 ) by Carneal, Johnston & Wright and the State Library and Supreme Court (1937–39; FIGURE 3.17 ) by Carneal Johnston & Wright and Baskervill & Son.

More aggressively Modern was a style we call Art Déco which, in the 1920s to 1930s, had several other names: Modernistic, Moderne, the vertical style, and the skyscraper style. Influenced in part by the world's fair from which its name was abbreviated, the *Exposition Internationale des Arts Décoratifs et Industriels Modernes* (Paris, 1925), and by American sources, especially new perceptions of the machine, architects of the period saw buildings and their details as parts or pieces arranged in complex patterns, their profiles stepped back, with intertwining foliate and geometrical ornament. Marcellus E. Wright, Jr., who studied architecture under Paul Cret at the University of Pennsylvania in the late 1920s, recalled, "There was little of Art Deco in school; some of my colleagues were playing around with these shapes—not shapes but more, well, I call it sort of wheat [and chaff], different ways of taking nuts and bolts and locking them, and seeing what they looked like. Everyone thought it was new and fun and a little different."[39] Tall, set-back skyscrapers became important symbols of America cities, and the Old Dominion's cities were no different. Both Central National Bank, Richmond ( SURVEY NO. 89 ) by New Yorker John Eberson, and the Allied Arts Building in Lynchburg ( SURVEY NO. 90 ) by

FIGURE 3.18. *In* **Richmond of the Future**, *an illustration for an advertisement placed by the Ralph L. Dombrower Advertising Company in 1929, the stepped-back skyscraper became an icon for growth, prosperity, and urban boosterism.* Richmond Magazine *(September 1929): 2.*

architects Johnson and Brannon, are the equals of any skyscraper built in the North. For Richmond businessmen and the Chamber of Commerce, the setback skyscraper became "Richmond of the Future" ( FIGURE 3.18 ). On a smaller scale, two-, three-, and four-story Art Déco structures were built throughout the state. Richmond architect Carl Lindner was especially successful in creating vibrant structures with abstract ornamentation derived directly from Paris ( FIGURE 3.19 ).[40]

FIGURE 3.19. *A French flavor in Art Déco ornament characterizes this 1928 drawing for* **306 East Grace Street**, *Richmond, Virginia, by Carl Lindner (1895–1973). (Reproduced from Randolph Williams Sexton,* American Commercial Buildings of Today *[New York: Architectural Book Publishing Co., 1928], 172.)*

FIGURE 3.20. **Model Tobacco Factory**, *Richmond, Virginia, 1938–40, by Schmidt, Garden & Erikson of Chicago, represents a hybrid blend of the International style with Art Deco.*

FIGURE 3.21. *Amaza Lee Meredith (1895–1984), circa 1930s. (Photograph courtesy of Virginia State University, Petersburg.)*

Modernism as it developed from the 1930s onwards tended toward simplification of forms, the avoidance of decoration, and sparse, geometrical elements. Streamlining and the International style were two of many idioms that were part of 1930s and 1940s Modernism. Smooth facades and rounded corners cropped up in the new roadside environments. Although "officially" introduced in 1932 at the Museum of Modern Art in New York, the International style did not appear in Virginia until later in the decade. The Model Tobacco Factory, Richmond (1938–40; FIGURE 3.20), by Schmidt, Garden and Erikson—a Chicago firm that originally worked in the Prairie style with Frank Lloyd Wright—is a hybrid of the International style, with its continuous horizontal fenestration and volumetric form, and Art Deco in the huge vertical signpost at its entrance.[41]

Of the few International-style houses in Virginia from the 1930s, the most interesting is the one Amaza Meredith designed for herself and her companion, Edna Meade Colson, next to the Virginia State University campus near Petersburg (FIGURES 3.21, 3.21A). Born in Lynchburg, Miss Meredith attended Virginia State College, a two-year college for black students, and then went north, to Columbia University, to earn both the bachelor's and the master's degrees in art. She later returned to Virginia State University, and taught art there for the rest of her life.[42] Her modest house of 1939, constructed of concrete block, illustrates her knowledge and sophistication with regard to the most advanced art currents of the period. Volume rather than mass, regularity rather than symmetry, and the avoidance of applied decoration—the principles of the

International style—define the exterior of her house.[43] A rounded corner, large picture windows, glass block, and a flat roof made it one of the most advanced residential designs in the state in its day. Extremely controversial because of its advanced design, it was scarcely appreciated by anybody.[44]

Virginia's basic conservatism was reflected in the results of a poll conducted by *Architectural Record* in 1940 of the buildings most admired in Richmond. Leading citizens (doctors, lawyers, businessmen, ministers, and the like) voted the State Highway Department Building as their favorite, and the Virginia State Library as runner-up. The Model Tobacco Factory took fourth place, and the next most modern structure, the new streamlined WMBG Radio Station by William H. Rhodes, tied for last place, eighth, with a Colonial Revival-style research laboratory by Francisco & Jacobus. The magazine summarized the results "A local preference in general for the architectural styles of tradition."[45]

FIGURE 3.21A. **Meredith-Colson House, "Azurest South,"** *Ettrick, Virginia, 1939, by African-American artist and teacher Amaza Lee Meredith, is one of the few International style houses in Virginia from the 1930s, and one of the most advanced residential designs in the state in its day. Drawing is in the Virginia State University Archives, Petersburg.*

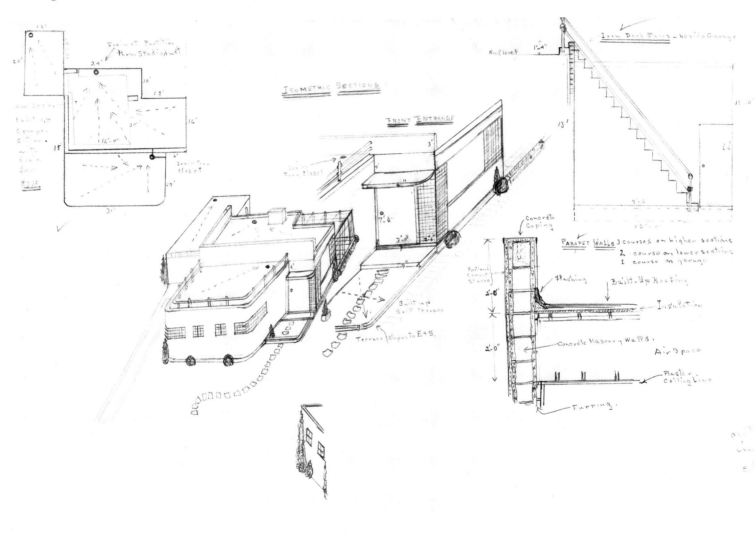

The International style finally arrived full blown in the 1950s when Skidmore, Owings & Merrill, with Gordon Bunshaft as the major designer, was commissioned to design the Reynolds Metals Building in Richmond (1953–58, FIGURE 3.22; SURVEY NO. 105). Crisp in form and elegantly detailed, the Reynolds building seems to sit on a pedestal while its symmetry and aluminum-clad steel supports evoke the air of a Greek temple.[46] Skidmore, Owings & Merrill would provide a number of other Modern-style buildings for Virginia, especially in the form of skyscrapers for banks and municipal institutions.

FIGURE 3.22. **Reynolds Metals Headquarters Building,** *main entrance and reflecting pool. (Photograph courtesy of Reynolds Metals Company.)*

From the 1950s onward the Virginia architectural landscape, like elsewhere across America, changed dramatically: cities were torn up internally with new high-rise structures replacing the old. On the outskirts, corporate headquarters, malls, and industrial parks appeared. Freeways were carved through cities, towns, and farmlands, and vast parking lots became ubiquitous. The new environments were in some ways alien and inhospitable, but the change was not so much caused by architecture as by new economic and technical forces at work. Changing land values in urban and rural areas alike, the need for consolidation of some businesses and dispersal of others, new types of white-collar employment, and new transportation systems were the root causes. The automobile provided freedom—supposedly because it allowed people to escape the city to the far suburbs. However, this harsh assessment of recent urbanism should be placed in a historical perspective. Americans tend to distrust the city, to bemoan their current problems, and to find greater virtue in some mythical city of the past. But the citizens of that historical city also saw it as a failure, and indeed in many ways it was. Violence, alienation, racism, endemic poverty, and class stratification have always been part of the American city. Colonial Williamsburg may appear wonderful to us now; Richmond of the 1910s and 1920s looks today like a decorated wonderland with its grand theatres, shops, skyscrapers, monuments, and Colonial Revival houses. But in each area, the same harsh features can be found, and most of the residents of the past would have preferred a house in the country.

Modern buildings and houses, many of them of very high quality, have been built across Virginia by out-of-state architects, among them Richard Neutra, Robert Anshen, and Edward Durrell Stone, and by Virginia architects Leonard J. Currie, Carlton Abbott, the firm of Glave Newman Anderson, and others. Frank Lloyd Wright returned to Virginia in the late 1930s with his special brand of Modernism that he called "organic" and designed a Usonian house for Loren Pope in Falls Church ( SURVEY NO. 96 ). Then, in the 1950s, he designed three more houses—two of which were built—for Andrew Cooke, Virginia Beach (1952–56), and Luis Marden, McLean (1952).[47] And there is much more. Schools in particular, by out-of-state firms like Caudill, Rowlett and Scott, and Virginia firms such as T. J. Collins and Son, are also part of a tremendous revolution in how people lived in twentieth-century Virginia.

Northern Virginia stands out for the significance of its Modern designs. Dulles Airport ( SURVEY NO. 106 ) marked a new, more expressive phase of Modernism, and became the new formal gateway to the nation's capital. Of perhaps more significance in actual living patterns is the work of Charles Goodman. Though born and trained elsewhere, Goodman's career has been primarily in Northern Virginia, where he designed a great many buildings, including the Hollin Hills subdivision ( SURVEY NO. 100 ).

## Postmodernism

Because Postmodernism, now informally called "PoMo," is a relatively recent development, its full historical contours (and of course its future) are not yet fully evident. Its roots can be traced to the 1960s and even earlier, to dissatisfaction with Modernism as it unfolded. Although some critics would claim that Postmodernism marks a fundamental break with Modernist orthodoxy, Modernism in fact was never monolithic and always encompassed many approaches. Similarly, Postmodernism does not encompass a single outlook, but ranges from aggressively abstract buildings, like Arquitectonica's Center for Innovative Technology in Herndon ( SURVEY NO. 115 ), to replays of historical models. One branch of Postmodernism reintroduced the validity of looking at historical models as a source of design and ornament. Early Postmodern work in Virginia, like Turnbull's Zimmerman residence in Great Falls ( SURVEY NO. 109 ) and Venturi's Newman Library addition at VPI ( SURVEY NO. 110 ), has an edgy, somewhat awkward quality. Some Postmodernists, like Michael Graves, have very explicitly recalled early Modernist works, especially Art Déco ( SURVEY NO. 116 ). Others—such as Wright, Cox & Smith for the University of Richmond ( SURVEY NO. 112 )—have veered toward historical recall, but with witty and critical overtones. And finally, some Postmodernists have gone the whole way towards a full-scale historical revival, as with recent work by Robert A. M. Stern of New York and Hartman-Cox of Washington, D.C., at the University of Virginia ( SURVEY NO. 117 and FIGURE 3.23 ).

FIGURE 3.23. **Perspective drawing for Monroe Hall Extension, University of Virginia,** *Charlottesville, 1982–87, by Hartman-Cox of Washington, D.C., represents the return to a Classical Revival in the work of some Postmodernists. Signed lower right:* Willard 85. *Pencil on tracing paper, 18 by 39 inches. (Photograph courtesy of Hartman-Cox.)*

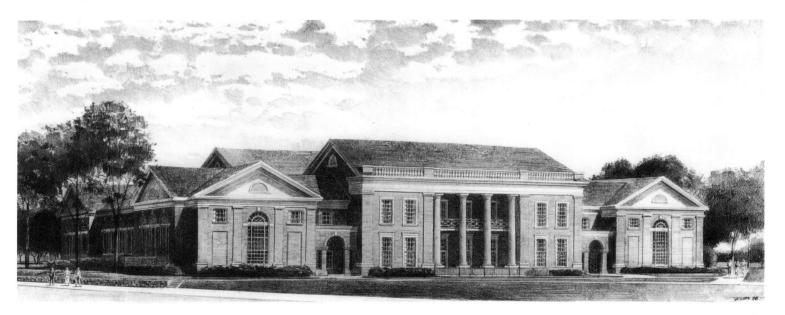

## The Historical Presence

When Virginia's Colonial Revival architecture is mentioned, many people think of those magnificent houses by Bottomley and Stanhope Johnson, or Cram's Carillon Tower or the Virginia Museum of Fine Arts by Peebles and Ferguson, ( SURVEY NOS. 80, 87, 92, 93 ). Usually forgotten are Stony Point ( SURVEY NO. 79 ) or Colonial Williamsburg ( SURVEY NOS. 83– 86 ), though they are equally valid examples of twentieth-century architecture. The Colonial Revival is the most obvious manifestation of a pattern of historicism that is fundamental to Virginia's architecture during the past century. In spite of stylistic Modernism and of the great changes in styles of living and working, buildings cloaked in historical styles have continued to dominate Virginia's architecture. The Virginia pattern of historicism is no different from many other areas of the United States, where historical designs continued all through the twentieth century, but in Virginia there is a special intensity. This pattern involves a complex interworking of preservation, of the research and writing of architectural history, and of architectural design itself.[48]

Virginia's place in American history, *sui generis*, has given it a past that could not be ignored. This history includes its status as the first colony, its preeminent role in the formation of a new nation, the presence of so many founding patriots—such as George Washington, Thomas Jefferson, James Madison, James Monroe, and George Mason—not to mention the substantial artifacts and buildings dating from its first two centuries. Equally important, the antebellum period and the Civil War itself also contribute to the perception of Virginia as a historical, indeed a mythological landscape. How could the present, the modern day, ever hope to compete with so much history?

The pattern of historicism can be seen emerging very early in the campaign to save Washington's home by the Mount Vernon Ladies' Association in the 1850s, a fight over Arlington House (the Custis-Lee Mansion) during the 1870s, the restoration of the Moore house as part of the Yorktown centennial in 1881, and the founding of the Association for the Preservation of Virginia Antiquities (APVA) in 1889. APVA's initial concerns were the preservation of the remains of Jamestown Island and the seventeenth-century church tower there, saving the home of Mary Washington, mother of the first president, in Fredericksburg, and the purchase of the old Powder Magazine in Williamsburg.[49] Homes of famous individuals and historical sites, from whatever period, became objects of interest. Preservationists were the first to define what architectural historians would study and what architects would refer to as models.

Most historical accounts have treated the Colonial Revival as a northeastern—Yankee—phenomenon that began in the 1870s around resorts like Newport, Rhode Island, and at the Centennial Exposition in Philadelphia. Heavily promoted by magazines and sophisticated young architects who had just returned from study abroad, the initial concerns of the nascent Colonial Revivalists lay in appreciating the seventeenth- and early eighteenth-century vernacular. Influenced by the contemporary Queen Anne and Olde English (or "Tudorbethan") that was being imported from England, American architects like Charles F. McKim and Stanford White created in the late 1870s and early 1880s a style that has been christened the "shingle style," though it was known at the time as Modernized Colonial.[50] By the mid 1880s McKim, White, and their followers turned to the more formal architecture of the eighteenth and early nineteenth century—the Georgian period—and were designing large symmetrical houses of clapboard and brick. A formalization in plan, shape, and sources of the Colonial Revival continued in the 1890s and into the twentieth century, while the earlier shingle-covered Colonial largely disappears into the Arts and Crafts Movement. Also beginning in the 1890s and gaining force in the 1900s and 1910s was the discovery of regional models for the Colonial style, such as the Dutch in New York, the French in Louisiana, the Spanish in the Southwest, and the plantation house in Virginia.

The role played by both Virginia architecture and her architects in the Colonial Revival has, for the most part, been ignored by architectural historians. The early shingle style, or Modernized Colonial, was imported and used by Virginia architects in the 1880s and 1890s, and examples can be found through-

FIGURE 3.24. *Most likely the first explicit reference to Southern motifs in the Colonial Revival was the design of* **The Commodore William Edgar House**, *Newport, Rhode Island, 1884–86, by McKim, Mead & White. Reproduced from George William Sheldon's* Artistic Country-Seats *(New York: D. Appleton and Company, 1887), 2:24.*

FIGURE 3.25. **Cobham Park**, *Albemarle County, Virginia, circa 1856, shows that certain building traditions usually associated with the 1790s to 1820s continued further into the nineteenth century. (Photograph courtesy of Virginia Department of Historic Resources.)*

out Virginia. The first explicit reference to Southern Colonial motifs probably came in McKim, Mead & White's Commodore William Edgar House, Newport, Rhode Island (1884–86; FIGURE 3.24 ), in which the extended wings and the arched chimneys are reminiscent of Stratford Hall, Westmoreland County.[51] Whether McKim and his partners were explicitly thinking of Stratford for their Newport mansion is unclear, for they never explained their sources, but unquestionably Virginian were the houses for James Breese in Southampton, New York (1898–1902) and Alfred A. Pope in Farmington, Connecticut (1898–1901), where the long porticoes recall Mount Vernon and were so noted by writers.[52] These later examples, however, come well after Virginia entered the Colonial Revival picture.

Virginia had long been interested in reviving its Colonial past. One of the earliest attempts was Bremo Recess in Fluvanna County (1834–36; SURVEY NO. 31 ) by John Hartwell Cocke, who specifically named Bacon's Castle in Surry County as a source for his Jacobean design.[53] Cocke's work parallels that of Washington Irving at Sunnyside in Irvington, New York, and this early explicit reference to the American past may indicate similar Colonial intentions by other architects of the day, such as Alexander J. Davis and A. J. Downing.[54]

Another element in the Virginia story is the question of Colonial survivals, such as Cobham Park, the Rives family summer home in Albemarle County (circa 1856; FIGURE 3.25 ). This residence well illustrates that certain building traditions usually associated with the 1790s to 1820s continued further into the nineteenth century.[55] Undoubtedly, similar examples will come to light. Bishop William Meade's *Old Churches, Ministers, and Families of Virginia* (1857), which described and illustrated early churches on the 250th anniversary of the Jamestown settlement, did much to popularize architecture of the colonial era through the history of Virginia's church buildings.

The years immediately following the Civil War are unclear, but interest in Virginia's colonial-period architecture can be inferred from paintings of Westover and Berkeley plantations by Edward Lamson Henry dating from the 1860s and 1870s.[56] A New Jersey architect, Van Campen Taylor (died 1906), measured Mount Vernon in 1876 ( FIGURE 3.26 ). His was apparently the first such attempt to do so, and parallels similar documentary projects in Rhode Island and Massachusetts.[57] Only a few articles on Virginia subjects appeared in the architecture press in the North in the 1870s; but more appeared in the 1880s. Among the first were Glen Brown's brief paragraphs and drawings of interior details from Northern Virginia; then came much more substantial articles by A. Burnley Bibb (see an architectural illustration by Bibb, FIGURE 4.44 ).[58] Photographs and drawings appear of Virginia monuments: Mills's Monumental Church, St. Luke's Church, and the Virginia Capitol.[59] Accompanying the Colonial Revival in the North in the 1870s were articles on travel and regional curiosities in the popular press—*Harper's, Scribner's* and *The Century* magazines—but only a few featured Virginia.[60] Reconstruction and the "bloody shirt" still dominated public conciousness of Virginia, but with their passing in the 1880s many more articles on Colonial Virginia began to appear in the

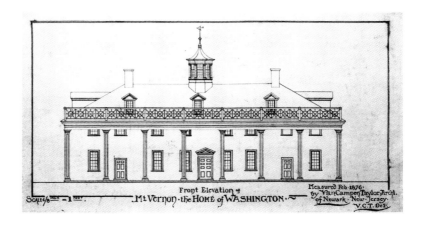

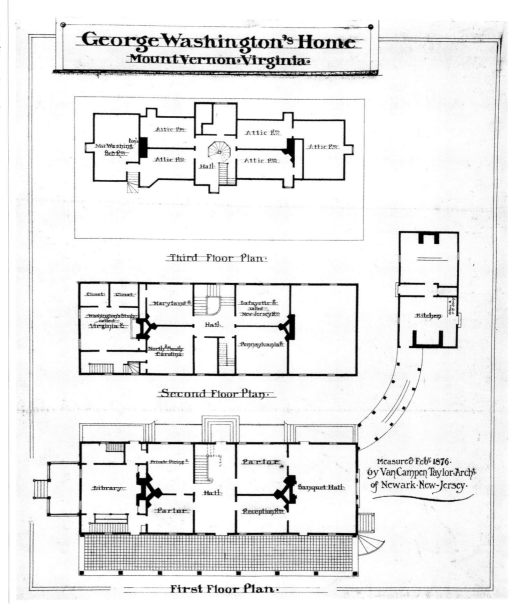

FIGURE 3.26. *Among the first attempts to pre-serve and document historic American buildings was this drawing of the* **East Elevation and Plans of George Washington's Home, Mount Vernon, Virginia,** *as measured and drawn February 1876 by architect Van Campen Taylor (died 1906) of New-ark, New Jersey. Ink on linen. (Photograph courtesy of Mount Vernon Ladies' Association.)*

FIGURE 3.27. *The first building with specific Virginia references by a Virginia architect was the* **Virginia Building for the World's Columbian Exposition**, *Chicago, Illinois, 1893 (demolished), by Edgerton Rogers (1860–1901). (Photograph by C. D. Arnold, courtesy of Ryserson & Burnham Libraries, The Art Institute of Chicago.)*

FIGURE 3.28. *Many buildings at the 1893 Chicago World's Fair were designed in what came to be called the Southern Colonial Revival style. The archetype was the* **Connecticut Building** *(demolished), by Warren R. Briggs (1850–1933). (Photograph by C. D. Arnold, courtesy of Ryerson & Burnham Libraries, The Art Institute of Chicago.)*

Northern popular press.[61] The stories, novels and historical studies of Thomas Nelson Page and others in the 1880s, 1890s, and 1900s mixed fact and fiction with the Colonial, antebellum, and Civil War past.[62] From the pages and illustrations of popularized historical romances, Americans fell in love with the glories of Virginia's architectural past.

The first building with specific Virginia references by a native Virginian (or an adopted son) is the Virginia Building at the World's Columbian Exposition in Chicago (1893; FIGURE 3.27) by Edgerton Rogers (1860–1901). The son of the sculptor Randolph Rogers, Edgerton had only a brief career in Virginia. Born in Rome, he had some foreign training and arrived in Richmond in 1888 with the commission from Major James H. Dooley for his Richmond estate, Maymont.[63] At the Chicago Fair, other states produced buildings based on their heritage: Massachusetts built a replica of the Hancock house, Pennsylvania had a confection based in part on Independence Hall, California produced a mission, and Virginia had Rogers's "exact reproduction" of Mount Vernon. Although some accounts sneered that "the state did not furnish a building architecturally the equal of those of some other commonwealths" (McKim, Mead & White had designed a replica of the Villa Medici, Rome, for New York), still "the historic interest attached to the house far more than compensated."[64] Surviving photographs of Rogers's Mount Vernon indicate that he embellished some of the details and added an entrance porch. It proved to be an extremely popular attraction, setting in motion the duplication of Washington's home for a tremendous variety of purposes. Already existing in that elite status as an American icon, Mount Vernon became an architectural form to be adopted, as we have seen, by Northern architects like McKim, Mead & White and many others, and reproduced indiscriminately as homes for the wealthy, insurance offices, and tract homes. The Commonwealth of Virginia itself revived Mount Vernon—with the assistance of Sears, Roebuck and Company—as the state building for national and international expositions in 1915, 1931, and 1932.[65]

The Chicago World's Fair also contributed to what came to be known as the generic type of Southern Colonial Revival, the giant-columned and porticoed two-story house that can be seen throughout the South and is well represented in Virginia. One example is H. H. Huggins's Mountain View, the Fishburn house (SURVEY NO. 69) in Roanoke. Several of the state buildings at the World's Columbian Exposition of 1893 were identified as "Southern," apparently because of their porticoes and columns.[66] The house that provided the specific model, however, was the Connecticut State Building, by Warren R. Briggs of Bridgeport. Briggs's imaginary confection had a projecting portico supported by paired columns of the colossal order, and behind it a single-story columned porch (FIGURE 3.28). This motif had no basis in Connecticut Colonial-style architecture, and was actually more reflective of French Beaux-Arts design. Paradoxically, and certainly because of the popular view of the South as the home of large-columned houses, the giant-columned portico became Southern in the popular mind. George Barber (1854–1915), the Nashville mail-order architect, picked up the motif and replicated it widely.[67] Great-columned porticoes following the Connecticut model or other configurations began to crop up throughout the South, especially in Virginia: Selma in Loudoun County by Noland and Baskervill (1902), and Ednam in Albemarle County by D. Wiley Anderson (1905), were two of the best known.[68] The equation of Colonial architecture in the South with giant columns would persist: as Thomas Mott Shaw, one of the restoration architects at Williamsburg recalled, "To a Southerner, colonial means columns—and of course here at Williamsburg there were practically no columns. I think that Jefferson was very disappointed in the College of William and Mary because it didn't have any columns."[69] Shaw reveals not only the common perception of what the Colonial style was in the South, but also the importance of Jefferson's post-Colonial, or early Republican architecture, with its large porticoes, in forming that view.

FIGURE 3.29. **Westover**, *originally built in 1735, was remodeled into an Edwardian country house in 1902 for Wm. McC. Ramsey, by Marion Johnson Dimmock (1824–1908) and George R. Tolman (active 1890–1906), with William H. Mersereau (1862–1933). Compare with 1992 photograph of Westover, figure 1.32. (Photograph of rendering courtesy Virginia Historical Society.)*

Red-brick and white-trim Colonial, or Georgian Revival, buildings began to appear in Virginia at the turn of the century. Restoration—or more properly, creative additions—were proposed and made to Westover, the most venerable of the James River houses, by William H. Mersereau of New York and by M. J. Dimmock and G. R. Tolman of Richmond. Arcaded hyphens, in what can best be called "Queen Anne" but thought to be in the same style as the original house, were built. As the rendering ( FIGURE 3.29 ) shows, the additions made Westover a turn-of-the-century Edwardian country house.[70] At the same time Cram, Goodhue & Ferguson of Boston began work on Sweet Briar College.

Ralph Adams Cram, who acted as the main designer for the project, found that "history, tradition, and architectural style pre-determined the course to follow," and that instead of his beloved medieval model, red-brick Georgian was the only appropriate image for the young ladies. Cram did not believe in archaeological reproduction, but that "historical precedent as a basis" could be expanded into a "romantic and pictorial form."[71] The extravaganza that Cram dreamed ( FIGURE 3.30 ) was only partially realized. It draws on Jefferson's University at Charlottesville, but is far more complicated with its cross axis. The scheme has a French flavor with the Pantheon-like lecture hall, and its English quotations recall James Gibbs in its towered chapel and Jones in its elevations. Colonnade piles up on colonnade.

FIGURE 3.30. *In his grand design for Sweet Briar College, architect Ralph Adams Cram envisioned a red-brick Georgian "romantic and pictorial" extravaganza that was never fully realized.* **Bird's-eye perspective of Sweet Briar College,** *Amherst County, Virginia, designed by Cram, Goodhue & Ferguson, 1901–02. Reproduced from* American Architect & Building News 77 *(August 23, 1902). (Photograph courtesy of Sweet Briar College.)*

FIGURE 3.31. *For the 300th anniversary of the Jamestown settlement, the focal point of what was advertised as a "Colonial City" was this enlarged and decorated variant on Monticello (compare with Survey no. 12).* **Auditorium and Convention Hall, Jamestown Tercentennial Exposition,** *Norfolk, Virginia, designed 1906–07 by John Kevan Peebles (1866–1934) and Parker & Thomas. (Photograph courtesy of the Library of Congress, Washington, D.C.)*

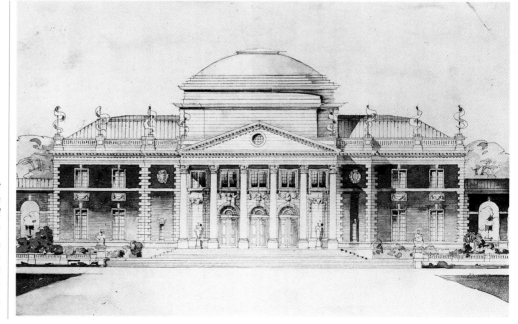

FIGURE 3.33. *The* **Virginia Building at the Jamestown Tercentennial Exposition**, *Norfolk, Virginia, 1906–07, by Breese & Mitchell, was built in what was called Southern Colonial style, with a giant two-story columned portico. (Photograph courtesy of the Library of Congress, Washington, D.C.)*

A similar free interpretation of Virginia's heritage can be seen at the Jamestown Tercentennial Exposition of 1907. John Kevan Peebles of Norfolk was chairman of the Board of Design; the other architects were Parker & Thomas of Baltimore and Boston; the landscape architect was Warren H. Manning of Boston; and Robert S. Peabody of Boston served as architectural advisor. This team produced what the promoters called a "Colonial City": large red-brick and white-trimmed facades and two-story columned porticoes. Peebles was probably responsible for the main ensemble on Raleigh Square, where the domed auditorium's source was obviously an enlarged and decorated Monticello ( FIGURES 3.31, 3.32 ). The Virginia Building, by the Norfolk architects Breese and Mitchell, was Southern Colonial with a giant two-story columned portico ( FIGURE 3.33 ).[72]

## Colonial Revival and American Renaissance

Several points must be made about the Colonial Revival wherever it developed. For although the details were carried out with archaeological and almost scientific exactitude, there was seldom wholesale reproduction. Instead, architects operated with a free-wheeling and creative reinterpretation of the past. The term "revival" is perhaps inappropriate; better would be "Colonial interpretation." What was viewed as Colonial was very broad and included the entire period from Jamestown through the 1820s. Considered as Colonial were the styles of Federal, Early Republican, Jeffersonian, and Greek Revival, or the entire period of late Georgian architecture from the 1780s to the 1820s. The line between Colonial and these other Classical idioms was very thin—if indeed it can be defined at all—and most architects, critics, and historians saw it all as part of the same architectonic and cultural system. The same architects who designed Colonial Revival buildings also did buildings in Italian Renaissance, French Renaissance, Jacobean, and other styles. Additions made to the University of

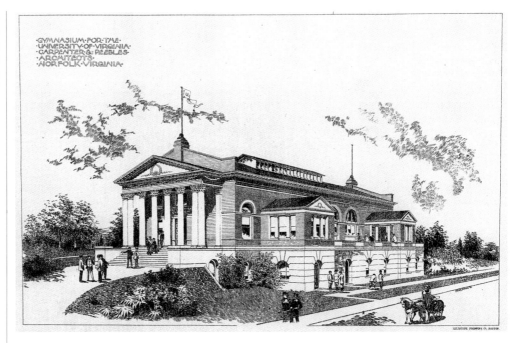

FIGURE 3.34. **Fayerweather Gymnasium, University of Virginia,** *Charlottesville, 1893–94, by James R. Carpenter and John Kevan Peebles, was a turn-of-the-century Beaux-Arts variation on the Roman Corinthian temple form. Reproduced from* American Architect and Building News, *no. 897 (March 4, 1893).*

FIGURE 3.35. **Aerial View of Monument Avenue,** *circa 1935. Reproduced from* the Work of William Lawrence Bottomley in Richmond *by William B. O'Neal and Christopher Weeks (Charlottesville: University Press of Virginia, 1985).*

Virginia illustrate the conjunction. John Kevan Peebles who, with his partner James R. Carpenter, designed Fayerweather Gymnasium ( FIGURE 3.34 ) in 1893, wrote one of the first articles on Jefferson as an architect. He disparaged Brooks Hall by John R. Thomas in 1876 ( SURVEY NO. 54 ) and the Gothic Chapel by Charles Cassel of 1885, and argued that Fayerweather Hall partook of the "Classic in feeling and in detail," but that the design was in no way a reproduction.[73] Peebles created a Roman Corinthian temple facade, raised up on a podium, that housed sweaty athletics. This is not the Roman architecture of Jefferson's Palladio, but a Beaux-Arts interpretation of it. Similarly McKim, Mead & White also "restored" and added to the University in what they considered to be compatible red-brick and light-colored-trim buildings, with large temple fronts—Cabell, Cocke, and Rouse halls. The idiom that Stanford White developed at the University came from his perceptions of Jefferson's work, which he explained: "They're wonderful and I am scared to death. I only hope I can do it right."[74] In his book of 1904, Joy Wheeler Dow made it very explicit that American Colonial and Georgian and their revivals, and the Classical architecture of Europe were all interrelated; in the United States it was the "American Renaissance."[75] The American Renaissance is the broader platform, a mental consciousness of the period from the 1870s into the 1930s, that attempted to place American culture on the same level as that of the Old World. Through the visual arts, painting, sculpture, and architecture, America would be glorified and extolled as the heir of Western civilization.[76]

The development of the Colonial Revival in Virginia went hand-in-hand with the creation of the myth of the "lost cause."[77] This is nowhere better seen than on Monument Avenue in Richmond ( FIGURE 3.35 ), where the Robert E. Lee monument (1890), the extension of the Avenue after 1900, and the placement of the other statues—J. E. B. Stuart and Jefferson Davis (1907),

Stonewall Jackson (1919), and Matthew Fontaine Maury (1929)—are in a setting of various architectural styles, especially Colonial Revival ( FIGURE 3.35A ).[78] Most of the Confederate monuments throughout Virginia were erected after 1900. They are the South's and Virginia's answer to a similar campaign that began in the North in the 1880s. One of the first big preservation battles in Richmond was over saving the White House of the Confederacy, which was threatened with demolition in 1889. Mrs. Joseph Bryan, a leader of the APVA, led a group that opened it as a museum in 1896.[79] The competition in 1910 for the Battle Abbey, the Confederate Memorial in Richmond, illustrates the conjunction: many of the ninety-seven entries in the competition were in various Colonial or Classical idioms. McKim, Mead & White's unsuccessful design adapted Jefferson's University Rotunda, but with a Doric order ( FIGURE 3.36 ). Bissell & Sinkler of Philadelphia won with a large temple-fronted design, then altered it. The building as erected in 1912–13 became much more specifically English in the style of the eighteenth century ( FIGURE 3.37 ).[80]

FIGURE 3.36. **Confederate Memorial Competition Entry** *(unbuilt), 1911, by McKim, Mead & White, adapted the form of Jefferson's Rotunda at the University of Virginia with a Doric order. (Photograph of lost drawing courtesy of Avery Library, Columbia University.)*

FIGURE 3.37. *The winning entry in the design competition for a memorial to the Civil War was based on a Classical Greek temple facade. The* **Confederate Memorial Institute** *(often called the Battle Abbey, now headquarters for the Virginia Historical Society), Richmond, Virginia, 1911–13, was designed by Philadelphia architects Bissell & Sinkler. (Photograph of architect's drawing, now lost, courtesy of the Virginia Historical Society.)*

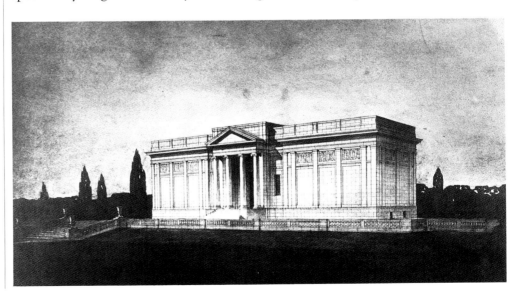

This memorializing and glorification of the War between the States, and by extension the mythologizing of "the olde South" and its antebellum, white-columned plantation culture, was a product of the American Renaissance, the quest to add a mythic dimension to American history. What events could give a more Homeric dimension to history than a battle of brother against brother, or the epic tragedy of a noble, agrarian-based culture trampled by mercantile industrialism?

So in Virginia there still exists a nostalgia for the past, a quest for the simplicity of "olde times" before the War, and even back to the noble days of the founding fathers; but there is also a complexity, for it was not all nostalgia. The Colonial Revival comes at the time of the "New South," a conscious quest by many Southern leaders to abandon the agrarian, poverty-stricken past, and to compete commercially and industrially with the North—to become, in effect, modern.[81] Progressive Virginia businessmen adopted the "New South" ethos and the architectural language of the American Renaissance. The tall office buildings, banks, markets, large estates, and even the addition to the State Capitol are all expressions of this new Southern sophistication. At a regional level it was the Colonial Revival and the monuments to Civil War heroes that provided the images for this New South. The Colonial Revival was urban in origin, created by urban sophisticates, who not only used it in cities but also for rural retreats.

The Colonial Revival was not an isolated movement, but part of a larger search for national identity that extends throughout most of the nineteenth and the twentieth centuries, first in the Western world, but more recently in other nations as well. Frequently interpreted as nostalgia, which can never be discounted, the nationalist quest for a style has other sources; it is intensely political and a product of the modern nation/state and its secular "religion" of patriotism. Nations throughout the past two centuries have excavated different styles and motifs of architecture to represent their national ethos. The Colonial Revival gave national identity to Americans, and provided unique personalities for regions and states. While historical and backward-looking, still the Colonial Revival is also a product of the modern mind, of a system of history that marks out the past in distinct epochs and periods, and seeks virtue in tradition. The Colonial Revival provided a canonical view of the American past, a hegemonic interpretation that was generally white, Anglo-Saxon, and Protestant. Other regions of the country modified this to suit their cultural roots, but the overriding perspective, aided and abetted by the ladies who supported historic preservation, was that of a WASP ethos. The Colonial Revival embodied the story and myth of America, of the colonists who created a new land, of a heroic generation of great leaders who created a new nation out of a wilderness. It symbolized and taught values to the young, to the immigrants, and to the citizens of all colors.

During the 1910s, 1920s, and 1930s, stylistic preferences in the Colonial Revival changed, as new views emerged about what was Colonial and appropriate for Americans and Virginians. John Russell Pope's John Kerr Branch House on Richmond's Monument Avenue ( FIGURES 3.38, 3.38A ) is one

FIGURE 3.38. *English Tudor and Elizabethan building forms are echoed in* **John Kerr Branch House** *at 2501 Monument Avenue, Richmond, 1918, designed by John Russell Pope (1874–1937). This elegant urban residence features historic antique woodwork and other construction details in the Tudor-Jacobean style.*

FIGURE 3.38A. Branch House, *north front, as it stands in 1992.*

FIGURE 3.39. **Virginia House** *was originally an English Tudor country house that was dismantled and reconstructed in Richmond, Virginia, in 1926–28, with extensive modifications by William Lawrence Bottomley (1883–1951) and Henry Grant Morse (1884–1934). The remodeled structure contains an addition designed to recall George Washington's ancestral home in England, Sulgrave Manor.*

FIGURE 3.40. **Agecroft,** *another fifteenth-century English antique relocated to Virginia, was dismantled and rebuilt in 1926–28 with extensive changes for Thomas C. Williams in his new residential development in Richmond, Windsor Farms.*

of the first instances of a new American birthright, though its roots can be traced all the way back to Bremo Recess (early 1830s; SURVEY NO. 31). The "Tudorbethan" style could be used on many different scales, as demonstrated in Richmond at Stony Point (SURVEY NO. 79), and the Williams house in Petersburg (SURVEY NO. 95). At Windsor Farms in Richmond's far West End during the mid 1920s, two English houses—the Tudor-style Virginia House and the fifteenth-century half-timbered Agecroft Hall (FIGURES 3.39, 3.40) were purchased in Britain, disassembled, shipped, and re-erected in Richmond with significant changes. William Lawrence Bottomley and Henry Grant Morse worked together on Virginia House and incorporated in it new features that recalled George Washington's ancestral home in England, Sulgrave Manor. The area known as Windsor Farms was developed by Richmond attorney and philanthropist Thomas C. Williams, who also owned Agecroft Hall. Williams had several of the community's structures done in similar styles, and the streets were laid out by city planner John Nolan in comforting curves. A promotional brochure for the development claimed that the English cottage "belongs as a sort of inherited right. . . . Virginia is bound . . . to the mother country where for centuries such splendid old houses have survived."[82] Most of the building at Windsor Farms was not "Tudorbethan", however, but Colonial Revival, including some of Bottomley's great works.

The giant-columned Southern Colonial never disappeared entirely in Virginia, but appeared in a more restrained and tasteful eighteenth-century form, rectangular and without columns. The models are many but the most popular is a form based on James River estates, or the more simple story-and-a-half, like Gunston Hall. A comparison of Bottomley's early work, such as the Coleman Wortham House (1917–25; FIGURE 3.41) with his later designs, such as Waverley Hill (1928–30; SURVEY NO. 87) illustrates how the free assemblage of many motifs from different periods is replaced by the more accurate and overall cohesive designs that are generally more faithful to a single style. In this case, the later house's facade is based largely on American examples from the 1750s and 1760s, while the earlier example is more Federal in origin,

FIGURE 3.41. *In one of his earlier residential designs in Virginia, William Lawrence Bottomley drew upon architectural motifs from many different periods.* **Front elevation, Coleman Wortham House,** *2301 Monument Avenue, Richmond Virginia, 1917–25, by William Lawrence Bottomley (1883–1951). Ink on linen, 19 by 18 inches. (Photograph of drawing courtesy of Carden McGhee.)*

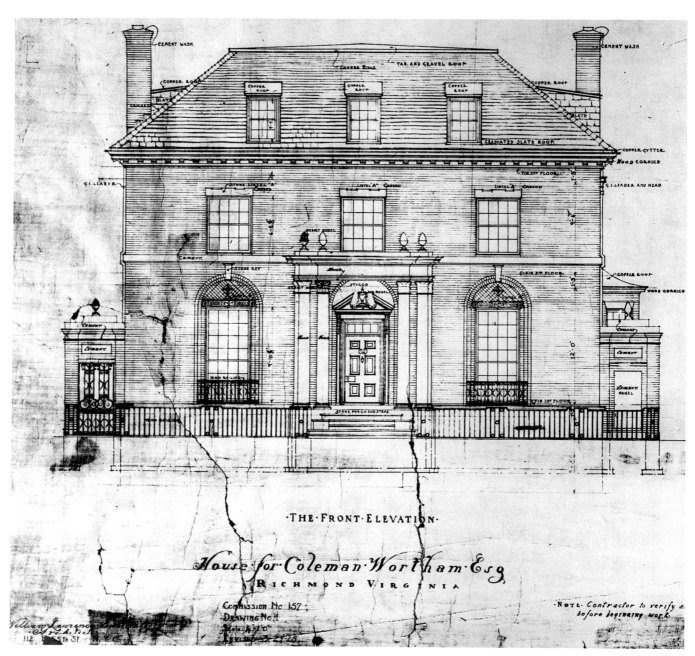

·THE·FRONT·ELEVATION·

*House for Coleman Wortham Esq*
RICHMOND VIRGINIA

FIGURE 3.42. *First built in 1751 for Carter Burwell by David Minitree, Carter's Grove has undergone extensive renovations. South (riverfront) facade of* **Burwell-Bisland-McCrea House, "Carter's Grove."** *The house was first remodeled in 1908 by W. W. Tyree (1874–1943) and then again in 1928–31 by W. Duncan Lee (1884–1952). (Photograph courtesy of Colonial Williamsburg Foundation.)*

with one of the largest porticoes Bottomley ever used—one inspired by the Roman Baroque architect Francesco Borromini—with Georgian pineapples.[83] Contributing to this trend toward simplicity was the Modernist rhetoric of elimination. Virginia-based Colonial Revival architects of these years are many; though the standouts would be John Kevan Peebles, Stanhope S. Johnson, and W. Duncan Lee (1884–1952). Lee designed several outstanding houses on Richmond's Monument Avenue and elsewhere. He had trained with Captain Marion J. Dimmock in Richmond, may have worked on the Westover plantation house, and did conduct a "restoration-plus" on Carter's Grove in the late 1920s ( FIGURE 3.42 ). At the turn of the century, the New York architect William W. Tyree (1874–1943) had done some restoration for a new owner, T. Perceval Bisland. Working for later owners, Molly and Archibald McCrea, Lee added the hyphens in a manner that, as he claimed, followed the intentions of the original designer. He also raised the roof and added dormers for more space. Carter's Grove's famous paneled hall had already lost its original paint: in the 1870s it had been painted red, white, blue, and green! Tyree stripped the paint in the hall and gave it a high-gloss dark stain varnish. Under Lee's direction the stain was lightened, and this contributed to the popular view that eighteenth-century Virginia interiors were left a natural wood finish.[84] For *House & Garden* magazine in 1934, Lee provided designs for a "James River Colonial," an adaptation of the main block facades of Carter's Grove. "The grand manner, of the wide-flung symmetrical wings" could not be used, but one small wing incorporated a garage.[85] Lee also served on the Advisory Committee for Colonial Williamsburg, and was involved with at least two, maybe three of the great architectural icons of the Commonwealth—Colonial Williamsburg, Carter's Grove, and Westover. Consequently he was also responsible for popularizing the image of Virginia as red-brick Colonial.

The shifts in perception in these years can be laid to several factors, but most importantly to the thousands of publications—books, articles, reports, and drawings—that appeared on the Colonial style in general, and on Virginia's Colonial style in particular. Among the books was Fiske Kimball's *Thomas Jefferson, Architect* (1916) and *Domestic Architecture of the American Colonies and of the Early Republic* (1922); the continuing *White Pine Series of Architectural Monographs* (1916–40); The Architects' Emergency Committee's *Great Georgian Houses of America* (1933, 1937), edited by William Lawrence Bottomley; and Thomas Tileston Waterman and John A. Barrows's *Domestic Colonial Architecture of Tidewater Virginia* (1932), which was a direct outcome of the Williamsburg restoration. Waterman's successive works, *Mansions of Virginia* (1946) and *Dwellings of Colonial America* (1950), became, and still remain, the canonical books defining Virginia's architectural contributions. Marcus Whiffen added to the Williamsburg canon with books on public buildings (1958) and houses (1960, 1970). These books all represent what might be called "advances," or greater knowledge on the subject, but they also represent a particular view of architecture founded on the Beaux-Arts system of education. The drawings published in the books by Kimball and

## Rosewell

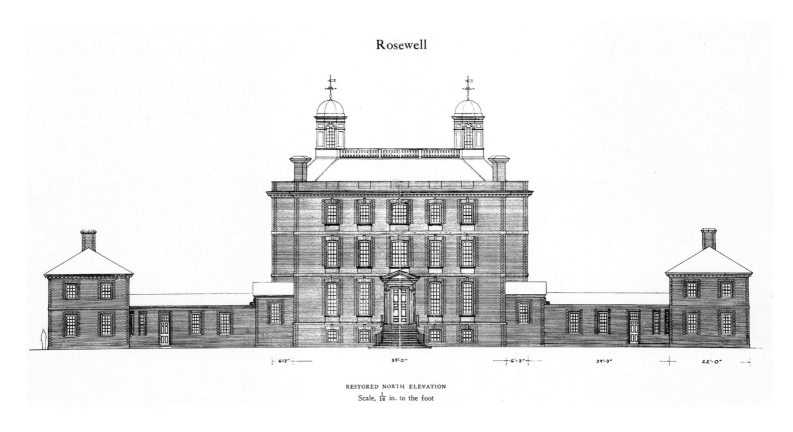

RESTORED NORTH ELEVATION
Scale, 1/16 in. to the foot

FIGURE 3.43. *The concept of tracing the European roots of American architecture and identifying the mastermind behind its creation has been a common theme in traditional architectural scholarship. A favorite model can be seen in this* **Reconstruction Drawing of Rosewell**, *Gloucester County, Virginia, in the 1930s by Thomas Tileston Waterman (1900–1950). Reproduced from Waterman and Barrows,* Domestic Colonial Architecture of Tidewater Virginia *(New York: Scribners, 1932), '94–5. [Compare the photograph of Rosewell in ruins: figure 1.23.]*

Waterman ( FIGURE 3.43 ) show that vision well: admired features are the center hall with symmetrical, balanced compositions; details are crisp; and their sources, along with those of the overall building, can be clearly traced to European models, giving them a pedigree. Great attention is paid to identifying the author of particular designs. This focus on a single master-mind at work is typical of nineteenth- and twentieth-century art history, but in actuality early

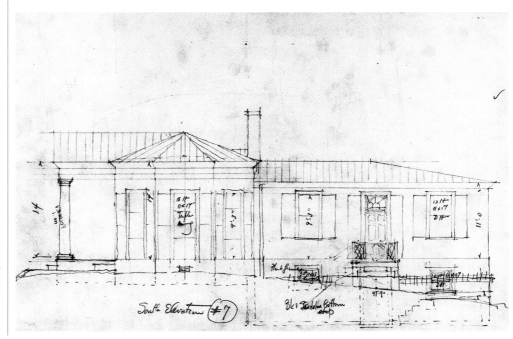

FIGURE 3.44. *Believing that historical precedent should guide creativity, scholar-architect Sidney Fiske Kimball (1888–1955) designed* **Tusculum**, *also called* **Shack Mountain**, *as his home in Charlottesville, Virginia, in 1934–35. South elevation, pencil on vellum, 11⅞ by 19 inches. (Photograph courtesy of the University of Virginia.)*

Virginia Colonial buildings were the products of many different talents and not a single designer. The authors of these latter books preferred brick buildings, which are more permanent and hence more architectonic. All of this is the result of how they had been taught to view architecture, or of how they were educated: academic and theoretical in the case of Kimball at Harvard, or practical and applied, with Waterman in Cram's office. They viewed themselves as scholar-architects and felt that a sound knowledge of historical precedent should be a guide to creativity. This approach can be seen in Shack Mountain (1935–36; FIGURE 3.44), Fiske Kimball's tour-de-force for himself and his wife, outside of Charlottesville. Drawing on his beloved Jefferson, Kimball created a single-story pavilion of amazing grace and at the same time with a large, Tuscan-columned portico that commands the landscape.[86]

The restoration of Colonial Williamsburg (SURVEY NOS. 83–86) beginning in the 1920s indicates how successfully the Colonial Revival summed up the quest for an American national style.[87] Such was its intention, as stated by its sponsor, John D. Rockefeller: "restoration of . . . a complete area entirely free from alien or inharmonious surroundings as well as to preserve the beauty and charm of the old buildings and gardens of the city and its historic significance. . . . It teaches of the patriotism, high purpose, and unselfish devotion of our forefathers to the common good."[88]

The Colonial Wiliamsburg restoration also culminates the Colonial Revival quest for accuracy or fidelity to original sources. Architecturally, it was important not so much for the larger structures such as the Capitol, the Governor's Palace, and the Wren Building, though they did become icons, but at the smaller, domestic scale, providing a new repertory of plans for houses and commercial buildings, along with appropriate paint colors, wallpaper designs, furniture, and other items for reproduction and sale. The project also provided a training ground for a large group of architects. There was the old guard, represented on the Advisory Committee by such leading figures as Fiske Kimball, Edmund S. Campbell (then chairman of the University of Virginia's architecture program), A. Lawrence Kocher, and others. There were also the many architects who worked on the project and went on to other jobs: Thomas Waterman as an architectural historian, Everette Fauber as a restoration expert, and Milton Grigg as an architect. In many ways restored Williamsburg became a paradigm of the twentieth-century garden suburb with its generous open space, its heavy vegetation and trees (some believe these are least forty percent more than in the 1770s), its overall cleanliness, its concealment of modern utilities, and its neat reproductions of historical buildings. The homemakers' press fell over itself praising the restoration and seeking lessons from its success. Hiram J. Herbert, writing for *Better Homes & Gardens* in 1936, felt that the business blocks of the town "offer an example of one way by which urban communities can be made ideal places in which to live." He found a hairy woodpecker in front of the small-paned, mullioned windows of the A&P store, "suggestive of a residence."[89] The only thing missing during daytime hours was the automobile, which arrived in the evening.

Yet the Colonial Revival does not stop in Williamsburg and the 1930s, for any look at Virginia's suburbs and countryside in the succeeding decades shows its strong continuance, including the work by Grigg and Johnson in Hollymead in 1935 ( SURVEY NO. 94 ). But a change does occur in the architectural press concerning the validity of designing in the historical styles, including the Colonial. This is most evident in the treatment of Williamsburg, which *Architectural Record* described as a "Restoration," with no relevance to contemporary design.[90] Only in the homemakers' press, in magazines like *House & Garden*—where architects Perry, Shaw & Hepburn provided house designs based on Williamsburg models—does the Colonial Revival remain a viable option.[91]

In spite of its conspicuous presence, the Colonial Revival went underground in the architectural press and in the schools. This is evident in the case of A. Lawrence Kocher (1885–1969), director of the University of Virginia's architecture program from 1926 to 1928, succeeding Fiske Kimball (1919–23) and Joseph Hudnut (1923–26). From Virginia, Kocher went to New York, where he became the managing editor of *Architectural Record* from 1928 to 1938, transforming it into the leading American epistle of Modernism. While he served on the architectural advisory board for Colonial Williamsburg, Kocher designed with Albert Frey several radically modern buildings. Later, in the early 1940s, he designed the main building at Black Mountain College in North Carolina, an institution devoted to Modernism in the arts, and also taught there. Kocher accepted the position of architectural records editor at Colonial Williamsburg in 1944, and remained there until his retirement in 1954. In 1947 Kocher designed "A Virginia House of Today" ( FIGURE 3.45 ) as part of *Your Solar House*, a project sponsored by Libby-Owens-Ford Glass Company. Architects representing every state were commissioned to show Americans how they could profit from the use of glass in their homes. Many of the designs were in the Modern style, and the contributors are a virtual roll-call of leading architects of the period. A few of the designs were in traditional styles, including Colonial, but not Kocher's for Virginia. Instead he provided a flat-roofed International-style derivative; even the so-called "Virginia brick" used for construction was painted. Here most graphically appears the bifurcated view of the Colonial: it was apparently considered appropriate for historical restorations, but not for Virginia homes which, Kocher explained, need only a few special provisions for shade and coolness, "Otherwise, the house of America is the same, whether it be north, south, east, or west."[92]

A full circle seems completed with the Postmodern rehabilitation of the Colonial Revival in the 1970s and 1980s. Architects who, a generation earlier, would have been designing in Modern idioms now used Colonial. The work of Robert A. M. Stern ( SURVEY NO. 117 ), Hartman-Cox ( FIGURE 3.23 ), and Allan Greenberg at the University of Virginia; Tony Atkin in Northern Virginia; and the new respect paid to older architects like Grigg & Johnson, are all indications of the shift. With the Postmodern revolution of the 1970s and 1980s came a new architectural history that examined all those styles that the Modernists had despised: Beaux-Arts, American Renaissance,

Colonial Revival, even High Victorian. Myers's old Richmond City Hall ( SURVEY NO. 58 ) became an object of praise and was saved from the wrecker's ball.[93] An aesthetic revolution occurred; the passage of time added distinction. One force behind these reevaluations was the historic preservation movement, which became official government policy in the 1960s. Actually, this shift in perceptions is in many ways a product of the modern consciousness: time is a succession of waves, or periods, and inherent values reside in the past.

FIGURE 3.45. *A non-traditional International style defined this perspective of* **A Virginia House of Today** *drawn in 1947 by Louis W. Ballou (1904– 1979), and designed by A. Lawrence Kocher (1885–1969), to illustrate how glass could add beauty and efficiency to the home. Reproduced from* Your Solar House, *a project sponsored by Libby-Owens-Ford Glass Company (New York: Simon & Schuster, 1947), 52.*

But such a sense of closure, with the Colonial Revival riding high, gives a false ending; for history does not end, it is open-ended, and a new, even more abstract, modern style, looms forth. Other alternatives exist. Those who write history create it, and in the past twenty years a new interest in the vernacular has emerged: the other side of Virginia's past, the log cabins, the ubiquitous I-houses, the barns and shacks, the buildings of the yeomanry who didn't live in James River estates, and the poor, both white and black. Historian Henry Glassie has been the leader of this group with his pioneering research on building types in western Virginia and in Louisa and Goochland counties.[94] Research by Edward Chappell, Dell Upton, Cary Carson, and Mark Wenger also explores Virginia's "other" past.[95]

The impact of this new scholarship on actual buildings has been most in obvious in museums: in Staunton, at the Museum of American Frontier Culture, and at Colonial Williamsburg, with the reconstruction of the Public Hospital, the Anderson Blacksmith Shop, and the Slave Quarter at Carter's Grove ( SURVEY NO. 118 ). Actually, architects have drawn from the vernacular since the nineteenth century; it is a continuing tradition. Virginia examples might include Floyd Johnson's small house in Charlottesville ( SURVEY NO. 101 ), and the structures Stanley W. Abbott designed in the mid 1930s for the Blue Ridge Parkway ( FIGURE 3.46 ). Abbott, a landscape architect, drew directly on the mountain vernacular of log cabins, shacks, and farm buildings to create gas stations, snack bars, and gift shops. His tightly composed designs, which used local stone for massive chimneys and foundations and relied on existing models, illustrate that even from the traditions of his early twentieth-century education he could look at the vernacular as well. More recently, Hartman-Cox's Immanuel Presbyterian Church in McLean (1978–80; FIGURE 3.47 ) draws on the idiom of barns and other rural structures. Conceived as a large barn behind a pre-existing house, the various additive forms recall vernacular churches while the side elevation comes from the Pennsylvania Germans at Ephrata. Certain features of Immanuel Church are later twentieth century: the large square window in the end elevation and the simulated board-and-batten siding (actually plywood sheets with battens added), which gives scale and

FIGURE 3.46. *A rural vernacular style was chosen for this design for a* **Typical Coffee Shop & Gas Station, Blue Ridge Parkway,** *(1936), by Stanley W. Abbott (1908–1975). Pencil on tracing paper, 9 by 12 inches. (Photograph courtesy of the Blue Ridge Parkway and the National Building Museum.)*

TYPICAL COFFEE SHOP & GAS STATION

BLUE RIDGE PARKWAY

DRVG Nº PKY—BR—GEN—2276

SWA
Nov 1936

FIGURE 3.47. **Immanuel Presbyterian Church,** *McLean, Virginia, 1978–80, by Hartman-Cox, is built in an updated version of the rural venacular style. (Photograph by Robert Lautman, courtesy of Hartman-Cox.)*

provides an economical exterior surface.[96] This "new" vernacular is still in its infancy, but if the pattern of history holds—that a dialogue does exist among preservationists, historians, and architects—then we might expect other "new" or different buildings that recall Virginia's architectural heritage.[97]

As we have seen, Virginia architecture of the past 125 years exhibits a multiplicity of images, forms, and intentions. While there is certainly a popular perception of Virginia's contribution to American design as residing in the early period, from 1607 to the 1820s, this view was created primarily by historians and the Colonial Revivalists. There is no one type of Colonial, or Colonial Revival, architecture for Virginia, but many: large-columned houses, extended-wing brick mansions, and more humble story-and-a-half builder's variety Colonial. So persuasive has the Colonial image become that the form of the eighteenth-century Virginia courthouse has been appropriated by the Commonwealth to serve as rest stops and "Welcome Centers" along Virginia highways ( FIGURE 3.48 ). This is the popular image, but there are other aspects of Virginia's architectural heritage that are equally worthy of study, preservation, and emulation, from High Victorian to Modern. The challenge is to recognize the values inherent in each and how those values represent who we are.

FIGURE 3.48. **Virginia Welcome Center,** *(circa 1970), Virginia Department of Transportation, follows the centuries-old tradition of an arcade passage seen first at the Capitol in Williamsburg and again in so many of Virginia's county courthouses.*

1. Kimball quoted in letter, Robert Tebbs to Philip Trammell Shutze, February 26, 1932, Atlanta Historical Society, quoted in Spencer Tunnell II, "Stylistic Progression Versus Site Planning Methodology: An Analysis of the Residential Architecture of Philip Trammell Shutze" (Master's thesis, University of Virginia, 1989), 9. See also Fiske Kimball, "Recent Architecture in the South," *Architectural Record* 55 (March 1924): 209–71.

2. H. L. Mencken, "The Sahara of the Bozart," in *Prejudices: Second Series* (New York: Alfred A. Knopf, 1920), 136–54.

3. These comments are generalized and refer to current surveys: David P. Handlin, *American Architecture* (New York: Thames & Hudson, 1985); Leland Roth, *A Concise History of American Architecture* (New York: Harper & Row, 1979); and Marcus Whiffen and Frederick Koeper, *American Architecture, 1607–1976* (Cambridge: MIT, 1981). Books claiming to treat the South are just as ignorant of the past, from the Civil War to World War II: Wayne Andrews, *Pride of the South* (New York: Atheneum, 1979) and Kenneth Severens, *Southern Architecture* (New York: E. P. Dutton, 1981).

4. The important studies are noted throughout this chapter or elsewhere in pertinent passages, but several should be singled out: William B. O'Neal, *Architecture in Virginia: An Official Guide to Four Centuries of Building in the Old Dominion* (New York: Walker Company, 1968), now out of print, is the only guidebook. Dell Upton, "New Views of the Virginia Landscape," *Virginia Magazine of History and Biography* 96 (October 1988): 403–70, while largely concerned with earlier architecture, is important for its perspective. Finally, and indispensable, is Calder Loth, ed., *The Virginia Landmarks Register,* 3rd ed. (Charlottesville: University Press of Virginia, 1986).

5. Cassie Moncure Lyne, "Historic Homes in Virginia Owned by the du Ponts . . ." *Richmond Magazine* 14 (November 1927): 19–22, 46. See also Mark Alan Hewitt, *The Architect & the American Country House* (New Haven: Yale University Press, 1990).

6. Studies for some of these cities exist and are noted in appropriate notes, but in addition see Royster Lyle, Jr., and Pamela Hemenway Simpson, *The Architecture of Historic Lexington* (Charlottesville: University Press of Virginia, 1977); W. L Whitwell and Lee W. Winborne, *The Architectural Heritage of the Roanoke Valley* (Charlottesville: University Press of Virginia, 1982); and K. Edward Lay, "Charlottesville's Architectural Legacy, *The Magazine of Albemarle County History* 46 (May 1988): 29–95.

7. S. Allen Chambers, *Lynchburg: An Architectural History* (Charlottesville: University Press of Virginia, 1981): 208, 214, 225, 238, 269.

8. Douglas McVarish, with K. Edward Lay and Boyd Coons, "Architectural Education at the University of Virginia," *Colonnade* 3 (Summer 1988) and 4 (Winter 1989): unpaginated; 4, no. 2 (Summer-Autumn 1989): 27–36. See also F. H. Bosworth and Roy Childs Jones, *A Study of Architectural Schools* (New York: Charles Scribner's Sons, 1932).

9. Chambers, *Lynchburg,* 153 and following, gives a picture of Robert Calhoun Burkholder (1826–1914), who began as a carpenter and later advanced to call himself an architect.

10. John Wells, Virginia Department of Historic Resources, provided some information, as did Tony Wrenn from the AIA Archives; see D. Adler, ed., *Proceedings of the Twenty-Sixth Annual Convention of the American Institute of Architects* [1892] (Chicago: Inland Architectural Press, 1893), 95–96; and *Proceedings* for 1893–98.

11. "Architects Form an Association," *Concrete Age* 15 (October 1911): 26. Letters in the AIA Archives indicate that the AIA tried to establish a Virginia chapter in 1900 but did not for lack of interest among Virginia architects themselves.

12. John Wells of Richmond has kindly supplied me with this information.

13. "The Virginia Chapter, AIA, A History," *Virginia Architect's Handbook* (Richmond: Virginia AIA, 1968): 19,21,23.

14. Turpin C. Bannister, ed., *The Architect at Mid-Century: Evolution and Achievement* (New York: Reinhold, 1954), 1:357.

15. This observation is based on an extensive survey of both magazines up to the 1920s.

16. This conclusion is based on examination of about 25 monthly issues of *The Southern Architect* from 1889 to 1932. Because complete collections of this periodical are scarce, it is difficult to base such a conclusion on any more thorough sampling. Stanislaw J. Makielski, who taught at the University of Virginia from 1919 to 1955 and practiced in the Charlottesville area, was on the editorial board of *The Southern Architect* during the 1920s. *Southern Architecture Illustrated* (Atlanta: Harman Publishing Company, 1931), by the same publisher as *Southern Architect,* illustrates 100 contemporary houses. Only six are from Virginia: three are by Duncan Lee, two are by Smithey & Tardy, and one is by Matthews & Short. Additionally, two Virginia Colonial-style designs are in the introduction, by Dwight James Baum: Chatham and Lower Brandon.

17. Beginning in 1953 the *Virginia Magazine,* later *Virginia and the Virginia Record,* and finally *The Virginia Record,* devoted one issue (sometimes several) to Virginia architecture. Poorly produced and with apparently few standards, the magazine was strictly a trade publication. In January 1990, the Virginia Society of Architects established *Inform,* a much more attractive publication, with the intention of appealing to a wider audience.

18. For background see Richard K. Dozier, "The Black Architectural Experience in America," *AIA Journal* 65 (July 1976): 162–68; Michael Adams, "Perspectives: A Legacy of Shadows," *Progressive Architecture* 72 (February 1991): 85–87; Peter H. Wood, "Whetting, Setting and Laying Timbers, Black Builders in the Early South" and Darryl Paulson, "Masters of It All, Black Builders in This Century," *Southern Exposure* 8 (Spring 1980): 3–13.

19. Giles B. Jackson and D. Webster Davis, *The Industrial History of the Negro Race of the United States* (Richmond: privately published, 1908), 171–87.

20. Interview with Harvey Johnson, Jr., Virginia Beach, February 16, 1990, and examination of materials in his possession.

21. Announcements of the winner were published in Norfolk's

*Virginian-Pilot* (November 17, 1938): 1,3; and *Richmond Times Dispatch* (November 17, 1938): 16. Moses' original drawings have been destroyed; however, reproductions of his winning entry can be found in Mentor A. Howe, "Come to the Fair!," *Phylon* 1 (no.4, 1940): 320–21; and the Newport News *Times Herald* (November 19, 1938): 2.

22.    A full report of the November 22 meeting, along with other matters relating to the design of the Virginia Room for the World's Fair, appeared in an article entitled "Restoration Would Decline Invitation of Fair Commission," *The [Williamsburg] Virginia Gazette* (February 17, 1939): 6.

23.    Quoted from Mary Tyler Cheek, "'An Island of Quiet in an Ocean of Noise'," *Virginia Calvacade* 35 (Summer 1985): 31–37, which contains both photos and descriptions of the completed room. See also Edward D. C. Campbell, Jr., "Fair Shadows: Virginia, Photographs, and the 1939 World's Fair," *Virginia Cavalcade* 41 (Summer 1991): 6–19. Extensive descriptions of Leslie Cheek's design are in the *Richmond News Leader* (January 27, 1939): 2; *Richmond Times-Dispatch* (February 10, 1939): 8; and the Norfolk *Virginian-Pilot* (February 10, 1939): 1, 9.

24.    Interview with William Moses, February 16, 1990. See *Richmond Times-Dispatch* (January 6, 1939): 9; and Norfolk's *Virginian-Pilot* (January 6, 1939), section 2: 8.

25.    "Moses Design for Fair Out," *Richmond News Leader* (January 27 1939): 1–2, includes the text of Hall's reply and a description of the substitute design proposal, prepared by Cheek.

26.    Norfolk *Journal and Guide* (February 4, 1939): 1.

27.    Mentor A. Howe, "Come to the Fair!" *Phylon* 1 (no. 4, 1940): 314–22. Many of the articles from the Norfolk and Richmond newspapers were reprinted in *The Southern Workman* 68 (January 1939): 14–18, and (April 1939): 102–05.

28.    The entire subject is just beginning to receive attention; among the few books are: Susana Torre, *Women in American Architecture: A Historic and Contemporary Perspective* (New York: Whitney Library of Design, 1977); and Ellen Perry Berkeley, and Matilda McQuaid, *Architecture, A Place for Women* (Washington, D.C.: Smithsonian Institute Press, 1989).

29.    Interview with Jane and Dan Duhl, current owners of the house, January 30, 1991.

30.    Mrs. William R. Massie and Mrs. Andrew H. Christian, comps., *Descriptive Guide Book of Virginia's Old Gardens* (Richmond: Garden Club of Virginia, 1929); Frances Archer Christian and Susanne Williams Massie, eds., *Homes and Gardens in Old Virginia* (Richmond: Garrett and Massie, 1931), known as "The Official Book of The Garden Club of Virginia."

31.    The connections between the Garden Club and noted architects' commissions in Virginia were pointed out by architectural historian Davyd Foard Hood.

32.    The Mount Vernon Parkway was later subsumed under the newer project, the George Washington Memorial Parkway; the final section of the Colonial Parkway in Williamsburg was completed in 1957. For the Blue Ridge Parkway see Harley E. Jolley, *Painting with a Comet's Tail* (Boone, N.C.: Appalachian Consortium, 1987); Jolley, *The Blue Ridge Parkway* (Knoxville: The University of Tennessee Press, 1969); Reuben Rainey, "The Blue Ridge Parkway; A Linear Park for the Automobile Age," *Utblick Landskad* (Stockholm: May 1991, forthcoming); and Rainey, "Stanley William Abbott," *Virginia Dictionary of Biography* (Richmond: Virginia State Library and Archives, forthcoming).

33.    Richard Guy Wilson and Joseph Dye Lahendro, "Larkin Company Jamestown Exhibition Pavilion," *Frank Lloyd Wright Newsletter* 3 (1980): 9; Paul V. Turner, "Frank Lloyd Wright's Other Larkin Building," *Journal of the Society of Architectural Historians* 39 (1980): 304–06; and Yukio Futagawa, ed., *Frank Lloyd Wright Monograph* (Tokyo: A.D.A. Edita, 1987): 46.

34.    *The Official Blue Book of the Jamestown TerCentennial Exposition* (Norfolk: Colonial Pub. Co, 1907): 505, 585.

35.    See Wendy Kaplan, ed., *"The Art that is Life": The Arts & Crafts Movement in America,* exh. cat. (Boston: Museum of Fine Arts, 1987).

36.    See Robert A. Reid, ed., *The Jamestown Exposition Beautifully Illustrated* (New York; Jamestown Official Photograph Corp., 1907), unpaginated. *The Official Blue Book*, p. 577, lists Tiffany Studios, who won a gold medal; and p. 474 lists Stickley Brothers of Grand Rapids, Michigan, who showed goatskin furniture and leather goods. However, in the Norfolk Public Library's copy of the Reid catalogue, cited above, the frontispiece has a hand-colored rendering of the L. & J. G. Stickley Library, done in the high Arts-and-Crafts mode, with a note that the furniture illustrated therein could be purchased at Willis-Smith-Crail Co., Norfolk, indicating that the latter had a display at the Tercentennial, as well.

37.    Chambers, *Lynchburg,* 414–15.

38.    William T. Frazier, "T. J. Collins: A Local Virginia Architect and his Practice at the Turn of the Century," (Master's thesis, University of Virginia, 1976), 38–42.

39.    Joseph Dye Lahendro interview with Marcellus E. Wright, Jr., November 8, 1979.

40.    Randolph Williams Sexton, *American Commercial Buildings of Today* (New York: Architectural Book Pub. Co., 1928), 172; and Robert Winthrop, *Architecture in Downtown Richmond* (Richmond: Junior Board of Historic Richmond Foundation, 1982), 113.

41.    "Tobacco Factory, Richmond, Virginia," *Architectural Record* 89 (April 1941): 50–57; also published in: *L'Homme et L'Architecture,* nos. 5–6 (May-June 1946): 22–25.

42.    Information on Amaza Meredith comes from conversations and correspondence with Lucious Edwards, Jr., archivist at Virginia State University. In addition to her residence, Meredith did a number of other architectural designs.

43.    See Henry-Russell Hitchcock and Philip Johnson, *The International Style: Architecture Since 1922* (New York: W. W. Norton Co., 1932); see also Richard Guy Wilson, "International Style: The MoMA Exhibition," *Progressive Architecture* 63 (February 1982): 92–105.

44.    Now owned by the Virginia State University Alumni Association, the house is currently restored after years of neglect.

45.    "The Record Poll," *Architectural Record* 88 (December 1940): 16–18. The *Record* conducted similar polls in other cities not only finding similar conservatism, but also finding much more Modernist sympathies.

46.    Carol Herselle Krinsky, *Gordon Bunshaft of Skidmore, Owings & Merrill* (New York and Cambridge: The Architectural History Foundation and MIT Press, 1988), 62–64.

47.    Yukio Futagawa, ed., *Frank Lloyd Wright Monograph* (Tokyo: A.D.A. Edita, 1988), 8: 39, 92, 98, 233. See also James A. D. Cox, "Frank Lloyd Wright and His Houses in Virginia" *Arts in Virginia* 13 (1972): 10–17.

48.    For suggestions regarding this topic I am indebted to Mark R. Wenger, "The Colonial Revival in Virginia," unpublished paper delivered at the Williamsburg Antiques Forum, sponsored by Colonial Williamsburg Foundation, February 3, 1987. Otherwise, the Colonial Revival in Virginia is largely untreated. For general background see William B. Rhoads, *The Colonial Revival* (New York: Garland Pub. Co, 1977), 2 vols.; Alan Axelrod, ed., *The Colonial Revival in America* (New York: W. W. Norton Co., 1985); and Jessie Poesch, "Architecture," and Davyd Foard Hood, "Georgian Revival Architecture," in *Encyclopedia of Southern Culture,* ed. C. R. Wilson and W. Ferris, (Chapel Hill: University of North Carolina Press, 1989), 55–57, 69–71.

49.    The APVA was formally organized on January 4, 1889, though its origins lie at least six months earlier. See Nancy Elizabeth Packer, *White Gloves & Red Bricks: APVA, 1889–1989,* exh. cat. (Richmond: Association for the Preservation of Virginia Antiquities, 1989): 5–7; and Charles B. Hosmer, Jr., *Presence of the Past* (New York: G.P. Putnam's Sons, 1965), chapters 2–3.

50.    See Vincent Scully, Jr., *The Shingle Style* (New Haven: Yale University Press, 1955); see also Richard Guy Wilson, "American Architecture and the Search for a National Style in the 1870s," *Nineteenth Century* 3 (Autumn 1977): 74–80; and "The Early Works of Charles F. McKim, Country House Commissions," *Winterthur Portfolio* 14 (Fall 1979): 235–67.

51.    See George William Sheldon, *Artistic Country-Seats,* (New York: D. Appleton & Co., 1886–87), 2: 25–28; Oliver Larkin, *Art and Life in America,* 247. A drawing of Stratford appeared in Mrs. Martha J. Lamb, *The Homes of America* (New York: D. Appleton & Co., 1879), 68.

52.    Some of the features of the Edgar house at Newport can be also interpreted as Philadelphian in style. Illustrations of all three houses appear in *A Monograph of the Works of McKim, Mead & White, 1879–1915* (New York: Architectural Book Pub. Co, 1915–20); reprinted as R. G. Wilson, ed., *The Architecture of McKim, Mead & White* (New York: Dover, 1990), pls.14, 146, 268–271. See also Mark A. Hewitt, "Hill-Stead, Farmington, Connecticut"

*Antiques* 134 (October 1988): 848–61. On the Breese house as Virginian see James A. Gade, "Long Island Country Places, Designed by McKim, Mead & White II—'The Orchard' at Southampton," *House & Garden* 3 (March 1903): 17.

53. See Tatiana S. Durilin, "Bremo Recess: A Colonial Jacobean Revival," (Master's thesis, University of Virginia, 1990).

54. Andrew Jackson Downing makes this suggestion in *The Architecture of Country Houses* (1850, New York: Dover, 1981): 264. See Arthur Channing Downs, *Downing & The American House* (Newtown Square, PA: Downing & Vaux Society, 1988), 24; and Downs, *Preliminary Report III: Brick & Architectural Terra Cotta (Part I), Brownstone (Downing and Upjohn), The Colonial Revival* (Newtown Square, PA: Downing & Vaux Society, 1990), 51–58. Downs is apparently the only scholar to have pursued this point.

55. Information provided by Calder Loth.

56. See Elizabeth McCausland, *The Life and Work of Edward Lamson Henry, N.A., 1841–1919* (Albany: New York State Museum, 1945).

57. Drawings by Taylor are in the Mount Vernon archives. In 1874–75 McKim had photographs taken of Newport antiquities and in 1877 McKim, Mead & White and William Bigelow took a sketching trip of Cape Ann, Massachusetts.

58. See T. Buckler Ghequiere, "Richmond County Court House, Virginia," *American Architect and Building News* 2 (June 23, 1877): 199. See also Glen Brown, "Old Colonial Work in Virginia and Maryland," *American Architect and Building News* 22 (October 22; November 19, 26, 1887): 198–99, 242–43, 254; reprinted in *The Georgian Period* parts 1–2 (New York: American Architect and Building News, 1898–1901), pls. 9–10. In his "Old Colonial Work of Virginia and Maryland," *American Architect and Building News* 24 (June 15, 1889), 279–281, A. B. Bibb began a six-part series that continued until November 1891. This series was reprinted in *The Georgian Period*, parts 5 and 6: 13–16, 17–54.

59. See "Old Brick Church, St. Luke's, Isle of Wight County, Virginia." *American Architect and Building News* 15 (April 19, 1884): 434; "Monumental Church," vol. 18 (November 14, 1885): 519; "The State Capitol of Virginia," vol. 22 (November 12, 1887): 235; "The Old State-House at Richmond, Virginia." vol. 23 (May 26, 1888):249.

60. See J. R. Chapin, "The Westover Estate," *Harper's* 42 (1871): 801–10. "Virginia: New Ways in the Old Dominion," *Scribner's* 5 (December 1872): 137–60, by Jed Hotchkiss, has illustrations of old architecture, while Edward King, "The Great South: A Ramble in Scribner's Virginia," 7 (April 1874): 645–74, does not.

61. Among the many articles found in *Century* with illustrations of early Virginia are F. H. Lungren and R. Blum, "An Old Virginia Town," vol. 21 (February 1881): 489–502; Thomas Nelson Page, "Old Yorktown," vol. 22 (October 1881): 801–16; Edward Eggleston, "Social Conditions in the Colonies," vol. 28 (October 1884): 848–71; J. G. Nicolay, "Thomas Jefferson's Home," and Frank B. Stockton, "The Later Years of Monticello," vol. 34 (September 1887): 642–53, 654–58.

62. Thomas Nelson Page, *The Old South* (New York: Scribner's, 1893); *In Ole Virginia* (New York: Scribner's, 1897); and *The Old Dominion* (New York: Scribner's, 1908), are but three of many such books and articles.

63. Information provided by Mary S. Boese, former curator, The Maymont Foundation, Richmond.

64. Quoted in *Buildings and Art and the World's Fair* (Chicago: Rand, McNally & Co., 1894), unpaginated. See also *Organizations, By-Laws, Plan of Work, Local and General, of the Board of World's Fair Managers of Virginia* (Richmond: publisher unknown, 1892); and Susan Prendergast Schoelwer, "Curious Relics and Quaint Scenes: The Colonial Revival at Chicago's Great Fair," in Axelrod, ed., *The Colonial Revival in America,* 189–90.

65. Drawings are in the Mount Vernon archives. Charles K. Bryant (1869–1933) of Richmond was in charge. Mount Vernon replicas were used as the Virginia Building at the Panama-Pacific International Exposition, San Francisco, 1915; the United States of America Building at the Exposition Coloniale Internationale de Paris, France, 1931; and as the City of New York Bicentennial Commission Building, Prospect Park, Brooklyn, New York, 1931. For the St. Louis Exposition of 1904, the Virginia building was based on Monticello.

66. The Kentucky, Delaware and West Virginia buildings were identified as "Southern" in *Buildings and Art and the World's Fair* (Chicago: Rand, McNally & Co., 1931), unpaginated.

67. I am greatly indebted to the research of Timothy Matthewson, former Chief of Interpretation and Education, McFaddin-Ward House, Beaumont, Texas, who has shared with me his information on this topic. The Barber catalogues that illustrate Southern Colonial are *Modern Dwellings* (Knoxville: S. F. Newman and Co., 1898–1907) and *Modern American Homes* (Knoxville: Gaut-Ogden Co., 1903–07). Rhoads, in *Colonial Revival* 1: 114, cites an article in the *American Architect* 48 (April 6, 1895): 5, on a design of Eames and Young in St. Louis for the David Francis house, which included a great two-story portico. This feature was described as "almost part and parcel of the southern colonial."

68. There may be some houses that predate the Connecticut example, such as Altha Hall (1889–1959, Fairfax), but its dates are uncertain. Also, there is the Doubleday Mansion of circa 1898. Both are illustrated in Eleanor Lee Templeman and Nan Netherton, *Northern Virginia Heritage* (privately published, 1966), 58–59.

69. "The Reminiscences of Thomas Mott Shaw," unpublished (Boston: Perry, Dean, Rogers & Partners, archives, 1956): 5.

70. The story of Westover is still unclear. Mark R. Wenger, "Westover: William Byrd's Mansion Reconsidered," (Master's thesis, University of Virginia, 1981), concentrates on the eighteenth-century elements of the house, but does consider some later work.

71. Ralph Adams Cram, *My Life in Architecture* (Boston; Little Brown & Co, 1936), 96, 124. See also Chambers, *Lynchburg*, 369–71; and views published by Cram's firm, in *American Architect and Building News* 77 (August 23, 1902), unpaginated; Sarah Drummond Lanford, "Ralph Adams Cram as College Architect," (Master's thesis, University of Virginia, 1981); H. Stafford Bryant, Jr.,

"Classical Ensemble," *Arts In Virginia* 11 (Winter 1971): 118–24; and Martha Lou Lemmar Stohlman, *The Story of Sweet Briar College* (Sweet Briar: Alumnae Assoc. of Sweet Briar College, 1956).

72. Quoted in *The Jamestown Exposition Illustrated* (Norfolk: Jamestown Official Photographic Corp., 1907); unpaginated [3]. The assignment of responsibilities of design are unclear. See Carl Abbott, "Norfolk in the New Century: The Jamestown Exposition and Urban Boosterism," *Virginia Magazine of History and Biography* 85 (January 1977): 86–96; Robert T. Taylor, "The Jamestown TerCentennial Exposition of 1907," vol. 65 (1957): 169–208; Warren H. Manning, "Jamestown Exposition, *Transactions of the American Society of Landscape Architects, 1899–1908* (1910), 1: 83–88; *The Official Bluebook of the Jamestown TerCentennial Exposition* (Norfolk: Colonial Publishing Co., 1909); and Betsy L. Fahlman, et al., *A Tricentennial Celebration: Norfolk, 1682–1982,* exh. cat. (Norfolk: Chrysler Museum, 1982), 149–56.

73. John Kevan Peebles, "Thos. Jefferson, Architect," *Alumni Bulletin [University of Virginia]* 1 (November 1894): 68–74; reprinted in *American Architect and Building News* 47 (January 19, 1895): 29–30. Fayerweather Hall appears in *American Architect* 43, no. 897 (March 4, 1893).

74. Quoted in Edward Simmons, *From Seven to Seventy* (New York: Harper & Brothers, 1922), 241.

75. See Joy Wheeler Dow, *American Renaissance* (New York: William T. Comstock, 1904).

76. Richard Guy Wilson, Dianne Pilgrim, and Richard Murray, *The American Renaissance* (Brooklyn and New York; The Brooklyn Museum and Pantheon, 1979); and Richard Guy Wilson, "Architecture and the Reinterpretation of the Past in the American Renaissance," *Winterthur Portfolio* 18 (Spring 1983): 69–87.

77. Gaines M. Foster, *Ghosts of the Confederacy: Defeat, The Lost Cause, and the Emergence of the New South, 1865 to 1913* (New York: Oxford University Press, 1987).

78. Richard Guy Wilson, "Monument Avenue, Richmond," in *Great American Avenues* (Washington, D.C.: AIA Press, forthcoming); and Carden C. McGehee, Jr., "The Planning, Sculpture, and Architecture of Monument Avenue, Richmond, Virginia" (Master's thesis, University of Virginia, 1980).

79. Hosmer, *Presence of the Past*, 68–69.

80. Virginius Cornick Hall, "The Virginia Historical Society: An Anniversary Narrative of Its First Century and a Half," *Virginia Magazine of History and Biography* 90 (January 1982): 100–105. Bissell & Sinkler's original entry and three others appear in the yearbook of the Philadelphia Chapter American Institute of Architects and the T-Square Club, *Seventeenth Annual Exhibition* (Philadelphia: Exhibition Board, 1911), unpaginated. Confederate Memorial Association, *Program of a Competition* (Richmond, 1910), listed the jurors as J. Taylor Ellyson, president of the Confederate Memorial Association, William C. Noland, and an architect yet to be selected. William M. S. Rasmussen, curator of art at the Virginia Historical Society, has discovered that James Knox Taylor, Supervising Architect of the U.S. Treasury, served as the outside architect on that jury.

81. The term "New South" comes from Henry Grady, editor of the Atlanta *Constitution* in the 1880s. See Henry Grady, *The New South, Writings and Speeches of Henry Grady* (Savannah: Beehive Press, 1971). The classic study is C. Vann Woodward, *Origins of the New South* (Baton Rouge: Louisiana State University, 1951).

82. From *The Black Swan,* quoted in Wenger, "The Colonial Revival." See also Marcus Binney, "An English Garden Suburb on the James," *Country Life* 177 (April 4, 1985): 912–14.

83. See William B. O'Neal and Christopher Weeks, *The Work of William Lawrence Bottomley in Richmond* (Charlottesville: University Press of Virginia, 1985).

84. W. Duncan Lee, "The Renascence of Carter's Grove," *Architecture* 67 (April 1933): 185–95. Apparently all of Lee's papers and drawings were destroyed by his widow after his death. See also Mary A. Stephenson, *Carter's Grove Plantation: A History* (city unknown: Sealantic Fund, 1964).

85. Henry H. Saylor, "James River Colonial-historic American style," *House & Garden* 67 (January 1935): 46–47, 58, 60.

86. Joseph Dye Lahendro, "Fiske Kimball: American Renaissance Historian" (Master's thesis, University of Virginia, 1982) is an excellent study, the best so far. See also, though flawed: George and Mary Roberts, *Triumph on Fairmont: Fiske Kimball and the Philadelphia Museum of Art* (Philadelphia: J. B. Lippincott Co., 1959), chapter 11.

87. The materials on Williamsburg are overwhelming. In addition to those cited elsewhere, the most important are Edward A. Chappell, "Architects of Colonial Williamsburg," in Wilson and Ferris, *Encyclopedia of Southern Culture,* 59–61; and Thomas H. Taylor, Jr., "The Williamsburg Restoration and Its Reception by the American Public: 1926–1942," (Ph.D. diss., George Washington University, 1989).

88. Quoted in George Yetter, *Williamsburg Before and After* (Williamsburg: Colonial Williamsburg Foundation, 1988), 54–55.

89. Hiram J. Herbert, "Williamsburg: The Ideal Home Town," *Better Homes & Gardens* 14 (July 1936): 15.

90. "Restoration of Colonial Williamsburg," *Architectural Record* 78 (December 1935), entire issue.

91. *House & Garden* 72 (November 1937) devoted the entire issue to Williamsburg, and published three house designs (pp. 69–80) by Perry, Shaw & Hepburn based on Williamsburg models.

92. Maron J. Simon, ed., *Your Solar House* (New York: Simon and Schuster, 1947), 53. On Kocher see introduction by Lawrence Wodehouse in Cynthia Zignego Stiverson, *Architecture and the Decorative Arts: The A. Lawrence Kocher Collection of Books at the Colonial Williamsburg Foundation* (West Cornwall, Connecticut: Locust Hill Press, 1989).

93. Carroll L. V. Meeks, "Character, Ugliness, Beauty and Time," *Historic Preservation* 14 (1962): 56–63; also published in: *Arts in Virginia* 2 (Spring 1962): 12–19.

94. Henry Glassie, *Pattern in the Material Folk Culture of the Eastern United States* (Philadelphia: 1968); and *Folk Housing in Middle Virginia* (Knoxville: University of Tennessee Press, 1975).

95. Among many publications see Edward Chappell, "Acculturation in the Shenandoah Valley: Rhenish House of the Massanutten Settlement," *Proceedings of the American Philosophical Society* 134 (1980): 55–89; Chappell, "Architectural Recording and the Open-Air Museum: A View from the Field," and Mark R. Wenger, "The Central Passage in Virginia: Evolution of an Eighteenth-Century Living Space," in C. Wells, ed., *Perspectives in Vernacular Architecture* 2 (Columbia: University of Missouri Press, 1986): 24–36, 137–49. See also Dell Upton, "Vernacular Domestic Architecture in Eighteenth-Century Virginia," and Cary Carson, Norman F. Barka, William M. Kelso, Garry Wheeler Stone, and Dell Upton, "Impermanent Architecture in the Southern American Colonies, *Winterthur Portfolio* 17 (Summer/Autumn 1982): 95–119, and vol. 16 (Summer/Autumn 1981): 135–96.

96. Interview with Warren Cox, February 21, 1991.

97. A few architects in the South have taken a clue from the vernacular; in particular see Mockbee-Coker-Howorth of Memphis, Tennessee, and Jackson, Mississippi; and Clark & Menefee of Charleston, South Carolina, especially their *Contempo Shotgun* (Jackson: Mockbee-Coker-Howorth, 1989) and other work; as well as Clark's "Noble Little Farmhouse," *Architecture* 78 (May 1989): 148–49. W. G. Clark now teaches at the University of Virginia.

# IDEA, TOOL, EVIDENCE
## *The Architectural Drawing as Instrument and as Artifact*

PART 1: Architectural Drawings and Design in the Virginia Colony

by WILLIAM M. S. RASMUSSEN

Only a handful of drawings survive from colonial Virginia, but these and the knowledge of lost examples provide some insight into the evolution of architectural design in the region. The evidence of these drawings is welcome, due to an almost equally poor survival rate of other documentation, much of which was lost with the burning of county records in the Tidewater region in the Civil War. In many more cases than not, from the simplest structures to famous mansions like Westover (Charles City County, late 1730s or 1750s), we are by no means certain as to how a design evolved, for the contributions of many different types of people—craftsmen, builders, and amateurs—seem to have been ever-varying and unpredictable. We can, at least, outline the range of their involvement.[1]

### The First Architects in the Colony

The drawings and their references suggest progressive phases of approach to design by a body of contributors that itself changed with the maturation and growth of the colony. Inevitably there were exceptions, but in the seventeenth century, building specifications, if recorded at all, seem to have been defined primarily in writing. If any drawing was appended, it was apparently the simplest of floor plans. This concise process, which left design largely in the hands of talented craftsmen, persisted throughout the colonial period: certainly the majority of Virginia buildings must have been made in this manner. A second, critical phase overlaps the first: at the time some Virginians began to see themselves as merely displaced Londoners and pursued appropriate trappings, we find an increased use of drawings, including elevations, now lost and known only through their being cited in references. We have no information about their characteristics. The most significant examples were those prepared for the turn-of-the-century public buildings of Williamsburg. Also introduced in this period

*Colonial architect-craftsman* **William Buckland** *(see figure 4.11).*

were a few plans and elevations from architectural books. Other early drawings are implied: the geometry of some surviving domestic buildings suggests that elevations, now lost, might have been used in their design. All of this evidence indicates that the architectural process in Virginia at the beginning of the eighteenth century was changing, as craftsmen were aided in design by contributions from new sources. A final phase began around 1750, when the increased availability of books caused their greater usage and contributed to the emergence of builders and craftsmen more accomplished in their ability to devise original designs and to offer to potential clients formal presentation drawings. From this last period also come the first surviving drawings by gentlemen amateurs.

The earliest Virginia drawing known to survive, a simple plan of 1719 for Swan Tavern in Yorktown ( SURVEY NO. 1 ), prepared by the carpenter-builder Richard King, has been preserved because it is drawn on the same sheet of paper as the legal contract that defines the commission. The document is a fairly late and probably elaborate example of a then century-old tradition in the colony of building from written specifications and with few or no drawings. In these early years, elevation drawings were easily avoided as unnecessary. Structural systems, preferences for building materials, and standard facade treatments too simple to warrant much delineation had been established in the colony in the seventeenth century and were transmitted among craftsmen probably by experience and from memory. If the carpenters and brickmasons did make any notations, these have not survived.

There is ample evidence that so practical a procedure of building persisted for much Virginia architecture throughout the colonial period. Vestries routinely announced the desired dimensions of proposed churches and invited proposals that they might accept, reject, or modify. Sometimes in the seventeenth century and certainly throughout the eighteenth, they may have received simple floor plans with the bids presented, but generally they saw little more until their church actually took form. In the same way, prisons were commissioned as buildings of specified sizes. Virginia courthouse designers, even after the Revolution, put dimensions into writing and drafted a simple plan, but tended to offer no elevation.[2]

The builders who contracted to undertake these public structures—which were numerous in colonial Virginia—were themselves many in number and different in type. Most ran small operations in their own parishes and were the craftsmen who performed the actual labor, aided by their helpers. Others were simply businessmen. Major Harry Gaines (died 1767) of King William County, for instance, following the example of his father, built churches and other buildings with the help of skilled craftsmen from his labor-force of some 200 slaves. Regardless of the type of builder, however, many throughout the colonial period and well beyond seem to have avoided elaborate drawings as unnecessary and unfamiliar.[3]

Without the use of elevation drawings, the appearance of a building was left almost entirely to the talents of craftsmen who followed the traditions of their time and place. The system undoubtedly produced results of varying quality.

FIGURE 4.1. *According to a vestry book for the year 1700, the design of* **St. Peter's Parish Church,** *New Kent County (1701–03), was the work of a carpenter, Will Hughes; the tower was built 1739–40. (Photograph courtesy of the Virginia State Library.)*

FIGURE 4.2. *One architectural drawing from colonial Virginia, found inscribed on the back of a piece of woodwork at Belle Farm in Gloucester County, dates to about 1775.* **Detail, Chimney-piece design, Belle Farm.** *Compare with survey no. 6. (Photograph courtesy of Colonial Williamsburg Foundation).*

However, it seems to have worked well enough for Richard King. His house type, already developed in Williamsburg, could be handsomely constructed in Yorktown as a tavern with only its essential elements defined on paper and its subtleties of design easily understood and remembered by a carpenter-builder. Proportions and detailing were generous, to the great satisfaction of the patron.[4]

The improved self-image of the local gentry underlies the second phase of design in the colony. Newly preoccupied with their architectural landscape, prominent Virginians began to change it. They initiated a greater use of drawings, including elevations. In Williamsburg they constructed impressive public buildings. Books on architecture made their way into the hands of some craftsmen, builders, and amateurs. Cultural sophistication developed in the colony, but due to the absence of critical information, the process of architecture in Virginia in the first half of the eighteenth century can only be loosely defined.

The new attention to architecture emerged in the later part of the seventeenth century. The fortunate survival of a vestry book of 1700 preserves a reference to "Sevrall Draffts" (now lost) for St. Peter's Parish Church (New Kent County; FIGURE 4.1) as the work of a carpenter. Will Hughes apparently drew more than a floor plan because his impressive, shaped-gable church presented elaborate and largely unfamiliar brickwork facades. His drafts may also have defined interior details. The additional drawings, however simple they may have been, informed the vestry and were a means to achieve a design of architectural distinction. The St. Peter's reference suggests that near-contemporary and earlier shaped-gable structures like St. Luke's Church (originally Newport Parish Church, Isle of Wight County, circa 1680) and Bacon's Castle (Surry County, circa 1665, FIGURE 1.5) probably also were the creations of brickmasons or carpenters responding to the call by an emerging aristocracy for fashionable English designs.[5]

Though none of the "Draughts" by Will Hughes survive, two late-eighteenth-century carpenter's sketches for Belle Farm (Gloucester County, circa 1775, demolished in the early twentieth century; FIGURE 4.2 and SURVEY NO. 6) have been preserved, only because they were drawn on the backs of boards installed in that house. Of the two, the chimney-piece design is particularly elaborate, though not an unusual feature for Virginia Georgian buildings of distinction after 1750. Like the lost St. Peter's drawings, the Belle Farm sketches prove that craftsmen could and did design complex detailing, which today would be the domain of the architect. That transfer of responsibility would not occur in colonial Virginia.[6]

### Public Buildings for the Colonial Capital

The question of who—or even what types of persons—produced the documented drawings for the large public buildings of Williamsburg is less easily answered. They were prepared because those buildings were important (even of interest to the Crown), and in contemporary England it was "usual . . . to have Designs or Draughts drawn" to alleviate any "need of Alteration."[7]

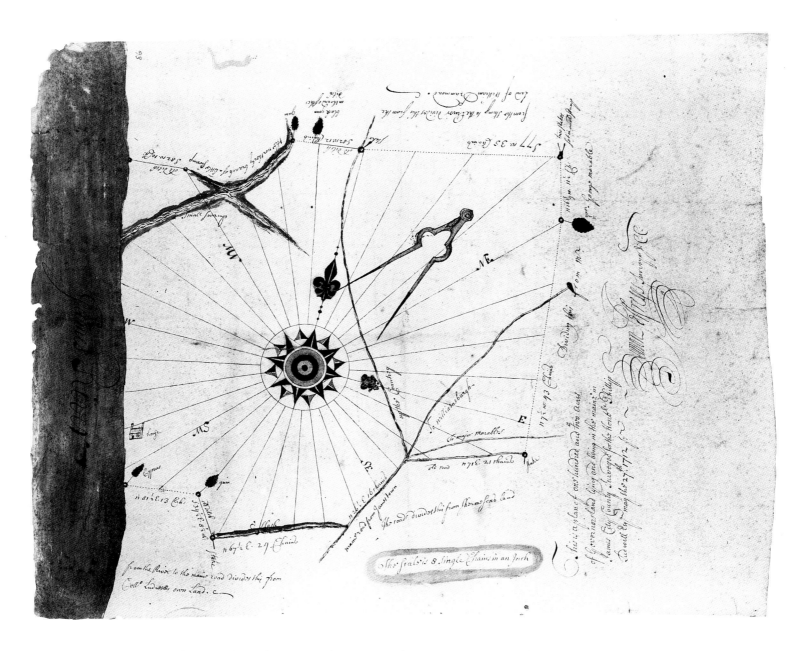

FIGURE 4.3. *Surveyors working in colonial Virginia may have produced architectural drafts.* **Land survey** *dated May 27, 1712, showing 102 acres of the Governor's Land tract in James City County, owned by Philip Ludwell, drawn by a "Simon Jeffreys." (Photograph courtesy of the Library of Congress, Washington, D.C.)*

No direct, strictly contemporary reference to drawings for the College of William and Mary (1695–1700) has been found. However, as a building of considerable size, it could scarcely have been constructed without the means of drawings, which are at least implied in a reference of 1694 to a garden design (and a gardener) sent to the College from Hampton Court. Drawings for the College could have been prepared in London in the office of the Surveyor General of Buildings for the Crown, Sir Christopher Wren, for the College was a project of the Queen. A generation later, in 1724, Hugh Jones wrote that the College was "modelled by" Wren. What Jones meant is by no means clear to us today: was the College drawn by Wren or in Wren's office, or was it only conceived in the style popularized by Wren? Jones adds without explanation that the design was "adapted to the nature of the country by the gentlemen there." The English surveyor Thomas Hadley, sent to supervise construction, could either have made drawings or brought drawings to Virginia. Whatever the case, the College must have been built with drawings, rendered by the hand of a type new to the colony (and one not to be seen again until the end of the century), a professional architect. No man native to the colony had the training to create it.[8]

The example of the College predictably influenced the building of the Capitol (1699–1705) with similar attention to planning and detail, though probably by local hands. Legislative records of May 1699 from Williamsburg mention a "Modell for the Statehouse" that was to be considered by the Governor's Council and the Burgesses and "a Plott or Draught of the building" that they viewed. Although expensive models made in England in this period survive, the term "model" usually meant a set of architectural drawings. In either case—and surely the latter—a significant development had occurred in Virginia: through the use of drawings a sizable building—albeit one with a number of provincial features (discussed in Chapter 1)—had been planned. Who produced the design we do not know. It may have come in whole or in part from the governor, Francis Nicholson, the probable architect of the Williamsburg town plan. Presumably after viewing the drawings, a committee of Burgesses was able to define the features of the structure in some detail, in an Act of the Assembly that survives. The building's construction was overseen by Henry Cary, Sr., a local planter of some prominence and probably the most accomplished of the new professional builders to emerge in response to the colony's increasing need for prominent public structures. But we can only speculate as to whether he might have been involved with the drawings or how Nicholson and the Burgesses may have contributed to the process, with or without the collaboration of English-trained craftsmen. We need also think of the surveyors then active in Virginia—unknown figures like "Simon Jeffreys," whose plat of 1712, of land owned by Phillip Ludwell near Jamestown ( FIGURE 4.3 ) reveals a surprising ability to provide an elegant draft, including a directional compass-pattern vividly colored in yellow, red, and black ink. As discussed in Chapter 1, the Capitol design was refined in a second Act, in 1701, obvious proof that the initial design and drawings—whatever they looked like—left room for improvement.[9]

The need for a governor's residence brought forth the same type of local planning, either by Burgesses, by craftsmen, or by Cary, who constructed the building. Again, we simply do not know. Earlier, in 1684, in response to royal instructions, the Virginia Burgesses ordered a model (drawings) of a proposed house for the governor. Presumably they sent the design to England for review. But neither the Crown nor the Burgesses would pay the cost of construction. In 1691, 1698, and 1706, further efforts were made by the London Board of Trade, and finally by the local Assembly, to secure a "draught" for such a house. On the latter date, Governor Edward Nott declined to produce a drawing and returned the problem to the Burgesses, from whose ranks a volunteer, probably an amateur designer, may have stepped forward. Presumably that drawing defined the design of the building sufficiently for its basic features to be specified in an Act of 1706. These documentary references for the governor's residence, like those for the Capitol, underscore the absence in Virginia of professional architects, a void—not unexpected on a frontier—that a seemingly undecipherable mix of craftsmen, builders, and amateurs by necessity were moved to fill.[10]

Another professional builder (or contractor) like Henry Cary, and one more closely tied by a documentary reference to drawings and design, is William Walker of Stafford County, who owned "many workmen," "many [building] Materials," and architectural books at his death in 1750. He had just won the commission that would have allowed him to rebuild the burned Williamsburg Capitol. In 1747 he had finished Cleve (King George County) for Charles Carter; in 1739 he had worked in some unknown capacity for Thomas Lee at Stratford (Westmoreland County). In 1740, when a tower was added to the shaped-gable facade of St. Peter's Parish Church, it was built "According to a Plan Delivered into the Vestry by the Sd: Walker." The "Plan" could have been an elevation, but whatever its nature it brought into being a design of distinction. Because it was prepared by a builder, it tells us a little more: it proves some shifting of design responsibility from the craftsman, now starting to lose at least part of his dominance as the primary source for architectural ideas. The documentation on Walker suggests that he and other "builders" played a major role in public and domestic design at mid century.[11]

### The Gentleman-Amateur as Architect in the Colony

Interest in their own domestic architecture logically provided incentive for gentlemen planters to contribute to the design process. From the first half of the eighteenth century, however, little evidence survives to indicate they responded with any frequency as amateur draftsmen: neither references nor actual sketches are known that would prove the point. But the phenomenon of the amateur did occur throughout contemporary England and her colonies, if only in scattered instances. And Governor Alexander Spotswood certainly set an example when he redesigned the burned College of William and Mary shortly after his arrival in Williamsburg in 1710 and then devised "a platt or draught of a Church" for Bruton Parish in 1711.[12]

If gentry involvement in early Virginia design is implied in Spotswood's actions, other evidence suggests the same. Gentlemen in the colony often owned prints of European buildings and would have remembered others from their travels. In the years immediately after the founding of Williamsburg, they could further turn for ideas to a few volumes then available, works like the earlier *Architettura* by an Italian, Sebastiano Serlio (republished in London in 1611, FIGURE 4.4), or Colen Campbell's contemporary *Vitruvius Britannicus* (London, 1715 and later). Some, like William Byrd II of Westover, owned a number of these rare and expensive volumes, which were beyond the means of most craftsmen. If, as seems probable, books provided ideas for a few of the early mansion plans and elevations (like Sabine Hall [Richmond County, circa 1733–42] and Stratford Hall [Westmoreland County, begun circa 1738]; see FIGURES 1.25, 1.28), then the Virginia gentry—as patrons—did make a significant contribution to the design process.[13]

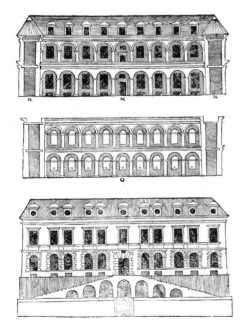

FIGURE 4.4. *Colonial landowners sometimes found ideas for their own homes in European books on architecture. The door on the building at the bottom of this drawing,* **"A Proposition for Building on a Hillside,"** *from Book VII, chapter 64, Sebastiano Serlio's* Architettura *(Venezia: 1547), is the probable source for the doorway built at Sabine Hall (compare figure 1.25).*

FIGURE 4.5. *Since no published sources can be found for elaborate woodwork such as this, the patterns and forms were probably brought to Virginia in the memory and experience of skilled English craftsmen.* **Detail of staircase at Rosewell,** *Gloucester County, 1721–41; destroyed by fire in 1916; see figure 1.23. (Photograph courtesy of the Virginia State Library and Archives.)*

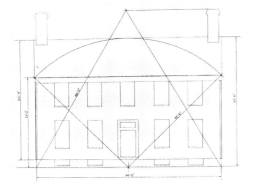

FIGURE 4.6. *Some colonial designers may have drawn line elevations based on simple geometrical relationships.* Modern elevation, **Archibald Blair House,** *Williamsburg, after 1716. Diagram showing system of proportion; reproduced with permission from Marcus Whiffen,* The Eighteenth-Century Houses of Williamsburg. *(Williamsburg: Colonial Williamsburg Foundation, 1960), 58, figure 15.)*

The early involvement of amateurs in Virginia architecture should not be overemphasized, however, for too little documentation survives to allow an accurate measure. To appreciate the vital role that was unquestionably retained by brickmasons and carpenters, we need only compare superbly crafted buildings like Sabine Hall ( FIGURE 1.25A ) or Stratford Hall ( FIGURE 1.28A ) to the simplistic plates in Serlio that may have provided raw ideas but little more for their gentlemen owners. Or we can turn to houses like Rosewell (Gloucester County, 1721–41; FIGURES 4.5, 1.23 ) or Tuckahoe (Goochland County, circa 1720s–30s; FIGURES 1.35, 1.35A ) to find lavish detailing that apparently has no source in architectural books and so must have been carried to the colony in the minds and notebooks of highly skilled English craftsmen. What the gentlemen did contribute to the process of architecture was the impetus to create designs of distinction, structures equal to or even better than the grand public buildings of the capital.[14]

## Tools of the Trade: Applied Geometry and Pattern-Books

As early as the first half of the eighteenth century a number of Virginia designers looked to geometry as a means to proportion the plans and facades of their Georgian structures. Drawings were apparently used in that process. The relevance of geometry had been demonstrated by the London mathematician-architect Sir Christopher Wren; in the available architectural books mathematics was discussed—sometimes at length—as fundamental to the discipline. Granted, many colonial buildings were constructed with no attention to geometry and for those that were, much proportioning could be accomplished without drawings. A small building, for example, could (and often did) have both its plan (sometimes a regular shape like a square-and-a-half) and its wall and roof heights (sometimes equal) defined in writing, with other decisions—any or all rooted in mathematics—left to the discretion of a craftsman. Larger buildings brought equally critical decisions—still answerable by geometry—about the placement of eaves, roof ridge, and chimney tops; the process, however, became more complex. For that reason, line elevations were brought into play—with undetermined frequency—by colonial designers. The practice seems to have enjoyed at least a degree of popularity, to judge from the evidence of some surviving mansion facades: when their elevations are reconstructed on paper, geometric shapes considered ideal to Georgian tastes—the square, square-and-a-half, double square, and equilateral triangle—can be tightly aligned over their facades ( FIGURE 4.6 ).

A late drawing in the Skipwith family papers (circa 1770; SURVEY NO. 2 and FIGURE 4.7 ) is important as rare evidence that Colonial designers—probably even an amateur in this case—did in fact sit down with paper and drafting tools and utilized ideas of geometry to develop architectural designs. Proportions of 1:1, 1:2, and 1:3 can be found throughout the drawing, though the arrangement is contrived and less than graceful (see SURVEY NO. 2 ). The proportioning might seem more the product of instinct than mathematics were it not for the evidence on this page of scored horizontal and vertical lines, pricking, and the scored arcs of a divider—physical traces of the design's geometrical development. The scored and pricked straight lines clearly facilitated the drafting of the elevation—the laying-in of the windows, roofs, and chimneys. Though the scored arcs defy explanation, they at least record the use of a divider. These barely visible marks—undeniably present—establish a factual basis for theories about the utilization of geometry in the design of Virginia architecture.[15] (For more on pricking and scoring, see pp. 150–52).

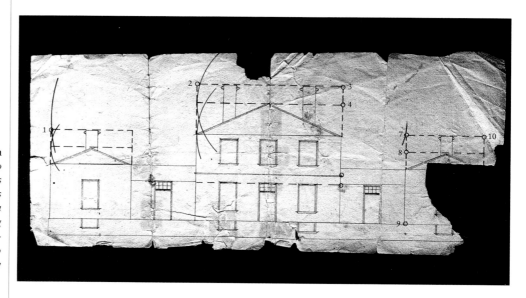

FIGURE 4.7. **Elevation of a Five-Part Palladian House** *(circa 1760; survey no. 2), with overlays to show the use of scoring and pricking. Pricking-holes that are evidence of the use of divider or compass appear at places numbered on the overlay. Broken lines are also superimposed to show where scoring lines, barely visible, appear on the original. Unexplained arcs that are scored on the original are also overlayed here. (Drawing from the Skipwith Family Papers, Virginia Historical Society, Richmond.)*

Of the several dozen English architectural books that were one product of that nation's Palladian Revival of the early eighteenth century, many had made their way by mid century to the American colonies. These gave professionals and amateurs much easier access than before to countless facade designs, plans, and examples of Classical detailing creatively adapted to uses in contemporary interiors and exteriors. So lucid and handsomely engraved are the plates that their designs were implemented in the colonies with enough frequency and skill to instill in the more costly American buildings a new aura of more sophisticated—though still provincial—formality. Instances in Virginia of direct reference to plates in pattern-books are well known. Plate 58 in James Gibbs's *A Book of Architecture* (London, 1728; FIGURE 1.40)—one of the more popular of the architectural volumes in both rural England and her colonies because of its easily adaptable designs—has long been recognized as the direct source used at Mount Airy (Richmond County, circa 1754–64; FIGURE 1.39). Owner John Tayloe did little more than eliminate two bays on the long facade and remodel the form of the quadrants and wings. Brandon (Prince George County, circa 1765; SURVEY NO. 2) is nearly as close to Plate 3 in a comparable pattern-book, Robert Morris's *Select Architecture* (London, 1755), unquestionably its source for both plan and elevation. More loosely derived from Gibbs, who offers several plates of its type, is Blandfield (Essex County, circa 1769–74; FIGURE 1.41).[16]

FIGURE 4.8 A. *The* **Small Dining Room** chimney piece, *Mount Vernon, also bears close resemblance to the Swan pattern-book. See figure 4.9 A.*

FIGURE 4.8 B. *For his* **Front (West) Parlor** chimney piece, *at Mount Vernon, George Washington must certainly have looked at English pattern-books. Compare with figure 4.9 B.*

On a smaller scale, the copying of Classical detailing from pattern-books was even more widespread because it was an easier undertaking. Mount Vernon (Fairfax County, enlarged after 1754; SURVEY NO. 5 ), whose owner, George Washington, is known to have taken a personal involvement in the intricacies of building, is a repository of examples of source-book adaptations. The chimney-piece designs of the small dining room and the front parlor ( FIGURE 4.8 A, B ), seem to be adaptations of plates 50 and 51 in Abraham Swan's *British Architect* (London, 1745; FIGURE 4.9 A, B ), while

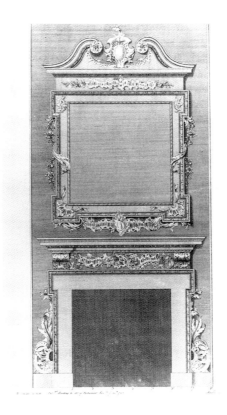

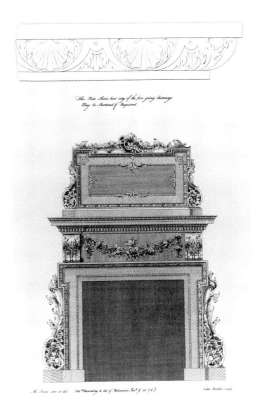

FIGURE 4.9 A,B. **Plates 50 and 51** *from Abraham Swan's* The British Architect *(London: 1745).*

the Palladian window of the banquet hall follows a design in Batty Langley's *Treasury of Designs* (London, 1740, plate 51), probably the same source for the Tuscan piers of Washington's two-story piazza. Examples from church architecture are just as well known. To cite but one, the altarpiece at nearby Falls Church (Fairfax County, 1767–70), specifically requested by an informed vestry to be in the Ionic order, derives from plate 110 in Langley's *Treasury of Designs*.[17]

### Colonial Architects Come of Age: Presentation Drawings by the New Professionals

The most immediate effect of the increased use of pattern-books was a greater formality in Virginia architecture, a change that is apparent to any viewer of the buildings just cited. Other results were just as significant. The books contributed to a new architectural awareness, evident from the knowledgeable involvement of the Falls Church vestry. They could inspire creativity, as seen in the 1770s at Kenmore, in Fredericksburg. Several of the ceilings there may derive their overall pattern from plates in Langley's *Treasury of Designs*, but within that framework is an explosion of original design and detail in the new style of Adamesque Neoclassicism. Pattern-books may also have encouraged gentlemen to draw: at least the few amateur efforts that survive date from after mid-century. One, the Skipwith drawing mentioned earlier (SURVEY NO. 2), a small sketch with a list of vegetables on the back of the paper, is of unknown origin but seems the work of an amateur, perhaps a member of the Skipwith family. And of course Thomas Jefferson's early study of Monticello (SURVEY NO. 8; early 1770s) dates from the end of the colonial period. Finally, the competition of the published plates inspired in the colony a local production of presentation drawings—finished elevations and plans prepared by a new generation of builder-designers and craftsmen-designers. To judge from the drawings that survive, these men eagerly contributed original ideas. Functioning as architects but probably never many in number, they helped to fill a void in the late colonial period.[18]

Their drawings are known from references, reproductions, and surviving examples. Builder James Wren of Northern Virginia followed in the tradition of earlier builders like Henry Cary of Williamsburg (and his son, Henry Cary, Jr.). But while we have no proof that either Cary prepared elevation drawings, we know of at least one by Wren. The builder of Falls Church, James Wren produced for that commission a "plan" (floor plan), now lost, that the parish also used at Christ Church, Alexandria (1767–73). Because Pohick Church (also Fairfax County, 1769–73) is essentially the same design, Wren very likely produced the presentation drawing for it (FIGURE 4.10), which survived at least until 1871, when it was published by Benson J. Lossing in *The Home of Washington*. Lossing redrew the original, "before me while I write," because he thought it the work of George Washington. Its style, detail, and combination of elevation and plan follow the published examples. But at the same time it is a unique Virginia church design, unlike all published English examples, a meld—

FIGURE 4.10. **Plan and Elevation of Pohick Church**, *Fairfax County, 1769–73, probably by James Wren, who provided the "plan" for Falls Church, a nearly identical building also in Fairfax County. Copy of a now-lost original drawing as published in Benson J. Lossing's* The Home of Washington *(Hartford: A. S. Hale and Company, 1871), 88. (Photograph courtesy of the Virginia Historical Society.)*

FIGURE 4.11. **William Buckland** *(1734–1774) was a highly talented London-trained joiner who created impressive woodwork for many homes in Virginia and Maryland. Portrait by Charles Willson Peale, 1773–1787. Oil on canvas, 36 ⅝ by 27 ½ inches. (Photograph courtesy of the Yale University Art Gallery, Mabel Brady Garvan Collection, acc. no. 1934.303.)*

as discussed in Chapter 1—of local architectural traditions with influences from neighboring colonies to the north.[19]

The best of the early presentation drawings to survive is that of Menokin (Richmond County, circa 1765–70; SURVEY NO. 3), the work of an accomplished hand better at drafting than at design—but expert at neither. The plan is darkly inked and a watery wash has been heavily applied to the elevations of three structures. Though the handling is uneven and awkward, a painterly, sensuous quality was developed from subtle gradations of white, grey, and black. Impressive for its time and place, this drawing successfully marketed a design that is not its equal; as constructed with ill-conceived proportions that are evident in the drawing, the building fell sadly short of nearby Mount Airy, its inspiration.

Menokin may well have been designed within the circle of (or even by) William Buckland (1734–1774; FIGURE 4.11). This highly talented joiner finished the interiors of Mount Airy and was the best Virginia example of the late colonial phenomenon of the craftsman-designer who could function as an architect. Buckland left London in 1755 as a young man indentured to George Mason, whose provincial Gunston Hall (Fairfax County, circa 1753–59; FIGURES 2.8, 2.9) he transformed with fashionable woodwork of exemplary design and craftsmanship. He gathered carvers and carpenters to form a team that was active in Virginia's Northern Neck throughout the 1760s, when Buckland produced at least a few drawings of building designs. In 1772 he relocated in Annapolis, where the next year he designed the Hammond-Harwood House, the commission on which he is shown working in his portrait by Charles Willson Peale. Buckland by then owned a dozen architectural books, but—as Peale was careful to record—he produced original designs. Though the tools to prepare finished drawings are present, Buckland is depicted in a moment of creativity, with a preliminary sketch before him.[20]

An earlier record of the development of an architectural idea is preserved on the back of an interior window frieze at Gunston Hall. Ten small and impromptu pencil sketches (FIGURE 4.12) have been convincingly attributed to Buckland, aided perhaps by George Mason, who knew Virginia legal rituals firsthand. In these the local architectural tradition is remembered in two prominent features—an apsidal end for the justices' bench and arcades for sheltered entrance. The polygonal forms so prominent in the sketches were current English fashion, well known to Buckland and favored by him throughout his career. Those, however, and the complex roof line sheltering second-floor jury rooms, were forms perhaps too avant-garde and extravagant for local interest; at least they are not known to have been implemented for a Virginia courthouse. But Buckland's novel idea for front and side arcades and corner jury rooms (FIGURE 4.13) apparently made its way to nearby Prince William County where, in 1759, a contract for a new courthouse was awarded. To judge from the excavated floor plan of the courthouse, which was abandoned in the nineteenth century, it was Buckland's contribution that allowed improved circulation through multiple entrances, at the front and at both sides.[21]

FIGURE 4.12. *The hand of William Buckland probably drew* **Sketches for a courthouse** *found on the back of an interior window frieze in the "Palladian Room" at Gunston Hall, circa 1759. (Copied by Hans Lorenz, Colonial Williamsburg Foundation; courtesy of Carl L. Lounsbury.)*

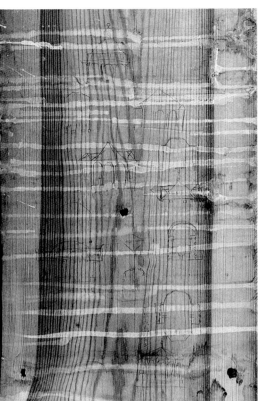

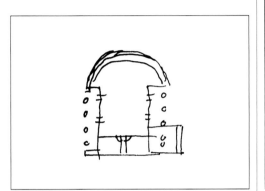

FIGURE 4.13. *Buckland's idea of front and side arcades provided the convenience of multiple entrances to a courthouse.* **Sketches for a courthouse,** *circa 1759, Gunston Hall. (Copied by Douglas R. Taylor, Colonial Williamsburg Foundation; courtesy of Carl R. Lounsbury.)*

Though by no means impressive, and not even intended to be seen after their entombment within a wall at Gunston Hall, the Buckland sketches demonstrate how a gifted joiner, who improvised with the forms he carved, apparently carried that same creativity into the larger realm of building design. He was well enough versed in the vocabulary and principles of the Georgian style that he had no need to copy blindly the published designs of others: he could devise his own. In that way Buckland, and a few others like him in the colony then—men like James Wren or John Ariss (who advertised his services through the newspaper)—moved Virginians closer to the modern era of the professional architect—the designer able to invent the new building forms needed by a growing nation.[22]

### The Past Lingers as the Present Strides Forth

Once the new republic was formed, old Georgian traditions were slow to be supplanted in Virginia. Nowhere is their survival more evident than in the collection of drawings (see SURVEY NO. 23), preserved among the Holladay Family Papers at the Virginia Historical Society. These drawings have been dated to around 1810, based on the various watermarks on the paper used for at least half of the group. Judging from the designs, John Crunden's *Convenient and Ornamental Architecture* (London, 1767) or a comparable later eighteenth-century pattern-book may have been an influence, as—probably—was James Gibbs's *Book of Architecture*, then more than eighty years after its publication date.

## PART 2: Architectural Drawings and Design, 1770–1870

by CHARLES E. BROWNELL

In Virginia architecture from just before the colonial War for Independence to just after the War between the States, no phenomenon stands out more prominently than the ascendance of the learned architect who exercised thorough control over a design by means of drawings. No matter what style(s) a given practitioner used, this unitary conception of architecture came out of the Classical tradition. The architects in question included Jefferson, the supreme American representative of the gentleman-amateur, in the tradition founded in Europe by Leon Battista Alberti (1404–1472), and they included other kinds of designers. But it is the professional architect who dominates this group.[23]

### An Example: Latrobe's Richmond Theatre Drawings

One set of drawings, the design for the Richmond Theatre by the first American giant of the profession, B. Henry Latrobe, will give us the basis for a series of useful generalizations. In the first part of this essay, we shall look at these drawings in respect to stage of realization, graphic form, and then technique. We shall see that the professional had at his fingertips an intricate, orderly, and refined graphic means of turning thoughts into buildings. In the second part of this essay, we can then fill in certain blanks between the 1770s and the 1870s. We shall see North Americans feeling their way toward improved graphic means in the late eighteenth and early nineteenth centuries, see Latrobe briefly expose Virginia to the standards of European professionalism just at the turn of the century, and see these standards from abroad thrive—not in Virginia, but in cities to the north. Virginia patronage of professional architects in those cities, taken with the work of Jefferson and Latrobe, makes the study of Virginia-related architectural drawings a rewarding way of studying the national development of architectural drawing during the nation's first century. One must recognize, though, that one has a long way to go yet before being able to reconstruct how, during the period in question, the architects and their delineators, or drafters, made their drawings. Because of this and because of other large gaps in our knowledge, the present essay offers no more than a first statement of its story.[24]

As to the stages of a design's realization, drawings by professionals during this period differ from earlier drawings so much that they require another set of terms. Those terms, in the approximate order of use of the drawings, include the preliminary sketch, the study, the presentation drawing, the working drawing, the contract drawing, the office record, and the topographical architectural drawing. These categories often overlap.

A design might well commence with the architect thinking out loud on paper in the form of a preliminary sketch—that is, a loosely handled drawing. According to John H. B. Latrobe, the architect's son, who had worked in his father's office during the 1810s, his father started with pen-and-ink sketches and carried a design very far "before the drawing board and Box of Instruments were resorted to." (No unquestionable preliminary sketch from the senior Latrobe's American career survives.)[25]

In the next step, Latrobe probably made ruled ink studies to sort out the design. Once he had brought the design to a state that he considered presentable, he made presentation drawings, such as the drawings he did for the Richmond Theatre ( SURVEY NOS. 18, 19 ). That is, he made formal, finely worked drawings, typically for display to the prospective clients. His presentation drawings usually do not show a fully buildable design, because the labor of working out the necessary details would not make sense until a patron contracted to pay the architect for such effort. In fact, Latrobe continued experimenting with the possibilities as he made such drawings, so that one can see his presentation drawings as a fancy form of study.

FIGURE 4.14. *The topographical architectural drawing, a record in perspective of an executed building:* **View of the old Richmond Theatre** *by B. Henry Latrobe from* "Designs of a Building . . . to contain a Theatre," *a volume of drawings prepared in 1797–98. (Photograph courtesy of the Library of Congress, Prints and Photographs Division.)*

If the support had arisen to build the Richmond Theatre, Latrobe would then have resolved all the discrepancies in the design and would have regulated construction with numerous working drawings on a larger scale using coarser paper. A set of such definitive drawings might become legally binding as contract drawings. For a design that went into execution, Latrobe needed graphic office records. He probably had a miscellany of these, such as annotated studies and duplicate presentation or working drawings, depending on whether he worked by himself (he worked alone in Virginia) or had pupils or other delineators in his office. Upon completion of the building, he might have made a perspective record, a topographical architectural drawing, of the building. He rarely recorded his buildings this way, though he drew the buildings of others a little more frequently (see drawing of the Old Richmond Theatre, FIGURE 4.14, and watercolor sketch of Mount Vernon, FIGURE 4.31 ) for a variety of reasons, sometimes because of the historic significance of a structure. Within our period, Latrobe and other architects did make geometric drawings of historic Virginia edifices, but they did so primarily in connection with proposed alterations.

FIGURE 4.15. *The preliminary sketch, a form of thinking out loud on paper:* "**Original Study for Va. Milty Institute—1848**," *Lexington, Virginia, by Alexander J. Davis, 1848. (Compare survey no. 39; photograph courtesy of Avery Architectural and Fine Arts Library, Columbia University in the City of New York, Davis Collection 1, F1–52.)*

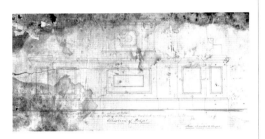

FIGURE 4.16 *The working drawing, a means of controlling the execution of a design:* **Elevation of the pulpit, Warrenton Baptist Church,** *Warrenton, Virginia, by Samuel Sloan, circa 1857. (Photograph courtesy of the Virginia Historical Society, Museum Collections, John R. Spilman Collection.)*

FIGURE 4.17. *The topographical architectural drawing:* **View of the Custis-Lee Mansion, Arlington, Virginia** *by Alexander J. Davis, 1831. (Photograph courtesy of Avery Architectural and Fine Arts Library, Columbia University in the City of New York, Davis Collection 1, V–3.)*

FIGURE 4.18. *The plan or floor plan, a "road map" of a building:* **Plan of the ground story, Richmond Theatre,** *by B. Henry Latrobe from "Designs of a Building . . . to contain a Theatre," 1797–98. (Photograph courtesy of the Library of Congress, Prints and Photographs Division.)*

Professionals differed in their graphic practices. The types of drawings are not hard and fast, and can obviously overlap. But now we have outlined how a professional might proceed. In this book are examples of almost all such types of drawings: the sketch ( FIGURE 4.15 ); the study ( SURVEY NOS. 7, 21, 33 ); the presentation drawing, which dominates this volume; the working drawing ( FIGURE 4.16 ); the office record ( SURVEY NOS. 24, 25, 39, 51 ); and the topographical architectural drawing ( FIGURE 4.17 ). Only the contract drawing, related to the Swan Tavern plan ( SURVEY NO. 1 ), does not appear.[26]

## Forms and Functions of Architectural Drawing

If we reshuffle the cards, we can examine the same set of drawings according to their graphic form—that is, the preliminary sketch, the orthogonal projection (or geometric drawing), and the perspective. In the sketch, the architect caught an idea on the wing, using whatever conventions suited him. To develop that idea, he picked up his straight-edge and moved on to the geometric (or measured) drawing, whether a study, presentation drawing, or working drawing. The measured drawings closely resemble exercises in geometry. They are drawn to a scale—the scale for the theater drawings remains a puzzle, as do the scales for quite a few early American drawings—and they permit the architect to measure every part of his design. They consist of the following:

*The Plan* ( FIGURE 4.18 ). A plan works much like a road map, and one should imagine oneself traveling through a plan along a thoughtfully chosen route, typically one that begins at the front entry. The set of theater drawings

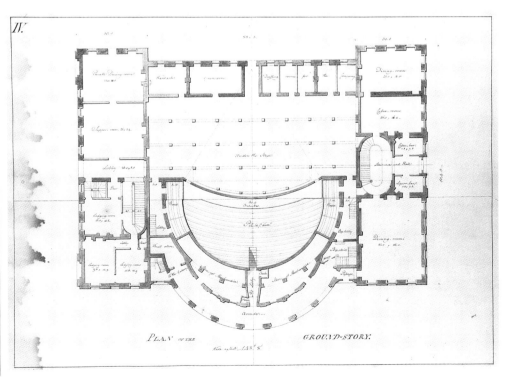

happens to include a Latrobe map of Richmond ( FIGURE 4.24 ), and the map naturally differs in no significant respect from the theater plans. Many maps, however, do not show elements as impenetrable, whereas an architectural plan treats walls as solids through which one can pass only at the doors. The plan comes closer to capturing the essence of a design than any other of the customary manners of representation. But plans tend to speak most clearly only to architectural professionals, and so are sparingly illustrated here.

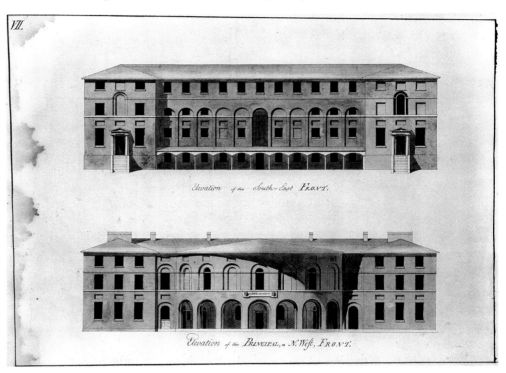

FIGURE 4.19. *The elevation, a diagram of an exterior wall of a building:* **Elevations of the front and rear facades, Richmond Theatre** *by B. Henry Latrobe from* "**Designs of a Building . . . to contain a Theatre,**" *1797–98. (Photograph courtesy of the Library of Congress, Prints and Photographs Division.)*

***The Elevation*** ( FIGURE 4.19 ). The elevation lays out a map of the building, not horizontally across a floor, but vertically up an exterior wall. It eliminates perspective effects (except for those of light and color, if the drafter chooses to pursue them, and except for elements in the foreground and background, where drafters often inconsistently introduced recession). Thus it permits the architect to measure expeditiously every element and relationship on a facade. By the same token, however, it may give a very false impression of how that facade will actually look.

***The Section*** (see Latrobe's drawing for the Richmond Theatre Auditorium, SURVEY NO. 18 ). A section shows the interior of a building in the same fashion as when one swings back the front wall of a doll's house. Unlike the view inside the doll's house, though, a section does not have effects of recession and diminution. The term "section" means "a cutting" (from the Latin *secare*, "to cut") and exists in the alternative form "sectional elevation." When an architect has envisioned a three-dimensional building on the basis of plans and elevations, the section literally permits him to cut into his conception. The process can expose all manner of conflicts. (It is a good question, though, how many of the discrepancies in Latrobe's badly-thought-out—actually unbuildable—theater this inexperienced, as-yet-immature architect was able to recognize from his sections.)[27]

*The Detail.* Such a drawing is a plan and/or elevation and/or section of part of a building. A detail drawing permits a designer to control the smallest molding in his conception. (John H. B. Latrobe rightly asserted of his father that "a moulding was rarely permitted to be used that was not first put by him upon paper.") We have no Latrobe details for his Richmond Theatre, with its Greek Doric porches, but the details of the Greek Doric order in FIGURE 2.27 make a serviceable stand-in.[28]

*The Perspective.* The new professionals probably had the most striking graphic ability in making drawings—full-color drawings—based on linear perspective. The plan, the elevation, the section, and the detail are technical diagrams. The perspective is a "picture"; it stands just inside the border that separates architectural drawing from landscape or topographical drawing. One can in fact distinguish between the topographical architectural drawing, recording a building after construction, and an architectural perspective, made before the construction of the building and requiring greater powers.[29]

Latrobe's theater drawings include two special kinds of architectural perspective, a before-and-after pair and an interior view. More precisely, Latrobe made only the first sketch for the "before" (or topographical) half of the pair, perhaps from memory ( FIGURE 4.14 ), but did a finished drawing for the interior perspective (Richmond Theatre Ballroom, SURVEY NO. 19 ). Some architects may have used perspectives to gauge the effect of a design in execution, but one suspects that the major figures have not needed this device to envision their results. The real, intended audience for the perspective was the lay viewer. As technical diagrams, geometric drawings require some effort for a nonprofessional to understand them. The perspective drawing, as a more pictorial image, allows a potential patron to form an idea of the executed effect much more readily than would a geometric drawing. The perspective can also seductively help an architect to sell a design.[30]

For a perspective by no means transcribes a faithful report on the visible world; instead, it interprets. Perspectives abound in conventions, graphic symbols that merely approximate the way our world looks. Most of us have two eyes, set at somewhat different angles, in a body that never stands stock-still, and we can swiftly collect far more data about a building than any perspective drawing—with its single, fixed viewpoint and restricted field—can begin to show. In such a drawing, the parallel horizontal lines converge toward one or several vanishing points; the parallel vertical lines, which should also converge, do not. Horizontals and verticals are drawn as having straight edges, not the subtle curves that our sight actually registers. An ever-invisible sun shines, customarily from the upper left-hand corner, at an obliging 45-degree angle that greatly simplifies the rendering of shadows. Compositional effect and convenience have often dictated the presence or absence of certain shadows. (So, for instance, the darkened foreground in the drawings for Clifton, Second Baptist Church, and Richmond Female Institute [ SURVEY NOS. 20, 35, 45 ] represents a compositional preference based on the way this dark area effectively sets off the main area of interest.) Notoriously, the exterior of a building may have a flair in a perspective drawing that it would not possess in execution. Interiors can suffer every bit as much. In his drawing for the Richmond Theatre Ballroom, for example ( SURVEY NO. 19 ), Latrobe carried the foreground beyond the planned limits of the ballroom, and this rendered the room more spacious than it would have been in reality. In later years Latrobe himself, writing to Maximilian Godefroy, his friend and collaborator on the Baltimore Exchange (1816–20), jocosely used Godefroy's expression "the habitual flippancy of professional Charlatanism," by which Godefroy referred to perspective drawings.[31]

Significantly, Latrobe's theater drawings constitute a coherent set. With a designer who meant to control his building throughout, drawings naturally came in closely related groups. If Latrobe had made the entire set of drawings on one sheet, he very likely would have drawn the plan first, would have used it to lift up—literally, elevate—the main front, and he would have applied the same economy of effort to arrive at any other elevations or sections. Latrobe originally had the set bound, a convenient measure to display the sheets. In a volume just as on a page, the representations belonged in a calculated order. Latrobe probably favored the sequence of exterior perspective (the image most easily understood), plans (the most essential), elevations, sections, and then nonessential representations, but in the bound volume of drawings for the Richmond Theatre, as in his others, circumstances led him to vary the pattern.

## Techniques of Architectural Drawing

As with the setting out of drawing categories according to the stage of realization of the design, looking at architectural drawings according to graphic techniques is a useful exercise. Drawings from the 1770s to the 1870s exhibit the major variations.

In technique, the Latrobe theater drawings again provide an excellent measuring-rod for drawings made during the next seventy-odd years (and for those of the preceding seventy, as well). As a professional, Latrobe brought a set of techniques from London to the United States. Through various agencies, these practices flourished for the remainder of this period. We can look at the media in roughly the sequence that a drafter would have used them: pricking and scoring, pencil, pen and ink, and watercolor.

*Pricking.* One of the principal offerings of this essay is the discovery of how widely drafters employed this technique. Pricking meant puncturing the paper at a set of points that would guide the delineator in laying out a drawing. Drafters used pricking for two purposes: to transfer key points from a drawing onto a blank sheet placed under it; and to lay out a drawing from scratch. The delineator employed one or another sharp instrument, called by such names as pricker, protracting pin, and needle holder ( FIGURE 4.20 ).[32]

Much about the process remains unknown, but the reason for its popularity is quite evident: architects used pricking because it guided them while remaining

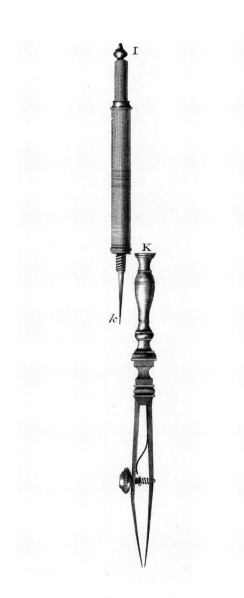

FIGURE 4.20. *The eighteenth- and nineteenth-century drafter typically laid out or duplicated a drawing by punching minute holes with a pricker or protracting pin at key points on the page.* **Pricker (I) with cap removed, and drawing pen into which it screws (K),** *from plate 1 of George Adams the Younger,* Geometrical and Graphical Essays, *1791 edition.*

virtually invisible, especially to lay eyes. In truth, the surfaces of drawings preserve a wealth of easily missed evidence as to how their architect made them and, more importantly, how he thought his way through his design. This evidence includes not only pricking but also scoring, pencil marks, and erasures. Drafters meant the viewer not to notice these elements, and historians of eighteenth- and nineteenth-American architecture have tended to oblige them.

Not all pricking challenges detection. Even in printed photographic reproductions one can see the coarse perforations that Major John Clarke made in order to work up his own drawing from Latrobe's penitentiary elevations ( SURVEY NO. 16 ). But drafters seem to have normally used an inconspicuous pricking technique, and one marvels at the eyesight that permitted a delineator to use pricking in its most refined form. Outstandingly deft performances include Robert Mills's Monticello elevation ( SURVEY NO. 12 ) and Thomas U. Walter's Mariner's Church project ( SURVEY NO. 36 ), drawings on which one can make out the tiny perforations only by taking great pains to do so.

Pricking has a long history in graphics. In architectural drawing, as well as in drawing and painting, it goes back at least to the Middle Ages. Work for this book and other recent research have brought to light dramatic evidence as to how standard the pricking technique became in North America. In essence, American drafters did not understand pen-and-ink or washes until the professionals came, but they were at home with pricking early on ( FIGURE 4.21 ). Such documents as Virginia platbooks and title books indicate that eighteenth-century Virginia surveyors made, at the minimum, widespread use of pricking. One suggests, as a working hypothesis, that the method was customary for American geometrical drawings in the eighteenth and nineteenth centuries, at least down to the Civil War. Pricking held on for some time after, as witness drawings from the offices of Alfred L. Rives (1867/8; SURVEY NO. 50 ), John R. Thomas (1876; SURVEY NO. 54 ), and George A. Frederick (1870s; SURVEY NO. 55 ).[33]

There are substantial exceptions to the process proposed here. Alexander Parris's sketchbook (see Wickham House, SURVEY NO. 24 ) has no pricking, but bound volumes are an iffy matter. So are perspectives which, as laborious and non-essential drawings, must have discouraged pricking for the end of duplication. A. J. Davis's drawings ( SURVEY NOS. 38–41 ) indicate that pricking may not have played an important part in his drafting.

In the present state of knowledge, one cannot discuss pricking with great certainty. Not the smallest problem is how seldom one can check properly for skillful pricking. Again and again, a page has revealed an abundance of tiny holes, but only after exacting inspection. Examining a sheet of paper against a light will often disclose the piercing, but if a drawing has been attached to a backing board, is framed under glass, or can only be examined in limited light conditions, the researcher is left fumbling. In any case, one can sometimes work as effectively by looking closely at the front of the drawing for indentations under a raking light of medium intensity. Alas, paper conservation itself can

FIGURE 4.21. *Detail, drawing of* **Menokin House** *(survey no. 3), circa 1765–70, showing holes made by pricking, visible along the right-hand side of the door (at the left edge of the mortar joints) and around the arch. The large hole within the archway (center) is not made by pricking but by the fixed leg of a compass.*

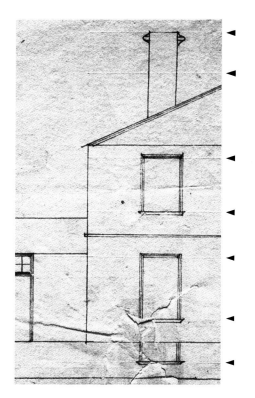

FIGURE 4.22. *Detail, drawing of* **Five-part Palladian House** *(survey no. 2), circa 1770, with arrows added to show the kind of guidelines called scoring. A drafter made scored lines by pressing into the surface of the paper with a sharp instrument.*

FIGURE 4.23. *B. Henry Latrobe's* "**Designs Of Buildings . . . in Virginia**," *a volume of drawings compiled circa 1799, contains an* **Elevation of a proposed church** *and a matching plan that have been misidentified as a proposal for replacing St. John's on Church Hill, Richmond. Marks on another Latrobe drawing establish the true identity of the unexecuted project (compare figure 4.24. Photograph courtesy of the Library of Congress, Prints and Photographs Division.)*

close up the holes. A drafter, as in the instance of George Frederick's Dulany project ( SURVEY NO. 55 ), did not have to pierce the paper in order to make useful guide points. And the holes made by a compass leg can create the false impression that a drawing has pricking. But the hole from a compass-point is normally larger than one made by pricking and, of course, always occurs at the center of a circular element.

*Scoring.* On close inspection, Latrobe drawings sometimes appear to have scored guidelines—that is, lines pressed into the drawing surface with a sharp instrument but without the application of pigment. On still closer inspection, those lines occasionally turn out to contain scarcely perceptible graphite particles from a very hard pencil. One must leave Latrobe's use of scoring an open question, but other Americans, such as Jefferson, did rely upon this barely visible technique for laying out elements of their design ( FIGURE 4.22 ). The process of scoring, in use since the days of ancient Rome, probably caught hold early on, like pricking, which it may accompany. So crude a diagram as the Swan Tavern plan ( SURVEY NO. 1 ) employs scoring to lay out the walls, almost certainly together with pricking. The combination occurs on a higher plane in Jefferson's drawings, such as the elevation and section of the University of Virginia Rotunda ( SURVEY NO. 27 ).[34]

*Pencil (Graphite).* A delineator typically laid in the outlines of a drawing in pencil, either by following pricked and/or scored notations, or by making the first marks on the page with graphite. Pencil had the irresistible advantages of gliding easily over a page and permitting ready erasure. On the minus side, it was vulnerable to smudging and rubbing away.

Important evidence about designs often passes undetected because it takes the form of light pencil underdrawing, light pencil overdrawing, imperfectly erased pencil lines or, for that matter, imperfectly erased ink lines. Latrobe's volume *Designs of Buildings Erected or Proposed To Be Built in Virginia* (Library of Congress) preserves the plan and the elevation of a church ( FIGURE 4.23 ) that earlier architectural historians, by educated guesswork, identified as a replacement for Henrico Parish Church, today's St. John's, on Church Hill (1739–41 and later). But in the Richmond plan among the theater drawings ( FIGURE 4.24 ), sketchy pencil overdrawing unmistakably locates the two-towered, apse-ended church in the middle of Broad Street at Twelfth (shaded detail, upper right of center), just south of the Richmond Theatre property (where, by a twist of fate, Robert Mills would later erect his Monumental Church [1812–17; see SURVEY NO. 21 ] to commemorate the victims of the disastrous 1811 Richmond Theatre Fire).

*Pen-and-Ink.* To give permanence to the lines laid down in pencil, the architectural delineator would use pen and ink. The choice of ink is one of the great marks of professionalism. The professional relied on so-called India ink (actually an ink from China), a richly black medium, impervious to water once it dries. At least well into the nineteenth century, less sophisticated delineators unfortunately often used ordinary writing inks, which in those days in nearly every case was iron-gall ink. A treacherous and highly unstable substance made

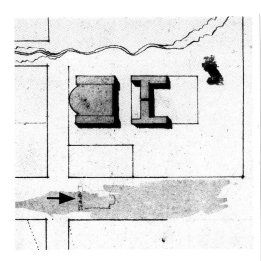

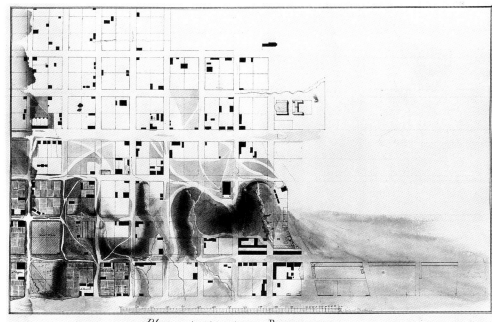

Plan *of part of the* CITY *of* RICHMOND, *shewing the Situation of the proposed* BUILDING.

FIGURE 4.24. "Plan of part of the City of Richmond . . . ," and Detail, *from Latrobe's* "Designs of a Building . . . to contain a Theatre," *1797–98. An added arrow points to the entrance front of Latrobe's lightly penciled plan of his church, which appears in the upper right center of the drawing, at Broad and Twelfth Streets. The architect meant the building to adorn the center of Richmond, far from St. John's. (Compare figure 4.23. Photograph courtesy of the Library of Congress, Prints and Photographs Division.)*

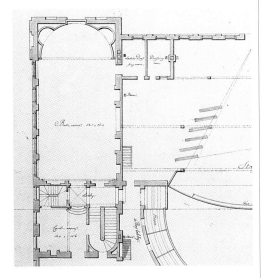

FIGURE 4.25. *Professionals have often lent their plans a three-dimensional quality by inking in the walls with thin* "face" *lines and thicker* "shadow" *lines.* Detail, Plan of the first floor of the Richmond Theatre *by B. Henry Latrobe from* "Designs of a Building . . . to contain a Theatre," *1797–98. (Photograph courtesy of the Library of Congress, Prints and Photographs Division.)*

according to various recipes (some of which include urine), iron-gall ink would eat into or even through the paper, would feather (that is, blur) if it came into contact with washes, and, over the years, would change from its original black or brownish-black to rust color. (Compare SURVEY NOS. 1, 7, 11. In the absence of a scientific analysis of the inks, the author cautiously used the label "writing ink" in listing media in the Survey of drawings, Chapter 6. But, in the text of some entries, when the evidence has warranted it, the ink is identified as iron-gall.)[35]

The professional could use the same line thickness throughout when inking a plan. Alternately, he might give the plan a modestly three-dimensional quality and hence more legibility by using so-called face lines and shadow lines, as Latrobe did for the first-floor plan of his theater (FIGURE 4.25). In this technique, the delineator would imagine a light source at a 45-degree angle from a corner of the drawing (often the upper left-hand corner). He then used a thin (face) line to define any surface details that faced toward the light and a thick (shadow) line for those on opposite surfaces, that is, those that faced away from the light.

*Watercolor.* With the outlines fixed in ink, Latrobe then filled in certain ones using a brush (called a "pencil" in the period) and with translucent watercolor. That is, he brushed on thin washes of water mixed with pigment suspended in a medium or binder, such as gum arabic. India ink laid on with a brush also qualifies in general terms as watercolor. As images made up of outlines filled in with the use of a brush, such works are referred to as tinted drawings or watercolor drawings, not watercolor paintings, which are made by an artist with touches of the brush. Using this medium amounts to applying translucent glazes over the reflective surface of a sheet of white or light-colored paper. After the washes dry, the layers remain translucent, trapping and diffusing light so as to achieve a subtle luminosity.[36]

Watercolor, of course, permitted the user to imitate natural appearances, especially in perspectives, elevations, and sections. It also permitted the drafter to code a drawing. As in the case of the Richmond Theatre floor plans ( FIG- URES 4.18, 4.25 ), Latrobe used a well-established European code for materials: yellow for wood, pink for brick, a cool or neutral color for stone, and black for iron. He coded plans with more arbitrary colors signifying period of construction, as in his main plan for the penitentiary (see SURVEY NO. 17 ). According to an inscription on the plan, he used a paler tint for the semicircular area to show that it should be built first, and a darker tone for the rectangular forecourts. He used other color differentiation as well: on the theater plans, the washes filling in the walls grow lighter as one moves up from story to story.

The initial hypothesis for this essay has held: from Latrobe to the Civil War, the professionally trained drafter typically gave a watercolor drawing its render- ing, or modeling, with a neutral tint before applying the local color over that. In other words, on the front elevation of the theater ( FIGURE 4.19 ), Latrobe first brushed on the shading (he used grey-blue washes), and then painted a rosy color for brickwork over that. Watercolorists thus built up compositions using gradations of color from light to dark, that is, as tonal compositions. The monochrome underpainting not only established the composition but also gave the overlying hues an understated quality. Squinting at a tonal composition filters the color out and reveals the broad, gray-to-white elements of the com- position. For convenience, the light normally falls from the upper left-hand corner at a 45-degree angle, as in the case of face and shadow lines.

To define a white or a light-colored area in a drawing, such as a highlighted wall or bright clouds, the watercolorist normally did not apply opaque white paint, but instead would use the reflective white surface of the paper itself, either leaving it untouched or brushing on a very thin wash. To do so demanded skill and enhanced the unique luminosity of the medium. The niche-heads, ceiling, main window, and looking-glasses in Latrobe's ballroom perspective ( SUR- VEY NO. 19 ) exemplify his ability to use the white of the paper and thin washes to capture the effects of light. His worthy successors include Thomas U. Walter (see drawing for Second Baptist Church, Richmond; SURVEY NO. 35 ) and Alexander J. Davis (drawing for Elk Hill; SURVEY NO. 40 ). For bright details an artist occasionally used a scraping technique: taking a knife blade or a device called a scraper to cut through the paint surface. (It may seem dangerously easy to damage a drawing in this way, but in practice it is done delicately and with little difficulty.) This technique enjoyed some popularity around the 1850s. It produced the highlights on the end of every bracket along the eaves of the anonymous Sweet Briar House elevation ( SURVEY NO. 44 ), the clouds in T. A. Tefft's perspective of the Richmond Female Institute ( SURVEY NO. 45 ), the reflected light on the windows of Norris Stark- weather's Camden perspective ( SURVEY NO. 46 ), and the fountain in the perspective of Morven Park ( SURVEY NO. 49 ).

The surfaces of translucent watercolor differ sharply from the more reflective, full-bodied, and often brightly colored surfaces of the medium called opaque watercolor, gouache, or body color. The latter enjoyed its strengths on the Continent, as at the hands of Jefferson's collaborator Charles-Louis Clérisseau. Among Virginia-related drawings before the Civil War, only touches of paint that appear to be gouache have come to light (see SURVEY NOS. 22, 28, 43).[37]

## The Architect's Model

Latrobe's presentation materials for the theater (like the rest of his projects) conspicuously lack a preliminary scale model. Like a perspective, the model approximates the effect of a design in execution, but a perspective drawing gets its results at a fraction of the cost of the notoriously expensive model. The French had a strong though certainly not absolute tradition of preferring the model—somewhat treacherous in its own way, because of the allure of miniatures—over the undeniably treacherous perspective. Hence in Paris Jefferson commissioned a plaster model for the Virginia State Capitol (SURVEY NO. 10). Hence Latrobe's Gallic friend Godefroy (SURVEY NO. 22), whose expression "the habitual flippancy of professional Charlatanism" played into the extinction of their relationship, had a model—probably of wood and some painted substance—made for his Battle Monument (Baltimore, 1815–25), although later, even he found himself making at least one architectural perspective, at the close of his American career. And hence, in the related area of instructional models of executed buildings, Jefferson's friend the Comte de Volney sent him a model of the Pyramid of Cheops. (One other Virginia-owned model of an executed building is known from our period, but of a different kind: from Paris, Washington had received a miniature of the Bastille made as a memento from one of the stones of the fallen prison.) The story of the instructional architectural model in Virginia in these years, of course, deals not with miniatures but with Jefferson's full-size exemplars.[38]

In addition to putting in an appearance in Latrobe's circle, the model caught on in at least one part of the United States in the early nineteenth century, winning partisans in New England. Virginia, however, turned a cold shoulder to model-making. One finds a few more stray references to one or another kind of architectural miniature. In a letter to Jefferson, for instance, Latrobe mentioned a model of a house that was burned to test the fireproofing of shingles for the State Capitol. But between the Fouquet model of the Capitol and the Civil War, no formal, full-fledged, preliminary scale model appears in the Virginia record except during the 1849–50 competition for the Virginia Washington Monument. At that time, John H. B. Latrobe saw "a collection of models" for the monument in the Virginia Capitol, though, except in the case of Thomas Crawford's "little plaster model" (compare FIGURE 2.38), the younger Latrobe's language leaves one guessing whether he meant model as miniature or as pattern.[39]

## Architectural Drawing and Virginia, 1770s to 1820s

Now that we have a good measuring-rod of forms and methods used in designing architecture during this period, let us look back to the 1770s and forward into the nineteenth century. We do well to begin with Jefferson. Contemplating what he saw as the unpromising prospects for good public buildings in Virginia, Jefferson wrote, significantly, that "it would not be easy to execute such an attempt, as a workman could scarcely be found here capable of drawing an order."[40] The full account of how Jefferson himself became capable of drawing remains to be written. One has much basic information. For instance, we know that Jefferson developed skill at pen-and-ink drawing from the late 1760s in the process of designing Monticello, and that in France as of 1785 he had added the use of the pencil and discovered the applicability of graph paper (see his elevation for the Virginia Capitol, SURVEY NO. 9). Assuredly, he had only the slenderest connection with the study of perspective. Whereas his promotion of the temple model and laminated wooden construction changed the architectural destiny of his nation, his drawing habits had little impact. But we still need to know how those habits grew to serve Jefferson's purposes, how he equipped himself with techniques such as scoring and pricking, and how he accumulated his repertory of conventions, which surely owed much to engraved plates in books. As yet we have only glimpses.

One of Jefferson's major options was the outline drawing in pen and ink, without pencil, with pricking, and sometimes with scoring. The manner, a basic one in the eighteenth century (see, for instance, the drawings for Skipwith, SURVEY NO. 2, and Mount Vernon, SURVEY NO. 5), would seem

FIGURE 4.26. (Below) *On Thomas Jefferson's* **Plan of the Rotunda,** *University of Virginia, Charlottesville, Virginia, circa 1817–21, the erased lines of an unworkable stage of the design remain recognizable. (Photograph courtesy of the Manuscripts Division, Special Collections Department, University of Virginia Library, Thomas Jefferson Papers.)*

FIGURE 4.27. (Right) **Rejected Plan of the Rotunda** *as reconstructed from Jefferson's erasures by Joseph Michael Lasala. For a time, before Jefferson decided on a smaller Order of paired columns, he was planning to use a ring of large columns spaced singly.*

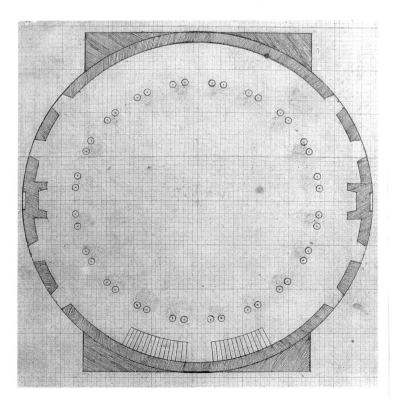

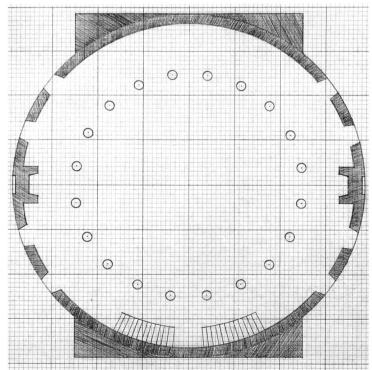

doomed to stiffness and scratchiness. Nonetheless, in certain Monticello drawings of the 1770s (see SURVEY NO. 8 and FIGURE 2.16), Jefferson brought this kind of drawing to a peak of purity and elegance, and these works remain beautiful even after the discoloration of the iron-gall ink and any soiling of the paper. Jefferson used this style to the end, despite learning about the fluidity of the pencil line, but he united the outline manner with graph paper. Unlike the choice Monticello I sheets, one would not call his Rotunda and Pavilion IX drawings (SURVEY NO. 27 and FIGURE 2.24) beautiful, but no doubt Jefferson did not intend them to be. An elderly man with a bad wrist that pained him when he wrote or drew, he made these as tools, tools that worked in creating one of the most demanding building complexes in the young country. The very limitations of these drawings have their benefits: since Jefferson reworked his ink drawings rather than start fresh when he changed a design, and since he could not erase ink lines completely, we can almost see his mind at work. Thus, on the Rotunda drawings one can make out the erased outlines of an unworkable phase of the design. The rejected scheme (FIGURES 4.26, 4.27) had different floor levels and a large Order of single columns (designated on the verso as Corinthian) rather than the smaller Order of paired Composite columns that went into execution.[41]

Sections, used to help visualize the interior spaces of a building that does not yet exist, had little to do with American design before the later eighteenth century. The three members of "J. Holland, and Company," a surveyor-builder firm newly arrived from London, advertised in the *Virginia Gazette* (6 August 1772) that they could draw "Plans, Elevations, and Sections" for erecting "any Building." In Jefferson's ambit, this kind of projection made more decisive early appearances. Jefferson himself explored the technique fairly early, as in the complex, inconsistently handled drawing for Monticello's South Outchamber (FIGURE 2.16). The drawings (lost two centuries ago) by Charles-Louis Clérisseau that Jefferson sent to Richmond in 1786 included sections for both Virginia's Capitol and its proposed prison. Probably as a result of Jefferson's exposure to French practice, the advertisement for the U. S. Capitol competition in the *Gazette of the United States* ([Philadelphia] 24 March 1792) called for "drawings . . . of the ground plats, elevations . . . , and sections through the building in such directions as may be necessary to explain the internal structure."[42]

Jefferson himself mastered the section (see his Rotunda at the University of Virginia; SURVEY NO. 27). He fared less well with another option, the monochrome wash drawing. In the eighteenth century, ink drawings with gray (or once-gray) washes enjoyed currency for ambitious designs all along the Atlantic seaboard, at the hands of such diverse figures as the unknown Menokin draftsman (SURVEY NO. 3), Charles Bulfinch, and John McComb, Jr. (see drawing for Cape Henry Lighthouse; SURVEY NO. 13). This usage represents a continuation of the European monochrome wash rendering. Unfortunately, many Americans, Jefferson included, not only could not render but also used writing ink that feathered into their uneven gray washes. Two hundred years later, the discolored brown ink, which may have begun to eat through the paper, and the smeary, dishwater-gray washes into which the ink has usually bled tend to lack in allure. Jefferson employed the manner only a few times, trying it out, with unlovely effect, for his early observation tower projects ( SURVEY NO. 7 ), and returning to it, with inconsistent results, in certain projects for Washington, D.C. (such as the Capitol, SURVEY NO. 11 ).[43]

The American-born delineators in Jefferson's circle exemplify the vigorous but uneven national development of architectural graphics as the eighteenth century gave way to the nineteenth. We need look only at three drawings that show their makers reaching. Samuel Dobie, the "adept in draughtmanship" who superintended the construction of the Virginia State Capitol, showed off in a set of three monochrome wash drawings (plan, elevation, section) for the colossal villa rotonda that he entered in the Capitol competition of 1792–93. The section ( FIGURE 4.28 ), portraying the interior down to the pegs of the roof framing, surely seemed a tour-de-force to Dobie and his contemporaries. But Dobie's

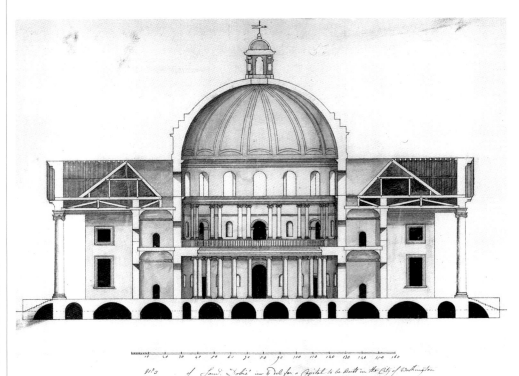

FIGURE 4.28. *This* architectural section, a 1792 competition project for the United States Capitol, *Washington, D.C., by Samuel Dobie, would have looked masterful to Americans. But such features as the use of writing ink and the extensive smearing of the rotunda, where the ink has run into the washes, hardly measure up to the European standards of the period. (Photograph courtesy of the Maryland Historical Society, Baltimore.)*

troubles give him away as a provincial: the feathering of the iron-gall ink into the washes, quite noticeable in the smeary rotunda; the paper's corrosion by the ink; the crumbling of the heavy washes around the roof trusses; and the inconsistent handling of the 45-degree-angle shadows.[44]

A jump of a decade takes us to the work of Robert Mills, who had studied with the Irish builder-architect James Hoban and who would become the premiere American-born professional architect. In 1803 Mills made another set of drawings (plans, elevation, and section) for a villa rotonda, Jefferson's "Building suited to a Public Officer." Surely Mills stretched himself in his drafting for the

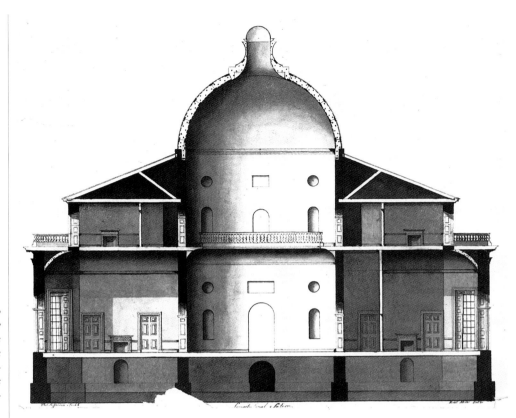

president, as in his section ( FIGURE 4.29 ), which he detailed minutely, down to dotting the nails for the Delorme ribs of the cove ceilings and the dome (compare FIGURE 2.20 ). The lighting still betrays uncertainty (in the dome and attics, for instance), but the medium is now the more stable India ink. In this adaptation of the monochrome wash style, Mills (with imperfect control of his washes) used yellow watercolor to signify wood where the section cuts through floors, partitions, and roofing. The companion elevation, like Mills's comparable, contemporary elevation of Monticello II ( SURVEY NO. 12 ), reaches a higher level, one of remarkable suavity.[45]

From two decades later comes an elevation (1823[?]; SURVEY NO. 28 ), one of numerous geometric drawings of the Lawn ascribable to John Neilson, a house carpenter with a passion for self-improvement and a keen interest in drawing. Neilson had very likely learned the rudiments of drafting in his native Ireland, but on some (other) occasions he used graph paper, à la Jefferson. Neilson (with some fumbling) built the elevation up from India ink lines and washes, but he moved toward full color and completed his drawing with a landscape setting inside a ruled border. (One must agree with recent scholarship in dismissing the quaint old misconception that Cornelia Jefferson Randolph made this and other geometric drawings at the knee of her grandfather, Thomas Jefferson. By that premise, Jefferson would have trained an amateur artist to make professional-looking architectural drawings based on a knowledge of ink, watercolor, and drafting conventions that he did not apply in his own drawings and no doubt did not himself possess.)

Traversing some three decades has rightly suggested certain historic patterns: the rise of architectural drawing per se, of orthogonal drawings in coherent sets, and of the uses of India ink, watercolor, and picture-like effects. As the examples intimate, one cannot separate the ascendancy of drawing from the rise of monumental Classicism in civic architecture, especially for the federal government. We get an inkling of a poorly studied subject, the impact of Ireland on architecture in this period. And all three examples bring us back to Latrobe, who preserved the federal competition drawings, whose tutelage transformed Mills in the years after 1803, and whose renderings in Jefferson's possession very likely excited the aspirations that Neilson's elevation discloses.[46]

FIGURE 4.30. **Title page vignette** *drawn by B. Henry Latrobe in 1799 for his volume* **"Designs Of Buildings . . . in Virginia."** *This architectural fantasy, showing the allegorical figure of Latrobe's imagination leaving Richmond for Philadelphia, can symbolize the fact that the young American architectural profession found its home not in Virginia but in the North. (Photograph courtesy of the Library of Congress, Prints and Photographs Division.)*

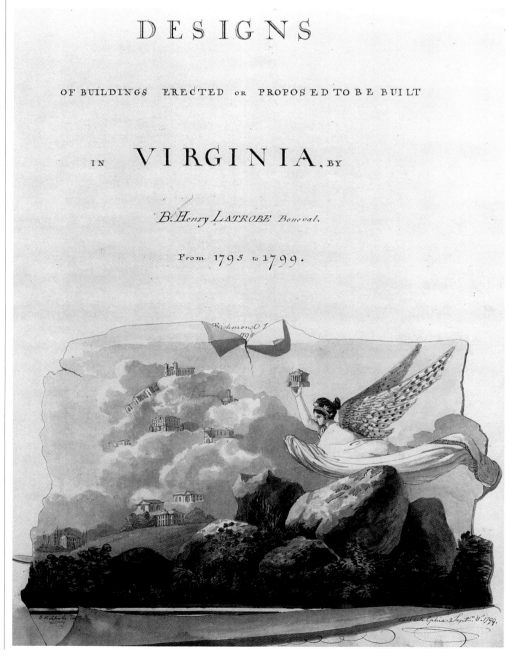

Latrobe was by no means the only drafter to bring professional standards from abroad just before the start of the nineteenth century. From the mid 1780s, figures as diverse as the French designer Etienne-Sulpice Hallet, the Irish builder James Hoban, and the English architect George Hadfield, a virtuoso at drawing, arrived with comparable skills. But Latrobe alone became a nationally eminent architect, with an important oeuvre of both buildings and drawings, and with prominent pupils to transmit his lessons.

In 1799, about nine months after moving from Richmond to Philadelphia, Latrobe prepared the title page for the volume of drawings "Designs of Buildings Erected or Proposed To Be Built in Virginia," with an allegorical vignette ( FIGURE 4.30 ). This watercolor drawing personifies Latrobe's imagination with a (no doubt fictitious) model of the Bank of Pennsylvania in her hand, taking flight for Philadelphia from the rocks of Richmond, while unrealized Virginia projects waft away as castles in the air. The Harvie-Gamble House (see SURVEY NO. 24 ) and Pennock House ( SURVEY NO. 15 ) alone rest solidly on the ground.

No single drawing better symbolizes Latrobe's role as a drafter. Enjoying his facility, he drew what are rarities in our period—in this case, an architectural fantasy; in other cases, records of buildings that he saw on his travels ( FIGURE 4.31 ). His fantasia depends on four fresh and intimately related British developments of the late eighteenth century: the intensification of the Picturesque movement, the flowering of landscape drawing and painting, advances in watercolor, and the acceptance of the architectural perspective, all of which had a lively future awaiting them in America.[47]

The drawing has special symbolic value in showing Latrobe departing from Virginia. Only after he left Virginia did he become a national figure and scale the heights of his creativity. Only after he left Virginia did he have access to the scanty American means for publishing drawings and exhibiting them institutionally. And only after he left Virginia did he take pupils, notably Robert Mills, William Strickland, William F. Small, and Frederick Graff, all of whom subsequently had designs of theirs executed in Virginia. One can probably even take his reestablishment in Philadelphia as the symbolic date for the emergence of the professional drafter. Strickland, for instance, worked in that capacity before his architectural career took off. Latrobe's move may have no significance in relation to the architect's ownership of his drawings and his charges for them, which remained vexing matters for the American Institute of Architects to address in the years after its foundation in 1857. But one can conclude that Latrobe became a force in American architectural drawing and, more broadly, American architectural professionalism only after he left Virginia. For the next seven decades, Virginia, briefly the home of a so-called father of the profession, played no part in the development of architectural drawing except to pay for some very good drawings by architects from outside.

Among the new professional graphic resources, easily the most beguiling one was the full-color perspective. One speculates, though, that of all these elements, India ink won the most endorsements the fastest. Still, writing ink

FIGURE 4.31. **View of Mount Vernon looking towards the southwest** *by B. Henry Latrobe, 1796. Latrobe, who widened American graphic horizons, indulged in such varied forms of expression as the topographical architectural drawing, represented by his* **View of Mount Vernon,** *and the architectural fantasy. (Compare figure 4.30. Photograph courtesy of the Maryland Historical Society, Baltimore.)*

FIGURE 4.32. *Nineteenth-century American and European engravings sometimes preserve the outlines of lost drawings for buildings that, in the end, took a significantly different form. An anonymous, undated* "Representation Of the New Church at Richmond Virginia" *purports to show Monumental Church as built, but, confusingly, it probably copies a lost engraving of a lost drawing that William Strickland had based on a semi-final stage of Robert Mills's design. (Compare survey no. 21, figure 1. Photograph of print courtesy of the Valentine Museum, Richmond; Hibbs Collection, print no. 45.28.21.)*

FIGURE 4.33. *As one engraver copied another, the descendants of William Strickland's perspective of Monumental Church grew into a bewildering family (compare figure 4.32). The undated engraving* "Episcopal Church, Richmond, Va.," *published in Boston by Samuel Walker, belongs to a sizable group of American and European derivatives that look deceptively like one another. (Courtesy of Jon and Stuart Halberstadt, Christiansburg, Virginia.)*

hung on for decades under some circumstances. As late as 1854, the Baltimore drawing instructor William Minifie had to caution inexperienced readers against using it for architectural and mechanical drafting because it destroyed metal pens. On occasion, too, the best professionals used writing ink, evidently when they did not have India ink at hand. For instance, Alexander J. Davis used writing ink to draw a plan and a perspective of an Italianate villa for the Richmond vicinity, probably in 1853. The ink subsequently began eating through the paper. But this topic has carried us away from the first decades of the nineteenth century, where we still belong for now.[48]

In the 1810s, architectural activity of high importance took place in Virginia, but the state was not becoming a stronghold of the architectural profession and architectural graphics. Architects of the historic status of Mills, Alexander Parris (Wickham House, SURVEY NO. 24), and Maximilian Godefroy (Washington Monument, SURVEY NO. 22) came to Virginia to work, but they did not stay. One understands Virginia's place better after tracking an important perspective image that took shape at this time. In 1812, Mills announced his plan to publish an aquatint of his Monumental Church design and promised that he would shortly display the drawing for the print in the State Capitol. Presumably Mills meant the drawing by William Strickland that in 1813 Strickland exhibited as "A View of the Monumental Church . . . from a design by R. Mills" in the annual exhibition at the Pennsylvania Academy of the Fine Arts, a Philadelphia institution founded in 1805. At some point, the Philadelphia engraver William Kneass issued the Strickland perspective as an aquatint, which today seems to be known only from derivatives that American and foreign publishers printed for decades (FIGURES 4.32, 4.33) after the actual building had taken a materially different form (see photograph, SURVEY NO. 21). Philadelphia, then the national artistic capital, did offer opportunities to exhibit and publish architectural drawings, but even though such opportunities were slender, they far exceeded any in Virginia. The Philadelphia publisher of Owen Biddle's *Young Carpenter's Assistant* (first edition Philadelphia, 1805) distributed the second, third, and fourth editions (1810, 1815, 1817) from their own bookstore in Richmond, but, in the words of Henry-Russell Hitchcock, the book "is hardly to be considered a southern imprint," and it has no Virginia content. (It did offer Virginia craftsmen a handy source for a modest amount of instruction on making modeled but uncolored drawings—plans, elevations, sections, and details, but not perspectives. It advised, for instance, that "no kind of ink should be used except Indian Ink.") Purely architectural publication did not take hold within the state, but Virginians did publish related literature, such as a sprinkling of builder's price books from the 1810s past the end of our period. Although in these same years Jefferson devised the University of Virginia buildings as models for architectural lectures, systematic architectural instruction did not begin at the University until a century later, when Fiske Kimball inaugurated the McIntire School of Fine Arts in 1919. Apparently the University did, however, offer lessons in technical drawing after it began providing instruction in civil engineering in 1833.[49]

The 1820s form a watershed nationally. B. Henry Latrobe, Thomas Jefferson, and William Thornton died, while Charles Bulfinch retired. The first generation of native professionals—those born in the 1780s, such as Robert Mills and William Strickland—found the second generation, those born around 1800—such as Alexander J. Davis and Thomas U. Walter—hot on their heels. Between the 1830s and the War between the States, the Old Dominion turned again and again to the good, the better, and the best professionals in the mid-Atlantic region, but during these decades no architect of the first rank lived in Virginia. Rather, many lived in New York City, which now challenged Philadelphia in architecture as it had in finance.

## Architectural Drawings in Virginia, 1830s to 1860s

Drawings by Virginia artisan-builders from the 1830s to the 1860s are much rarer than those by the Northern professionals. In particular, from after the 1820s, no drawings have come to light by the workmen who had served Jefferson and, from a very different architectural family tree, none have come to light by Otis Manson, the Yankee builder who came south in 1810 and became the leading architect in Richmond. These men, however, did not need drawings in the way that the professional architects did. One suspects that artisan-builders—who, after all, designed the lion's share of good buildings in Virginia during the period in question—continued to operate largely without drawings. The increased availability of builder's guides, which left their mark on Virginia detailing, must have facilitated the persistence of this method of working. Latrobe, from his arrival in Virginia in 1796, had met with builders who would not forsake their ideas on detail for his (and patrons who did not insist on adherence to his conceptions). From the late 1830s to the 1860s, as outsider-architects sent designs in numbers to Virginians, Latrobe's experiences must have had interesting sequels.[50]

The Virginia drawings by these outsiders offer valuable evidence about the development of architectural drawing nationally, as in the case of inks and reproductive techniques. By the mid nineteenth century, colored inks, previously used only in exceptional cases, had become a medium to reckon with. Very likely, though, architects normally used these inks ornamentally, in subordination to India ink. A selection of Virginia drawings suggests the probable place of the colored inks. As early as 1843 in Philadelphia, Thomas U. Walter used a tan ink for the leading of the windows in his Mariner's Church project for Norfolk ( SURVEY NO. 36 ). In his perspectives for the Richmond Female Institute (circa 1853; SURVEY NO. 45 ) and the First Baptist Church in Alexandria (circa 1854; FIGURE 4.34 ), the Providence architect T. A. Tefft sketched the mortar joints of the bricks in brown ink. A little later in Philadelphia, Walter made extensive use of red ink—one suspects that this enjoyed the greatest popularity of the colored inks—for the brickwork in his unexecuted 1859 project ( FIGURE 4.35 ) for the United States Arsenal in Harper's Ferry, then in Virginia. (As opposed to Tefft's animated handling, Walter took the

FIGURE 4.34. **Perspective of "Mr. Tucker's Church"** (**First Baptist Church**), *Alexandria, Virginia, by T. A. Tefft, circa 1854. The brown of Tefft's mortar joints reflects the rise of colored ink at the middle of the nineteenth century, and the freehand drawing of these joints looks forward to a scintillating style of draftsmanship later in the century. (Compare survey no. 59. Photograph courtesy of Brown University Library, Tefft Drawings, Ch(AlV)1.1.)*

FIGURE 4.35. **Elevation of the United States Arsenal,** *Harper's Ferry, Virginia, by Thomas U. Walter, 1859. The red of Walter's mortar joints in this unexecuted design represents the vogue for colored ink at the middle of the nineteenth century, and the ruling of these joints moves toward an elegantly linear style of drawing popular in the 1870s. (Compare survey nos. 52–55. Photograph courtesy of the Athenaeum of Philadelphia Archives, no. WTU\*066\*002.)*

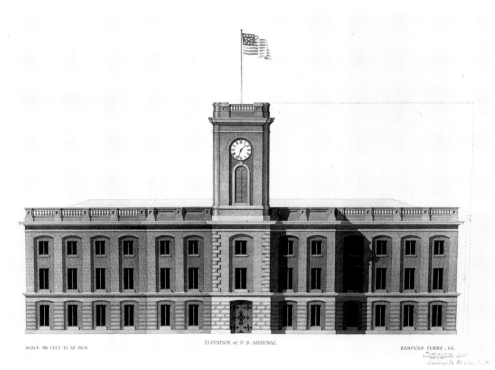

SCALE VIII FEET TO AN INCH      ELEVATION OF U.S. ARSENAL      HARPERS FERRY . VA.

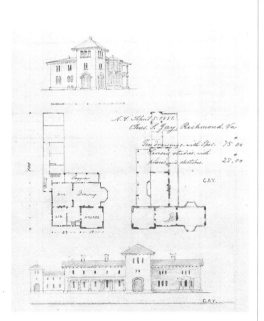

FIGURE 4.36. **Two Projects for the Charles S. Gay House,** *Richmond, Virginia, by Alexander J. Davis, 1851. At mid-century, Davis experimented with a variety of colored inks, using both sepia and green for the unexecuted Gay designs. From Davis's Journal, p. 125. (Photograph courtesy of the Department of Prints and Photographs, Metropolitan Museum of Art, New York, Davis Collection.)*

tighter approach of ruling the mortar joints of the wall with red ink: Walter's manner here looks forward to a geometrically detailed drafting style popular in the 1870s [as in SURVEY NOS. 52–55 ], whereas Tefft's style anticipates the still later preference for sparkling effects like those seen in etchings [see the drawing for the Hotel Altemonte, SURVEY NO. 59 ].) In these drawings, the color made a contribution, but Walter and Tefft used India ink for the basic lines. A little differently in New York, Alexander J. Davis tried out a small spectrum of inks in his Journal. For instance, an 1851 page of unexecuted designs for Charles S. Gay of Richmond ( FIGURE 4.36 ) employs both sepia ink (of which Davis used a good deal in his Journal) and green ink. The sizable body of Davis's Virginia and non-Virginia drawings examined during research for this book indicates that India ink remained fundamental for Davis. But his reliance on blue and brown inks for most of the outlines in his 1870 elevation for the Virginia Military Institute Barracks ( SURVEY NO. 39 ) laid the groundwork for the vibrancy of this beautiful drawing.[51]

As to reproductive techniques, at the approach of mid century one finds architects considering alternatives to pricking. In the case of the only known set of drawings by Robert Cary Long, Jr., for the Virginia School for the Deaf and the Blind (1839–46), Long pricked both his studies and his presentation drawings ( SURVEY NO. 33 ). The only details in this set, however, are elements of the orders traced, it would appear, onto two sheets of thin paper ( FIGURE 4.37 ). Translucent paper, available abroad since the early eighteenth century, enjoyed increasing popularity internationally from the 1840s. In the later nineteenth century, while pricking declined, the use of vellum or tracing paper became a standard option, side-by-side with tracing cloth, made of linen coated

FIGURE 4.37. *When Robert Cary Long, Jr., designed the* **Virginia School for the Deaf and the Blind,** *in Staunton, Virginia, 1839–46 (survey no. 33), he used tracing, an all-important method for the future, for the* **Details of the Orders.** *(Photograph courtesy of the Winterthur Library, Joseph Downs Collection of Manuscripts and Printed Ephemera.)*

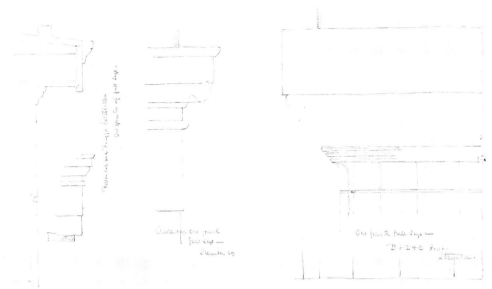

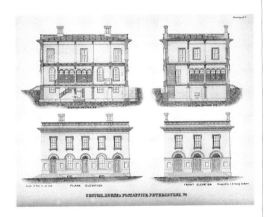

FIGURE 4.38. *In standardizing the buildings erected by the Treasury Department, Captain Alexander H. Bowman and Ammi B. Young lithographed the working drawings.* **Drawing no. 2, "Custom-House & Post-Office, Petersburgh, Va.,"** *was printed in 1855 for the commission of 1856–59. (Photograph courtesy of the National Archives, Cartographic and Architectural Branch, Record Group 121: Records of the Public Buildings Service, Folder 1 of 4.)*

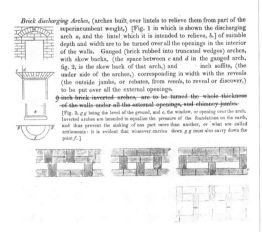

FIGURE 4.39. *In 1845, Alexander J. Davis printed his* **Specification of the Materials and Works . . . at Belmead** *(survey no. 38), with such illustrations as this* **Detail of Brickwork.** *Thereafter he made a practice of printing specifications. (Photograph courtesy of the New York Public Library, A. J. Davis Papers, Box 6, Folder 1.)*

with a wax-like finish. In the next turn of the wheel, these materials, used as negatives, made blueprinting possible.[52]

Another alternative did not bear this kind of fruit. In the prolific Office of Construction of the United States Treasury Department, Captain Alexander H. Bowman and Ammi B. Young standardized the designs for custom houses and post offices in the 1850s and put these designs on lithographic plates ( FIGURE 4.38 ). They only printed working "drawings" in the necessary quantity for a given building. They had so far standardized these designs that they could also print details for multiple buildings from a single plate, with merely a change in the inscription. This mechanization of graphics, in an age when publishing had become a major industry, is on a par with Bowman and Young's use of industrially fabricated building elements. It has a forerunner in Alexander J. Davis's innovative use of printing to produce multiple copies of his specifications ( FIGURE 4.39 ). Virginia had a part in that practice: the long-distance nature of the Belmead commission ( SURVEY NO. 38 ) prompted Davis to begin printing his specifications in 1845.[53]

Virginia fostered no such innovations in publishing drawings or architectural literature during the same years. The state remained on the receiving end in the expansion of architectural publication between the 1840s and 1861, the beginning of the Civil War: as before, many elements in Virginia architecture came out of published sources, while few went in. By the 1840s, architecture had found in the agricultural journal one modest outlet in print appropriate to an agrarian state. In the first installment of this development, the *Southern Planter* of Richmond published on architectural topics intermittently between 1844 and 1859 and illustrated a handful of designs. All of the latter came from outside the state, although John Hartwell Cocke unsuccessfully tried to get an engraving of Bremo Recess ( SURVEY NO. 31 ) published in 1844. He and his son Philip St. George Cocke (owner of Belmead, SURVEY NO. 38 ) saw houses of theirs into print in other journals.[54]

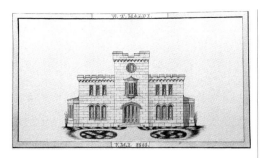

FIGURE 4.40. *In teaching mechanical drawing at the Virginia Military Institute, Thomas Hoomes Williamson sometimes had his students copy Alexander J. Davis's drawings for the campus buildings (compare with survey no. 39). W. T. Hardy's* "V. M. I. 1855" *is probably a copy of a Davis elevation for Williamson's own house. (Photograph courtesy of VMI Archives, Preston Library, Lexington, Virginia.)*

Virginia's graphic horizons do seem to have widened perceptibly in the two decades before the firing on Fort Sumter in 1861. In 1841, the engineer Thomas Hoomes Williamson joined the faculty at the new Virginia Military Institute, where his subjects included architecture and mechanical drawing. He evidently regarded Davis's watercolors as suitable models for his pupils to copy, including the elevation of Williamson's own faculty residence ( FIGURE 4.40 ). In the 1850s, Richmond benefited from a little-studied national phenomenon of this period, the incursion of German-born architects. Richmond acquired the abilities of Albert Lybrock (who designed the Miller School, SURVEY NO. 52 ) and Oswald J. Heinrich (who made a splendid presentation drawing of Lybrock's design for the tomb for James Monroe, SURVEY NO. 48 ). Heinrich not only designed buildings and worked as a drafter but also gave lessons in perspective drawing. The arrival of these and other dimly known figures, such as Henry Exall and Albert L. West, must have meant major increments in graphic skills in the city.[55]

The second installment on architectural images published by the Virginia agricultural press takes us past the years 1861–65. In 1866–67 in Richmond, the new journal *The Farmer* began publishing architectural designs very nearly as a regular feature. Most of these came from the truly crude Philadelphia architect Isaac H. Hobbs. Hobbs's projects, almost all of which may live up to their billing as designed "Expressly for *The Farmer*," reflect Hobbs's attempt to design for the "prostrate and destitute condition" of Virginia. Three of his designs (for instance, FIGURE 4.41 ) subsequently reached a wider public in *Godey's Lady's Magazine* and/or the two editions of Hobbs's *Architecture*

FIGURE 4.41. *In the absence of a nineteenth-century Virginia architectural press, Virginia agricultural journals occasionally published on architectural topics. This* **"Perspective View of a Cheap Country Cottage,"** *from a series of designs made by the Philadelphia architect Isaac H. Hobbs to meet the needs of postwar Virginians, appeared twice in a Richmond publication,* **The Farmer** *(volume 1, October 1866: 377, and volume 2, March 1867: 67), before reappearing in three Northern imprints. (Photograph courtesy of the Virginia State Library.)*

FIGURE 4.42. **The Farmer** *also published a* **Perspective View of "A Country Cottage, Designed . . . by a Gentleman of Charlotte, N. C."** *(volume 2, June 1867: 181). The anonymous amateur architect had applied more understanding to meeting the needs of "Southern people in their present poverty stricken condition." (Photograph courtesy of the Virginia State Library.)*

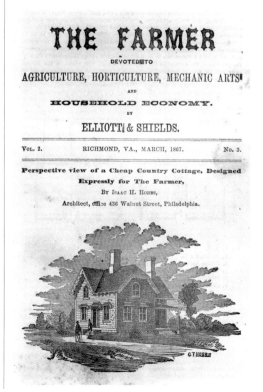

(Philadelphia, 1873 and 1876). But a cottage carefully devised for *The Farmer* by an anonymous North Carolina gentleman "with special reference to the wants of the Southern people in their present poverty stricken condition," drawn by Albert L. West, and engraved on wood by the Richmond artist William Ludwell Sheppard ( FIGURE 4.42 ), easily upstaged Hobbs. Whatever the effect these offerings had on building in Virginia, in 1868 *The Farmer* merged with *The Southern Planter* to form *The Southern Planter and Farmer,* which did not publish building designs. With this minor instance of the publication of architectural drawings, this chronicle ends.[56]

## *In Summary*

Even with all the cautions appropriate to an early study, this review of architectural drawing in Virginia supports the simple, and not very surprising, conclusions suggested at the beginning. In 1796–98, the first three great American architects—Thomas Jefferson, Charles Bulfinch, and B. Henry Latrobe—were all at work. Two of the three lived in Virginia (Jefferson did so whenever he was not fulfilling his duties as vice president in Philadelphia), and any serious account of American architectural drawings must pay close attention to what these men drew here. The Old Dominion would not, however, shape the course of American architectural graphics in the next seventy-odd years. Jefferson's individual synthesis of possibilities from home and abroad did nothing of the sort. Professional practice instead embraced the orthodox use of pencil and pen, stable inks, watercolor, and picture-like effects, especially in perspective renderings. This practice took its direction to a significant extent from Latrobe, but even so only after Latrobe escaped to Philadelphia from the rocks of the James. To a greater extent, professional practice took its course from the European standards that Latrobe conveyed and that reached North America by way of other immigrants, publications from abroad, imported drawing supplies, and perhaps other agencies as well. Apart from the Jefferson-Latrobe circle, Virginia does matter in the history of American architectural drawing between the Revolution and the Civil War because of her patronage of outside architects. From Boston to Charleston, from even as far west as Nashville in the case of William Strickland's Grace Episcopal Church (Cismont, designed 1847), but most of all in the rival architectural centers of Philadelphia, Baltimore, and New York, a phenomenal array of major architectural designers responded to the opportunities promised by Virginia patronage. The surviving drawings of this diverse band provide valuable evidence not only about Virginia architecture but also about the national evolution of architectural graphics in these decades. The combination of these sheets with the handiwork of Jefferson and Latrobe gives us an unsurpassable means of studying the history of American architectural graphics from the onset of monumental Classicism to the first flourishes of High Victorian taste.[57]

## PART 3

## Drawings, Models, and the Making of Architecture in Virginia since 1870

by RICHARD GUY WILSON

Architecture is ultimately a physical act of making a permanent place, of attempting to symbolize in built form a particular world view. The road to that final, built form can be long and arduous. Central to the constructed house, office building, or state capitol has been a process that encompasses a world of negotiation, a world that is initially revealed to us through drawings and models. In many cases the drawing or model can reveal the original intention of an architect and the development of a design. However, above all, the primary purpose of architectural drawing is to help in the visualization and the actual making of architecture.

The French saying, *plus ça change, plus c'est la même chose* (the more things change, the more they stay the same), might be an appropriate epigram for discussing architectural drawing in Virginia since the 1870s. Although there are some obvious differences in appearance and in how architectural drawings have been made between those of the recent past and those of, say, the 1850s, still the fundamentals remain the same. Reginald Blomfield, a turn-of-the-century English architect, summed it up nicely: "Generally, the object of architectural drawing is the representation of architecture."[58] Most buildings are still designed in a time-honored manner: an architect develops a mental concept, then tries to communicate it by graphic or other visual means to the client, the draftsmen in the office, the builders, and anybody else concerned—neighbors, review committees, zoning boards, or real estate editors. Drawings will always be needed, as visual approximations of what a building will look like—floor plans, elevations, and construction details. The differences between drawings of earlier decades and more recent ones result from many factors, including different views of what the drawing is intended to accomplish, the type of drawing or presentation style, and the relationship of the architect to the building and to the documents of the building.

### Drawing as Art

Architectural drawings and models can exude a fascination; they can cajole, seduce, and impress, and many are indeed intended to accomplish this end. The drawing produced by an unknown renderer for G. V. Stone and Donald Drayer's Arlington Towers Apartments ( FIGURE 4.43 ) is a masterpiece of perspective. With charcoal and pencil, the artist has the viewer floating a few thousand feet above the apartment towers, with the city of Washington, D.C., the Mall, and Arlington Memorial Bridge stretching off into the horizon. Who wouldn't be impressed? While the apartment towers in the foreground appear large, their scale is minimized by the panorama in which they are placed. Yet when one examines the buildings carefully, the buildings themselves have no architectural distinction. They are not simply grossly over-scaled for human occupation and identity, they lack any redeeming architectural qualities. They are boring, dull, and uninspired, mere money-making ventures. But the tour-de-force of the composition minimizes architectural detail for the glory of the scene. Art serves promotion in this case and brings forth the ongoing argument of not just a drawing's ability to impress a client, but the very question of architectural drawings as art.

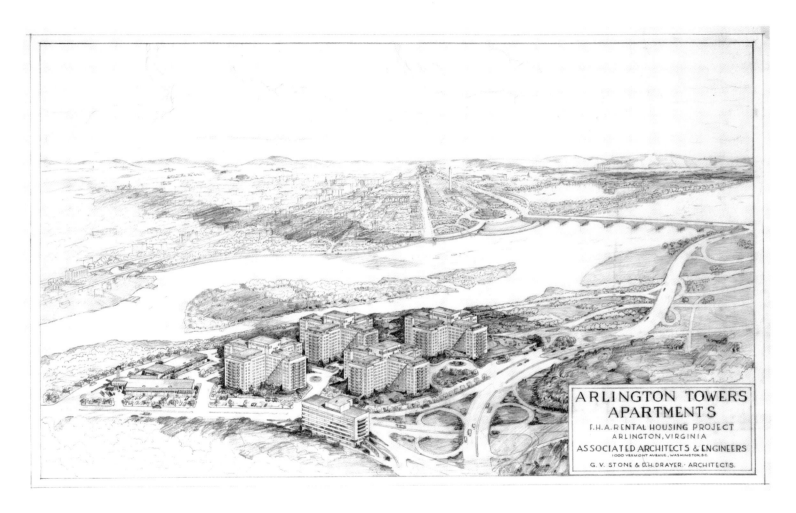

FIGURE 4.43. **Arlington Towers Apartments,** *FHA Rental Housing Project, Arlington, Virginia, circa 1950, by Donald H. Drayer, is a masterpiece of perspective. Inscribed:* Associated Architects and Engineers, 100 Vermont Ave., Washington, D.C., G. V. Stone and D. H. Drayer, Architects. *(Photograph courtesy of the Library of Congress, Prints and Photographs Division.)*

Not all architectural drawings are art objects. Many architects, including some of America's and Virginia's most important designers, have not viewed their drawings as art even though we may disagree with them. Drawings, to many architects, are simply tools for getting a building built.

The artistic value of architectural drawings has long been an issue. An editorial in the February 1876 issue of *The American Architect and Building News* bemoaned the low state of architectural drawing in America, claiming it was more than straight lines and construction. Architecture, the author claimed, "must be pre-eminently an art of form if it is to be an art at all; and it cannot be properly represented when accuracy of form is slighted."[59] However, there was an even greater issue: "The good draughtsman must have the eye and feeling of an artist; and the eye of an artist is only to be developed by a serious training," meaning an education that went beyond the usual office routine. Only by studying ornament and by drawing the figure from life could the architectural draftsman develop the required skills. This emphasis on training the architect as an artist was indicative of the professional concerns of the late nineteenth century—that the architect was different from the mere builder—but it also points to the revival of architectural drawing as an art form. According to Reginald Blomfield, again quoting from his book of 1912, "Architectural draughtmanship has fallen from the high place it once occupied, and has been cut off from the main stream of Art."[60] However, Blomfield fell into the time-honored tradition of condemning the taste of one's parents but finding great virtue in one's grandparents, for he claimed that mid-nineteenth-century architectural drawing, which he characterized as "unprofitable emptiness" springing out of "nothing," had ended. To him there was a resurgence in architectural draftsmanship both in England and America that followed "the French tradition." Blomfield's point can be illustrated by examples of architectural drawing in this book. For example compare any drawings by Thomas Jefferson (see SURVEY NOS. 7, 8, 9, 11) to the splashy presentation drawings done at the turn of the century by architects such as William Noland or Hughson Hawley. Not every architect agreed that the so-called French or *Beaux-Arts* technique marked an advance. Indeed, J. Stewart Barney, who was not above using such drawings for the Handley Library in Winchester (SURVEY NO. 66), lambasted the "false atmospheric effects" and a system in which too much emphasis was placed, he felt, upon the drawing, until it, rather than the building, became the goal.[61]

This tension between the architectural drawing as an instrument for getting a building designed and built, versus its existence as an art object in its own right, has continued—with occasional lapses—throughout the twentieth century. Many of the no-frills Modernists of the 1940s and 1950s viewed architecture as a pragmatic, problem-solving, technological art, and they eschewed the highly colorful, self-consciously arty drawing. Agreeing with Barney, they felt that drawing itself should not be their concern. Certainly not all Modernists agreed with this; several leading architects viewed their drawings as art, and some, such as Frank Lloyd Wright, developed a distinctive style (see the Pope-Leighey House, (SURVEY NO. 96). But still children rebel against their fathers, and many aspects of the architectural drawing revival of the 1890s to 1920s were tossed out: color, highly charged atmospheric effects, and false approximations.

The wheel of rebellion by the younger generation has turned again, and in the 1970s and 1980s came a resurgence of architectural draftsmanship as art. Or, as one critic breathlessly exclaimed, "drawings—the visual language of design—are back!"[62] Of course, architectural drawings as such had never disappeared, but as will be explained further on, architects did find other methods by which to visualize and study design. The big breakthrough in the national revival of architectural drawing in America came with the Museum of Modern Art's large *Ecole des Beaux-Arts* exhibit of 1975–76. Here, enshrined in the command-post of high Modernism in the United States, was the old enemy: the nineteenth century's eclectic-classical *Beaux-Arts* tradition, complete with all of its highly colorful drawings.[63] Actually, a revival of the architectural drawing as art had already been taking place among who those who would soon be labeled Postmodernists. This can be seen in drawings by Robert Venturi ( SURVEY NO. 110 ), Michael Graves ( SURVEY NO. 116 ), and other architects, whose work is exhibited and sold by commercial art galleries. The revival of architectural drawing as art spread to historical examples and a spate of exhibits has taken place, along with catalogues and books on the topic—of which this book is yet another example.[64] But what is art and what architectural drawings mean has changed dramatically.

## The Architect and Architectural Drawing in the Twentieth Century

One trend has been a diminishing relationship of the designing architect to the actual drawings associated with a building. With the increasing complexity of the building industry and the increasing size of buildings themselves, the designing architect might only do a few initial sketches and then see them worked up and elaborated by assistants. E. E. Myers certainly did not sit down with pen, ink, T-square, triangle, and other apparatus to execute the drawing illustrated for Richmond City Hall ( SURVEY NO. 58 ). One, probably several, unrecorded draftsmen in Myers's office worked many hours at its execution. Myers himself would have been far too busy to spend his time creating such a detailed elevation. The drawing by the office of Carrère & Hastings for the Hotel Jefferson ( SURVEY NO. 62 ) represents one of many drawings that would be needed for such a complex job. In some ways, architectural offices became factories, the main designer only doing a few preliminary sketches, to be developed by assistants, and then the staff in the drafting rooms creating the myriads of drawings required for detail and fixture. With this separation of skills and responsibilities, the size of architectural offices changed enormously. Before the Civil War, an office of ten would be considered large; in many cases one or two individuals were enough. Then it was entirely possible that the principal designer actually did the drawings from which a building was to be constructed. But in the years following the war, everything in America gets bigger: government bureaucracy grows, big business comes into being, and buildings become very large and complex. Some architectural offices, such as Carrère & Hastings and McKim, Mead & White employed more than 100 people by the turn of the century. The trend in these offices was toward specialization, a production-line mentality, and to try to streamline, to make the production of drawings more efficient. In offices of any size the tendency toward systematization meant that individuals became specialists in certain types of drawings, such as presentation drawings or working drawings. Given the American penchant to have machines do all sorts of manual labor in the early decades of the twentieth century, even architectural drawings would have been produced by machine if that had been possible.

The increasing size of architectural offices at the beginning of the twentieth century meant that the office staff would learn the principal designer's characteristics or styles, then imitate them, creating an office style. Another innovation has been the "talking" of design, in which the principal designer would simply describe what he wanted to an assistant, who would then assign the drawings thus specified to a team of drafters. A former employee in the office of McKim, Mead & White recalled Charles McKim: "He liked to sit down at a draftsman's table, usually [wearing] his hat and immaculate shirtsleeves, and design out loud . . . cyma recta; cyma reversa; fillet below; dentils; modillions; and so on."[65] This is increasingly true today. Many of the leading figures in the world of corporate architecture never touch a pencil.

As the complexity of buildings increased, they not only grew larger but the mechanical and structural systems also became more technical. The relation of the architect to the construction of a building completely changed. Instead of an intimate relationship to the builder, in which the workers either knew what to do or could be directed verbally to carry out an instruction, everything was minutely detailed in contract documents, specifications, and drawings. A factor seldom mentioned is the increased availability of paper at lower prices. In the eighteenth and early nineteenth centuries paper was expensive. Jefferson hoarded it. But since the 1870s, paper became so plentiful that it could be used and discarded freely. The general contractor appeared in the 1890s and further altered the relationship of the architect to the project. Prior to the 1890s the architect, or his assistant, also acted as coordinator of the job, scheduling the various tradesmen and material suppliers, and overseeing the building. After 1900 the general contractor assumed these duties and the architect only needed to ensure that the design was properly executed and to oversee any changes in the drawings.

The accurate reproduction of drawings so they could be disseminated and used at the building site and for other purposes was a never-ending quest. Up to the 1880s many architects produced original drawings that would then be used on the site. Photo-duplication, blue-printing, or the other reproduction processes were invented in France in the 1840s, but as late as the 1870s such duplication was still being described as an innovation in office practice.[66] Architectural offices did not begin to use blueprints widely until the 1890s. A number of different duplicating processes were in use for years. The shift from ink-on-vellum to ink-on-linen occurred in the 1880s, as the new duplicating processes demanded that drawings be executed on opaque white surfaces. The inherent limitations of the gradations of tone in blue-printing led to the use of stark black ink and the development of different symbols for various textures and materials. Frequently color would be added, through either wash or pencils. This has been an ongoing process, as can be seen in the Bottomley drawing for Waverley Hill ( SURVEY NO. 87 ), a reproduction to which color has been added.

## Types of Architectural Representation

The increasing amounts of paper and drawings and the shift to specialization in the architect's office have given rise to attempts to categorize architectural drawings according to their use or purpose. The usual orthographic projections remain: plan, elevation, and details. But not all plans or elevations are the same, and they can have different purposes. Reginald Blomfield divided architectural drawings into two categories based on their "intention": the objective and the subjective. According to Blomfield, "objective" drawings were always geometrical, accurate, and clear; they are the usual plan, elevation, and details. They are drawings, Blomfield explained, "which can be carried out in the building [process] by other hands." He described "subjective" drawings as the making of a picture or "the impression" of a project as a whole, or of a fantasy, in order to communicate its ideas to other individuals.[67] Robert A. M. Stern attempted to modify Blomfield's ideas by claiming that objective drawings were the conceptual working drawings, intended only for the use of the architect or his/her office. This type of drawing is personal and difficult for the layman to understand. In contrast, Stern claimed that the subjective category was "perceptual." It is a "picture" and easy for all to understand, the common type is a perspective, or presentation drawing.[68]

Another method of classifying architectural drawings is by their purpose, whether they are intended for an actual building project or are done as travel sketches, illustrations, student drawings, or merely theoretical or fantasy drawings.[69] Travel sketches done by an architect can be either for relaxation or as a source for further study. Illustrations are just that: views of buildings used for not for construction but as accompaniments to a text, such as those A. B. Bibb drew for a series of articles on early Virginia architecture ( FIGURE 4.44 ). Bibb used a style of pen-and-ink sketch popularized by the English renderer E. Elden Deane, that shows old Virginia buildings populated by Virginians in colonial dress. Student drawings are obviously learning-tools and are not meant to be used to construct a building. They are allied with polemical (theoretical) or fantasy drawings, which are not for real buildings, but are merely intended as speculation.

Another way of viewing architectural drawings is by describing how they are used in the design process. (Note the use of the word *process*, which implies that there may be an orderly development in the design. But this is not always so evident). Such drawings can be classified as 1) the initial study sketches; 2) study and development drawings; 3) working drawings; and 4) presentation drawings. Sometimes the different types are combined in a single sheet, as for instance Frank Lloyd Wright's drawing for the Pope-Leighey House ( SURVEY NO. 96 ), which has presentation perspectives and the elements of a working drawing.

Initial sketches are drawings done for the architect's own purposes. They are simply ideas recorded on paper and often have little meaning and make little sense to anyone besides the architect and his or her colleagues. These are the

FIGURE 4.44. *Architectural drawing becomes illustration in this* **Interior, Shirley,** *by A. Burnley Bibb (active 1880s–90s) for a series of articles on early Virginia architecture. Pen and ink (?) on paper, published in* American Architect and Building News 25 (June 15, 1889): 281.

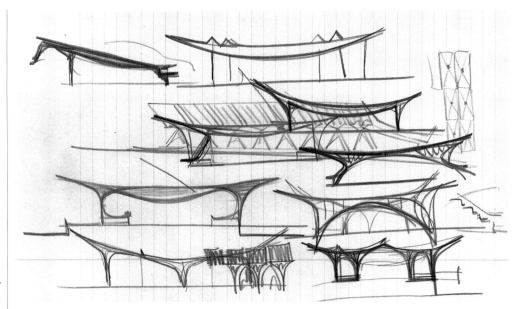

rarest type of drawings—the ones done on an envelope, on the proverbial napkin, or in the margin of a letter. Because this type of drawing is of necessity crude, they are seldom saved, but from them flow the initial ideas. In the case of Dulles Airport ( SURVEY NO. 107 ), Eero Saarinen preserved several very rough sketches in which he experimented with structure and form ( FIGURES 4.45, 4.46 ). Here is perhaps the closest one can get to the creative process, as the architect struggles with putting on paper ideas in his mind. The concern is not with beautiful artistic drawings; but in this case, the sixteen sketches that have been saved show us how Saarinen tried out a number of solutions. While there is a crudity to the initial sketch, such drawings need not be entirely plan and elevation. The small perspective drawing, in order to study the concept in a representation of three dimensions, can occur at any point in the design process.

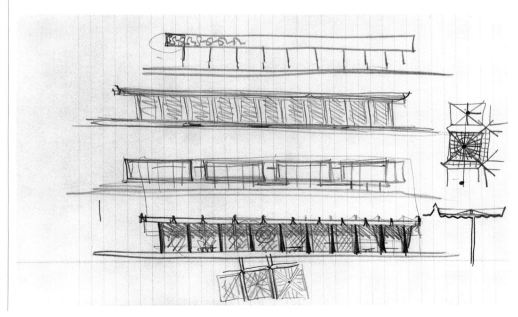

Study and development drawings are those in which the architect begins to elaborate on the initial solution(s), as can be seen in Johnson & Brannon's Allied Arts Building in Lynchburg ( SURVEY NO. 90 ), where the architects experimented with facade treatment and site—in this case, placing the building on the opposite side of the street. Saarinen's drawing for Dulles Airport ( SURVEY NO. 107 ) is an example of a development drawing. Here the architect works out the building in three dimensions, though this would not be the final solution. Drawings are, however, but one means of studying a design's development, and architects frequently resort to models. The use of the model by architects has a long history that is not fully understood. In many cases models were used as demonstrations and as three-dimensional presentation pieces, as can be seen with the model for the Virginia Capitol ( SURVEY NO. 10 ), more a miniature than a part of the design process. Evidence does exist that, in the 1890s, architects such as McKim, Mead & White began to use plaster-of-Paris models as a method of studying and checking massing and the relationship of elevations.[70]

With the advent of Modernism in the 1910s and thereafter, models came to be used more often as a method of design development. Especially popular became the cardboard or chipboard model, which emphasized a building's form almost exclusively at the expense of detail and materials. In some ways these chipboard-thin models rather accurately summed up the changing technology of most buildings—that the "art" or design aspect was, in reality, only skin deep; that the architect was a sort of "exterior decorator," deftly placing different facades around steel or concrete armatures or skeletons. This shift in what a building was really made of had been true for years, as can be observed in the construction photographs of the Handley Library in Winchester, where the steel frame is in fact the real structure of the dome ( FIGURE 4.47 ). The increasing use of models in the twentieth century also corresponded with the distrust many Modernists held toward architectural drawings in general. The model for the Chemistry Building at the University of Virginia by Louis Kahn ( SURVEY NO. 108 ) is one example, though Kahn himself was known as a distinguished architectural renderer. The model illustrates his major preoccupation with form; there is no indication that the scale of the building would be significantly different when it was built out of brick. Many architects continue to depend on models as a design development tool. George Hartman and Warren Cox, who designed the 1985 additions and renovations for the Chrysler Museum, Norfolk ( SURVEY NO. 114 ) have been very important in the reintroduction of scale and craft in recent architecture, and their firm still uses models almost exclusively. However in this case the model was also a means of studying the urban context, an attempt to understand the scale of the building in its setting.

Working drawings are, as noted earlier in Blomfield's terms, subjective; they are always geometrical, and they are the drawings that are intended, along with the written specifications, to communicate to the builder and the workmen some of the facts necessary to get a building erected. Working drawings show how a building is to be erected, as can be seen in shop drawings from the Guastavino

FIGURE 4.47. *This photograph of the* **Handley Library, Winchester, Virginia, during construction,** *circa 1910, designed by J. Stewart Barney (1869–1924), reveals that the essence of a building's design is not its surface decoration but the volumes and spaces defined by its skeletal armature. (Compare the rendering of the library, survey no. 66. Photograph by Fred Barr; courtesy of the Handley Library, Winchester, Virginia.)*

Company for the vaulting at the University of Virginia's Rotunda during McKim, Mead & White's restoration ( FIGURE 4.48 and SURVEY NO. 63 ). As indicated earlier, the number of working drawings has greatly increased over the years as buildings have grown more complicated and the architect becomes further removed from the actual construction process.

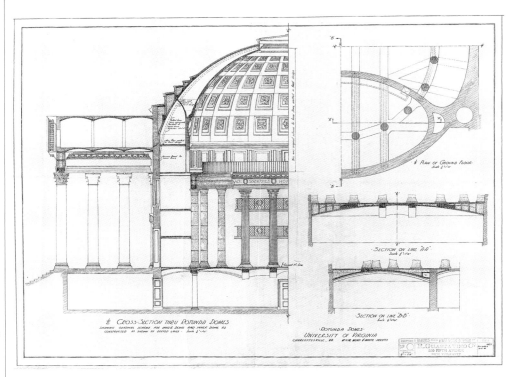

FIGURE 4.48. *A clear example of a working drawing is this sheet of* **Construction Drawings for the restoration of the Rotunda Dome** *at the University of Virginia, 1897, by R. Guastavino Co. of New York City for McKim, Mead & White. Ink on linen; 26 ½ by 37 ¼ inches. (Photograph courtesy of Avery Architectural Library, Columbia University, New York.)*

Although working drawings are the pragmatics of building, still they can have a beauty all their own. The evident attention to the composition of the sheet—the interworking of sections, elevations, and plans with a dynamic diagonal running down the center—is apparent in a drawing from the office of the Supervising Architect of the Treasury Department for the iron staircase ( FIGURE 4.49 ) at the U.S. Courthouse and Post Office in Lynchburg from 1886. What is amazing from our perspective more than a century later is not just the care taken—the art—of the drawing, but that this would be the document from which the cast ironwork would be manufactured and built. While no exact comparison can be made, since such staircases have not been made since the early twentieth century, such a project today still would require many more drawings than just this single sheet. Similarly, a working drawing from the Carneal & Johnston office for terra-cotta detailing on the Chamber of Commerce building in Richmond ( FIGURE 4.50 ) is a work of art. Its quality can be seen in the draftsman's evident care and pleasure in drawing each separate element of the upper floors and how they fit together. This drawing illustrates a level of confidence between the architect, the builder, and the suppliers of terra-cotta tiles and bricks.

The last category for consideration in this chapter, presentation drawings and models, is also subjective, in that they are impressions of the entire building,

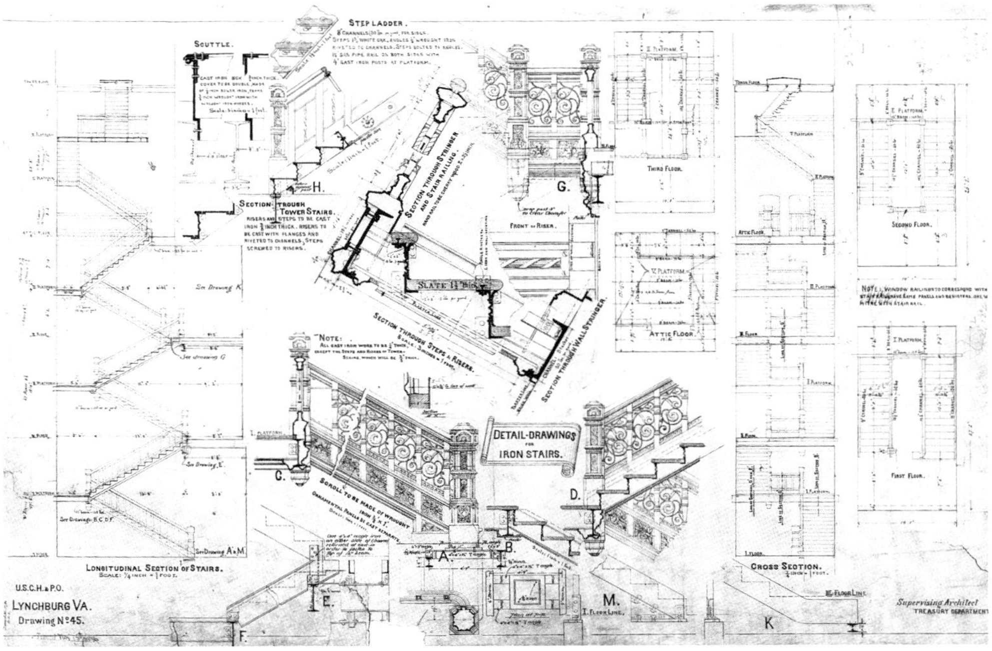

FIGURE 4.49. *The artistry and dynamic symmetry of the finest working drawings can be seen in this sheet of* Detail drawings for Iron Stairs, drawing no. 45 for United States Court House and Post Office *(demolished), Lynchburg, Virginia, 1885–88, by Miffin E. Bell (1846–1904). Multicolored inks, 24 by 36 inches. (Photograph courtesy of the National Archives, Washington, D.C.)*

FIGURE 4.50. *The art of architectural drawing is apparent in this drawing of terra-cotta tiles on the* Elevation, 9th and 10th floors, Chamber of Commerce Building, Main and Sixth Streets, *Richmond, Virginia, by Carneal & Johnston dated January 18, 1912. Colored inks on linen, 21 ½ by 28 inches. (Photograph courtesy of Carneal & Johnston.)*

intended to convey information about the building to someone other than those involved in the design or construction. The presentation drawing is done when the architect has worked out what is thought to be a design solution and the design needs to be shown to the client and/or to the public. By mid 1959, when Eero Saarinen felt he had arrived at a successful design for Dulles Airport, he had Jay Barr, a draftsman in the office, created a perspective drawing ( FIGURE

FIGURE 4.51. *The drama and presence of the proposed structure comes alive in this* **Presentation drawing of Dulles Terminal,** *Chantilly, Virginia, by Jay Barr, circa June 1959, for a design by Eero Saarinen. Colored pencil on vellum, 14 7/16 by 12 1/2 inches. (Photograph courtesy Kent Cooper, Cooper-Lecky Partnership, Washington, D.C.)*

4.51). A few changes would still be made to the design, but this drawing is close to the final version. With drama, Barr captured the monumental front of this airport, showing the rush of arrivals and departures, and the importance of automobiles to the design. A short time later a large model of the terminal was also made, to demonstrate more clearly what the building itself would look like (SURVEY NO. 107). As can be seen in the case of Dulles Airport, presentation drawings are valuable sales aids; they help promote the project to individual clients or committees. Because many architects had found that their clients could not read architectural drawings or understand floor plans and elevations, they realized that greater fidelity to the completed building was needed; hence, elaborate models and presentation drawings.

Presentation drawings are what most people think of when they think of architectural drawings as "art." Their scheme can be either orthogonal—at right angles to the picture plane—or perspective—drawn with certain angles to give an impression of depth, by means of a vanishing-point formula. The *Ecole des Beaux-Arts*—which, as Blomfield claimed, so influenced American design at the turn of the century—assisted in the revival of artistic architectural drawings. Architects came to prefer orthogonal projections (or the elevation, plan, and section) without rendering the building in context. Examples include Richard Morris Hunt's drawing for the Second Academic Building at Hampton Institute (SURVEY NO. 57), or Peebles & Ferguson's drawing for the Virginia Museum of Fine Arts (SURVEY NO. 93), both of which are in color, or McKim, Mead & White's large ink-on-linen drawing for the Rotunda restorations at the University of Virginia (SURVEY NO. 63). But far more popular with architect and client alike was the presentation drawing that did include the site context, either in elevation—such as Frye and Chesterman's City Auditorium and Market in Lynchburg (SURVEY NO. 71)—or in perspective, such as the dramatic rendering for Arlington Towers Apartments (FIGURE 4.43) illustrated earlier in this essay. Such drawings gave verisimilitude, a feeling that this drawing would show how the building will look when it is completed.

Presentation perspectives have a noble lineage. Early examples include those by B. Henry Latrobe and A. J. Davis (SURVEY NOS. 18, 41). But specialization has occurred since 1880 and the appearance of the professional renderer. Individuals like Eldon Deane and Hughson Hawley did not work in an architect's office; instead they operated independently, producing perspective renderings for whoever could pay. It is estimated that Hawley produced more than 11,000 architectural renderings. Frequently such perspectives are described as French or *Beaux-Arts* in style, because the buildings depicted reflect the classicism of the design itself. But, as has been noted, the doctrine of the *Ecole* itself actually discouraged the use of perspective rendering, and encouraged instead the orthographic (non-perspective) projection. We can only conclude that the source for this use of flashy and contextual perspectives and elevations is apparently not France but England. Perspective and contextual presentations were inherently picturesque, revealing the architect's concern with the relationship between a building and its setting. The major makers of presentation perspectives in America—Hawley and Deane—were English, or had their training in England. Hawley was English-born and -trained; Deane's background is uncertain, but apparently he trained in London.[71]

Eldon Deane began as a pen-and-ink perspective artist, doing sketches for architectural periodicals. He gradually developed into doing full-scale perspectives, as for Yarnall & Goforth's Hotel Altemonte, Staunton ( SURVEY NO. 59 ) and finally did full-color renderings, as he did for Winchester's Handley Library ( SURVEY NO. 66 ). Aspects of a diluted French-Impressionism, especially in atmospheric techniques, did appear in the work of Hughson Hawley and his followers (see Boxley Building, SURVEY NO. 77 ), though some of the same features were present in both English and American watercolor painting. Far more important was the fact that these artist-draftsmen brought a sense of drama to the perspective: they showed automobiles, birds, clouds, and people, including the recurring girl or woman in a red dress. It should be noted that Hawley had first trained as a scenic artist or backdrop painter for the theater in England before he came to the United States in 1879. Many professional renderers like Hawley demanded that the architect provide a drawing of the building in perspective, and then he would enlarge it and add atmosphere. The fact that this decidedly non-French type of presentation drawing was used by Americans even for Classical structures at the turn of the century indicates the inherently picturesque nature of even the American Renaissance. Not all perspectives were done as sales aids. Some were drawn after the fact, to record the finished building, and as illustrations of the architect's work. The drawing for the Dining Hall additions at the University of Virginia, created by Robert A. M. Stern's office ( SURVEY NO. 117 ) was done several years after the building itself was completed. Many of Frank Lloyd Wright's famous perspectives were done from photographs after the building was completed.[72] His rendering for the Larkin Company Building at the Jamestown Tercentennial was probably done from a photograph.

Perspective drawings of interiors, such as the small sketch by T. J. Collins ( FIGURE 4.52 ), or the one by Frye and Chesterman for the First National Bank, Lynchburg ( SURVEY NO. 70 ), are relatively rare. Most architects prefer elevations for interiors; they are, of course, easier to draw. But interior drawings, by and large, are not very common compared to the many exterior elevations and perspectives that have survived. This indicates that while architects may think in terms of space, still their common preoccupation is with the building as a form in space, not as a spatial enclosure in which people live or work. The Collins sketch is very unusual and may possibly have been copied from a plan book.

Some architects, such as Frank Lloyd Wright, Milton Grigg, or James Wines (SITE), did continue to do their own presentations, but increasingly the splashy presentation was done by either an office specialist or a free-lance renderer. At times these professional renderers became very influential. Hugh Ferriss, for example, helped create an entire look for the 1920s and 1930s (see his perspective for National Airport, SURVEY NO. 97 ). There are today many firms

FIGURE 4.52. *Among the rarest types of architectural drawings is the* **Interior** perspective, *such as this one drawn by William M. Collins (1874–1953) for the* **C. W. Miller House,** *Staunton, Virginia, circa 1900. Watercolor, 5 ½ by 7 inches. (Photograph courtesy of T. J. Collins & Son, Staunton.)*

such as Brackett, Zimmermann Associates (see Center for Innovative Technology, SURVEY NO. 115 ) that specialize in producing presentation renderings for architects, or for the building's clients.

## *The Future of Architectural Drawing*

Beginning tentatively in the 1970s and growing with force in the succeeding decades has been the introduction of computers into the architect's office. The field is expanding so rapidly and contains so many complexities that any sort of judgment must be tempered by both the unknown future and the superficial knowledge of the recent past. Computer-aided design has tended towards several changes in the architect's relation to the drawing process. The first and most obvious has been the increasing use of computers to produce working drawings, more often in larger offices, which have more resources at their disposal. The laborious and time-consuming drawing of every detail by hand has been replaced by computers. While this has spared the draftsman this task, it has also replaced him or her. The use of the computer not only means fewer entry-level jobs, but also the absence of an opportunity by which young architects could traditionally learn how a building is constructed. This trend toward computerization of drawing fits with the trend toward further removal of the architect from the actual building process and the growing trend toward mechanization in many professions and industries. The other recent shift has been toward actual designing with the aid of a computer, no longer using the older method of pencil on paper. This speeds up the process since square-footage requirements and zoning regulations for a particular site can be contained in the computer program. Within a matter of minutes a variety of building forms, massing solutions, and other factors are presented in a series of graphic displays on the computer screen, and the design options can be explored. The presentation on the CRT screen or video monitor can be amazingly accurate, as good as any draftsman can achieve through many hours of work. Using this system, clients may not even need a paper printout (known as "hard copy") since telephone-interface modems and computer networks allow the clients to see what the architect has done, right on their own terminal monitor. They might even make suggestions as the building is being designed. Still in its infancy, total design of buildings by computer depends on some sort of standardization of program. This seems to imply that only certain parameters can be explored. In other words, the architect would be bound by what the computer allows and certain flights of fancy would no longer be possible. Of course, architects have always been bound by some constraints: paper is only a two-dimensional medium, models can never be full-scale, and the architect can perhaps never realize the dream that exists only in his or her mind.

With computer-aided design at its present stage of development, one traditional element still remains: paper printouts of the computer-generated drawings are still needed by the builder or contractor. What the future may bring could be the absence of anything in tangible form. Eventually, all the components of a structure—and this is certainly far in the future—might be ordered and assembled through computer-generated directions.

But this is speculating. For now, the goal of most architects is safely conservative. The preferred office size is, for the most part, relatively small, six to eight persons which precludes any "gee-whiz" science-fiction futurology. But where computer-aided design does create problems is that more and more of Virginia's landscape—malls and shopping centers—are not designed by architects in small local offices, but by large out-of-state developers who have no knowledge of local building traditions, much less any sensitivity or loyalties to precedent. And that is precisely where the difficulty lies. Whether this new technological tool can be harnessed to the production of responsible architecture is the challenge of the future.

Looking back on these historic drawings and the buildings that resulted from them, we can see that architectural drawings are but one entry into the world of architecture. In many cases they are also compelling and wonderful as drawings. In some cases they show what a building might have been, what the architect intended before the realities of budgets, construction costs, workmanship, and other impediments intervened. In some cases they are better than the completed building. But they are never substitutes.

1. The colonial buildings cited in this essay are in most instances discussed at greater length in Chapter 1.

2. Dell Upton, *Holy Things and Profane: Anglican Parish Churches in Colonial Virginia* (New York and Cambridge: Architectural History Foundation/MIT Press, 1986), 11, 14, 23–24; Carl Lounsbury, "The Structure of Justice: The Courthouses of Colonial Virginia," in *Perspectives in Vernacular Architecture* 3 (Columbia: University of Missouri Press, 1989), 3:214–26.

3. A few craftsmen-undertakers were extremely successful: Larkin Chew (died 1729) built so many public structures in the Tidewater area that he was elected a justice, sheriff, and Burgess (Upton, *Holy Things and Profane,* 23–28, 357.)

4. For examples of the one-and-a-half story wooden houses built in Williamsburg, see Marcus Whiffen, *The Eighteenth-Century Houses of Williamsburg, A Study of Architecture and Building in the Colonial Capital of Virginia* (Williamsburg: Colonial Williamsburg, 1960).

5. Upton, *Holy Things and Profane,* 33–34.

6. Whiffen, *Houses of Williamsburg,* 28–30.

7. J. Moxon, *Mechanick Exercises; or the Doctrine of Handy-Works. Applied to the Art of Bricklayers-Works* (London, 1700), 15–16.

8. James D. Kornwolf, in his thorough study of the College (*"So Good A Design," The Colonial Campus of the College of William and Mary: Its History, Background, and Legacy* [Williamsburg: Joseph and Margaret Muscarelle Museum of Art, College of William and Mary, 1989], 33–56, 109–11) presents a strong argument that Jones's attribution of the building to Wren should be accepted as fact until proven incorrect. Hugh Jones, *The Present State of Virginia,* ed. Richard L. Morton (Chapel Hill: University of North Carolina Press, 1956), 67. See also Marcus Whiffen, *The Public Buildings of Williamsburg, Colonial Capital of Virginia: An Architectural History* (Williamsburg: Colonial Williamsburg, 1958), 28–32.

9. Whiffen, *Public Buildings of Williamsburg,* 34–48; Carl R. Lounsbury, "Beaux-Arts Ideals and Colonial Reality: The Reconstruction of Williamsburg's Capitol, 1928–1934," *Journal of the Society of Architectural Historians* 49 (December, 1990), 373–89; Kornwolf, *"So Good A Design,"* 126–29. The plat by "Mr. Jeffery" is in volume 2 of the Ambler Family Papers (1709–1809), Library of Congress.

10. *Journals of the House of Burgesses of Virginia, 1659/60–93,* 208, cited in Henry Chandlee Forman, *Jamestown and St. Mary's, Buried Cities of Romance* (Baltimore: Johns Hopkins Press, 1938), 120; Whiffen, *Public Buildings of Williamsburg,* 53–58; Kornwolf, *"So Good A Design,"* 134–35. The earliest known reference in any of the Tidewater settlements to the use of a plat, draft, or plan is in 1680 in Talbot County, Maryland (information from Colonial Williamsburg courtesy of Carl Lounsbury).

11. William Walker is identified in the St. Peter's Parish vestry book as "of the Parish of St. Paul in the County of Stafford Builder" (Whiffen, *Public Buildings of Williamsburg,* 134–35); Upton, *Holy*

*Things and Profane,* 34. Walker also supervised construction of Marlborough (Stafford County), the home of John Mercer, and built several prisons in the Northern Neck. I am grateful to Carl Lounsbury for sharing with me his knowledge of Walker and other early Virginia builders.

12. Whiffen, *Public Buildings of Williamsburg,* 98, 77.

13. Some of the prints that hung in Virginia gentry houses are cited in Wayne Craven, *American Portraiture: The Economic, Religious, Social, Cultural, Philosophical, Scientific, and Aesthetic Foundations* (Cambridge: Cambridge Univ. Press, 1986), 197; Marcus Whiffen, "Some Virginia House Plans Reconsidered," *Journal of the Society of Architectural Historians* 16 (May 1957): 17–19.

14. For a consideration of how craftsmen in England utilized notebooks, see Daniel D. Reiff, *Small Georgian Houses in England and Virginia* (London and Toronto: University of Delaware Press, 1986), 44–45.

15. See Whiffen, *Houses of Williamsburg,* 56–59 for his theories that both plans and elevations of some Virginia Georgian mansions have in common a sense of proportioning based on simple mathematical ratios or elementary shapes. It has been convincingly argued elsewhere by Whiffen (*Public Buildings of Williamsburg,* 80–82) that Alexander Spotswood devised the design of Bruton Parish Church as an exercise in geometry. Though the governor could have worked with numbers alone, it seems unlikely that he would not have sketched at least a simple plan and elevation to see the results of his mathematics. For a discussion of the geometric proportioning at Westover, see Mark R. Wenger, "Westover: William Byrd's Mansion Reconsidered" (M.A. thesis, University of Virginia, 1981), 108–21.

16. Examples of close borrowing from the plates of architectural books are found throughout New England and the South, whereas in Philadelphia—where some of the best craftsmen were located—direct copying was generally avoided. The English sources for Mount Airy and Brandon were pictured in 1945 by Thomas Tileston Waterman in *The Mansions of Virginia, 1706–1776* (Chapel Hill: University of North Carolina Press), 255, 366. Sources for Blandfield are cited in William M. S. Rasmussen, "Palladio in Tidewater Virginia: Mount Airy and Blandfield," in *Building by the Book* (Charlottesville: University Press of Virginia for the Center for Palladian Studies in America, 1984), 1:88.

17. Scott Campbell Owen, "George Washington's Mount Vernon as British Palladian Architecture" (M.A. thesis, University of Virginia, 1991); Matthew John Mosca, "The House [Mount Vernon] and Its Restoration," *The Magazine Antiques,* 135 (February 1989): 462–73; Waterman, *Mansions of Virginia,* 271–97; Upton, *Holy Things and Profane,* 128–32, 247–48.

18. Waterman, *Mansions of Virginia,* 322–23; Mills Lane, *Architecture of the Old South: Virginia* (Savannah: Beehive, 1987), 84–89.

19. Fairfax Parish, which commissioned Falls Church, paid James Wren to use his plan again, with alterations, at Christ Church, Alexandria (1767–73). Upton, *Holy Things and Profane,* 33–34; Lossing, *The Home of Washington* (Hartford: A. S. Hale and Company, 1871), 88.

20. Lane, *Virginia,* 64. Buckland's skills as a designer may have been slower to develop than his talents as a carver. His career is comparable to that of the contemporary and equally gifted Philadelphia carpenter Robert Smith, who designed large, impressive structures in a city renowned for distinctive architecture. One early house plan by Buckland that is documented (though now lost) was drawn in 1766 for Robert Wormeley Carter (William M. S. Rasmussen, "Sabine Hall, a Classical Villa in Virginia," *Journal of the Society of Architectural Historians* 39 (December 1980): 295.

21. Carl Lounsbury, "An Elegant and Commodious Building: William Buckland and the Design of the Prince William County Courthouse," *Journal of the Society of Architectural Historians* 96 (September 1987): 228–40. Buckland designed a polygonal porch for the Gunston Hall garden facade and used polygonal bays for the Hammond-Harwood house dependencies.

22. Ariss advertised his architectural services in *The Maryland Gazette* (May 15, 1751; cited in Lane, *Virginia,* 62). See also Upton, *Holy Things and Profane,* 34, 240, note 27.

23. The most celebrated statement of this unitary conception of architecture is Leon Battista Alberti's definition of beauty. The English translation used in our period gives it as "a Harmony of all the Parts, . . . fitted together with such Proportion and Connection, that nothing could be added, diminished or altered, but for the Worse"; see *The Architecture of Leon Batista [sic] Alberti, In Ten Books,* trans. into Italian by Cosimo Bartoli and into English by Giacomo Leoni, 3rd ed. (1755; reprint, with emendations, as *The Ten Books of Architecture,* New York: Dover Publications, 1986), Bk. 6, chap. 2. For important recent examinations of the early years of the profession in the United States, see Mary Woods, "The First American Architectural Journals: The Profession's Voice," *Journal of the Society of Architectural Historians* 48 (June 1989): 117–38, and Dell Upton, "Pattern Books and Professionalism: Aspects of the Transformation of Domestic Architecture in America, 1800–1860," *Winterthur Portfolio* 19 (Summer/Autumn 1984): 107–50.

24. The literature on the history of architectural drawing is extensive but scattered. I know of no modern, extended discussion of the international development. For a good recent introduction to architectural drawing and its history, see Jill Lever and Margaret Richardson, *The Architect as Artist,* exh. cat., Royal Institute of British Architects (New York: Rizzoli, 1984). On technique, see two indispensable sources, Maya Hambly, *Drawing Instruments, 1580–1980* (London: Sotheby's Publications, 1988); and Albert O. Halse, "A History of the Developments in Architectural Drafting Techniques" (D.Ed. diss., New York University, 1952). Books, especially exhibition catalogues, on American architectural drawings have appeared in some numbers during the last three decades. They have produced their most fruitful results in the form of the catalogue devoted to a particular locale, but they tend to ignore the drawings as drawings, and no synthesis of these volumes exists. I have derived much benefit from reports on early American architectural drawings by two University of Virginia graduate students in architectural history, Margaret M. Maliszewski in 1987 and Christina K. Hough during the 1989–90 academic year. For a major research tool, see George S. Koyl, comp. and ed., with Moira B. Mathieson, *American Architectural Drawings: A Catalog of Original and Measured Drawings of Buildings of the United States of America to December 31, 1917,* 5 vols. (Philadelphia: Philadelphia

Chapter, American Institute of Architects, 1969), supplemented by James M. Goode, comp., *Addendum to American Architectural Drawings* (Washington, D.C.: no publisher, 1977). For Virginia in the period under discussion, the two most important general works are William B. O'Neal's landmark exhibition catalogue *Architectural Drawing in Virginia, 1819–1969* (Charlottesville: University of Virginia, School of Architecture, 1969) and, to the extent that it illustrates a wealth of drawings, Mills Lane's *Architecture of the Old South: Virginia,* with editorial assistance by Calder Loth (Savannah: Beehive Press, 1987). In the United States, women began to make at least the occasional architectural drawing in the period 1770–1870. This author uses the non-sexist words *drafter, delineator,* to refer to an individual who draws.

25. Quotation from John H. B. Latrobe, "Memoir of Benjamin Henry Latrobe, 1st," Latrobe Family Journal, p. 50, collection of F. C. Latrobe III, Baltimore; photocopy, Papers of Benjamin Henry Latrobe, Maryland Historical Society. Charles E. Brownell and Jeffrey A. Cohen's two-volume study *The Architectural Drawings of Benjamin Henry Latrobe,* in *The Papers of Benjamin Henry Latrobe,* Series 2, Architectural and Engineering Drawings (New Haven: Yale University Press, for the Maryland Historical Society, forthcoming) analyses its subject in detail. On the closely related topic of Latrobe's landscape and figural drawings, see Brownell, "An Introduction to the Art of Latrobe's Drawings," in *Latrobe's View of America, 1795–1820, The Papers of Benjamin Henry Latrobe,* Series 3, Sketchbooks and Miscellaneous Drawings (New Haven: Yale University Press, for the Maryland Historical Society, 1985).

26. I have E. Lee Shepard, Senior Archivist at the Virginia Historical Society, to thank for tracking down the Warrenton Baptist Church drawings (fig. 4.16), or rather, the John R. Spilman Collection. Spilman appears to have been a nineteenth-century Warrenton builder and to have constructed the church. The Spilman Collection contains almost a hundred Warrenton architectural drawings, largely of quite utilitarian character, dating roughly from the 1850s to the 1880s. The scope and interest of the collection became apparent too late to do the materials justice in this book. On Warrenton Baptist Church, see Edna M. Stephenson, *History of the Warrenton Baptist Church, 1849–1988* (Warrenton, Virginia: Warrenton Baptist Church, 1988); Lane, *Virginia,* p. 223; and Harold N. Cooledge, Jr., *Samuel Sloan, Architect of Philadelphia, 1815–1884* (Philadelphia: University of Pennsylvania Press, 1986), 245. Construction of the church appears to have begun in 1860 (Stephenson, 18), the war interrupted the work, and the spire reached completion about 1870 (Stephenson, 23). Successive remodelings make it difficult to know whether the original form of the pulpit matched Sloan's drawing for it (fig. 4.16).

27. For etymology see *Oxford English Dictionary* under "section."

28. Quotation from Latrobe, "Memoir," 50.

29. Gavin Stamp, *The Great Perspectivists* (London: Trefoil Books, in association with the Royal Institute of British Architects Drawings Collection, 1982), 9, argues convincingly for the distinction between the *topographical architectural drawing* and the *architectural perspective.* As he points out, one occasionally has trouble telling to which class a drawing belongs. For more on this subject, see *Latrobe's View,* 27–28, and nos. 105, 119, 128, and 141.

30. Interior perspectives had begun to appear in England in the 1770s, and the line of descent appears to run from Adam to Joseph Bonomi to Latrobe. See Stamp, *Great Perspectivists,* p. 11 and no. 7, a Bonomi drawing strikingly like Latrobe's perspective for the Richmond Theatre Ballroom. One suspects that Latrobe took a good look at the variant Bonomi drawing exhibited at the Royal Academy in 1790.

31. Quotation from Latrobe to Godefroy, 27 May 1816, in Latrobe, *The Correspondence and Miscellaneous Papers of Benjamin Henry Latrobe,* ed. John C. Van Horne et al., 3 vols., *The Papers of Benjamin Henry Latrobe,* Series 4 (New Haven: Yale University Press, for the Maryland Historical Society, 1984–88), 3: 780–82, with further references.

32. For recent comments on pricking, a neglected subject, see Hambly, *Drawing Instruments,* 28, 47, 57–58, 125, 127. Prickers appear in many of Hambly's illustrations, not always with identification. Halse, "History," apparently confused pricking with the pouncing process used in painting when he attempted to account for the reproduction of architectural drawings (pp. 402–03).

33. For an example of pricking in Medieval architectural drawing, see Robert Branner, "Drawings from a Thirteenth-Century Architect's Shop: The Reims Palimpsest," *Journal of the Society of Architectural Historians* 17 (Winter 1958): 9–21. George Pastor, a University of Virginia graduate student in the Department of Architecture, made the discoveries about Virginia surveyors in a seminar of mine in the spring of 1991 and will, one hopes, publish his excellent work.

34. William L. Beiswanger, Director of Restoration, The Thomas Jefferson Memorial Foundation, Inc., originally drew my attention to Jefferson's use of scoring. On the technique see Hambly, *Drawing Instruments,* 11, 19, 57; and 127 on a similar tracing technique.

35. Once again I am indebted to the research of George Pastor, who has experimented with re-creating eighteenth-century inks.

36. The use of watercolor for architectural drawings by Latrobe and his successors depended upon the flowering of the medium in Britain. For a rewarding recent introduction, see Scott Wilcox, *British Watercolors: Drawings of the 18th and 19th Centuries from the Yale Center for British Art,* exh. cat. (New York: Hudson Hills Press, in association with the Yale Center for British Art and the American Federation of Arts, 1985). For more detail, see Marjorie B. Cohn and Rachel Rosenfield, *Wash and Gouache: A Study of the Development of the Materials of Watercolor* (Cambridge, Massachusetts: The Center for Conservation and Technical Studies, Fogg Art Museum, 1977), and Martin Hardie, *Water-colour Painting in Britain,* ed. Dudley Snelgrove with Jonathan Mayne and Basil Taylor, 3 vols. (London: B. T. Batsford, 1966–68).

37. Thomas J. McCormick, in *Charles-Louis Clérisseau and the Genesis of Neo-Classicism,* An Architectural History Foundation Book (Cambridge, Massachusetts: MIT Press, 1990), concentrates on Clérisseau, a master of gouache, as a painter of architectural views and fantasies. Chapter 8, however, permits one to sample Clérisseau's work in geometrical drawing in gouache and in watercolor; see especially notes 9–10, 12–14, 26.

38. I have not found a publication that draws together the newer literature on scale models, such as John Physick and Michael Darby, *"Marble Halls": Drawings and Models for Victorian Secular Buildings,* exh. cat. (London: Victoria and Albert Museum, 1973), and John Wilton-Ely, "The Architectural Model," *Architectural Review* 142 (July 1967): 26–32. On Godefroy see Robert L. Alexander, *The Architecture of Maximilian Godefroy* (Baltimore: The Johns Hopkins University Press, 1974), 102, 114–19, 145–46, 208; also Brownell and Cohen, *Architectural Drawings of Latrobe.* For Jefferson's lost pyramid, see Harold E. Dickson, "Jefferson as Art Collector," *Jefferson and the Arts: An Extended View,* ed. and with introduction by William Howard Adams (Washington, D.C.: National Gallery of Art, 1976), 121. For a 1798 description of Washington's lost Bastille, see Julian Ursyn Niemcewicz, *Under Their Vine and Fig Tree: Travels through America in 1797–1799, 1805,* trans. and ed. by Metchie J. E. Budka, Collections of the New Jersey Historical Society at Newark, vol. 14 (Elizabeth, New Jersey: Grassmann Publishing Company, 1965), 96.

39. For a sample of the evidence concerning the liking for models in Rhode Island and Massachusetts, see William H. Jordy, Christopher P. Monkhouse, and contributors, *Buildings on Paper: Rhode Island Architectural Drawings, 1825–1945,* exh. cat. (Providence: Bell Gallery, List Art Center, Brown University, et al., 1982) 9–11. On the model used to test the fireproofing of the Capitol shingles, see Latrobe to Jefferson, 28 November 1806, in Latrobe, *The Papers of Benjamin Henry Latrobe,* microfiche edition, ed. Thomas E. Jeffrey (Clifton, New Jersey: James T. White & Company, for the Maryland Historical Society, 1976), 51/E9 or 186/G1. On the 1849–50 competition entries, see John E. Semmes, *John H. B. Latrobe and His Times, 1803–1891* (Baltimore: Norman, Remington Company, 1917), 445–47.

40. Quotation from Jefferson, *Notes on the State of Virginia,* ed. with an introduction and notes by William Peden (1955; reprint, New York: W. W. Norton and Company, 1972), 153. On Jefferson and graph paper, see Peter Collins, "The Origins of Graph Paper as an Influence on Architectural Design," *Journal of the Society of Architectural Historians* 21 (December 1962): 159–62, and the exchange of letters between Sibyl Moholy-Nagy and Collins in the *Journal* 22 (May 1963): 107.

41. Joseph Michael Lasala dramatically enlarged the study of Jefferson by disclosing and analysing the erasures on the Rotunda drawings in "Comparative Analysis: Thomas Jefferson's Rotunda and the Pantheon in Rome," *Virginia Studio Record* 1 (Fall 1988): 84–87. The 1991 draft for his University of Virginia Master of Architectural History thesis, "Thomas Jefferson's Designs for the University of Virginia," carries the revelations much further.

42. On the South Outchamber, see William L. Beiswanger, "The Temple in the Garden: Thomas Jefferson's Vision of the Monticello Landscape," *Eighteenth Century Life,* n. s. 8 (January 1983): 170–88. For Clérisseau's section, see his bill in *The Papers of Thomas Jefferson,* ed. Julian P. Boyd et al., 23 vols. to date (Princeton: Princeton University Press, 1950–) 9: 603–4.

43. For a monochrome wash drawing by Bulfinch, see James F. O'Gorman, *On the Boards: Drawings by Nineteenth-Century Boston Architects,* exh. cat, Wellesley College Museum (Philadelphia: University of Pennsylvania Press, 1989), no. 1 and color plate 1.

44. On Dobie, see Lisa Marie Tucker, "Samuel Dobie's Design for the U.S. Capitol and Architectural Literature" (Master of Architectural History thesis, University of Virginia, 1990), which brings fresh insight to its subject but needs correction. For the characterization of Dobie's adeptness, see Edmund Randolph to Jefferson, 12 July 1786, in Jefferson, *Papers,* 10: 133–34; see also Dobie's advertisement in the *Virginia Gazette,* 25 and 26 October 1786. For the Capitol and President's House competition designs in the Maryland Historical Society, I have consulted a set of helpful technical reports at the Society, which the Library of Congress Examination Records prepared for these drawings in 1975.

45. The drawings are nos. 411–13 in Frederick Doveton Nichols, *Thomas Jefferson's Architectural Drawings . . . with Commentary and a Check List,* 5th ed. (Boston: Massachusetts Historical Society, 1984). Several scholars have connected the design with the "Bill of Particulars for a Building suited to a Public Officer as design'd by Thomas Jefferson—President of the U Sts.," Robert Mills Papers, Howard-Tilton Memorial Library, Tulane University. I am specially indebted to William L. Beiswanger and Douglas J. Harnsberger, who made a copy of the the bill available to me in 1982, and to Pamela Scott, who discussed the project in 1989 in "Thomas Jefferson and Robert Mills," a paper presented at "The South in Architecture," the Second Annual Symposium on Architectural History at the University of Virginia. With characteristic generosity, Scott has shared her manuscript with me and with Donald Matheson, who fruitfully studied these drawings for a 1990 seminar of mine.

46. For brief but significant comments on the preservation of the federal competition drawings, see John H. B. Latrobe, "Construction of the Public Buildings in Washington," a paper read when this Latrobe presented the drawings to the Maryland Historical Society in 1865; printed in *Maryland Historical Magazine* 4 (September 1909): 221–28. One would like a clear statement from his father as to why he saved these documents.

47. Architectural perspectives go back to antiquity by way of the Italian Renaissance; Vitruvius described one kind when he discussed architectural drawing in *On Architecture* 1.2.2. But perspective technique became established in British design practice only in the later eighteenth century. There, however, it enjoyed a unique flowering between the 1770s and World War II. See Stamp, *Great Perspectivists,* introduction.

48. For Minifie's remark, see his *Essay on the Theory of Color and Its Application to Architectural and Mechanical Drawings* (Baltimore: William Minifie, 1854), 150. For Davis, see the drawing inscribed "Wm. O. Yeatman. Richmond. Va." in the Metropolitan Museum of Art, A. J. Davis Collection, under letter Y (24.66.1569).

49. All the Monumental Church drawings vanished long ago. On the perspective, see George D. Fisher and Thomas H. Ellis, *History and Reminiscences of the Monumental Church, Richmond, Va., from 1814 to 1878* (Richmond: Whittet & Shepperson, 1880), 28; Anna Wells Rutledge, comp. and ed., *Cumulative Record of Exhibition Catalogues: The Pennsylvania Academy of the Fine Arts, 1807–1870; The Society of Artists, 1800–1814; The Artists' Fund Society, 1835–1845* (Philadelphia: American Philosophical Society, 1955), under "Mills, Robert," and "Strickland, William"; also Alexander Wilbourne Weddell, *Richmond, Virginia, in Old Prints, 1737–1887*

(Richmond: Johnson Publishing Company, under the auspices of the Richmond Academy of Arts, 1932), 45–47. For different readings of the evidence, see John M. Bryan, ed., *Robert Mills, Architect* (Washington, D.C.: The American Institute of Architects Press, 1989), 11, 13, 31 nn. 36–37, 56, 71 n. 38. Hitchcock's comment on Biddle's book comes from Hitchcock, *American Architectural Books: A List of Books, Portfolios, and Pamphlets on Architecture and Related Subjects Published in America before 1895,* new expanded ed., with contributions by divers hands (New York: Da Capo Press, 1976), entry no. 177. Biddle's counsel on ink comes from the 1810 reissue of *The Young Carpenter's Assistant; or, A System of Architecture, Adapted to the Style of Building in the United States,* 6. On the intertwined Alexandria and Washington price books, see Penny Morrill, *Who Built Alexandria?: Architects in Alexandria, 1750–1900,* exh. cat. (Alexandria: Carlyle House Historic Park, 1979), 28–29, 42–43. The price book lived on at least as late as *The Architect and Builder's Vade-Mecum and Book of Reference* (Richmond: Woodhouse and Parham, 1872) by the Richmond architect Albert L. West (copy in the Virginia State Library). F. H. Boyd Coons, a Ph.D. candidate in architectural history at the University of Virginia, has kindly allowed me to read his manuscript history of the School of Architecture. On the civil engineering program at the University before the War, see Philip Alexander Bruce, *History of the University of Virginia, 1819–1919: The Lengthened Shadow of One Man,* 5 vols. (New York: The Macmillan Company, 1920–22), 2: 126; 3: 48–49.

50. On Jefferson's workmen see K. Edward Lay, "Charlottesville's Architectural Legacy," *Magazine of Albemarle County History* 46 (1988): 28–95, especially 28–59, and Richard Charles Cote, "The Architectural Workmen of Thomas Jefferson in Virginia," 2 vols. (Ph.D. diss., Boston University, 1986). On Manson see Sarah Shields Driggs, "Otis Manson and Neoclassicism in Central Virginia" (Master of Architectural History thesis, University of Virginia, 1988). For an outline of architectural publication in the period see "Chronological Short-Title List," comp. under the direction of William H. Jordy, in Hitchcock, *American Architectural Books,* 137–41.

51. For a sampling of different evidence adding up to the same pattern of use, see O'Neal, *Architectural Drawing,* 28–29, 36–37, 56–57, 64–69, 72–73. This includes evidence from France in the Alfred Landon Rives Drawings, Special Collections Department, University of Virginia Library. In the early-to-mid 1850s Rives, a future engineer and occasional architect (see survey no. 50), was finishing his education at the Ecole Nationale des Ponts et Chaussées and made extensive use of what are now vivid cerise and blue-green inks on his India-ink engineering drawings. I have chiefly examined Oversize Tray 41, Folder 4. The apparently unpublished First Baptist Church perspective is in the Brown University Archives, Tefft Collection, Ch(AIV)1.1; for the literature on the commission, see survey no. 45, n. 3. Dr. Roger W. Moss kindly called my attention to Walter's Arsenal drawings in The Athenaeum of Philadelphia Archives, WTU*066. The pertinent drawings under this number are *002 and *004, with brown ink for the brickwork on *003. Davis's Journal is volume 1 of the Davis Collection in the Department of Prints and Photographs at The Metropolitan Museum of Art in New York; the Gay drawings appear on p. 125. The excellent research on Gay's patronage by Martin C. Perdue, a Ph.D. candidate in architectural history at the University of Virginia, deserves to see publication.

52. On the last years of pricking and the dating of translucent papers, see Hambly, *Drawing Instruments,* 125, 127. Halse discusses tracing paper, tracing cloth, and the blueprint in "Drafting Techniques," 402–03, 406–13; see also "The 'Blue' Copying Process," *American Architect and Building News* 4 (3 August 1878): 44.

53. An account of the rise and fall of Bowman and Young's procedures appears in Bates Lowry, *Building a National Image: Architectural Drawings for the American Democracy, 1789–1912* (Washington, D.C.: National Building Museum, 1985), 51–59. For a more detailed examination of their great building campaign, see Daniel Bluestone, "Civic and Aesthetic Reserve: Ammi Burnham Young's 1850s Federal Customhouse Designs," *Winterthur Portfolio* 25 (Summer/Autumn 1990): 131–56. On Davis's adoption of printed specifications for Belmead, see Patrick Alexander Snadon, "A. J. Davis and the Gothic Revival Castle in America, 1832–1865," 2 vols. (Ph.D. diss., Cornell University, 1988), 209–10; see also Marian Card, "A. J. Davis and the Printed Specification," *College Art Journal* 12 (Summer, 1953): 354–59.

54. For a wealth of evidence on the impact of outside publications during this period, see Lane, *Virginia,* chaps. 5–6. On the Richmond periodical, see Donald W. Matheson, "Design Harvest from the *Southern Planter,* 1841–1861: An Annotated Index to Articles on Home Design, Construction, Maintenance, and Other Aspects of Domestic Economy," Studies in Vernacular Architecture, under the direction of K. Edward Lay, University of Virginia, 1991 (one copy of which will be assigned a study number and deposited in the Fiske Kimball Fine Arts Library, University of Virginia). On the Cocke publications see, in addition to survey nos. 31 and 38, Calder Loth and Julius Trousdale Sadler, Jr., *The Only Proper Style: Gothic Architecture in America* (Boston: New York Graphic Society, 1975), 71; see also M. Boyd Coyner, Jr., "John Hartwell Cocke of Bremo: Agriculture and Slavery in the Ante-Bellum South" (Ph.D. diss., University of Virginia, 1961), 48–51, a reference patiently located for me by Bess T. Brownell.

55. The accounts of the Virginia Military Institute tell little about the history of drawing instruction, traditionally an important part of a military education. On Williamson and drawing, see pp. 36–37 in Edwin L. Dooley, Jr., "Gilt Buttons and the Collegiate Way: Francis H. Smith as Antebellum Schoolmaster," *Virginia Cavalcade* 36 (Summer 1986): 30–39, and Francis H. Smith, *The Virginia Military Institute: Its Building and Rebuilding* (Lynchburg, Virginia: J. P. Bell Company, 1912), 76. What appear to be student exercises after various sources survive in the Museum of the History and Traditions of the Virginia Military Institute and in the collection of Pamela Scott, Washington, D.C.

56. In an invaluable 1988 paper, my student Dana Reed sorted out the Hobbs story. My quotations come from *The Farmer* 1 (February 1866): 50, and 2 (June 1867): 182.

57. For Strickland's drawings of Grace Church, Cismont, made after his move from Philadelphia to Nashville, see O'Neal, *Architectural Drawing,* 34–39; also Lane, *Virginia,* 206.

58. Reginald Blomfield, *Architectural Drawing and Draughtsmen* (London: Cassell & Co., 1912), 4.

59. "Architectural Drawing," *American Architect and Building News* 1 (February 19, 1876): 58–59.

60. Blomfield, *Architectural Drawing,* 1, 3–4.

61. J. Stewart Barney, "Our National Style of Architecture will be Established on Truth not Tradition," *Architectural Record* 24 (November 1908): 384–385.

62. Richard Oliver in " America Now: Drawing Toward a More Modern Architecture," ed. R. A. M. Stern, *Architectural Design* 47 (June 1977): 445.

63. Arthur Drexler, ed., *The Architecture of the Ecole des Beaux-Arts* (New York: Museum of Modern Art, 1977).

64. Among the first (if not the first) exhibitions that treated architectural drawings was William B. O'Neal's *Architectural Drawing in Virginia, 1819–1969* (Charlottesville: School of Architecture, University of Virginia, 1969). In addition to those cited in the notes, there has also been David Gebhard and Deborah Nevins, *200 Years of American Architectural Drawings* (New York: Whitney Library of Design, Watson-Guptill, 1977); William H. Jordy and Christopher Monkhouse, *Buildings on Paper: Rhode Island Architectural Drawings, 1825–1945,* exh. cat. (Providence: Brown University, The Rhode Island Historical Society, 1982); Richard Guy Wilson, *Honor and Intimacy: Architectural Drawings by AIA Gold Medalists, 1907–1983,* exh. cat. (Washington, D.C.: The Octagon, 1984); Bates Lowery, *Building a National Image: Architectural Drawings for the American Democracy,* exh. cat. (Washington, D.C.: National Building Museum, 1985); James F. O'Gorman, et al., *Drawing Toward Building: Philadelphia Architectural Graphics, 1732–1986,* exh. cat. (Philadelphia: Pennsylvania Academy of the Fine Arts and University of Pennsylvania Press, 1986); Heinrich Klotz, *20th Century Architecture Drawings-Models-Furniture* (New York: Rizzoli, 1989); James F. O'Gorman, *On the Boards: Drawings by Nineteenth-Century Boston Architects,* exh. cat. (Philadelphia: University of Pennsylvania Press, 1989).

65. H. Van Buren Magonigle, "A Half Century of Architecture," *Pencil Points* 15 (March 1934): 16.

66. "The 'Blue' Copying Process," *American Architect and Building News* 4 (August 3, 1878): 44; J. Norman Jense, "The Early History of Blueprinting," *Architectural Forum* 71 (May 1932): 33.

67. Blomfield, *Architectural Drawing,* 5–6.

68. Robert A. M. Stern, "Introduction," in Stern and Deborah Nevins, *The Architect's Eye: American Architectural Drawings from 1789–1978* (New York: Pantheon, 1979), 11–13.

69. With some modifications I developed this categorization in Richard Guy Wilson, Dianne Pilgrim, and Richard Murray, *The American Renaissance, 1876–1917* (Brooklyn and New York: The Brooklyn Museum and Pantheon Books, 1979), 95–101. The list has also been modified by John Zukowsky and Pauline Saliga in *Chicago Architects Design,* exh. cat. (Chicago and New York: Art Institute of Chicago and Rizzoli, 1982), 20–31.

70. Egerton Swartwout, "An Architectural Decade" (Unpublished ms., circa 1930, copy in possession of author), 33.

71. "Hughson Hawley: Scenic Artist and Architectural Painter," *Pencil Points* 9 (December 1928): 761–774. Information on Deane is more difficult. See Eileen Michels, "Late Nineteenth-Century Published American Perspective Drawings," *Journal of the Society of Architectural Historians* 31 (December 1972): 302; and Michels, "A Developmental Study of the Drawings Published in *American Architect* and in *Inland Architect* through 1895" (Ph.D. diss., University of Minnesota, 1971), 97.

72. H. Allen Brooks, "Frank Lloyd Wright and the Wasmuth Drawings," *Art Bulletin* 48 (June 1966): 193–202.

CHAPTER 5

# THE HISTORIAN'S CHALLENGE

## The Search for Virginia's Architectural Drawings

by CALDER LOTH

FIGURE 5.1. *This detail of the drawing of* Sweet Briar House, *photographed before recent conservation, shows the irreversible signs of age and wear that have been the fate of so many architectural drawings. Such artifacts are often all that remain to tell the history of American architecture. (Compare with the restored drawing, survey number 44.)*

The survey of architectural drawings in the next chapter tells the story of Virginia's architectural heritage not through the buildings themselves but in the drawings and documents behind them. This sampling represents only the tiniest fraction of the wealth of Virginia-related drawings scattered throughout the nation and abroad. Assembling it has been no easy task. The absence of any organized, consistent approach toward the preservation of architectural drawings has hampered the study not only of the architecture of Virginia, but also of the nation as a whole.

To say that drawings and related records are essential to the task of piecing together architectural history would be an understatement. Some effort to solve the various problems of architectural record-keeping was initiated in 1973 with the formation of COPAR (Cooperative Preservation of Architectural Records), a national clearinghouse of information on the location, preservation, and cataloguing of this important facet of our nation's cultural history. But now, nearly two decades later, COPAR has been successful only in isolated instances in the monumental task of seeking out such documents and finding safe homes for them.

The barriers to preserving collections of architectural drawings are many, the main one being their bulk. The typical architect or architectural office produces an extraordinary quantity of drawings and related records. Holding on to such a volume of work is problematic. It is the exception rather than the rule for the archives of an architect or an architectural firm not to be destroyed when the architect dies or the firm goes out of business. Also, there is the problem of attitude. For most architects, and understandably so, the final product is the finished building. Drawings as well as models are usually seen as simply a means towards that end, not necessarily as items worthy of preservation for their own sake. Hence, architects can be very casual about keeping drawings. In many cases the best drawings, the presentation drawings, end up the property of the client, who can also be casual about their preservation.

Virginia, like many other places, has suffered the disappearance of original drawings for many of its most famous landmarks. If one could assemble a wishlist of lost or destroyed drawings for Virginia works it would include Sir Christopher Wren's drawings (or those of his office) for the Wren Building at the College of William and Mary; any drawings known to be the hand of a colonial architect such as William Buckland, Richard Taliaferro, James Wren, or John Ariss; Robert Mills's drawings for Monumental Church; George Hadfield's drawings for Arlington House; James Dinsmore's drawings for Estouteville; John E. Johnson's drawings for the Bruce family mansions Berry Hill and Staunton Hill; Minard Lefever's drawings for Richmond's Second Presbyterian Church; William M. Poindexter's drawings for Randolph Macon Woman's College in Lynchburg; and Duncan Lee's drawings for the restoration of Carter's Grove.

Fortunately, for one reason or another, many architectural drawings and related records are sometimes preserved. Frequently it is simply by chance. Someone instinctively realizes that there is archival or artistic value either in individual pieces or in a whole collection, and has them turned over to an appropriate repository. Likewise in some situations, particularly when the government is the client, the drawings become classified as official documents and are preserved as government records.

Yet there remains no thorough guide to the myriad locations of architectural drawings. One important exception, compiled by George S. Koyle and published in 1969, is *American Architectural Drawings: A Catalog of Original and Measured Drawings of Buildings of the United States of America to December 31, 1917.* This pioneering work, a project of the Philadelphia Chapter of the American Institute of Architects, provides an excellent model for more extensive endeavors. Koyle's catalog lists drawings in the collections of seventy-three principal but selected repositories across the country. The catalog was invaluable as a primary reference for this work, particularly for locating items out-of-state. But Koyle's document is a very limited guide to drawings located in Virginia, because it covers the collections of only two Virginia institutions: the Virginia State Library and the University of Virginia. Many other important repositories, such as the Virginia Historical Society and The Valentine Museum, are not included.

The search for Virginia-related architectural drawings thus differs little from the hunt for leads in any research project. One has to think of as many likely sources as possible and then to visit each one, painstakingly looking through catalogues, indexes, and the collections themselves, which frequently are inadequately inventoried. A starting-point for this project has been the archives of the Virginia Department of Historic Resources. While this agency does not collect original drawings, in the course of preparing research reports leading to the nomination of buildings as historic landmarks, the department's staff has noted the existence of numerous original drawings. Often it might be a single document in private ownership, such as the drawing of Melrose ( survey no. 4 7 ), still in the possession of the builder's descendants. More than two decades ago, one of the department's field staff located the impressive rendering of Morven Park ( survey no. 4 9 ), also in private ownership, and since then held by the Westmoreland Davis Foundation. Only recently, research undertaken by the department on Virginia Episcopal School in Lynchburg, revealed the existence of the original working drawings of the school complex by the prominent Washington architect Frederick H. Brooke, who worked with Sir Edwin Lutyens on the British Embassy.

The Virginia Historical Society's holdings of architectural drawings are not extensive, but it does possess some of the oldest and indeed rarest Virginia architectural drawings, including those few, other than Thomas Jefferson's, that date from the eighteenth century. These drawings have generally come to the Society as individual items, usually among family papers, such as the Menokin drawings ( survey no. 3 ), which were found among the Tayloe family manuscripts. Nor has the Virginia State Library made a point of collecting architectural drawings, but still it holds some very significant pieces, including Latrobe's drawings of the Virginia State Penitentiary and the drawings for the Washington Monument competition ( survey nos. 1 6, 1 7, 2 2 ).

Amazingly, the extensive output of drawings by Thomas Jefferson, B. Henry Latrobe, and Alexander Jackson Davis—three major early American architects who worked in Virginia—does survive, though spread among various institutions. The fact that the scores of Jefferson drawings have been preserved probably marks the first instance in this country of the recognition that such drawings have historic value. Nearly all of Jefferson's drawings for the University of Virginia remain at that institution. The largest body of Jefferson drawings, however, are in the Massachusetts Historical Society, donated by Thomas Jefferson Coolidge, a Jefferson descendant. The drawings of both Latrobe and Davis are in themselves of great artistic merit and may have been saved in no small part because of their aesthetic quality. Many of Latrobe's beautiful renderings are in the collections in the Library of Congress, the Maryland Historical Society and, as already noted, the Virginia State Library. Davis's many elegant drawings, including a significant number for Virginia commissions, are housed primarily in the Metropolitan Museum of Art, New York; the New York Public Library; the New-York Historical Society; and the Avery Architectural and Fine Arts Library at Columbia University. Also, among the vast architectural collections at Avery Library are Virginia-related drawings by Ralph Adams Cram, Calvin Pollard, Richard Upjohn, and Napoleon LeBrun.

It never ceases to amaze what turns up where. That drawings for Virginia projects are scattered far and wide results mainly from the fact that Virginians so often turned to architects outside the state for their designs. Among other institutions that hold Virginia drawings is Brown University, with its drawings by the Rhode Island architect Thomas Tefft for the Richmond Female Institute ( survey no. 4 5 ) and the First Baptist Church in Alexandria ( figure 4 . 3 4 ). The Athenaeum of Philadelphia has within its outstanding architectural collections drawings for Virginia commissions beautifully rendered by Thomas U. Walter, part of the large assemblage of Walter drawings the Athenaeum was fortunate to acquire from Walter's descendants. Also in the Athenaeum are drawings by Thomas S. Stewart for the Egyptian Building of the Medical College of Virginia ( SURVEY NO. 37 ); records relating to the construction of St. Paul's Episcopal Church, Richmond; and John Notman's proposal for the Washington Monument in Richmond ( SURVEY NO. 42 ). The American Antiquarian Society in Worcester, Massachusetts, has among its Alexander Parris documents the drawings for Richmond's Wickham House ( SURVEY NO. 24; now part of The Valentine Museum), and Parris's floor plan for the Virginia Governor's Mansion.

The National Archives in Washington, D.C., is a treasure-trove for drawings of buildings and works sponsored by the federal government, including post offices, courthouses, customs houses, and even the Pentagon. The Library and Archives of the American Institute of Architects, also in Washington, has various drawings by Washington architects for projects in northern Virginia. Recently noted in Delaware, at the Winterthur Museum, were drawings by Baltimore architect Robert Cary Long, Jr., for the Virginia School for the Deaf and the Blind ( SURVEY NO. 33 ). Lastly, one can even go abroad in the search for Virginia architectural documents. In the archives of London's Royal Institute of British Architects are C. A. Busby's drawings for the long-gone Bollingbrooke Theater (1817; SURVEY NO. 25 ) in Petersburg.

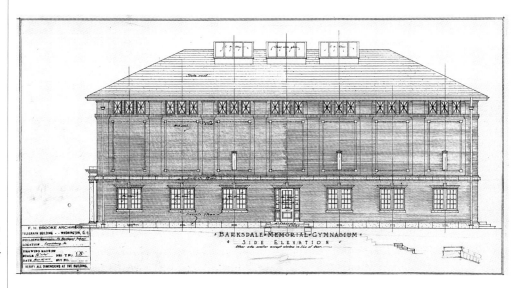

FIGURE 5.2. *This working drawing (1917) by Frederick H. Brooke for* Barksdale Memorial Gymnasium, *was recently discovered in the archives of Virginia Episcopal School, Lynchburg.*

Naturally, in seeking out Virginia architectural drawings, the search will be more fruitful inside the state. Probably the most active patrons of quality architecture are Virginia's colleges and universities. By visiting key educational institutions across the state, researchers have brought forth a variety of significant documents. Some schools have diligently preserved original drawings of their buildings simply as part of good record-keeping ( FIGURE 5.2 ). The University of Virginia, of course, stands out with its important assemblage of Jefferson's drawings for the original building complex, and has kept the drawings for many of its other buildings, including John R. Thomas's delineations for Brooks Hall ( SURVEY NO. 54 ), the drawings for various proposals for the rebuilding of the Rotunda (most notably those of McKim, Mead, & White; SURVEY NO. 63 ) and, of course, has the drawings for nearly all of its recent buildings. Important special collections owned by the University are the Cocke Family papers, with their many intriguing drawings relating to Bremo, the Cocke estate in Fluvanna County ( SURVEY NO. 29 ). Found within the diverse holdings of the University's Rives manuscripts are the original drawings of Grace Church, Cismont, the only building in Virginia designed by William Strickland.

Washington and Lee University has been diligent in preserving architectural drawings related both to its own buildings and to buildings in the town of Lexington. Likewise one of the treasures of the neighboring Virginia Military Institute is the collection of drawings by Alexander Jackson Davis for the original V.M.I. complex.

Although one would hope for an equally extensive set of drawings by Richard Morris Hunt for his works at Hampton University, such is not the case. Fortunately at least one Hunt drawing is preserved—not there, but in the American Institute of Architects Foundation in Washington, D.C. Hampton does, however, hold drawings for some of its other buildings, including those by Hilyard R. Robinson, one of Virginia's pioneering African-American architects.

An obvious and unusually rich source of Virginia architectural drawings is the architects' offices themselves. As already noted, the preservation of architectural office records is inconsistent. When firms close down, records, drawings, and models, more often than not are discarded or scattered. Especially lamentable is the loss of the archives of Duncan Lee, who produced many of Virginia's finest Colonial Revival buildings and who was involved with the restoration of numerous historic houses. The main out-of-state firms that suffered the loss of the major part of their drawings are Carrère and Hastings and John Russell Pope. By mere chance did many of Carrère and Hastings' working drawings for the Hotel Jefferson ( SURVEY NO. 62 ) survive in the hotel basement. Regrettably, there are no known original drawings by Pope for his two outstanding Virginia commissions: Broad Street Station (now the Virginia Science Museum) and the Branch House, both in Richmond. Only blueprints survive. An exception to the usual loss of a firm's records are the preserved papers and drawings of Lynchburg architect Stanhope Johnson, preserved and catalogued by S. Allen Chambers as a special project of the Jones Memorial Library.

Fortunately, a number of Virginia architectural firms have excellent archives of their own output since their founding in the beginning of the century. The most extensive and impressive is that of the Richmond firm presently known as Baskervill & Son, whose office is a treasury of drawings of elegant houses, churches, and institutional buildings by the firm's early partners: Henry Baskervill, A. Gary Lambert, and William C. Noland. Two other venerable Richmond firms—Wright, Cox & Smith, and Carneal & Johnston—have extensive archives of their work. Outside Richmond, the drawings of T. J. Collins have been preserved by the firm he founded in Staunton in the late nineteenth century. Also, the output of the remarkable career of Milton T. Grigg, one of the state's foremost restoration and residential architects, is maintained by his successor firm, Browne, Eichman, Dalgliesh, Gilpin & Paxton. Other noteworthy firms could be named, and it is hoped that the majority of them will eventually have their papers safely preserved and accessible in archival repositories.

Outstanding among the specialized collections of drawings in the state are the archives of the Colonial Williamsburg Foundation, which has carefully preserved the records of all its restorations, reconstructions, and new buildings, as well as working drawings, sketches, perspectives, photographs, and models. The elegant draftsmanship of many of the drawings (see SURVEY NOS. 83–86, for example) marks them as interesting documents of the style and technique of a past era. But these are especially significant documents, not only because of their association with many prominent architects, but because the buildings in Williamsburg have been viewed and enjoyed by more people than any other group of buildings in the state and have had a profound and far-reaching influence on American taste.

It should be noted that many noteworthy drawings are still spread out among homes, churches, businesses, small museums, historical societies, and private collections. Some are treasured and well cared for; others remain forgotten or neglected in piles of old records, still waiting to be discovered. Churches are often fruitful sources for drawings and usually are responsible caretakers. In Norfolk, Christ and St. Luke's Episcopal Church proudly displays its richly colored rendering by Watson and Huckel (SURVEY NO. 72), as well as drawings for earlier churches of its parish. Another store of Watson and Huckel drawings, together with drawings by the great Gothic Revivalist Philip Frohman, is maintained by St. Stephen's Episcopal Church in Richmond. In the tiny community of Rapidan, the extraordinary Waddell Memorial Presbyterian Church, a landmark of the style known as Carpenter Gothic, preserves its drawings by John Danforth (see SURVEY NO. 51). In Roanoke, the city parks department has diligently held onto H. H. Huggins's ink-on-linen drawings for Mountain View, and the W. W. Boxley Company still has its cheerful rendering of the Boxley Building (SURVEY NOS. 69, 77). The list could continue *ad infinitum;* it is sufficient to observe that while many likely sources have been sought out for this project, scores more await the scholar's perusal.

In considering the scope of the Survey that follows, it is also important to note that what has been selected for illustration and discussion in this book represents but a handful of the hundreds of drawings and related items searched out and considered by the principal contributors and many other individuals who kindly shared their knowledge and assistance. Let us simply state that the search for Virginia architectural drawings is an ongoing process. It is hoped that this book, though unavoidably limited in its scope, will serve as a constant reminder of the inherent value of these documents in the study of our architectural heritage. May it also serve as a reminder of the vital necessity to preserve them and to make known their whereabouts.

FIGURE 5.3. *The Italian-Villa-Style plantation house,* Winterham, *to be built in Amelia County, was designed by Virginia architect Thomas Tabb Giles around 1840. This* Front Elevation *for Winterham was only recognized as a historic document when discovered in an antique shop in Richmond, more than 150 years later.*

*Front Elevation.*

Finally, there is a sense of drama and surprise in this book and the years of research that brought it into being. Even as this book was going to press, a set of original drawings from circa 1840 surfaced in an antiques shop in Richmond. The drawings—by Thomas Tabb Giles, a little-known Virginia-born architect— are for Winterham, an Italian Villa-style plantation house in Amelia County. ( FIGURE 5.3 ).The drawings were promptly acquired by the Virginia Historical Society as its first effort toward establishing a formal collection of Virginia architectural records. This very incident reveals that a heightened awareness and concern for documentation and preservation of such materials can turn the historian's endless and diligent search into fruitful reality.

# 6

# THE SURVEY

*A Selection of Virginia Architectural Drawings, Studies, and Models, 1719–1990*

## EDITOR'S NOTES

Measurements are given by height, then width and, if appropriate, by depth.

When a drawing bears the maker's signature, the survey entry begins with the name of the maker; when a drawing does not bear the maker's signature, the survey entry begins with the phrase "Attributed to".

Drawings not described as signed or inscribed should be considered unsigned.

In those entries in which a list of References follows the Notes, both references cited and additional relevant sources are included.

Short titles that appear in the lists of References are cited in full in the Bibliography.

## CONTRIBUTING AUTHORS

| | |
|---|---|
| CCL | Calder C. Loth, Senior Architectural Historian, Virginia Department of Historic Resources |
| CEB | Charles E. Brownell, Associate Professor of Architectural History, Virginia Commonwealth University, Richmond |
| CRL | Carl R. Lounsbury, Architectural Historian, Colonial Williamsburg Foundation, Williamsburg, Virginia |
| DAD | David A. Dashiell III, M.A. Candidate, Architectural History, University of Virginia, Charlottesville |
| DDMcK | David Duane McKinney, Ph.D. Candidate, Architectural History, University of Virginia, Charlottesville |
| DMcV | Douglas C. McVarish, Architectural Historian, Charlottesville, Virginia |
| EAC | Edward A. Chappell, Director of Architectural Research, Colonial Williamsburg Foundation, Williamsburg, Virginia |
| JP | Jane B. Preddy, Theatre Historian and President "Architecture On Stage," New York City |
| MBC | Martha B. Caldwell, Professor, American Art & Architecture, James Madison University, Harrisonburg, Virginia |
| MCH & JA | Michael C. Henry, Watson & Henry Associates, Bridgeton, New Jersey; Janet Averill, Architectural Historian and Architect, Keswick, Virginia, and New York City |
| MEG | Mathew E. Gallegos, Ph.D. Candidate, Architectural History, University of Virginia, Charlottesville |
| MM | Michael McDonough, Architectural Historian, Chicago Architecture Foundation |
| MPC | Michael Patrick Corrigan, Architectural Historian, Richmond, Virginia |
| PCP | Peter C. Papademetriou, Professor of Architecture, New Jersey Institute of Technology, Newark |
| RGW | Richard Guy Wilson, Chairman, Department of Architectural History, University of Virginia |
| SAK | Susan A. Kern, Archaeologist, Monticello, Charlottesville, Virginia |
| SCO | Scott Campbell Owen, Architectural Historian, Seabrook, Texas |
| SSD | Sarah Shields Driggs, Architectural Historian, Richmond, Virginia |
| ST | Sergei Troubetzkoy, Architectural Historian, Tourism Coordinator, City of Staunton, Virginia |
| WMSR | William M. S. Rasmussen, Curator of Art, Virginia Historical Society, Richmond |

# 1.

# SWAN TAVERN

*Plan*

Yorktown
Presentation sketch, 1719
Scoring, pricking(?), pen and iron-gall ink on paper;
12 by 7 ⅜ inches, on folded page 12 by 14 ¾ inches
Collection of Clerk's Office, Northampton County Circuit Court,
Eastville, Virginia, loose papers

FIGURE 1. **Swan Tavern** *as it looks today, reconstructed on its original foundation in 1935.*

Richard King was a successful Williamsburg carpenter and builder who owned nine half-acre lots in that city and "2 books of Architecture."[1] By 1720, however, even with the spectacular Governor's Palace nearing completion, the new capital saw less building activity than did the major port of Yorktown, which grew from its founding in 1691 to a town of about 200 houses by the time of the Revolution.[2] A visitor in 1736 noted a "great Air of Opulence" in the town, houses of "Magnificence," a spirit of "unbounded Licentiousness," and "many" taverns "much frequented."[3]

Swan Tavern, which King built from this drawing, was commissioned on July 9, 1719 by two wealthy Yorktown merchants, Thomas Nelson—whose handsome brick house in the city is known by his name—and Joseph Walker. In the same year they purchased city lot number 25 where the tavern, destroyed in the Civil War, is now rebuilt on its surviving foundations (52 feet 10 inches by 31 feet 6 inches).[4] In "Articles of Agreement," written on the same folded page with the drawing, King agreed to construct for Nelson and Walker a one-and-a-half-story "Dwelling House," 51 by 31 feet, with a "12 foot pitch" (probably from the eaves to the roof ridge and from the ground to the eaves), "mundillion Eves" (a modillioned cornice), "12 sash windows," and "10 dormant [dormer] Windows." Thus the building was to be five bays long (four ground-floor windows and a door), with two ground-floor windows on each side elevation.

King, rather than his employers, must have designed Swan Tavern, for the contract is written in his hand. His "books of Architecture," whether English or Continental, would have emphasized the mathematical basis of the discipline, which King, as a carpenter, would also have noticed in the Williamsburg public buildings. Thus his drawing is determined by that discipline: the corner rooms, which vary considerably in size as do others in colonial Yorktown,[5] are three squares and a square-and-a-half, all based on multiples of the number six. Conversely, King's cross-passage—used as a wide living space and air-draught for ventilation—is a distinctly regional feature.[6]

King was to begin construction by 1 August 1719—three weeks after the signing of the agreement—and was to "continue . . . on the said Work [and no other project] until the same shall be perfected and finished." Nelson and Walker agreed to provide building materials ("such material and Scantlings as the said Richard King shall from time to time Direct") and to furnish "Lodging" for King and his "two other able Workmen." Typically for colonial Virginia, the important proportioning of elements and most details of construction and finish—much of the appearance of the building—were left to King's discretion to "Build Artfully & Substantially." He would be paid eighty pounds "within One Month" after completion of the work, but if that sum proved to be "not sufficient" for the work performed, he could bring in other builders (specified as Henry Cary, recent overseer of the Williamsburg Capitol and Palace, and Henry Pow-

ers) to appraise the finished structure. Without detailed drawings, which would have defined the intricacies of the building, its cost was as difficult to predict as was the duration of construction. Those matters would unfold as the structure went up.[7]

King's avoidance of elevation drawings and his use instead of the simplest floor plan with a written contract is evidence of a concise building procedure that was undoubtedly the one most often followed in Virginia throughout the Colonial period. However, of all the Virginia drawings before 1750, a number of which are known from documentary references, King's appears to be the only one that survives.

Even so rudimentary a drawing makes more use of craft than first meets the eye. The walls were laid out by scoring and almost surely by pricking before they were inked. In fact, the scoring and probable pricking facilitated the process by which the iron-gall ink (before conservation) bit into the paper and in many areas ate right through it. WMSR

NOTES

1. York County Records: XVI, Orders, Wills, 504, 588; III, Deeds and Bonds, 217–18. Cited in Marcus Whiffen, *The Eighteenth-Century Houses of Williamsburg, A Study of Architecture and Building in the Colonial Capital of Virginia* (Williamsburg: Colonial Williamsburg Foundation, 1960), 22, 40. In the Swan Tavern document King lists himself as "Richard King of Williamsburg Carpenter."

2. The town was significantly destroyed during the Revolutionary War. In 1796 traveler Isaac Weld described Yorktown as then containing about seventy houses and only one-third its former size *(Travels through the States of North America and the Provinces of Upper and Lower Canada. during the Years 1795, 1796, and 1797* [London: J. Stockdale, 1807], 1:163, cited in John W. Reps, *Tidewater Towns, City Planning in Colonial Virginia and Maryland* [Williamsburg: Colonial Williamsburg Foundation, 1972], 84).

3. "Observations in Several Voyages and Travels in America in the Year 1736," from *The London Magazine* (July 1746), *William and Mary Quarterly*, 1st ser., 15 (April 1907):222.

4. When the Nelson-Walker partnership was dissolved in 1722, Swan Tavern was described as "built by the said Thomas Nelson and Joseph Walker" (York County Records: III, Deeds and Bonds, 394). Information about Swan Tavern has been kindly provided by Jane N. Sundberg and James N. Haskett of the National Park Service, Yorktown.

5. The Augustine Moore house outside of Yorktown, for example, has on either side of its passage rooms of 17 feet 9 inches by 18 feet 5 inches, 17 feet 9 inches by 5 feet 3 inches, 15 feet 8 inches by 13 feet, and 15 feet 8 inches by 10 feet 9 inches.

6. See discussion of the cross-passage in Chapter 1.

7. The building business in early eighteenth-century Virginia was so newly established that accurate cost projections were beyond the abilities of most in the colony. In 1712, while overseeing construction of the governor's residence, Alexander Spotswood complained that "it was very Difficult to make Computations in this Country" (Marcus Whiffen, *The Public Buildings of Williamsburg, Colonial Capital of Virginia* [Williamsburg: Colonial Williamsburg Foundation, 1958], 90), further evidence that the use of detailed drawings and detailed planning were not the norm and that local craftsmen had devised no other means to project costs adequately.

REFERENCES
Wenger, Mark R. "The Central Passage in Virginia: Evolution of an Eighteenth-Century Living Space." In *Perspectives in Vernacular Architecture*, edited by Camille Wells, 2:137. Columbia: University of Missouri Press, 1986.

Articles of Agreement made and Concluded on this Ninth Day of July in the Year of our Lord One Thousand Seaven hundred and Nineteen Betweene Richard King of Williamsburgh Carpenter of the One part And Joseph Walker and Thomas Nelson Gent. of the other part as follow (viz:)

Imprimis the said Richard King for the Consideracons hereafter mentioned Doth Covenant and Agree to and with the said Joseph Walker and Thomas Nelson by these presents That he the said Richard King shall and will at or before the first Day of August ensueing the Date of these presents begin continue to perfect and finish a Dwelling House in the Town of York According to the fforme and Dimensions hereunto Annexed Which he doth hereby Oblige himself to Build Artfully & Substantially as soon as conveniently may be and to continue himself and two other able Workmen on the said Work untill the Same shall be perfected and finished as aforesaid.

Item The said Joseph Walker and Thomas Nelson Do and each of them Doth Covenant promiss and Agree to and with the said Richard King by these presents That they the said Joseph & Thomas on or before the said first Day of August shall & will ffind and provide Such materialls and Scantlings as the said Richard King shall from time to time direct and so continue to do untill the said House shall be perfected and finished And that the said Richard King shall not at any time be hindred in the said Building for want of materialls for himself or Workmen And also shall & will ffind & provide for the said Richard & Workmen all necessary [...] and [...] untill Such Work shall be compleated And also within two Month after the said Work shall be perfected & finished will and truly pay or Cause to be paid unto the said Richard King or his Assigns the Sume of Eighty pounds Curr. money of Virginia In Wittness whereof the partys to these presents have interchangeably Set their hands & Seals the Ninth day of July in the year of our Lord One thousand Seaven hundred & Nineteen

Rich. King      Thos. Nelson      Jo Walker

# 2.
# A FIVE-PART PALLADIAN COUNTRY HOUSE

*Elevation*

Prince George or Dinwiddie County (?)
Presentation drawing, circa 1770
Scoring, pricking, pen and iron-gall ink on paper;
5 ⅛ by 11 ⅝ inches
Collection of the Virginia Historical Society, Richmond,
Mssl Sk366 a151

The modest scale and appearance of this elevation—on the back of which is given a short list of vegetables—suggest the hand of an amateur architect. Yet on the drawing undeniable evidence can be found of scoring, pricking, and the use of a divider (see FIGURE 4.7), proof not only that its draftsman was familiar with current drafting techniques but also that such skills were more widespread in Colonial Virginia than previously supposed. Perhaps the designer of this house was a member of the Skipwith family, with whose papers it has descended. If so, it is akin to George Washington's elevation of Mount Vernon (SURVEY NO. 5): both project the appearance of a house planned for construction.

The Skipwith design, which may not have been built because a floor plan is conspicuously absent from the page, shows a single-pile, five-part Palladian country villa of an unusual type, derived ultimately from a plate (no. 3) in Robert Morris's *Select Architecture* (London, 1755; FIGURE 1) The Morris villa enjoyed some popularity in central Virginia, for the type lent itself well to a regional need for rural dwellings impressive in their length, well ventilated, easily constructed, yet not so large as to be overly expensive. The Skipwith variation closely resembles Battersea (Dinwiddie County [now Petersburg], circa 1765–75, FIGURE 2) and to a lesser extent Brandon (Prince George County, circa 1765; built by Nathaniel Harrison II), the handsomest of the group and the closest to Morris's in its use of seven parts instead of only five. Both houses must have been known to the Skipwith family, which lived and owned property in those counties: one member, William Skipwith (1707–1764), even listed his address in 1755—a decade before the present Harrison house was built—as "Brandon, Prince George County."[1] A lost "Brandon" in the same county, listed in an insurance policy of 1810 (FIGURE 3) as an immediate neighbor of the grander brick house with the same name, was a wooden five-part Morris type.[2] Though its design differs in proportions from the Skipwith drawing, it shares similarities. Both were surely second-generation Morris designs, influenced less by the book than by existing Virginia buildings. The dimensions of the wooden Brandon of 30 by 30 feet (center house), 18 by 18 feet (hyphens), and 20 by 20 feet (wings) probably approximate those measurements absent from the Skipwith drawing. The Skipwith elevation, in turn, provides a clue to the probable appearance of the wooden Brandon.

Morris, like many English authors, stressed the mathematical basis of architecture, known to Virginia builders from the earliest Williamsburg designs. Following that approach, the Skipwith designer devised an exercise in geometry which—as best one can reconstruct it—is a contrived arrangement of both modules and standard units of measure into 1:1, 1:2, and 1:3 proportions. The total expanse—possibly determined arbitrarily—is divided into thirds, making the center building unusually long, equal to the length of each hyphen and wing combined. Apparently the length of that module was then further divided, for one third of it is the height of the center building's first floor, and one half of it is a height in the end wings—the distance from the ground to the eaves and from the floor level to the peak of the gable. Other dimensions seem to have been determined by English measure: the height of the second floor is one inch, the width of each end wing is two inches, and the distance from the first floor of the center section to the peak of its gable is three inches.[3] Scoring lines allowed the draftsman to ink in easily the chimney tops, gable peaks, windows, and doors. Those bays are placed at one-, two-, and three-inch distances from walls. The scored arcs of a divider (compass), also visible on this drawing, show how little we know about colonial drafting. They may simply represent ideas not carried out.

This drawing—its traces of scoring and pricking never before recognized—proves that at least some builders in colonial Virginia used drafting tools and geometry to develop architectural designs. Since no similar drawing is known to survive from the colony, this example is significant.[4]                    WMSR

NOTES
1.  Extract on Skipwith genealogy from the *Richmond Times-Dispatch* (not dated), Skipwith Family Papers, Section 14, Virginia Historical Society. In the *Virginia Gazette* of 7 March 1755, William Skipwith of "Brandon" advertised for a runaway slave.

2.  Mutual Assurance Society policy no. 2182, dated August 3, 1810, for the "Plantation called Brandon," then owned by John Edloe, situated in Prince George County beside the "Lands of Benjamin Harrison on the East & South" (Richmond: Virginia Department of Historic Resources Archives). I am indebted to Calder Loth for bringing this policy to my attention. The use of the name "Brandon" for more than one house is explained by the term "Martin's Brandon" given to the early seventeenth-century patent of thousands of acres of land that eventually included both the famous home of the Harrison family and many other plantations.

3.  The distance of two inches also determines the placement of chimney tops (from the window bottoms on the wings and from the window tops on the center section); and the bottoms of windows are drawn at ¼ inch above floor levels.

4.  I thank Charles Brownell for coaching me on the subtleties of scoring and pricking, the marks of which—as intended—are barely visible to the untrained eye.

FIGURE 2. **Battersea,** *Dinwiddie County (now Petersburg), built circa 1765–75.*

FIGURE 3. *Detail,* **Mutual Assurance Society Policy of 1810, "Brandon,"** *Prince George County. (Photograph courtesy of Virginia State Library, Virginia Department of Historic Resources.)*

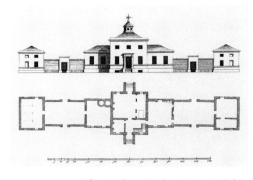

FIGURE 1. *Plate 3 from Robert Morris,* **Select Architecture** *(London: 1755).*

# 3.
# MENOKIN
## *Plan and Elevation*

Near Warsaw (Richmond County)
Presentation drawing, circa 1765–70
Pricking, pencil, pen and India ink with India ink wash on
paper; 13 by 16 inches
Collection of the Virginia Historical Society, Richmond,
Tayloe Family of Richmond County, Virginia, Papers 1650–1970,
Mss1 T2118 d 163

FIGURE 1. *Vintage photograph of* **Menokin,**
taken by Frances Benjamin Johnston in the 1930s.

Menokin was a thousand-acre plantation in Richmond County, Virginia, that John Tayloe II (1721–
1779) of Mount Airy deeded around 1769 to his
daughter Rebecca (1752–1797), wife of Francis Lightfoot Lee (1734–1797). The main house at Menokin
( FIGURE 1 ) was completed circa 1770; two
flanking dependencies were completed shortly thereafter. Abandoned for several decades, the house now
stands in very poor condition. The west dependency
has been demolished and the east dependency is in
ruins. Restoration remains quite feasible because of
the construction (rubble and stucco), the excellent documentation, and the survival of the interior woodwork, which is in the custody of the Association for
the Preservation of Virginia Antiquities.

The grouping is one of a handful of grand domestic complexes erected in stone in colonial Virginia,
among them Menokin's "parent," Mount Airy in
Richmond County, circa 1754–64 ( FIGURE
1.39 ). The main house is a three-bay, double-pile,
two-story structure with a central entrance and hip-
on-hip roof. Its basic form derives from the "detached
house" that had developed in late-seventeenth-century
England.[1] Numerous eighteenth-century Virginia
houses evolved from this prototype, though five-bay
examples predominate. As built, the plan and basic
form of the main house closely resemble the drawing.
In the plan, the off-center stair passage between two
rooms of unequal size runs only one bay in depth,
thereby allowing the rear-bay dining room to be the
largest room in the house. This scheme also appears at
Kenmore (Fredericksburg, 1752–circa 1756) and several eighteenth-century Maryland Tidewater houses.

Colonial American houses are characterized by
irregular architectural details, but the exterior details
of Menokin's main house are particularly idiosyncratic. The designer was likely influenced by pattern-
books, but he did not understand how Classical details
could fit together in coherent hierarchical compositions. Unorthodox relations exist among the windows
on the main facade (where the seven windows have no
fewer than four different patterns): the second-floor
and basement windows are more elaborately framed
than are those of the main floor, and the side-window
frames on the second floor are more elaborate than
those on the central window. Another detail appears
particularly awkward when seen from an oblique
angle: two belt courses are used on the main facade
and only one on the other facades. A more successful
departure from precedent is the incorporation of a
raised molding in the water table at the base of the
corner quoins that allows the quoins to be seen as
disappearing pilasters. This device occurs in the stone-
work of a number of Virginia buildings, such as the
main house at Mount Airy and at Pohick Church
(Daniel French, undertaker; Fairfax County, 1769–
74), and it may point to a related group of stonemasons. The visual importance of these details is heightened by their execution in dark sandstone, which
contrasts dramatically with white plaster walls.

Most of the internal decoration of the main

house is typical of Virginia plantation houses of the
period. The decorative program and scale of the dining
room defined it as the center of hospitality.[2] The exterior door in the dining room, which is on axis with the
main entrance, allowed for cross-ventilation. The interior details of the south dependency at Mount Airy
resemble the interior of the main house at Menokin.
Perhaps the same artisans worked at both houses.

Drawings for only a rare few eighteenth-century
American houses survive, and the Menokin sheet commands attention even in that select group. Its nameless
maker was not urbane and did not handle ink washes
skillfully, though the handwriting is reputed to be Tayloe's. But he did have the proficiency to use stable India
ink rather than the usual writing ink, to pull elevations
up from plans, and to draw dotted lines for elements
overhead. (With a touch of individual vivacity, he made
the two center chimneys emit smoke.) The remarkable
variety of window frames in the house postdates this
elevation, which shows orthodox, consistent decoration. But, both as drawn and as built, the grouping,
made of costly materials richly adorned, vividly
expresses the power of a family of grandees.     MM

NOTES
1.    See Reiff, *Small Georgian Houses,* and Upton, "Vernacular Domestic Architecture."

2.    For a discussion of the increasing importance of the dining room in eighteenth-century Virginia, see Wenger, "Dining Room."

REFERENCES
Lane. *Virginia.*

Lee, Francis Lightfoot, to Landon Carter, 23 July 1778. Virginia Historical Society,
Mssl L51f400 Lee.

"A List of Lands Belonging to the Honble. John Tayloe in the Northern Neck."
Virginia Historical Society, Mssl t2118d 161–162.

Loth, Calder. "Menokin: Concern for the Future of a Historic Landmark." *Discovery*
[publication of the Association for the Preservation of Virginia Antiquities] 18
(1986):6–7.

"Menokin." *Occasional Bulletin, Virginia Historical Society,* no. 21 (October 1970):
1–3.

Reiff, Daniel D. *Small Georgian Houses in England and Virginia.* Cranbury, New
Jersey: Associated University Presses, 1986.

Richmond County Deed Books: Book 2:501; Book 21, Part 2:495; Book 24:334;
Book 34:233; Book 120:107.

Richmond County Will Books: Book 9, Part 1: 62, 82; Book 11, Part 2: 661; Book 14:
222.

Tayloe, Rebecca Plater. Accounts, 1780–1782. Virginia Historical Society, Mss1
T2118b 15–19.

United States Department of the Interior. Historic American Buildings Survey, No.
VA-156 (Menokin).

Upton, Dell. "Vernacular Domestic Architecture in Eighteenth-Century Virginia." In
*Common Places: Readings in American Vernacular Architecture,* edited by
Dell Upton and John Michael Vlach. Athens: University of Georgia Press,
1986.

Virginia, Commonwealth of. Virginia Landmarks Register, File No. 79–11 (Menokin).

Waterman, Thomas Tileston. *The Mansions of Virginia, 1706–1776.* 1946. Reprint.
New York: Bonanza Books, 1965.

——— and John A. Barrows. *Domestic Colonial Architecture of Tidewater Virginia.*
1932. Reprint. New York: Dover Publications, 1969.

Wenger, Mark R. "The Central Passage in Virginia: Evolution of an Eighteenth-
Century Living Space." In *Perspectives in Vernacular Architecture,* vol. 2,
edited by Camille Wells. Columbia, Missouri: University of Missouri Press,
1986.

———. "The Dining Room in Early Virginia." *Perspectives in Vernacular Architecture,* vol. 3, edited by Thomas Carter and Bernard L. Herman. Columbia,
Missouri: University of Missouri Press, 1989.

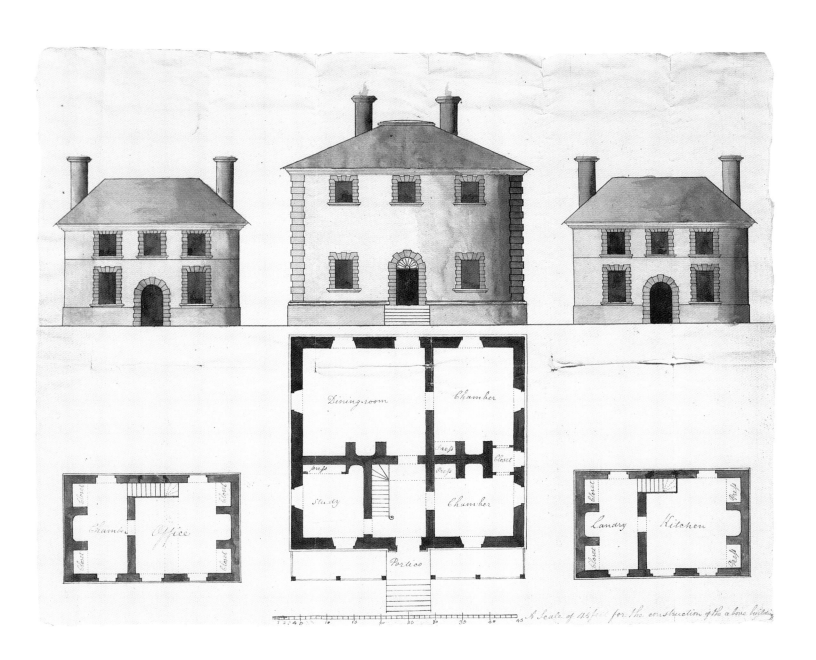

Dining-room

Chamber

press

press

closet

Study

press

Chamber

Portico

Chamber

Office

closet

closet

closet

closet

Landry

Kitchen

closet

press

closet

press

A Scale of 45 feet for the construction of the above building

Attributed to CHRISTOPHER FORD, died 1788

# 4.
# AMELIA COUNTY COURTHOUSE

*Plan with Specifications on Verso*

Amelia Court House (demolished)
Working drawing, 1767
Pen and ink on paper; 6 ½ by 14 inches
Collection of the Amelia County Circuit Court, Clerk's Office,
Loose Papers, 29 May 1767

In early Virginia, drawings played an important role in planning major public buildings. The design of most churches, courthouses, and jails was a collaborative effort, the product of a subtle interplay of ideas among a number of individuals working within a common building tradition. The form of these structures, initially developed in design sketches, was the result of the deliberations of building committees composed of magistrates or vestrymen who worked in conjunction with professional builders and craftsmen.

In the case of county buildings, the design process began with discussions among the magistrates about the overall size, shape, materials, and finish of a proposed structure. Generally, the bench authorized a number of its members to form a committee, whose task it was to develop a "suitable and convenient" plan. Most of these committees were content to agree on the basic size and materials of a new building and to leave the more detailed specifications in the hands of craftsmen who might submit their own plans for consideration. Once a committee had agreed with a particular "undertaker," or contractor, they might renegotiate with him specific design and construction details, which would then be ratified in a written set of specifications.

Integral to this debate over the design of a new church or courthouse were design drawings. The 1767 plan of a wooden courthouse for Amelia County is typical of most of the dozen or so public-building drawings that survive from the eighteenth and early nineteenth centuries. Nearly all courthouse sketches consist of simple floor plans, which indicate the location of doors, windows, partitions, and courtroom furnishings such as the magistrates' bench, sheriff's boxes, and lawyers' bar. Although the Amelia design was drawn by the undertaker, the carpenter Christopher Ford, others were often drafted by members of a building committee and reveal little regard for scale or drafting conventions.[1] A number are merely rough sketches with the major dimensions scrawled across the design. Representative of this latter type is the sketch for the design of an early-nineteenth-century jail in Westmoreland County, in which the elevational features are superimposed on the plan, a convention frequently employed in both England and the other American colonies for both design schemes and presentation drawings.[2] Drawings such as these were generally used in developing or confirming design decisions and, because of their diagrammatic nature, were not meant as working guides for craftsmen on the site.

The earliest evidence in Virginia of the use of drawings to convey design ideas for public buildings occurs in the first years of the eighteenth century. In 1702, for example, carpenter Larkin Chew submitted a "Mapp Platt or Draugh" to the Essex County magistrates to illustrate his proposed layout of a new courthouse.[3] By the second quarter of the eighteenth century, the use of a simple floor plan to convey information about the configuration of the building had become fairly common. Many specifications make reference to a now-lost "plan hereto annexed."[4]

Virginians seldom depended upon elevational drawings to convey design concepts. When they did appear they were used to show the size and relationship of openings as well as roof configurations on elaborate or unusual buildings. Elevations were drawn to clarify structural information, particularly in prison designs where the concern for security often required the employment of many unusual building techniques. In 1765 Orange County magistrates depended upon a plan and sectional drawing to illustrate their proposal for the complex construction of triple-thick prison walls capped by a solid brick roof covered with clapboards.[5] Because Virginians worked within the familiar patterns of well-defined regional building practices that needed little explication, drawings provided a useful medium to convey unusual ideas.   CRL

NOTES
1.    At the time of the letting of the courthouse, Christopher Ford was a resident of Amelia County. He had moved there in 1759 or 1760, after working as a carpenter in Williamsburg the previous decade. Little is known about his early training and building activities.

2.    Westmoreland County Clerk's Office, Loose Papers, 22 May 1826.

3.    Essex County Suit Papers, 11 April 1702. Dell Upton has noted a similar appearance of the use of drawings for Virginia churches about the same time. Upton, *Holy Things and Profane*, pp. 32–33.

4.    See, for example, Fauquier County Order Book 1763–1767, p. 111, 24 April 1764; and Orange County Loose Papers, Virginia State Library, Richmond, 28 November 1765.

5.    Orange County Loose Papers, 28 November 1765.

REFERENCES
Lounsbury, Carl R. " 'An Elegant and Commodious Building': William Buckland and the Design of the Prince William County Courthouse." *Journal of the Society of Architectural Historians* 46 (September 1987):228–40.

———. "The Structure of Justice: The Courthouses of Colonial Virginia." In *Perspectives in Vernacular Architecture vol. 3*, edited by Thomas Carter and Bernard Herman. Columbia: University of Missouri Press, 1989.

Upton, Dell. *Holy Things and Profane: Anglican Parish Churches in Colonial Virginia*. Architectural History Foundation Books, 10. New York, 1986.

Whiffen, Marcus. *The Public Buildings of Williamsburg, Colonial Capital of Virginia: An Architectural History*. Williamsburg Architectural Studies, vol. 1. Williamsburg: Colonial Williamsburg Foundation, 1958.

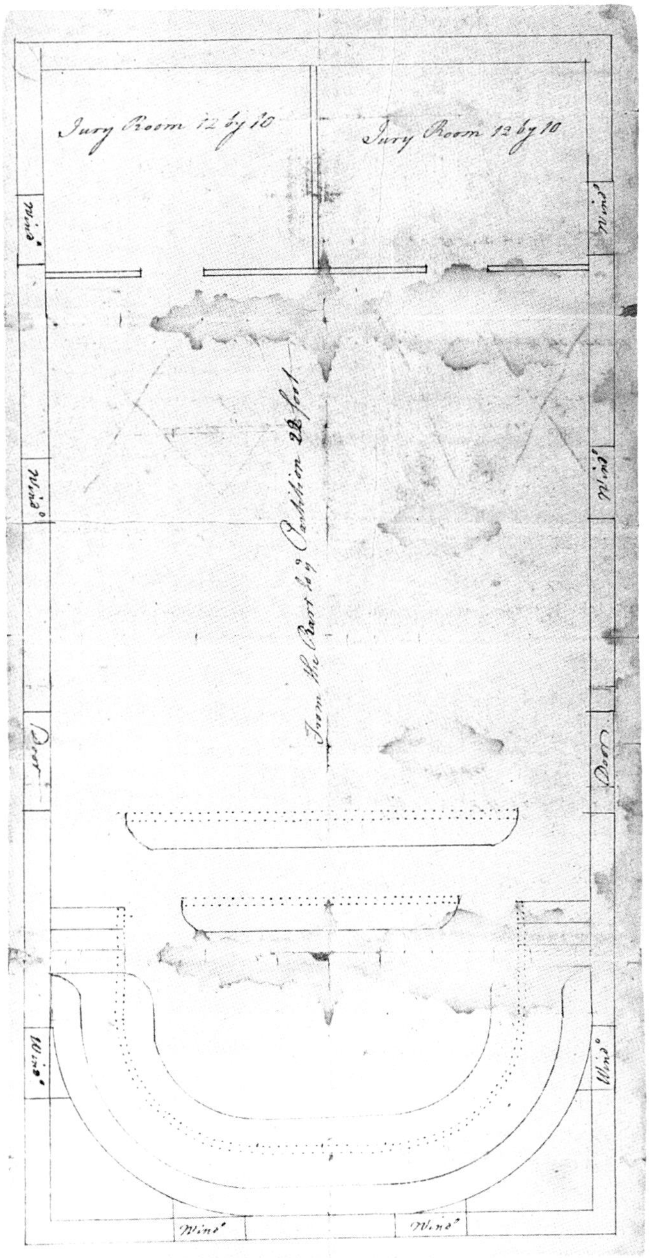
Jury Room 12 by 10
Jury Room 12 by 10
Wind°
Wind°
Wind°
Wind°
Door
Door
From the Barr to ye Partition 28 foot
Wind°
Wind°
Wind°
Wind°

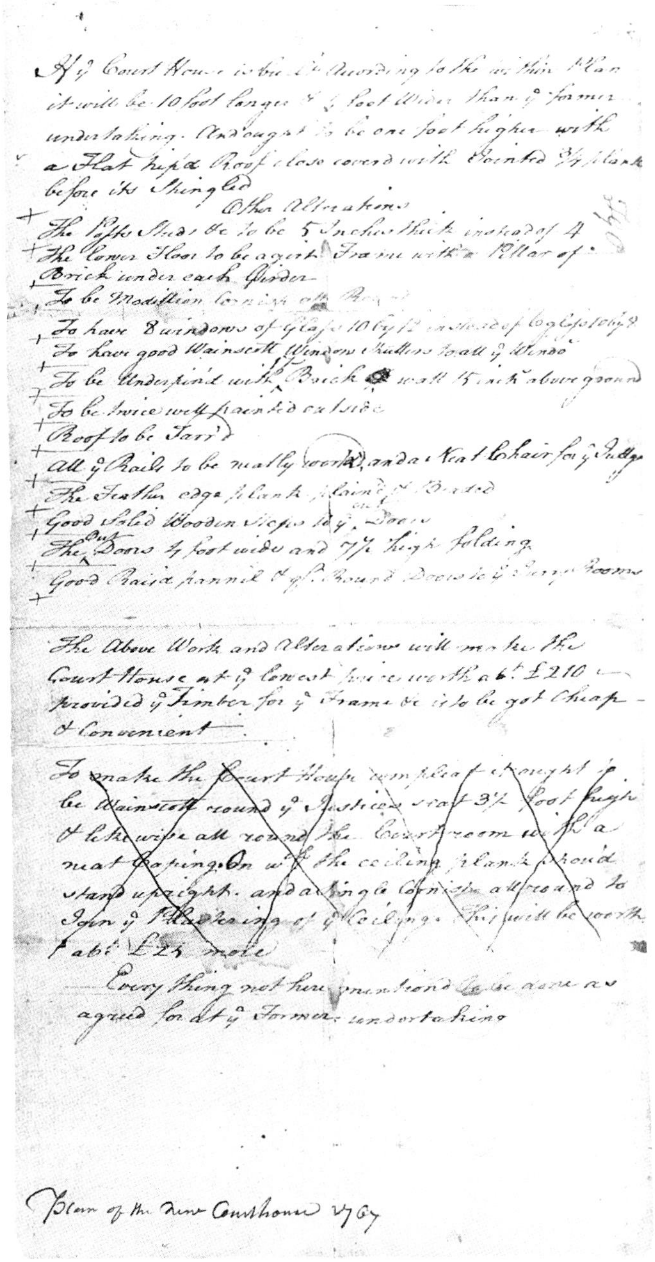
If ye Court House is built According to the within Plan
it will be 10 foot Longer & 4 foot Wider than ye former
undertaking. And ought to be one foot higher with
a Flat hip'd Roof close coverd with Pointed 3/4 Plank
before its Shingled

Other Alterations

+ The Posts Studs &c to be 5 Inches thick instead of 4
+ The Lower Floor to be a girt Frame with a Pillar of
Brick under each Girder
+ To be Modillion Corniss all Round
+ To have 8 windows of Glass 10 by 12 instead of 6 of 8 glass 10 by 8
+ To have good Wainscott Window Shutters to all ye Windo
+ To be Underpin'd with Brick ye wall 15 inch above ground
+ To be twice well painted outside
+ Roof to be Tarr'd
+ All ye Rails to be neatly work'd, and a Neat Chair for ye Judge
+ The Feather edge plank plain'd & Beaded
+ Good Solid Wooden Steps to ye out Doors
+ The Out Doors 4 foot wide and 7 1/2 high folding
+ Good Rais'd pannel & 1/2 Round Doors to ye Jury Rooms
+

The Above Work and Alterations will make the
Court House at ye Lowest price worth abt £210 —
provided ye Timber for ye Frame &c is to be got Cheap —
& Convenient.

~~To make the Court House compleat it ought to
be Wainscott round ye Justices seat 3 1/2 foot high
& likewise all round the Courtroom with a
neat Caping. On wch the ceiling plank should
stand upright. and a single Cornish all round to
join ye Plaistering of ye Ceiling. This will be worth
abt £24 more~~

Every thing not here mentiond to be done as
agreed for at ye Former undertaking

Plan of the New Courthouse 1767

# 5.
# MOUNT VERNON

*Elevation of West Front,
with Cellar Plan on Verso*

George Washington Memorial Parkway, near Alexandria
(Fairfax County)
Elevation drawing, 1774 or later
Pricking, pen and writing ink on paper; 6 ⅜ by 8 inches
Collection of the Mount Vernon Ladies' Association, W-1369/A

FIGURE 1. *Site photo,* **Mount Vernon,** *west front.*

Farmer, soldier, and statesman, the "Father of His Country," George Washington is the *other* U. S. president who functioned as an amateur Palladian architect. Washington's architectural role has remained far more poorly understood than Jefferson's, not only in respect to how he shaped Mount Vernon, but also in respect to how far he set the architectural terms for the city of Washington.

George Washington transformed Mount Vernon from an unpretentious farm equipped with an assortment of vernacular buildings into one of the grand American estates of the eighteenth century. At the outset of this process, his family's plantation had a story-and-a-half wooden house, very likely erected in the 1730s. The outbuildings included a set running diagonally off each end from the west, or landward, front of the dwelling.[1] In his first rebuilding of 1758 to 1763 and later, Washington raised the dwelling to two stories and an attic, and he developed the geometric layout adjacent to the house. The sweeping second rebuilding of 1774 to 1787 roughly doubled the length of the house while increasing the height to three stories. It added the celebrated east "piazza," the cupola, the west pediment, and the arcaded quadrants leading to two new western outbuildings. Washington now flanked the house with irregular groves overlooking the Potomac, and he replaced the geometric western approach with an "English garden": a bowling green set within a serpentine walk, "shrubberies," and "wildernesses," which screened out utilitarian structures and areas laid out formally behind them. He also replaced most of the outbuildings, an enterprise that continued into the 1790s. In the late 1790s, furthermore, he had to refurbish his house.

In the present connection, Mount Vernon matters for three reasons above all others: first, in the eighteenth century Washington memorably translated at Mount Vernon a group of ideas in the British Palladian orbit into local terms (see below); second, in the nineteenth century, the nation found there one great answer to the problem of how to honor Washington's memory and how to treat his remains (see chapter 2 for its discussion of Washington monument, and compare SURVEY NOS. 22, 42, 43 ); and third, the revival of "Colonial" architectural elements there has a history going back more than 130 years.

A comprehensive account of Mount Vernon would have to acknowledge the remarkable way that phase after phase in the fortunes of British Palladianism left its mark there, from the achievement of Inigo Jones through the early Neoclassical reactions to the Palladian legacy. Such an account would likewise have to acknowledge the remarkable ways in which North American traits surfaced here, such as the adaptation of the timber-building tradition to styles meant for masonry construction, or the use of porches as outdoor rooms. Such an account would also have to acknowledge that all this mixing at Mount Vernon had a number of incongruous results. In this mixture, however, the high points come in the reunion of British Palladianism with its great complement, the taste for

Picturesque settings, at an American site remarkable for its scenic beauty.[2]

Washington responded to the Picturesque movement with feeling. Writers have often remarked on one or another of his Picturesque tastes, especially because of the landscaping for his second rebuilding of Mount Vernon. The features of this landscaping (such as axially balanced "wildernesses") show only a tentative response, extremely old-fashioned by British standards.[3] The curved arcades from the same rebuilding represent the discovery of the landscape in a more distinguished way: whereas from Palladio onward, such wings normally had at least one closed side, and often served specifically to hide what lies beyond, Washington's arcades open up all the way through, delectably framing the scenery of the Potomac and its Maryland shore ( FIGURE 2 ). The "transparency" of the arcades seems to be Washington's inspired, Picturesque rethinking of a Palladian feature. His extraordinary piazza, an outdoor room for enjoying the same view—and the climax of Mount Vernon as an essay, it seems, in Tuscan themes—has a less straightforward relation to Palladian tradition. Its genesis, however, is unthinkable without British Palladian publications.[4]

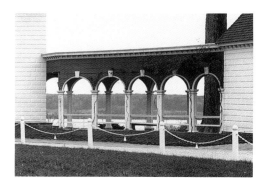

FIGURE 2. *Detail of arcade, showing "transparent" effect.*

Mount Vernon raises questions about Washington's intentions. Did he have in mind the principle that the Tuscan order suited architecture in the countryside, or the intimate associations between liberty and the English discovery of natural beauty?[5] In 1785 he wrote two of the earliest American documents connecting architecture with an ideal of importance for the next eighty years, the "republican style" of living, but the meaning of this ideal still awaits an authoritative interpreter.[6] To what extent did Washington, a man keenly conscious of how he appeared to an ever-larger world, base his designs on principles?

The Mount Vernon Ladies' Association owns three sheets of Washington's rudimentary architectural drawings. They are rare records of a Virginia planter's work in design, an area where Washington's neglected achievements retain a fresh appeal lacking in his military and political careers. The date and purpose of the severely faded example reproduced here remain uncertain. Washington probably first drew the cellar

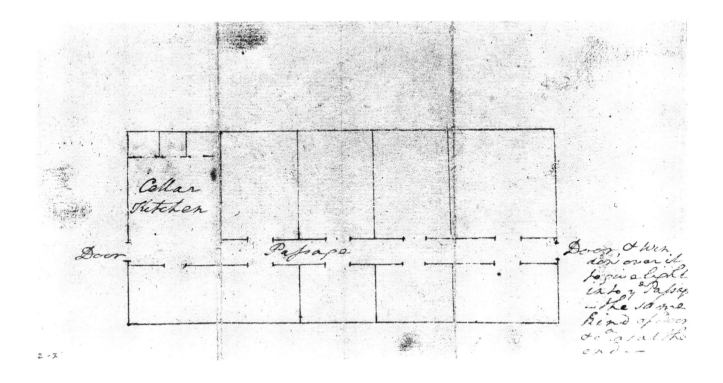

Cellar
Kitchen

Door                    Passage

Door & Win-
dow over it
to give a light
into ye Passage
in the same
kind of Door
to equal the
ends —

plan that appears on the back of the sheet and at some later point used this set of lines to make the elevation, partly by pricking guide points through the page. He may have made the elevation chiefly for some purpose connected with the cupola, which he drew in the most detail, along with numbers on each side, to match a lost key. Certainly the elevation records Washington's attempt to make his west front approximate a domestic manner somewhat overly associated in the eighteenth century with Inigo Jones ( FIGURE 3 ). Such houses typically have a simple, classicizing, horizontal body, with or without a pedimented center pavilion, under a dominantly northern European skyline, with a hipped roof, dormers, chimneys, and often a cupola.[7] The drawing differs extensively from the front as executed, above all because the irregularity of the old house prevented Washington from achieving this degree of axial symmetry.[8]                            CEB

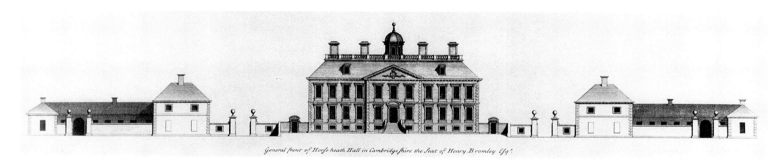

General front of Horse heath Hall in Cambridgeshire the Seat of Henry Bromley Esq.

FIGURE  3.  **Horse Heath Hall,** *elevation, from Colen Campbell et al.,* **Vitruvius Britannicus** *(London: 1715–1806).*

## NOTES

1.  The Mansion actually stands at an angle to the compass points. Thus the so-called west front faces northwest.

2.  The leading ideas in the discussion that follow have grown during exchanges with Scott Owen in the course of various graduate-level projects that have led to "Washington's Mount Vernon," his excellent Master's thesis, at the University of Virginia, Charlottesville. For more detail see that essay, which puts the design of Washington's plantation squarely into the realm of modern scholarship.

3.  Washington's response to the discovery of the Picturesque or, more broadly, of the landscape, expressed itself more strikingly in his acquisition of paintings and prints. The story runs from at least 1757, when his order of a "Neat Landskip" from London brought him a copy reputed to be "after Claude Lorrain," to the 1790s, when he bought not only a quantity of prints after Claude and other European landscapists, but also four paintings of American scenery by William Winstanley and two by George Beck. His attraction to landscape subjects stands out in an artistically narrow culture dominated by the tyranny of the portrait. Even beyond that, his interest in American scenes in the 1790s was altogether precocious. For the 1757 purchase, see *The Papers of George Washington*, Colonial Series, 4:132–35, 401–2; 5:49–51; for the copies in the 1790s see Wendy Wick Reaves, "The Prints," in *The Magazine Antiques* 135 (February 1989):502–11; for the American subjects (in relation to the aesthetic categories of Edmund Burke), see Nygren, *Views and Visions*, pp. 28, 49, 236, 304.

4.  For a 1796 commentary on the beauty of the site, the mingling of the formal and Picturesque traditions, and the use of the piazza, see Latrobe, *View*, pp. 22–24, 92–93, and Latrobe, *Virginia Journals* 1:161–72. For a complementary description of 1798, see Niemcewicz, *Under Their Vine*, chapter 4.

5.  For a valuable discussion of the Tuscan order and its great proponent among British Palladians, see Summerson, "Jones." For two classic statements on the tie with liberty, see Pevsner and Wittkower as cited in Chapter 2, note 7.

6.  See Washington, *Writings* 28:62–64; also Bailey, "New Room."

7.  The type appeared in some quantity in the first three volumes of Campbell, et al., *Vitruvius Britannicus*; see esp. vol. 2, plates 36, 38, 46, 85; vol. 3, plates 70, 91–92. Roger Pratt rather than Jones established this compromise between northern and southern Europe. See Reiff, *Small Georgian Houses*, chapters 1–2.

8.  Dennis J. Pogue, Chief Archaeologist, and Barbara A. McMillan, Librarian, Mount Vernon Ladies' Association, kindly assisted me in compiling the sources on Mount Vernon. Mr. Pogue generously shared his own unpublished manuscripts.

## REFERENCES

*The Magazine Antiques*, Mount Vernon no. 135 (February 1989).

Bailey, Worth. "General Washington's New Room." *Journal of the Society of Architectural Historians* 10 (May 1951):16–18.

———. "Growing Pains of a Great House: Mount Vernon, Period 1757–1787." [1947]. Ms. on file, Mount Vernon Ladies' Association.

Beckerdite, Luke. "William Buckland and William Bernard Sears: The Designer and the Carver." *Journal of Early Southern Decorative Arts* 8 (November 1982):6–41.

Boyd, Sterling M. "The Adam Style in America, 1770–1820." Ph.D. diss., Princeton University, 1966. Published in *Outstanding Dissertations in the Fine Arts*, New York: Garland Publishing, 1985.

Campbell, Colen, et al. *Vitruvius Britannicus, or The British Architect.* 5 vols. 1715–1808. Reprint. New York: Benjamin Blom, 1972.

De Forest, Elizabeth Kellam. *The Gardens & Grounds at Mount Vernon: How George Washington Planned and Planted Them.* Mount Vernon, Virginia: The Mount Vernon Ladies' Association of the Union, 1983.

Johnson, Gerald W. *Mount Vernon: The Story of a Shrine.* With extracts from the diaries and letters of George Washington selected and annotated by Charles Cecil Wall. Rev. ed., with an epilogue by Ellen McCallister Clark. Mount Vernon, Virginia: The Mount Vernon Ladies' Association, 1991.

Latrobe. *View.*

———. *Virginia Journals.*

Macomber, Walter M. "Mount Vernon's 'Architect.'" *Historical Society of Fairfax County, Virginia* 10 (1969):1–10.

*Mount Vernon: A Handbook.* New ed. Mount Vernon, Virginia: The Mount Vernon Ladies' Association of the Union, 1985.

Niemcewicz, Julian Ursyn. *Under Their Vine and Fig Tree: Travels through America in 1797–1799, 1805.* Translated and edited by Metchie J. E. Budka. Collections of the New Jersey Historical Society at Newark, vol. 14. Elizabeth, New Jersey: Grassmann Publishing Company, 1965.

Nygren, Edward J. "From View to Vision." In Nygren, Edward J., et al. *Views and Visions: American Landscape before 1830,* exh. cat. Washington, D.C.: Corcoran Gallery of Art, 1986.

O'Malley, Therese. "Landscape Gardening in the Early National Period." In Nygren, Edward J., et al. *Views and Visions: American Landscape before 1830.*

Owen, Scott Campbell. "George Washington's Mount Vernon as British Palladian Architecture." Master of Architectural History thesis, University of Virginia, 1991.

Pogue, Dennis J. "Archaeology at George Washington's Mount Vernon: 1931–1987." Mount Vernon Ladies' Association, Archaeology Department, File Report No. 1. Mount Vernon, Virginia, 1988.

———. "Mount Vernon: Transformation of an 18th-Century Plantation System." Ms. 1989.

———. "Washington's View of Mount Vernon: Transformation of an 18th-Century Plantation System." Unpublished paper presented at the conference *Re-Creating the World of the Virginia Plantation, 1750–1820,* University of Virginia, 1990.

Reiff, Daniel D. *Small Georgian Houses in England and Virginia: Origins and Development through the 1750s.* Newark, Delaware: University of Delaware Press, 1986.

Summerson, Sir John. "Inigo Jones." British Academy Lecture on a Master Mind. *Proceedings of the British Academy* 50 (1965):69–92.

Wall, Charles C. "Notes on the Early History of Mount Vernon." *William and Mary Quarterly*, 3rd ser., 2 (April 1945):173–90.

Washington, George. *The Papers of George Washington.* Colonial Series, edited by W. W. Abbot, et al. 6 vols. to date. Charlottesville: University Press of Virginia, 1983–.

———. *The Writings of George Washington . . . 1745–1799.* Edited by John C. Fitzpatrick. 39 vols. Washington, D.C.: U. S. Government Printing Office, 1931–44.

Waterman, Thomas Tileston. *The Mansions of Virginia, 1706–1776.* Chapel Hill: University of North Carolina, 1946.

Williams, Morley Jeffers. "Washington's Changes at Mount Vernon Plantation." *Landscape Architecture* 28 (January 1938):63–73.

# 6.
# BELLE FARM

*Detail, Arch and Doric Pilaster Base*

Gloucester County (demolished and partly reconstructed in Williamsburg)
Drawings labeled "Arch Section" and "Pedestal Design," circa 1775–1800
Scribed and inked on heart pine board; 13 ¼ by 31 ⅜ by ⅞ inches. Probably reused as a shelf below the stair.
Collection of the Colonial Williamsburg Foundation, Williamsburg, Virginia, Department of Architectural Research

FIGURE 1. **Belle Farm,** *arched doorway at rear of front passage, circa 1930. T. Leyton. (Photograph courtesy of the Colonial Williamsburg Foundation.)*

It is evident from court record-books and vestry minutes that rudimentary design sketches accompanied written specifications as a method of conveying to builders and clients the general configuration intended for some public buildings in eighteenth-century Virginia. These drawings were seldom as detailed as the modern observer would expect, given the wide spectrum of finishes found among buildings of the day, even within single structures. Generally, they were roughly sketched plans and elevations that provided dimensions and located doors and windows. While a few of the architectural drawings were done to scale, most produced in Virginia before the Revolutionary War were characterized by stick-like cartoons more akin to the labored sketches of freshman architectural surveyors than some provincial Christopher Wren.

Within a general framework of stylistic change, architectural decoration—mantels, cornices, staircases, and the like—was formulaic in the pre-Revolutionary Chesapeake. Decorative design involved settling the degree of elaboration more than exercising the imagination, so that woodwork could be assembled without even rough sketches. Much woodwork designed for substantial houses in the new Republic expanded the decorative vocabulary beyond the familiar conventions of the earlier period. Such innovation may well have made it necessary to develop designs with more detailed sketches in the joinery shop or on site before work began.

It is interesting, then, that three of the earliest woodworking sketches found in Virginia date from about 1775–1800 but are relatively conventional and old-fashioned in design. All three were found on hidden surfaces of planed boards at Belle Farm, a late-eighteenth-century farmhouse in Gloucester County. One, a design for a mantel with a familiar architrave surround topped by an entablature block and pedimented overmantel, is executed in ink largely with a straightedge (see Chapter 4, FIGURE 4.2). The other two, shown here, are designs for a Doric base and an arched doorway surround of the kind sometimes used to decorate the spaces flanking internal chimneys or the openings between contiguous circulation spaces. These sketches are scribed into the board with dividers, a straightedge, and some freehand effort, but without the use of such instruments as a triangle or a square.

When the Perry, Shaw & Hepburn architects working on the Williamsburg restoration visited Belle Farm in 1928, they found an eccentric structure, a sizable two-story, central-passage house whose three-bay facade was capped by a giant gable, and to the rear a lower wing with a picturesque mansard roof.[1] The first floor had two front rooms separated by a corridor leading to a broad stair passage in the wing. Beyond the rear passage was a single room, completing the three-room suite (hall, dining room, and chamber) that typified substantial gentry houses of the period.[2] The ink drawing was the basis for the best fireplace treatment, that which survived in the front left room (FIGURE 2), while the scribed arch resembles

FIGURE 2. **Belle Farm Parlor,** *1930. (Photograph courtesy of the Colonial Williamsburg Foundation.)*

those flanking the fireplace and more closely resembles the treatment of the opening that links the passages ( FIGURE 1 ). Both principal sketches vary in proportion from the executed woodwork, and the stages evident in construction of the base detail indicate that this was in part a design exercise. Yet if the drawings were intended simply as a practical means of composing the parts of the design, why were details like flutes and spandrel panels included and why were various parts like "Key" (keystone) and "Capital" (impost block) labeled?

It may be, then, that the artisan was concerned with illustrating for the client how the features would look in some detail. One is reminded of mail-order architects George and Charles Palliser's acerbic remark a hundred years later about the design techniques of traditional American builders: "Had the

builder been any sort of draughtsman, we presume our client would never have come to us, but would have had his builder scratch out his ideas on paper, or perhaps on a board, and then commenced building without any regard to taste or proportion or anything else."[3]

This serendipitous survivor shows that even with familiar elements, developing a complex decorative design may have required Virginia builders and house owners to employ some kind of graphic exercise. Given the number of historic buildings pulled apart since the 1920s, it is surprising that more sketches on wood have not come to light.　　　　　EAC

NOTES

1.　The plan came within less than a foot of matching the description of the main building at Belle Farm included in an 1802 Mutual Assurance policy: "A wooden Dwelling house 46 feet by 23 feet 2 Story high And underpin[n]ed with Brick / A wood wing 23 feet by 16 / 1 story high / And underpinned with Brick." The owner and occupant in 1802 was Thomas Lewis.

2.　Upton, "Vernacular Architecture," pp. 95–119. For a more detailed description of the house, its unhappy fate, and relevant circa 1930 drawings, see Edward Chappell, "Belle Farm: A Brief Assessment," unpublished, Colonial Williamsburg Foundation, 1991.

3.　Palliser's Model Homes, 17.

REFERENCES

Lounsbury, Carl R. "'An Elegant and Commodious Building': William Buckland and the Design of the Prince William County Courthouse." Journal of the Society of Architectural Historians 46 (September 1987):228–40.

Mutual Assurance Society of Virginia Policy, February 1802, transcription, site file, Colonial Williamsburg Foundation Library.

Palliser's Model Homes, 2nd. ed., rev. Bridgeport, Conn.: Palliser & Palliser, 1878.

Upton, Dell. "Vernacular Domestic Architecture in Eighteenth-Century Virginia." Winterthur Portfolio 17 (Summer-Autumn 1982).

Whiffen, Marcus. The Eighteenth-Century Houses of Williamsburg: A Study of Architecture and Building in the Colonial Capital of Virginia. Williamsburg Architectural Studies. Revised. Williamsburg: Colonial Williamsburg Foundation, 1984.

# 7.
# MONTICELLO, OBSERVATION TOWER

*Plan and Elevation*

Near Charlottesville (Albemarle County; unbuilt)
Study, circa 1768 to 1778
Scoring, pricking, pencil, pen and writing ink with gray wash
on paper; 14 ⅜ by 9 ⅛ inches
Massachusetts Historical Society, Boston, Coolidge
Collection, Jefferson Papers, No. 21

*The West end*

Statesman and universal man, Thomas Jefferson is also the first American-born architect of international stature, although he designed only a modest number of executed buildings.[1] His architecture, a unique, late outgrowth of Anglo-Palladianism, does contain other elements. Jefferson, who began as an architect by designing his own house (circa 1768 and later), became one of the profound forces upon American civic architecture.

Jefferson made four drawings of an unexecuted tower for Montalto, the mountain that rises over Monticello on the southwest. He devised the tower primarily as a Picturesque landscape ornament and secondarily as an element from which to take the awe-inspiring kind of view that he and his contemporaries called *Sublime*.[2] In two drawings the tower displays the five Orders, to be cut from flat planks and to rise from Tuscan to Composite, according to Jefferson's notes on the back of the pages. The other two studies show a crenellated tower. Scholars have dated the pair with the Orders to various points between about 1768 and 1778. The two, the work of a painfully inexperienced designer and drafter, seem most at home toward the early end of this span.

The drawing featured here is a clumsy first attempt at a tower, modeled on steeples illustrated in Gibbs's *Book of Architecture* (London, 1728; FIGURE 1). The plan shows the Tuscan order as a vertical plank inserted into the ground, a startling echo of earlier perishable-post construction that Virginians had used almost exclusively for their buildings until the 1720s and that Jefferson surely despised.[3] Jefferson raised the Tuscan onto a substructure when he improved the scheme in his second drawing but then noted, on the back of the study, that he preferred a 200-foot-tall column, which would have loomed almost 1,200 feet above the valley.[4]

It seems probable that, like the British Palladians and Palladio himself, Jefferson thought that he was practicing the one, true architecture that the Greeks and Romans had founded on the unchanging Laws of Nature. It seems probable that, like many of his contemporaries, Jefferson believed that the "moderns" (the architects from the renewal of antiquity in the Renaissance onward) had never equaled the ancients. And it seems probable that Jefferson meant his estate as a re-creation of a Roman villa.[5] His Observation Tower may reflect references in Roman literature to towers on country estates.[6]

Like other followers of Palladio, Jefferson subscribed to an extreme form of the belief that the Orders were the principal ornament in architecture. The idea of exhibiting the best Orders persisted throughout his career and reached its zenith with his designs for the University of Virginia (1817 and later; SURVEY NOS. 26–28). Between the clumsy tower and the masterpiece, Jefferson developed his thoughts on a canon of the orders. He accepted many of the views of the French Palladian Fréart de Chambray, who exercised a potent influence on British Palladianism, partly via Robert Morris. Fréart argued that the Doric, Ionic, and Corinthian orders gave an architect all the expressive scope that he needed. Jefferson did not sacrifice the cheap, useful Tuscan. But from some time after the observatory projects until the eleventh hour, he seemingly made one of the major tenets of his canon the Fréart-Morris rejection of the Composite.

This crude sheet fits squarely into the family of American drawings done in iron-gall ink and gray wash, an unpleasant provincial counterpart to European monochrome renderings. A comparison with the Menokin sheet (SURVEY NO. 3), which makes competent use of India ink, underscores the failings of the tower drawing. Not surprisingly, Jefferson largely laid aside the use of washes in his subsequent drawings.

CEB

NOTES

1. This publication offers a view of Jefferson different from the popular ones. See Chapter 2 for a summary of my thinking about Jefferson, and note 4 therein for an acknowledgement of my most pressing debts.

2. For the Picturesque views through the tower from Monticello and the Sublime panorama from its summit, as well as for fresh findings on Jefferson's use of Gibbs for this design, see Reed, "Observatory Tower."

3. For an introduction to post construction in the Chesapeake Tidewater, see Carson, et al., "Impermanent Architecture." On Jefferson's contempt for perishable wooden buildings, see his *Notes*, pp. 152–54.

4. For the data on height (other than what Jefferson wrote on the back of the drawing), see Beiswanger, "Temple," p. 175.

5. See Lehmann, *Jefferson*, pp. 51–53 and chapter 11, and Prothro, "Monticello," 1989, a revision of the 1988 thesis.

6. For example, Pliny the Younger, *Letters*, 2.17.12–13.

REFERENCES

Beiswanger, William L. "The Temple in the Garden: Thomas Jefferson's Vision of the Monticello Landscape." *Eighteenth Century Life*, n.s., 8 (January 1983):170–88.

———. "Thomas Jefferson's Designs for Garden Structures at Monticello." Master of Architectural History thesis, University of Virginia, 1977. Pp. 13–16 and appendix III.

Carson, Cary; Norman F. Barka; William M. Kelso; Garry Wheeler Stone; and Dell Upton. "Impermanent Architecture in the Southern American Colonies." *Winterthur Portfolio* 16 (Summer/Autumn 1981):135–96.

Donnelly, Marian C. "Jefferson's Observatory Design." *Journal of the Society of Architectural Historians* 36 (March 1977):33–35.

Jefferson, Thomas. *Notes on the State of Virginia*. Edited with an introduction and notes by William Peden. 1955. Reprint. New York: W. W. Norton and Company, 1972.

Kimball. *Jefferson, Architect*. No. 38.

Lehmann, Karl. *Thomas Jefferson, American Humanist*. 1947. Reprint. Foreword by Dumas Malone. Charlottesville: University Press of Virginia, 1985.

Nichols. *Jefferson's Architectural Drawings*. No. 65.

Pliny the Younger. *Letters*. 2.17; 5.6.

Prothro, Kimberly. "Monticello: A Roman Villa?" Master of Architectural History thesis, University of Virginia, 1988.

———. "Monticello as Roman Villa: The Ancients, Architecture, and Jefferson." *Virginia Cavalcade* 39 (Summer 1989):10–21.

Reed, Helen Scott Townsend. "Jefferson's Observatory Tower Projects for Montalto and the University of Virginia." Master of Architectural History thesis, University of Virginia, 1991.

Sommer, Frank H., III. "Thomas Jefferson's First Plan for a Virginia Building." *Papers on American Art*. Edited by John C. Milley. Maple Shade, New Jersey: Edinburgh Press, for The Friends of Independence National Historical Park, 1976.

Waddell, Gene. "The First Monticello." *Journal of the Society of Architectural Historians* 46 (March 1987):5–29.

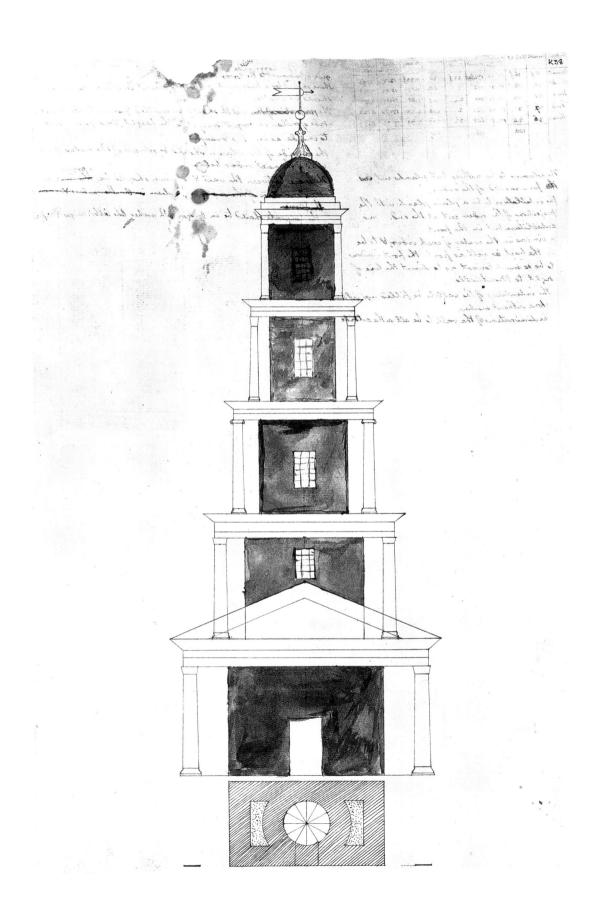

# 8.
# MONTICELLO, FIRST HOUSE

*Elevation*

Near Charlottesville (Albemarle County; unbuilt)
Study or presentation drawing, early 1770s
Scoring, pricking, pen and writing ink on paper; 13 ½ by 18 ⅞ inches
Collection of the Massachusetts Historical Society, Boston, Coolidge Collection, Jefferson Papers, No. 289.

FIGURE 1. **Villa Cornaro,** *from Giacomo Leoni, ed.,* **The Architecture of A. Palladio** *(Florence: 1721). (Photograph courtesy of the Virginia State Library.)*

Jefferson made his second house at Monticello (beginning 1796) an incomparable essay in the use of space and light. The conception for Monticello I began, however, as an assemblage of boxes with openings cut through the sides. By degrees the first villa opened up as the design acquired polygonal bows and became joined to service wings embracing the crest of the hill. This drawing, Jefferson's third and last measured elevation for Monticello I, shows a handsome house approaching its executed form. But, with its largely solid wall surfaces and its lack of polygonal bows, the drawing gives a foretaste of the dazzling lightness and openness of Monticello II only in its portico.

The metamorphosis of this house into unforgettable architecture owes profoundly to Jefferson's taste for what he found light and airy, both literally and figuratively. This preference runs through his lifetime. Thus, when he gave the second Williamsburg Capitol (beginning 1751) his very qualified praise, he called it "a light and airy structure," no doubt largely because of its two-tiered Palladian portico.[1] Again, when Colonel Isaac Coles relayed Jefferson's advice to John Hartwell Cocke concerning the design of Bremo (SURVEY NO. 29), Coles reported that "he is a great advocate for light and air—as you predicted he was for giving you Octagons. They were charming. They gave you a semicircle of air & light."[2]

Jefferson took the idea of using a light and airy two-tiered temple portico on a house from Giacomo Leoni's reinterpretation of Palladio's *Four Books* (FIGURE 1). He meant Leoni's version of Palladio when he told Coles that "Palladio . . . 'was the Bible' "; he apparently never read Leoni's preface, where Leoni boasted of how much he had changed Palladio's plates for the better.[3]

In adopting his two-level porch, Jefferson accepted the division of a facade into pronounced layers, and he used such articulation until the end of his life for parts of the "academical village" at the University of Virginia (see SURVEY NO. 26). But, at the Virginia Capitol (SURVEY NOS. 9–10), Monticello II (SURVEY NO. 12), parts of the University (SURVEY NOS. 27–28) and elsewhere, he adopted the alternative of unifying two stories with a single Order (with or without a basement). Much of the development of nineteenthcentury Western architecture centered on the rivalry between the facade composed of emphatic tiers and the facade with stories subordinated to a monumental pattern.[4]

Jefferson had plans for making Monticello I something like a museum of the Orders, that paramount element in his architecture. The present elevation illustrates three of his choices (to ignore the door- and window-cases): Palladio's Doric; a derivative of Palladio's Ionic; and a so-called Attic order, which dictates the second-story moldings on the wings. Eighteenth-century British and American Palladians characteristically preferred the "modern Ionic" capital of Palladio's pupil Scamozzi to Palladio's (SURVEY NO. 10, FIGURE 1).[5] Jefferson's lifelong attraction to Palladio's Ionic is one of his unusual ties to that

master. But Jefferson never learned the authentic features of Palladio's order, because he depended on unreliable material (compare FIGURES 2.13, 2.14).[6]

Jefferson cannot have taken his museum-of-the-orders notion very far at Monticello I, which did not reach a highly finished state. But the idea achieved three important realizations: the United States Capitol, Monticello II, and, above all, the University of Virginia.

In a period of few and rudimentary American architectural graphics, this drawing shows a mind using measured ink lines to achieve architectural precision and purity, down to the last molding. Its self-taught drafter had taken impressive strides since drawing the observation tower. Pen and ink, Jefferson's basic medium before he went abroad, made erasing difficult, as witness the erasure marks above the Ionic cornice and various sills.

CEB

NOTES

1. Jefferson, *Notes,* p. 152.

2. Coles to Cocke, 23 February 1816.

3. Quotation from Coles to Cocke, 23 February 1816. On Leoni's Palladio and Jefferson's ownership, see Chapter 2, note 28. The Villa Cornaro (Leoni's pl. 38) seems the most likely model; see Ackerman, *Villa,* p. 191.

4. On the tug-of-war, see Chapter 2.

5. Kalbian, "Ionic," 1990, takes the Ionic story much beyond her thesis on the same topic. We both have debts to valuable papers on the Ionic by University of Virginia students Daniel Lee Kaplan, Catherine L. Ribble, and Leon McKinley.

6. Comparison of Book 1, chapter 16 (on the Ionic), in Palladio's *Quattro Libri* and in the 2nd ed. of Leoni's *Architecture,* reveals a range of Leoni "corrections." The Ionic in the present elevation seems to be some form of derivative from Leoni, perhaps via an intermediary publication.

REFERENCES

Ackerman, James S. *The Villa: Form and Ideology of Country Houses.* The A. W. Mellon Lectures in the Fine Arts, The National Gallery of Art, 1985; Bollingen Series XXXV, 34. Princeton: Princeton University Press, 1990.

Adams, William Howard. *Jefferson's Monticello.* New York: Abbeville Press, 1983.

Beiswanger, William L. "The Temple in the Garden: Thomas Jefferson's Vision of the Monticello Landscape," *Eighteenth Century Life,* n. s. 8 (January 1983):170–88.

Coles, Colonel Isaac A., to General John Hartwell Cocke, 23 February 1816, University of Virginia Library, Special Collections Department, Cocke Papers, No. 640 etc., Box 21.

Jefferson, Thomas. *Notes on the State of Virginia.* Edited with an introduction and notes by William Peden. 1955; reprint ed., New York: W. W. Norton and Company, 1972.

Kalbian, Maral S. "The Ionic Order and the Progression of the Orders in American Palladianism before 1812." Master of Architectural History thesis, University of Virginia, 1988.

———. "The Ionic Order in America before 1812." Lecture, Third Annual Architectural History Symposium, "Classicism: Visions and Revisions, 1740–1990." University of Virginia, 1990.

Kimball. *Thomas Jefferson, Architect.* No. 23.

Lucas, Ann M. "Ordering His Environment: Thomas Jefferson's Architecture from Monticello to the University of Virginia." Master of Architectural History thesis, University of Virginia, 1989.

McLaughlin, Jack. *Jefferson and Monticello: The Biography of a Builder.* New York: Henry Holt and Company, 1988.

Nichols. *Jefferson's Architectural Drawings.* No. 48.

Palladio, Andrea. *The Architecture of A. Palladio; in Four Books.* Translated by Nicholas Dubois and edited by Giacomo Leoni. 2nd ed. 2 vols. London, 1721.

———. *I Quattro Libri Dell' Architettura Di Andrea Palladio.* 1570; reprint ed., with Ottavio Cabiati, "Nota al Palladio," 1945, laid in, Milan: Ulrico Hoepli, 1968.

Prothro, Kimberly, "Monticello as Roman Villa: The Ancients, Architecture, and Jefferson," *Virginia Cavalcade* 39 (Summer 1989):10–21.

Waddell, Gene. "The First Monticello." *JSAH* 46 (March 1987):5–29.

Attributed to THOMAS JEFFERSON, 1743–1826

with

CHARLES-LOUIS CLERISSEAU, 1721–1820

# 9.
# VIRGINIA STATE CAPITOL

*Side Elevation*

Capitol Square, Richmond
Study, 1785
Scoring, pricking, and pencil on paper; 10 ⁵⁄₁₆ by 15 inches
Collection of Massachusetts Historical Society, Boston,
Coolidge Collection, Jefferson Papers, No. 63.

FIGURE 1. *Vintage photo,* **Virginia Capitol Building,** *southeast view, circa 1890. (Photograph courtesy of The Valentine Museum, Richmond.)*

As Jefferson recalled the story of the Virginia State Capitol in his "Autobiography" in 1821,

> I was written to in 1785 (being then in Paris) . . . to advise . . . as to a plan, and to add to it one of a Prison. Thinking it a favorable opportunity of introducing into the State an example of architecture, in the classic style of antiquity, and the Maison Quarrée of Nismes . . . being considered as the most perfect model existing of what may be called Cubic architecture, I applied to M. Clerissault, who had published drawings of the Antiquities of Nismes, to have me a model of the building made in stucco, only changing the order from Corinthian to Ionic, on account of the difficulty of the Corinthian capitals. I yielded, with reluctance, to . . . Clerissault, in his preference of the modern capital of Scamozzi to the more noble capital of antiquity. . . . To adapt the exterior to our use, I drew a plan for the interior. . . . These [the model and the drawings] were . . . carried into execution, with some variations, not for the better, the most important of which, however, admit of future correction.[1]

Previously, Jefferson had amplified the matter of prototypes when he wrote in his "Account of the Capitol in Virginia" that the Richmond building

> is the model of the Temples of Erectheus at Athens, of Balbec, and of the Maison quarrée. . . . All of which are nearly of the same form and proportions, and are considered as the most perfect examples of cubic architecture, as the Pantheon of Rome is of the spherical.[2]

No one has ever satisfactorily explained what Jefferson meant by "cubic" and "spherical" architecture. Moreover, commentators have tended to pass over his interest both in Greek precedent and in Roman precedent other than the Maison Carrée. But his thinking obviously belongs to the family of square and circular proportional systems of which both Vitruvius and Palladio had written, and that the Jones circle and its eighteenth-century followers had employed in Britain. Jefferson had explored such possibilities at Monticello.[3] Thus, he had made a project (circa 1778; FIGURE 2.16) for transforming his square south pavilion (1770) into a variation on Lord Burlington's miniature Pantheon at Chiswick (by 1727; FIGURE 2.17). According to his notes on the back of this tantalizing study in square and circular geometry, Jefferson meant to draw details from four models that emphasize the design's relation to speculation about ideal proportions: three circular buildings—the Choragic Monument of Lysicrates (Athens, 334 B.C.), a Greek building of lasting interest to him; Bramante's Tempietto (Rome, 1502; FIGURE 2.18); and an extraordinary round design attributed to Jones—as well as a fourth centrally planned building, Palladio's Villa Rotonda (Vicenza, 1565/66 and later; FIGURE 2.11).[4] Shortly afterward, probably in 1780, he designed a rectangular Ionic temple (or "cubic" tem-

ple, one suspects) to house the Virginia legislature in Richmond, and he probably meant the judiciary to occupy a matching building.

Before Jefferson ever left North America, then, old books—especially British publications—had taught him about the Vitruvian tradition of square and circular proportional possibilities and about the use of the temple in modern times. One has no reason to search among the French avant-garde to understand the design in this later elevation. Jefferson expressly stated that he had trouble finding a Parisian architect to assist him, "the style of architecture in this capital being far from chaste."[5] He sought no radical and, in the antiquary and decorative master Clérisseau, he found nearly enough what he wanted.

In France, Jefferson made two discoveries of lifelong value for his drawing practice. He encountered squared paper, manufactured—originally for silk weavers—with a scaled grid (in this case a waffle-like grid raised from the surface). And he discovered the facile, easily erased pencil. His tight, amateur's pencil lines contrast with the free, fluid touches added by Clérisseau, such as the elliptical surrounds under the entablature. Like Jefferson's admiration of the "light and airy," Clérisseau's decorative details, such as the delicate consoles that he sketched under certain window sills, have nothing to do with the avant-garde possibilities that such architects as Claude-Nicolas Ledoux were probing in 1785.　　　　CEB

NOTES

1. Quoted in Kimball, *Capitol,* p. 11. Poffenberger, in "Jefferson's Design," will carry the interpretation of the Capitol a full step beyond the present book.

2. Quoted in Kimball, *Capitol,* p. 13.

3. On Jefferson, "cubic" and "spherical" proportions, and the south pavilion, see Chapter 2.

4. I have profited from a 1989 essay on Jefferson's interest in the Lysicrates Monument by John Alexander, a University of Virginia graduate student.

5. Jefferson to Buchanan and Hay, 13 August 1785, in *Papers,* 8:366–68.

REFERENCES

Beiswanger, William L. "The Temple in the Garden: Thomas Jefferson's Vision of the Monticello Landscape." *Eighteenth Century Life,* new series 8 (January 1983):170–88.

Collins, Peter. "The Origins of Graph Paper as an Influence on Architectural Design." *Journal of the Society of Architectural Historians* 21 (December 1962):159–62.

Jefferson. *Papers.*

Kimball. "Jefferson and the Public Buildings of Virginia." *Huntington Library Quarterly* 12 (February 1949):115–20; (May 1949):303–10.

———. "Thomas Jefferson and the First Monument of the Classical Revival in America." *Journal of the American Institute of Architects* 3 (September 1915):371–81; (October):421–33; (November):473–91.

———. "Thomas Jefferson and the First Monument of the Classical Revival in America." 1915; rev. ed., as *The Capitol of Virginia: A Landmark of American Architecture,* edited by Jon Kukla, with Martha C. Vick and Sarah Shields Driggs. Richmond: Virginia State Library and Archives, for the General Assembly of Virginia, 1989.

———. *Jefferson, Architect.* No. 115.

Kummer, Karen Lang. "The Evolution of the Virginia State Capitol, 1779–1965." Master of Architectural History thesis, University of Virginia, 1981.

McCormick, Thomas J. *Charles-Louis Clérisseau and the Genesis of Neo-Classicism.* An Architectural History Foundation Book. Cambridge, Massachusetts: MIT Press, 1990.

Nichols. *Jefferson's Architectural Drawings.* No. 48.

Poffenberger, Brien J. "Thomas Jefferson's Design for the Virginia State Capitol." Draft, Master of Architectural History thesis, University of Virginia, 1991.

Scale 1 Square = 1 foot.

Virginia Capitol. Side Elevation - Study

Cols. 3?

# 10.
# VIRGINIA STATE CAPITOL

*Model*

Capitol Square, Richmond
Model, 1785–86
Plaster; 13 ¾ by 29 ¼ by 17 ¼ inches
Collection of the Virginia State Library and Archives,
Richmond, courtesy of the Virginia General Assembly

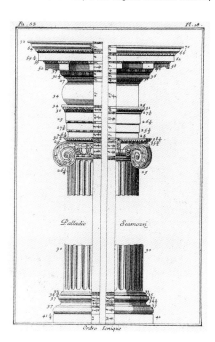

FIGURE 1. **Ionic capital of Palladio and Scamozzi** *from* **Parallèle de l'Architecture** *by Fréart de Chambray (Paris: 1766). (Photograph courtesy of the Virginia Historical Society.)*

For some reason, Clérisseau made a first and then a second set of drawings for the Capitol. In January 1786, Jefferson sent to Richmond a plan and elevations for the building along with his prison design, also drawn by Clérisseau. The model followed in June. In 1791, all the Clérisseau drawings were sent to Pierre-Charles L'Enfant for use in making a design for the Washington, D.C., Capitol, and they soon disappeared.

Jefferson wished to use the Virginia Capitol to set a model in the Ionic order. In his elevational study (SURVEY NO. 9), he proposed a version of Palladio's Ionic, or, rather, of Palladio's Ionic as altered by Leoni, with a flattened frieze (compare FIGURES 1 and 2). Palladio's capital belongs to the so-called ancient type. That is, it resembles a scroll of paper laid over the top of the column, with identical principal faces on the front and the back, and rolled sides of not much interest. Jefferson's flank elevation shows him struggling unhappily to bring the order around the sides of the portico and to join it to the body of the building. Awkwardly, this facade shows only the sides of the Ionic capitals, not the scrolled fronts.

The model, however, unites an Ionic entablature of somewhat unclear detail with a variant Ionic capital that Jefferson knew from what his age called the Temple of Fortuna Virilis (the Temple of Portunus, Rome, late second century B.C.). In this alternative, the scrolled face of the capital looks outward along the front of a portico, as usual, and then, turning the corners, it also looks outward along the side. Turning the corner this way exacts a double price: the scroll at the angle has to project on the diagonal, aligning with neither its mate on the left nor its mate on the right; and the two leftover rolled "sides" are forced around to the rear, where they collide (FIGURE 2). Although Palladio admired and used this corner capital, eighteenth-century Palladians rarely employed it.[1] Jefferson betrayed a striking affinity with Palladio in loving this Ionic.

According to Jefferson, he "yielded, with reluctance" to Clérisseau's preference for "the modern capital of Scamozzi to the more noble capital of antiquity."[2] Palladio's pupil Scamozzi published an Ionic capital (the so-called modern Ionic) that did not suffer from the corner problems of the two "ancient" varieties just mentioned.[3] This capital, the favorite of the British-Palladians, has all its scrolls on the diagonal (like four fronds curling out of a vase rather than like a roll of paper) and four identical faces in between (FIGURE 1). This is the Order of the Capitol as executed. The decision to use it may have occasioned the making of the second set of Clérisseau drawings. Presumably the decision came at a point when Jean-Pierre Fouquet had the costly model too far along to change.[4]

Jefferson failed to set the example of the Ionic that he preferred for Richmond, but he succeeded in giving his country a specimen of "cubic" architecture on a uniquely grand scale. Americans had rarely built temple porticoes. In the 1780s and 1790s, such portals

first arose in numbers along the Atlantic seaboard, but none of the others could compete in grandeur with Jefferson's deep and lofty Richmond frontispiece. Thanks most of all to this portico, Jefferson's conception for the Capitol retains great power despite the clumsy execution of his design (by Samuel Dobie, beginning 1786), the rebuilding and enlargement of the Capitol (by John Kevan Peebles and others, 1904–06), and the erection of taller buildings around Capitol Square. The Capitol, a landmark in the Temple Revival, is likewise a landmark in the rise of the taste for buildings wrapped in one grand Order.

Until recently this model was mistakenly ascribed not to Fouquet, an important model-maker, but to one of his assistants, by the name of Bloquet. In turning to Fouquet, Jefferson subscribed to the very strong French preference for models over perspectives. But architectural models, expensive and demanding to make, did not catch on in Virginia. We do not hear of further preliminary scale models here until the Washington Monument competition of 1849–50.[5]    CEB

NOTES
1. Palladio, *Architecture*, Bk. 1, chap. 16, p. 28; Bk. 2, chap. 14, p. 80; Bk. 4, chap. 13, pp. 65–66.

2. Kimball, *Capitol*, p. 11.

3. It had ancient precedent in what Palladians called the Temple of Concord (Temple of Saturn, Rome, [A. D. 284]).

4. For the reconstruction of this model-maker's career, see Cuisset, "Fouquet."

5. On the model tradition, see Chapter 4, part 2.

REFERENCES
Cuisset, Geneviève. "Jean-Pierre et François Fouquet, Artistes Modeleurs." *Gazette des Beaux-Arts* 115 (May-June 1990):227–40.

———. *Jefferson, Architect.* No. 117.

Nichols. *Jefferson's Architectural Drawings.* No. 280.

Palladio, Andrea. *The Architecture of A. Palladio* in *Four Books.* Trans. Nicholas Dubois; ed. Giacomo Leoni. 2nd ed. 2 vols. London, 1721.

See additional references on Jefferson's architecture, the Virginia Capitol building, and on Clérisseau's architecture in survey no. 9.

FIGURE 2. *Detail of model, inner angle showing unusual juncture of scrolls.*

# 11.
# UNITED STATES CAPITOL

*Proposed Plans*

Washington, D.C. (unbuilt)
Presentation drawing, circa 1791
Pricking, pen and writing ink, and gray wash on paper; 7 5/16 by 7 1/8 inches
Collection of the Massachusetts Historical Society, Boston, Coolidge Collection, Jefferson Papers, No. 257, piece 1, recto and verso

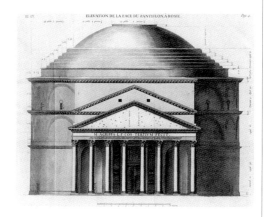

FIGURE 1. *Main elevation,* **Pantheon,** *Rome, from Antoine Desgodetz,* **Edifices Antiques de Rome** *(Paris: 1682).*

Between 1790 and 1800, George Washington and other American leaders prepared a city on the banks of the Potomac for the new federal government. The creation of this capital set a challenge that American architecture was ill-prepared to meet. Washington, D.C., required not only practical public buildings but also monumental ones. Faced with shaping the new building types of the modern age, Americans, like Europeans, repeatedly turned to domestic and sacred architecture for models.

In 1791–92, Pierre Charles L'Enfant had the responsibility of designing the new city and its buildings. As secretary of state, Jefferson, who played an immense role in molding Washington and its architecture, wrote him to promote adopting, for the exterior of the Capitol, "some one of the models of antiquity which have had the approbation of thousands of years."[1] His standard, as usual, was the *consensus gentium,* the agreement of all enlightened human beings.[2]

Having set a model of "cubic" architecture in Richmond, Jefferson wished now to imitate the Pantheon, thereby giving the country a model of "spherical" architecture. He tried to get better reconstructions of the Pantheon than he owned; he succeeded in acquiring the 1779 edition of Antoine Desgodetz' *Edifices antiques de Rome* (Paris, 1682), which corrected the errors in Palladio's Pantheon illustrations ( FIGURE 1 ).[3] And he made a Roman Pantheon Capitol design. Three problematic and highly schematic drawings, one perhaps not by Jefferson, survive; two of them are virtually unknown to scholars.[4] (The one shown here, for example, was not photographed until 1990.) Jefferson wished to insert elliptical rooms (à la Racine de Monville and François Barbier's column house at the Désert de Retz [1774]) inside an enlargement of the Pantheon. On the front of the sheet shown here he drew a version of his design with an elliptical central hall. On the back, he drew a revised version with a rectangular center hall.

Why would the admirer of the sphere accept the ellipse, a deformed circle? It had the ancient authority of the Colosseum (Rome, 70–82 and later) and, as a shape for rooms, it had the modern authority of numerous staircases designed by Palladio. (One wonders, though, whether an instinctive attraction to the form does not lie at the root of the matter.) Jefferson experimented with ellipses inside a circle, on the example of the column house, at least as early as a design of around 1785 for remodeling his Paris house, the Hôtel de Langeac (demolished).[5]

Over the floor with the elliptical chambers had to come some kind of enormous domed space with a span of some 164 feet. Jefferson may have failed to find any purpose for this room, which he had no credible way of covering. Until the great iron train sheds of the 1850s, few architects equaled the 142-foot span of the Pantheon, and none surpassed it.[6] In Paris, Jefferson had become enamored of the dome that Legrand and Molinos had put over the Halle au Blé (demolished) in 1782–83 and of the Delorme construction ( FIGURE 2.20 ) that they had used.[7] But the dome of the Halle

au Blé spanned a mere 120 feet, and Jefferson had never built any dome at all. It took three decades before he found an application for his conception, at the head of the University of Virginia Lawn ( SURVEY NO. 27 ). Almost surely, though, his spherical temple idea influenced not only the Capitol schemes of L'Enfant, Etienne Sulpice Hallet, and William Thornton, but also the Capitol Rotunda as executed.

Another drawing attributed to Jefferson, a slight sketch plan and elevation, has an uncertain relation to the Capitol story. It owes at least as much to churches illustrated in Colen Campbell's *Vitruvius Britannicus* (London, 1715–25) as to Jacques Germain Soufflot's Panthéon (Paris, 1757–90), with which architectural historians usually associate it.[8]                      CEB

NOTES

1. Jefferson to L'Enfant, 10 April 1791, *Papers* 20:86–87.

2. For a recent statement on the principle, see Harris and Savage, *British Architectural Books,* pp. 31, 159.

3. See, for instance, Jefferson to William Short, 16 March 1791, in *Papers* 19:578–79; O'Neal, *Jefferson's Library,* under "Desgodetz, Antoine Babuty."

4. They are the present two plans and no. 257, piece 2. Kimball seemingly overlooked all three. Nichols catalogued all three as his no. 388.

5. William L. Beiswanger drew my attention to Jefferson's love of the ellipse. Maria Lourdes Solera sorted out the authority for the form in a 1989 seminar report.

6. On these spans, see Meeks, *Railroad Station,* pp. 36ff., 169.

7. See Chapter 2.

8. These observations depend upon an unpublished 1989 report by Scott Owen, a graduate student of Architectural History at the University of Virginia.

REFERENCES

Adams, William Howard, ed. *The Eye of Thomas Jefferson.* Exh. cat. Washington, D.C.: National Gallery of Art, 1976. Cat. no. 434 (by Frederick Doveton Nichols).

Allen, William C. *The United States Capitol: A Brief Architectural History.* 101st Congress, 1st Session, House Document 101-144. Washington, D.C.: U.S. Government Printing Office, 1990.

Bowling, Kenneth R. *Creating the Federal City, 1774–1800: Potomac Fever.* Octagon Research Series, 1. Washington, D.C.: American Institute of Architects Press, 1988.

Brownell and Cohen. *Architectural Drawings of Latrobe.*

Butler, Jeanne F. "Competition 1792: Designing a Nation's Capitol." *Capitol Studies,* special number, vol. 4, no. 1 (1976):83–85.

Collins, Peter. "The Origins of Graph Paper as an Influence on Architectural Design." *Journal of the Society of Architectural Historians* 21 (December 1962):159–62.

Harris, Eileen, assisted by Nicholas Savage. *British Architectural Books and Writers, 1556–1785.* Cambridge: Cambridge University Press, 1990.

Jefferson. *Papers.*

Kimball. *Jefferson, Architect.* Pp. 52–56 and no. 132.

Meeks, Carroll L.V. *The Railroad Station: An Architectural History.* New Haven: Yale University Press, 1956.

Nichols. *Jefferson's Architectural Drawings.* No. 388.

O'Neal. *Jefferson's Library.*

FIGURE 2. *Daguerreotype, by John Plumbe, of* **U. S. Capitol,** *as built circa 1846. (Photograph courtesy of the Library of Congress.)*

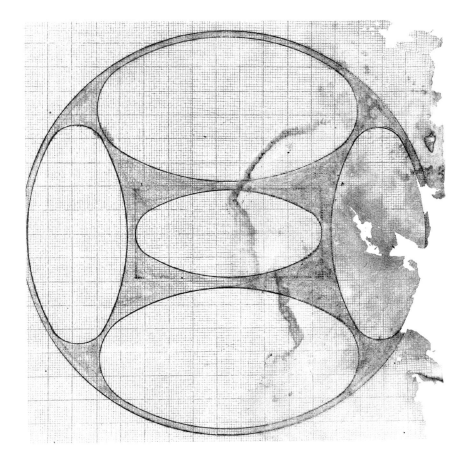

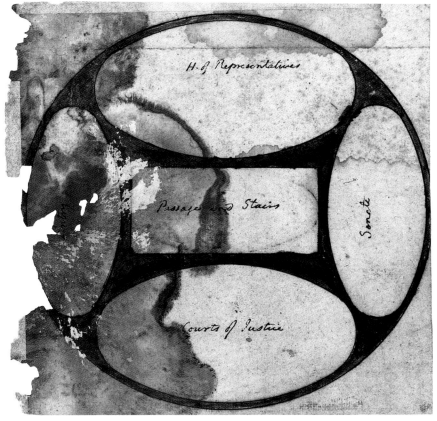

THOMAS JEFFERSON, 1743–1826

Drawing attributed to ROBERT MILLS, 1781–1855

# 12.
# MONTICELLO,
# SECOND HOUSE

*West Elevation*

Near Charlottesville (Albemarle County)
Presentation drawing, 1803 (?)
Pricking, pencil(?), pen and India ink, and India ink washes on
paper; 8 ⅜ by 14 ½ inches
Collection of the Massachusetts Historical Society, Boston,
Coolidge Collection, Jefferson Papers, No. 126

FIGURE 1. **Monticello II** *showing Jefferson's
"caged bow," a bow-front inside a temple portico.*

Robert Mills served as Jefferson's draftsman for this elevation. After working under James Hoban, Mills received employment and encouragement from Jefferson, who helped him enter Latrobe's office in late summer 1803. As Hoban's and, far more important, Latrobe's pupil, Mills rightly claimed to be the first professionally trained American-born architect. At the same time, Jefferson left his mark on Mills.

The garden front of Monticello II (1796 and afterward) employs two quintessentially Jeffersonian elements. First, the placing of a bow, especially a polygonal bow, inside a temple portico is one of Jefferson's most engaging devices, and he may have invented the treatment when he applied it to Monticello I ( FIGURE 1 ). It did not find many imitators, unlike the second element. Jefferson capped the bow at Monticello II with a dome framed on the simple, light, inexpensive Delorme system of laminated plank ribs ( FIGURE 2.20 ). After discovering this technique in Paris, he spent forty years—down to the University of Virginia Rotunda ( SURVEY NO. 27 )—establishing its use in America. Because of him the technique entered the repertories of both Mills and Latrobe, who in time integrated the Delorme method with his own specialty, masonry vaulting, best of all at his Roman Catholic cathedral in Baltimore (1806–10; 1817–21 and later).[1]

No form of architectural drawing could or can do justice to how space unfolds at Monticello II, where Jefferson carried his pursuit of lightness and airiness to an unforgettable level. A comparison with his elevation for the first Monticello ( SURVEY NO. 8 ) gives a mere inkling of the effect by revealing how Jefferson opened the first two windows left and right of the center down to the floor ( FIGURE 2 ). In looking at those spaces today, however, one must remember that the house has lost much of Jefferson's accumulation of possessions. Jefferson's extraordinary *sanctum sanctorum*, for instance, once held the boxes that contained thousands of documents from his public life.[2]

Comparing the two Monticello elevations does convey another change successfully: the shift from a facade of tiered Orders to one bound together by a single Order, a form of Palladio's Doric. In 1808, a guest partly inventoried the Orders in Jefferson's private collection of good examples. J. E. Caldwell wrote that Monticello's interior

> contains specimens of all the different orders, except the composite, which is not introduced; the hall is in the Ionic, the dining room, in the Doric, the parlour, in the Corinthian, and dome [room] in the Attic; in the other rooms are introduced several different forms of these orders, all in the truest proportions, according to Palladio.[3]

In fact, since Monticello I, Jefferson had acquired a new authority in his Palladian program, in addition to Fréart de Chambray (whose prohibition of the Composite underlies the fact that it "is not introduced"). For his richest Ionic and Corinthian orders Jefferson

used friezes from Desgodetz' *Edifices*.[4] He apparently learned that Desgodetz had corrected many of the mistakes in Palladio's and Fréart's plates.

This elevation, like its predecessor ( SURVEY NO. 8 ), has extraordinary distinction among American architectural drawings of its period (the work of foreign-trained architects excepted). Mills spared no efforts in this rendering for his eminent patron. The way that he used the white surface of the paper for the nearest planes and graded washes for the more distant ones exemplifies the impressive skill that he had attained. But still the standards for refinement here are provincial, and confused details (such as the blurry shading under the pediment, rather than crisp 45-degree shadows) show that Mills lacked full command of drafting skills. This elevation probably predates his exposure to the cosmopolitan standards of Latrobe's office. Mills exhibited this or another drawing of the "Garden Front of Monticello House" in the annual exhibition of the Pennsylvania Academy of the Fine Arts in 1812. CEB

NOTES

1. On the "caged" bow and the Delorme method, see Chapter 2.

2. Susan R. Stein, Curator, the Thomas Jefferson Memorial Foundation, has kindly pointed this out to me.

3. *Tour*, p. 27. Caldwell's description circulated via popular journals. On 4 January 1817, *Niles' Register* (Baltimore) reprinted it from the *Cape Fear Recorder* (Wilmington, North Carolina).

4. On Jefferson's use of this book at Monticello, see O'Neal, *Jefferson's Library*, under "Desgodetz, Antoine Babuty."

REFERENCES

Adams, William Howard. *Jefferson's Monticello*. New York: Abbeville Press, 1983.

Bryan, John M., ed. *Robert Mills, Architect*. Washington, D. C.: The American Institute of Architects Press, 1989. Esp. pp. 10–11.

[Caldwell, John Edwards.] *A Tour through Part of Virginia, in the Summer of 1808 [with] an Account of . . . Monticello, . . .* New York: for the author, 1809.

Kimball. *Jefferson, Architect*. No. 23.

McLaughlin, Jack. *Jefferson and Monticello: The Biography of a Builder*. New York: Henry Holt and Company, 1988.

Nichols. *Jefferson's Architectural Drawings*. No. 48.

O'Neal. *Jefferson's Library*.

Prothro, Kimberly. "Monticello as Roman Villa: The Ancients, Architecture, and Jefferson," *Virginia Cavalcade* 39 (Summer 1989):10–21.

Rutledge, Anna Wells, comp. and ed. *Cumulative Record of Exhibition Catalogues: The Pennsylvania Academy of the Fine Arts, 1807–1870; The Society of Artists, 1800–1814; The Artists' Fund Society, 1835–1845*. Philadelphia: American Philosophical Society, 1955.

Scott, Pamela. "Thomas Jefferson and Robert Mills." Lecture, Second Annual Architectural History Symposium, "The South in Architecture." University of Virginia, 1989.

FIGURE 2. **Parlor, Monticello** *(Photograph courtesy of David King Gleason, Baton Rouge, La.)*

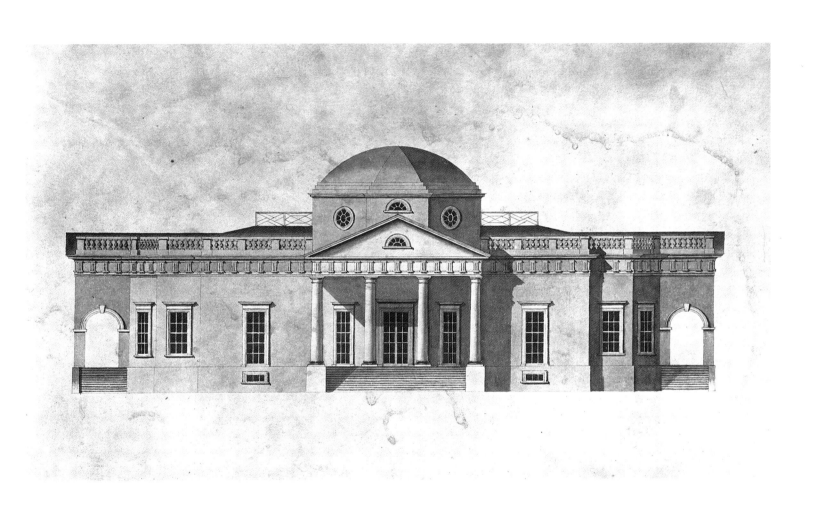

# 13.
# CAPE HENRY LIGHTHOUSE

*Plan, Elevation, and Section*

U. S. Route 60, Virginia Beach
Presentation drawing, circa 1792
Signed: *John MComb* [sic] *Junr.*
Pricking, pencil, pen, and writing ink, with watercolor on paper, mounted on board; 35 ⅛ by 20 ¾ inches
Collection of the New-York Historical Society, John McComb, Jr., Collection, Drawing No. 77

FIGURE 1. *Site photo,* **Cape Henry Lighthouse.**

John McComb, Jr., was an American-born architect who worked in the late Colonial tradition of the master builder. He was listed simply as "mason-builder" in the New York City directories of 1790, the last year he worked for his father, an established builder-architect and Surveyor of the City of New York. The younger McComb apparently received no formal architectural training and was probably self-taught. By 1808, his library included more than fifty-two books on architecture, construction, and fortifications. His memoranda books contain technical information, geometric formulae, and recipes for materials.

Having just begun his own practice in 1790, McComb replied to a solicitation from the new United States government for proposals for a lighthouse at Cape Henry. It was the first lighthouse commissioned in the first session of the First Congress of the United States of America in 1789, and was an important federal project. Duties on shipped goods were essential to the federal reserve, and lighthouses were necessary to safe shipping. Cape Henry was unprotected, since an earlier attempt at construction of a lighthouse by the Commonwealth of Virginia had failed.

Treasury Secretary Alexander Hamilton endorsed McComb's $15,200 proposal over six others, including a lower bid. President George Washington approved the bid, the contract was awarded in March 1791, and construction was completed in October 1792. McComb's uncle, William Pers, worked with him on the project.

Hamilton's confidence in McComb was well-placed. McComb had already been commissioned to design Government House (1790; demolished), the planned residence for the President in New York City. Tench Coxe, in recommending that McComb be awarded the contract for the lighthouse at Montauk Point, New York, stated that "this is the same person who built that [lighthouse] on Cape Henry. . . . His attention, skill, and fidelity in that case inspire confidence on this occasion."[1] McComb subsequently built the Montauk Point Lighthouse (1796), the Eton's Neck, New York, Lighthouse (1797–98), and Hamilton's country house, The Grange (New York, 1801–02). His finest hour came with New York City Hall (1803–12), one of the preeminent American commissions of the early nineteenth century, designed with Joseph-François Mangin. In 1817, the elder James Renwick solicited McComb's interest in succeeding Latrobe, with Bulfinch, as architect of the United States Capitol.

McComb's drawing for the Cape Henry Light shows a seventy-two-foot-high octagonal-pyramidal tower carried by a spread foundation twenty feet deep. As executed, the tower has an exterior of hammer-dressed Rappahannock sandstone ashlar, with foundations, door surrounds, and window surrounds of Aquia sandstone. The tower is mounted with a wrought-iron framed octagonal lantern, set on a projecting platform with a copper-clad cornice. The lantern is capped with a domed roof, also sheathed in copper. The ventilator, shaped like a man's head and turned by a vane, was not mere whimsy; McComb designed it to comply with the literal requirements of the specifications.

Cape Henry, patterned on the Cape Henlopen, Delaware, Lighthouse (1767), and the Sandy Hook, New Jersey, Lighthouse (1764), was the model for McComb's Montauk Point and Eton's Neck lighthouses and for his shot tower in Baltimore (1822). The octagonal-pyramidal form had material efficiency and structural strength. It had less surface area and material yet more rigidity than a square pyramid; it approached the strength and economy of a conical tower, yet could be laid in straight courses of flat-faced masonry. The present condition of the structure (today maintained as a museum by the Association for the Preservation of Virginia Antiquities) testifies to the integrity of the design.

There are five extant lighthouse drawings by McComb, all are in the collection of the New-York Historical Society. This drawing, though untitled, is identifiable as Cape Henry because its major dimensions and features approximate Cape Henry more closely than they do Montauk Point or Eton's Neck. The foundation measurements approximate the final depth at Cape Henry, suggesting that the drawing postdates construction. A separate drawing of the lantern (New-York Historical Society Collection No. 78) is identifiable as Cape Henry by similar analysis. A drawing comparing the as-contracted and as-executed foundations at Cape Henry (No. 75) was apparently used by McComb to substantiate a contract change-order.

MCH and JA

NOTES
1.  Henry, "Old Cape Henry," 7.

REFERENCES
Gilchrist, Agnes Addison. "Notes for a Catalogue of the John McComb (1763–1853) Collection of Architectural Drawings in the New-York Historical Society." *Journal of the Society of Architectural Historians* 28 (October 1969):201–10.

————. "John McComb, Sr. and Jr., in New York, 1784–1799." *Journal of the Society of Architectural Historians* 31 (March 1972):10–21.

Hamilton, Alexander. *The Papers of Alexander Hamilton.* Edited by Harold C. Syrett and Jacob E. Cooke. 27 vols. New York: Columbia University Press, 1961–87.

Hamlin, Talbot. *Greek Revival Architecture in America: Being an Account of Important Trends in American Architecture and American Life Prior to the War between the States.* 1944. Reprint. New York: Dover, 1964. Pp. 122–23.

————. "McComb; John." *Dictionary of American Biography.*

Henry, Michael C., with Janet Averill. "Old Cape Henry Lighthouse." Historic Structure Report. Watson and Henry Associates, 1990.

McComb, John, Jr. Memorandum Book. 1792–98. New-York Historical Society, John McComb, Jr., Collection.

Stillman, Damie. "Artistry and Skill in the Architecture of John McComb, Jr." Master of Arts thesis, University of Delaware, 1956.

————. "McComb, John, Jr.," in *Macmillan Encyclopedia,* 1982.

# 14.
# NEWMARKET, NEW HOUSE

*Proposed Elevation*

Caroline County (unbuilt)
Presentation drawing, late eighteenth century
Pricking(?), pencil(?), pen and India ink, and watercolor on
paper, with added watercolor; 11 ¾ by 17 ⅞ inches
Collection of the Virginia Historical Society, Richmond, bound
in *The Architecture of M. Vitruvius Pollio*, Rare Book, NA 340
V5 1771, copy 2, oversize

His father, a prominent horse-breeder, and his younger brother, George, a colonel in the Revolutionary War, both overshadow John Baylor (1750–1808), who is said to have acquired self-indulgent tastes during his education in England. His claim on history rests on his intention to replace his family's house at Newmarket plantation in Caroline County (demolished; FIGURE 1 ) with one of the grandest mansions ever proposed for a Virginia site up to that time.[1]

At some unknown date, Baylor acquired a set of drawings for the new house from a professional architect and began construction. The design and the style of the drawings indicate that he almost surely turned to an architect in Great Britain, as did a number of his contemporaries. Rubble from the unfinished endeavor remained visible on the site at least into the mid 1960s.[2] Two drawings—a roof plan and the present elevation—survive, tipped in on the back flyleaves of Baylor's copy of *The Architecture of M. Vitruvius Pollio* (London, 1771). This volume was the first half of the first English edition (1771, 1791) of Vitruvius's *Ten Books*, translated by the architect William Newton.[3] The presence of these two drawings in the book does not argue for an attribution to Newton because the design does not especially resemble his work and because the Baylors used the Vitruvius for a scrapbook.[4] In 1946 the architect and preservationist A. Lawrence Kocher, then at Colonial Williamsburg, promoted the idea of copying the design in Waco, Texas, at Baylor University, a school named for a nephew of John Baylor's; but nothing came of this idea.[5]

Insofar as one can tell without a plan, the Newmarket design amounts to an English country house transported to America. The scale looks particularly out of place in comparison with the more modest size of eighteenth-century Virginia mansions. At least one other design for so ambitious a Virginia house survives from the late eighteenth century, a Latrobe project of around 1796–98 for an estate identified only as "Mill Hill."[6] But, with the rarest of exceptions, not until the early twentieth century did Virginians build mansions of this size.

The conception, with its colonnaded wings and temple portico, develops the British Palladian past in an Adamesque manner. The colonnades are screens through which to view the landscape. (Straight "transparent" wings have an Anglo-Palladian precedent, but Robert Adam surely popularized the Picturesque columnar screen [ FIGURE 2.25 ].)[7] The portico, which combines features from a variety of Orders, fully embodies Adam's rejection of the laws that the Palladians had expected to pass on to posterity. The binding of Baylor's book preserves two antithetical representatives of the Classical tradition, the text of Vitruvius and a house designed in Adam's anti-Vitruvian vogue, brought together, one suspects, by the wish to live like an English gentleman, with a grand house and a learned library.

The refined inking, fluent washes, and facile modeling, unremarkable by English standards, represent a level probably never attained in the eighteenth century by an American-born drafter. A later hand added to the originally muted elevation such features as the lurid foliage and the coarse reinforcing of the lines and shadows. Two copies of the elevation are known.[8]

CEB

NOTES

1. The old house belonged to a group of H-plan Virginia houses, such as Tuckahoe in Goochland County (by 1723 and later). Ellen Bruce Baylor's commonplace book, pp. 24, 26–27, gives an account of the building with a site plan. Michael McDonough, a Ph.D. candidate in architectural history at the University of Virginia, called this drawing and the Baylor commonplace book to my attention.

2. On the fragments, see "Grandeur in Caroline," p. 3.

3. Baylor's copy of Vitruvius also has textual annotations, probably by two individuals.

4. Damie Stillman, John W. Shirley Professor of Art History at the University of Delaware, graciously evaluated the possibility of a Newton attribution.

5. Kocher to Pat M. Neff, President, Baylor University, 14 February 1946; carbon preserved inside the front flyleaves of *The Architecture of . . . Vitruvius*. Kathy Hinton, Secretary, Texas Collection, Baylor University, kindly helped me to determine that Kocher's suggestion did not bear fruit.

6. On "Mill Hill," see Brownell and Cohen, *Architectural Drawings*.

7. On the Picturesque use of veil-like wings, see Chapter 2.

8. In 1886 Ellen Bruce Baylor made one copy in her commonplace book, p. 31. Baylor and Baylor, *Baylor's History*, p. 15, and Wingfield, *History*, p. 371, illustrate another, unlocated, derivative.

REFERENCES

Baylor, Ellen Bruce. Commonplace book. Virginia Historical Society, late nineteenth century. Pp. 17–31, 47–48, 50–51, 57–58, 59–61, 128, 180, 185–88.

Baylor, Orval Walker, and Henry Bedinger Baylor, eds. *Baylor's History of the Baylors: A Collection of Records and Important Family Data.* [LeRoy, Illinois]: LeRoy Journal Printing Company, [ca. 1915]. Pp. 2 n. 13, 10 n., 11–12, 15, 50, 54.

Boyd, Sterling M. "The Adam Style in America, 1770– 1820." Ph.D. diss., Princeton University, 1966. Published in *Outstanding Dissertations in the Fine Arts.* New York: Garland Publishing, 1985.

Decatur, Stephen, and Vera Walker Morel. "Baylor of Virginia." *Historical Southern Families* 17 (1972):60–80.

"Grandeur in Caroline." *Occasional Bulletin, Virginia Historical Society* no. 9 (October 1964):2–4.

Stillman, Damie. *English Neo-classical Architecture.* 2 vols. from the series *Studies in Architecture,* 26. London: A. Zwemmer, 1988.

Stiverson, Cynthia Zignego. *Architecture and the Decorative Arts: The A. Lawrence Kocher Collection of Books at the Colonial Williamsburg Foundation.* West Cornwall, Connecticut: Locust Hill Press, 1989.

Wingfield, Marshall. *A History of Caroline County, Virginia, from Its Formation in 1727 to 1924.* Richmond: Trevvet Christian & Co., 1924. Pp. 86, 371–79.

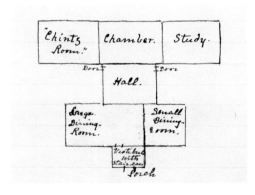

FIGURE 1. **"Baylors Folly," New Market, old house plan.** *Sketched some time before 1899 by Ellen Bruce Baylor in her commonplace book, after demolition. (Photograph courtesy of the Virginia Historical Society.)*

# 15.
# WILLIAM PENNOCK HOUSE

*Interior Perspective*

16 Main St., Norfolk (demolished)
Presentation drawing, probably late 1790s
Signed on title page of bound volume of drawings: *B. Henry Latrobe, Boneval*
Pencil, pen and India ink, and watercolor on paper; binding size 21 by 14 ⅝ inches
Collection of the Library of Congress, Washington, D.C., Prints and Photographs Division, "Designs of Buildings . . . in Virginia," folio 6

A professionally trained English architect and engineer, the thirty-one-year-old B. Henry Latrobe spent most of his first three American years (1796–98) in Virginia before leaving for Philadelphia, the American metropolis. On his arrival in Virginia, Latrobe was both a universal man with a magnificent education and an immature member of the international architectural avant-garde, essentially the practitioners of the second phase of Neoclassicism. To his modest British practice, his Virginia stay added only three buildings, all mutilated in execution by others. Thereafter, between 1799 and 1820, Latrobe took his place as one of the towering figures in American architecture, a designer who balanced profound self-discipline with great imaginative power. Only Jefferson did more to establish monumental Classicism in the young nation.

The William Pennock House (Norfolk, 1796; demolished) was Latrobe's first American building.[1] In March 1796 the architect won a wager with Pennock (circa 1752–1816), a wealthy merchant, by planning a house that fit certain accommodations into a restricted space without throwing the main entry off-center. After Latrobe left Norfolk, Pennock decided to execute the design from the small drawing that Latrobe had given him. The project stalled, apparently for lack of working drawings. When Latrobe came to the rescue, he discovered simple bungling along with major changes made by both the family and the builders. (He indicated that the builders had introduced elements of "the heavy wooden taste of the last century," apparently a reference to British Palladianism.) Throughout the rest of Latrobe's career, the elements of this little drama recurred, particularly the drastic modification of designs built at a distance, and Latrobe's activity in training artisans to follow his ideas.

The staircase says a great deal about the Pennock design.[2] Latrobe's hall brought to America some of the most exhilarating features from the great development of staircase design in later eighteenth-century Britain. Latrobe won the architectural wager by devising an asymmetrical version of an *imperial* staircase, the staircase that rises to a landing in one flight and then, splitting in half and reversing direction, ascends to the next floor in two flights ( FIGURE 1 ). By eliminating the left-hand upper flight, Latrobe made room so that the main doorway would come in the center of the principal facade. Simultaneously, he designed these stairs as a *geometric* (or "flying") staircase. Self-consciously bringing new ideas to a provincial society, Latrobe invented for Pennock a room of spectacular novelty.

The novelty of the drawing, however, exceeds that of the hall. To a world that knew architectural drawing as the occasional geometric diagram, Latrobe brought a stunning graphic repertory. His resources began with those of the European professional (such as the clean, stable India ink line) and culminated in the full-color perspective rendering, where his extra abilities as an amateur artist came into play. Theoretically, a perspective—an architectural drawing that is a picture rather than a diagram—permits the layman to understand what the actual building will look like. But perspectives have at least as great a value for simply selling a design, and none of Latrobe's known perspectives can surpass the spectacle of forms shooting through space in Captain Pennock's hall. Indeed, rather than giving good information, this drawing, like many perspectives, deceives the viewer. The room must have looked tame next to it, and Latrobe had to take out a wall in the foreground to make the scene possible.

The drawing is a tour-de-force of modeling and color, as well as perspective. The color scheme is by no means as simple as it first appears. Thus, up through the string course Latrobe made the woodwork white with light yellow panels. But above that he made the woodwork yellow with pale sunk areas, perhaps of light blue on the doors.

Latrobe incorporated four leaves of Pennock materials into a volume called "Designs of Buildings . . . in Virginia," with a title page dated 1799, after his move to Philadelphia. The volume poses many puzzles, including how to date the execution of the individual pages. Latrobe assembled several such volumes to display his abilities to prospective clients. — CEB

NOTES
1.   On Pennock, see Latrobe, *Virginia Journals*, 2:550. For the documents of the "commission," see 1:79–80, and Latrobe, *Correspondence*, 1:147–50.

2.   On English Neoclassical staircase types, see Stillman, *English Neo-classical Architecture*, pp. 286–96.

REFERENCES
Brownell and Cohen. *Architectural Drawings of Latrobe*.

Fahlman, Betsy L., et al. *A Tricentennial Celebration: Norfolk, 1682–1982*, exh. cat. Norfolk: Chrysler Museum, 1982.

Hamlin. *Latrobe* Pp. 68, 92, 95–98, 103, 116.

Kimball, Fiske. "Some Architectural Designs of Benjamin Henry Latrobe." *Library of Congress Quarterly Journal of Current Acquisitions* 3 (May 1946):8–13.

Latrobe, B. Henry. *Correspondence*.

——. *Virginia Journals*.

Stillman, Damie. *English Neo-classical Architecture*. 2 vols. from the series *Studies in Architecture*, 26. London: A. Zwemmer, 1988.

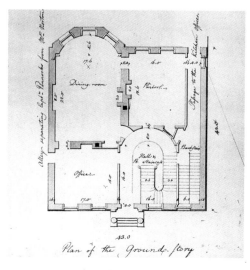

FIGURE 1. **Plan of the Ground Story, Pennock House.** *(Photograph courtesy of the Library of Congress.)*

# 16.
# VIRGINIA STATE PENITENTIARY

*Proposed Elevations*

Belvidere and Spring Sts., Richmond (demolished)
Presentation drawing
Signed and dated: *B. H. Latrobe, Architect, 1797*
Pricking, pencil, pen and India ink, and watercolor on paper;
20 1/16 by 14 7/8 inches
Collection of the Virginia State Library, Richmond

Latrobe's first American commission in civic architecture, the Virginia State Penitentiary, sprang from an international late-eighteenth-century spirit of rationalized and humanitarian penology. Although Jefferson had attempted to revise the "sanguinary code" of Virginia, reform did not come until 1796. In that year, Virginia restricted capital punishment to first-degree murder; substituted a program of imprisonment, labor, and partial solitary confinement for all other felonies, with segregation of the sexes; and provided for a "gaol and penitentiary house" (a building with cells for the solitary confinement that suppposedly induced repentance), with provision for light, air, and security from fire. In all this, the legislature followed the model of recent reforms in Pennsylvania.

In 1796–97, at least four designers competed unofficially for the prison: Samuel Dobie; George Hadfield; Jefferson, who sent a new drawing of his prison design in case the drawings sent in 1786 (see SURVEY NOS. 9, 10) had disappeared, as indeed they had; and Latrobe, whom the governor and the Executive Council picked unaminously. Latrobe's scheme ( FIGURE 2 ) had two parts, a rectangular front area of three forecourts, and the main, semicircular prison area, for male offenders, whom Latrobe separated from the women. He meant to build the curved part first, to serve as the prison until he could add the forecourts. He provided workshops, infirmaries, and a variety of sleeping quarters. He meant to use partial vaulting. He planned the bow windows of the central keeper's house to survey the curved range, and he felt sure enough about his provisions for confinement and surveillance to make all the screen walls remarkably low. This surely reflects a concern to distribute air as a preventive against the dreaded "jail fever," or typhus, and no doubt it reflects a concern to distribute light.

Latrobe's design agreed only at certain points with the provisions of the law. It did not grow out of Jefferson's design (as Jefferson himself thought)[1]; it answered, not to Jefferson's principle of labor in solitude, but to Virginia's Pennsylvania-inspired program of partial solitary confinement. Evidently Latrobe owed many principles to his friendship with John Howard, the British crusader for prison reform. Latrobe's layout probably derived from William Blackburn, the prison architect whom Howard

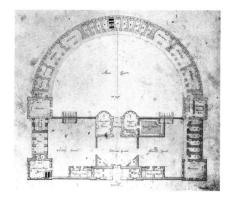

FIGURE 2. **Richmond Penitentiary, ground plan.** *(Photograph courtesy of the Virginia State Library.)*

favored, and/or the gifted Neoclassicist Thomas Harrison. From the English philosopher Jeremy Bentham and his brother Sir Samuel Bentham, Latrobe may have borrowed the principle that, because of the security that central surveillance would provide, prison walls could be relatively low for good ventilation.

Latrobe worked on the prison in 1797–98, starting with the forepart. The effort gives an ominous taste of the challenges to his professionalism that the future would bring. In 1798, the great commission for the Bank of Pennsylvania (1799–1801; demolished, FIGURE 2.39 ) bore him off to Philadelphia.

All the prison drawings by Latrobe and other architects have disappeared except for seven sheets of Latrobe's preliminary proposals in the Virginia State Library. The top elevation shows the flat south face of the semicircular unit that Latrobe meant to build first, with the keeper's house at the center. The middle elevation depicts the south front of the forecourts, which Latrobe meant to add. The bottom elevation represents the west side of the forecourts. The fact that the state gave him the very large, unexpected gratuity of $100 for the drawings *before* choosing the design for execution suggests the impact of Latrobe's drawings (which he submitted bound as a volume).[2] Unfortunately, this action also suggests the erratic treatment of Latrobe and the other early professionals. Far more typical of their fortunes, Latrobe in the long run accepted a remuneration less than the professionally proper five percent for design and supervision of the penitentiary.

CEB

NOTES
1.   Jefferson, "Autobiography," p. 65.

2.   See Latrobe to James Wood and the Council of State of Virginia, 12 May 1797, in Latrobe, *Correspondence*, 1:45.

REFERENCES
Brownell and Cohen. *Architectural Drawings of Latrobe.*

Hamlin. *Latrobe.* Pp. 92, 120–26, 149, 534, 560, 589.

Jefferson. "Autobiography." In *The Writings of Thomas Jefferson.* Comp. and ed. by Paul Leicester Ford. 10 vols. New York: G.P. Putnam's Sons, 1892–99. 1:62–66.

Keve, Paul W. *The History of Corrections in Virginia.* Charlottesville: University Press of Virginia, 1986.

Latrobe, B. Henry. *Correspondence.*

———. *Virginia Journals.*

FIGURE 1. *Vintage photo,* **Virginia Penitentiary,** *by Dementi Studios, circa 1929. (Photograph courtesy of The Valentine Museum, Richmond.)*

*Elevation of the South Front of that part of the Building which is proposed to be first erected, as shown in N: II.*

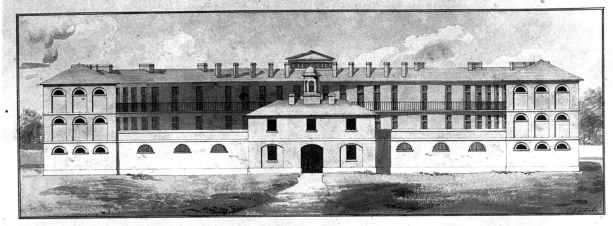

*Elevation of the South Front as it will appear on completion of the Whole Design, as shown in the plan N: I.*

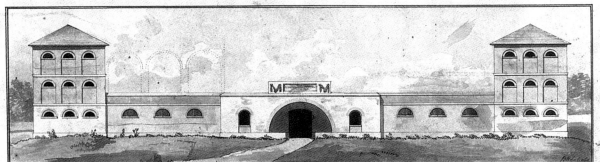

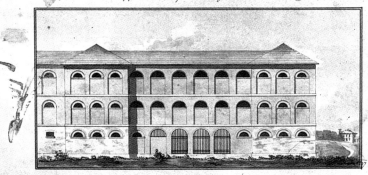

*Elevation of the West Flank, see N: I.*

# 17.
# VIRGINIA STATE PENITENTIARY

*Proposed Elevations and Perspective*

Belvidere and Spring Sts., Richmond (demolished)
Presentation drawing
Signed and dated: *B. H. Latrobe Architect 1797* and *B. H. Latrobe Arch. del. 1797*
Pricking, pencil, pen and India ink, and watercolor on paper; 19 ¹⁵⁄₁₆ by 14 ³⁄₁₆ inches
Collection of the Virginia State Library, Richmond

FIGURE 1. *Photo of 1991 archaelogical excavations prior to demolition of the Penitentiary, showing foundations of original gatehouse. (Photograph by Action Photo, courtesy of Ethyl Corporation.)*

In May of 1797, when Latrobe thanked the governor and the Council of State for the surprise gift of $100 for his drawings, he wrote of adding less essential drawings "of the square part of the building," and he sent two more sheets on 1 June.[1] The page of drawings illustrated here is probably one of these. Its three drawings are less essential, but they all display the hand of Latrobe the reforming designer. The middle elevation shows the women's court on the east side; separation of the sexes was one of the most fundamental articles of the new penology. The top elevation, inside the west court, shows the infirmary, designed for women on the third story, men on the second, and a grill on the first to give this unit of the prison not only good ventilation but even a view. An especially telling image, however, occurs on the bottom of the page.

From the late eighteenth century to the late nineteenth, the prison presented one of the supreme test cases to architects concerned with expressing the nature of buildings. Latrobe, for whom this expression came under the heading of *character,* made his perspective into a classic illustration of the possibilities.[2] His handling of the Penitentiary reflects his close study of the works of a master, George Dance the Younger. Dance's Newgate Prison (London, 1770–80 and later; Chapter 2, FIGURE 2.49) won him international acclaim for the way its somber, rusticated walls, adorned with garlands of chains over the portals, conveyed the nature of the building and issued a dire threat to wrongdoers. Latrobe had shown such festoons on his earlier elevation (SURVEY NO. 16). Now he converted the walls to the logical Virginia counterpart of rustication, rough stone, which he later argued would "add to the Solemn character of the building."[3] (Unfortunately neither this rubble masonry nor the festoons of chains made it into execution.) For the only known time in an architectural drawing, Latrobe portrayed a stormy background; he chose to harmonize Nature with the gloom of incarceration. In his interest in stamping his building with a threatening character, he represents the love of those awesome effects that he and his period called "Sublime."

Latrobe's successor, Major John Clarke, an important amateur architect, made many changes to the design (FIGURE 2). Several of these evidently stemmed from doubts about the security that surveillance would provide. Clarke set the keeper's house on top of the gateway and linked the resultant element to the wings by grilled arcades to increase security without cutting off ventilation. The prison began receiving inmates in 1800, but work on the building dragged on into 1806.

Despite all the high purpose that entered into the creation of this penitentiary, and despite all the important names that belong to its story, the future of prison design lay in Pennsylvania and New York, not in Virginia. During the early nineteenth century, the Richmond Penitentiary severely disappointed expectations as to its wholesomeness, security, reformative power, and capacity to support itself. The problems sprang primarily from the newness of the Virginia State Penitentiary as an institution. The sketchy portrait one has of Latrobe as its architect shows us an immature designer, dedicated to advanced ideas and, despite his limitations, able to combine those ideas from an impressive range of sources.

Major Clarke's changes affected Latrobe's drawings as well as his building. Although no architectural drawing from his hand has come to light, it appears that he used Latrobe's drawings in an attempt to render his own proposals as impressively. Thus, Latrobe's main elevation (SURVEY NO. 16) has clumsy pricking that marks out Clarke's arcade. And its surface is disfigured with practice strokes that make no sense at all on a beautiful presentation drawing, unless one concludes that Clarke, in trying to make his own colored drawings, used Latrobe's for wiping his brush.

CEB

NOTES
1.  See Latrobe to James Wood and the Council of State of Virginia, 12 May 1797, in Latrobe, *Correspondence,* 1:45.

2.  On the theory of character, Dance's Newgate Prison, and the Sublime, see Chapter 2.

3.  See Latrobe to James Wood and the Council of State of Virginia, 12 July 1797, in Latrobe, *Papers,* microfiche ed., 156/A6.

REFERENCES
Brownell and Cohen. *Architectural Drawings of Latrobe.*

Hamlin. *Latrobe.* Pp. 92, 120–26, 149, 534, 560, 589.

Jefferson. "Autobiography." In *The Writings of Thomas Jefferson.* Comp. and ed. by Paul Leicester Ford. 10 vols. New York: G. P. Putnam's Sons, 1892–99. 1:62–66.

Keve, Paul W. *The History of Corrections in Virginia.* Charlottesville: University Press of Virginia, 1986.

Latrobe, B. Henry. *Correspondence.*

———. *Virginia Journals.*

FIGURE 2. *Detail,* **Penitentiary at Richmond, main front,** *aquatint by J. Wood, circa 1825. (Photograph courtesy of The Valentine Museum, Richmond.)*

*Internal Elevation of the Infirmary in the West Wing.*

*Internal Elevation of the Women's Court, or of the East Wing.*

*View in perspective of the Gate of the Penitentiary House.*

B. H. Latrobe Architect 1797.

# 18.
# RICHMOND
# THEATRE

*Section of Proposed Auditorium*

Richmond (unbuilt)

Presentation drawing, 1797–98

Inscribed on title page of bound volume of drawings: *B. Henry Latrobe Boneval, Architect & Engineer. Begun Dec^r 2d 1797. finished Jan^y 8th 1798.*

Pricking, pencil, pen and India ink, and watercolor on paper; 15 ¾ by 21 ¹⁵⁄₁₆ inches

Collection of the Library of Congress, Washington, D.C., Prints and Photographs Division, "Designs of a Building ... to contain a Theatre, Assembly-Rooms, and an Hotel," folio 5

During December 1797 and early January 1798, Latrobe produced another major design for a Richmond public building, one that would have combined a theater, assembly rooms, and a hotel.[1] Had he succeeded in executing the scheme, such a building—in the United States, with its modest development of public architecture—would have at once become a landmark. Even in Britain the ensemble would have stood out, at least to the historian. And the theater per se, executed anywhere in the western world, would hold a significant place because of how the scheme serves as an example of Neoclassical thinking about character in architecture.

So far there has come to light no earlier design by an English-speaking architect for a composite building devoted to exactly the same three purposes. Nonetheless, Latrobe's conception grew logically out of the eighteenth century. Precedent had developed in Britain for making such combinations as an assembly house with a theater, an assembly house with a hotel, and an opera house with assembly rooms and a tavern. As to the United States, Latrobe surely knew that Virginians sometimes housed the functions that he had in mind under one roof, for the ballroom, or "long" room, of the tavern/hotel often accommodated theatrical performances.

Latrobe chose a Neoclassical plan-type ( FIGURE 4.25 ), the H-plan which, in his handling, points to the influence of reconstructions of Roman baths, as does the prominent bow. In this bow Latrobe placed the theater, the *raison d'être* of the design and the real measure of his ambition. In the auditorium he took an exceptional step when he classicized British theatrical tradition by wedding the pit, the box, and the gallery to a neo-antique semicircular plan. He drew on Henry Holland's two new theatres royal in London—in Drury Lane (1791–94, demolished) and Covent Garden (1792, demolished)—which had introduced a splendor virtually unprecedented in English theaters. From Covent Garden in particular Latrobe took the idea of cantilevering, an innovation in the Anglo-American world. In accord with the theory of character, the curved theater found external expression in the bow, an important but rarely executed Neoclassical treatment. (Charles A. Busby's bowed porch for the Bollingbrook Street Theatre [ SURVEY NO. 25 ] very likely reflects the same principle.) In this case, the treatment owes to reconstructions of the baths; perhaps to the Théâtre Feydeau (Paris, 1788–91; demolished) by Legrand and Molinos; and surely to an almost forgotten work by George Dance, the surgeon's theater at St. Bartholomew's Hospital in London (1791; demolished). The design unmistakably exhibits Latrobe's determination to create avant-garde architecture.

But the project falls painfully short of its architect's aspirations. The multiple levels of the building confused Latrobe. He lost control over the design inside and out. He showed thorough indifference to fire precautions. And he erred acoustically.

Latrobe's auditorium discloses another limitation, his uncertainty with ornament at this date. Delicate, small-scale motifs from the First Phase of Neoclassicism (such as the garlands and scrolls on the parapets) mingle unhappily with the bold forms of the Second Phase (such as the broad-planed, coffered ceiling). The rising influence of ancient Greece appears in the mixture, as in the adaptation of a Greek Doric order, or in an element of the kind often called "Etruscan" in the period, the black and terra-cotta parapet panels inspired by Greek painted vases. In later years, Latrobe's interest in this kind of Neoclassical decoration may have led the way to certain of the painted decorations at the John Wickhams' Richmond mansion ( SURVEY NO. 24 ).

Latrobe's whimsy makes the drawing hard to resist. At one end of the upper parapet, on a scaffold that Rube Goldberg might have concocted in collaboration with M.C. Escher, a painter finishes his decorations; at the other, the workmen are still stretching the linen ground on which the artist paints. Right of center, a figure who must be Latrobe himself gives instructions to a carpenter.

Latrobe made this section as part of a magnificently conceived volume of drawings that, typically, he did not finish. In the end, he moved this section and his perspective of the ballroom (see next entry) from the back to the front, presumably because he thought that they had the greatest attraction for lay eyes. The book held fourteen sheets of drawings, all now in the Library of Congress.                                                           CEB

NOTES

1. For Latrobe's comments on the enterprise, see his *Virginia Journals*, 2:332–33, 340. For the advertisement to prospective subscribers that appeared in the Richmond press, see Latrobe, *Correspondence*, 1:66–68.

REFERENCES

Brownell and Cohen. *Architectural Drawings of Latrobe.*

Hamlin. *Latrobe.* Pp. 87–88, 117–20.

Kimball, Fiske. "Some Architectural Designs of Benjamin Henry Latrobe." *Library of Congress Quarterly Journal of Current Acquisitions* 3 (May 1946):8–13.

Latrobe, B. Henry. *Correspondence.*

——. *Virginia Journals.*

Leacroft, Richard. *The Development of the English Playhouse: An Illustrated Survey of Theatre Building in England from Medieval to Modern Times.* New ed. New York: Methuen, 1988.

Shockley, Martin Staples. *The Richmond Stage, 1784–1812.* Charlottesville: University Press of Virginia, 1977.

Stillman, Damie. *English Neo-classical Architecture.* 2 vols. from the series *Studies in Architecture*, 26. London: A. Zwemmer, 1988.

FIGURE 1. *Latrobe,* **Richmond Theatre,** *elevation (view of the stage). (Photograph courtesy of the Library of Congress.)*

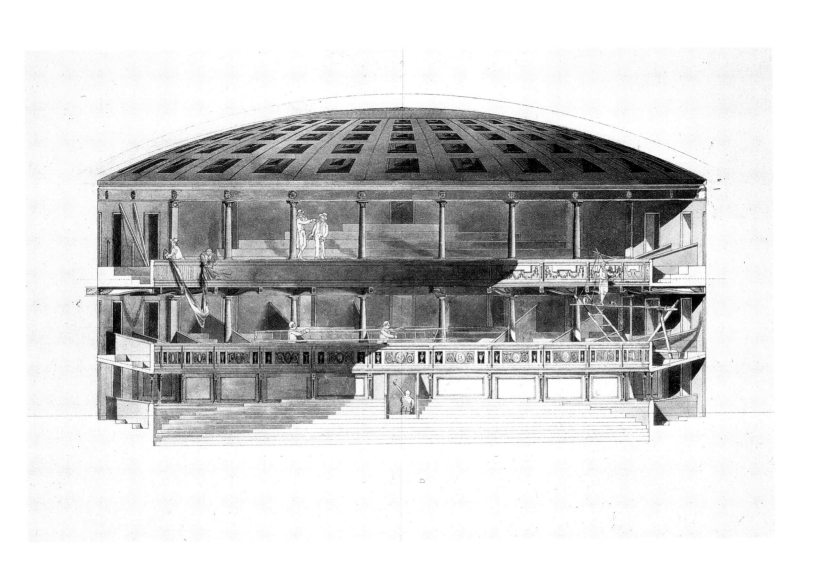

# 19.
# RICHMOND
# THEATRE

*Proposed Ballroom Perspective*

Richmond (unbuilt)
Presentation drawing, 1798
Inscribed on title page of bound volume of drawings: *B.Henry Latrobe Boneval, Architect & Engineer. Begun Dec ʳ 2d 1797. finished Janʸ 8th 1798.*
Pricking, pencil, pen and India ink, and watercolor on paper; 15 ¾ by 21 ¹⁵/₁₆ inches
Collection of the Library of Congress, Prints and Photographs Division, "Designs of a Building . . . to contain a Theatre, Assembly-Rooms, and an Hotel," folio 6

Latrobe envisioned his theater complex as a replacement for the decaying frame building that Alexandre Quesnay de Beaurepaire had built in 1786 ( FIGURE 4.14 ), the year after Quesnay founded his ill-fated Académie des Sciences et Beaux Arts des Etats-Unis de l'Amérique, in actuality an academy/theater scheme. In 1790 Thomas Wade West and John Bignall, two newly arrived British actors, took over the building. In time, the West and Bignall company had theaters in four other Virginia cities as well as one in Charleston, South Carolina (1792–93, demolished) that James Hoban built. The latter structure was the first of the stylish American theater buildings of the 1790s that left behind the inelegant accommodations of the past— such as Quesnay's academy building. Latrobe had close ties with the West and Bignall company to the point that, just after making his design, he wrote his lost play, *The Apology,* for a member of the troupe.

Little less captivating than Latrobe's auditorium section is his ballroom perspective, an ambitious essay in ornamental design. It took him roughly another decade to discover the kind of reformed decoration that matched his conception of architecture, and this happened only when he discovered the pages of Thomas Hope's *Household Furniture and Interior Decoration* (London, 1807). In his ballroom, bold chimneypieces, consonant with the Second Phase of Neoclassicism, keep company with dainty looking-glasses and settees perhaps suggested by the third edition of George and Alice Hepplewhite's *Cabinet-Maker and Upholsterer's Guide* (London, 1794), a book that popularized the First Phase after it had fallen from high fashion.

One can miss neither the importance of color in this drawing nor the importance of light, but a twentieth-century eye may find the festive coloring hard to take. The color scheme—principally pale yellow, radioactive pink, and white—conforms with eighteenth-century standards that seem puzzling two hundred years later. Latrobe's concern for light poses no such problems. Here, as in the Pennock stairhall ( SURVEY NO. 15 ), one can enjoy his skillful rendering of effects, such as light bouncing up onto a ceiling (a favorite touch of Latrobe's) and the cool, sketchy reflections in the looking-glasses. In this third-story assembly room, the overmantel glasses would have

faced windows and reflected the sky. Most likely, Latrobe here deliberately used the Picturesque technique of placing a looking-glass to catch a living picture through a window, a practice that already enjoyed currency in America. In the contemporary rebuilding of Monticello (begun 1796), Jefferson used the technique in all three rooms along the garden front, and Latrobe would propose it for the President's House in Washington a decade later.[1]

The Latrobe of the Richmond Theatre project had miles to go before reaching maturity (and the mature Latrobe had far too busy a life to make intricate drawings such as this). No doubt the imperfections in the incompletely digested presentation drawings for the theater had nothing to do with the failure of the scheme, which died even though the Quesnay building burned in early 1798. West meant to build the interior of Latrobe's theater, but the rest of the structure required investors, and they did not come forth. After makeshifts, the West and Bignall company opened a new theater on the same site. This building, too, went up in flames in the disastrous Richmond Theatre Fire of 1811. It fell not to Latrobe but to his pupil Robert Mills to raise the monument over the graves of the victims. Mills's Monumental Church (1812–17; see SURVEY NO. 21, FIGURE 1 ) is in fact the successor to three Latrobe proposals: the Theatre; a roughly contemporary church design for the middle of Broad Street ( FIGURE NO. 4.23 ); and an 1812 mausoleum proposal ( SURVEY NO. 21 ). The twentieth century thwarted one more "Latrobe" project, the 1964–69 endeavor to build a version of Latrobe's theater as adapted by Conover Fitch, Jr., of Perry, Shaw, Hepburn and Dean.     CEB

NOTES
1.   For the proposal, see Latrobe to Dolley Madison, 21 April 1809, in Latrobe, *Correspondence,* 2:711–13.

REFERENCES
Brownell and Cohen. *Architectural Drawings of Latrobe.*

Hamlin. *Latrobe.* Pp. 87–88, 117–20.

Kimball, Fiske. "Some Architectural Designs of Benjamin Henry Latrobe." *Library of Congress Quarterly Journal of Current Acquisitions* 3 (May 1946):8–13.

Latrobe, B. Henry. *Correspondence.*

———. *Virginia Journals.*

Leacroft, Richard. *The Development of the English Playhouse: An Illustrated Survey of Theatre Building in England from Medieval to Modern Times.* New ed. New York: Methuen, 1988.

Shockley, Martin Staples. *The Richmond Stage, 1784–1812.* Charlottesville: University Press of Virginia, 1977.

Stillman, Damie. *English Neo-classical Architecture.* 2 vols. from the series *Studies in Architecture,* 26. London: A. Zwemmer, 1988.

FIGURE 1.   B. Henry Latrobe, **Richmond Theatre,** *elevation of the principal, or northwest front. (Photograph courtesy of the Library of Congress.)*

Attributed to BENJAMIN HENRY LATROBE, 1764–1820

# 20.
# CLIFTON, BENJAMIN JAMES HARRIS HOUSE

*Proposed South Front, Perspective*

Fourteenth St. and Apricot Alley, Richmond (demolished)
Presentation drawing, circa 1807
Pencil, pen and India ink, and watercolor on paper; 10 ¼ by 16 ⅞ inches
Collection of the Library of Congress, Washington, D.C., Prints and Photographs Division

FIGURE 1. *Drawing of* **Clifton Hotel**, late 1800s, shows Clifton after its conversion to a hotel, and after re-grading the street to foundation level. (Photograph courtesy of the Virginia State Library.)

When the Richmond tobacconist Benjamin James Harris built his house, Clifton (1808–09, demolished), he brought the unhappy story of one Latrobe set of designs to its close. A decade before, Latrobe had offered his Richmond patron, Colonel John Harvie, a distillation of his ideas on villa design ( SURVEY NO. 24, FIGURE 2 ). Latrobe proffered a winged design founded on the principles of orientation that guided him throughout his American career. Unsympathetic execution of the Harvie-Gamble House (1798–99, demolished; see SURVEY NO. 24 ) seems to have replaced many of the Latrobean qualities with a commonplace handling while robbing the villa of its wings.

Shortly after moving to Philadelphia, Latrobe proposed a grander variation on the Harvie-Gamble themes for the Baron Henri-Joseph Stier who, as a descendant of Peter Paul Rubens, had brought to Maryland an art collection without precedent on this side of the Atlantic.[1] In this design Latrobe incorporated one of his favorite themes, a rotunda, to serve as a painting gallery, and doubled the bows on the garden front. Stier had the design modified extensively as Riversdale (Bladensburg, 1801–02 and after), the house that he built for his daughter Rosalie and her husband, George Calvert. In the process, the rotunda, the bows, and Latrobe's artistic "handwriting" succumbed.

With a little editing, Latrobe offered the Riversdale design anew to Harris, apparently as a consequence of Latrobe's 1807 trip to Richmond to attend the trial of Aaron Burr. The provincial execution of Clifton modified Latrobe's proposal nearly past recognition.[2] Harris's narrow house certainly had no rotunda, and, as commonly happened when Latrobe could not supervise execution, the house acquired the traits of the early Neoclassicism that he found obsolete. But Clifton did keep Latrobe's pair of bows and thus belonged to a group of Neoclassical Richmond dwellings with polygonal projections. No one has yet analyzed the origin of this distinctive local preference.

From its hilltop, Latrobe's Neoclassical villa serenely surveys a superb view. In the absence of a floor plan for this house, the cupola provides the guarantee that Latrobe had retained the rotunda of the Stier project. Even before the Stier drawings surfaced, it was obvious that Latrobe had applied his consistent theory of orientation.[3] The principal rooms face south to have the advantage of the sun in the unhealthy winter season. On the Stier plan, behind the opposite facade— the one subject to winter winds—Latrobe located spaces not meant for protracted occupancy, and the Harris project must have had a quite similar layout. Latrobe took pains to protect the interior from the hot light of a summer morning and the hotter light of the afternoon. For instance, to judge from the Stier plan, the seeming windows on the west of the main block in the perspective are in fact false windows when they occur in the wall of a major room.

The perspective, preserved with a site plan, emphasizes the Picturesque constituent in Latrobe's Neoclassicism. Using elements once popularized by the British Palladians—rotunda core, colonnaded wings, garden bows—Latrobe here proposed a villa chastened by an ideal of Greek simplicity, even though it uses only a few specifically Greek elements. Latrobe meant this house to compose a good picture with its landscaping, which his site plan roughs out as winding walks and Picturesque groups of trees. Latrobe never dematerialized the walls of a house in the dazzling, profoundly personal way that Jefferson did at Monticello (see SURVEY NO. 12 ). But for Clifton, as elsewhere, he proposed to adorn a landscape with rich architectural "scenery," from the varied spaces within the house to the east pavilion, which opens on the north to permit a peep into the distance. By enabling the architect to suggest the relation between building and setting, an exterior perspective such as this fulfilled an important function.

CEB and SSD

NOTES
1. On the Stier-Calvert house and Clifton, see Latrobe, *Correspondence*, 3:12–13, n. 2.

2. One might doubt that any connection existed, specially given the puzzling fact that Latrobe's copious papers evidently contain no written evidence of a commission from Harris. But the site plan that accompanies the perspective matches the site of Harris's house, thereby confirming the identification of the perspective that Scott proposed in *Old Richmond Neighborhoods*, p. 122. See esp. Beers, *Atlas*, sec. L, p. 52.

3. For two major statements of this theory, see Latrobe to Hugh Henry Brackenridge, 18 May 1803 (*Correspondence*, 1:297–301), and Latrobe to Jefferson, 12 August 1817 (*Correspondence*, 3:928–34).

REFERENCES
Brownell and Cohen. *Architectural Drawings of Latrobe.*

Beers, F. W. *Illustrated Atlas of the City of Richmond, Virginia.* Richmond: Southern and Southwestern Surveying and Publishing Company, 1876.

Hamlin. *Latrobe.* Pp. 103, 105, 115.

Latrobe. *Correspondence.*

Scott, Mary Wingfield. *Old Richmond Neighborhoods.* 1950. Reprint. Richmond: Valentine Museum, 1984. Pp. 120–22.

Stillman, Damie. *English Neo-classical Architecture.* 2 vols. from the series *Studies in Architecture*, 26. London: A. Zwemmer, 1988.

# 21.
## RICHMOND MONUMENT AND CHURCH

*Elevation Sketch*

Richmond (unbuilt)
Study, probably late January or early February 1812
Pricking, pencil, pen and India ink, and watercolor on paper; 19⁵⁄₁₆ by 13¾ inches
Collection of the Maryland Historical Society, Baltimore

On 26 December 1811, a catastrophic fire in the Richmond Theatre claimed more than seventy lives. The victims, many of them prominent citizens, including the governor, were buried on the site. Latrobe became involved in planning a memorial in connection with such men as John Wickham and his architect Alexander Parris (see SURVEY NO. 24). The prevailing idea in Richmond called for the city to build a monument over the common grave and for a special association to erect a long-desired church behind the tomb. Latrobe did not believe that Richmonders could afford both buildings. He indulged in the possibility in this study, and then eliminated the church. In his three subsequent drawings (also in the Maryland Historical Society), he made the monument successively smaller and more simple, to reach a design that he could build for $10,000, the minimum budget for erecting a respectable public building. The commission, however, went to his pupil, Robert Mills, who created Monumental Church (1812–17; FIGURE 1). By combining a monument with a church and incorporating other novel features, the conception exhibits a Millsian love of ingenuity. The design exceeded Richmonders' means, so that its tower remains unfinished. But whatever Mills's imperfections or those of Parris, in the Richmond of the 1810s these two architects born in the 1780s prepared to take over from the generation of 1760 (led by Latrobe, Bulfinch, and Thornton). Mills thus began his ascendancy over Latrobe as a molder of the American civic monument.

As usual, Latrobe drew upon his previous work for a starting point in this design. In the late 1790s, he had proposed an ungainly twin-towered church (FIGURE 4.23) near the Richmond Theatre, but the church in the present drawing derives from his masterpiece, the Roman Catholic Cathedral in Baltimore (1806–10, 1817–21 and later). For the monument, Latrobe rethought his unexecuted project for George Washington's tomb, which he had designed in 1800 as a 100-foot-tall pyramid (see SURVEY NO. 22).[1] Writing Wickham before making the present drawing, he set down two principles for the Richmond memorial: permanence and the handing on of a written record.[2] Permanence had led him back to the pyramid, this time a smaller one in granite, holding a chamber with inscribed marble tablets set in freestone walls. Typically for this period, the steep pyramid in his drawing probably takes its ratio of height to width from the first-century-B.C. pyramid of Cestius at Rome, not from any Egyptian model. At some time, Latrobe marked possibilities for a dome lightly in pencil across the pyramid. This drawing itself may have made him question the wisdom of taking the pyramid theme—associated with colossal marvels from antiquity—and reducing it to a building only some forty-five feet tall. In simplifying his conception, Latrobe later replaced the pyramid with a dome, and he eliminated the freestanding order along with all specifically Egyptian details.

This drawing speaks eloquently of Latrobe's role in elevating the standards for American architectural graphics. With its crisp delineation and luminous watercolor washes, this sheet is handsome—far handsomer than many eighteenth-century American presentation drawings (see SURVEY NOS. 3, 13; Chapter 4, FIGURE 4.28). But it is only a study, a tool for Latrobe to use in thinking out loud.　　CEB

NOTES
1. For an outline of the story of monuments to Washington, see Chapter 2.

2. Latrobe to Wickham, 21 January 1812, in Latrobe, *Correspondence*, 3:230–36.

REFERENCES
Brownell and Cohen. *The Architectural Drawings of Latrobe.*

Bryan, John M., ed. *Robert Mills, Architect.* Washington, D.C.: The American Institute of Architects Press, 1989. Pp. 11–12, 16, 54–57, 144–46, 155–57.

Carrott, Richard G. *The Egyptian Revival: Its Sources, Monuments, and Meaning, 1808–1858.* Berkeley: University of California Press, 1978. See especially pp. 19, n. 14; 76–77, n. 8.

Latrobe. *Correspondence.*

Mickler, Margaret Pearson. "The Monumental Church." Master of Architectural History thesis, University of Virginia, 1980.

FIGURE 1. **Monumental Church** *(1812–17), 1224 East Broad Street, Richmond, designed by Robert Mills.*

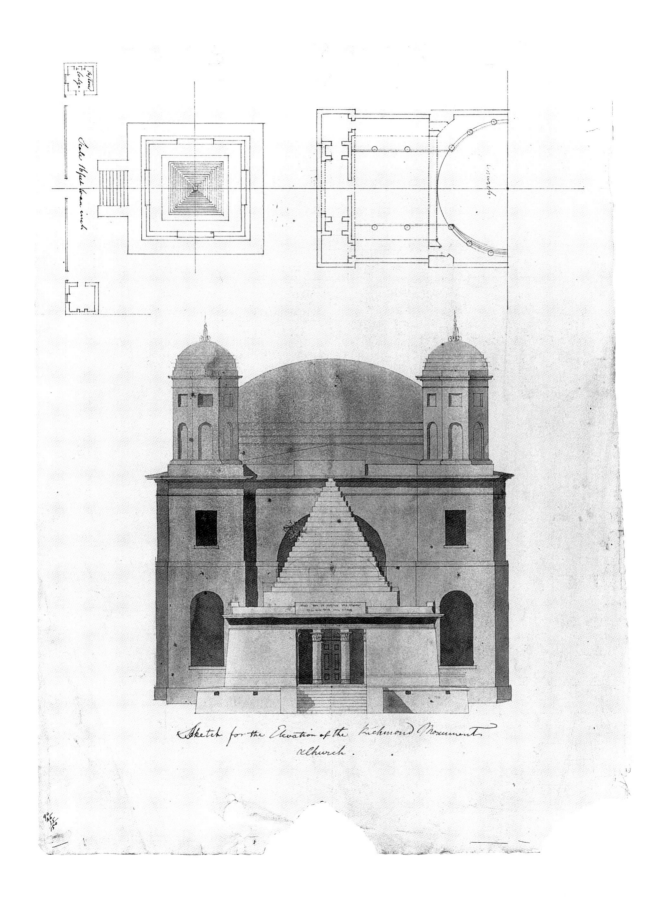

Sketch for the Elevation of the Richmond Monument & church.

# 22.
# DESIGN FOR A WASHINGTON MONUMENT

*Elevation*

Unbuilt
Presentation drawing, 1810
Signed and dated: *Max^an. Godefroy invenit et Delineavit 1810*
Inscribed: *Elevation of the front of a Triumphal Arch of the Roman Doric Order designed to accompany a pedestrian or Equestrian Statue of Washington Upon the Place where the Old Court House now Stands in Baltimore*
Pricking, pencil, pen and India ink, with brown ink, watercolor, and touches of gouache on paper; 17 ⅞ by 24 ½ inches
Collection of The Peale Museum, Baltimore City Life Museums, acc. no. CB 5471

FIGURE 1. **La Porte St. Denis,** *engineered by Adam Perelle, plate 42 from Perelle's* **Collection of Views of Paris . . . ,** *1680s. (Photograph courtesy of the John Work Garrett Library, Special Collections Department, The Johns Hopkins University.)*

Maximilian Godefroy spent the years 1805–19 in the United States as a French political refugee. Shortly before leaving France he began teaching himself architecture. Like the other French Neoclassical architects who tried to establish themselves in this country, he met with insuperable cultural differences, and a problematic personality increased his troubles. Nonetheless, he erected in Baltimore one of the most important American *oeuvres* of the early nineteenth century.

In 1816 Richmond briefly held out promise to Godefroy. He had made a series of designs for a Washington monument in Baltimore and, in the 1813–14 competition for that commission, had pinned his hopes on a triumphal arch project. Robert Mills's proposal for a giant column won over Godefroy's arch, an arch by Joseph Jacques Ramée, almost certainly a Latrobe pyramid, and other projects.[1] In 1816, after the failure of his collaboration with Latrobe on the Baltimore Exchange (1816–20, demolished), Godefroy received the commission to landscape and renovate Jefferson's Capitol (see SURVEY NOS. 9, 10). Other projects in this vicinity came his way, including designing a facade to unite the banks of John Wickham (see SURVEY NO. 24) and John Brockenbrough.

In 1815, the Virginia General Assembly had appointed commissioners to receive donations for a Washington monument in Virginia. This group of men brought the campaign to fruition, but not for almost half a century (see SURVEY NOS. 42, 43).[2] Godefroy publicly displayed his triumphal arch design, received encouragement, and perhaps even chose a site in front of the Capitol.[3] When he exhibited the design in London in 1822 and Paris in 1827, he claimed that Virginia would execute it shortly. But nothing of the sort happened—the governor had in fact advertised a now-mysterious competition for a $100,000 Washington monument in 1818—and time has swept away Godefroy's Richmond works.[4]

Godefroy's elevation combines an equestrian figure with a triumphal arch, two kinds of monuments whose hour had not yet come in the United States. Apart from Joseph Wilton's *George III* for New York (unveiled 1770, demolished), such sculpture began to appear only in the 1850s; when Virginia commissioned its Washington monument from Thomas Crawford in 1850, it gave the second American commission for an equestrian monument. The arch had longer to wait. Designers intermittently proffered the idea, but it appears that, aside from temporary arches for festivities, no example reached execution before the Civil War.[5] Behind Godefroy's and Ramée's selection of this theme lie two-and-a-half centuries of French experience with the triumphal arch. Godefroy combined ideas from two Parisian works in his project: François Blondel's mighty Porte St. Denis (1671; FIGURE 1),[6] a product of the *grand siècle* of Louis XIV, which Neoclassicists accepted as one of the great ages of patronage; and the triumphal portal of an early work by Claude-Nicholas Ledoux, the reconstructed townhouse for the martial Duc d'Uzès (finished 1769; demolished).

In the drawing, Washington rides in glory, amidst such symbols of triumph as the arch and the trophies on the columns. In the attic story, a relief portrays the leader whom power could not corrupt, in the act of resigning his military commission in 1783. Godefroy's design reflects his abiding concern for appropriate expression. Thus, in honor of so robust a hero, he made the Doric order unfluted and, under the influence of recent discoveries about Greek architecture, he replaced the triglyphs with wreaths.[7]

The drawing illustrated here, inscribed "1rst. Sketch" twice at lower left, is the only known drawing of the arch and comes from the Baltimore competition. Godefroy was willing to make an elevation this picture-like. He subscribed, however, to a strong French tradition of rejecting perspective renderings as deceitful and of relying instead on models.[8]        CEB

NOTES
1. For the development of the American public monument see Chapter 2.

2. On the continuity of the effort, see Brumbaugh, "Evolution," pp. 4–6.

3. In September 1816, Godefroy wrote to Ebenezer Jackson that "les Virginiens . . . paraissent determinés" to give him the commission. For the documentation of the episode, see Alexander, *Architecture*, p. 132.

4. I know of the competition only through the advertisement in the *Raleigh [North Carolina] Register*, 10 July 1818.

5. For triumphal arch projects, see George Bridport's 1816 proposals for Philadelphia in Cohen, "Bridport," and an anonymous entry into the 1849–50 Richmond competition in O'Neal, *Architectural Drawing*, pp. 52–53.

6. A variety of contradictory engravings of this project existed.

7. For the wreaths, compare the Choragic Monument of Thrasyllus as illustrated in Stuart, Revett, et al., *Antiquities of Athens*, vol. 2, chap. 4.

8. See Chapter 2.

REFERENCES
Alexander, Robert L. "Architecture and Aristocracy: The Cosmopolitan Style of Latrobe and Godefroy." *Maryland Historical Magazine* 56 (September 1961):229–43.

———. "The Drawings and Allegories of Maximilian Godefroy." *Maryland Historical Magazine* 53 (March 1958):17–33.

———. "Maximilian Godefroy in Virginia: A French Interlude in Richmond's Architecture." *Virginia Magazine of History and Biography* 69 (October 1961):420–31.

———. "The Public Memorial and Godefroy's Battle Monument." *Journal of the Society of Architectural Historians* 17 (March 1958):19–24.

———. *The Architecture of Maximilian Godefroy.* Baltimore: The Johns Hopkins University Press, 1974.

Brownell and Cohen. *Architectural Drawings of Latrobe.*

Brumbaugh, Thomas B. "The Evolution of Crawford's 'Washington.'" *Virginia Magazine of History and Biography* 70 (January 1962):3–29.

Cohen, Jeffrey A. "George Bridport." In James F. O'Gorman et al., *Drawing Toward Building: Philadelphia Architectural Graphics, 1732–1986.* Philadelphia: published for the Pennsylvania Academy of the Fine Arts by the University of Pennsylvania Press, 1986.

Godefroy, Maximilian. Autobiographical memoir. Translated by Gilbert Chinard and edited by Carolina V. Davison. *Maryland Historical Magazine* 29 (September 1934):175–212.

——— to Ebenezer Jackson, 7 September 1816. Photocopy of an unlocated original. Maryland Historical Society, MS 1289.

Mordecai, Samuel. *Virginia, Especially Richmond, in By-Gone Days; with a Glance at the Present: Being Reminiscences and Last Words of an Old Citizen.* 2nd rev. ed., Richmond: West and Johnston, 1860. Pp. 264–65 and chap. 36.

O'Neal. *Architectural Drawing.* Pp. 52–53.

*Raleigh [North Carolina] Register,* 10 July 1818.

Stuart, James; Nicholas Revett; et al. *The Antiquities of Athens.* 3 vols. 1763–95. Reprint. New York: Arno Press, 1980.

Elevation of the front of a Triumphal Arch of the Roman Doric Order
designed to accompany a pedestrian or Equestrian Statue of
WASHINGTON
Upon the Place where the Old Court House now stands in Baltimore

# 23.
## HOLLADAY FAMILY PLANTATION HOUSE

*(Prospect Hill?)*
*Elevations and Plans*

Spotsylvania County (unbuilt)
Presentation drawing, circa 1810
Pricking, pencil, pen and India ink, iron-gall ink, and
watercolor on paper; 15 ⅝ by 12 ¾ inches
Collection of the Virginia Historical Society, Richmond,
Mssl H7185c 123–141

An extraordinary group of fifteen architectural drawings is preserved among the 2,300 papers given to the
Virginia Historical Society over the past twenty-five
years by the Holladay family of Spotsylvania County.
Only one has been previously published.[1] The drawings are not only impressive in their scope, detail, and
appearance; they also reflect the hand of a draftsman
accomplished in technique. Most present an elevation
and a floor plan; a few offer multiple plans and even a
side elevation, pulled up—like the front—from an
adjacent floor plan. The faintest of horizontal and vertical pencil lines—still visible—functioned like scoring,
to aid the draftsman in placing walls, roofs, chimneys,
windows, and doors. Pricking was used extensively
for the same purpose and to locate fireplaces and the
risers of stairs. A compass was used to draft circular
columns and curved exterior stairs. Watercolor washes
were applied—a bold brown color for roofs and
doors—and some shadows were drawn. The techniques used here rival those of English Georgian pattern-books from which they are obviously derived.
They are sufficiently consistent throughout the group
to suggest the hand of a single draftsman, probably at
work over a period of years. Yet none of the drawings
is in any way identified.

Several designs are exceptional, a surprise for
what might be expected to survive from the earlier
settlements of north-central Virginia. One drawing
shows a three-part doorway, an even number of bays,
and an almost square plan, more characteristic of
English country houses than any built in Virginia.
Another drawing offers a design that must be
unique—a twelve-sided house with two large rooms
of 20 by 34 feet each, separated by a central passage.
It and one other elevation present a Neoclassical doorway with lunette and sidelights. All of those ideas are
close enough to designs in John Crunden's *Convenient
and Ornamental Architecture* (London, 1767) to suggest that it or a similar pattern-book of the late colonial
period could have made its way to Spotsylvania
County. Other designs in the Holladay group are akin
to those in the more popular *Book of Architecture* by
James Gibbs (London, 1728), a volume known to have
been used in colonial Virginia. One design, a five-part
house plan and elevation,[2] is a curious adaptation of a
large English Palladian villa—a type popularized by
Gibbs—to the local one-and-a-half story, double-pile
Virginia building. Another, a design for a garden pavilion to be a 14 ½-foot-square, two-story double-
cube—certainly an ambitious design for the colonies—follows illustrations in Gibbs of more than
twenty types of similar "summer houses" and
"rooms" with Classical detailing.

The reliance on English Georgian pattern-books
by the Holladay family architect—apparent as much
in his drafting style as in his use of borrowed motifs—
would suggest a late colonial date for the drawings
were it not for watermarks on eight of the pages that
firmly date them to after 1805, 1806, and—in one
instance—1811.[3] That information conforms with the
similarity of seven of the drawings with Prospect Hill

(FIGURE 1), the Holladay family home in Spotsylvania County that was built in 1810–14. These
seven drawings, the most elaborate of which is illustrated here, all seem to be variations on a theme: all
show the same central-passage, four-room house type
that is Prospect Hill, but with differing roof types and
with either a five- or six-bay facade. One (not pictured)
has the same roof as Prospect Hill and the same five
bays, and the dimensions of its front rooms are within
a foot of being identical. The U-shaped plan, placement of chimneys on the passage walls, and the use of
masonry construction were eliminated, probably for
reasons of practicality.

An unusually large house for its time and place,
Prospect Hill was built by planter and politician Waller Holladay shortly after he inherited substantial
wealth from a prominent half-brother. He engaged as
his builder Spotswood Dabney Crenshaw, whose
sketchy career in Spotsylvania County, Lynchburg,
and Richmond now appears to be that of a carpenter
who acquired property and wealth. His dated and
detailed statement and bill of $1,355.44 for building
a house for Waller Holladay survives in the family
papers. Because he married a cousin of Waller Holladay, Crenshaw may well be the unknown drafter of the
fifteen drawings that the family saw fit to preserve.[4]

The names of architect-craftsmen capable of
such drawings appear earlier—in the late colonial
period—in public and private records in northern and
north-central Virginia, regions where new settlement
was then developing and where domestic and church
designers increasingly added Classical details to their
buildings.[5] Out of that tradition the Holladay family
architect emerged. That he turned to outdated books
and ideas is no more surprising than Thomas Jefferson's similar use of Gibbs's *Book of Architecture* after
the turn of the century for detailing at Monticello.
Both document the perpetuation of Georgian architecture in Virginia beyond the Georgian period.   WMSR

NOTES
1.   A five-part Palladian house by the Holladay family architect is illustrated in
Mills Lane, *Architecture of the Old South: Virginia* (Savannah: The Beehive Press,
1987), 68.

2.   Ibid.

3.   The watermarks are: "RG" (for Baltimore merchant Robert Gilmore, involved
with paper mills in Delaware in 1805 and Philadelphia in 1816); an American eagle
(used by mills in Massachusetts and Delaware in 1805 and 1806); and "PJK" (for
Philip Jacob King, whose Pennsylvania mill was in operation by 1811). See Thomas
L. Gravell and George Miller, *A Catalogue of American Watermarks, 1690–1835*
(New York and London: Garland Publishing, Inc., 1979), 125, 138, 118. (There are no
watermarks on seven of the pages.)

4.   References to Crenshaw are found in the Holladay Family Papers, Virginia
Historical Society, Richmond; the Prospect Hill file at the Virginia Department of
Historic Resources; and Files 56572 and 56442 in the Museum of Early Southern
Decorative Arts, Winston-Salem, North Carolina. These sources identify Crenshaw
as living in a "Dwelling house & Carpenter's shop" in Lynchburg in 1816. See also
H. W. Flourney, ed., *Calendar of State Papers* 10 (Richmond, 1892): 436, which
mentions Crenshaw's ownership of at least one slave in 1816. I thank Sarah Driggs
for pointing out the MESDA files to me.

5.   See Chapter 4, part 1, for mention of the activities in northern Virginia of
architect-draftsmen James Wren, William Buckland, and John Ariss. Another was
Mardun Eventon, active in Prince William County, whose dozen architectural books
were announced for sale in *The Virginia Gazette* at his death on 11 December 1779
(cited in Mills Lane, *Virginia*, 62).

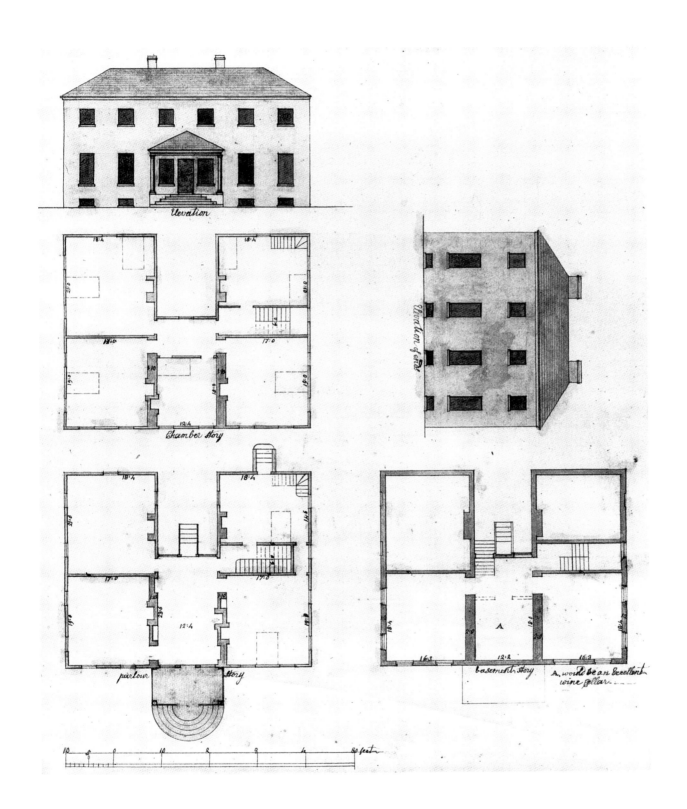

Elevation

Elevation of end

Chamber Story

parlour Story

basement Story    A. would be an excellent wine cellar.

# 24.
# JOHN WICKHAM
# HOUSE

*Proposed Front Elevation*

1015 East Clay St., Richmond
Office record, 1811
Pencil, pen and India ink on paper; 7 ⅞ by 9 ⅞ inches
Collection of the American Antiquarian Society, Worcester,
Massachusetts, Manuscript Collections, Octavo Volumes "P,"
Alexander Parris Sketchbook

FIGURE 1. *Site photo,* **Wickham Valentine House** *as it looks today.*

Alexander Parris, a member of that first generation of American-born professionals that included Robert Mills, William Strickland, and Ithiel Town, began his career as a New England house-wright in the early Neoclassical ambit of Charles Bulfinch and Asher Benjamin. Like other Yankee artisans hard-pressed by the consequences of Jefferson's Embargo Act of 1807 against Britain and France, Parris ventured south and spent something less than two years in Richmond, 1810 to 1812. Exposure to Latrobe's influence in Richmond, Washington, and Philadelphia played the determining role in Parris's metamorphosis into a professional and a practitioner of the Second Phase of Neoclassicism. He brought the newer Classicism back to New England, where he erected some of the most important of all specimens of the Temple Revival, even while some of his old associates made a new home for the New England Adamesque in central Virginia.[1]

Parris designed two extant Richmond buildings (both 1811–13): the Governor's Mansion and the Wickham House (now part of The Valentine Museum; FIGURE 1). In turning to Parris to design a lavish town residence, the attorney and banker John Wickham (1763–1839) gave him one of the great domestic commissions of American Neoclassicism. The house caught Parris midway in his stylistic transformation. In general, the paths of the First Phase of Neoclassicism (in both its Adam and its Chambers varieties) and the Second Phase intersected at this building. Many of the three-dimensional ornaments match the plates of the first edition of the *American Builder's Companion* (Boston, 1806) by Asher Benjamin and the stucco-worker Daniel Raynerd (see FIGURES 2.29, 2.32). Raynerd himself may have executed the Wickhams' stucco. The interior painted decorations (largely discovered in the 1980s) echo the plates of the Neoclassical British reformers John Flaxman and Thomas Hope; they probably also draw upon Stuart and Revett's *Antiquities of Athens* (London, 1763–95); and they most likely owe a good deal to certain Latrobe designs. Latrobe's favorite decorative painter, George Bridport, may have executed this ornament. Despite the incompatibility of the several species of Neoclassicism, the application of the Classical principle of fitness, or decor, lent the house cohesion. Thus, the public rooms have representational ornament that refers to their functions.

Parris's elevation shows the semifinal stage in the evolution of the main front. As in the executed house, the basic articulation follows Latrobe's precedent. For instance, Parris used a three-bay scheme with triple openings and a shallow central pavilion, rather than arranging five openings across one plane in accord with his New England past. (One wonders whether Parris had access to Latrobe's drawings for the Harvie-Gamble House [Richmond, 1798–99, demolished; FIGURE 2], which Latrobe disavowed because of its mutilation in execution.) But, as in the finished house, the recognizable details square with New England Adamesque taste. Thus the first-floor arches take an elliptical curve rather than a Latrobean seg-

ment of a circle.[2] Parris adapted this facade for the entry front of his domestic masterwork, the David Sears House (Boston, 1819–21; now the Somerset Club).

One suspects that Wickham, the president of the Farmer's Bank of Virginia, and his neighbor Dr. John Brockenbrough, the president of the Bank of Virginia, had Parris design their adjacent banks (both now demolished). An 1835 plan of Richmond shows that both halves of the pair had apsidal ends, an unusual treatment that Parris had used for his lost Portland Bank (Portland, Maine, 1806, demolished).[3]

Parris saved the present elevation and three other pages of Wickham drawings in a sketchbook that shows his impressive progress as a draftsman. He relied on India ink; he developed skill in modeling with washes; and he made a beginning at using color for simulating appearances and for coding. His workaday Wickham elevation has, on the second floor of the pavilion, almost undecipherable pencil sketching for a different treatment from the one that Parris inked in.

CEB

NOTES

1. On Parris, the generation of the 1780s, the Wickham House, and the exchange of architectural taste between North and South, see Chapter 2.

2. For Latrobe's dislike of the ellipse, see, among many statements, his "Report on the U. S. Capitol," 4 April 1803, in Latrobe, *Correspondence*, 1:272.

3. See Alexander, *Godefroy*, fig. III–4 (Micajah Bates's 1835 plan of Richmond) and pp. 130–31 (the banks, for which Godefroy designed a single, unifying facade in 1816); Zimmer and Scott, "Parris," p. 205 (the Portland Bank); and Zimmer, "Architectural Career," vol. 1, pp. 103–12.

REFERENCES

Alexander, Robert L. *The Architecture of Maximilian Godefroy.* Baltimore: The Johns Hopkins University Press, 1974.

Benjamin, Asher, and Daniel Raynerd. *The American Builder's Companion: Or, A New System of Architecture, Particularly Adapted to the Present Style of Building in the United States of America.* 1806. Reprint. New York: Da Capo Press, 1972.

Bishir, Catherine W., and Marshall Bullock. "Mr. Jones Goes to Richmond: A Note on the Influence of Alexander Parris' Wickham House." *Journal of the Society of Architectural Historians* 43 (March 1984):71–74.

Giles, Leslie A. "Decorative Paintings at the Wickham House, Richmond, Virginia: Their Sources, Their Author, and *Decor.*" Master of Architectural History thesis, University of Virginia, 1990.

Latrobe. *Correspondence.* 1:272; 3:42–44, 62–64, 230–36, 264–68.

Zimmer, Edward Francis. "The Architectural Career of Alexander Parris (1780–1852)." 2 vols. Ph.D. diss., Boston University, 1984.

———, and Pamela J. Scott. "Alexander Parris, B. Henry Latrobe, and the John Wickham House in Richmond, Virginia." *Journal of the Society of Architectural Historians* 41 (October 1982):202–11.

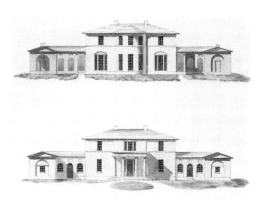

FIGURE 2. *Henry Latrobe's design for the* **Harvie-Gamble House** *(1789–99; demolished. Photograph courtesy of the Library of Congress.)*

# 25.
# BOLLINGBROOK STREET THEATRE

*Front Elevation*

Near the northeast corner of Bollingbrook and Phoenix Sts., Petersburg (demolished)
Office record, 1817
Signed and dated: *C. A. Busby, Archt./N. York Sepr. 1817*
Pen on paper; 15 ½ by 19 ½ inches
Collection of the British Architectural Library, Royal Institute of British Architects, London; Drawings Collection

FIGURE 1. *Vintage photo (circa 1865) of* **Bollingbrook Street Theatre,** *Petersburg. Originally built around 1818, the building reveals newer brickwork on its roof-line, which was altered after a fire. (Photograph courtesy Fred R. Bell, Arlington, Va.)*

The English architect Charles Augustin Busby began exhibiting drawings at the Royal Academy when he was only thirteen years old. By 1810 he had published two pattern-books and was soon designing commercial and residential buildings. This ambitious early career came to an abrupt halt with a declaration of bankruptcy, and he subsequently traveled in America for two or three years. He made this theater design in New York in 1817. He returned to England about 1820 and gained fame there through his extensive work in Brighton and the surrounding area.[1]

Petersburg had been the home of two previous theaters. Little is known of the first; the second burned in a devastating fire that destroyed much of the downtown area on 15 July 1815. Yet the city recovered quickly, and in fact flourished: about 300 handsome buildings, largely of brick, replaced those lost.[2] The plans for the Bollingbrook Street Theatre were presented to the public by James H. Caldwell, an English actor and stage manager, and the building was erected by subscription in 1818.[3] It is not known how Caldwell obtained the plans, but Busby may never have actually visited Virginia. The theater, a rare example of an English architect's work in early-nineteenth-century Virginia, enjoyed immediate success. In 1821 Junius Brutus Booth made his second American appearance there, and his brilliant performance ended rumors that he was an impostor. A gala ball celebrating Lafayette's visit to Petersburg took place there in 1824. After two decades of decline, the theater burned in mid century, but another was built on its ruins.[4]

The stylish Neoclassical facade that Busby designed provided the booming city of Petersburg with a source of civic pride. Latrobe's design for the Richmond Theatre (SURVEY NOS. 18, 19) included an assembly room, but during the nineteenth century, hotels and taverns, such as Petersburg's Niblo's Hotel, became the primary public gathering-places. The Bollingbrook Street Theatre was built to function only as a theater. Its arcaded windows on the second floor, accenting a refreshment room, and the bowed porch, which created a covered entrance for theater-goers, articulated the necessary social spaces.

The plan (FIGURE 2) reflected Busby's knowledge of contemporary theater design. In section, three cantilevered tiers were exposed. The first two tiers above the pit contained boxes, each with a separate entrance. The third tier contained side boxes and a center gallery with a separate entrance for the holders of lower-priced tickets. Several features indicate that Busby had weighed many options before arranging the theater. A horseshoe-shaped plan, like that at Sir Robert Smirke's Covent Garden Theatre (London, 1808–09), was a controversial choice at a time when many designers argued that a nearly circular plan would maximize visibility.[5] Curving front boxes had been generally accepted in England to improve the view, and a domed ceiling was thought by some, including Latrobe, to improve acoustics.[6] The building's numerous exits were probably inspired by universal concern about fire safety rather than Virginia's particular fears since the disastrous Richmond theater fire of 1811.

A cache of more than 300 Busby drawings came to light in the attic of an English farmhouse in the late 1980s and was deposited at the Royal Institute of British Architects. Seven sheets of drawings for Petersburg's theater survive in this collection, all of them office records of the project. For this purpose Busby needed only utilitarian geometric diagrams, but his talent and training as a professional graphic artist lent the sheets some of the dash of spontaneous sketches.

SSD

NOTES
1. For the most reliable information on Busby's life, see Colvin, *Dictionary*, under "Busby, Charles Augustus." See also Bingham, "Rare Regency Find."

2. For an excellent history of Petersburg's eighteenth- and nineteenth-century theaters, see Wyatt, "Three Petersburg Theatres."

3. Wyatt, "Theatres," pp. 101–02.

4. Wyatt, "Theatres," pp. 101–10. See also Wyatt and Scott, *Petersburg's Story.*

5. Leacroft's *Development of the English Playhouse* provides a detailed discussion of the design problems that Busby's contemporaries were debating.

6. Latrobe's design for the Richmond Theatre (survey nos. 18, 19) is important comparative material for Busby's design. For a thorough discussion of Latrobe's project, see Brownell and Cohen, *Architectural Drawings.*

REFERENCES
Bingham, Neil R. "Rare Regency Find: The Busby Drawings." *Country Life* 182 (14 April 1988):138–39.

Brownell and Cohen. *Architectural Drawings of Latrobe.*

Colvin, Howard. "Busby, Charles Augustus." *A Biographical Dictionary of British Architects, 1600–1840.* 2nd ed. London: John Murray, 1978.

Leacroft, Richard. *The Development of the English Playhouse.* London: Methuen, 1988.

———, and Helen Leacroft. *Theatre and Playhouse: An Illustrated Survey of Theatre Building from Ancient Greece to the Present Day.* London: Methuen, 1984.

Shockley, Martin Staples. *The Richmond Stage, 1784–1812.* Charlottesville: University Press of Virginia, 1977.

Tidworth, Simon. *Theatres: An Architectural and Cultural History.* New York: Praeger Publishers, 1973.

Wyatt, Edward A., IV. "Three Petersburg Theatres." *William and Mary Quarterly,* 2nd series, 21 (April 1941):83–110.

———. *Along Petersburg Streets: Historic Sites and Buildings of Petersburg, Virginia.* Richmond: The Dietz Printing Co., 1943.

———, and James G. Scott. *Petersburg's Story: A History.* Petersburg: privately printed, 1960.

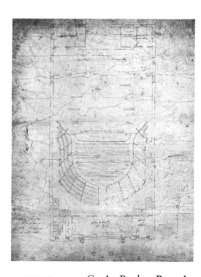

FIGURE 2. *C. A. Busby,* **Petersburg Theatre, Virginia,** *first floor plan. (Photograph courtesy of the British Architectural Library, Royal Institute of British Architects, London. Copyright RIBA).*

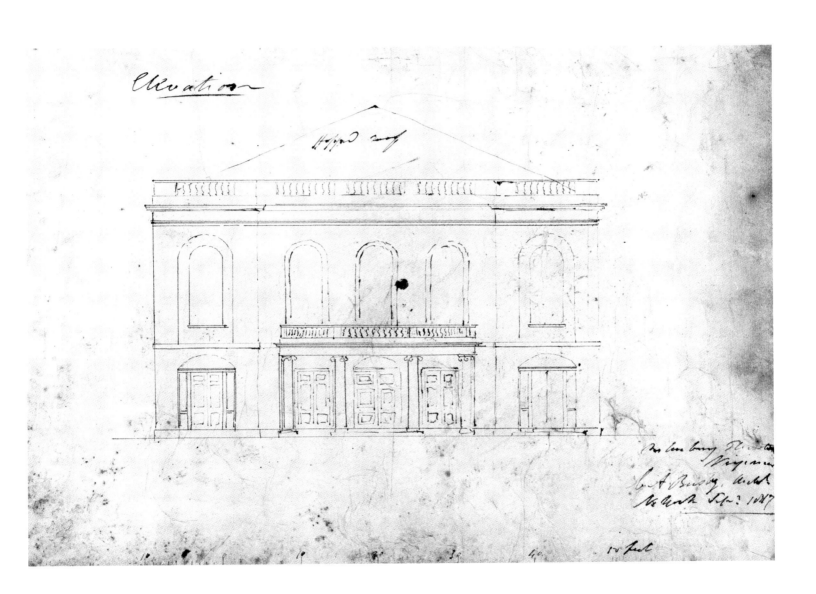

Elevation

Attributed to WILLIAM THORNTON, 1759–1828

for

THOMAS, JEFFERSON, 1743–1826

# 26.
# CENTER AND END PAVILIONS, COVERED WALKS

*University of Virginia*
*Proposed Elevations*

University Ave., Charlottesville
Presentation drawing, 1817
Pricking, pencil, pen, India ink and writing ink with gray wash on paper; 9 ½ by 7 ⅝ inches
Collection of the University of Virginia Library, Charlottesville, Special Collections Department, Jefferson Papers, N352

FIGURE 1. *Site photo,* **Pavilion VII,** *now the faculty's Colonnade Club.*

Among American amateur architects, Dr. William Thornton ranks second after his friend Jefferson, whom Thornton resembled in his sweeping range of interests. He belonged, however, to the younger generation of Charles Bulfinch, the amateur who became a professional, and B. Henry Latrobe, the architect who transferred the emerging standards of professionalism from Britain. Thornton's importance lies foremost in his contributions to the all-important building that the other three men also molded, the U.S. Capitol (1793–1829). Thornton founded his work on British Palladianism, but he increasingly accepted Neoclassical ideas, including the freedom popularized by the iconoclast Robert Adam. His writings enunciate the Picturesque ingredient in his designs.

Thornton briefly but decisively entered the story of the University of Virginia. Jefferson devoted the last decade of his life to creating this institution, one of only three achievements that he wished to have listed on his tombstone.[1] In his mid seventies he became the architect for one of the most ambitious building programs on the Atlantic seaboard (at least outside commercial speculation), and he did this in the Virginia Piedmont, a region with no tradition of erecting monumental public buildings. Some of his sources remain debatable, but he unquestionably turned to a Palladian domestic conception that he had developed for Monticello I, Monticello II, and the President's House in Washington: a one-story, single-pile string of rooms, fronted by a covered walk, and interrupted by two-story pavilions.[2] As he wrote Thornton on 9 May 1817, he wished to make the upper stories of the pavilions "models of taste & good architecture . . . no two alike, so as to serve as specimens for the Architectural Lectures," and he asked Thornton to sketch a few facades. That is, he requested patterns in which to arrange specimens of correct orders because, surprisingly enough, he had run short of models. Still more surprisingly—even astonishingly—Jefferson had decided to break with one of the most fundamental tenets of orthodox architecture: he proposed an axially asymmetrical building complex. Thornton obliged with this single sheet of elevations, which he sent with a letter of 27 May 1817.[3]

Thornton recommended the logical sequence of two Doric end pavilions, two Ionic corner pavilions, and a pedimented, Corinthian central pavilion. He advised building among clumps of trees "to produce a perfect Picture." Seemingly he understood Jefferson's mind well enough to propose using the temple portico theme for the models on the upper stories of the pavilions. But he thoroughly misunderstood Jefferson's intentions concerning the Orders and drew unorthodox examples. (His Doric, for instance, has, instead of an architrave and a frieze, a cross between the two, penciled with Adamesque trios of fluting in place of true triglyphs.) Jefferson had no interest in displaying unorthodox Orders such as Thornton's, but he found useful material in Thornton's suggestions. Above all, Jefferson took over the pattern of a temple portico on an arcaded basement for his first pavilion

(FIGURE 1), to which he ultimately gave the number VII. (He had found the pattern acceptable at least as early as a reputed preliminary study for Monticello.)[4] But in setting the first of his models for the Lawn, he gave Pavilion VII a Portico order, simplified from Leoni's adaptation of Palladio's Doric.          CEB

NOTES

1.  In tackling the evolution of the University designs, I have had the luck to have had students whose own work greatly modifies (in some cases, transforms) the subject. Those statements available to the reader—the important theses of Lasala, Lucas, Riddick, and Wigren—appear in the references that follow. Among other materials I must single out the two seminar reports of 1990–91 in which Patricia C. Sherwood has set the dating of the Jefferson drawings on a scholarly basis.

2.  On this wing plan, see Chapter 2.

3.  The present drawing is probably Thornton's only one for the University. Drawing no. 310 in Nichols, *Jefferson's Architectural Drawings*, seems unlikely to have any connection either with the University or with Thornton.

4.  Kimball, *Jefferson, Architect*, no. 6; Nichols, *Jefferson's Architectural Drawings*, no. 28. Waddell, "First Monticello," p. 27, has disputed the identification of the design.

REFERENCES

Brown, Glenn, ed. "Letters from Thomas Jefferson and William Thornton, Architect, Relating to the University of Virginia." *AIA Journal* 1 (January 1913):21–27.

Brownell, Charles E. Under "Thornton, William." In *Encyclopedia of Architecture: Design, Engineering, and Construction*. 5 vols. New York: John Wiley & Sons, 1988–89.

Bruce. *History of the University of Virginia.*

Jefferson, Thomas, to William Thornton, 9 May 1817. Jefferson Papers. Special Collections Department, University of Virginia Library.

Kimball, Fiske. "The Genesis of Jefferson's Plan for the University of Virginia." *Architecture* 48 (December 1923):397–99.

———. *Jefferson, Architect.* No. 212 and pp. 74–80, 186–92.

Lasala, Joseph M. "Thomas Jefferson's Designs for the University of Virginia." Draft, Master of Architectural History thesis, University of Virginia, 1991.

Lucas, Ann M. "Ordering His Environment: Thomas Jefferson's Architecture from Monticello to the University of Virginia." Master of Architectural History thesis, University of Virginia, 1989.

Malone, Dumas. *Jefferson and His Time.* 6 vols. Boston: Little, Brown and Company, 1948–81. Vol. 6, *The Sage of Monticello.*

Nichols. *Jefferson's Architectural Drawings.* No. 352 (catalogued also as no. 303).

O'Neal, William B., comp. "An Intelligent Interest in Architecture: A Bibliography of Publications about Thomas Jefferson as an Architect, together with an Iconography of the Nineteenth-Century Prints of the University of Virginia." *American Association of Architectural Bibliographers, Papers,* 6 (1969).

———. *Pictorial History of the University of Virginia.* 2nd ed. Charlottesville: University Press of Virginia, 1976.

O'Neal, William Bainter, and Frederick Doveton Nichols. "An Architectural History of the First University Pavilion." *Magazine of Albemarle County History* 15 (1955–56):36–43.

Ridout, Orlando, V. *Building the Octagon.* Octagon Research Series, 2. Washington, D.C.: American Institute of Architects Press, 1989.

Riddick, Susan C. "The Influence of B. H. Latrobe on Jefferson's Design for the University of Virginia." Master of Architectural History thesis, University of Virginia, 1988.

Stearns, Elinor, and David N. Yerkes. *William Thornton, A Renaissance Man in the Federal City.* Washington, D.C.: A.I.A. Foundation, 1976.

Thornton, Anna Maria. "Diary of Mrs. William Thornton, 1800." *Columbia Historical Society Records* 10 (1907):88–226.

Thornton, William, to Thomas Jefferson, 27 May 1817. The Thomas Jefferson Papers of the Library of Congress, microfilm reel no. 49, Special Collections Department, University of Virginia Library.

Turner, Paul Venable. *Campus: An American Planning Tradition.* The Architectural History Foundation/MIT Press Series, 7. New York, 1984.

Waddell, Gene. "The First Monticello," *Journal of the Society of Architectural Historians* 46 (March 1987):5–29.

Wigren, Christopher. "Thomas Jefferson's Chinese Designs." Master of Architectural History thesis, University of Virginia, 1989.

Woods, Mary N. "Thomas Jefferson and the University of Virginia: Planning the Academic Village." *Journal of the Society of Architectural Historians* 44 (October 1985):266–83.

## 27.
# ROTUNDA

*University of Virginia*
*Section and Elevation*

University Ave., Charlottesville
Study/presentation drawing, circa 1817–21
Pricking, scoring, pen and writing ink, and added pencil on
paper; 8 ¾ by 17 ½ inches
Collection of the University of Virginia Library, Charlottesville,
Special Collections Department, Jefferson Papers,
N328–N329

After receiving Thornton's design suggestions for the University (see previous entry), Jefferson wrote Latrobe (12 June 1817) with the same request. Here, Jefferson compared his scheme with his design for the White House wings, which Latrobe had partly executed in 1805–11 (partly demolished). Why he waited to approach Latrobe remains a question, but their correspondence had become infrequent. Having plagued Latrobe for six years (1803–09) with his recourse to models for the Capitol and the President's House, Jefferson now, ironically, sought models from his old associate. The renewed correspondence continued until 19 May 1818, when Jefferson saluted Latrobe for the last time.

With his letter of 6 October 1817, Latrobe sent Jefferson a large sheet of drawings, now long lost. Only a sketch in Latrobe's letter to Jefferson of 24 July 1817 survives to illustrate his thoughts. Clearly, however, Jefferson found much to use in Latrobe's drawing. Clearly, too, Latrobe's suggestions came from decades of consistent work in designing institutions; he took pains to suit his friend's taste, and he accepted Jefferson's startling principle of asymmetry. And clearly — last of all — after taking any idea from Latrobe, Jefferson absorbed it altogether into his own brand of Palladianism.

Leaving aside some debatable practical issues, which of Latrobe's suggestions found their way into Jefferson's museum of the Orders? The use of giant Orders came from him: only with Latrobe's participation did Jefferson deviate from the idea of stacking the Orders above the covered walk. Latrobe despised this tiered effect and had, in the case of Jefferson's White House wings, compared the appearance to "a litter of pigs."[1] Jefferson took over an indeterminate number of Latrobe's facade patterns. The use of giant Orders to make temple fronts also came from a Latrobe who wished to give his old hero what he knew Jefferson liked. Latrobe had counseled the addition of a "Center building which ought to exhibit in Mass & details as perfect a specimen of good Architectural taste as can be devised." He sketched one with a portico and a dome treated the way Jefferson had once asked him to treat the dome over the Hall of Representatives: that is, lightened with the windows that Leoni had added when he doctored the design of the Villa Rotonda ( FIGURE 2.11 ).[2] Jefferson's specification-book shows that, by 18 July 1817, he had begun to consider "some principal building" at the north end of the school, but he saw his Rotunda as the product of Latrobe's suggestion, even though he recast the idea as the Pantheon with elliptical rooms, a revision of his design for the U.S. Capitol ( SURVEY NO. 11 ). Writing Latrobe about the anticipated buildings on 19 May 1818, he mentioned "your central one, which would be reserved for the Center of the ground."[3] More strikingly, the previously ignored inscription struck out at upper right reads "Latrobe No [illegible]."[4] Latrobe's influence assisted Jefferson in creating his architectural masterpiece and, just at the same period, Jefferson's influence assisted Latrobe in

perfecting his chef d'oeuvre, the Roman Catholic cathedral in Baltimore (1806–10, 1817–21 and later).[5]

The elevation and section were originally on one sheet, later split into two. Unlike Latrobe the professional, Jefferson never had the facility to produce drawings rapidly, and the "stiffening wrist" that he mentioned to Latrobe (19 May 1818) surely made drawing, like writing, "slow & painful." To change a design, it made more sense to work the drawings over than to start afresh, and he worked the present drawings over heavily. One can easily see his erasures, especially where he eliminated the original floor levels from the section. The drawing shows an internal Corinthian order. Ultimately, breaking from the Fréart tradition in order to complete his museum of the Orders, Jefferson shifted to the Composite. Before conservation, his ink had bitten far enough into the paper to reproduce most of the design on the back of the page.     CEB

NOTES
1.   Latrobe to John Lenthall, 3 May 1805, in Latrobe, *Papers*, microfiche ed., 39/E8 and 178/F13. On giant Orders vs. tiers, see Chapter 2.

2.   Jefferson to Latrobe, 8 September 1805, in Latrobe, *Correspondence*, 2:139–40.

3.   Latrobe, *Correspondence*, 3:987–89.

4.   The author and Joseph Lasala examined the inscription on 29 November 1990, with the kind assistance of Richard H.F. Lindemann, then Head of Public Services, Special Collections, Alderman Library. Fluorescent light and magnification made it possible to sort out the lighter original inscription from the darker superscription. In "Jefferson's Designs," Lasala's study of Jefferson's annotations and erasures opens up uncharted territory.

5.   On the cathedral, see Brownell and Cohen, *Architectural Drawings of Latrobe*.

REFERENCES
Dickey, John. Review of *Thomas Jefferson's Rotunda Restored, 1973–76*, by Joseph Lee Vaughan and Omer Allan Gianniny, Jr. *Journal of the Society of Architectural Historians* 41 (May 1982):167–68.

Jefferson, Thomas. [University of Virginia] Specifications Book. Jefferson Papers, N318. Special Collections Department, University of Virginia Library.

Lasala, Joseph. "Comparative Analysis: Thomas Jefferson's Rotunda and the Pantheon in Rome." *Virginia Studio Record* 1 (Fall 1988):84–87.

Latrobe. *Correspondence*, 2:62–68; 3:705, 899–910, 914–17, 928–34, 955–56, 975–77, 987–89.

Nichols. *Jefferson's Architectural Drawings*. Nos. 328–29.

O'Neal. *Architectural Drawing in Virginia*. Pp. 14–21.

———. *Jefferson's Buildings at the University of Virginia*. Vol. 1, *The Rotunda*. Charlottesville: University of Virginia Press, 1960.

Vaughan, Joseph Lee, and Omer Allan Gianniny, Jr. *Thomas Jefferson's Rotunda Restored, 1973–76: A Pictorial Review with Commentary*. With a foreword by Frederick Doveton Nichols. Charlottesville: University Press of Virginia, 1981.

For additional references on Jefferson's work as an architect, see survey no. 26.

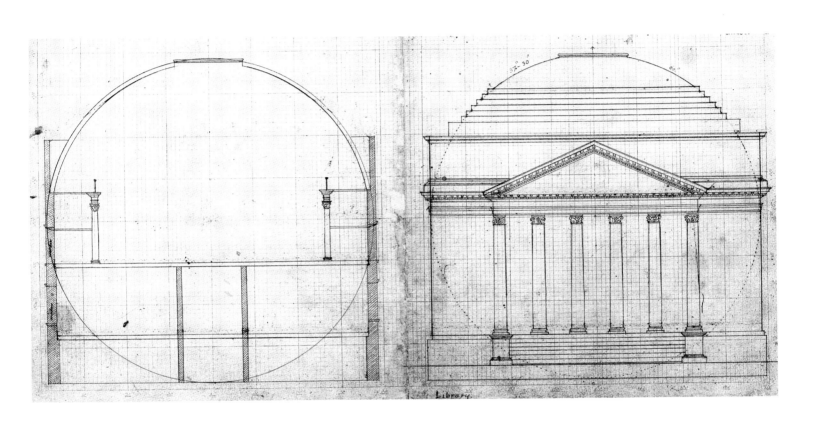

Library

THOMAS JEFFERSON, 1743–1826

Drawing attributed to JOHN NEILSON,

before 1775–1827

# 28.
# ROTUNDA, PAVILION IX, AND PAVILION X

*University of Virginia Elevations*

University Ave., Charlottesville
Presentation drawing, 1823(?)
Pricking, pencil, pen and India ink with writing ink, watercolor, and touches of gouache (?) on paper; 10 ¾ by 17 ¼ inches
Collection of the University of Virginia Library, Charlottesville; Special Collections Department, Jefferson Papers, N354

FIGURE 1. *Site photo*, **Rotunda and Pavilions.**

A pair of Northern Irish house-joiners, John Neilson and James Dinsmore (circa 1771–1830), worked on Monticello, Montpelier, and Upper Bremo before becoming the chief builders at the University of Virginia. Here they collaborated on the Rotunda and the Anatomical Hall (demolished), and Neilson was the master carpenter for Pavilions IX and X. His inventory reveals him to be a man of property and diverse interests. His remarkable collection of drawings and drawing instruments included two of the most important of all American architectural drawings, however acquired: the perspective of the U. S. Capitol (now in the Library of Congress) that Latrobe made as a gift for Jefferson in 1806, and "Latrobe's plan for university of Virginia."[1]

Neilson, who probably studied drawing in Ireland, seems to have had a large role as a draftsman at the University. He most likely made the drawings for the first (1822) and second (1825) states of the university plan that Peter Maverick engraved ( FIGURE 2 ).[2] A newly discovered 1823 letter from Neilson to John Hartwell Cocke, a key member of the Board of Visitors, may refer to the present rendering when it speaks of "an elevation of the Pantheon with the flank [view?] of Pavillions No. 9 and 10 for Miss Cocke[.] I was ashamed to tell of it as it fell so far below my intentions, . . ."[3] One can no longer entertain the century-old misconception that attributed this elevation and other equally professional drawings to Jefferson's granddaughter Cornelia Jefferson Randolph.[4]

Although Neilson's elevation eliminates the terracing of the buildings, probably predates construction of the Rotunda, and shows the Lawn before various final decisions, it admirably illustrates the zenith of Jefferson's reinterpretation of Palladian tradition, with correctness invigorated by an almost incomprehensible freedom. Jefferson used two kinds of Orders: "modern", which means Palladio in every case except Pavilion IX, and "ancient". He relied on only two books—Leoni's *Palladio* and Fréart's *Parallèle*—for authoritative models, and he used even these books most selectively. After a complicated evolution, he gave the core of the Lawn the form of western, eastern, and northern triads of the Doric, Ionic, and Corinthian orders, threaded onto an essentially Tuscan string. (Of the triads, we see only the Rotunda, the apex of the northern trio, beneath a dome executed on the Delorme method.) Pavilions IX and X came fairly late in the design and belong at least one rung down the ladder of Jefferson's preferences. On the "ancient" side, Pavilion X, with its baseless Roman Doric, probably exemplifies antique architecture before its maturity. The much-misunderstood Pavilion IX, based on a Latrobe design, seems to be Jefferson's experiment with a "modern" Ionic hybrid. The vastly more important freedom, however, has largely gone unnoticed, although this drawing underscores it. By 1817 Jefferson (uniquely among major Western architects, it seems) could conceive of displaying the orders on a major public building laid out with explicit axial asymmetry. In following his principle of contrasting

pavilions ("no two alike"), he did not display an unerring hand at massing, but one cannot deny the vitality that this variety gives the group.

Despite discoloration, the elevation shows Neilson stretching his graphic abilities, which leave the standards of eighteenth-century Virginia far behind. The dependence on India ink (except for a few areas of writing ink in the Chinese rails), the skillful use of a crow-quill pen, the modeling, the presence of color, the reserving of the white of the paper for the trim, and the use of a landscape setting replete with trees and clouds—all these place the drawing within the developing professional standards of the nineteenth century. In some details, such as the over-ambitious cast shadows—labored, not smoothly washed—Neilson's aspirations outran his abilities. It seems likely that Latrobe's University drawings prompted him to aim here for a new level of accomplishment.[5]       CEB

NOTES
1.   Albemarle County, Will Book 9, p. 278. K. Edward Lay and Joseph Lasala helped me with this document. See also Lay, "Architectural Legacy," p. 39; Cote, "Architectural Workmen," pp. 85–86; and Brownell and Cohen, *Architectural Drawings.*

2.   O'Neal, "Intelligent Interest," pp. 75–78.

3.   Neilson to Cocke, 22 February 1823. C. Allan Brown, a consultant to the Center for Palladian Studies at the University of Virginia, kindly shared this discovery of his. It is unclear whether Neilson made more than one such drawing. His inventory (p. 274) lists "Rotunda & Two Pavillions."

4.   For the reattribution, see Cote, "Architectural Workmen," pp. 84–89; see also Lay, "Architectural Legacy," p. 39.

5.   I owe this excellent suggestion to my student Donald W. Matheson.

REFERENCES
Albemarle, County of. Will Book 9, pp. 269–80.

Cote, Richard Charles. "The Architectural Workmen of Thomas Jefferson in Virginia." 2 vols. Ph.D. diss., Boston University, 1986.

Lay, K. Edward. "Charlottesville's Architectural Legacy." *Magazine of Albemarle County History* 46 (1988):29–95.

Neilson, John, to John Hartwell Cocke, 22 February 1823. University of Virginia Library, Special Collections Department, Cocke Papers, No. 640 etc., Box 38.

Nichols. *Thomas Jefferson's Architectural Drawings.* No. 354.

O'Neal. *Architectural Drawing in Virginia.* Pp. 22–23.

For additional references to Jefferson's work as an architect, see survey nos. 26, 27.

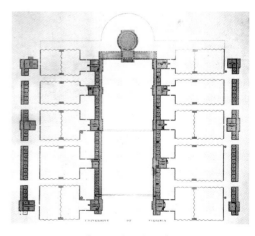

FIGURE 2. *Plan,* **University of Virginia,** *engraving by Peter Maverick, 1825. (Photograph courtesy of the Thomas Jefferson Papers, Special Collections Department, Manuscripts Division, University of Virginia Library.)*

# 29.
# BREMO

*Elevation and Plan*

Near Bremo Bluff (Fluvanna County)
Presentation drawings, circa 1817
Inscribed at top of elevation: *North front of Gen'l J. H. Cocke's house Upper Bremo*; inscribed at top of plan: *plan of the principal story*
Ink and wash on paper; 14 by 20 inches
Collection of the University of Virginia, Charlottesville; Alderman Library

FIGURE 1. *Vintage photo,* **Bremo,** *circa 1930–36 by Frances Benjamin Johnston, for the WPA. (Photograph courtesy of the Virginia State Library).*

The crisply executed drawings of the Palladian mansion Thomas Jefferson built for his close friend Gen. John Hartwell Cocke have been the subject of much mystery and controversy. The drawings were apparently included among a collection of drawings by John Neilson that came into the possession of the University of Virginia soon after Neilson's death. Among these was Neilson's drawing of the Rotunda (see SURVEY 28).[1] Although it is difficult to prove conclusively, Neilson's plan and elevation of Bremo are very likely the drawings discovered in the early twentieth century by Dr. William Alexander Lambeth in the University of Virginia Library (then housed in the Rotunda), which Lambeth took to be drawn by Thomas Jefferson. It was this "find" which led Lambeth to assign authorship of the design of Bremo to Jefferson in his pioneering work *Thomas Jefferson as an Architect* (1913). The drawings subsequently disappeared, but the ones illustrated here were discovered around 1966 among Dr. Lambeth's papers following the death of his widow, and were handed over to the University.[2] A plausible explanation is that Dr. Lambeth was working with the drawings while writing his book and inadvertently misplaced them among his papers where they remained forgotten for fifty years.

The issue is further complicated by the fact that these drawings, along with the those of the original buildings at the University of Virginia, drawn and rendered in similar style on the same type of paper, and preserved in the University's manuscript collection, have been attributed by various scholars to Jefferson's granddaughter Cornelia Randolph. Now that the inventory of Neilson's effects listing "a book of drawings of the U.Va. by Jno. Neilson"[3] make it evident that the University drawings are Neilson's, the Cornelia Randolph attribution is no longer a consideration. Because the elevation illustrated here shows Bremo as proposed, with stepped parapets—and not as actually built, with a straight parapet—it would be highly unlikely that it is the work of Cornelia Randolph in any case, since she supposedly only made drawings of completed works.[4]

John Neilson was born in what is today Northern Ireland and became a naturalized citizen of the United States in Philadelphia in 1804. That same year he was engaged by Thomas Jefferson for the construction of Monticello, where he lived and worked until 1808. From that year until 1810, he was hired by James Madison to execute alterations to Montpelier. Although principally a master builder, Neilson was also a skilled architect and was well-read. His library, at his death, contained 248 titles, including many works on architecture.[5] In 1817, he and his fellow Irish builder, James Dinsmore, were hired by Gen. John Hartwell Cocke to assist him in designing and building a new mansion for Bremo, a Fluvanna County plantation.[6] Cocke had been planning the house since 1815 and had sought advice from numerous builders and architects. He had hoped to have the assistance of Thomas Jefferson, but Jefferson passed up this opportunity to become formally involved with Bremo and

thus what would have been one of his most important commissions. Jefferson did give Cocke many helpful suggestions but resisted providing drawings since he had recently sold his architectural books to the Library of Congress. To compensate, Jefferson recommended that Cocke seek guidance from Dinsmore and Neilson. Both men had become thoroughly familiar with Jefferson's Classical idiom and were competent to give Cocke the services he required.

Thus both Dinsmore and Neilson contracted with General Cocke on December 23, 1817. However, because of previous commitments, Dinsmore soon turned the whole project over to Neilson. Having responsibility for preparing the final plans and supervising the construction, and the credit for Bremo's ultimate appearance, including its careful proportions and flawless detailing, belongs to Neilson.[7] Even though Cocke, through his sketches as well as his various consultations, had already determined what the basic form of Bremo was to be, it was Neilson who synthesized the many ideas into a cohesive design following Jefferson's Palladian tenets. In the cornerstone record for Bremo prepared July 8, 1818, General Cocke erased any doubt of Neilson's role when he stated: "John Neilson of Albemarle Architect—and execute(s) the Carpentry at the same terms for which he finished the late President Madison's House at Montpelier. . . . "[8]

Neilson also likely produced numerous working drawings for Bremo, none of which are known to exist. However, what must be regarded as Neilson's formal record of his design, the ink-and-wash drawings illustrated here, survives as testimony of the talent of one of Virginia's foremost but least-known architects.
                                        CCL

NOTES
1. K. Edward Lay, "Charlottesville's Architectural Legacy." *The Magazine of Albemarle County History* 46 (1988): 38–39.

2. For a more complete discussion of the complicated story of the disappearance of the drawings see Peter Hodson, "The Design and Building of Bremo: 1815–1820," (Master of Architectural History thesis, University of Virginia, 2–4.

3. Quoted in Lay, "Architectural Legacy," 39.

4. The parapets and flat roof leaked badly and were replaced by General Cocke in 1836 with a balustrade and hipped roof.

5. Lay, 39.

6. Bremo plantation was subdivided by General Cocke into three separate farms: Upper Bremo, Lower Bremo, and Recess, each with its own distinctive residence. The design discussed here is for Upper Bremo, although it is generally referred to as simply Bremo.

7. Formal credit for the design of Bremo to John Neilson with the close involvement of General Cocke was first given by Peter Hodson in his thesis, "The Design and Building of Bremo: 1815–1820."

8. Hodson, "Building of Bremo," 11, 48.

REFERENCES
Adams, William Howard, ed. *The Eye of Thomas Jefferson.* Washington, D.C.: The National Gallery of Art, 1967. P. 383.

Hodson, Peter. "The Design and Building of Bremo." Master of Architectural History thesis, University of Virginia, 1967.

Kimball, Sidney Fiske. "The Building of Bremo." *The Virginia Magazine of History and Biography,* January 1949.

Lay, K. Edward. "Charlottesville's Architectural Legacy." *The Magazine of Albemarle County History* 46 (1988): 38–39.

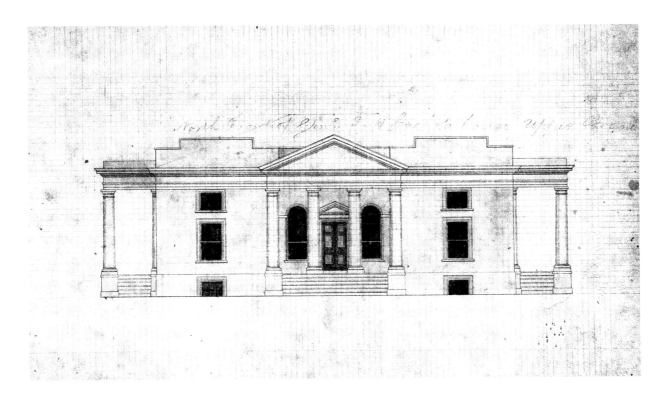

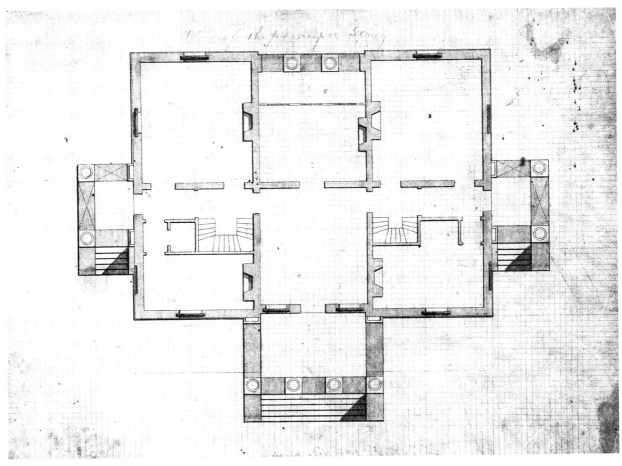

# 30.
# REID-WHITE HOUSE

*(now called Evergreen House)*
*Elevation and Sections*

208 West Nelson St., Lexington
Study, 1821
Inscribed on reverse: *Saml. McD Reid / Ballenfalls [?] / plan / House*
Ink and watercolor on paper; 14 by 11 ⅛ inches
Collection of the McCormick Library, Washington and Lee University, Lexington, Virginia

FIGURE 1. *Site photo,* **Reid-White House (Evergreen House)** *as it looks today.*

The preparation of architectural drawings has become such a specialized craft that today it is left almost exclusively to professionals. Because professional architects were essentially nonexistent in early-nineteenth-century Virginia, some would-be clients had to do their own designing. Indeed, not a few of these amateur or gentlemen architects showed a high degree of competence, but unfortunately their drawings are exceedingly rare. One individual undaunted by the execution of proper plans was the Lexington lawyer and landowner Samuel McDowell Reid, who succeeded his father as Clerk of Rockbridge County Court from 1831 until 1852. Reid's interest in architecture was demonstrated by his serving on the building committees for several important Lexington structures, including the committee that selected Thomas U. Walter to design the Rockbridge County jail.

In the process of planning his own house in 1821, Reid—with unusual proficiency for an amateur—prepared a set of gaily colored drawings, including an elevation, two sections, and a floor plan. The resulting design shows a carefully proportioned but architecturally conservative Federal house, a type that was favored by the professional and landholding classes of the region. Lending it refinement are the three-part facade windows, properly diminished in proportion on the second floor. That it was to be an above-average residence was signaled by its two-room-deep floor plan, a departure from the more standard single-pile plan.

The house is not elaborate; Reid employs no fancy cornice, merely a molded brick cornice, a feature typical of the vernacular dwellings of the area. Although the elliptical-arch doorway is shown unembellished on the drawing, Reid did indulge himself when he noted in his specifications: "fancy doors with sidelights."[1] The one-story porch currently on the house may be original, for Reid also instructed his carpenter to provide fluted Ionic columns on the entrance.[2] Reid obviously wanted to see the effect of brick walls, since he painstakingly penned the brickwork on the elevation, not in the fine Flemish bond of which the house was actually built, but in a simple running bond. The sections also show Reid's interest in detail. The hierarchy of spaces is indicated by the treatment of the woodwork. The main first-floor rooms are given turned corner blocks in the architrave frames and panels under the windows. The lesser first-floor rooms have no corner blocks and no panels, while the main rooms upstairs have panels but no corner blocks. Mantels are shown on the drawing as simple outlines, but Reid's written specifications call for two fancy chimney-pieces on the first floor, with the ones above to be "finished in middleing style."[3] Reid was knowledgeable enough in structural matters to show the floor joists in the wing and the collar beam in the attic.

It is difficult to point to any specific design source for Reid's house. While the elevation is vaguely similar to a facade design published in Owen Biddle's *Young Carpenter's Assistant* (1810), the house is more typical of the provincial Federal idiom of the region. Its exterior was dressed up in the 1840s when stepped parapets were added to the gables and the original cornice was replaced with a larger wooden one with a deep stuccoed frieze. The Lee Avenue view of the house was lost in 1913 when the United States Post Office was built in its front yard. CCL

NOTES
1. Royster Lyle, Jr., and Pamela Hemenway Simpson, *The Architecture of Historic Lexington* (Charlottesville, The University Press of Virginia), 84–86.

2. Ibid.

3. Ibid., 86.

REFERENCES
Lyle, Royster, Jr., and Simpson, Pamela Hemenway. *The Architecture of Historic Lexington.* Charlottesville: The University Press of Virginia, 1977. Pp. 21–24, 84–86.

*Architectural Drawing in Lexington, 1799/1926.* An exhibition presented by Washington and Lee University in cooperation with Virginia Military Institute and the Lexington/Rockbridge County Bicentennial Commission. Lexington: Washington and Lee University, 1978. Pp. 3–4.

Sect 1st          Sect 2nd

Sect 3rd          Sect 4th

# 31.

## BREMO RECESS

*Proposed Plan and Elevations*

Near Bremo Bluff (Fluvanna County)
Presentation drawing, mid 1830s
Pricking, pencil, pen and India ink with writing ink and India
ink wash on paper; 13 ⅛ by 16 ½ inches
Collection of the University of Virginia, Alderman Library,
Charlottesville; Special Collections Department, Cocke
Papers, No. 640 etc. (acc. no. 5685–a), Oversize Box 3

John Hartwell Cocke had engaged in building at Bremo plantation (SURVEY NO. 29) before he created his Palladian villa at Upper Bremo. (Cocke had divided the inherited property into Upper and Lower Bremo, on the James, and Bremo Recess, set back from the river.) In 1807–08, Cocke erected a story-and-a-half wooden dwelling at Bremo Recess, to replace a log house. In 1834–36, after his son John Hartwell Cocke, Jr., had assumed management of the Recess plantation, Cocke enlarged the house there and wrapped it in a brick Jacobean Revival facade.

Cocke, without clearly claiming authorship of the design, named the models in a letter to Charles Tyler Botts, editor of the *Southern Planter*. In 1844, proposing unsuccessfully that Botts publish a drawing of the "cottage," Cocke stated that "the stile is copied from the only two specimens of the like building I ever saw—the well remembered, old Six-chimney House in Wmsburg once the property of the Custis Family—and Bacons Castle. . . . The dimensions & cheapness of this Building bring it within the means of any Gentleman who can afford to lay out $2500 or 3000 . . . and its accommodations are sufficent for any family of temperate habits & moderate desires in a republican age & Country."[1] Whatever form the lost Custis house took, the cottage at Bremo Recess derived from it and the Arthur Allen House (Surry County, circa 1665) authentic Tudor-Stuart features: the projecting frontispiece with a chamber over a porch, shaped gables, and columnar chimney stacks set diagonally. The designer, however, by no means produced an archaeological essay and blended into the design such openly medieval elements as the Gothic arches. The design may well have owed additionally to John Claudius Loudon's *Encyclopaedia of Cottage, Farm and Villa Architecture* (London, 1833), which Cocke acquired in 1834.[2] The experiment with style at Bremo Recess pleased Cocke, who built a second essay in the same taste for another son at Lower Bremo in 1839–40.

It appears that Cocke chose the style he used at the Recess and at Lower Bremo to display the Cocke pedigree as an established family in the American republic. The family traced its history back two centuries in America and had, by marriage, acquired Bacon's Castle, where Cocke grew up. Within a decade, a third son built a house that again evoked the Tudor-Stuart world, but with opulence (SURVEY NO. 38).

This positive response to the architectural legacy of the North American past seems exceptional in the period. Cocke's undertaking does have a counterpart at Sunnyside in Tarrytown, New York, where Washington Irving, aided by the painter George Harvey and the architect Calvin Pollard (see SURVEY NO. 34, St. Paul's Church, Petersburg), converted a small Dutch house into an interpretation of early Netherlandish taste in the New World (1835–37 and later).[3] The journalist Anne Royall reported in 1826 on a less elegant parallel. The owner of the first house built on the site of present-day Washington, D.C., had carefully protected the century-old dwelling, "this sacred relic

of antiquity," and had "turned it into a stable for her favorite horse, who . . . appeared to participate in our pleasure" at viewing the historic treasure.[4]

Two known drawings for Bremo Recess survive.[5] The present sheet shakily approximates professional standards. Thus, the drafter relied on India ink as the primary medium, and his layout shows the front elevation (top left) as pulled out from the plan, and the rear elevation (top right) as pulled out from the front. The maker lacked skill with India ink and furthermore suffered from confusion about the convention of face lines and shadow lines (see Chapter 4). Apparently he did not recognize that the thick or shadow lines belong on the two sides of a rectangle away from the imagined light source and that the thin or face lines belong on the two opposite sides, for he used the two thicknesses with no apparent order. He or someone else tested options in pencil, such as gabled dormers on the front elevation. In the final version of the house, the gabled frontispiece shown here at the rear became the centerpiece of the entry facade.                CEB

NOTES
1.   John Hartwell Cocke to Charles Tyler Botts, 1844. According to Loth and Sadler, *Only Proper Style*, p. 71, Cocke published a version of this text in the *Richmond Enquirer*, 1844, but the citation is elusive.

2.   On this point, see Durilin, "Bremo Recess," pp. 30–32.

3.   On Sunnyside I have used Snadon, "Davis," pp. 293–96, and Zukowsky and Stimson, *Hudson River Villas*, pp. 78–79.

4.   [Royall], *Sketches*, pp. 170–71.

5.   Lane, *Virginia*, p. 205, speaks of a "rough sketch, in Cocke's distinctive style and on his usual drawing paper," but does not locate this.

REFERENCES
Cocke, John Hartwell, to Charles Tyler Botts. 1844. Cocke Papers, No. 640 etc., Box 112. Special Collections Department, University of Virginia Library.

Durilin, Tatiana S. "Bremo Recess: A Colonial Jacobean Revival." Master of Architectural History thesis, University of Virginia, 1990.

Hodson, Peter. "The Design and Building of Bremo: 1815–1820." Master of Architectural History thesis, University of Virginia, 1967.

Kimball, Fiske. "The Building of Bremo." *Virginia Magazine of History and Biography* 57 (January 1949): 2–13.

Lane. *Virginia*. Pp. 203–05.

Loth, Calder and Julius Trousdale Sadler, Jr. *The Only Proper Style: Gothic Architecture in America*. Boston: New York Graphic Society, 1975. Pp. 71–74.

Miyagawa, Ellen. "John Hartwell Cocke's Architectural Legacy to Fluvanna County." *Bulletin of the Fluvanna County Historical Society* no. 40 (October 1985): 3–46.

Pevsner, Nikolaus. Chap. 9, "'Good King James's Gothic.'" *Studies in Art, Architecture and Design*. 2 vols. London: Thames and Hudson, 1968.

[Royall, Anne.] *Sketches of History, Life, and Mannners, in the United States*. 1826. Reprint. New York: Johnson Reprint Corporation, 1970.

Snadon, Patrick Alexander. "A. J. Davis and the Gothic Revival Castle in America, 1832–1865." 2 vols. Ph.D. diss., Cornell University, 1988.

Virginia, Commonwealth of. *Virginia Landmarks Register*. File Nos. 32–1 (Lower Bremo), 32–2 (Bremo Historic District), and 32–6 (Bremo Recess).

Zukowsky, John, and Robbe Pierce Stimson. *Hudson River Villas*. New York: Rizzoli, 1985.

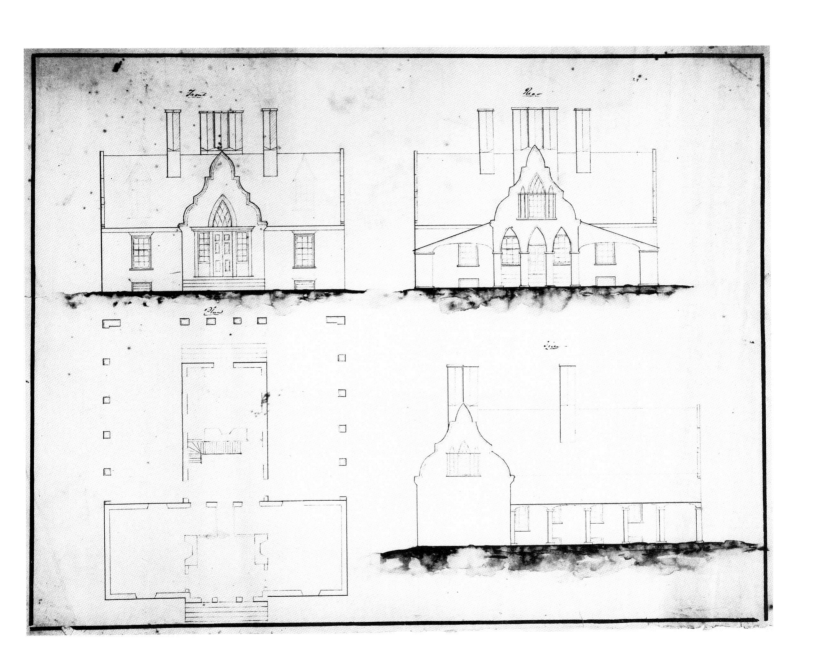

# 32.
# COURT-HOUSE FOR ALEXANDRIA

*Elevation of Facade*

Columbus between Queen and Princess Sts., Alexandria (demolished)
Presentation drawing, 1838
Signed and dated: *Robt. Mills/Archt. Pub. Bldgs/City. Washington July 17.1838*
Pricking, pencil, pen and India ink with watercolor on paper; 15 by 20 ¼ inches
Collection of the National Archives, Cartographic and Architectural Branch, Alexandria, Virginia; Record Group 42: Records of the Office of the Public Buildings, NCP–0–29

FIGURE 1. **Alexandria Courthouse before demolition,** *circa 1905. (Photograph courtesy of the Alexandria Library, Lloyd House, Alexandria, Va.)*

Like other founders of the American architectural profession, Mills repeatedly found himself hard put to make a living. He labored in various East Coast cities for two decades, spent the 1820s in his native South Carolina, and became a permanent Washingtonian in 1830, six years before his appointment as architect of the Treasury Building (1836–42) and the Patent Office (1836–40; 1849–51). (Both buildings incorporate the work of other architects.)

In 1838–39 Mills designed and erected the Alexandria courthouse. During the Colonial period, Virginia had possessed only a few towns and two main kinds of public building, the Anglican parish church and the courthouse, the latter functioning as a "rural forum."[1] The rise of towns meant the multiplication of secular building-types to serve community life, such as early-nineteenth-century Alexandria's markethouse, town hall, banks, theater, library, museum, and bathhouse.[2]

With the Alexandria courthouse, Mills made a synthesis of varied experiences. He put the rooms necessary for the court upstairs and those for the offices on the ground floor. Upstairs, the differentiation of space has well-established Virginia features. Raised, apsidal seating for magistrates went back a little over a century to the rise of brick courthouses over those of perishable earth-fast construction. The same pedigree stretches behind the lawyer's bar across the center of the space and the placement of two jury rooms opposite the bench. One can probably track the judge's apse back to Inigo Jones's introduction of High Classicism into Britain.[3] Surely the form percolated from a few royal projects to wider use in late Stuart architecture, exemplified by the first Williamsburg Capitol (1701–05, demolished), which established the use of the apse in Virginia judicial architecture.

The immediate precedent for Mills's raised courtroom lies with his practice in South Carolina during the 1820s. There, in place of the established local type, a wooden courthouse with ground-floor courtroom, he had built courthouses with raised, vaulted basements for offices and fireproof record storage. Latrobe, a master at vaulting, had trained Mills in the techniques of arcuation.

The courtroom itself does not simply conform to Virginia custom. Mills reshaped the apse-ended tradition on the model of the Classical theater and its adaptations at the U.S. Capitol, where Latrobe had built a series of chambers reinterpreting this antique source, notably the first Courtroom (1807–09, demolished) and the second (1816 and after), which served the Supreme Court and the District of Columbia Circuit Court. (With the theater plan, too, Mills had experimented before in South Carolina and Virginia.) Unlike Latrobe's chambers, the Alexandria courtroom has its bench in the curve, in accord with Virginia custom, not on the straight side.

Mills obviously planned to cover the courtroom with a light wooden half-dome, not a masonry one. One suspects that this covering (part of which caved in in 1851) employed the Delorme method (FIGURE 2.20).[4] Mills had learned of this laminated plank construction from Jefferson (FIGURE 4.29); had assisted Latrobe to instate the method at the Capitol, at Jefferson's behest; and had used Delorme construction extensively, for instance in the dome on Monumental Church (Richmond, 1812–17; SURVEY NO. 21, FIGURE 1).

Mills's portico, with its lateral staircases, also echoes his South Carolina work. The widely spaced columns are a far cry from the muscular peristyle of the Parthenon, though they have a measure of Hellenic precedent.[5] This portal serves as a reminder that Mills, not Latrobe, introduced the Greek orders into use in Virginia. Latrobe's Greek orders had met with indifference in Virginia for more than fifteen years when Mills executed the Doric and Ionic shafts of Monumental Church.

A sheet of Mills's plans for the courthouse survives with the "Facade" (National Archives, NCP-0-30). The professionalism in which Latrobe instructed Mills puts the elevation in revealing contrast with Mills's Monticello elevation of thirty-five years before (SURVEY NO. 12). The luminous use of watercolor is the most apparent debt to Mills's great mentor. In such features as the still-detectable pencil guidelines for washing-in the courthouse shadows, one recognizes that the naive perfectionism of the Monticello elevation has given way to a hard-pressed professional's discrimination between what has a telling effect and what does not.

CEB

NOTES

1. Quoted from Lounsbury, "Structure of Justice," p. 214.

2. Royall, *Sketches,* pp. 100–13, gives an animated description of Alexandria a decade before Mills built his courthouse.

3. See, for instance, Harris and Higgott, *Jones,* 98–100, 108–11, 114–15. On the apse and other points concerning courthouse architecture, I have profited from extended discussions with my student Bryan Clark Green.

4. On the collapse, see *Alexandria Gazette,* 26 February 1851; on the Delorme method, see Chapter 2 and survey no. 13.

5. For examples of wider Greek Doric intercolumnations, see Stuart, Revett, et al., *Antiquities of Athens,* vol. 1, chap. 1; vol. 2, chap. 5; vol. 3, chap. 10.

REFERENCES

Alexander, Robert L. "Mills, Robert." In *Macmillan Encyclopedia.*

*Alexandria Gazette,* 26 February 1851.

Bryan, John M., ed. *Robert Mills, Architect.* Washington, D. C.: The American Institute of Architects Press, 1989.

Caton, James R. *Legislative Chronicles of the City of Alexandria.* Alexandria: Newell-Cole Company, 1933. Pp. 130–33.

Harris, John, and Gordon Higgott. *Inigo Jones: Complete Architectural Drawings.* Exh. cat. New York: The Drawing Center, 1989.

Lounsbury, Carl R. "Beaux-Arts Ideals and Colonial Reality: The Reconstruction of Williamsburg's Capitol, 1928–1934." *JSAH* 49 (December 1990):373– 89.

———. "The Structure of Justice: The Courthouses of Colonial Virginia." In *Perspectives in Vernacular Architecture.* Vol. 3. Edited by Thomas Carter and Bernard L. Herman. Columbia, Missouri: University of Missouri Press, 1989.

Morrill, Penny. *Who Built Alexandria?: Architects in Alexandria, 1750–1900.* Exh. cat. Alexandria: Carlyle House Historic Park, 1979. Pp. 13, 22–24.

[Royall, Anne.] *Sketches of History, Life, and Manners, in the United States.* 1826. Reprint New York: Johnson Reprint Corporation, 1970.

Stuart, James; Nicholas Revett; et al. *The Antiquities of Athens.* 3 vols. 1762–94. Reprint New York: Arno Press, 1980.

Waddell, Gene, and Rhodri Windsor Liscombe. *Robert Mills's Courthouses and Jails.* Easley, South Carolina: Southern Historical Press, 1981.

Whiffen, Marcus. "The Early County Courthouses of Virginia." *Journal of the Society of Architectural Historians* 18 (March 1959):2–10.

FAÇADE of the COURT - HOUSE for ALEXANDRIA.

NCR - O - 29

# 33.
## VIRGINIA SCHOOL FOR THE DEAF AND THE BLIND

*Front Elevation, Main Building*

East Beverley St., Staunton
Study, probably 1839
Pricking, pencil, pen and India ink with watercolor on paper;
15 ¼ by 21 ¼ inches
Collection of The Winterthur Library, The Henry Francis
du Pont Winterthur Museum, Winterthur, Delaware; The
Joseph Downs Collection of Manuscripts and Printed
Ephemera, 68x198.53a

FIGURE 1. *Site photo,* **Virginia School for the Deaf and the Blind,** *Staunton.*

The Long family illustrates how the artisan-architect of one generation could sire the professional architect of the next generation. The Baltimore builder Robert Cary Long, Sr. (1772–1835), was an ambitious popularizer of the innovations in Latrobe's orbit. Long's son, after training in the circle of Ithiel Town and Alexander J. Davis in New York, became Baltimore's leading architect and an intellectual figure. He fared so well professionally that he reestablished himself in New York in 1848, only to die the next year. The reputation of his important early commission in Staunton survived him.

A bill to establish a state school for the deaf was first introduced in the State Legislature in 1826 but was postponed. By the 1830s, a growing movement to create a school for the blind joined forces with advocates for a school for the deaf, and persuaded the General Assembly to create a joint institution. In 1839, Staunton was selected as the location. Reporting on the construction contract with William Donoho of Albemarle County, the *Staunton Spectator & General Advertiser* noted that these buildings "are to be made of brick, with stone foundations, and . . . there shall be an absolute separation of the two classes of pupils from each other, that the care and instruction of each may be committed to their appropriate teachers, while the supplies of food, &c. for both, can be furnished by some common steward." In 1839, Long was selected as the architect, at a cost not to exceed $250.00, including the expense of a visit to Staunton by him. The cornerstone ceremony took place on 9 July 1840; construction continued to 1846.

The resemblance of the school to a large house gives away the ancestry of its planning. In the early modern era, as institutional buildings multiplied, they often took the form of enlarged houses. Robert Cary Long, Jr., employed one of the most important of these patterns ( FIGURE 2 ), a cross-axial arrangement, with an oblong body served by a corridor and, at right angles to that, a central element with a formal entry in front and an assembly hall behind. (Like many other designers, Long used additional rear wings as well.) This layout had reached North American educational architecture no later than the much-imitated Nassau Hall at Princeton (by Robert Smith and Dr. William Shippen, 1754–56).[1]

Long's plan is at odds with the possibilities that Jefferson unveiled at the University of Virginia, where he avoided the large, concentrated, expensive "magnificent house," which he considered all too vulnerable to fire and the spread of disease.[2] But the pattern that Long used, not the Jeffersonian one, surfaced again and again for Virginia schools, in such diverse guises as the Richmond Female Institute ( SURVEY NO. 45 ) and the Miller School ( SURVEY NO. 52 ).

While Long worked on the school (1839–40) he also worked at Staunton's Western State Hospital, begun in 1825 by another Baltimorean, Latrobe's pupil William F. Small.[3] It is not clear which project came first, although there is a common factor in that Dr. Francis T. Stribling, Superintendent of Western

State Hospital, also served on the school's Board of Visitors and its building committee. The hospital's North Building sits on a hill facing the school across the valley, and its facade incorporates a Doric central pavilion. This treatment, variously attributed to Long and to Thomas Blackburn, the hospital's Building Superintendent, seems to have been designed to harmonize with its elegant neighbor.

Long's elevation approximates his final facade. In addition to this elevation, Winterthur also has five sheets of plans (three studies, two presentation drawings) and two identifiable sheets of details for this commission. These drawings partly reveal Long's interest in Greek refinements, and thus disclose that he spaced the two outer columns closer than the rest, presumably to strengthen the look of the corner. They do not show that he gave the executed columns *entasis*, a curved taper not accepted as authentically Greek Doric by most American and many British Neoclassicists, who tapered their shafts on a straight line.          CEB and ST

NOTES
1.    On the original form of this building, see Paul Norton, chap. 1, and Robert C. Smith, chap. 3, in Savage, ed., *Nassau Hall.*

2.    Jefferson to Latrobe, 12 June 1817, in Latrobe, *Correspondence,* 3:901.

3.    Bryan Clark Green, a Ph. D. candidate in Architectural History at the University of Virginia, has unearthed a wealth of information on Western State, which he presented in a 1990 seminar report.

REFERENCES
Bass, R. Aumon. *History of the Education of the Deaf in Virginia.* Staunton: Virginia School for the Deaf and Blind, 1949.

Florence, Camille. "Grandeur in the Wilderness: The Architects and Architecture of Western State Hospital and the Virgina School for the Deaf and Blind." Paper, Mary Baldwin College, 1969. (Copy in the Fiske Kimball Fine Arts Library, University of Virginia.)

Ghequiere, T. Buckler. "The Messrs. Long, Architects." *American Architect and Building News* 1 (June 1876): 207.

Lane. *Virginia.* P. 192.

Latrobe. *Correspondence.*

McCue, Elizabeth Bray. *Staunton, Virginia: A Pictorial History.* Staunton: Historic Staunton Foundation, 1985.

Savage, Henry Lyttleton, ed. *Nassau Hall, 1756–1956.* Princeton: Princeton University, 1956.

Stanton, Phoebe B. "Long, Robert Cary." In *Macmillan Encyclopedia.*

*Staunton Spectator & General Advertiser.* 11 July 1839.

Streeter. "Virginia School for the Deaf and Blind." *Architecture in Virginia,* under the direction of K. Edward Lay, no. 37, University of Virginia, 1986. (Copy in the Fiske Kimball Fine Arts Library, University of Virginia.)

Turner, Paul Venable. *Campus: An American Planning Tradition.* The Architectural History Foundation/MIT Press Series, VII. New York, 1984.

Virginia, Commonwealth of. Virginia Landmarks Register, File. No. 132–8 (Virginia School for the Deaf and the Blind, Main Building).

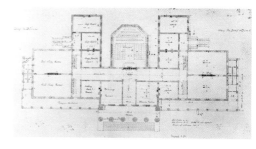

FIGURE 2. *Plan of the principal story,* **School for the Deaf and the Blind.** *(Photograph courtesy of the Winterthur Library, Joseph Downs Collection of Manuscripts and Printed Ephemera.)*

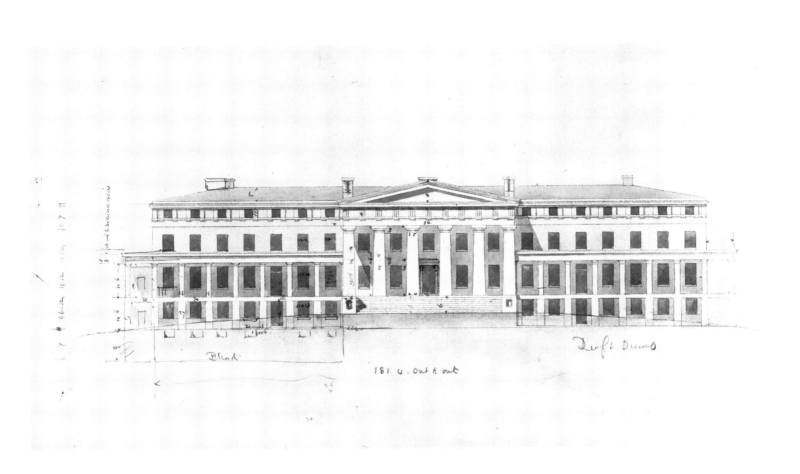

Blind

181. 4. Out & out

# 34.
# ST. PAUL'S CHURCH
# PETERSBURG

*Front Elevation*

Sycamore St. opposite Franklin St., Petersburg (demolished)
Presentation drawing, late 1830s
Signed: *Calvin Pollard Archt. New Yo[rk]/March 13th. 1 - - -* [torn]
Pencil, pen and India ink with watercolor and gold paint on paper; 26 ½ by 18 inches
Collection of Columbia University, New York City,
Avery Architectural and Fine Arts Library, Pollard Collection

The obscure Manhattan architect Calvin Pollard has had two holds on history. His architectural drawings (consisting of a large collection at the New-York Historical Society and a small one at Avery Library) have attracted historians at least since Talbot Hamlin (1889–1956). Pollard's work in Petersburg, such as the Courthouse (1838–40), has likewise secured him a place in American architectural history. With St. Paul's Church, a Petersburg building best known from the present elevation, the two reasons for remembering Pollard overlap.[1]

Before the Disestablishment of the Anglican Church in Virginia in 1784, its congregations met (by urban British standards) in unpretentious buildings. None boasted a temple portico; only a handful had towers; and many were of wood. In the nineteenth century, the church survived challenges from its Baptist, Methodist, and Presbyterian rivals and underwent a renewal. Between the 1830s and the Civil War, a major period for church-building in Virginia, all these Protestant groups adopted for their town churches the architectural display that their eighteenth-century houses of worship had lacked.

The congregation of Bristol Parish has erected a succession of buildings since its formation in the mid seventeenth century. Its third church, today called Blandford Church (1734–37; Colonel Thomas Ravenscroft, undertaker) was the first one called St. Paul's. Calvin Pollard designed the fifth church (built circa 1837–39) just at the time of a "general awakening" among Petersburg Protestants.[2] After Pollard's building burned in 1854, the Baltimore firm of Niernsee and Neilson designed the present church (1855–57). Bishop William Meade (1789–1862), the great restorer of the Episcopal Church in Virginia, dedicated that structure, which was an adaptation of the Gothic for Protestants.

Pollard's design shows the originally Jeffersonian Temple Revival returning south with alterations: a belfry and a special kind of temple-shaped front. The pattern of the latter, here called *distyle-in-muris*, has two columns standing between sections of wall.[3] Those wall bays maintain the effect of a temple facade, but they have pressed forward to take the place of the other columns needed for an orthodox portico. No doubt Pollard used this treatment because these bays gave him a place to put the gallery staircases near the entry, the standard reason for using this pattern in America. This Neoclassical scheme reached immense popularity in the United States between the 1820s and the 1860s. The Manhattan firm of Town and Davis had much to do with popularizing it, and Pollard's interest in the format may well reflect their practice.

Pollard's drawing seems to show a blue-gray granite basement under stuccoed brick walls scored, along with the columns, in no evident overall pattern. The blind windows and the unmolded pilaster strips lend novelty to the distyle theme, which here has a box-within-a-box quality. Neither this refreshing variation on a basic theme, nor the appeal of the elevation as a drawing, conceals Pollard's uncertainty over harmonious design and the refinements of Greek detail. (Infelicitous details, such as the overly attenuated Doric columns and the off-center triglyphs over the middle pilasters, betray his unsureness.) Thomas U. Walter and, still more, Alexander J. Davis exhibited a superior command of the type. Pollard's articulation of his facade and the anthemion-trimmed, domed octagon of his belfry suggest that he made use of a design by the British handbook writer Peter Nicholson, who must have done much to popularize this pattern (compare FIGURE 2.43).

This elevation, with its skillfully graded washes, has exercised an understandable attraction for half a century, though it does not attain the finesse of a drawing by Davis or Walter. The Petersburg amateur artist William Skinner Simpson, Sr. (1795–1868), copied a closely similar, lost Pollard elevation.[4]                    CEB

NOTES

1. The elevation has appeared in print repeatedly; for example in Hamlin, *Greek Revival*, p. 191n. and pl. 49, and Parks, "Avery" p. 68 (in color).

2. Marshall Bullock, Adult Services Librarian at the Petersburg Public Library, kindly helped with the documentation of Pollard's building. For the documentation, see the Virginia Landmarks Register File No. 123–41 (on the Niernsee and Neilson church) and its condensation in *Notes on Virginia*, and Lunsford, "History," p. 1. On the "awakening," see Meade, *Old Churches*, vol. 1, pp. 443–44.

3. On this pattern, see Chapter 2.

4. Now on loan to the Virginia Historical Society from St. Paul's Church. See Bailey, *Pictures*, p. 34, and color plate p. 26.

REFERENCES

Bailey, James H. *Pictures of the Past: Petersburg Seen by the Simpsons, 1819–1895*. Loc. unknown: Fort Henry Branch, Association for the Preservation of Virginia Antiquities, 1989.

Davis, Vernon Perdue, and James Scott Rawlings. *Virginia's Ante-Bellum Churches: An Introduction with Particular Attention to Their Furnishings*. Richmond: Dietz Press, 1978.

Francis, Dennis Steadman. *Architects in Practice, New York City, 1840–1900*. [New York]: Committee for the Preservation of Architectural Records, [1980?]. Under "Pollard, Calvin."

Hamlin, Talbot. *Greek Revival Architecture in America: Being an Account of Important Trends in . . . Architecture and . . . Life Prior to the War between the States. 1944*. Reprint. New York: Dover Publications, 1964. Pp. 127, 130n., 133n., 140, 151–52, 191n.; pls. 29–30, 33, 49.

Lane. *Virginia*. Pp. 179–83.

Lunsford, Charles, Jr. "History of St. Paul's Church, Petersburg, Virginia." Typescript, 1965. Laid into the binding of *His Holy Temple: Another Century in the Life of St. Paul's Episcopal Church, Petersburg, Virginia*. [Petersburg]: [St. Paul's Episcopal Church], 1956. Research Room, Petersburg Public Library.

Meade, Bishop William. *Old Churches, Ministers, and Families of Virginia*. 2 vols. Philadelphia: J. B. Lippincott & Co., 1857. Vol. 1, pp. 438–45.

*Notes on Virginia*, no. 29 (Fall 1986): 8–9.

Oles, James. "The Petersburg Courthouse (1838–40): An Important Example of the Greek Revival in Virginia." *Architecture in Virginia*, under the direction of K. Edward Lay, no. 62, University of Virginia, 1987. (Copy in the Fiske Kimball Fine Arts Library, University of Virginia.)

Parks, Janet. "Avery." *American Heritage* (April/May 1984): 65–79.

Turner, Paul Venable. *Campus: An American Planning Tradition*. The Architectural History Foundation/M.I.T. Press Series, VII. New York, 1984.

Virginia, Commonwealth of. *Virginia Landmarks Register*. File No. 123–41 (St. Paul's Episcopal Church).

. FRONT ELEVATION .

OF 1                    URCH . PETERSBURGH VA .          CALVIN POLLARD ARCH.T NEW YOR
                                                                        MARCH 13.th 1

# 35.
# SECOND BAPTIST
# CHURCH
# RICHMOND

*Perspective*

Sixth and Main Sts., Richmond (demolished)
Presentation drawing, 1840
Signed and dated: *T. U. Walter, Archt. 1840*
Pricking (?), pencil, pen and India ink, with watercolor on paper; 23 ½ by 18 inches (image size)
Collection of The Athenaeum of Philadelphia Archives, WTU*029*001

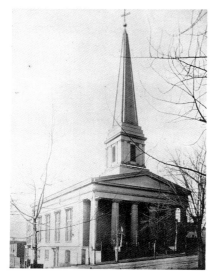

FIGURE 1. *Vintage photo,* **Second Baptist Church** *(second building), built 1841, demolished 1906. (Photograph courtesy of The Valentine Museum Richmond.)*

The Philadelphian Thomas U. Walter belongs to the populous generation of architects born around 1800, such as Henry Austin, Alexander J. Davis, Minard Lafever, Calvin Pollard, Thomas S. Stewart, Richard Upjohn, and Ammi B. Young. Walter combined a practical background—he belonged to a family of Germanic builders—with professional skills that he developed in the office of Latrobe's pupil William Strickland and at the Franklin Institute. Walter was very much Latrobe's successor: as designer of the climax of the Temple Revival (Founder's Hall, Girard College for Orphans, Philadelphia, 1833–48); as reshaper of the U. S. Capitol (wings and dome, 1851–65); and as one of the founders of the architectural profession (second president of the American Institute of Architects, 1876–87).

In the late 1830s and the 1840s, Walter made numerous designs for Virginians. His executed work in the Old Dominion included five exercises in the Temple Revival. The temples, in various kinds of Greek Doric on the exterior, consist of the Norfolk Academy, an amphiprostyle temple (designed 1839), and four Protestant churches.[1] To the churches, Walter (himself a Baptist churchman) gave the form of an auditory inside a temple-like box with a spire. The earliest is Second Baptist Church, Richmond (designed 1839, demolished 1906; FIGURE 1), a *distyle-in-muris* temple now lacking its steeple. Walter then devised three prostyle temples closely related to each other: Second Baptist Church, Richmond (designed 1840, the only Walter temple in Virginia to have perished; the Tabb Street Presbyterian Church in Petersburg (designed 1841), now missing its steeple; and the Presbyterian Church in Lexington (designed 1843). In these churches, the Temple Revival fused with the tradition established in London by James Gibbs (1682–1754) of uniting the Northern European spire with the temple portico. (Unlike eighteenth-century Gibbsian churches, however, the portico runs the full width of the building, creating a more literal approximation of a temple.) The portals and spires denied to Virginia's Anglican churches in the eighteenth century became disseminated among Virginia's Protestant sects in the nineteenth century.

Walter's three churches look so similar as to invite confusion. In fact, the present drawing has passed as a drawing of the Tabb Street church. But if one can trust the inscribed date, Walter drew this perspective in 1840, whereas he did not receive the Petersburg commission until after an 1841 fire had destroyed the Presbyterian church there. A list of projects drawn up by his biographer, Robert B. Ennis, shows no other ecclesiastical projects for 1840.[2] And the perspective answers well to the executed church, if one allows for familiar kinds of minor discrepancies between a presentation drawing and a finished building. (For instance, the actual church had fluted columns in the portico.) It seems appropriate, then, to reidentify the sheet, pending a full investigation of primary sources.

Finished in 1841, Second Baptist Church occupied a distinguished location amidst Neoclassical dwellings and actually shared the block with Moldavia (1800 and later, demolished), the villa that had briefly been the home of the young Edgar Allan Poe.[3] In an expression of the contest between Classicism and Mediavalism as well as the rivalry between Philadelphia and New York, Minard Lafever's Gothic-style Second Presbyterian Church (1846–48) soon rose across the way. The Second Baptist congregation remained loyal typologically even when they abandoned Walter's building in 1906; they had the Richmond firm of Noland and Baskervill build a more magnificent Corinthian temple on Franklin Street.

In Walter's perspective, irregular edges on the coloring and unerased penciling betray some haste, unlike the finer finish of the elevation of the Tabb Street church. Even so, the perspective testifies to Walter's accomplishments. For instance, he used sophisticated conventions to suggest how light reflects: he suffused the shadowed areas with radiance and picked out the undersides of moldings in these areas with brightness. As a draftsman, Walter was Latrobe's heir, too. According to John H. B. Latrobe, the architect's son and Walter's friend, Walter even declared that studying Latrobe's 1818 competition drawings for the second Bank of the United States in Strickland's office (now in the Library of Congress) had "aided in making him the admirable draftsman that he is."[4]     CEB

NOTES
1.   On the terminology for classical temples, see Chapter 2.
2.   Ennis, "List of Projects," in Tatman and Moss, under "Walter, Thomas Ustick."
3.   On the church see Scott, *Old Richmond Neighborhoods,* pp. 135, 139, 141, 183.
4.   Latrobe to McAllister, 22 June 1867.

REFERENCES
Allen, Mary Lee Link. "Thomas U. Walter's Greek Revival Church in Richmond, Virginia." Master of Arts thesis, Virginia Commonwealth University, 1978.

Davis, Vernon Perdue, and James Scott Rawlings. *Virginia's Ante-Bellum Churches: An Introduction with Particular Attention to Their Furnishings.* Richmond: Dietz Press, 1978.

Ennis, Robert Brooks. "Thomas Ustick Walter, Architect." Exh. handlist. Mimeographed. Philadelphia: Athenaeum of Philadelphia, 1979.

———. "Walter, Thomas U." In *Macmillan Encyclopedia.*

"Historical Sketch of the Tabb Street Presbyterian Church, Petersburg, Va." In East Hanover Presbytery, *Minutes,* 25 April 1932, pp. 56–62.

Lane. *Virginia.* Pp. 184–87, 208, 210.

Latrobe, John H. B., to John A. McAllister, Jr., 22 June 1867. Historical Society of Pennsylvania, Society Collection.

Laverty, Bruce, comp. Under "Walter, Thomas Ustick, Tabb Street Presbyterian Church, Petersburg, Virginia." *Catalog of Architectural Drawings: The Athenaeum of Philadelphia.* 2 vols. Boston: G. K. Hall & Co., 1986.

Ruffin, Sally Walthall. "History of Tabb Street Presbyterian Church." *One Hundredth Anniversary Celebration of the Dedication of Tabb Street Presbyterian Church, Petersburg, Virginia, January 23–25, 1944.* [Petersburg: Virginia Printing Company, 1944?]. Pp. 4–15.

Scott, Mary Wingfield. *Old Richmond Neighborhoods.* 1950. Reprint. Richmond: Valentine Museum, 1984.

Tatman and Moss. Under "Walter, Thomas Ustick."

Virginia, Commonwealth of. Virginia Landmarks Register. File No. 123–43 (Tabb Street Presbyterian Church).

# 36.
## MARINER'S CHURCH
*Proposed Front Elevation*

Norfolk (unbuilt)
Presentation drawing, 1843
Signed and dated: *T. U. Walter Archt. 1843*
Pricking, pencil, pen and India ink with tan ink, watercolor, and added pencil on paper; 26 ½ by 20 inches
Collection of The Athenaeum of Philadelphia Archives, WTU*039*001

The sustaining element in Walter's life was perhaps his ardent faith and his active participation in the life of the Spruce Street Baptist Church, Philadelphia, which he designed and built in 1829. Because of his close ties to the church, Walter (who was named for Thomas Ustick, the Baptist preacher who baptized both of Walter's parents) was approached for many church designs, such as the one for the Mariner's Church in Norfolk. The details of this "mail-order" undertaking are sketchy at best; in his diary for 1842–43, Walter made only two rather cryptic mentions of a set of drawings for a Gothic church for Norfolk. According to the diary entry for 13 January 1843, the drawings consisted of a front elevation, a flank elevation, a transverse section, a plan of the basement, one of the principal story, and one of the gallery. An entry made a week earlier records that Walter sent two perspectives of the church to a Dr. Babcock "to be returned." In an entry dated 8 July 1841 in Walter's account book, he recorded having sent to a Rev. W. Harris a strikingly similar list of drawings "for a Gothic Church," and an "embellished perspective, a descriptive letter and an estimate . . . [$] 20.00."[1] On the facing page, where Walter recorded receipts, the corresponding block has been left blank.

The Mariner's Church was to be a rather modest Gothic church in the English "decorated style," with a central tower, single lancet windows, and very restrained ornament, relying on an almost classical emphasis on massing and form rather than on surface ornament. The Mariner's Church contrasts markedly with Walter's 1848 design for the Freemason Street Baptist Church of Norfolk ( FIGURE 1 ), with its exuberant wooden decoration in the form of monumental pinnacles and buttresses. The two designs can be seen as brackets on the 1840s, and exhibit very clearly Walter's change in interpretation of the Gothic style over the course of the decade. Although the Mariner's Church was never built, Walter perhaps made good use of his essays in designing it. He was working at the same time on a design for "the Episcopalian Church" (Chapel of the Cross) at Chapel Hill, North Carolina, which is remarkably similar in its chaste English Gothic form.[2] Walter's design for the Norfolk Church may also have influenced his old teacher's interpretation of the Gothic style for a church in Virginia; William Strickland's 1847 design for Grace Episcopal Church in Cismont, Albemarle County, betrays some of the same qualities of restrained ornament and emphasis on form that Walter had used nearly six years before in the Mariner's Church design.[3]

Revising a previous phase of the design, Walter skillfully erased some form of superstructure that rose roughly six inches higher up the sheet. In a Picturesque manner characteristic of the mid century, his elevation luxuriates in the effect of crisp ashlar blocks in a random arrangement of contrasting browns. The exact alignment of the vertical joints in every second course was an ideal achievable at this date by simulating ashlar in stucco, as presumably Walter meant to do. But,

through the first half of the nineteenth century and beyond, it eluded stonemasons time after time (as witness Walter's Founder's Hall at Girard College for Orphans [1833–48] or John Notman's Athenaeum of Philadelphia [1845–47]). MPC

NOTES
1. Walter, *Diary,* 8 July 1841 and 13 January 1843.
2. Walter, *Diary,* 24 September and 1 October 1842.
3. For Strickland's drawings, see O'Neal, *Architectural Drawing,* pp. 34–39.

REFERENCES
Corrigan, Michael Patrick. "Puritans in Priestly Garb: The 'Gothic Taste' in Antebellum Virginia Church Architecture." Master of Arts thesis, Virginia Commonwealth University, 1988.

Davis, Vernon Perdue, and James Scott Rawlings. *Virginia's Ante-Bellum Churches: An Introduction with Particular Attention to Their Furnishings.* Richmond: Dietz Press, 1978.

Ennis, Robert Brooks. "Thomas Ustick Walter, Architect." Exh. handlist. Mimeographed. Philadelphia: Athenaeum of Philadelphia, 1979.

———. "Walter, Thomas U." In *Macmillan Encyclopedia.*

Lane. *Virginia.* Pp. 184–87, 208, 210.

Stanton, Phoebe B. *The Gothic Revival and American Church Architecture: An Episode in Taste, 1840– 1856.* The Johns Hopkins Studies in Nineteenth-Century Architecture, Baltimore, 1968.

Tatman and Moss. Under "Walter, Thomas Ustick."

Walter, Thomas U. Account Book, 1831–42, 1858. Athenaeum of Philadelphia Archives.

———. Diary, 1842–43. Athenaeum of Philadelphia Archives.

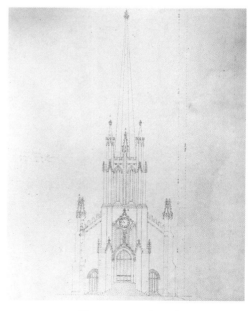

FIGURE 1. *Thomas U. Walter, design for* **Freemason Street Baptist Church,** *Norfolk, Virginia. (Photograph courtesy of the Atheneaum of Philadelphia.)*

T.U.WALTER *anno 1843*

Attributed to THOMAS SOMERVILLE STEWART,
1806–1889

# 37.
# MEDICAL COLLEGE
# OF RICHMOND

*(now Egyptian Building,*
*Medical College of Virginia)*
*Front Elevation and*
*Miscellaneous Sketches*

College and East Marshall Sts., Richmond
Study, mid 1840s
Pricking, pencil, and pen and [India?] ink on paper; 15 ⅞ by
10 ⅞ inches
Collection of The Athenaeum of Philadelphia Archives,
STW*003

FIGURE 1. *Site photo,* **Egyptian Building,**
*south front.*

Thomas S. Stewart, born in Scotland and trained in Philadelphia as a carpenter, designed a handful of large buildings between the late 1830s and 1845. He later made his income as an investor, dying a wealthy man. During his brief practice as an architect, he gave Richmond two monuments of later Neoclassicism. With the first, St. Paul's Episcopal Church (1843–45), for a congregation that split off from Monumental Church, he built a Temple Revival building modeled on his own St. Luke's in Philadelphia (1839–40). Reinterpreting the Gibbs vein, Stewart designed steeples for both temples, and he employed a florid manner that is one of the late manifestations of the Greek taste.

His work at St. Paul's seemingly led to a nearby second commission. In 1837, Hampden-Sydney College founded a medical department in Richmond. This "Medical College of Richmond, Va." represented a reaction against the limitations of medical instruction at the University of Virginia. Richmond would grow into a great medical center and the institution would evolve into today's Medical College of Virginia. Stewart created a lofty Egyptian edifice for the school (1844–45) and apparently modeled the facade on an unexecuted proposal of his from the mid 1830s for the Athenaeum of Philadelphia.[1] In 1938–39, Baskervill and Son modified the exterior and rebuilt the interior, inserting a splendid neo-Egyptian auditorium.

Stewart envisioned the school not as a large house, unlike many early modern architects such as Robert Cary Long, Jr. (see School for the Deaf and the Blind, Staunton, SURVEY NO. 33), but as an assembly hall with many ancillary rooms inside a temple-like casing. The building bears a pregnant likeness to the *distyle-in-muris* buildings of the period. Subscribing to the widespread "aesthetic of the temple," Stewart minimized the presence of tiers of windows and, as far as possible, gave the building—a five-story edifice—the monumental unity of a giant Order.[2]

A strong literary tradition declares that the Egyptians invented many branches of learning or, at the least, conveyed various kinds of wisdom to the Greeks.[3] In the nineteenth century, this association made Egyptian architectural inspiration seem appropriate for institutions of learning. Richard G. Carrott has connected Stewart's design with the tradition that the Egyptians excelled in medical learning, as in the legend of Imhotep, who supposedly invented architecture and practiced medicine.[4] In a different vein, an 1845 article in the *Richmond Times and Compiler* found the "mystery" of the style appropriate to "this temple of the medical science."

The popular conception of the so-called Egyptian Revival sees it simply as an alternative to Greco-Roman influence. It ignores the notion (influential though not universal in the period) that Classical architecture originated in what the Egyptians learned and then taught to the Greeks, a view of history in which Egyptian, Greek, and Roman architecture belonged to one continuum. Given the primitive connections of distyle porches, the Egyptian Building poses a question.[5] Does its form rest on a belief that the Egyptians

invented architecture and medicine, then passed these discoveries along to Western Civilization?

Stewart created a landmark of the Egyptian taste in the United States. Not only did he build an occupiable building (as opposed to the more common Egyptian cemetery gateway) but he also designed an enclosure to match, with granite obelisks for gateposts and a cast-iron railing running between herm figures (often mistaken for mummy-cases; FIGURE 2). A New England patron might have executed the design in almost imperishable granite, hammered by virtuoso masons, but the maturity of the Richmond quarries came only in the late nineteenth century. And Stewart evidently built the school (like his two churches) on a budget. Instead of challenging the ages, he depended mainly on stuccoed brick and timber.

FIGURE 2. *Detail,* **cast iron railing** *with herm figures, designed for the Egyptian Building.*

The elevation shows the essentials of the Medical College but not its exact final features. On the front and back of this page, Stewart roughed out plans, a section, and less identifiable sketches, along with notes on the building program. His ledger has at least two more sketch plans and a rough section. The more gifted nineteenth-century draftsmen disdained to make studies like this messy page, with its uncertain inking and its coarse penciling. In making presentation drawings, however, Stewart functioned at a professional level.                                              CEB

NOTES
1. On the prototype see Carrott, *Egyptian Revival,* pp. 111, 144, and figure 101; Steele, "Egyptian Building," pp. 27, 97, 106, 127, and 140; and Laverty, *Catalogue,* under "Stewart, Thomas Somerville, Athenaeum of Philadelphia, Pennsylvania."
2. On this aesthetic, see Chapter 2.
3. See, for example, Herodotus, 2.4; Diodorus Siculus, 1.69, 96–98.
4. *Egyptian Revival,* pp. 111–12. On the Egyptian Building, see also pp. 71, 145.
5. On the primitivist connections of the distyle front, see Chapter 2.

REFERENCES
Carrott, Richard G. *The Egyptian Revival: Its Sources, Monuments, and Meaning, 1808–1858.* Berkeley: University of California, 1978.
Lane. *Virginia.* Pp. 186, 189–91, 210–11.
Laverty, Bruce, comp. Under "Stewart, Thomas Somerville, Medical College of Richmond, Richmond, Virginia." *Catalog of Architectural Drawings: The Athenaeum of Philadelphia.* 2 vols. Boston: G. K. Hall & Co., 1986.
O'Gorman, James F., et al. *Drawing toward Building: Philadelphia Architectural Graphics, 1732–1986.* Exh. cat. Philadelphia: published for the Pennsylvania Academy of the Fine Arts by the University of Pennsylvania Press, 1986. Pp. 97–98.
*Richmond Times and Compiler,* 11 July 1845.
Shoemaker, Mary McCahon. "Thomas Somerville Stewart, Architect and Engineer." Master of Architectural History thesis, University of Virginia, 1975.
Steele, Karen Dallison. "The Egyptian Building: A Study." Master of Arts thesis, Virginia Commonwealth University, 1979.
Stewart, Thomas Somerville. Ledger. 1829 ff. The Athenaeum of Philadelphia Archives.
Tatman and Moss. Under "Stewart, Thomas Somerville."
Virginia, Commonwealth of. Virginia Landmarks Register, File No. 127–87 (Egyptian Building).

Facade 65 feet

Attributed to ALEXANDER JACKSON DAVIS,
1803–1892

# 38.
# BELMEAD

*East Elevation*

Route 684, Powhatan County
Study, 1845
Pencil, pen and India ink with watercolor on paper;
9 ⅛ by 12 ¼ inches
Collection of the New-York Historical Society,
A. J. Davis Collection, Drawing Number 274e

FIGURE 1. *Vintage site photo,* **Belmead,** *river front. (Photograph courtesy of The Valentine Museum, Richmond.)*

The Manhattanite Alexander J. Davis came to architecture from drawing via the office of Ithiel Town. His gift for pictorial effect shone, both in the Greek designs for public buildings that brought him fame in the early 1830s, and in the Picturesque houses that dominated the rest of his career.[1] The charm of his houses should not blind one either to Davis's practicality or to his reformative intentions as a specialist in the Picturesque and in *character,* the expression of the nature of a building.[2]

In 1845, Davis met one of his great patrons, Philip St. George Cocke (1809–1861), son of John Hartwell Cocke and a wealthy agricultural reformer (see SURVEY NOS. 29, 31).[3] The younger Cocke wished to build a Gothic house at his Belmead plantation because, he wrote, the "irregular or Gothic style" suited "rural scenes" and domestic life better than the "stiff" Classical taste.[4] He had found Davis's work alluring in A. J. Downing's *Cottage Residences* (New York, 1842) and had picked as a model an asymmetrical villa from J. C. Loudon's *Encyclopaedia* (London, 1833).[5] His intentions in building a manorial house, suggestive of his father's Jacobean Revival houses at Bremo (SURVEY NO. 31), are not entirely clear.[6]

The meeting of the two men was fateful. Davis designed for Cocke one of the great American mansions (1845–48) of the Gothic Revival (along with outbuildings, now lost), while Cocke opened Virginia to Davis as one of his largest fields of employment.[7] The long-distance Belmead commission prompted Davis to begin his habit of having standard specifications printed, perhaps for the first time in the United States. The Davis-Cocke relationship flourished until the War, which drove Cocke to suicide. Cocke's estate became St. Emma's (1895–1972), an historic Roman Catholic school for African-Americans, now Blessed Sacrament High School at Belmead.

In 1850, in his journal the *Horticulturist,* A. J. Downing published an article on Belmead based on a Davis description, with a perspective that Davis used for his own letterhead.[8] The article described Belmead as Tudor Gothic, of brick stuccoed and "coloured with warm grey tints" to match the trim of local granite. At Cocke's wish,[9] the drawing room commanded a view "across the valley of the James river, and the distant hills—the river meandering in the midst, its silver line lost in the distance." The details that gave the building its character included motifs that referred to the Belmead crops (FIGURE 2.52).[10] The mansion had a picture gallery and a furnace, a "museum" and running water.

Davis's elevation (one of five Belmead drawings at the New-York Historical Society catches the house near the end of its evolution. (Only traces of the model in Loudoun survived.) The design became increasingly "scenic," although the east wall never wholly lost a boxy quality. On the riverfront, Davis replaced a three-sided bay with a square tower that provides exhilarating views. On the opposite side, Davis inked the archway of a one-bay entry before substituting a two-bay porch. Thus the house grew more cross-axial, more varied as "architectural scenery," and more open to its setting via arches that Davis treated as frames for passages of loosely brushed landscape. This muted elevation does not show Davis at his vivacious best, but this degree of finish on a study aptly demonstrates his facility.

CEB

NOTES

1. The indispensable biographical account is Jane B. Davies, "Alexander Jackson Davis, in *Macmillan Encyclopedia.*" Mrs. Davies has graciously shared her unique knowledge of Davis with me since 1965.

2. For Davis's reformative intentions, see his *Rural Residences,* "Advertisement," no pagination.

3. For Cocke's biography, see Couture, *Powhatan,* and Gordon, "Cocke". I thank John Page Elliott, Cocke's great-grandson, for helping me learn about Cocke and Belmead.

4. Cocke to Maxwell, 1 May 1845.

5. For a discussion of the chivalric "plantation myth" and the poles of Cocke's character, see Snadon, "Davis," pp. 189–96, 201–02. I thank Snadon warmly for sharing his findings on Davis with me over the years.

6. For the documentation of the Belmead commission I have used Snadon, "Davis," pp. 162–67, 194–213; also Davis, Journal, pp. 82, 89, 148, and the numerous references in Davis, Daybook I. I owe John Richardson of Richmond an enormous debt for his exertions in enabling me to study Davis's Powhatan County buildings.

7. On Davis's authorship, see Chapter 2. Cocke meant to publish the house with the same illustration in the *Virginia Historical Register* but the idea fell through. See Snadon, "Davis," p. 197.

8. Cocke to Maxwell, 1 May 1845.

9. On Belmead and character, see Chapter 2.

REFERENCES

Cocke, Philip St. George, to William Maxwell, 1 May 1845. University of Virginia Library, Special Collections Department, Cocke Papers, No. 640 etc., Box 189, Letterbook.

Couture, Richard T. *Powhatan: A Bicentennial History.* Richmond: Dietz Press, 1980.

Dabney, William Pope, to Alexander J. Davis, 10 May 1871. Metropolitan Museum of Art, A. J. Davis Collection, vol. 18, leaf 148–148v.

Davies, Jane B. *A. J. Davis and American Classicism.* Exh. cat. Tarrytown, New York: Historic Hudson Valley, 1989.

———. "Davis, Alexander Jackson." In *Macmillan Encyclopedia.*

———. "Davis and Downing: Collaborators in the Picturesque." In *Prophet with Honor: The Career of Andrew Jackson Downing, 1815–1852.* Edited by George B. Tatum and Elisabeth Blair MacDougall. Dumbarton Oaks Colloquium on the History of Landscape Architecture XI. Washington, D. C., 1989.

———. "Gothic Revival Furniture Designs of Alexander J. Davis." *The Magazine Antiques* 111 (May 1977):1014–27.

Davis, Alexander J. Daybook. Vol. 1, October 1827–September 1853. Rare Books and Manuscripts Division, New York Public Library.

———. Journal. Metropolitan Museum of Art, A. J. Davis Collection, vol. 1.

———. *Rural Residences . . . Consisting of Designs . . . with Brief Explanations, Estimates, and a Specification of Materials . . . Published . . . with a View to the Improvement of American Country Architecture.* 1838. Reprint. New York: Da Capo Press, 1980.

———, and A. J. Downing. "Belmead, Va." *The Horticulturist* 4 (April 1850):479–81 and frontispiece facing p. 441.

Gordon, Armistead Churchill, Jr. "Cocke, Philip St. George." *Dictionary of American Biography.*

Lane. *Virginia.* Chap. 6.

Loth, Calder, and Julius Trousdale Sadler. *The Only Proper Style: Gothic Architecture in America.* Boston: New York Graphic Society, 1975. Pp. 71–74.

Loudon, John Claudius. *An Encyclopaedia of Cottage, Farm, and Villa Architecture and Furniture.* London: Longman, Rees, Orme, Brown, Green, & Longman, 1833. Bk. 3, Des. 21.

Obituary of Philip St. George Cocke. *Richmond Whig,* 28 December 1861.

Snadon, Patrick Alexander. "A. J. Davis and the Gothic Revival Castle in America, 1832–1865." 2 vols. Ph.D. diss., Cornell University, 1988.

Virginia, Commonwealth of. Virginia Landmarks Register, File No. 72–49 (Belmead).

# 39.
# VIRGINIA MILITARY INSTITUTE BARRACKS

*(Claytor Hall)*
*Proposed West Elevation*

Institute Hill, north of Main St., Lexington
Presentation drawing, 1870
Signed: *Alexander J. Davis. Archt.*
Pencil, pen and India ink with colored inks and watercolor on paper; 8 ⅞ by 13 ½ inches
Collection of the Virginia Military Institute Archives, Lexington; Preston Library, A. J. Davis Collection, Number 18

FIGURE  1.  *Site photo,* **VMI Barracks,** *south front.*

Davis's work at Belmead ( SURVEY NO. 38 ) had many sequels (see SURVEY NO. 40 ), but the Virginia Military Institute heads the list. The school crystallized in the 1830s, with Francis H. Smith as its first superintendent. Philip St. George Cocke, a member of the Board of Visitors and a West Point graduate, wished to make the school into the great southern polytechnic institute and to house it in a fine, unified architectural complex. His influence brought the commission to Davis, who had a specialty in designs for academic institutions.

For a hilltop site of outstanding potential, Davis proffered the castellated Gothic, which had the compelling advantages of economy and expressive fitness. (VMI is one of the earliest examples, if not the first, in the United States of a campus designed in the Gothic by a professional architect.) In the years 1848 to 1861, Davis created six buildings for the school, all of brick stuccoed to simulate stone: the Barracks, the Gilham House, and the Superintendent's Quarters, which survive, and the Williamson house, the Mess Hall, and a porter's lodge, which do not.[1] After Union troops burned the school, the buildings rose again (1866–69) in their original form while Davis—now in his professional decline—looked on hopefully from Manhattan. The Davis buildings reached their present state via a complicated series of events that conspicuously features the sensitive intervention of Bertram Grosvenor Goodhue in 1914 to 1916.

For the Barracks, Smith specified a quadrangle with tiers of piazzas around the court to connect the rooms. Davis devised probably the first large-scale quadrangle ever built for an American college.[2] Thus, although the genealogy of the Barracks includes previous Davis plans for schools in the "big-house" genre, this building departed from such predecessors. By the War, the Institute had built the original main or south front ( FIGURE 1 ) and, on the west front (today's main or parade front), the portion between the two right-hand towers in the present drawing. To the left Davis planned a dramatic central chapel or assembly hall and then the remainder of the wing, meant as a museum, under the name Claytor Hall. In the rebuilding, he strove to see the previously unexecuted parts of his plan realized, and he made the present drawing in that futile attempt. The Barracks only became a complete quadrangle, through the agency of various architects, in 1923. Davis's Barracks design had no imitators in its own time, for Americans preferred the native tradition of the open campus until the close of the century.

Davis had a brilliant gift for composing irregular groupings, but his Classical background led him to find such informality inappropriate for a public building.[3] He not only gave symmetrical fronts to the Barracks but he also reined in asymmetry in respect to the other VMI buildings. It remained for his rivals, such as James Renwick and Henry Austin, to develop the secular public building with an irregular front.[4] The "aesthetic of the temple" led Davis to counteract the stratified effect of multiple stories with his renowned vertical groupings of windows.[5] Here, typically, he pulled four stories together as if a giant Classical order governed the facade.

VMI retains twenty-seven of Davis's drawings. Despite soiling, the one reproduced here has the brightness and definition of a faceted gemstone. Its freshness owes much to Davis's artful use of the white paper to represent the areas of wall and cloud lit by the sun. Davis largely drew the facade in brown and blue inks. This vibrant play of warm and cool pervades the drawing, carrying through the billowing clouds and the myriad touches of color that evoke a wall of figured stone. Despite its miniature size, the elevation conveys the monumentality of a commanding building. Appropriately, the cadets were sometimes assigned to copy Davis's drawings in their drawing classes (see Chapter 4, part 2).                                    CEB

NOTES
1.  For the documentation of VMI, I have used Mackie, "Designs," and Lyle and Simpson, *Architecture*, pp. 209–76; also Davis, Journal, 105, 117–18, 140, 200–01, 235, and Davis, *Daybook* 1, here and there.

2.  On Davis, the quadrangle, and the open campus, see Turner, *Campus*, 124–25.

3.  I owe this important line of thought to Mackie, who made a somewhat different version of it the thesis of his "Designs." For more on the subject, see Brownell, "Italianate."

4.  On the "aesthetic of the temple," see Chapter 2.

5.  What appear to be student exercises after various sources survive in the Museum of the History and Traditions of the Virginia Military Institute and in the collection of Pamela Scott, Washington, D.C.

REFERENCES
*Architectural Drawing in Lexington, 1779–1926.* Exh. cat. Lexington, Virginia: Washington and Lee University, 1978.

Brownell, Charles E. "The Italianate Villa and the Search for an American Style, 1840–1860." In *The Italian Presence in American Art, 1760–1860.* Edited by Irma B. Jaffe. New York: Fordham University Press, 1989.

Davies, Jane B. "Davis, Alexander Jackson." In *Macmillan Encyclopedia of Architects.* Ed. Adolf K. Placzek. 4 vols. New York: Free Press, 1982.

Davis, Alexander J. Daybook. Vol. 1, October 1827–September 1853. Rare Books and Manuscripts Division, New York Public Library.

———. Journal. Metropolitan Museum of Art, A. J. Davis Collection, vol. 1.

Dooley, Edwin L., Jr. "Gilt Buttons and the Collegiate Way: Francis H. Smith as Antebellum Schoolmaster." *Virginia Cavalcade* 36 (Summer 1986):30–39.

Lane, Mills. Chapter 6. *Architecture of the Old South: Virginia.* With editorial assistance by Calder Loth. Savannah: Beehive Press, 1987.

Loth, Calder, and Julius Trousdale Sadler. *The Only Proper Style: Gothic Architecture in America.* Boston: New York Graphic Society, 1975. Pp. 71–74.

Lyle, Royster, Jr., and M. W. Paxton, Jr. "Architecture of the VMI Barracks." *Virginia Cavalcade* 23 (Winter 1974):14–29.

———, and Pamela Hemenway Simpson. *The Architecture of Historic Lexington.* Charlottesville: University Press of Virginia for the Historic Lexington Foundation, 1977.

Mackie, Osborne Phinizy. "The Designs by Alexander Jackson Davis for the Virginia Military Institute: Their Place in the American Gothic Revival." Master of Architectural History thesis, University of Virginia, 1982.

Snadon, Patrick Alexander. "A. J. Davis and the Gothic Revival Castle in America, 1832–1865." 2 vols. Ph. D. diss., Cornell University, 1988.

Turner, Paul Venable. *Campus: An American Planning Tradition.* The Architectural History Foundation/M.I.T. Press Series, VII. New York, 1984.

Virginia, Commonwealth of. Virginia Landmarks Register, File No. 117–17 (Virginia Military Institute Historic District).

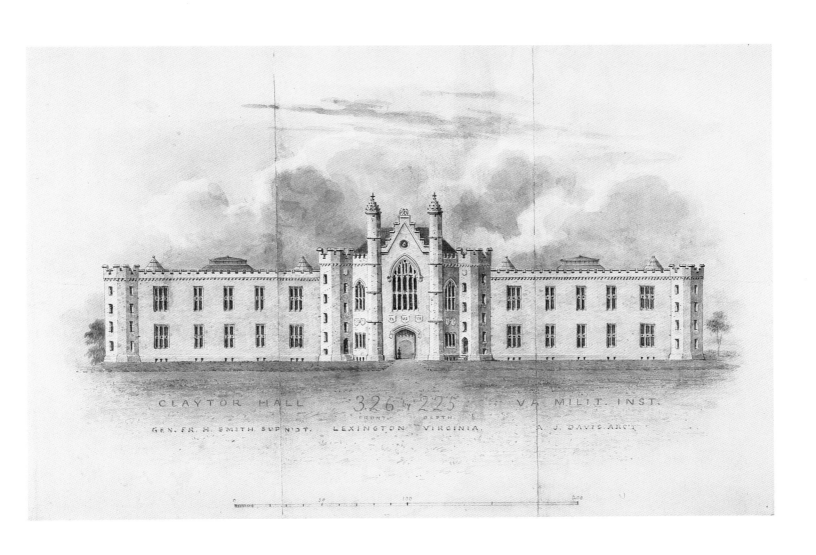

CLAYTOR HALL     326 by 225     VA. MILIT. INST.

FRONT    DEPTH

GEN. FR. H. SMITH SUP'N'DT.     LEXINGTON VIRGINIA.     A. J. DAVIS ARC'T.

Attributed to ALEXANDER JACKSON DAVIS,
1803–1892

# 40.
# ELK HILL

*(also called Red Lodge)*
*Plantation Mansion*
*of William S. Archer*
*South Front Elevation*

Genito Rd. and Rte. 609, Amelia County (demolished)
Office record, probably 1850 or 1851
Pricking, pencil, pen and India ink with watercolor on paper;
13 ⅞ by 17 inches
Collection of the New-York Historical Society,
A. J. Davis Collection, Drawing Number 271a

FIGURE 1. **Elk Hill,** *also known as, "Red Lodge," as illustrated in* **Old Homes and Buildings of Amelia County, Virginia,** *by Mary Armstrong Jefferson, 1964. (Photograph courtesy of the Virginia Historical Society.)*

Clearly delighted with Davis's work for him on Belmead (SURVEY NO. 38), Philip St. George Cocke promoted commissions for him at every turn.[1] Cocke may well stand behind every one of Davis's Virginia projects. Through him, Davis received commissions in a spectrum of expression that runs through the Doric Powhatan County Courthouse (1848–49; FIGURE 2.40), one of his best surviving Greek works, despite its modesty; the castellated Virginia Military Institute (Lexington, 1848–61; SURVEY NO. 39), a milestone not only in American academic architecture but also in the Gothic Revival; the Italianate Hawkwood (Green Springs, 1851–54; SURVEY NO. 41), easily one of the choicest embodiments of the Tuscan villa manner in the United States; and Elk Hill, which resists categorization. Smaller-scale works aside, Cocke and his contacts elicited from Davis an even more varied array of unexecuted projects, such as three proposals for the Richmond Washington Monument competition of 1849–50 (see SURVEY NOS. 42–43); institutional projects, including a Richmond "agricultural hall" (1856) that Cocke planned with Davis in New York; all sorts of domestic designs; and the promising but ill-timed schemes for a hotel, a bath, and a church at White Sulphur Springs (then in Virginia) in 1859–60.[2]

In the case of Elk Hill, Senator William S. Archer (1789–1855), who served in the Virginia and national legislatures for some thirty-five years, wished a mansion to house himself and a domestic entourage of somewhat uncertain makeup, on a plantation that has gone by various names.[3] This major undertaking entailed endless correspondence, a puzzling sequence of designs, visits from Archer to New York, and even a site visit. In the course of a Davis trip south in 1850, the architect spent 21–24 November at Archer's in viewing the grounds and planning with the family. Two basic Davis records, his Journal and his Daybook, indicate that construction began in 1851 and neared completion in 1852.[4] The family got all too little pleasure from their house; Archer died in 1855 and, as of 1871, a Virginia correspondent wrote Davis that the mansion had burned and "the old ladies are living in a cabin as badly ruined as their house."[5] The walls survived into the twentieth century.[6]

Twentieth-century taste has responded less favorably to adventuresome design in the years 1760–1860 than in periods before and after, at least when such design mixes non-Classical styles. But the stature of a George Dance the younger, a Latrobe, or a Davis requires that we look seriously at their work of this sort. In a series of drawings for Archer's villa (six of them in the New-York Historical Society), Davis proposed variants on the novel house with an axially symmetrical, single-towered facade.[7] His *South Front* boldly combines such diverse elements as Romanesque corbels; a parapet pierced, Hardwick-Hall-like, with Archer's name; and maize columns à la Latrobe. This offering makes the most sense as an atypical, eclectic experiment in devising an American style. It will take future research to establish the exact final form of Elk Hill, particularly of the top of the tower. But much of the conception shown here did reach execution, including a maize order.[8]

A Davis inscription in the upper right ("Copy to keep") identifies this elevation as merely an office record. Nonetheless, the page not only displays the fresh color and crispness that distinguish Davis's drawing; it also displays evocative touches, particularly the blooming plants that show through the conservatory windows. Even a handsome Davis drawing may not make such a facade easy on the eyes. But the elevation does summon up tantalizing impressions of a lost enclave of luxury and exoticism.
CEB

NOTES

1.  My knowledge of Davis's Virginia work owes a great deal to the extensive unpublished findings of my former student Stephen J. Schottler.

2.  Lane, *Virginia*, chap. 6, handsomely demonstrated what a wealth of Virginia projects by Davis survives. I have also used Davis's *Daybook* 1, and his Journal, pp. 182 (agricultural hall; White Sulphur projects), 200, 202, 203 (White Sulphur).

3.  On Archer and his plantation, see, in addition to Stanard, "Archer," Hadfield and McConnaughey, *Historical Notes*, esp. pp. 181, 282–83, 370, 377. *Lodge* and *Red Lodge* occur as variant names for the plantation.

4.  *Daybook*, (mainly September 1850–September 1851); Journal, p. 120.

5.  Dabney to Davis, 10 May 1871.

6.  For a photograph, see Jefferson, *Old Homes*, p. 69.

7.  Davis had just introduced the type; see Davies, "Blandwood."

8.  For the documentation of the maize and wheat order, see Davis, *Daybook* 1, 28 July, 2 August, and 27 October 1852.

REFERENCES

Dabney, William Pope, to Alexander J. Davis, 10 May 1871. Metropolitan Museum of Art, A. J. Davis Collection, vol. 18, leaf 148–148v.

Davies, Jane B. "Blandwood and the Italian Villa Style in America." *Nineteenth Century* 1 (September 1975):11–14.

Davis, Alexander J. Daybook. Vol. 1, October 1827–September 1853. Rare Books and Manuscripts Division, New York Public Library.

———. Journal. Metropolitan Museum of Art, A. J. Davis Collection, vol. 1.

Hadfield, Kathleen Halverson, and W. Cary McConnaughey, eds. *Historical Notes on Amelia County, Virginia.* Amelia: Amelia County Historical Committee, 1982.

Jefferson, Mary Armstrong. *Old Homes and Buildings in Amelia County, Virginia.* Vol. 1. Amelia, 1964.

Lancaster, Clay. "Oriental Forms in American Architecture, 1800–1870." *Art Bulletin* 29 (September 1947):183–93.

Lane. *Virginia.* Chap. 6.

Stanard, Mary Newton. "Archer, William Segar." *Dictionary of American Biography.*

ELK HILL
SOUTH FRONT.
PLANTATION MANSION OF WM. S. ARCHER, AMELIA, VA.
1850.

# 41.
# HAWKWOOD

*Plantation Mansion
of Richard O. Morris
Elevation and Plan of
Lower Ground Floor*

U.S. Rte. 15, near Zion Crossroads (Louisa County)
Presentation drawing, 1851
Signed and dated: *Davis. Arc. 1851*
Pencil, pen and India ink, with watercolor on paper;
11 ¾ by 8 ½ inches
Collection of the New-York Historical Society,
A. J. Davis Collection, Drawing Number 94

FIGURE 1. *Vintage site photo, Morris Mansion,*
**Hawkwood,** *circa 1950s. (Photograph courtesy of
the Virginia State Library.)*

Hawkwood, the "Plantation Mansion" of Richard Overton Morris (1825–1897), has undergone extraordinary vicissitudes. Morris, a wealthy planter, belonged to a well-established Louisa County family and to the circle of Philip St. George Cocke.[1] Davis's Italianate villa for Morris supplanted a vernacular frame house of the eighteenth century, which Morris had remodeled into a Gothic cottage in 1848. Morris built his Italianate villa in 1852–54, employing such craftsmen as the distinguished Richmond stonecutter John W. Davies and George Gill of New Haven, Connecticut, a specialist in exterior stucco.[2] The design pleased Davis so much that he imitated it as Arcade Cottage (circa 1859; demolished) when he compiled an anthology of his domestic ideas at Llewellyn Park in New Jersey, the premier romantically landscaped suburb in the United States.[3] During the Civil War and thereafter, Morris's means suffered disastrously, but he managed to remain at Hawkwood until his death. The house became forgotten, then rediscovered in time to figure at the center of a successful and nationally important preservation battle in 1970, in the face of an insensitive proposal to locate a penal facility in the Green Springs area. In 1982, a fire gutted the house, but painstaking restoration work is, by degrees, assuring its future.[4]

This house, regarded by Davis scholar Jane B. Davies as "probably the finest of Davis's surviving Tuscan villas," exhibits its designer and its style in an admirable light.[5] The simplicity of the building illustrates why it seemed to many that an "American style" could grow out of the Italianate villa manner. The plan, an improved version of a Davis layout that A. J. Downing had published in his *Architecture of Country Houses,* shows Davis as one of Jefferson's worthiest successors in opening the American house from room to room and from indoors to outdoors.[6] Double doors open the hall, parlor, dining room, and library to each other in an internal landscape of subtly different polygons. One of the finest touches represents Davis's (presumably independent) discovery of that engaging Jefferson invention, the bay window encased within a porch. The exterior massing builds to its finale on the south front ( FIGURE 1 ), a crisp combination of a polygonal pavilion and a square tower that is a Davis signature and one of the most beautiful devices in his architecture. Rising on its mount, this delightful Picturesque conception commands idyllic views over rolling ground as far as the violet ridges of the Southwest Mountains.

In the present drawing, Davis tentatively revised his design after execution. He thus shifted the tower from the left of the dining room to the right, added dormers to the roof, and brushed in an imaginary river background as well. The plan (with much erasure on the right) betrays his uncertainty. The color scheme suggests a date late in Davis's life, long after commissions for mansions had evaporated. Although he had been a vigorous innovator in the 1830s, the sources of his architecture were growing dated by the 1850s, and after the Civil War he faced an increasingly alien archi-

tectural world. He kept his office until 1878, but his professional activity revolved around copying and revising old designs (with, at times, bewildering consequences for the scholar), imagining projects that no one wanted, and drafting architectural jeremiads for which he did not have an aptitude. In such buildings as Hawkwood, however, the sheer delight that he infused into his designs has outlasted his embittered old age by a century.                    CEB

NOTES
1.   For Morris, I have relied on Allen, "Hawkwood."

2.   On the excellent construction documentation, see Allen, "Hawkwood," chap. 6 and appendix B. On the commission I have also used Davis, *Journal*, pp. 128, 238, 250, and Davis, Daybook I, 10 and 14 June 1851; 13 April 1853.

3.   See Davies, "Llewellyn Park."

4.   I thank Hawkwood's owner, Rae H. Ely, for generously sharing her house and her information with me.

5.   Davies, "Llewellyn Park," p. 147.

6.   Downing, *Architecture*, Design 30. Allen made this connection in "Hawkwood," p. 45.

REFERENCES
Allen, William C. "Hawkwood: A Country House in the Tuscan Villa Style." Master of Architectural History thesis, University of Virginia, 1974.

Brownell, Charles E. "The Italianate Villa and the Search for an American Style, 1840–1860." In *The Italian Presence in American Art, 1760–1860.* Edited by Irma B. Jaffe. New York: Fordham University Press, 1989.

Davies, Jane B. "Davis, Alexander Jackson." In *Macmillan Encyclopedia.*

——. "Davis and Downing: Collaborators in the Picturesque." In *Prophet with Honor: The Career of Andrew Jackson Downing, 1815–1852.* Edited by George B. Tatum and Elisabeth Blair MacDougall. Dumbarton Oaks Colloquium on the History of Landscape Architecture XI. Washington, D.C., 1989.

——. "Llewellyn Park in West Orange, New Jersey." *The Magazine Antiques* 107 (January 1975):142–58.

Davis, Alexander J. Daybook. Vol. 1, October 1827–September 1853. Rare Books and Manuscripts Division, New York Public Library.

——. Journal. Metropolitan Museum of Art, A.J. Davis Collection, vol. 1.

Downing, A. J. *The Architecture of Country Houses; Including . . . Cottages, Farm Houses, and Villas, . . . Interiors, Furniture, and . . . Warming and Ventilating.* 1850. Reprint. New York: Da Capo Press, 1968.

Lane. *Virginia.* Chapter 6.

Wilson, Richard Guy. "Idealism and the Origin of the First American Suburb: Llewellyn Park, New Jersey." *American Art Journal* 11 (October 1979): 79–90.

PLANTATION MANSION OF RICHARD O MORRIS. VA. 1851.

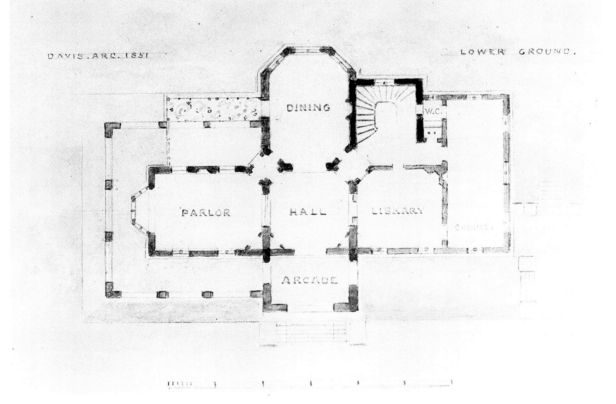

DAVIS, ARC. 1851

LOWER GROUND.

DINING

W.C.

PARLOR

HALL

LIBRARY

ARCADE

# 42.
## PROPOSED WASHINGTON MONUMENT

*Elevation*

Richmond (unbuilt)

Presentation drawing, 1850

Signed and dated: *John Notman Architect/Philad[a] Jan[y] 4th 1850*; inscribed: *Elevation [,] Washington Monument. Richmond. Vacinia.*

Pencil, pen and India ink, with watercolor on paper; 20 ¾ by 13 ¾ inches

Collection of The Athenaeum of Philadelphia Archives, on deposit from the American Institute of Architects, Philadelphia Chapter

FIGURE 1. **Washington Monument competition entry** *by Edward B. White (1806–1882). (Photograph courtesy of the Virginia State Library.)*

John Notman, a Philadelphian born and trained in Scotland, was one of the leading innovators in the Picturesque movement, the importation of Anglo-Italianate influences, and the Gothic Revival. His ecclesiological churches held no appeal for Virginia's evangelical Protestants, and Virginia deserves only a footnote in the story of his Italianate designs. But two major works, Hollywood Cemetery (1848) and his replacement of Godefroy's layout in Capitol Square (1850–circa 1860; see SURVEY NO. 22) in Richmond, along with Spring Hill Cemetery (1855) in Lynchburg, testify to his artistry at Picturesque landscaping.

In 1849, the campaign to create a Virginia Washington Monument began to bear fruit (see SURVEY NO. 43).[1] The announcement of a competition reached the newspapers by mid October.[2] The architectural monument had dominated in the United States since the second decade of the century, and the commissioners' wording indicates that they had this kind of memorial in mind. The $500 premium and the commission for a $100,000 monument attracted an array of professional architects including Alexander J. Davis; Henry Exall; possibly John P. Gaynor; Napoleon Le Brun (see next entry); Detlef Lienau; John McArthur, Jr.; Robert Mills (FIGURE 2.36); Calvin N. Otis; James Renwick, Jr.; and Edward B. White (FIGURE 1); as well as Notman.[3] The competition also lured ideas from other quarters and the non-professionals made some startling offerings (FIGURE 2.37). The commissioners extended the deadline to 8 January 1850.

This seems to have been Virginia's second formal architectural competition, the first being the ill-documented Washington Monument competition of 1818. In 1850, by a turnabout, sculpture vanquished architecture (despite Mills's best attempts in the aftermath). Thomas Crawford (1813–1857) won with his equestrian proposal (1850–69; completed by Randolph Rogers; FIGURE 2.38). Crawford's was the second in the wave of equestrian monument commissions that washed over the nation at mid century, marking a turning-point in the maturation of American sculpture. Such commissions represent the ascendancy of the sculptural monument over the architectural one. Moreover, the pedestals of some of these schemes, including Crawford's, also represent the ascendancy of a Picturesque taste for layering over Neoclassical monumentality.

Well before the competition, Notman had acknowledged the possibility of building Virginia's Washington Monument at Hollywood Cemetery, on the site later used for the Monroe tomb (SURVEY NO. 48).[4] In the competition Notman, like several of his rivals, proposed a column in an Americanized order. Allegorical figures flank the basement story, which probably would have opened into a central staircase leading to a viewing platform atop the capital. Military trophies and escutcheons—of the original states?—rise over the basement, beneath a relief of Washington, apparently accepting the surrender of Cornwallis at Yorktown. The shaft has a capital adorned with American eagles. Above, on a pedestal containing the staircase door or a niche, an allegorical female figure rises to a height of more than 200 feet. She seems to extend the olive branch of peace (changed, it seems, from a sword) with her right hand, while she extinguishes the torch of war with her left. In breaking the lower portion into tiers and in elaborating the silhouette, the design carries the column away from Neoclassicism and into Victorian taste. (White's simple pedestal represents the older fashion.) Though Notman lost in the competition, the construction of the monument led to his appointment to relandscape Capitol Square.

Only this drawing of Notman's conception has come to light.[5] In 1990, conservation revealed the fragmentary plan at the bottom of the sheet. For unclear reasons, Notman had glued the label, a separate piece of paper, over it. The elevation, somber in its lack of color and muddy in its details, is an unprepossessing entry for a competition. But the date on it—"Jany 4th 1850"—just four days before the extended deadline, explains a good deal, including Notman's failure to complete the G's and his misspelling of *Virginia* in the inscription.[6]

CEB

NOTES

1. For an outline of the story, see Chapter 2.

2. *Richmond Enquirer*, 19 October 1849 (advertisement and editorial).

3. The *Richmond Enquirer* for 5 and 8 February 1850 gives the total number of entries as sixty-four rather than the forty-one or seventy sometimes given as the figure. See also Brumbaugh, "Evolution," n. 24, with a list of the competitors known as of 1962. For surviving entries in addition to those illustrated here, see O'Neal, *Architectural Drawing*, 40–53 (selections from the roughly twenty-five sheets of drawings in the Virginia State Library), and Lane, *Virginia*, pp. 240–41. Marsha Oates Ellis helped me by making a rough catalogue of the State Library drawings.

4. Notman, "Report," p. 21.

5. See Chapter 2.

6. Goode, *Addendum*, p. 94, lists a supposed Notman drawing for the Richmond Washington Monument in the Virginia State Library, but this drawing has not been found.

7. "Jan" has formerly been misread as "Aug."

REFERENCES

Brumbaugh, Thomas B. "The Evolution of Crawford's 'Washington.' " *Virginia Magazine of History and Biography* 70 (January 1962):3–29.

Gale, Robert L. *Thomas Crawford, American Sculptor.* Pittsburgh: University of Pittsburgh Press, 1964. Esp. chaps. 5–7.

Goode, James M., comp. *Addendum to "American Architectural Drawings."* Washington, D.C.: no pagination, 1977.

Greiff, Constance M. *John Notman, Architect, 1810–1865.* Exhibition catalogue. Philadelphia: Athenaeum of Philadelphia, 1979. Esp. pp. 28–29; nos. 34, 44, and 45.

Lane. *Virginia.* Pp. 212, 240–41.

Mordecai, Samuel. *Virginia, Especially Richmond, in By-Gone Days; with a Glance at the Present: Being Reminiscences and Last Words of an Old Citizen.* 2nd ed., rev. and enl. Richmond: West and Johnston, 1860. Pp. 264–65 and chap. 36.

Nye, W. A. R. *Historical Account of the Washington Monument in the Capitol Square, Richmond, Virginia.* Richmond: no pagination, 1869.

Notman, John. "Report Accompanying Plan of Holly-wood Cemetery, Richmond, Va." In *Historical Sketch of Hollywood Cemetery, from the 3d of June, 1847, to 1st Nov., 1875.* Richmond: Baughman Brothers, Printers, 1875.

O'Neal. *Architectural Drawing.* Pp. 40–59.

*Richmond Enquirer*, 19 October 1849; 5, 8, 15 February 1850.

Scott, Pamela. "Robert Mills and American Monuments." In *Robert Mills, Architect.* Edited by John M. Bryan. Washington, D.C.: The American Institute of Architects Press, 1989.

Semmes, John E. *John H. B. Latrobe and His Times, 1803–1891.* Baltimore: Norman, Remington Company, 1917. Pp. 445–47.

Tatman and Moss. Under "Notman, John."

ELEVATION

WASHINGTON MONUMENT.

RICHMOND . VAGINIA .

NAPOLEON EUGENE HENRY CHARLES LE BRUN,
1821–1901

# 43.
## PROPOSED
## WASHINGTON
## MONUMENT

*Perspective*

Richmond (unbuilt)
Presentation drawing, 1850
Signed and dated: *NLeBrun Archt./Philadelphia 1850*
Pricking (?), scoring (?), pencil, pen and India ink with
watercolor and touches of gouache on paper;
26 ⅛ by 20 ⅝ inches
Collection of Herbert Mitchell, New York

Through Napoleon Le Brun, a chain of transmission stretches from B. Henry Latrobe ( SURVEY NOS. 15–21 ) into the twentieth century. The Philadelphia-born son of French émigrés, Le Brun studied with Thomas U. Walter ( SURVEY NOS. 35, 36 ), the pupil of William Strickland, whom Latrobe had trained at the beginning of the nineteenth century. At the close of the century, having moved to New York City, Le Brun and his sons designed a string of important skyscrapers. In between, Le Brun had probed the Renaissance and Baroque at two major public buildings in Philadelphia, the Roman Catholic Cathedral of Saints Peter and Paul (1846–51, 1860–64; partly by John Notman and John T. Mahony) and the Academy of Music (1855–56; with Gustav Runge).

The perspective illustrated here, the sole Le Brun survivor from the competition, has surfaced only recently. The architect's cover letter of 11 January 1850 provides valuable information. Le Brun submitted two projects, both crowned with figures of Washington: a 160-foot-tall, thirteen-column circular memorial, estimated at $90,000; and the present 180-foot tower, estimated at $95,000. In preference to the Gothic and the Egyptian, Le Brun had selected the "Roman style . . . of the Restoration" (that is, he had chosen the Renaissance tradition), partly because it embraced the architecture of Washington's own time. Rushed like Notman to complete his entry before the deadline, he apologized because pressure had compelled him to submit some drawings of poor quality, but this apology does not apply to his fine perspective.

Seeking to make the tower in a style appropriate to Washington's day, Le Brun—unwittingly echoing Jefferson's observatory ( SURVEY NO. 7 )—treated the monument as a spire in the tradition of London architect James Gibbs (compare St. Martin's Church, FIGURE 2.6 ). (One notes the irony that eighteenth-century Virginia churches normally did not have steeples.) This precocious experiment in Colonial Revivalism very likely reflects both Strickland's 1828 rebuilding of the Independence Hall steeple and Arthur Gilman's 1844 essay "Architecture in the United States" in the *North American Review*. In attacking the Greek taste, Gilman renewed an older argument about the incompatibility between the temple and the steeple. Gilman praised the Wren-Gibbs tradition in American architecture before evaluating a series of American Gibbsian spires by the Gibbsian criterion of graceful diminution from one stage to the next. Le Brun worked uncertainly toward those elegant eighteenth-century transitions by which the stages, as Gibbs had put it, "gradually diminish, and pass from one Form to another without confusion."[1]

Le Brun subscribed to the rising preference for breaking large bodies into tiers. He made his proposal a tower of three Greek orders with additional attic or pedestal zones. Atop the first story (identifiable as Doric by wreaths in the frieze, after the Thrasyllus Monument in Athens), personifications allude to the achievements of Washington, whom Le Brun represented as a bust. Le Brun made the candelabra, fasces,

and wreaths bronze color, and perhaps he meant to cast them in bronze (rather than in a cheaper metal with a "bronzed" surface). Ornaments of solid cast bronze would have been a novelty, for this medium was just about to take its place in American public monuments, chiefly as equestrian sculpture.

The second story (presumably reached by narrow stairs) appears to provide a raised platform for taking the view. Le Brun originally penciled in the third full story as an open circular temple, which he meant to have thirteen shafts. The columns at the back of this ring remain unerased and just visible. But perhaps recognizing the incongruity of so airy an element beneath the heavy plinth of the next stage, he decided on a solid cylinder for the third floor, though his modeling of the areas suffers from confusion. The figure of Washington is probably shown resigning his military commission atop this secular steeple, but one has trouble seeing what he holds in his right hand. This problem highlights a basic flaw with the scheme which, like many other proposals for Washington monuments, reduces a hero to a poorly visible finial. Recognizing this problem, Le Brun offered the alternative of displaying the statue within the arched story. Whatever can be criticized in his design, his freestanding Gibbsian tower remains a powerful conception, and a remarkably fresh one for its period.

The acid in bad paper has destroyed most of the color in this ambitious rendering. Nonetheless one can still enjoy the skillful handling of such details as the grove, the candelabra, the carved moldings, and the seal of Virginia on the first-story keystones.    CEB

NOTES
1.   Gibbs, *Book of Architecture*, viii. Compare Gilman, "Architecture," pp. 461–63.

REFERENCES
Brumbaugh, Thomas B. "The Evolution of Crawford's 'Washington.'" *Virginia Magazine of History and Biography* 70 (January 1962):3–29.

Gale, Robert L. *Thomas Crawford, American Sculptor*. Pittsburgh: University of Pittsburgh Press, 1964. Esp. chaps. 5–7.

Gibbs, James. *A Book of Architecture, Containing Designs of Buildings and Ornaments*. 1728. Reprint. New York: Benjamin Blom, 1968. Esp. pls. 1, 3, 7–8, 14–15, 29–30.

Gilman, Arthur Delavan. "Architecture in the United States." *North American Review* 58 (April 1844):436–80.

Lane. *Virginia*. Pp. 212, 240–41.

Le Brun, Napoleon. Letters to William F. Ritchie, 9 November 1849 and 5 January 1850; to Governor John B. Floyd, 7 January 1850; to the Commissioners of the Virginia Washington Monument, 11 January 1850. Virginia State Library, Capitol Square, Washington Monument Funds, Box 16.

Mordecai, Samuel. *Virginia, Especially Richmond, in By-Gone Days; with a Glance at the Present: Being Reminiscences and Last Words of an Old Citizen*. 2nd ed., rev. and enl. Richmond: West and Johnston, 1860. Pp. 264–65 and chap. 36.

Nye, W. A. R. *Historical Account of the Washington Monument in the Capitol Square, Richmond, Virginia*. Richmond: no pagination, 1869.

O'Neal. *Architectural Drawing*. Pp. 40–59.

*Richmond Enquirer*, 19 October 1849; 5, 8, 15 February 1850.

Scott, Pamela. "Robert Mills and American Monuments." In *Robert Mills, Architect*, ed. John M. Bryan. Washington, D. C.: The American Institute of Architects Press, 1989.

Semmes, John E. *John H. B. Latrobe and His Times, 1803– 1891*. Baltimore: Norman, Remington Company, 1917. Pp. 445–47.

Tatman and Moss. Under "Le Brun, Napoleon."

# 44.

# SWEET BRIAR HOUSE

*Proposed Front Elevation*

Sweet Briar College, Amherst County
Presentation drawing, circa 1851
Pencil, pen and India ink, with watercolor and scraping on paper; 7 by 10 ⅝ inches
Collection of Sweet Briar College, Amherst, Virginia

FIGURE 1. *Site photo,* **Sweet Briar House.**

The Vermont schoolteacher Elijah Fletcher (1789–1858) prospered in Virginia. After marrying well, he became a prominent public figure in Lynchburg and was publisher of the Lynchburg *Virginian*. In 1851–52, agreeing to "a project of my Daughters," Indiana and Elizabeth, he remodeled the family's Neoclassical brick house at Sweet Briar plantation, roughly twelve miles north of the city.[1] The Fletchers thereby gave Lynchburg its first Italianate villa. Half a century later one of these daughters, Indiana Fletcher Williams (1828–1900), left most of her estate to found the school for young women that shortly acquired the name "Sweet Briar College."

In the anonymous elevation of circa 1851, one readily distinguishes the old house—the central, hip-roofed block—from the new towers and one-story porch. The two-tier central loggia replaced a two-tier gabled portico, and thus the regional feature of a double porch survived in the new design. Execution brought many changes, such as towers of identical size.

Taken together, the drawing and the house represent an immediate, provincial, but successful response to a reformative book, A. J. Downing's *Architecture of Country Houses* (New York, 1850). Downing illustrated an avant-garde house by Richard Upjohn, the Edward King villa (Newport, Rhode Island, 1845–47; FIGURE 2), and Downing praised this dwelling as "one of the most successful specimens of the Italian style in the United States."[2] The Fletchers took their facade pattern of two non-matching towers and two tiers of triple-arched loggias from Downing's plate, although they stretched the pattern out. The clearest giveaway occurs as a novel feature in which the left-hand Fletcher tower clearly imitates the left-hand King tower. Both towers break from the Classical principle of making windows on different stories line up with one another vertically, so that solids rest on solids and voids come over voids (compare Menokin, Monticello I, and Reid-White House, SURVEY NOS. 3, 8, 30). This new freedom from the Classical grid at the King villa appealed to Downing for its "beauty of . . . expression." Downing liked "the great variety of forms in the windows . . . which denotes different uses in various apartments." This expression of "varied enjoyments" contributed to the expressive character of the house as "a gentleman's residence."[3]

The Kings and the Fletchers accepted a facade treatment that had a remarkable history of satisfying householders. The pattern began as a provincial Roman villa with a central loggia between projecting blocks, and it received a fresh lease on life beginning in fifteenth-century Italy.[4] Whatever towerless variants may have reached America previously, the King villa quickly established the pattern with two asymmetrical towers, thanks to Downing. Important derivatives appeared throughout the country, and Upjohn designed quite a few of these himself, probably including Ben Dover (1854–56; altered beyond recognition), the Stanard House in Goochland.[5] The asymmetrically two-towered front had many progeny in Virginia,

down to Elijah E. Myers's Richmond City Hall (1887–93; SURVEY NO. 58), which reached completion just as the American Renaissance renewed the tower-and-loggia pattern from its Italian sources in such works as Carrère and Hastings's Hotel Jefferson (1895 and later, Richmond; SURVEY NO. 62).

This elevation is by a trained drafter who knew standard conventions, such as a light source at 45 degrees in the upper left, face lines (thin ink lines for edges facing the light) and shadow lines (thick ink lines for the opposite edges). But the drawing falls well below the best urban standards and very likely originated close to home. The extensive pencil markings include preliminary outlines for taller towers.   CEB

NOTES
1. Elijah Fletcher to Calvin Fletcher, 18 April 1851, in Fletcher, *Letters*, p. 228.

2. The villa appears as Design 27, pl. facing p. 317 and pp. 317–21. The quotations come from pp. 317–19.

3. The Sweet Briar elevation also owes to Downing's *Cottage Residences*, in particular to Design 6 (pp. 113–26) for the handling of the lower two stories of the righthand tower.

4. See Ackerman, *Villa*, esp. pp. 29, 61, 86, 90–91, 97. He here tempers his argument in his "Sources" of 1963.

5. Space prohibits surveying the fresh discoveries concerning the towered loggia-house in the United States. On the attempt to have Alexander J. Davis provide a design for the Stanards based on the King Villa, see Weeks, "Ben Dover." But Upjohn almost at once made plans for the family; see Upjohn, *Upjohn*, p. 215.

REFERENCES
Ackerman, James S. "Sources of the Renaissance Villa." In Vol. 2, *The Renaissance and Mannerism*, pp. 6–18 of *Studies in Western Art: Acts of the Twentieth International Congress of the History of Art*. Ed. Ida E. Rubin. 4 vols. Princeton: Princeton University Press, 1963.
———. *The Villa: Form and Ideology of Country Houses*. The A. W. Mellon Lectures in the Fine Arts, The National Gallery of Art, 1985; Bollingen Series XXXV, 34. Princeton: Princeton University Press, 1990.
Brownell, Charles E. "The Italianate Villa and the Search for an American Style, 1840–1860." In *The Italian Presence in American Art, 1760–1860*. Edited by Irma B. Jaffe. New York: Fordham University Press, 1989.
Chambers, S. Allen, Jr. *Lynchburg: An Architectural History*. Charlottesville: University Press of Virginia, 1981. Pp. 95, 100, 189–92.
Downing, A. J. *The Architecture of Country Houses; Including . . . Cottages, Farm Houses, and Villas, . . . Interiors, Furniture, and . . . Warming and Ventilating*. 1850. Reprint. New York: Da Capo Press, 1968.
———. *Cottage Residences: or, A Series of Designs for Rural Cottages and Cottage Villas, and Their . . . Grounds, Adapted to North America. . . .* 4th ed. [1852?]. Reprint. Watkins Glen, New York: American Life Foundation, 1967.
Fletcher, Elijah. *The Letters of Elijah Fletcher*. Edited by Martha von Briesen. Charlottesville: University Press of Virginia, 1965.
Upjohn, Everard M. *Richard Upjohn, Architect and Churchman*. 1939; reprint ed., New York: Da Capo, 1968.
Virginia, Commonwealth of. Virginia Landmarks Register, File No. 05–18 (Sweet Briar House).
Weeks, Elie. "Ben Dover." *Goochland County Historical Society Magazine* 4 (Autumn 1972):2–9.

FIGURE 2. *Perspective,* **King Villa,** *Newport, Rhode Island, published as "Villa in the Italian Style" in A. J. Downing's* **Architecture of Country Houses,** *1850.*

# 45.
# RICHMOND FEMALE INSTITUTE

*Perspective*

Tenth St. between Marshall and Clay, Richmond (demolished)
Presentation drawing, circa 1853
Signed: *T. A. Tefft, Archt.*
Pencil, pen and India ink with brown ink, watercolor, and
scraping on paper; 15 1/8 by 19 1/2 inches
Collection of the Brown University Archives, Providence,
Rhode Island; Tefft Collection, Inv. No.-Sch(Ri) 1.1(1)

FIGURE 1. *Vintage photo,* **Richmond Female Institute.** *(Photograph courtesy of The Valentine Museum, Richmond.)*

A former schoolteacher and a protégé of the educational reformer Henry Barnard, T. A. Tefft took a degree at Brown University and studied in the Providence office of Tallman and Bucklin. His early death abroad deprived his country of a designer with rare educational advantages, an appetite for the challenges of modern life, and a great gift for the round-arched Picturesque styles.

Tefft's reputation in school design (and probably, his ties as a highly placed Baptist) brought him the commission for the Richmond Female Institute building (1853–54; demolished 1924), one of his few chances to create a monumental public edifice. The founders of this Baptist-sponsored institution (incorporated in 1853) strove to create a women's "seminary" comparable with the University of Virginia.[1] The school survived to merge with the University of Richmond (1914). For Tefft the commission led to a far grander sequel, the design for Vassar College (1856), but at his death, that undertaking went to James Renwick. The main building at the College of William and Mary, in its third incarnation (by Henry Exall and Eben Faxon, 1859; burned 1862), imitated Tefft's Richmond building.[2] Tefft also made a design (1854; FIGURE 4.24) that seems to underlie the 1858 remodeling of the First Baptist Church in Alexandria.[3]

Tefft evolved at least one proposal in detail (FIGURE 2) before his final design.[4] For the executed conception he employed one of the fundamental school patterns (compare SURVEY NOS. 33, 52). That is, he used a long block, of domestic ancestry, with a corridor running its length and a central, cross-axial wing, providing a gabled frontispiece at the front and an assembly hall at the rear. He also included end pavilions that the Institute could (but did not) add later. Tefft developed his conception as an Italianate essay; unbeknownst to him, his loggia framed by towers has a pedigree back through fifteenth-century Italy to a Roman villa pattern (see Sweet Briar House, SURVEY NO. 44). Tefft made paired towers in a round-arch style nearly his signature. Here, one held a bell and the other "an observatory, commanding an extensive view of a most beautiful landscape, . . . suited also for astronomical observations."[5]

In 1853 Tefft called expression of purpose "the primal law of design."[6] Despite its domestic ties, this school "reads" as an institution. Thus it has too regular a massing, too many stories, and too uniform a fenestration to be mistaken for a house.

The Brown University Archives has fifty-four other sheets of drawings for the Institute, many of these on deposit from the Museum of Art, Rhode Island School of Design. In its catalogue, the Institute used a perspective related to the drawing shown here. In this one, the Picturesque, animated effect of the articulated bricks looks forward to the scintillating surfaces shown in late-nineteenth-century drawings. The Tefft drawings seen while preparing this text suggest that Tefft and his office excelled at line drawings and monochrome wash drawings.[7]                    CEB

NOTES

1. See Richmond Female Institute, *Catalogue,* esp. pp. 5, 7.

2. See Whiffen, *Public Buildings,* fig. 84.

3. On this church see *Tefft,* pp. 222–25 (cf. Katherine M. Long, "Style and Choice in . . . Church Architecture," pp. 79–94); and Morrill, *Who Built Alexandria?,* pp. 10, 19, 25–26. The Tefft Collection at Brown has two drawings, a perspective (Ch[AIV]1.1), and a sheet of geometrical drawings (-Ch[AIV]1.2).

4. Tefft Collection, Inv. No.-Sch (Ri) 1.1(2).

5. Richmond Female Institute, *Catalogue,* p. 9.

6. Quoted by David A. Brenneman, "Innovations in American Library Design," in *Tefft,* p. 75, n. 39.

7. The literature (for example, *Tefft,* p. 160) notes that one Charles P. Hartshorn executed some of Tefft's perspectives but does not offer a means of distinguishing his hand.

REFERENCES

Alley, Reuben E. *History of the University of Richmond, 1830–1971.* Charlottesville: Published for the University of Richmond by the University Press of Virginia, 1977. Pp. 94–95, 112–15, 119–22, 124, 138–42, 181–82.

Brownell, Charles E. "The Italianate Villa and the Search for an American Style, 1840–1860." In Irma B. Jaffe, ed. *The Italian Presence in American Art, 1760–1860.* New York: Fordham University Press, 1989.

Curran, Kathleen. "The German Rundbogenstil and Reflections on the American Round-Arched Style." *JSAH* 47 (December 1988):351–73.

Downing, A. J. *The Architecture of Country Houses.* 1850. Reprint. New York: Da Capo Press, 1968.

Jordy, William H.; Christopher P. Monkhouse; and contributors. *Buildings on Paper: Rhode Island Architectural Drawings, 1825–1945.* Exhibition catalogue. Providence: Bell Gallery, List Art Center, Brown University, et al., 1982. Pp. xi–xii, 12, 14–15, 16, 38–40, 150–53, 157–73, 234–35.

Morrill, Penny. *Who Built Alexandria?: Architects in Alexandria, 1750–1900.* Exh. cat. Alexandria: Carlyle House Historic Park, 1979.

O'Neal. *Architectural Drawing.* Pp. 74–75.

Richmond Female Institute. *Catalogue of the Richmond Female Institute, Richmond, Virginia.* Richmond: H. K. Ellyson's Steam Presses, 1855.

"Richmond Female Institute." *American Baptist Memorial* (September 1854):205–6.

"Richmond Female Institute." *The Southern Planter,* 20 (November 1860):679–80.

Scott, Mary Wingfield. *Old Richmond Neighborhoods.* 1950; Reprint. Richmond: Valentine Museum, 1984. Pp. 91, 114–15, 117.

*Thomas Alexander Tefft: American Architecture in Transition, 1845–1860.* Exh. cat. Providence: Brown University, 1988.

Turner, Paul Venable. *Campus: An American Planning Tradition.* The Architectural History Foundation/MIT Press Series, VII. New York, 1984.

Whiffen, Marcus. *The Public Buildings of Williamsburg, Colonial Capital of Virginia: An Architectural History.* Williamsburg Architectural Studies, Vol. 1. Williamsburg: Colonial Williamsburg, 1958.

Wriston, Barbara. "Tefft, Thomas Alexander." In *Macmillan Encyclopedia.*

FIGURE 2. *Thomas A. Tefft,* **Richmond College,** *preliminary perspective. (Photograph courtesy of Brown University Archives, Tefft Collection, Providence, Rhode Island.)*

PERSPECTIVE VIEW
OF THE
RICHMOND FEMALE INSTITUTE
RICHMOND VA.

T. A. Tefft, Arch.

# 46.
# CAMDEN

*Perspective*

Near Port Royal, Caroline County
Presentation drawing, 1856
Watercolor and ink on paper; 20 by 36 inches
Collection of Mrs. Richard T. Pratt, Camden

This colorful perspective of one of the nation's purest examples of the Italian Villa style was executed by Norris G. Starkwether, an able designer who worked out of both Baltimore and Washington. Born in Vermont, Starkwether (who also spelled his name *Starkweather*) practiced in Philadelphia before settling Baltimore in the 1850s. Starkwether's design for a Virginia plantation house on the banks of the Rappahannock River was commissioned by William Carter Pratt, to be erected on the site of the eighteenth-century Pratt house that was demolished to make way for the present structure, a present for Pratt's bride. The exuberant structure, with its fancy brackets, ornamented porches and balconies, and arch-eaved tower, all in the latest taste, must have made a strong impression not only on the new bride but on the whole neighborhood as well, for nothing like it had ever been seen before in the conservative Rappahannock River Valley. Not only was its architecture very up to date, so were its many appointments. It was equipped with running water in every bedroom, central heating, gas lighting, and an attached conservatory. A guest writing from Camden in 1864 stated: "The immediate grounds contain twenty acres, and are laid out with much taste, beautified with trees, shrubbery, arbors, and seats. . . . Each room is furnished with and finished with a different kind of wood—oak, rosewood, mahogany, walnut, etc. The room I occupied was the rosewood. The mantles are all of white marble, and the locks and knobs of heavy silver plate."[1]

Camden remains a remarkable document of mid-nineteenth-century taste and life-style, for it has survived almost unchanged from the time it was originally occupied. Still preserved are most of the original furnishings, including carpeting, curtains, and light fixtures, not to mention Starkwether's set of architectural drawings, which includes the perspective discussed here.[2] Remarkably, the original water-basins remain intact with their taps still operable, and elements of the original heating system are still in service. The amazing untouched quality of the place is due in no small part to the fact that Camden has had only one change of ownership since it was completed; its current occupant is the daughter-in-law of the builder. The major change the house has suffered is the loss of its tower, which was destroyed when fired upon by a Union gunboat during the Civil War.

Starkwether's perspective gives a somewhat misleading impression of Camden's situation. The people strolling and riding about, the boat passing by, and the line of houses on the opposite shore, all in a happy, verdant landscape, lead one to think that Camden is a suburban villa amid much coming and going. Actually it is a more lonely place, the core of a plantation still containing hundreds of acres. The rendering technique also gives a false impression, suggesting that the house was built of stuccoed masonry. Instead it is a wooden house covered with flush boarding painted pale pink. Yet Camden remains a monument of its style and received official recognition as such when it was designated a National Historic Landmark in 1971.

Although Starkwether is well represented by works in the Washington and Baltimore areas, he has only one other documented Virginia work, the original complex of the Virginia Theological Seminary in Alexandria. Mayhurst, near Orange, Virginia, a house similar in style to Camden, is variously attributed to Starkwether, but no documentation has surfaced to confirm his involvement. CCL

NOTES

1. Quoted in William B. O'Neal, *Architecture in Virginia*. (New York: Walker & Co. for the Virginia Museum, 1968), p. 97.

2. The other drawings preserved at Camden are a sheet showing the north (river) and south (drive) elevations and a sheet showing west (side) elevation. Both are signed "N. G. Starkweather ARCHITECT BALTO & WASH."

REFERENCE

Howland, Richard Hubbard. "Tuscan Transplant." *Arts in Virginia* 9 (Fall 1968): 2–9.
O'Neal, William B. *Architectural Drawing in Virginia, 1919–1969*. (School of Architecture of the University of Virginia, Charlottesville and The Virginia Museum of Fine Arts, Richmond, l969). pp. 76–79.

FIGURE 1. *Site photo of* **Camden,** *river facade.*

Attributed to EDMUND GEORGE LIND, 1829–1909

# 47.
## MELROSE

*(also called Murray's Castle)*
*Perspective*

Casanova (Fauquier County)
Presentation drawing, circa 1857–58
Watercolor and ink on paper; 9⅝ by 12⅜ inches
Collection of E. W. Bridgeman, Jr., Harwood, Maryland

FIGURE 1. **"Dr. Murray's House, Fauquier County, Virginia, with Tents. November 1863."** *Vintage photograph by T. H. O'Sullivan, (Photograph courtesy of the Library of Congress.)*

The impact of the Romantic movement on mid-nineteenth-century Americans, especially on landed Southern families, is well illustrated in numerous antebellum dwellings whose architecture is dominated by historical allusion. Probably the strongest influence came from the novels of Sir Walter Scott and the medievalism he popularized. With their vivid historical narrative, heroic characters, and detailed descriptions of Gothic buildings, Scott's novels electrified American imaginations and opened American eyes to medieval pageantry and color. Indeed, during his lifetime Scott was the perhaps the most widely read author in America. He made Americans realize that the glory of the Middle Ages was the common heritage of all English-speaking people. Thus was kindled our desire to surround ourselves with the trappings of the past, both authentic and reproduced.

A prime example of Scott's sway on our romantic aspirations is the design for Melrose, one of Virginia's most important expressions of the castellated mode of the Gothic Revival. This crenelated country house was commissioned in 1857 by Dr. James H. Murray of Maryland for a large Fauquier County farm he purchased in 1856. Murray chose the name Melrose for his new house in honor of Melrose Abbey in Scotland, which he claimed as an ancestral home. The name was also likely inspired by Scott, who uses Melrose Abbey as a setting for several stories. The architect for the project was Edmund George Lind of Baltimore, whose commission from Dr. Murray is listed by Lind in a catalogue of his works.[1]

Lind was born in England and studied architectural drawing in the Government School of Design at Somerset House under C. M. Richardson. Before coming to America in 1855, he served as apprentice draftsman to John Blore from 1849 to 1852. Upon settling in Baltimore, he worked for six months in the office of Norris G. Starkweather. At the time he was engaged to design Melrose, Lind was associated with William Turnbull Murdoch, a partnership which lasted until 1859. Although the authorship of the watercolor rendering of Melrose is unknown, the careful delineation of its details and the professional handling of the perspective indicates that it is the work of an architect. It could have been executed by either Lind or Murdoch, as both were trained draftsmen. It could also be the work of William T. Richards, who was chief draftsman in their firm.

The Murray family did not long enjoy their new castle. With the outbreak of the Civil War, Dr. Murray enlisted in the Confederate army medical corps. The property had been completely vacated by April 1862 when it was occupied by federal troops. Murray sold Melrose in 1863 to Horace L. Kent of Richmond, but kept the watercolor rendering of his evocative creation. It remains in the possession of Murray family descendants. Still preserved on the interior of a closet at Melrose is this threatening message, inscribed by a lieutenant in the Indiana Volunteers: "Dear Sir, I think you would have saved the destruction of your beautiful house by remaining at it. I am much pained to see so fine a place destroyed. Yet I presume you think it none of my business either yet. My desire is that all good citizens shall enjoy their homes, of course, you do not fall under the above either." [2] Fortunately, Melrose was not destroyed, and except for an expanded service wing it remains essentially as originally designed. CCL

NOTES
1.   Mills Lane, *Architecture of the Old South, Virginia* (Savannah: The Beehive Press, 1987), 227.

2.   "Melrose," *National Register of Historic Places Inventory-Nomination Form* (United States Department of the Interior: May 10, 1982), section 8.

REFERENCES
Lane, Mills. *Architecture of the Old South, Virginia.* Savannah: The Beehive Press. 1987. pp. 223, 227.

Loth, Calder. *The Virginia Landmarks Register,* third edition. Charlottesville: The University Press of Virginia. 1987. P. 146.

Withey, Henry F., and Elsie Rathburn Withey. *Biographical Dictionary of American Architects (Deceased).* Los Angeles: Hennessey & Ingalls, 1970. Pp. 372–73.

Melrose

# 48.
## TOMB OF JAMES MONROE

*Perspective*

Hollywood Cemetery, 412 S. Cherry St., Richmond
Presentation drawing by Oswald J. Heinrich (1828–1886), 1858
Signed and dated: *O. Heinrich. fec./1858.*
Pricking, pencil, pen, India ink, brown ink, and watercolor on paper; 25 ¾ by 20 inches
Collection of The Valentine Museum of the City of Richmond, V:65.16.5

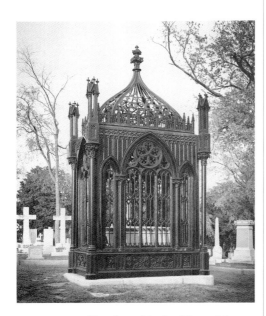

FIGURE 1. *Site photo,* **Tomb of James Monroe** *at Hollywood Cemetery, Richmond.*

Albert Lybrock was born on January 11, 1827, at St. Johann, Rhein-Provinz, Germany. After studying architecture at the Polytechnic School of Karlsruhe, Germany, he immigrated to the United States in 1848. For the next five years he lived and worked in New York, where he spent at least a portion of the time working in the office of Trench and Snook, one of the leading New York architectural firms of its day. The firm had introduced the Italian *palazzo* style of commercial architecture to the United States with the design of the A. T. Stewart Store in New York City in 1845–46. Lybrock cited his role in the design of two of the firm's major commissions, the Metropolitan Hotel (1850–52, demolished) and the St. Nicholas Hotel (1851–54, demolished), as well as "several of [New York's] finest Churches, and a large number of the best dwellings and stores."[1]

When Lybrock moved to Richmond, Virginia, in 1853, the city had a substantial German populace, accounting for almost one-quarter of the city's pre-War white population. Lybrock first worked in the office of Henry Exall, a native of Reading, England, who, according to his obituary, had designed "fully one half of the houses built in Richmond prior to the War".[2] During Lybrock's employment, Morson's Row on Governor Street was completed (1853), and was probably designed by either Exall or Lybrock.

Later in the 1850s, Lybrock worked on three important civic commissions in Richmond. The first, in 1857, was the supervision of construction of the Richmond Custom House, designed by Ammi B. Young, Architect of the Treasury. The second, in the same year, was the preparation of measured drawings of the Virginia State Capitol and the drafting of proposed enlargements of the building. The third, in 1858, was the design of the tomb of President James Monroe.

Throughout most of his career, Lybrock continued to use the same Italianate vocabulary employed in the office of Trench and Snook. His buildings, most of which are now demolished, helped define the character of the Main Street commercial district in Richmond, which he designed either alone or in partnership with other architects. These included the Ballard Hotel (1855), Shafer's Building (ca. 1870), Levy Brothers Dry Goods Store (1872), State Bank Building (1874), and the Mozart Academy of Music (1885). Lybrock also designed buildings outside of Richmond; he may have been the architect for Sabot Hill (1855–56), the Goochland County home of James Morson, Secretary of War for the Confederacy, and he is known to have been the architect of the main building (1878–84) and Superintendent's House (1883) of the Miller Manual Labor School ( SURVEY NO. 52 ).

Lybrock died on January 11, 1886, the same day that the grand opening concert was held in the Mozart Academy of Music, his last commission.[3] He is buried in Hollywood Cemetery in Richmond not far from his best known work, the tomb of James Monroe.

James Monroe, fifth president of the United States and a native of Virginia, had died on July 4, 1831, in New York City. In 1858, as the centennial of his birth approached, many Virginians lobbied to erect a proper monument for the president and to reinter his remains in his home state. The governors of both New York and Virginia were agreeable to the plan.

The *Richmond Daily Dispatch* of 24 December 1858 reported that Governor Henry A. Wise "has at length decided on the style of Monument to be erected in Hollywood Cemetery, over the remains of James Monroe, and orders have been given for the execution of the work. From the number of styles furnished him, he has selected the 'Gothic Temple' prepared by A. Lybrock, Esq. This temple is to be of cast iron, 12 by 7 foot square and 20 feet to the top of the dome, the whole of which is to be enriched with Gothic ornament. Messrs. Wood and Perot of Philadelphia have contracted for the cost; and we understand that the whole cost of the temple will not exceed $1,700."[4] Wise may have become acquainted with Lybrock as a result of his designs for the enlargement of the Virginia State Capitol, prepared the previous year.

The contract with Wood and Perot provided that the monument be installed by June 1, 1859, and be primed with a coat of white lead oil paint. It was later painted with at least two finish coats. The Monroe Tomb, which resembles a tiny chapel, stands on a stone base on a hill overlooking the James River.

Oswald J. Heinrich (1828–1886), the draftsman for this perspective, was born in Dresden and studied architecture and drawing in Germany. After coming to Richmond in 1855, he worked as an architect, a drawing master, and a draftsman. He ended his days as a mining engineer in the West. Heinrich adorned this outstanding presentation drawing with a panoramic background, an extraordinary glimpse of Richmond and Manchester—from their church spires to their industrial chimneystacks—in the year 1858.

DMcV

NOTES
1. "Architect's Office, Opposite the Exchange Bank—Henry Exall," *The Richmond Dispatch*, 11 February 1853.

2. "Henry Exall Dead," *The Richmond Dispatch*, 6 August 1891.

3. "It Is Dedicated: Mozart Academy of Music," and "The Hand of Death: Captain Albert Lybrock," *The Richmond Dispatch*, 12 January 1886.

4. "The Monroe Monument," *The Richmond Dispatch*, 24 December 1858.

REFERENCES
Gayle, Margot. "Cast-Iron Masterpiece: Gothic Revival Tomb of President James Monroe." *Nineteenth Century* 7 (Summer 1981): 62–64.

Lee, Ann Carter. "Architectural Ironwork on Main Street, Richmond, Virginia." Master of Architectural History thesis, University of Virginia, 1970.

Mitchell, Mary H. *Hollywood Cemetery: The History of a Southern Shrine.* Richmond: Virginia State Library, 1985.

———. "'With Appropriate Honors': The Reburial of James Monroe." *Virginia Cavalcade* 35 (Autumn 1985): 52–63.

O'Neal, William B. *Architectural Drawing.* Pp. 32–33, 60–61, 80–85, 102–03.

Raymond, R. W. "Oswald J. Heinrich." *The Engineering and Mining Journal*, issue no. 144 (1886): 1–3.

Virginia, Commonwealth of. *Virginia Landmarks Register*, File No. 127–221 (Hollywood Cemetery).

Winthrop, Robert P. *Architecture in Downtown Richmond.* Edited by Virginius Dabney. Richmond: Junior Board of Historic Richmond Foundation, 1982.

EDMUND G. LIND, 1829–1909

WILLIAM TURNBULL MURDOCH, dates unknown

for

LIND AND MURDOCH, Baltimore

# 49.
# MORVEN PARK

*Thomas Swann House*
*Perspective*

Leesburg (Loudoun County)
Presentation drawing, 1861
Inscribed lower left: *LIND & MURDOCH ARCHts*; lower
center: *MURDOCH & RICHARDS, DELs 1861*
Pricking, pencil, pen, India ink, brown ink, watercolor, and
scraping on paper; 22 ¾ by 36 ¾ inches
Collection of Morven Park, Westmoreland Davis Memorial
Foundation, Inc., Leesburg, Virginia

FIGURE   1.   *Site photo of* **Morven Park.**

This remarkable design for a country house in Loudoun County is a proposed remodeling of an architecturally complex structure, the north wing of which
incorporates the walls of an eighteenth-century stone
dwelling. The property was acquired in 1808 by Judge
Thomas Swann, who erected the two-story center section with its massive Doric portico and flanking two-
story dependencies in the 1830s. The architect of this
relatively sophisticated essay in the Greek Revival
idiom has not been determined. In 1858 Swann's son,
Thomas Swann, Jr., a Baltimore banker, employed the
architect Edmund G. Lind, also of that city, to greatly
enlarge his country seat.[1] The scheme called for wings
connecting the dependencies, four Italianate towers of
unequal heights, and various service areas. The resulting design, with its jumble of elements, has more of
the air of a fantasy pastiche than anything actually
built. Its diverse towers vaguely recall Osborne, Queen
Victoria's country house on the Isle of Wight, a structure that helped make the Italian Villa style fashionable
on both sides of the Atlantic in the mid nineteenth
century. In this country, however, the standard Italian
Villa house in nearly every case had only one tower,
usually placed in the center of the composition. A
house with four towers may be unique among the
American expressions of the style.

Although Lind's proposed enlargements for the
body of the house were carried out, apparently only
one of the small towers was constructed, and it was
removed during a remodeling following the purchase
of Morven Park in 1903 by Virginia governor Westmoreland Davis.[2] Because Loudoun County was
caught in the cross-fire of the Civil War, it is likely that
hostilities caused construction to cease before the principal towers were begun.

At the time Lind was commissioned to remodel
Morven Park in 1858, he was in partnership with William Turnbull Murdoch. The partnership broke up a
year later, in 1859. Apparently Lind's involvement
with Morven Park ceased with the dissolution of the
partnership. In 1860 Murdoch took on as his new
partner William T. Richards, who had been chief
draftsman for the original firm.[3] Because the architectural rendering is signed Murdoch and Richards, it is
presumed this new firm was kept by Swann for the
Morven Park project in place of Lind. Whether it was
Murdoch or Richards who executed the carefully
delineated watercolor is unknown, but William T.
Richards, continuing his role as draftsman, is a safe
guess. The fact that the building never received its towers makes the rendering a valuable record of a most
extraordinary concept, one probably without parallel
in this country. It is also a rare example of a polished
presentation drawing of the antebellum period.[4]   CCL

NOTES
1.   Mills Lane, *Architecture of the Old South, Virginia.* 227.

2.   According to the administrator of the Westmoreland Davis Foundation, Governor Davis, following his acquisition of Morven Park, donated the fountain shown
in the foreground to the Commonwealth of Virginia, whereupon it was placed in
Capitol Square. The fountain shown in the rendering indeed strongly resembles
one of the two fountains in Capitol Square today.

3.   I am grateful to Mills Lane for providing information on the firms of Lind &
Murdoch and Murdoch & Richards.

4.   I am grateful to John G. Lewis for bringing the existence of this drawing to
the attention of the Virginia Department of Historic Resources.

REFERENCES
Lane, Mills. *Architecture of the Old South, Virginia.* Savannah: The Beehive Press.
1987. Pp. 220, 227.

Loth, Calder. *The Virginia Landmarks Register, Third Edition.* Charlottesville: University Press of Virginia. 1987. P. 244.

Sale, Marian Marsh. "Morven Park." *Commonwealth*, November, 1969.

Withey, Henry F., and Withey, Elsie Rathburn. *Biographical Dictionary of American
Architects (Deceased).* Los Angeles: Hennessey & Ingalls, Inc., 1970. Pp.
372–373.

MURDOCH · RICHARDS Del. 1862

# 50.
## COMMERCIAL BUILDING, 1101–1103 EAST MAIN STREET

*Elevation*

Richmond (demolished)
Presentation drawing, circa 1866
Pricking, pencil, pen and India ink, with watercolor on paper;
23 ⅛ by 17 ¾ inches
Collection of the University of Virginia Library, Charlottesville;
Special Collections Department, Alfred Landon Rives
Drawings, Oversize Box N-17, Folder 2313–22 to 2313–26

FIGURE 1. *Site photo of an* **Ironfront** *building on East Main Street, Richmond. (Photograph by Sergei Troubetzkoy.)*

Alfred L. Rives was born in Paris, France, on March 25, 1830, while his father, William Cabell Rives, was serving as minister to France from the United States. The family left France in 1832, but returned to Paris while the elder Rives served once again as U.S. minister, from 1849 to 1853. It was during this period that Alfred Landon Rives received training in architecture and engineering at the Ecole Impériale des Ponts et Chaussées in Paris, graduating at the head of his class in 1854. He served as assistant engineer for the completion of the Capitol in Washington, D.C. before returning to Virginia with the outbreak of war in 1861. He served as a colonel of engineers in the Confederate Army; following the war, he settled in Richmond and spent most of his career working on a variety of railroad projects around the world.

More than nine hundred commercial and industrial buildings were destroyed in Richmond as the result of the Evacuation Fire of April 2 and 3, 1865. The area was rebuilt with numerous substantial commercial structures, many with cast-iron ornamentation or, in a few cases, even complete facades of cast iron. Cast iron was erroneously believed to be fireproof, so its use in a neighborhood which had recently been destroyed by fire seemed appropriate. Perhaps even more important, however, was the fact that cast iron could save both time and money to the builder.

William Cabell Rives wrote to his son on December 22, 1865:

> I think you are in a fair way of becoming the *homme indispensable* [sic] in all the enterprises of improvement about Richmond, if you turn, as I trust you will, your opportunities to good account. . . . I think the governor, by his complimentary introduction of your name in his message to the legislature, will have been of service to you. . . . In short, I cannot but hope . . . that you are to play an important part in the great problem of *reconstruction*, in its best sense. It is a career which unites motives of the highest patriotism with a just and necessary regard to private interests.[1]

Rives's design for 1101–1103 was constructed by Thomas Randolph Price, with whom Rives had a distant family connection. According to Price's account book, it was begun in 1866 and was certainly completed by December 1867. The Richmond Land Books for 1868 note an important addition to the property, which is assessed at $32,000 and the land at an additional $8,000. According to the statement, submitted by Alfred L. Rives to Thomas R. Price in December of 1867, the total cost for constructing this building was $63,255.97. Price died a year later on December 7, 1868.

The Thomas R. Price Co., a drygoods firm, apparently moved to this location in 1868 from 229 East Broad Street and continued in operation for many years under a variety of names well into the twentieth century. The 1869 City Directory (which also carries the date of 1868) lists William C. Dunham & Company, commission merchants, as being located on the "upper floors" of this building.

Alfred L. Rives is listed in two different places in the 1869 City Directory, and each listing gives him a different address: over 1113 East Main and over 1117 East Main. In any case, he had an office in the very same block as this building, which he designed. It is possible that he might have had business associations with two major architects of the day as well, for the same directory lists architect Albert West as being located above number 1117 and architect Marion Charles Dimmock as having offices above number 1113, the two addresses listed for Rives. Since Rives's listing in the directory gives his Albemarle County address for his residence and not a local address, the association with West and/or Dimmock is a real possibility. The 1870 City Directory lists three occupants at 1101–1103 East Main: Thomas R. Price & Co. Dry Goods; the YMCA; and the State Bank of Virginia. Because the State Bank of Virginia received its charter in January 1870, this would have been their first location. This bank later merged into the Merchants National Bank, later First and Merchants National Bank—which demolished the building in 1971—then became Sovran, now merged with NationsBank.

In designing this building, Rives seems to have followed the prevailing Italianate style of architecture, which was being used almost exclusively along Richmond's Main Street during the Reconstruction period. Like many of his contemporaries, Rives chose to use cast iron extensively on the street level of the facade, and only modest cast-iron details on the upper levels, as was often done on area buildings. The decorative cast-iron elements used on this building were made in Richmond, by Snyder and Bowers.

This drawing appears to be an early version, and the design was later altered somewhat by Rives before construction. Rives extended the building to two bays in depth, eliminated the exterior basement entrances, and made the four center bays project as a unit.

The Rives Collection preserves at least four other slightly scattered drawings for this commission: two plans and a section [Oversize Box N–17, Folder 2313–15 to 2313–20] and the flank elevation [Oversize Tray 1, Folder 14]. The present elevation, despite its naive representation of the sidewalk in perspective, has various refinements. (For instance, broader shadows set the plane of the bottom half of each window further back than the plane of the top half.) One has difficulty, however, in pointing to any feature that indicates Rives's French training.                  ST

NOTES
1.  Unpublished manuscript letter dated 22 December 1865 from William Cabell Rives to his son Alfred Landon Rives. University of Virginia collections.

REFERENCES
O'Neal. *Architectural Drawing.* xii, 34, 36, 38, 62–69, 72–73, 96–101.

Moore, John H. "Judith Rives of Castle Hill." *Virginia Cavalcade* 13 (Spring 1964): 30–35.

Price, Thomas Randolph. *Accounts, 1860–68.* Virginia Historical Society, Mss1 P9318 a 34–42.

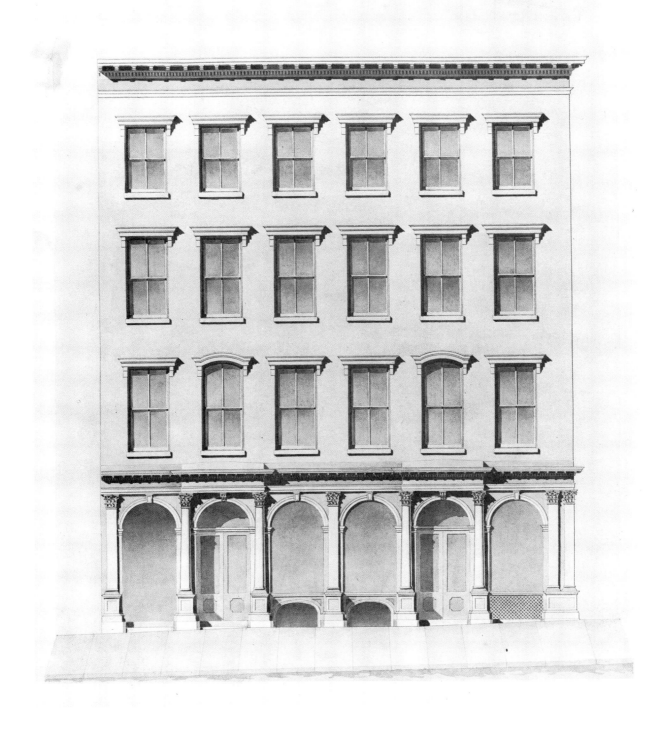

# 51.
# WADDELL
# MEMORIAL
# PRESBYTERIAN
# CHURCH

*Elevation and Transverse Section*

Route 20, near Rapidan (Orange County)
Office record, 1870s
Inscribed, left center: *J B Danforth, Amateur*; under left
center: *Tracing from original/by J* [illegible] *Gibson June
[Junr?] 187[2?]*
Pen and India ink with writing ink on tracing cloth;
18 ¼ by 21 ½ inches
Collection of the Waddell Memorial Presbyterian Church,
Orange County

<figure>FIGURE   1.   *Site photo of* **Waddell Church.**</figure>

In his obituary, the amateur architect J. B. Danforth was extolled as "an accomplished draughtsman, and [a man] of decided skill and taste in architecture [who] often drew plans for public and private edifices in this city."[1] Unfortunately, the obituary does not specifically mention any of Danforth's Richmond architectural work, leaving to the Waddell Memorial Presbyterian Church ( FIGURE   1 ) the distinction of being his sole known contribution to the architecture of nineteenth-century Virginia.

For many years Danforth served as chief clerk at Richmond's Mutual Assurance Society. His eldership in Grace Street Presbyterian Church most likely brought him into contact with officials of the Virginia Synod, which was regaining strength after the devastation of the War. By 1870, a number of new congregations were being organized outside of Richmond and Petersburg, and the general health of the Synod seemed much improved.[2]

With the encouragement of their pastor, the Reverend J. C. Dinwiddie, six members of the Orange Presbyterian Church decided in 1871 to organize a new congregation at the "Rapid Ann Station," on the border bewteen Orange and Culpeper counties. The new church was to be named for James Waddell, the famous colonial "Blind Preacher" of Orange. In order to raise funds for the church building, Waddell's descendents in June, 1872, prepared a circular to solicit money for "Waddell Memorial Chapel." As chairman of the building committee, Dinwiddie endorsed this solicitation with an added appeal, noting that an acre of land had been procured and half the funds raised.[3]

Danforth submitted the drawings for the church building on 13 August 1872, "the first lumber was delivered on September 30, 1872 [and] on April 9, 1873, the last shipment was delivered consisting of the doors which would be used throughout the building."[4] The completion of the building in the fall of 1874 was recorded by George Q. Peyton, longtime Clerk of Session and maker of the altar woodwork, pulpit, and chairs.[5]

Although the present appearance of Waddell Memorial Presbyterian Church is a somewhat reduced version of Danforth's original design, the naive exuberance of this Carpenter Gothic building is unmatched in Virginia Gothic Revival church architecture. Danforth obviously knew both the growing number of neo-Gothic Virginia church buildings and the illustrated builder's manuals so popular at the time. His design for Waddell Memorial Church is most probably a synthesis of his own vision of the Gothic and his borrowings from one or more architectural manuals.

That a small, rural congregation would choose the Gothic Revival for their new church building in the early 1870s indicates the level of acceptance and desirability that the neo-Gothic had attained in once-Classical Virginia. The use of Gothic Revival for a Presbyterian church building further underscores the extent of the change of heart among Virginia's adamantly Protestant clergy and laity who, not thirty years before, had characterized the Gothic style as "Romish" at best, and the work of the devil at worst. Danforth's design and the finished building offer a testimony to the pervasive influence of the romantic yearning for "a more morally upright, chivalrous age, and for some material way to express it."[6]

An inscription at the the bottom of this drawing identifies it as a "Tracing from original" by John Gibson, a carpenter-architect from an important Richmond family of builders.[7] Gibson participated in erecting the Richmond Female Institute ( SURVEY NO.   45 ) and worked in association with Albert Lybrock ( SURVEY NOS.   48,   52 ), but only the drawing documents his connection with Danforth's church. Gibson used a new material, tracing cloth, to make his own coarse copy of a set of Danforth's presentation drawings. The appearance of the scale and the inscription "J B Danforth, Amateur" under both the elevation and the section suggests that Gibson traced two separate originals onto one sheet.   MPC

NOTES
1.   *Richmond Enquirer*, 3 July 1875. For basic biography, see also Danforth and Claiborne, *Historical Sketch*, 124–25.

2.   Thompson, "From Civil War to World War," 103–17.

3.   "History of Waddell," no pagination.

4.   "History of Waddell," no pagination.

5.   Shotwell, *History*, 5.

6.   Corrigan, "Puritans," 54.

7.   On the Gibson family, see Lane, *Virginia*, 228. The editions of [Sheriff and] Chataigne's Richmond *Directory* for the 1870s and early 1880s list a whole troop of John Gibsons who had livelihoods related to architecture.

REFERENCES
Corrigan, Michael P. "Puritans in Priestly Garb: The 'Gothic Taste' in Antebellum Virginia Church Architecture." Master of Arts thesis, Virginia Commonwealth University, 1988.

Danforth, John Buchanan, and Herbert A. Claiborne. *Historical Sketch of the Mutual Assurance Society of Virginia.* Richmond: William Ellis Jones, 1879.

"A History of Waddell Memorial Presbyterian Church." *Anniversary Service Bulletin.* Orange, Virginia: Waddell Memorial Presbyterian Church, 1974.

Obituary of J. B. Danforth. *Richmond Enquirer*, 3 July 1875.

Shotwell, Alan J. *History of Rapidan Station.* N. p.: Alan Shotwell, 1989.

Thompson, Ernest Trice. "From Civil War to World War (1861–1914)." In *Virginia Presbyterians in American Life: Hanover Presbytery (1755–1980)*, ed. Patricia Aldridge. Richmond: Hanover Presbytery, 1982.

Virginia, Commonwealth of. Virginia Landmarks Register, File No. 68–54 (Waddell Memorial Presbyterian Church).

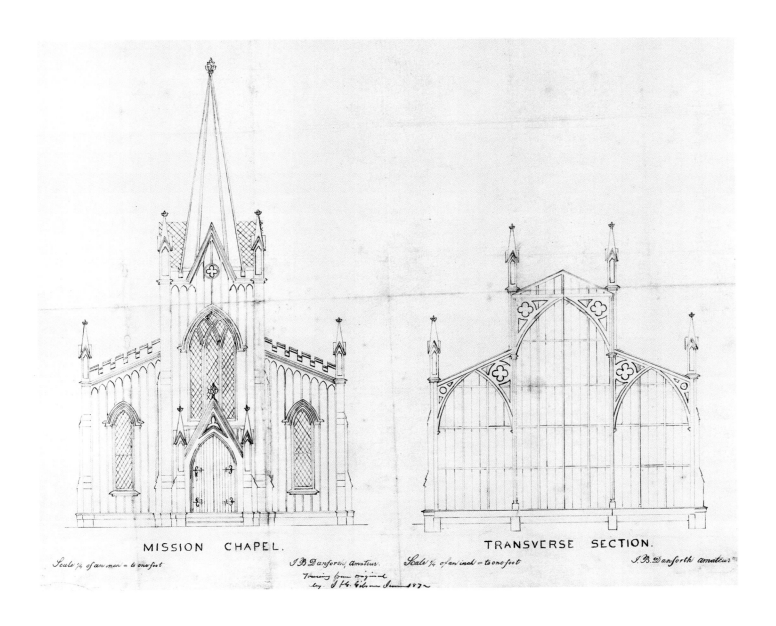

MISSION CHAPEL.

TRANSVERSE SECTION.

Scale ¼ of an inch = to one foot

J. B. Danforth, Amateur.
Tracing from original
by J. G. Gibson June 187~

Scale ¼ of an inch = to one foot

J. B. Danforth Amateur

# 52.
# THE MILLER MANUAL LABOR SCHOOL

*Front Elevation*

Near Batesville (Albemarle County)
Presentation or working drawing, circa 1876
Inscribed: *Brown, for Albert Lybrock, Architect./*
*Richmond, Va.*
Pencil, pen, India ink, and red ink on tracing cloth (?);
16 ⅜ by 36 inches
Collection of The Miller School of Albemarle, Charlottesville, Virginia

FIGURE 1. *Site photo*, **The Miller School.**

The Miller School of Albemarle (originally the Miller Manual Labor School) was established by bequest of Samuel Miller, a native of Albemarle County who became a very successful merchant and trader of agricultural commodities in Lynchburg.

Born June 30, 1792, in a small cabin on Ragged Mountain near Batesville, Virginia, Miller attended the local public school, and later taught there. His impoverished upbringing and his interest in education led him to provide for the establishment of a free school near the site of his birth.

By the time of his death in 1869, Miller had amassed a fortune of close to two million dollars. Shortly before his death he donated $100,000 to the University of Virginia, for the "establishment, maintenance and support of a school of experimental and practical agriculture." In his will he provided for several small gifts to relatives, and a gift of $151,000 to the Lynchburg Female Orphan Asylum. He designated that the remainder of his estate be used for "the founding, establishment and perpetual support of a School on the Manual Labor Principle—to be superintended by competent teacher or teachers . . . and wholly free of expense to the pupils."[1] The school would combine academics, industrial arts, and manual labor.

The School Commissioners of Albemarle County were given the responsibility of selecting the "poor orphans and other children" who were to be admitted to the school. The will also provided that "there shall be erected . . . such buildings of brick and other durable materials as shall be sufficient for the comfortable accommodation of one hundred pupils and their teachers" and that "the County Court of . . . Albemarle is hereby authorized and directed to employ some skillful and experienced architect to superintend the erection of the said building."

Miller's will was the subject of protracted litigation, but the provisions were upheld and in February 1874 the General Assembly of Virginia established the Miller Manual Labor School of Albemarle. Early in 1876, advertisements requesting submission of plans for the building were placed in Richmond and Washington newspapers. By the spring of the year, the design by the Richmond-based architect Albert Lybrock had been chosen and construction was begun.

In design, the building is a long, two-and-a-half-story brick block, with wings projecting from the center and two ends. The plan has the same extraction as those of Long's Virginia School for the Deaf and the Blind in Staunton ( SURVEY NO. 33 ) and Tefft's Richmond Female Institute ( SURVEY NO. 45 ). The polychromed brick building is topped with a steeply pitched mansard roof; its closely spaced gabled dormers provide light for the third floor. Construction was completed in phases: the central section in 1878, the southern wing in 1881, and the remaining work in late 1884. The total construction cost was $140,000.

In 1878 a Richmond journalist described the first phase with great enthusiasm:

The only term by which we could describe the building would be to call it a Magnificent Structure. Rising three stories of high pitch in height, presenting a front of 228 feet, in shape of a T, running back 220 feet, of composite architecture, combining Gothic and Elizabethan styles, its grandeur strikes the beholder at once with astonishment, and the exclamation of every one is, What a pity this splendid building should be in such an inaccessible place![2]

Located on a hillside in a rural area southwest of Charlottesville, the Miller School main building is one of the best examples of High Victorian Gothic architecture remaining in Virginia. Its polychromy, use of varying textures of brick and stone, stacked massing, and Gothic ornament are all characteristics of the style.

High Victorian Gothic was widely used for monumental institutional buildings, including Withers and Vaux's 1875 design for New York's Jefferson Market Courthouse and Elijah E. Myers's 1886 design for Richmond City Hall ( SURVEY NO. 58 ), and was often used for the main academic or administrative building at land-grant colleges. Since Lybrock's main building at the Miller School is an early example, it may have been the model for many "Old Mains" on land-grant college campuses in the midwestern and western United States.

This building was originally designed as a classroom, dormitory, and dining facility for the school. The Miller School, now a private military school for boys, continues to use the building as classroom, office, and dining facility.

"Brown," Lybrock's drafter for this elevation, remains unidentified. No other drawing for the Miller School except this, "Sheet No. 1," is known to survive. Whereas renderers in watercolor used paler or cooler colors to represent elements at a distance, here Brown used thinner ink lines to indicate the recessed parts of the building. DMcV

NOTES
1. For the documentation of the school, see Runk, "Brief History."
2. "Miller Manual-Labor School," *Richmond Dispatch.*

REFERENCES
Browne, Henry J. "A Feasibility Study for the Preservation of Miller School of Albemarle County, Virginia." Charlottesville: Browne, Eichman, Dalgliesh, 1978.

Chamberlain, Bernard. "Samuel Miller, 1792–1869: Albemarle Philanthropist." *Magazine of Albemarle County History* 28 (1970):119–27.

"Miller Manual-Labor School of Albemarle," *Richmond Dispatch,* 9 August 1878.

Runk, B.F.D., "A Brief History of the Early Years of the Miller Manual Labor School." *Magazine of Albemarle County History* 31 (1973):31–50.

Virginia, Commonwealth of. Virginia Landmarks Register, File No. 02–174 (Miller School of Albemarle).

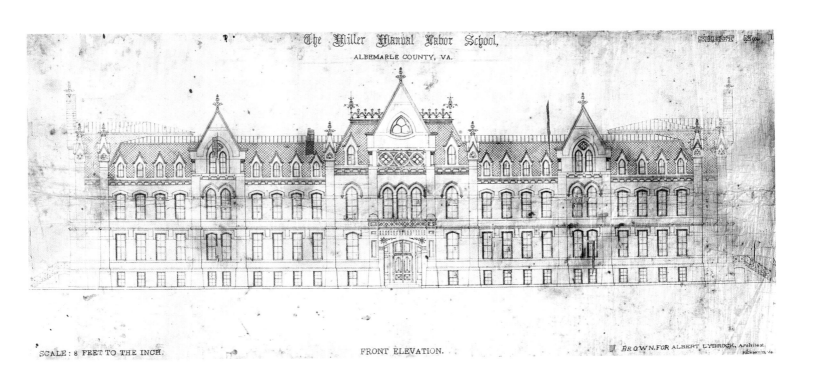

The Miller Manual Labor School,
ALBEMARLE COUNTY, VA.

SHEET No. 1

SCALE : 8 FEET TO THE INCH.

FRONT ELEVATION.

BROWN. FOR ALBERT LYBROCK, Architect.

# 53.
## GATEKEEPERS' LODGES AND GATE, MOUNT VERNON

*Plan, Elevation, Details*

George Washington Memorial Parkway near Alexandria
(Fairfax County)
Presentation drawing, 1875
Signed and dated: *July 7th 1875/Samuel Bootes./Civil Engr. &
Architect./Washington, D.C.*
Pen and India ink with pink wash on tracing cloth;
23 5/8 by 28 3/4 inches
Collection of the Mount Vernon Ladies' Association,
Mount Vernon, Virginia; Cat. No. G9

FIGURE 1. *Site photo,* **Mount Vernon Gate and Gatekeeper's Lodges.**

Little is known about Samuel Bootes, who signed this drawing as a civil engineer and architect, except that he was probably born and raised in Washington, D.C. The name of Samuel Bootes that appeared as early as 1820 in the national census records for Washington is probably that of the father or grandfather of the architect involved in this project. After 1853 the elder Bootes (or his son) was listed in the Washington directory as a clerk in the Treasury.[1] Samuel Bootes the architect was first listed in the City Directory in 1870. He appeared in the directories of both Washington and Georgetown intermittently until 1899, variously listing his occupation as draftsman for the Quartermaster's Department, engineer, architect, and clerk at the War Office.[2]

Two western gate lodges (or "porter's lodges") facing the road to Alexandria were originally built by Bushrod Washington between 1810 and 1812.[3] These lodges required periodic repairs and alterations throughout the nineteenth century, and eventually fell into ruin by 1858.[4] The Mount Vernon Ladies' Association began thinking of restoring the lodges in 1874, and by 1876 the project was completed.[5] Bootes submitted his restoration plan in 1875, and in an inscription in the lower right-hand corner he asserted that his buildings "can be built & finished [in] the best manner for $800.00 . . . All the trimmings are to correspond with the trimmings and finish on the buildings on the place." It remains a question whether Bootes actually received the commission. If the Ladies' Association did rebuild the lodges according to the 1875 plan, the ones that exist today have been substantially altered. (The block cornices are missing, the lodge entrances have been shifted to the center of their walls, and the actual gate is a simple horizontal rail fence that does not abut the lodges).

What becomes clear, however, is the remarkably early re-creation of colonial architectural forms at Mount Vernon. In 1858 the Ladies' Association began the purchase of the estate, then in a disastrously decayed condition, and began the restoration work in 1859. They rebuilt all of Washington's original piazza in 1860[6] (the new pillars rotted quickly and were replaced in 1894).[7] Shortly thereafter, when the south arcade blew down in 1861, the Association rebuilt it, and repaired its northern mate in 1875.[8] The nineteenth-century reconstructions apparently were not accurate, so the Ladies began rebuilding both the so-called colonnades in 1956 based on an 1853 photograph of the mansion's south end, which showed the south arcade in its original configuration.[9]

The drawing illustrated here clearly shows us two sides of a "Victorian" coin. On the one hand, much of what one sees passes for eighteenth-century taste; on the other hand, certain elements betray the date of 1875. In an intricate case, the cornice matches exactly the block cornice on the principal Mount Vernon buildings, a cornice that Batty Langley had associated with the Tuscan order (in *The Builder's Jewel*, London, 1746). On the other hand, Bootes's drawing puts this cornice on the lodge chimneys in a fashion that

belongs as thoroughly to its period as elaborate bargeboards.

Bootes's drawing, representative of the precise, highly detailed, linear style popular in the 1870s, is in no way remarkable for its date. But when compared with Washington's own elevation for the main house of just a century before ( SURVEY NO. 5 ), it exhibits a striking increase in control. The dissemination of training in draftsmanship has permitted a drafter of no particular distinction to pull the facade of a building out of its plan, to peel away wall and roof in the form of a section, and to zoom in on major details in a fashion rarely dreamed of along the Atlantic seaboard in the eighteenth century.          SCO

NOTES
1.    Albert Hunter, ed., *The Washington and Georgetown Directory* (Washington, D.C.:1853), 10, 95.

2.    I have used William H. Boyd, ed., *Boyd's Directory of Washington, Georgetown, and Alexandria* (Washington, D.C.: 1870–71); and *Boyd's Directory of the District of Columbia* (Washington, D.C.: 1872–1881). Matthew B. Gilmore, Reference Librarian, Washingtoniana Division, District of Columbia Public Library, was so kind as to track Bootes through the later directories.

3.    "Porter's Lodge" file, Mount Vernon Ladies' Association, Mount Vernon, Va.

4.    Benson J. Lossing, *Mount Vernon* (New York: 1859) 196.

5.    Charles C. Wall, "Early Restoration, 1859–1885," abstracts from Early Records of the Mount Vernon Ladies' Association, (Mount Vernon, Va.: 1956), 31.

6.    Wall, *Early Restoration,* 19.

7.    "Piazza" file, Mount Vernon Ladies' Association, Mount Vernon, Va.

8.    Wall, *Early Restoration,* 20.

9.    "Colonnades" file, Mount Vernon Ladies' Association, Mount Vernon, Va.

REFERENCE
Johnson, Gerald W. *Mount Vernon: The Story of a Shrine.* With extracts from the diaries and letters of George Washington selected and annotated by Charles Cecil Wall. Revised, with an epilogue by Ellen McCallister Clark. Mount Vernon, Virginia: The Mount Vernon Ladies' Association, 1991.

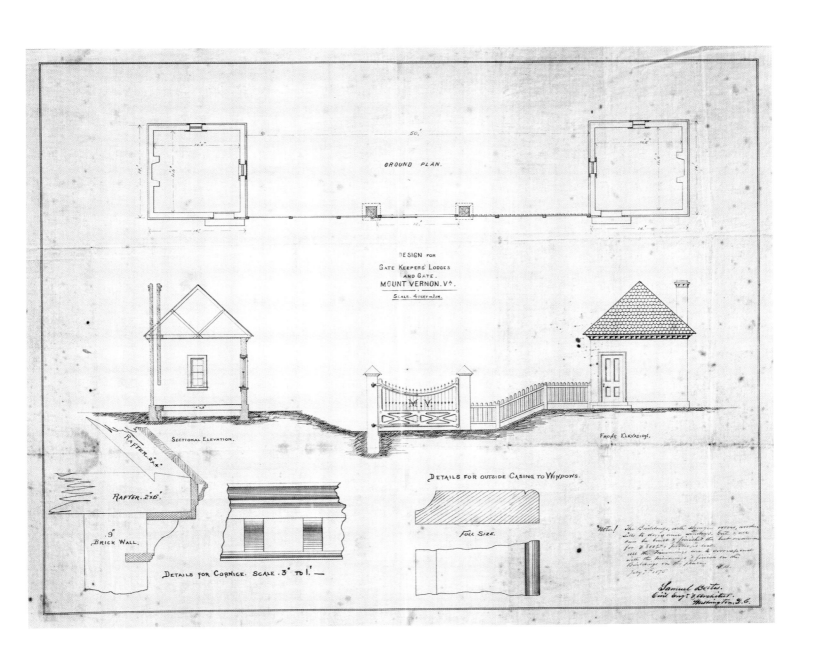

GROUND PLAN.

DESIGN FOR
GATE KEEPERS' LODGES
AND GATE.
MOUNT VERNON. VA.

Scale. 4 FEET = 1 IN.

SECTIONAL ELEVATION.

FRONT ELEVATION.

RAFTER. 2×4".

RAFTER. 2×6".

9"
BRICK WALL.

DETAILS FOR CORNICE. SCALE. 3" TO 1'.—

DETAILS FOR OUTSIDE CASING TO WINDOWS.

FULL SIZE.

Samuel Beiles.
Civ'l Eng'r & Architect.
Washington, D.C.

# 54.
# LEWIS BROOKS HALL

*University of Virginia*
*Side Elevation*

University Ave., Charlottesville
Presentation drawing, 1876
Signed and dated: *J. R. Thomas / Architect / Rochester N.Y. / May 1876.*
Pricking, pencil, pen and India ink and watercolor on paper; 14 ⅞ by 21 inches
Collection of the University of Virginia Library, Charlottesville; Special Collections Department, Brooks Museum Drawings, 6846–P

FIGURE 1. *Vintage site photo,* **Brooks Hall,** *University of Virginia. (Photograph courtesy of Prints Collection, Special Collections Department, University Archives, University of Virginia Library.)*

Born in Rochester, New York, John R. Thomas practiced there until 1882, when he moved to New York City.[1] He specialized in public buildings, where he often displayed his bent for engineering. He gave Virginia two of its principal High Victorian buildings, the Lewis Brooks Hall of Natural Science, and Lynchburg's High Victorian Gothic First Baptist Church (1884–86 and additions). Thomas capped his career with a major work of the American Renaissance, the New York City Hall of Records (1899–1911), which won the praise of the eminent critic Montgomery Schuyler.

The textile manufacturer Lewis Brooks belonged to the Rochester intellectual circle around Lewis Henry Morgan, the "father of American anthropology." This circle included Henry A. Ward, naturalist and founder of Ward's Natural Science Establishment. Ward, suffering after the Panic of 1873, tried to interest Brooks in funding natural history collections. Brooks took Ward's counsel about making such a gift to the University of Virginia, and John Thomas was commissioned to design Brooks Hall to house one of the best American natural history museums of the period ( FIGURE 1 ).[2]

In this elevation, the building nears its final form. The design owes much to library typology: thus the main hall takes the library-like pattern of an oblong with alcoves and galleries along the sides.[3] With its chief space openly framed in iron inside a highly symbolic masonry shell, Brooks Hall descends from Henri Labrouste's Bibliothèque Ste.-Geneviève (Paris, 1838–50). The symbolism conveys the nature of the building and takes three forms: a band of inscriptions names great natural historians; sculpted animal heads in the keystones represent zoology, a branch of natural history; and the unusual articulation traces the interior of the building on its exterior.[4]

Thomas here designed in the experimental spirit of the 1870s. For his sources he looked chiefly at the Classical tradition: at the Italian Renaissance and its Northern European sequels; at antiquity ( FIGURE 2.54 ); and at new work, such as the Bibliothèque Ste.-Geneviève and Richard Morris Hunt's Lenox Library (New York, 1870–77, demolished FIGURE 2.48 ). Like the libraries by Labrouste and Morris, Brooks Hall drew on the past to achieve not a revival but an assertively modern style. In all three buildings, the hand of the reformer shows plainly in a series of dwarf pilasters. Powerless to support a load or regulate a mass, these diminutive strips embody a thorough reaction against the costly, free standing giant Order— the kind of Order that had triumphed a few feet away on the Lawn some sixty years before.

More at home with ideas than form, Thomas did not approach the level of the great Victorian experimenters, but Brooks Hall has an ingratiating combination of vitality and earnestness. Shorn of its original function since the 1940s, today it awaits the care it deserves as a distinguished work of architecture.

The University of Virginia has originals (or, in one case, a photograph) of twelve drawings by

Thomas for Brooks Hall. They seem to belong to two groups. One set of presentation drawings includes the elevation shown here. A set of working drawings comes closer to the hall as executed. The sharp, bright quality of the present elevation, with its ruled ink brick joints and its contrasts of red, cream, and blue, underscores that Thomas and his world meant this as a modern style.

CEB

NOTES
1.  I thank my undergraduate students Leslie Claytor and John C. Pachuta for invaluable help in beginning the study of Brooks Hall.

2.  This paragraph condenses the findings in Hantman, "Brooks Hall." For Brooks's similar 1876 gift to Washington and Lee University and J. Crawford Neilson's floor plans for housing it, see Lyle and Simpson, *Lexington,* pp. 168, 193.

3.  I owe the library connection to McHugh, "Form and Fitness," p. 17. McHugh and Hantman provide the most up-to-date discussions of Brooks Hall.

4.  For details, see Chapter 2.

REFERENCES
Bruce. *History of the University of Virginia.* 3:361–63, 4:317–18; 5:148–49, 229–30.

Hantman, Jeffrey L. "Brooks Hall at the University of Virginia: Unraveling the Mystery." *Magazine of Albemarle County History* 47 (1989):69–92.

James, Anthony O. "Brooks Museum at the University of Virginia: An Architectural, Historical, and Adaptive Use Study." Seminar paper, AR H 824, University of Virginia, 1975. (Copy in Virginia Landmarks Register, File No. 104–63).

Levine, Neil. "The Romantic Idea of Architectural Legibility: Henri Labrouste and the *Néo-Grec.*" In *The Architecture of the Ecole des Beaux-Arts.* Edited by Arthur Drexler. New York: Museum of Modern Art, 1977.

"The Lewis Brooks Hall of Natural Science—University of Virginia." *Jeffersonian Republican* (Charlottesville, Virginia), 9 January 1878.

"The Lewis Brooks Museum of Natural Science." *Frank Leslie's Illustrated Newspaper,* 9 March 1878.

McHugh, Kevin. "Form and Fitness: John Rochester Thomas and Brooks Museum at the University of Virginia." Master of Architectural History thesis, University of Virginia, 1987.

"The New Museum." *Virginia University Magazine* 14 (June 1876):494–95.

*National Cyclopaedia of American Biography* 9:329.

Obituary of John R. Thomas. *American Architect and Building News* 73 (7 September 1901):74.

Schuyler, Montgomery. "The New Hall of Records, N.Y.C." *Architectural Record* 17 (May 1905):383–87.

Southall, James Cocke. *Opening of the Lewis Brooks Museum at the University of Virginia, June 27th, 1878: Address on Man's Age in the World.* Richmond: printed by order of the Board of Visitors, 1878.

Virginia, Commonwealth of. Virginia Landmarks Register, File No. 104–63 (Brooks Hall).

Wilson, Richard Guy. "The French Architectural Connection." *Daily Progress* (Charlottesville, Virginia), 21 September 1982.

FIGURE 2. *Vintage photograph of* **Interior, Brooks Hall.** *(Photograph courtesy of the Prints Collection, Special Collections Department, University Archives, University of Virginia Library.)*

SIDE ELEVATION.
OF PROPOSED
Natural History Building
FOR
UNIVERSITY OF VIRGINIA.

Scale 8 Ft. to an Inch.

BUFFON.    HUMBOLDT.    AGASSIZ.    LYELL.    ST HILAIRE.    PLINY.

# 55.
# HOUSE FOR
# HENRY GRAFTON
# DULANY, JR.

## *Proposed Elevations and Plans*

Upperville (Fauquier County), (unbuilt [?])
Presentation drawing, circa 1870s
Signed: *Geo A Frederick Archt./Baltimore Md.*
Pricking, pencil, pen, brush, and India ink on paper;
16 ¾ by 29 ¼ inches
Collection of the Maryland Historical Society, Baltimore;
George A. Frederick Collection, acc. no. 19.7.56.4

The Baltimore architect George A. Frederick, who studied in the office of Lind and Murdoch (see also SURVEY NOS. 47, 49), laid his claim to fame with a youthful triumph, Baltimore City Hall (1867–75), in what is commonly known today as the "Second Empire" style. The building's reputation rests on reasons tangential to its architectural quality, above all on Frederick's feat in staying well under the budget. He actually designed more winningly in his maturity. Frederick was active in the American Institute of Architects and published many articles on architecture.

His drawings at the Maryland Historical Society include two otherwise undocumented villa projects for H. Grafton Dulany, Jr. (1854–1890?), son of Richard Henry Dulany, who founded the Upperville Colt and Horse Show, the oldest in the country.[1] One scheme, recorded on a single sheet, calls for a palatial Italianate villa with a towering central observatory. That project should predate the other scheme, illustrated here. In this alternative, on three sheets, Frederick used a plan not unlike his first one and compensated for decreasing the size of the house by increasing the High Victorian Picturesqueness of his conception. Dulany turned elsewhere by May 1884, when Cabot and Chandler of Boston published a manorial design for his country house in the *American Architect and Building News* (FIGURE 1).[2]

Frederick based the present design on a block with a tower centered on the axially symmetrical main front. This format had become a standard one among American designers ever since Alexander J. Davis and A. J. Downing published an Italianate villa version in the 1840s.[3] Frederick developed this conception in combination with other well-established patterns: a central hall running back from the tower, and a cross-axis created by placing a service wing at one side. On an Italianate villa body Frederick set three kinds of high Northern European roofs, with a true mansard over the body of the house. He and his contemporaries commonly acknowledged a great kinship between postmedieval Italian and French architecture. Frederick wrote of his City Hall that "the style . . . is the 'Renaissance.'"[4] He presumably saw his second Dulany design (where he even used a variation on his City Hall *oeil-de-boeuf* dormers) in the same light.

In the United States, the Italianate and French tastes of this period did not rest on revivalism or scholarship but rather on free interpretation and innovation. At their best, such mansions as the second Dulany proposal offered luxurious living for a family, inside a scenic architectural mass hung with some of the most shapely ornament ever used in North America. Frederick's design deserves a middling rating. He planned for the new comforts of life, but not brilliantly: for instance, providing a furnace does not outweigh the problem that, if the best rooms face south as they should, then the babies have to sleep in a nursery facing into the chilling winds from the north. Frederick massed the house dramatically, but important relationships went awry. (The compression of the main floor by the porch leaves something to be desired, particularly in relation to the elongation of the upper

stories of the tower.) And, below the cresting, the ornament on the body of the building, although well-shaped, holds no great interest in itself, unlike the detailing of other regional masters (for instance, the exuberantly stylized ornament in *Progressive American Architecture* [New York, 1875] by the provincial New York State architect G. B. Croff). Reservations aside, one regrets the presumed absence of so vigorous a building from the Virginia countryside.

The weightless elegance of the ink lines on this handsome sheet represents one side of taste in the 1870s. In execution, splashed with sun and shadow, this robust and plastic conception would have represented another, heartier side of taste. CEB

NOTES
1. For a characterization of Dulany, a dim figure despite his wealth and his descent from the eminent Maryland family of the same name, see Hagey and Hagey, *Hagey Families*, pp. 608–09.
2. My students David Thompson and Donald Matheson discovered the Cabot and Chandler design.
3. On the history of this pattern, see Davies, "Blandwood," 13–14.
4. Frederick and John J. Purcell, "Description of the City Hall," 127, in Forrester, *City Hall.* See also Chapter 2.

REFERENCES
*American Architect and Building News* 15 (17 May 1884): unnumbered plate.
Brownell, Charles E. "The Italianate Villa and the Search for an American Style, 1840–1860." In Irma B. Jaffe, ed. *The Italian Presence in American Art, 1760–1860.* New York: Fordham University Press, 1989.
Davies, Jane B. "Blandwood and the Italian Villa Style in America." *Nineteenth Century* 1 (September 1975):11–14.
Dorsey, John, and James D. Dilts. *A Guide to Baltimore Architecture.* 2nd ed. Centreville, Maryland: Tidewater Publishers, 1981. Pp. xxxiii–xxxiv, xxxvii, 55–56, 86–88, 98, 100–01, 126, 191–94, 249–50, 270, 273.
Forrester, Allen E., comp. *The City Hall, Baltimore: History of Construction and Dedication.* Baltimore: The Mayor and City Council, 1877.
Frederick, George A. "Recollections of George A. Frederick; to Mr. J. B. Noel Wyatt, President, and the Baltimore Chapter, A.I.A." 10 October 1912. Maryland Historical Society Library, Manuscripts Division, Vertical File.
"George A. Frederick, F.A.I.A." *American Institute of Architects Journal* 12 (1924):494.
Hagey, King Albert, and William Anderson Hagey. *The Hagey Families in America and the Dulaney Family.* Bristol, Tennessee: King Printing Company, 1951.
Lacina, Thomas M., and William C. Thomas. *A History of Sacred Heart Parish.* Boyce, Virginia: Carr Publishing Company, 1953.
*National Cyclopaedia of American Biography* 9: 334.
Semmes, John E. *John H. B. Latrobe and His Times, 1803–1891.* Baltimore: Norman, Remington Company, 1917. Pp. 444, 566.
Virginia, Commonwealth of. Virginia Landmarks Register. File No. 30–46 (Oakley).

FIGURE 1. **Design for Country House for H. G. Dulany, Jr.,** *Upperville, Virginia. Cabot & Chandler Architects, Boston, Massachusetts, as published in* **American Architect & Building News,** *15 May 1884, no. 458. (Photograph courtesy of Avery Architectural and Fine Arts Library, Columbia University, New York City.)*

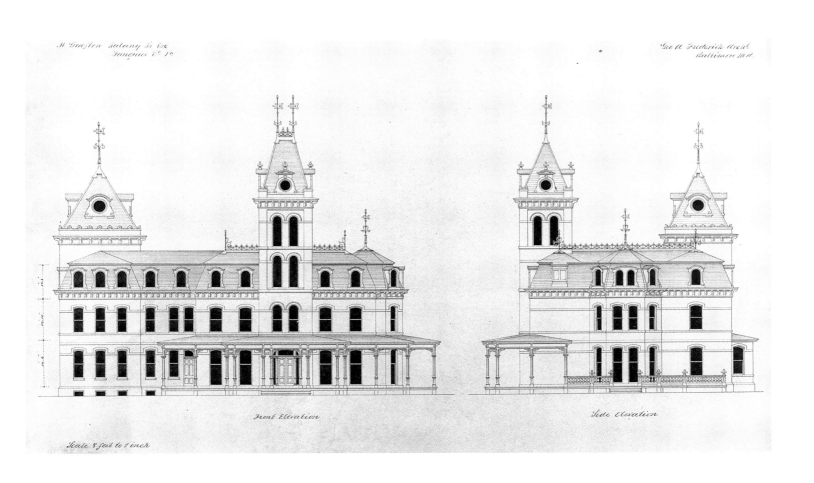

M. Grafton Dulany Jr Esq
Fauquier Co Va

Geo A Frederick Arch[t]
Baltimore Md.

Front Elevation

Side Elevation

Scale 8 feet to 1 inch

# 56.
## SECOND ACADEMIC BUILDING

*Hampton Institute Elevation*

On Hampton Creek, Hampton
Presentation drawing, circa 1879
Watercolor on tissue, mounted on board; 23 ⅝ by 17 ½ inches (irregular)
Collection of the American Architectural Foundation, Washington, D.C., acc. no. 80.5665

FIGURE 1. *Vintage photo of the* **Second Academic Building** *at* **Hampton University.** *(Photograph courtesy of Hampton University Archives.)*

In 1869 General Samuel C. Armstrong, the superintendent and one of the founders of the new Hampton Normal and Agricultural Institute, invited Richard Morris Hunt to design the first permanent buildings for the school. The intent of the new school was to provide education in manual labor and teaching for the newly freed blacks, as well as for Native Americans. General Armstrong had grown up in the Hawaiian Islands and had seen missionaries working among the natives there. During the War he had commanded black troops in the Peninsular Campaign and later headed the Freedmen's Bureau in Virginia. His new enterprise was sponsored by the American Missionary Association and the Freedmen's Bureau. The site he selected fronted on Hampton Creek, with a commanding view of Hampton Roads, was where freed men had gathered around the Emancipation Oak Tree after the War. It was adjacent to a National Soldier's Home and a National Cemetery. Believing that environment played a role in education, General Armstrong also selected his architect with care.[1]

Forty-two-year-old Richard Morris Hunt was already one of the most important architects in the United States. Born in Vermont, Hunt had spent much of his youth abroad and had been the first American to attend the prestigious Ecole des Beaux-Arts in Paris, where he studied architecture. After working on additions to the Musée du Louvre for Napoleon III, Hunt gave up the possibility of an eminent architectural career in France to return to the United States, with the express intention of assisting in the development of American architecture. Hunt rose rapidly to the top of the American architectural profession with important commissions for houses in New York, Boston, and Newport, and for institutional and commercial buildings as well. He briefly ran an architectural school in New York and served as secretary of the newly established American Institute of Architects. While he escaped the Civil War by returning to France, Hunt had strong connections with liberal reformers in the 1860s and 1870s and was a natural choice for the Hampton Institute commission. Later, in the 1880s, Hunt's career would take a different direction and he became known for the large and luxurious palaces he designed for the Vanderbilt family in New York, Newport, Asheville, and elsewhere. The esteem in which Hunt was held by his contemporaries is attested to by several notable accomplishments: he was asked to design the Administration Building, the centerpiece for the World's Columbian Exposition in Chicago, 1893; he was the first American to receive the Royal Gold Medal of the British Institute of Architects; and he was widely considered "the dean of American architects."[2]

Hunt's work at Hampton encompassed three buildings and a span of more than a decade. The earliest, referred to as the First Academic Hall (1869–70), was a three-story wooden structure covered in red brick. It served as an all-purpose building, with assembly rooms, offices, a library, instructional spaces, and dormitory rooms. Virginia Hall, Hunt's second building, was much larger and took longer: it was designed from late 1872 through early 1873; construction began shortly thereafter; and while it was dedicated in mid 1874, the interior was not complete until 1879; finally, a porch was added in 1885. A massive French Second Empire structure, Virginia Hall bristles with tall mansard roofs, dormers, and displays of elaborate wood bracing. No architectural drawings survive for either of these projects.

After First Academic Hall burned in November 1879, Hunt was asked to provide plans for a fireproof structure on the same site. For this project Hunt designed a slightly smaller brick building with an attached tower or campanile. The watercolor rendering for the project, illustrated here—probably by Hunt—emphasizes the picturesque qualities of the design, the emphasis on polychrome brickwork, the contrast of colors of the reddish brick and white stucco infill panels, the elaborate tower with the American flag snapping in the breeze, and the shadows cast by the different projections. Stylistically Hunt drew upon the wide windows of his earlier Studio Building in New York (1857–58), and in the elaborate brackets, wide eves, and shallow, sloping roof of the Swiss chalets he had designed in Newport and elsewhere. The revealed brick of the window arches and bands emphasizes its structural nature. When built, the tower and some of the brackets were eliminated, and the brick corner piers were emphasized. The result was a simple and straightforward building, utilitarian in appearance and befitting its intention, to serve as a center for unpretentious education. RGW

NOTES
1. For background I have relied on Helen W. Ludlow, "The Hampton Normal and Agricultural Institute," *Harper's New Monthly Magazine* 47 (October 1873): 672–85; Francis Peabody, *Education for Life: The Story of Hampton Institute* (New York: Doubleday, 1918); and Thelma Robins Brown, "Memorial Chapel: The Culmination of the Development of the Campus of Hampton Institute, Hampton, Virginia, 1867–1887," M. A. thesis, University of Virginia, 1971.

2. The standard source on Hunt is Paul Baker, *Richard Morris Hunt* (Cambridge: MIT Press, 1980). See also Susan Stein, ed., *The Architecture of Richard Morris Hunt* (Chicago: The University of Chicago Press, 1986); and Montgomery Schuyler, "The Works of the Late Richard M. Hunt," in his *American Architecture and Other Writings*, W. Jordy and R. Coe, eds. (Cambridge: Harvard University Press, 1961): vol.2, 502–55.

# 57.
# YORKTOWN
# MONUMENT

*Perspective*

Yorktown
Architect's sketch, circa 1884
Signed lower right: *RMH* [Richard Morris Hunt]
Watercolor on paper, mounted on board; 37 ⅝ by 23 ¾ inches
Collection of the American Institute of Architects Foundation,
Washington, D.C., acc. no. 78.163

The excitement of construction, of seeing a creation that has existed only on paper or as a model finally begin to emerge, is a thrill seldom shown or noted in American architecture. And yet for an architect to see a dream take form, to watch the dismantling of the cranes, derricks, and scaffolding that have dominated the designer's creation, is a special event. Poets and writers sometimes note the drama of construction, but the creator's point of view has normally gone unrecorded. In this rare watercolor, Richard Morris Hunt perfectly captures the aesthetic of building, the pure functional forms of the construction site, and especially his excitement at its conclusion. Hunt, accompanied by the sculptor John Quincy Adams Ward, visited the site in August 1884 when the crowning figure of *Victory* was put in place and recorded the construction in a small pencil sketch.[1] Back in New York he worked up a larger watercolor, depicting himself in the lower right-hand corner. Here he has controlled the atmosphere so that the clouds have providentially parted to allow sun to stream down on the white marble monument to the American victory at Yorktown more than a hundred years before.

In 1781 Congress ordered a marble column to be erected at Yorktown, but the plan was never carried out. Consequently, on the eve of the centennial of the American (and French) victory over Cornwallis at Yorktown, Congress approved a new monument in June 1880 and appropriated $100,000 for its execution. In July 1880, the Secretary of War, Alexander Ramsey, asked the architects Richard Morris Hunt and Henry Van Brunt, and the sculptor John Quincy Adams Ward, to serve as a Commission for the Monument. By 1880 Hunt had become one of America's leading architects. Henry Van Brunt (and his partner William Robert Ware) of Boston had studied with Hunt in the late 1850s and had designed Memorial Hall at Harvard and other buildings.[2] John Quincy Adams Ward (1830–1910) was considered the "dean" of American sculptors in the years after the Civil War; Hunt designed bases or pedestals for many of his projects.

Rather than oversee a competition, the three artists decided to design the monument themselves and had it approved by a Joint Congressional Committee in March 1881. The cornerstone was laid in October 1881 with full Masonic rites, followed in the next few days by speeches by President Chester A. Arthur and others, an army and naval parade and review, with ex-presidents Grant and Hayes, several governors, the Supreme Court justices, and other notables in attendance. Construction dragged on the monument and the crowning figure was not set into place until August 12, 1884, when Hunt visited the site and did the watercolor. The unveiling took place on October 10, 1884.

As a collaboration between Hunt, Van Brunt, and Ward, several variations were submitted for the Victory figure at the top.[3] The basic form of a column surmounted by a figure draws on many precedents, from Trajan's column in Rome to the Victory Monument in Trafalgar Square, London. However, the elab-

oration of this basic form with the pedimented and inscribed podium, the sculpted drum, and the banded column, owes a debt to several contemporary French monuments. The *American Architect* published a plate of these designs next to a rendering of the Yorktown Monument in October 1881.[4] The Yorktown Monument had four parts: an elaborate podium with inscriptions of the siege, the alliance with France, and the peace; the drum containing thirteen female figures, to represent the original states, carved by Ward; the column, with bands of laurel wreaths and stars in high relief, and the composite capital with eagles in each of the four faces; and finally, the Victory figure, with arms outstretched. The total height was about one hundred and fifty feet.

Its remote location and the fact that the centennial of the surrender had taken place three years earlier conspired to leave the Yorktown Monument relatively unknown. But its elaborate and obvious symbolism were part of a growing sentiment to monumentalize America, to create an American Renaissance comparable with the earlier European Renaissance.    RGW

NOTES

1.   The small sketch is in the collection of the American Institute of Architects Foundation and is reproduced in Paul Baker, *Richard Morris Hunt* (Cambridge: MIT Press, 1980), fig. 77, see also 302–03. For other background material see: Lewis Sharp, *John Quincy Adams Ward: Dean of American Sculpture* (Newark: University of Delaware Press, 1985), 201–04; and Susan R. Stein, ed., *The Architecture of Richard Morris Hunt* (Chicago: University of Chicago Press, 1986): pl. 11, 117; 133–34.

2.   For illustrations, see Henry Van Brunt, *Architect and Society, Selected Essays of Henry Van Brunt,* W. Coles, ed. (Cambridge: Harvard University Press, 1969).

3.   Related materials, including drawings and photographs, can be found at the American Institute of Architects Foundation, Washington, D.C.; documents are kept at the National Archives, Washington, D.C.

4.   "Competitive Designs for a Monument Commemorative to the Constituent Assembly, to be erected at Versailles," and "The Design for the Yorktown Monument," *American Architect and Building News* 10, no. 303, (October 15, 1881) between pages 182 and 183; the French designs were taken from *Moniteur des Architects.*

# 58.
## RICHMOND
## CITY HALL

*Elevation*

1001 East Broad St., Richmond
Presentation elevation, circa 1886
Signed lower right: *E. E. Myers*
Ink on linen; 53 by 40 inches
Collection of The Valentine Museum, Richmond, Virginia

FIGURE 1. *Site photo of* **Richmond City Hall.** *(Photograph courtesy of Richard Cheek, Belmont, Massachusetts.)*

No drawing better illustrates the self-confidence and hubris of High Victorian architecture than this oversize rendering by Elijah E. Myers. Architects like Myers found American cities low-rise: two, three, and four stories in height; they left them as cities of towers, of exclamation points. In Richmond this was the first building to challenge the state capitol as the focus of the city; rising immediately behind it dwarfs Jefferson's temple. Although the building—with its rough-faced granite, vivid ornament, large corner tower and excited roof-line—gives the impression of picturesque asymmetry, the drawing illustrates that it was in reality a very rationally planned structure with symmetrical entrances and a logical floor plan. In sheer size, scale, and delineation of detail, Myers's rendering was intended to impress and it did, gaining for him one of the most controversial commissions of its time.

The erection of large and impressive civic buildings was a feature of late-nineteenth-century America. In Richmond, the City Council's concern over the safety of Richmond's old City Hall (constructed in 1816–18 after a design by Maxmilian Godefroy and Robert Mills), and its outmoded style, caused them in 1874 to order its demolition and replacement. However, economic and political circumstances brought a delay, and a competition was not held until 1883. Though Myers won, his plans were deemed to be too expensive, and after a series of disputes, he was discharged and a new competition ordered in 1885. After selecting a design by a Boston firm, the City Council again changed its mind, and in August 1886 reinstated Myers as the architect. Myers's new victory was owed in some manner to the recent election of a "reform" city government and, ironically, some influence-purchasing by agents on his behalf, which came out in a newspaper investigation. Myers also claimed that the new City Hall would cost less than $500,000; when construction was completed in 1894 the final tally was $1,369,588.43.[1]

"Colonel" (apparently the title was honorary) Elijah E. Myers of Detroit was one of the most successful High Victorian, or Gilded Age, architects; indeed his career and actions seem to sum up some of the unsavory aspects of that period. Born in Philadelphia, Myers learned architecture from the promient Samuel Sloan (1815–1884), and moved west during the 1860s, first to Springfield, Illinois, and then, in the 1870s, to Detroit. Charges of corruption, graft, cost overruns, and professional malfeasance followed Myers throughout his long and very profitable career. He was never a member of any professional architectural organizations, whose members loathed him. Yet Myers designed all types of buildings, from residential to commercial, but his specialty was public commissions: courthouses, city halls, hospitals, and especially state capitols. He was the architect for the capitols of Colorado, Texas, Michigan, and Idaho.[2]

Richmond City Hall is one of the best surviving examples of Myers's High Victorian Gothic style; he preferred Classical styles for state capitols. Built of James River granite and cast iron made in Richmond by Asa Snyder, the building is aggressive and solid in form and detail. Some elements, such as the tower, have direct European prototypes, especially the English Victorian architecture of Alfred Waterhouse.[3] Myers was not loathe to use similar designs for other buildings, and his contemporary Grand Rapids (Michigan) City Hall (1885) was a slightly reduced version of his Richmond design. This did not bother Richmond's citizens (if they even knew of it); the president of the Chamber of Commerce proclaimed at its dedication that the new City Hall represented "a standing advertisement to the world of our taste in architecture."[4]

RGW

NOTES

1. Dwight L. Young, "The Building of the Richmond City Hall, 1870–1894" (M. A. thesis, University of Virginia, 1976); and Marlene Elizabeth Heck, "The Politics of Architecture in the Gilded Age: The Practice of Elijah E. Myers" (M.A. thesis, University of Virginia, 1977). The Valentine has other drawings for this project. This drawing has been illustrated with commentary in: William B. O'Neal, *Architectural Drawing in Virginia*, exh. cat. (Charlottesville: School of Architecture, University of Virginia, 1969), 104–05; and Travis C. McDonald, *The Art of Architecture in Downtown Richmond, 1798–1989*, exh. cat. (Richmond: Second Presbyterian Church, 1989), 13–14.

2. Myers's career has not been fully documented, and as Paul Goeldner claimed in his 1976 unpublished paper, "Elijah E.Myers, Politics, Patronage and Professionalism," Myers's style "was a rare mixture of flamboyance and secrecy which can mislead scholars as it sometimes misleads clients." Commentary cited in "Proceedings of Thematic Sessions of the Twenty-ninth Annual Meeting of the Society of Architectural Historians," *Journal of the Society of Architectural Historians* 35 (December 1976): 285. See also, Paul Goeldner, "New Introduction & Commentary," in *Bicknell's Village Builder* (Watkins Glen: American Life Foundation & Study Institute, 1976 [1872]), unpaginated, which also contains seventeen of Myers's early designs. See also: Henry-Russell Hitchcock and William Seale, *Temples of Democracy: The State Capitols of the U. S. A.* (New York: Harcourt Brace Jovanovich, 1976).

3. Although there are notable differences, it is obvious that Myers had looked at Alfred Waterhouse's Manchester Town Hall, 1868–77, a mixture of English and French Gothic. See Roger Dixon and Stefan Muthesius, *Victorian Architecture* (London: Thames and Hudson, 1978), 166.

4. Quoted in *The State*, 16 February 1894, cited by Young,"Richmond City Hall": 3. Myers's Grand Rapids City Hall is illustrated in Constance M. Greiff, *Lost America: From the Atlantic to the Mississippi* (Princeton: Pyne Press, 1971), 35. Richmond built a new City Hall in 1972 and after a protracted preservation battle the old City Hall was adapted for use as an office building.

ALBERT ELLIS YARNALL, died 1928

WILLIAM DAVENPORT GOFORTH, 1866–1899

for

YARNALL & GOFORTH, Philadelphia, Pennsylvania

# 59.
## PROJECT FOR HOTEL ALTEMONTE

*Perspectives*

Staunton (unbuilt)
Presentation drawings, circa 1890, attributed to E[dward].
Eldon Deane
Inscribed lower right: *Yarnall & Goforth*
Ink on paper; each 15 ½ by 37 ½ inches
Collection of Historic Staunton Foundation, Staunton, Virginia

Pure fantasy, dreamland, and the Bavarian castles of Mad King Ludwig come to mind when looking at this extravagant project for Staunton. And certainly it was a dream, for although the Staunton Development Company published an aerial map of the town in 1891 showing the Hotel Altemonte as erected, ground was never broken and the hotel was never constructed. This sad fate was common to a number of grand schemes in the Shenandoah Valley during the late nineteenth century, however some projects did come to fruition as can be seen with the "grand" hotels built in Roanoke, Buena Vista, and Lexington.

While several east-west railroads had come into the Shenandoah Valley earlier, it was only in 1888 that the Valley was opened up. In that year the Shenandoah Railroad completed its line from Hagerstown, Maryland, through Waynesboro, Virginia, with connections to the Chesapeake and Ohio Railway, and terminating at Roanoke with the Norfolk and Western Railway. A land boom ensued and schemes were announced for more than a hundred projects of all types, from coal- and iron-producing company towns to resorts and the expansion of existing cities.[1]

The luster soon wore off the boom and the national depression of the 1890s laid most of the plans in an early grave. Common to many of the schemes was a large grand hotel that would promote the aspirations of the financial backers. One of the failures, the Staunton Development Company, projected great ideas for this hotel on its land in northeast Staunton.

The firm of Yarnall & Goforth of Philadelphia was formed by Albert Ellis Yarnall and William Davenport Goforth in 1890. Yarnall had studied drawing at the Franklin Institute in Philadelphia, then entered a building firm and rose to the position of chief designer. Goforth had studied architecture at the University of Pennsylvania between 1884 and 1886. Both partners were members of the Philadelphia T-Square Club. Much of their work was done for land development companies in Pennsylvania, Alabama, and Virginia. In Virginia they designed projects (few of which apparently were erected) in Goshen, Waynesboro, Charlottesville, Shendun, Hot Springs, Warm Springs, Harrisonburg, and other places.[2]

Better known though more enigmatic is the draftsman for these drawings, Edward Eldon Deane, whose work is one of the high points in American architectural delineation during the 1880s and 1890s. The upper drawing, the entrance perspective for the hotel, is signed with the draftsman's cipher, "ED." Apparently Deane was born in England; at least he took courses at the London Architectural Association. Deane worked in the Boston area in the 1880s producing eye-catching renderings for architects like H. H. Richardson and Peabody and Stearns, and working for the magazine *The American Architect and Building News*.[3] After he lived in New York in the late 1890s and 1900s, Deane can no longer be traced, although his hand is recorded in the brilliant presentation perspective for the Handley Library in Winchester, circa 1904 ( SURVEY NO. 66 ). His renderings for the

Hotel Altemonte are a tour-de-force of texture and incidents, for with a few pen lines he subtly indicated stone, brick, and shingles.[4]

As a design the Hotel Altemonte represents a synthetic eclecticism, an assimilation of a variety of different and very generalized sources treated in a free, or uncanonical manner. Such eclecticism, typical of a number of Philadelphia architects who clustered around the T-Square Club in the 1880s, reflects the influence of Wilson Eyre. The primary source for the Hotel Altemonte seems to be French, with its large towers and tourelles from chateaus used as picturesque exclamation points. The half-timbering and the bracing in the extended gables comes from Northern European vernacular buildings. The design has an accumulative character with different forms, roofs, and wall textures creating a panoramic picture. What it lacks in overall coherence it makes up for with its tremendous verve. While similar grand hotels were built elsewhere at nearly the same time—from Coronado, California, to Mohonk, New York—this one lived only on paper.[5]                      RGW

NOTES
1.    Stuart S. Sprague, "Investing in Appalachia: The Virginia Valley Boom of 1889–1893," *Virginia Cavalcade* 241 (Winter 1975):134–143.

2.    Sandra L. Tatman and Roger W. Moss, *The Biographical Dictionary of Philadelphia Architects: 1700–1930* (Boston: G. K. Hall Co, 1985), 310–311, 889–891.

3.    Eileen Michels, "Late Nineteenth-Century Published American Perspective Drawings," *Journal of the Society of Architectural Historians 31* (December 1972):302.

4.    A front perspective drawing also exists at the Historic Staunton Foundation.

5.    See Richard Guy Wilson, ed., *Victorian Resorts and Hotels* (Philadelphia: The Victorian Society, 1982).

"HOTEL ALTEMONTE"
to be erected.
ON THE GROUND OF THE STAUNTON DEVELOPMENT CO.
STAUNTON, VIRGINIA.

YARNALL & GOFORTH
ARCHITECTS
14 SOUTH BROAD ST. PHIL.

— HOTEL ALTEMONTE —
to be erected.
ON THE GROUND OF THE STAUNTON DEVELOPMENT, CO.
STAUNTON, VIRGINIA.

YARNALL & GOFORTH
ARCHITECTS
14 SOUTH, BROAD, ST. PHILA, PA.

# 60.
## PROJECT
## FOR A HOUSE

*Perspective*

Staunton or Augusta County (unbuilt)
Presentation drawing, circa 1891
Signed lower right: *T. J. Collins*
Watercolor and ink on paper; 19 ¾ by 27 inches
Collection of J. Joseph Johnson, Mt. Sidney, Virginia

T. J. Collins is inescapably associated with the city of Staunton where, for more than a hundred years he, his sons, and grandsons have been the reigning architectural dynasty. The range of their work mirrors the changing fashions of American architecture and reflects how popular currents were interpreted for small-town America.

Thomas Jasper Collins came from the Washington, D.C., area, where his family had been in construction since the 1790s. His grandfather, John Collins, had placed second in the White House competition of 1792 behind James Hoban. T. J. Collins served in the Union Army during the Civil War and then entered the family construction business. Between 1867 and 1883 Collins worked for the U.S. Postal Service as an engineer, and through this experience and the family construction business he decided to become an architect; by 1876 he listed himself as "architect" in the Washington, D.C., City Directory.[1] Hoping to profit from his governmental contacts, Collins, with a nephew, formed a building company in 1883 and secured a commission for a federal building in Kentucky. Mismanagement led to their losing the contract and Collins had to forfeit two houses he owned in Georgetown. Needing employment, he joined the Staunton Development Company as a draftsman in 1890, and moved to town (see SURVEY NO. 59). Discovering that the Company was insolvent, Collins—with another draftsman named Hackett—set up an architectural practice that lasted from 1891 to 1894. William M. Collins (1874–1953), a son by Collins's first marriage, joined his father shortly thereafter, and the firm name became T. J. Collins & Son. In 1906, Samuel J. Collins (1881–1953), a son by his second marriage who had been practicing in North Carolina, also joined the firm, followed in 1910 by T. J. Collins, Jr. (1891–1943) and even later by one more son, Harry J. Collins (1896–1968). Two grandsons, Richard E. Collins (born 1910) and J. Joseph Johnson, Jr. (born 1926), subsequently joined the firm, and the latter continues it today. Staunton and the Shenandoah Valley were the scene of intense economic development during the 1890s and 1900s, and the Collins firm profited.[2] When T. J. Collins retired in 1911, his firm had designed approximately two hundred commissions of all types. Their impact went beyond Staunton to the surrounding counties and included courthouses for Augusta County in Staunton (1900) and Rockingham County in Harrisonburg (1896); churches like St. Francis in Staunton (1895) and St. Peter's in Harpers Ferry, West Virginia (1895); as well as office buildings of all types and many houses. The Collins firm used a variety of architectural expressions ranging from Richardson Romanesque to Eastlake, Colonial Revival, and others. T. J. Collins's personal preference was for the more rugged and picturesque idioms. After the turn of the century, his sons' interests led the firm's designs toward the newer Classicism emanating out of New York and the Arts and Crafts Movement.

This brilliantly colored rendering for an unidentified house, apparently drawn by T. J. Collins himself, reveals his Picturesque sensibilities. Stylistically, it is a hybrid that, at the time, would have been labeled Queen Anne, Olde English, Eastlake, or Colonial. The first three of these stylistic idioms were English in origin and were hybrids themselves, using combinations of motives ranging from Medieval vernacular to late-seventeenth-century English red-brick Classicism, along with elements of oriental design. The uncanonial origins of these expressions were further diluted by transatlantic travel and their adaptation to American materials, construction conditions, and building types. Features like the large wrap-around porches or piazzas, and the Colonial details—as on the porch and the widow's walk—were pure Americanizations. The roof form contains many peaks and Jacobean chimneystacks. The smooth red brick of the walls is interrupted by half-timbering, molded brick, and terra-cotta panels in the chimney, shingles, and large oriel windows. Wooden spindles, brackets, columns, basket-weave panels, and other details add to the accumulative and synthetic character of the design. As a drawing it is compelling, and Collins built several houses in Staunton that are similar. The house is uniquely American suburban and intended for the upper middle class.

The probable source for the design is a pattern-book similar to those of Shoppell, Holly, or the Pallisers that Collins would have known. The difference between the high degree of competence in the handling of the perspective of the house and the naive and amateur treatment of the garden and drive may indicate that Collins copied or traced the design for the building out of a book and then added his own color and landscape.[3] Collins's drawing is a rarity for this period and style in American architecture, for apparently very few colored perspectives were used.　　　　RGW

NOTES
1.　　William T. Frazier, "T. J. Collins: A Local Virginia Architect and His Practice at the Turn of the Century" (Master of Architectural History thesis, University of Virginia), 1976, 5. I have relied for most of my data on this pioneering study, still the only one done on T. J. Collins and his sons, and also on interviews with T. J. Collins's grandson, J. Joseph Johnson, Jr.

2.　　Stuart S. Sprague, "Investing in Appalachia: The Virginia Valley Boom of 1889–1893," *Virginia Cavalcade* 24 (Winter 1975): 134.

3.　　The exact source for Collins's design has not been located, but similar houses appear in *Shoppell's Modern Houses*, a series of catalogues and portfolios published in the 1880s and reprinted as R. W. Shoppell, et al., *Turn-of-the-Century Houses, Cottages and Villas* (New York: Dover, 1983); and *Shoppell's Modern Houses* (Rockville Centre, N.Y.: Antiquity Reprints, 1983); Henry Hudson Holly, *Modern Dwellings in Town and Country* (New York: Harper & Brothers, 1878); and *Palliser's New Cottage Homes and Details* (1887; reprint, New York: Da Capo, 1975).

# 61.
## UNITED STATES POST OFFICE, ROANOKE

*Elevations*

Church Ave. at First St., Roanoke (demolished circa 1933)
Cabinet sketch, presentation elevation, 1893
Signed lower right: *Jeremiah O'Rourke, July 8, 1893*
Ink on paper; 18 ½ by 24 ½ inches
Collection of the National Archives, Washington, D.C.,
Record Group 121

Part of the reintegration of the South after Reconstruction was the building of federal courthouses and post offices in southern cities. Virginia received several of these: Danville, 1881; Harrisonburg and Lynchburg, 1885; Staunton and Roanoke, 1893. All were built under the auspices of the Office of the Supervising Architect of the Treasury, often a political appointment that changed rapidly in these years. Jeremiah O'Rourke occupied the Office of the Supervising Architect of the Treasury from April 1893 to early 1895.[1] Although his tenure was short he was responsible for a number of federal buildings in Taunton, Massachusetts; Buffalo and Newburgh, New York; and Kansas City, Missouri. O'Rourke's accession to the highest architectural office in the federal government illustrates the coming into power of a new ethnic group, the Irish. Born in Dublin, Ireland, O'Rourke was trained there in the Government School of Design, taking courses in painting, sculpture, and architecture. He emigrated to the United States in 1850 and established a practice in Newark, New Jersey, in 1856. In the course of his long career he designed many buildings, including a great number of Catholic churches.[2]

For the growing city of Roanoke, Virginia, O'Rourke's office produced this highly competent and compact design. Stylistically, his preference was for the medieval revivals, Gothic and Romanesque. The Roanoke design owed a debt to Henry Hobson Richardson's small suburban libraries like the Ames Memorial Library in North Easton, Massachusetts, or the Winn Library in Woburn, their horizontal massing opposed by a vertical tower. Equally Richardsonian are the banked windows over the entrance and in the gable. O'Rourke favored the Gothic arch over the Romanesque, however, and while his arches do resemble Richardson's round forms, still they have a slight point at their apex. Although not a large structure, the Roanoke Post Office did lend presence to the street with its large corner tower. Yet O'Rourke was swimming against the tide with a design such as this, for in the summer of 1893 the World's Columbian Exposition opened in Chicago and set in motion a new Classical Revival. Within a few years the Roanoke Post Office would look like the Dark Ages.                    RGW

NOTES
1.    There is no good overall study. See Darrell Hevenor Smith, *The Office of the Supervising Architect of the Treasury: Its History, Activities, and Organization* (Baltimore: Johns Hopkins Press, 1923); *History, Organization, and Functions of the Office of the Supervising Architect of the Treasury Department* R. H. Thayer, comp. (Washington, D. C.: Government Printing Office, 1886); and Bates Lowery, *Building a National Image: Architectural Drawings for the American Democracy, 1789–1912*, exh. cat. (Washington, D. C.: National Building Museum, 1985).

2.    Obituary, *Journal of the American Institute of Architects* 4 (1916): 267. See also Henry F. and Elsie Rathburn Withey, *Biographical Dictionary of American Architects (Deceased)* (Los Angeles: New Age, 1956), 449.

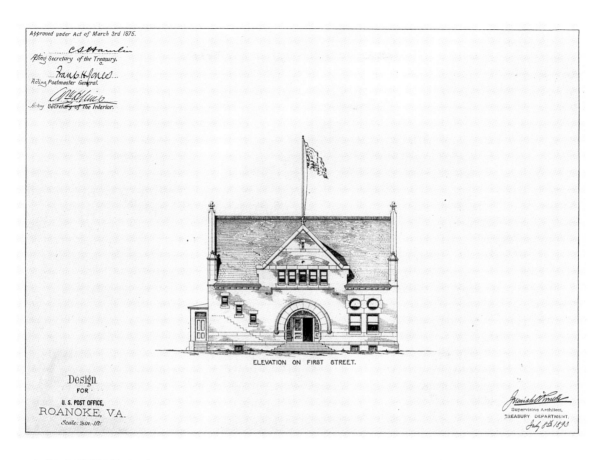

Approved under Act of March 3rd 1875.

*C S Hamlin*
Acting Secretary of the Treasury.

*Frank H Jones*
Acting Postmaster General.

*W M Sims*
Acting Secretary of the Interior.

ELEVATION ON FIRST STREET.

Design
FOR
U. S. POST OFFICE,
ROANOKE, VA.
Scale: ⅛ in.-1ft.

*Jeremiah O'Rourke*
Supervising Architect,
TREASURY DEPARTMENT.
July 8th 1893

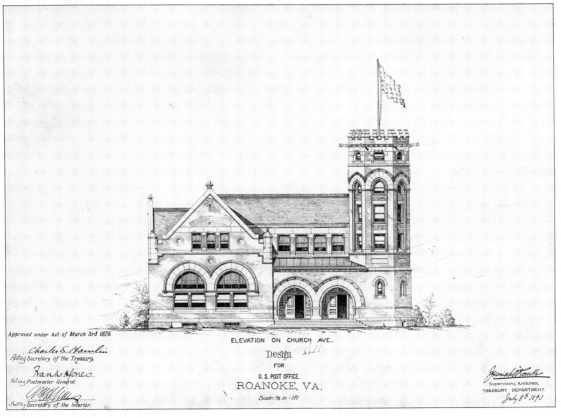

Approved under Act of March 3rd 1875.

ELEVATION ON CHURCH AVE.

*Charles S. Hamlin*
Acting Secretary of the Treasury.

*Frank H Jones*
Acting Postmaster General.

*W M Sims*
Acting Secretary of the Interior.

Design
FOR
U. S. POST OFFICE,
ROANOKE, VA.
Scale: ⅛ in.-1ft.

*Jeremiah O'Rourke*
Supervising Architect,
TREASURY DEPARTMENT.
July 8th 1893

JOHN MERVIN CARRERE, 1858–1911

THOMAS HASTINGS, 1860–1929

for

CARRERE & HASTINGS, New York

# 62.
# THE JEFFERSON HOTEL

*Section through Porte-Cochère*

Franklin and Jefferson Sts., Richmond
Working drawing, 1893
Inscribed and dated: *Drawing No. 261, November 10th, 1893,*
*Longitudinal Section through Porte-Cochère;* signed and
dated lower right: *Carrère & Hastings, Architects. 44 & 46*
*Broadway, New York.*
Ink on linen; 32 ½ by 40 inches
Collection of The Valentine Museum, Richmond, Virginia

The opulence of America's Gilded Age was given full play in the grand hotel commissioned by Richmond tobacconist Major Lewis Ginter. For its design, Ginter engaged the prestigious New York firm of Carrère & Hastings—a leading practitioner of the Beaux-Arts style specializing in hotels, churches, and estates—and charged the architects to provide the finest hostelry in the South. They met their task "working with freedom and enthusiasm in their personal Edwardian, eclectic manner."[1] Completed in 1895, the building is an architectural extravaganza, exhibiting an exuberance seldom seen in commercial buildings. Built of a pearly white brick with white terra-cotta Classical decorations and granite details, the building's towers, loggias, and pavilions are reminiscent of Rome's Villa Medici. The magnificent interior, with its regal progression of public rooms, was complemented by such advanced technological devices as service telephones, electric lighting, central heating, and hot and cold running water for each of its 342 guest rooms. A fire destroyed the central and south portions of the building in 1901, but it was sympathetically rebuilt in 1907 by Norfolk architect J. Kevan Peebles, who replaced the original glass-and-iron court with the present Edwardian Baroque lobby and its famous grand stair.

The drawing shown here, of a detail of the hotel's porte-cochère is evidence that by the end of the nineteenth century the practice of architecture had entered the Modern Age. No longer was the architect a lone artist producing a plan and an elevation or two, letting the contractor deal with construction and details. At its height, a large New York firm such as Carrère & Hastings would have up to a hundred employees, including architects, draftsmen, engineers, accountants, and clerks. Every feature of construction and decoration would be painstakingly drawn, usually in ink on linen, and then be reproduced in blueprints for on-site use by the various contractors. Many individual elements such as a piece of carving would be drawn full-size so that every nuance of contour and proportion could be completely understood. Although the firm's principals normally oversaw all aspects of the design, the delineator of this drawing most likely was among the firm's many now-anonymous draftsmen.

For a building of the scale and elaboration of the Jefferson,[2] hundreds of drawings were required, in this case more than five hundred. Two hundred and sixty drawings had been produced by the time the masonry details of the porte-cochère were considered. Since this was a construction drawing, it is covered with notes, instructions, and dimensions. Of particular interest is the notation giving the Perth Amboy as the source for the bricks. That it was used on site is confirmed by the fact that it was found among a barrel of nearly two hundred drawings and blueprints stored in the hotel basement just prior to its restoration in the 1980s. Such was truly a fortunate discovery since the archives of Carrère & Hastings have been destroyed, and very few of their drawings survive.[3]

John Mervin Carrère and Thomas Hastings both studied at the Ecole des Beaux-Arts, Paris, and both began their professional careers in the New York offices of McKim, Mead & White. In 1884 they decided to begin architectural practice together and formed the partnership of Carrère & Hastings. Their first important client was Henry M. Flagler, developer of Florida's east coast, for whom they designed a number of buildings in St. Augustine, including the Hotel Ponce de Leon and the Alcazar Hotel. Among the most conspicuous of the firm's extraordinary output are the New York Public Library (commissioned 1897, completed 1911) and the House and Senate office buildings (completed 1905 and 1906) in Washington, D.C., both in a restrained Classical idiom sharply contrasting with their more festive luxury hotels.          CCL

NOTES
1.    William B. O'Neal, *Architecture in Virginia* (New York: Walker & Company, 1968), 35.

2.    Although the drawing is titled "Jefferson Hotel," the name by which the building has been known historically is The Hotel Jefferson.

3.    The Hotel Jefferson drawings were donated to the Valentine Museum in June 1990 by R.W.S. Partners, principal owners of the hotel.

REFERENCES
Howland, Richard Hubbard. "Echoes of a Gilded Epoch." *Arts in Virginia* 5 (Fall 1964): 2–9.

Loth, Calder, ed. *The Virginia Landmarks Register*, 3rd ed. Charlottesville: University Press of Virginia, 1987, p. 373.

O'Neal, William B. *Architecture in Virginia*. New York: Walker & Company, Inc., 1967, p. 35.

Withey, Henry F., and Withey, Elsie Rathburn. *Biographical Dictionary of American Architects (Deceased)*. Los Angeles: Hennessey & Ingals, Inc., 1970, pp. 109–10, 269–70.

"The Works of Carrere & Hastings." *Architectural Record* 27 (Jan 1910): 1–120.

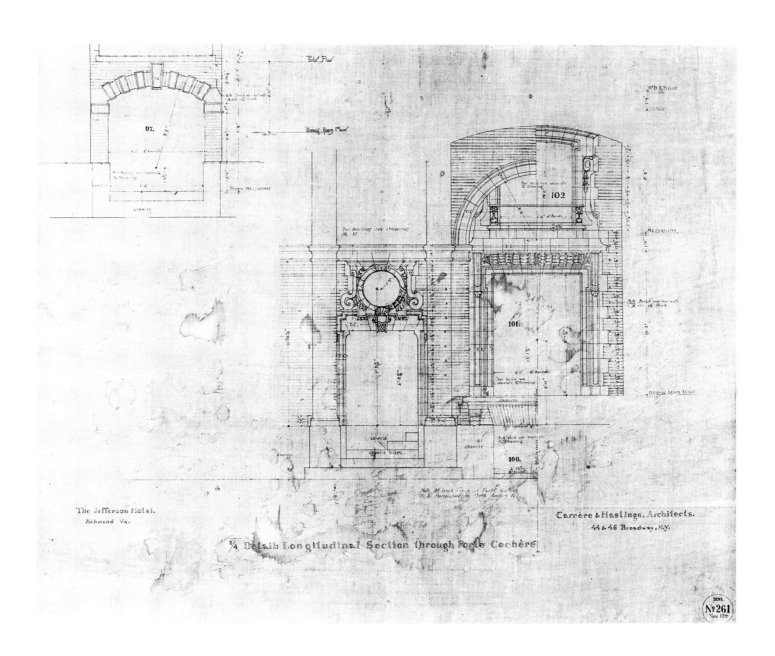

97.

102.

101.

100.

The Jefferson Hotel.
Richmond Va.

Carrère & Hastings, Architects.
44 & 46 Broadway, N.Y.

¾ Detail: Longitudinal Section through Porte Cochère

Nº 261

# 63.
## RESTORATION OF ROTUNDA

*University of Virginia*
*Front [North] Elevation*

Charlottesville
Working drawing, 1896
Inscribed lower center: *McKim, Mead & White*; signed and
dated, lower right: *[William J.] Haase, April 9, 1896*
Blueprint transfer with watercolor on linen;
26 ½ by 32 ¼ inches
Collection of the University of Virginia Library, Charlottesville,
the University Archives

Although one speaks of Jefferson's composition for the University of Virginia as "The Lawn," and his concept was a spacious, small village, the prime symbol and centerpiece was always the library or the Rotunda. Hence when the Rotunda burned on October 27, 1895, there was never any question but that it should be restored to approximately its original shape as designed by Jefferson. Not to be restored was the much-despised and ugly addition designed by Robert Mills in 1850, located on the north side, where the fire had started. Since Jefferson's original design a great reorientation had taken place with "the grounds" (as the campus is called). A new, formal entry from the north and off of the major east-west highway was needed. But how this was to be undertaken and by whom brought forth controversy. Initially it was up to the University Rector to hire the architects, McDonald Brothers and the Spooner Construction Company, both of Louisville, Kentucky. Unfortunately, their proposal was uninspired and when some preliminary construction was found faulty, the University leaders were persuaded to look elsewhere. John Kevan Peebles, a University alumnus and Norfolk architect (and designer of Fayerweather Hall, 1893), appears to have given some advice and helped persuade the University Rector, W. C. N. Randolph, to contact McKim, Mead & White of New York.[1]

McKim, Mead & White, comprised of Charles Follen McKim (1847–1909), William R. Mead (1846–1928), and Stanford White (1853–1906), were the leading architects in America in their time. From their first work in the late 1870s and early 1880s designing shingle-covered and Colonial Revival "cottages" in Newport, Rhode Island, and other watering-spots of the wealthy, they had progressed toward an architecture based on Italian Renaissance, Roman, Georgian, and other Classical precedents. Enriched with murals and sculpture, the firm's Villard houses (1882–86) and Metropolitan Club (1891–94), both in New York; the Boston Public Library (1887–95) with decoration added until 1917; and scores of other buildings, seemed to indicate that America was experiencing a Renaissance equivalent to that of the Old World.[2] The firm knew well the work of Jefferson; McKim had been asked to design a seal for the University in 1890 and apparently had visited the area in the spring of 1895.[3] Stanford White was in the office when the telegram arrived asking their participation, and he had readily agreed to become the main designer on the project for the firm.[4] White's architectural training had been in the office of H. H. Richardson; he had not attended the Ecole des Beaux-Arts as had McKim.[5] Although White's personal style tended toward elaborate—and flamboyant—ornamental excess in contrast to McKim's restraint, White's designs for The Rotunda and the Cabell, Cocke, and Rouss Hall additions at the end of the Lawn are notably restrained and show McKim's influence. (Garrett Hall and Carr's Hall were also designed by the firm, but after White's death.) White balked at placing buildings across the end of the Lawn and closing Jefferson's original

entrance and vista and so drew up an alternative. However, the University Building Committee directed their placement to screen unsightly development.[6]

For the Rotunda, White essentially duplicated Jefferson's original on the south—Lawn—facade, and then on the north designed a new shallow portico and basement wing, which was connected along the sides by colonnades and terraces to the original south wing. On the interior a Gustavino vaulted dome replaced Jefferson's Delorme system, and the upper floor of the library was eliminated to create a dramatic, well-like space. A Corinthian order duplicating the south portico was used on the new north portico which, with a steep flight of steps, created a new monumental entrance to The University. The drawing, by one of White's assistants, William J. Haase, was intended to convey through size and level of detail some of the intended effect.[7]                                    RGW

NOTES

1.   The University had considered Carrère & Hastings, J. Stewart Barney (of Barney and Chapman), and Shepley, Rutan & Coolidge. The basic story of the rebuilding is George Humphrey Yetter's "Stanford White at the University of Virginia: The New Buildings on the South Lawn and the Reconstruction of the Rotunda in 1896" (M. A. thesis, University of Virginia, 1980). See also his "Stanford White at the University of Virginia: Some New Light on an Old Question," *Journal of the Society of Architectural Historians* 40 (December 1981): 320–25; and William B. O'Neal, *Pictorial History of the University of Virginia* (Charlottesville: University Press of Virginia, 1968).

2.   See Richard Guy Wilson, Dianne Pilgrim, and Richard Murray, *The American Renaissance, 1876–1917* (Brooklyn and New York: The Brooklyn Museum and Pantheon, 1979); Richard Guy Wilson, *McKim, Mead & White, Architects* (New York: Rizzoli, 1983); Leland Roth, *McKim, Mead & White, Architects* (New York: Harper & Row, 1983).

3.   Letter from McKim to William M. Thornton (Chairman of Faculty), August 6, 1890, McKim, Mead & White Collection, The New-York Historical Society; and letter from McKim to Augustus Saint-Gaudens, May 6, 1895, McKim Collection, Library of Congress.

4.   Telegrams from White to William M. Thornton and to W. C. N. Randolph, January 22, 1896, in The New-York Historical Society.

5.   On White, see Charles Baldwin, *Stanford White* (New York: Dodd, Mead, 1931), and Paul R. Baker, *Stanny: The Gilded Life of Stanford White* (New York: The Free Press, 1989).

6.   A few weeks before his death White actually submitted some sketches for the President's house, Carr's Hall; however the design was later modified considerably. Materials relating to the work and alternative designs are in the University Archives, University of Virginia Library.

7.   Other drawings for the Rotunda and other structures on the campus are kept at the University Archives and at The New-York Historical Society. A duplicate drawing appeared in William B. O'Neal, *Architectural Drawing in Virginia, 1819–1969*, exh. cat. (Charlottesville: School of Architecture, University of Virginia; and Richmond: Virginia Museum of Fine Arts, 1969), 117 and 120–21. In addition to Haase, apparently a draftsman who specialized in large linens, White was assisted by Bert Fenner and William Mitchell Kendall in the design phase, while Theodore H. Skinner was the job captain in Charlottesville.

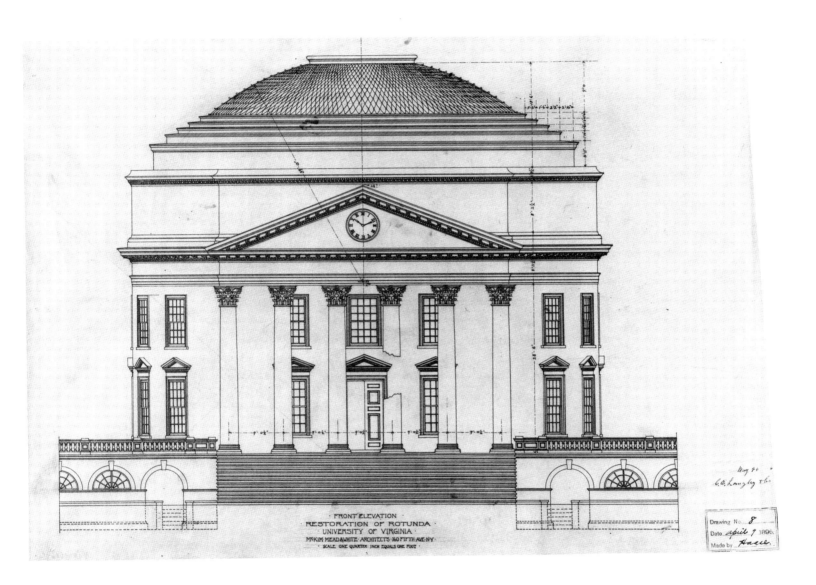

FRONT ELEVATION
RESTORATION OF ROTUNDA
UNIVERSITY OF VIRGINIA
McKIM MEAD & WHITE ARCHITECTS · 160 FIFTH AVE · NY ·
SCALE ONE QUARTER INCH EQUALS ONE FOOT

Drawing No. 8
Date April 7 1896
Made by Hart.

# 64.
# CATHEDRAL
# OF THE
# SACRED HEART

*Interior Sections*

Monroe Park at Floyd and Laurel Sts., Richmond
Presentation drawing, 1902
Signed and dated lower right: *J.L.C.; September 2, 1902,*
with subsequent revisions
Ink on linen; 23 ½ by 42 ½ inches
Collection of The Valentine Museum, Richmond, Virginia

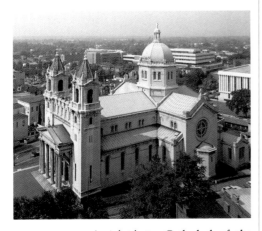

FIGURE 1. *Aerial photo,* **Cathedral of the Sacred Heart,** *Richmond.*

Richmond's prominently sited, monumental, and lavish Sacred Heart Cathedral, dedicated in 1906, is a sectarian, social, and aesthetic anomaly. Although largely accepted by their Protestant neighbors, Virginia's Catholics in the nineteenth century were generally few in number, of modest means, and concentrated in the Norfolk, Portsmouth, and Martinsburg areas. Upon the request of Norfolk's Catholics, Rome established Virginia as a diocese in 1820, but designated Richmond as the seat of the diocese in spite of Richmond's small and relatively poor Catholic population.[1] A cathedral and episcopal residence were not established in Richmond until 1841, when the city's first Catholic church, St. Peter's (1834) at Eighth and Grace streets, along with a private residence nearby, were adopted to serve that function. Construction of a more appropriate cathedral and episcopal residence was first proposed in 1867, but the site at Monroe Park was not completely secured until 1886. A shortage of funds prevented further work on the project until 1901, when Thomas Fortune Ryan and his wife Ida offered to fund the project's entire cost.[2] The Cathedral's design expresses many personal and social factors: Ryan's wealth, the Parisian training of its architect, the Roman domination of American Catholicism following papal condemnation of American Catholic liberalism in 1899, and the distinctive character of American Catholic architecture.[3] The design does not express the peripheral social status of most Virginia Catholics in the nineteenth century, nor does it acknowledge the state's highly developed Classical architectural heritage.

Ryan (1851–1928), born in poverty in Nelson County, Virginia, was a self-made man who became one of New York City's wealthiest and most controversial business tycoons.[4] Ryan owned controlling interests in American Tobacco Company; Equitable Life Assurance Association; gold, copper and diamond mines in the Congo; and the street railway and lighting systems of New York and Chicago. The Ryans' prodigious philanthropy included more than 20 million dollars given to various Catholic institutions. Their architectural patronage in Virginia included additions to Oakridge, their Nelson County residence (circa 1909), expansion of the Lynchburg Hospital (1905), murals in Richmond's Battle Abbey Memorial (1921), Sacred Heart Parish church in Richmond (1901), and the Cathedral project (1901–1906). The Cathedral of the Sacred Heart is credited as being the only cathedral ever "constructed by the sole munificence of one family."[5]

The training of New York architect Joseph Hubert McGuire, the Cathedral's designer, was typical of American Renaissance designers, including study in New York and at the Ecole des Beaux-Arts, Paris (1888–1891).[6] Like other Americans who attended the Ecole, McGuire was active in the American Institute of Architects and the Society of Beaux-Arts Architects, and designed numerous monumental public and private buildings in a variety of historical styles during his fifty years in practice, from 1892 to 1940. Many were Catholic churches and institutional buildings. His obituary identifies Richmond's Cathedral as one of his major accomplishments.[7]

The Cathedral was constructed of the elegant materials favored by American Renaissance designers. American Renaissance bravura and Ryan's generosity are especially evident in the portico's monumental fluted Corinthian columns, the nave arcade's monolithic marble columns, deep vault paneling, wrought iron grillwork, brass bas-relief tableaux, mosaic and terrazzo floors, chandeliers, and pipe organ. The facade design, a synthesis of Gothic verticality with Antique, Renaissance, and Baroque Classical forms, revives a favorite theme of early-nineteenthcentury French Academic architectural theory. The design's symmetry, twin-towered facade, numerous references to Mediterranean architecture, and coursed dressed-faced ashlar masonry stand as a distinctly Roman Catholic expression. This Roman and American Catholic character is especially noticeable in its context, that of a Protestant and secular Virginia, with its highly refined, classically rooted architectural heritage.

This drawing's high numerical pagination (76), early original dating, and subsequent revisional datings suggest that its purpose was to convey initially to the client, and then to the contractor, the relationship between the Cathedral's horizontal and vertical components; its foundation, vaulting, and roof construction; and its interior and exterior finishes and ornamentation.[8] Except for his initials, the draftsman in McGuire's office has remained anonymous. The high quality of this drawing is typical of American office production in the early twentieth century. MEG

NOTES
1. Francis Joseph Magri, *The Catholic Church in the City and Diocese of Richmond* (Richmond: Whittet and Shepperson, 1906). Prominent Catholics such as Joseph Gallego, founder of the Gallego Flour Mills, and Anthony Keiley, Richmond's mayor and editor of the *Richmond Examiner* during the 1870s, were exceptions within nineteenth-century Richmond's largely labor- and merchant-class Catholic population. A substantial increase in Virginia's Catholic population did not occur until after World War II.

2. The Ryan donation, just under $500,000, paid for the Cathedral, its furnishings, the Episcopal residence and Rectory, which were all connected by an arcade enclosing a garden.

3. Thomas T. McAvoy C.S.C., *The Great Crisis in American Catholic History: 1895–1900* (Chicago: Henry Regnery,1957).

4. Max Lerner, "Thomas Fortune Ryan," *Dictionary of American Biography* (New York: Scribner's, 1963), 8: 265–68.

5. Magri, *The Catholic Church,* 10.

6. See Richard Guy Wilson, Dianne Pilgrim, and Richard Murray, *The American Renaissance, 1876–1917* (Brooklyn and New York: The Brooklyn Museum and Pantheon, 1979) and Arthur Drexler, ed., *The Architecture of the Ecole Des Beaux-Arts* (New York: Museum of Modern Art, 1977).

7. Obituary: *New York Times,* November 24, 1928, and Francis W. Kervick, *Architects in America of Catholic Tradition* (Rutland, VT: Charles E. Tuttle, 1962), 92.

8. Correspondence between McGuire and the Cathedral's bishop at that time, Rt. Rev. Augustine Van De Vyver, in the archives of the Diocese of Richmond, reveals the project's construction contract was signed in 1903 and suggests that McGuire's involvement with the project ended in 1907.

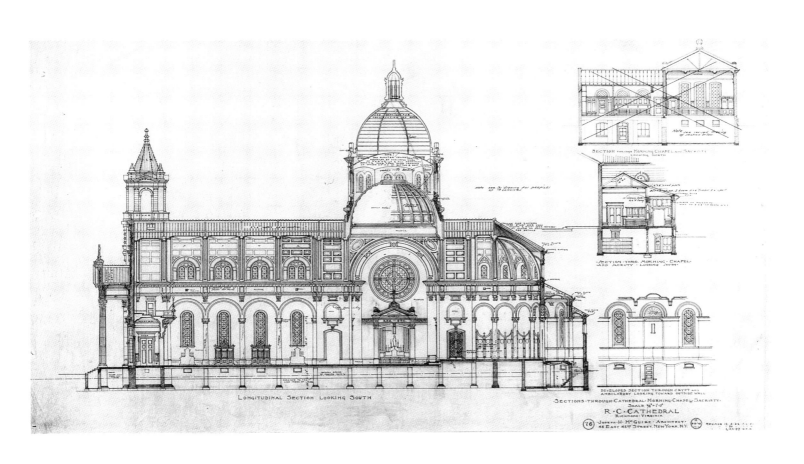

LONGITUDINAL SECTION LOOKING SOUTH

SECTIONS THROUGH CATHEDRAL MORNING CHAPEL & SACRISTY
SCALE ⅛" = 1'-0"
R·C·CATHEDRAL
RICHMOND·VIRGINIA

JOSEPH·H·McGUIRE·ARCHITECT·
45 EAST 42ND STREET, NEW YORK, N.Y.

# 65.
## NEWPORT NEWS BAPTIST CHURCH

*(First Baptist Church)*
*Perspective*

29th St. at Washington, Newport News
Presentation drawing, 1902
Signed lower right: *W. M. Campbell* and *R. H. Hunt Architect*
Watercolor and ink on brown paper; 35 ½ by 27 ½ inches
Collection of First Baptist Church, Newport News

FIGURE 1. *Site photo,* **Newport News Baptist Church.**

Reuben H. Hunt of Chattanooga, Tennessee, designed three large Baptist churches in the Hampton Roads area in the early twentieth century: the First Baptist (a black congregation) on Bute Street in Norfolk, 1904–06; the one on Court Street in Portsmouth, 1903; and the Newport News Baptist Church in 1902 to 1903. All three draw upon the Romanesque Revival style developed by H. H. Richardson and are built of similar rough-faced pink New England granite; all have similar massing, with tall corner towers and a broad nave. The architectural imagery of the Romanesque that had been developed by Richardson, most notably for the Episcopalian Trinity Church, Boston (1872–77), and other public buildings such as the Allegheny County Courthouse in Pittsburgh (1883–88), had fallen into disfavor in the cosmopolitan centers of New York and Boston by the turn of the century. However in more provincial areas, such as the South and the Midwest, reinterpretations of Richardson's Romanesque—drawing upon the Southern French—still found great favor and became especially associated with preaching denominations: Baptist, Presbyterian, and Methodist.

The architect Reuben H. Hunt, in his circular printed in 1907, claimed designs for sixty churches in Georgia, Kentucky, Alabama, Mississippi, Arkansas, Louisiana, North and South Carolina, and Tennessee.[1] The majority were for the denominations cited above, with only two Episcopal churches, one Catholic church, and two Jewish synagogues appearing. His position for many years as chairman of the board of deacons of the largest Baptist church in Chattanooga certainly helped him in obtaining these commissions, as did his location in Chattanooga, a major railroad center for the South.

Hunt was born in Georgia and had learned architecture while working for an architecture and construction firm in Chattanooga. He set up a partnership in 1886, and by 1892 he had set up his own firm, R. H. Hunt and Company. Known for his political acumen, Hunt soon established branch offices in Jackson, Mississippi, and Dallas, Texas, that specialized in churches and civic, school, and commercial buildings. Stylistically Hunt was conservative, following broad national trends and, besides Richardson Romanesque after the turn of the century, he adopted various forms of Classicism. Widely known in the South, Hunt was virtually ignored by the Northern architectural press, though obviously he followed it closely.

By 1902 First Baptist Church of Newport News, Virginia, had a new pastor, the Reverend J. W. Porter, D.D., whose sermons were drawing capacity audiences. The church had been established in 1881, shortly after Collis P. Huntington chose the city as the eastern deepwater terminus of the Chesapeake and Ohio Railway, turning a small farming community into a major port city. The First Baptist congregation had occupied a small brick building on Twenty-Ninth Street that was demolished to make way for the new edifice. The cornerstone for the new church was laid in 1902 with great ceremony. As a contemporary account explained, "The local Masons and Hampton

Commandery Knights Templar, headed by the Old Point Band, were out in regalia."[2] The church was completed and dedicated in time for Christmas, 1903. The cost was approximately $50,000. Two years later, in January 1906, a great portion of the new church was consumed by fire; only the thick masonry walls survived. A portion of the old walls were used in the rebuilding, which was completed by May 1907.

The beautiful rendering for the 1902 structure was apparently done in Hunt's Chattanooga office. The delineator, W. M. Campbell, is unknown, but he has successfully adopted the atmospheric style developed by Hughson Hawley in New York. The requisite "girl in a red dress" appears, as do luminous clouds. The rendering indicates that the church was to be constructed of a relatively smooth-faced ashlar; however, during the rebuilding after the fire, pink Maine granite was laid up with a rough face. While the broad high roof and large front gable recall Richardson's consolidation of form, the various pointed roofs and the exuberant tower are more picturesque and indicate a creative departure. The tower's flamboyant corner tourelles probably owe more to the drawings of Harvey Ellis, an extremely popular draftsman whose work appeared extensively in architectural periodicals in the 1890s.[3] As rebuilt, the tower was considerably tamed and the tourelles shortened. The treatment of the three porch arches, as shown both in the rendering and as built, is much simpler and more austere than in any Richardson building. Their thin linearity recalls the earlier Romanesque or Italianate of the 1850s and 1860s, and overall the exterior lacks the embellishment typical of Richardson.

One feature the rendering does not reveal is the versatile and spacious interior. The large rose window in the front gable lights one side of a large auditorium, with the baptistry located to the right rear. The first floor of the auditorium seated 450, the gallery 250, and the rear wall then had a large door which could be lifted to open the Sunday-school room, which seated 500, giving an overall capacity of 1,200. The interior was plain, executed in quarter-sawn white oak.[4] RGW

NOTES
1. Advertisement, "R. H. Hunt Architect," *Chattanooga Star,* August 31, 1907; entry on Hunt in *The National Cyclopedia of Biography*; and obituary, "Noted Architect, R. H. Hunt is Dead," *The Chattanooga Times,* May 29, 1937, sec. 1: 6–7. For additional information on Hunt I have relied on materials supplied by Robert Franklin, of Selmon T. Franklin Associates, Architects, Inc. (successor to the firm of R. H. Hunt); Gavin Townsend, Department of Art, University of Tennessee at Chattanooga, who is preparing a study on Hunt; and Professor Martin A. Davis, Clemson University, who is also preparing a study on Hunt and kindly lent me his paper "The Eclectic Architecture of Reuben Harrison Hunt," Southeast Chapter Society of Architectural Historians, presented in Tuscaloosa, Alabama, November 1–2, 1986.

2. *The Times* of Richmond, Virginia, 8 November 1902, quoted in Lewis Peyton Little, *History of the First Baptist Church of Newport News Virginia from 1883 to 1933* (Newport News: Franklin Printing Company, 1936), 125.

3. Jean France, *A Rediscovery-Harvey Ellis: Artist, Architect,* exh. cat. (Rochester: Memorial Art Gallery of the University of Rochester and Margaret Woodbury Strong Museum, 1972).

4. In 1917 the name was changed to the First Baptist Church of Newport News. A large educational building was added in 1930. By the mid 1950s the downtown area of Newport News was in decline, and by the mid 1970s a satellite ministry was begun that by the mid 1980s became the main church. In 1988 the downtown church was closed and put up for sale.

R.H. HUNT, ARCHITECT.
CHATTANOOGA, TENN.

J[JAMES]. STEWART BARNEY, 1869–1924

for

BARNEY & CHAPMAN, New York

# 66.
# HANDLEY LIBRARY

*Perspective*

Braddock and Piccadilly Sts., Winchester
Presentation drawing, circa 1904
Signed lower left: *E. Eldon Deane*
Watercolor and ink on paper, mounted on canvas and
stretcher; 23 ½ by 29 ½ inches
Collection of Handley Library, Winchester, Virginia

FIGURE 1. *Site photo,* **Handley Library,** *Winchester.*

The Handley Library is the result of a bequest of Judge John Handley (1835–1895) to the city of Winchester. Born in Ireland, Handley came to the United States in 1854 and prospered in coal, banking, and real estate in Scranton, Pennyslvania. He began visiting Winchester, Virginia, in the 1870s and became enamored with the area and the myth of the Old South. In his will he left a large sum to the town for the erection of schools and a library.[1] In 1902 the Handley Board of Trustees purchased land near the center of town at a major intersection and began searching for an architect. They selected J. Stewart Barney of New York and in May 1904 preliminary plans were approved, although bids for construction and working drawings were not complete until December 1906.[2] The cornerstone was laid on May 28, 1908, in an elaborate Masonic ceremony, and the library was opened to the public on August 21, 1913.

Barney had a substantial reputation and his work was regularly illustrated and noted in the architectural press. He trained in the office of George B. Post and then attended architecture school at Columbia University before setting up practice in New York in the early 1890s. He entered into partnership with Henry Otis Chapman (1863–1929) around 1894, but Barney remained the head designer. That his name appears alone on some of the drawings for the Handley Library indicates that it was his project. He retired prior to World War I and went to Paris, where he studied painting and gained a reputation as a landscapist.[3] Montgomery Schuyler, one of the best known critics, considered Barney a leading architect and praised him for his Gothic "temperament," though he noted Barney's work was so wide-ranging as to be "eclectic."[4] Barney himself wrote and condemned the recent American infatuation with Beaux-Arts design methods and especially the quickly drawn plan. He claimed that an American "National Style" could not come from importation but from internal sources.[5] While Barney as a writer sounded relatively progressive, his work as an architect was stylistically based, and he designed in American Colonial, Italian and French Renaissance, and various forms of English and French Gothic. His All Saint's Church (demolished) and Grace and Holy Trinity Church, both in Richmond, are examples of his very original Gothic, while the Hart Memorial Library in Troy, New York, resembles a Roman Renaissance *palazzo.*

At first glance the Handley Library seems to belie some of Barney's writings, for it is Classical with some Beaux-Arts elements. The most apparent element is the large triple-arched entrance portico, which recalls the almost contemporary portico of the New York Public Library. Barney's unconventional temperament, however, is shown in the placement of the entrance at the corner, not the more usual *palazzo*-type front. This placement allows the building to relate to several adjacent structures and orients it to the center of town. So while Handley Library is a monumental structure—indeed far beyond anything else in Winchester—it is a design that understands its specific context. Certainly very French are the dome and the elaborate sculptural program. Robust and very active sculptures cover the side entrances. Yet there is a non-doctrinaire feeling to the sculpture and to the entire building; it is not reminiscent of any historical prototype but rather a very original solution. Frequently interpreted as Beaux-Arts is the elaborate rendering by E. Eldon Deane (compare SURVEY NO. 59), a type of flashy drawing that Barney would condemn in an article a few years later.[6] Deane however, was English, not French, and in spite of any reservations Barney may have had about it, the rendering succeeded, for it won him the commission. The library as completed lacks some of the sculptural embellishment that appears in the drawing, but remains nonetheless one of Virginia's most spectacular buildings of the twentieth century.                                              RGW

NOTES

1.  Background information can be found in Garland R. Quarles, *John Handley and The Handley Bequests to Winchester, Virginia* (Winchester: The Farmers and Merchants National Bank, 1969); the bequest was originally for schools for the poor, but this was changed to a public school system in 1918.

2.  Working drawings are in the Handley Archives Room. They are variously signed "J. Stewart Barney, Arch." and "Barney & Chapman, Architects."

3.  Obituary, *The Journal of the American Institute of Architects* 14 (January 1926): 46.

4.  Montgomery Schuyler, "The Work of Messrs. Barney and Chapman," *Architectural Record* 14 (September, 1904): 203–96, see especially 233 and 248; and Montgomery Schuyler, "Recent Church Building in New York," *Architectural Record* 13 (June 1903): 508–34.

5.  J. Stewart Barney, "The Ecole des Beaux Arts, Its Influence on Our Architecture," and "Our National Architecture Will Be Established on Truth Not Tradition," *Architectural Record* 22 and 24 (November 1907 and November 1908): 333–42 and 381–86.

6.  Barney, "Our National Architecture," 386.

NOLAND & BASKERVILL, Richmond

FRYE & CHESTERMAN, Lynchburg

JOHN KEVAN PEEBLES, Norfolk

# 67.
# VIRGINIA STATE CAPITOL

*Additions and Reconstruction
Perspective*

Capitol Square, Richmond
Presentation drawing, circa 1904
Watercolor and ink on board; 24 ¾ by 40 inches (by sight)
Collection of Richard P. Hankins, Richmond

FIGURE 1. *Aerial photo,* **Virginia Capitol Building,** *Richmond.*

In the years between 1890 and 1914 many state governments became preoccupied with either the construction of large new capitols or the significant remodeling and expansion of existing ones. Among the reasons was the tremendous expansion in state bureaucracy and governmental functions. Equally important was a belief common to the spirit of the American Renaissance of the period that large, impressive edifices would inspire civic virtue and decorum. A rivalry existed between different states as a building binge took place and new or vastly expanded capitols were built across the country, from Rhode Island to Washington, and from Texas to Minnesota. In their study of state capitols, Henry-Russell Hitchcock and William Seale noted: "No capitol in the United States went unaffected by the American Renaissance."[1]

The Virginia State Capitol, designed by Thomas Jefferson (see SURVEY NOS. 9, 10), had not weathered the nineteenth century well. Maintenance had been deferred and the interior had been cut up. The historical associations connected with the old building mitigated against its complete replacement, though even that extreme measure had its advocates. Beginning in 1895 every governor's annual message to the General Assembly included a plea for rebuilding and new quarters. Governor A. J. Montague (1862–1937) wrote in February 1902: "The condition of the Capitol Building is a reproach to the State."[2] The Governor's message found a receptive ear and the Assembly made an appropriation of $100,000 for restoration and enlargement, with the proviso that "there be no alteration in the general design of this historic building any further than may be necessary."[3] A five-member Capitol Building Commission announced a competition for May 1902 and invited all Virginia firms and five out-of-state firms—McKim, Mead & White of New York; Paul J. Pelz, and W. M. Poindexter, both of Washington, D.C.; Frank P. Milburn of Columbia, South Carolina; and George F. Barber of Knoxville, Tennessee—to submit drawings. None of them responded. The commission then interviewed six firms who did submit plans: Philip T. Marye of Newport News, D. Wiley Anderson, M. J. Dimmock, and Noland & Baskervill, all of Richmond; John K. Peebles of Norfolk; and Frye & Chesterman of Lynchburg. All were eliminated except for Frye & Chesterman and Noland & Baskervill, who were asked to submit a composite plan. Their composite plan proposed extending the senate chamber out fifteen feet into the portico with entrances to either side, and adding a broad stairway across the front following Jefferson's original scheme.[4] This scheme met with much opposition, and construction bids came in over the appropriation. Meanwhile John Peebles's competition entry, which called for expansion through two wings at either side, resurfaced. The architects were asked to submit new plans for the wings, but no consensus could be reached and the commission was disbanded. In March 1904 a new appropriation of $250,000 was made specifically for restoration and enlargement by the erection of wings.

The General Assembly Act named as architects John Kevan Peebles, Frye & Chesterman, and Noland & Baskervill. Construction began in August 1904 and the building was occupied by January 1906.

The composite partnership for the Capitol effectively covered the state geographically and linked together the three leading firms. Peebles's original design was the basis for the additions, though modifications were made. The undated rendering by an unknown hand—though similar to the work of Hughson Hawley—was probably commissioned by the Noland firm in 1904 to spur interest in the project.[5] It represents an intermediate version of the design; in execution, changes would be made to the wings, and the second floor entrances in the hyphens would be eliminated. Because Noland and Baskervill were located in Richmond they had more responsibility for construction supervision and final details. The wings, linked by hyphens, were kept lower and subservient to the original structure. An Ionic order of engaged columns and pediments and a high podium echoed the main building. The House of Delegates was placed in the west wing and the Senate in the east wing, and provision was made for committee rooms and other spaces. To carry out the project, the original Jefferson structure was gutted; only the exterior masonry walls and columns were left standing. Structural steel and fireproofing were installed. Only the woodwork for the rotunda and select portions of the pilasters and cornices in the original Senate and House chambers were saved and reinstalled. On the exterior broad steps were built.[6] The new State Capitol illustrated that a continuity of Classicism existed between the past and the present in Virginia, which could stand up to other states in the rivalry of public buildings.     RGW

NOTES

1.   Henry-Russell Hitchcock and William Seale, *Temples of Democracy: The State Capitols of the U. S. A.* (New York; Harcourt Brace Jovanovich, 1976), 226.

2.   *Senate,* 20 February 1902: 150; for background see Karen Lang Kummer, "The Evolution of the Virginia State Capitol, 1779–1965" (M. A. thesis, University of Virginia, 1981).

3.   *Acts,* 1901–1902, chapter 452.

4.   Discussion of the plans can be found in: *The Richmond Times,* May 15, November 30, and December 12, 1902; *The Richmond Dispatch,* December 6, 12, and 14, 1902. D. Wiley Anderson's plan is reproduced in his portfolio, *Short Reviews, A Few Recent Designs* (no pagination, no date; circa 1904), photocopy at Virginia Department of Historic Resources. The composite plan of Noland & Baskervill and Frye & Chesterman shown in figure 2 is a photograph of the original rendering, which has been lost.

5.   The rendering was rescued by the present owner from a trash pile in the Baskervill office in 1959. Additional drawings exist for this project.

6.   *Specifications for Fireproofing and Additions to the Virginia State Capitol* (Richmond: no date).

Attributed to WILLIAM COLLINS, 1874–1953
for
T. J. COLLINS & SON, Staunton

# 68.
# C&O DEPOT

*North Elevation*

Middlebrook at S. Augusta Ave., Staunton
Working drawing, 1905
Signed lower right: *T. J. Collins and Son, Archts.*;
dated: *May 22, 1905*
Ink on linen; 24 by 34 inches
Collection of T. J. Collins & Son, Architects, Staunton, Virginia

The railroad first came to Staunton in 1854 and the first station was built by 1857. A second was built in 1890 and this, the third, of 1905, reflects the growing importance of Staunton to the economic development of the Shenandoah Valley. This depot was part of a larger complex of freight depot, water tower, signal tower, pedestrian bridge, and warehouses in this section of town.

The design of the C&O Depot reflects the interests of T. J. Collins's sons, especially William (Will) Collins. The elder Collins was still active in the firm, but Will became more evident as both a draftsman and, one can assume, as a designer since the firm's styles begin to change. The new direction is towards an American Renaissance Classicism and the Arts and Crafts, and away from the rugged Picturesque favored by the elder Collins. Several designs were developed for the station. "Design No. 2" ( FIGURE 2 ) and "Design No. 3," which survive, show more orthodox Classicism in which ornamental details are more correct.[1] These schemes were discarded for a new design completed on May 22, 1905, which was subsequently erected with some small changes ( FIGURE 1 ).[2]

The accepted design is more of a hybrid and, while containing Classical forms, is more generically a railroad station. The overall proportions are horizontal and stretched out, and the broad encompassing and dominant roof and the heavy corner piers reflect an innate American preference for form that appeared in these years in places as diverse as California, Chicago, and New York. The bungalows of Gustav Stickley and Harvey Ellis and others have the same solidity and long, linear orientation. Although Frank Lloyd Wright's designs are more abstract, the Collins design shows a similar concern for enclosed forms and deep, overhanging eves, an almost archaic American Classicism. Another contemporary style, California Mission Revival, can be seen as having a very direct influence on the C&O Station design, especially in the quatrefoil windows shown in the rendering. The drawing for the west elevation has a dormer reminiscent of contemporary Mission Revival stations for western railroads, such as the Union Pacific and the Santa Fe. These Mission features were expurgated when the depot was constructed. The south front is the concourse side, where a 400-foot-long covered platform is carried on iron Tuscan columns. Staunton's C&O Depot reflects an American Classicism deeply rooted in the architectural climate of its day. RGW

NOTES
1. Two drawings are in the archives of T. J. Collins & Son.

2. An unpublished ms. by John Wells, "The Architects of Virginia," notes that reports on the projected design of the C&O Depot appeared in the *Manufacturer's Record* in early 1904 through 27 July 1905, and that the estimated cost was approximately $30,000.

FIGURE 1. *Site photo,* **C&O Depot,** *Staunton.*

FIGURE 2. *Design No. 2, proposed* **C&O Depot.** *(Photograph courtesy of T. J. Collins & Son, Staunton.)*

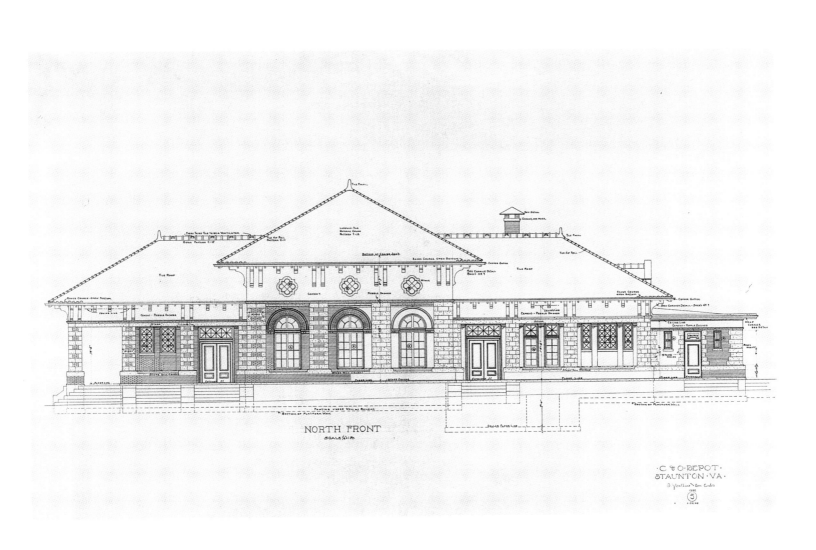

NORTH FRONT

SCALE ⅛ = 1 FT.

·C & O· DEPOT·
STAUNTON · VA·

# 69.
## MOUNTAIN VIEW

*(Junius Blair Fishburn House)*
*Section*

714 13th Street S.W., Roanoke
Presentation and working drawing, 1907
Inscribed upper left: *Residence for Mr. J.B. Fishburne.*
*Roanoke, Va. H. H. Huggins—Architect. Roanoke, Va. March*
*6th. 1907. Design No. 2405—Sheet No. 9 Line A-B.*
Ink on linen; 26 by 36 inches
Collection of the City of Roanoke, Virginia

Mountain View, the sprawling mansion erected for Roanoke businessman and civic leader Junius Blair Fishburn,[1] was regarded by its architect, H. H. Huggins, as an object of great personal pride. In one of Huggins's advertisements in the 1908 *Roanoke City Directory* he boldly stated: "Under my plans and direction, there has been erected in Roanoke one of the finest residences in the State of Virginia. A card from you or a verbal request will entitle you to a pictorial proof of the above assertion."[2] Huggins, a native of Darlington, South Carolina, attended South Carolina College, where he studied civil engineering. The unprecedented building boom taking place in Roanoke at the turn of the century attracted Huggins to take up the practice of architecture, and in 1891 he joined fellow Darlington County native Charles C. Wilson to form the office of Wilson and Huggins in the so-called Magic City. The partnership was dissolved by 1893. Although he proved to be a competent designer, Huggins won commissions largely through aggressive self-confidence, as seen in numerous advertisements extolling his talent and accomplishments. Typical of his brashness is this statement, from in the *Roanoke City Directory* of 1900: "Roanoke is proud of her school buildings. I planned the four best ones. How's that?" In the 1909 directory Huggins advertised "HURRAH! Roanoke has over 40,000 people, and more of them live in Huggins-designed buildings than in buildings designed by any other twelve architects. A bold assertion, but I can prove it."[3] Huggins's overconfidence eventually caught up with him, for when he died at the age of forty-eight in Richmond, newspaper investigations revealed that he had been leading a double life: "H.H. Huggins, highly respected architect, with wife and child in Roanoke, lived here under the name of Johnston with a woman known as his wife. . . ."[4]

Like many architects of the period, Huggins worked in the increasingly fashionable Colonial or Georgian Revival style, which was ideally suited for the many suburban and small-town houses being erected around the turn of the century. Unlike many architects of the mid-Atlantic and New England states, who created almost literal copies of authentic models, Southern architects were generally much freer in their interpretations of the style. Indeed, H. H. Huggins exhibited in his own way some of the same creativity and panache as one of the style's originators, Stanford White. Georgian forms and motifs were thrown about: a scrolled broken pediment more suitable for a grandfather's clock found itself capping a dormer, and no opportunity for a colonnette or pilaster was missed. In the principal elevation of Mountain View, however, Huggins followed a scheme that was to find popularity throughout the South, that is, a facade fronted by a pedimented portico with paired or clustered columns, over a one-story porch extending across the entire front. This format, frequently referred to as "Southern Colonial," satisfied the Southerner's desire for both monumentality and neighborliness. The stately portico signaled the fact that a person of importance dwelled there, while the one-story porch acknowledged that that person was "folks," an ordinary individual who could relax comfortably in full view, rocking and greeting his neighbors. Southerners acquired their taste for columns in the antebellum era and never got over it. The fact that columns were rarely, if ever, found on true colonial houses mattered little; anything that smacked of antiquity was "colonial."

In this section drawing we see that Huggins emphasized grandeur by employing a central stair that divides at a landing. Classicism is carried into the interior with the use of Ionic doorways. The glassed-in rear wing and the conservatory on the opposite side are typical of the quality appointments of a mansion of the period.

Huggins's client, Junius Blair Fishburn (1865–1955), was ideally suited for the mansion created for him. A self-made banker and newspaper executive, as well as officer and director of more than thirty corporations during his lifetime, Fishburn was a leading figure in the phenomenal growth of Roanoke. He was also a foremost philanthropist, donating thousands of acres of land for parks and other public facilities. At his death, Mountain View itself was bequeathed to the Roanoke Department of Parks and Recreation.   CCL

NOTES
1.   The correct spelling for the Fishburn family of Roanoke is without a final *e.* Huggins was apparently not aware of that spelling.

2.   *Roanoke City Directory,* 1908, 413.

3.   I am indebted to John E. Wells of the Virginia Department of Historic Resources for biographical information on H. H. Huggins, as well as for the quotes from the city directories.

4.   *Richmond Times-Dispatch,* December 9, 1912.

REFERENCES
Loth, Calder. *The Virginia Landmarks Register, Third Edition.* Charlottesville: University Press of Virginia, 1987. p. 403.

"Roanoke's First Citizen." *Roanoke Times,* September 27, 1945, sec.1: p. 1.

Whitwell, W. L., and Lee W. Winborne, *The Architectural Heritage Roanoke Valley.* Charlottesville: University Press of Virginia, 1982. (pp. 139–140).

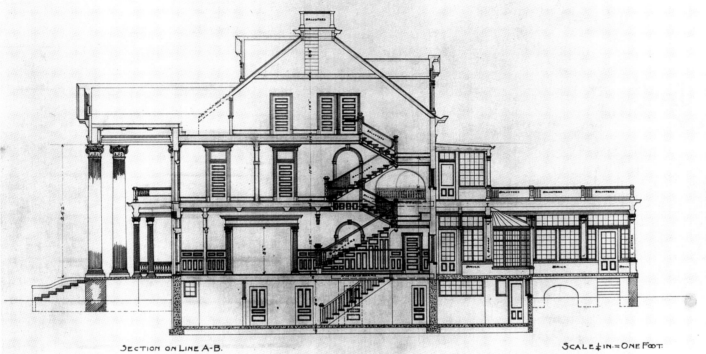

RESIDENCE FOR
MR. J. B. FISHBURNE.
ROANOKE, VA.
H.H.HUGGINS · ARCHITECT.
ROANOKE, VA. MARCH 6TH 1907.
DESIGN No. 2405 — SHEET No. 9.

SECTION ON LINE A-B.

SCALE ¼ IN.= ONE FOOT.

EDWARD GRAHAM FRYE, 1870–1942

AUBREY CHESTERMAN, 1874–1937

for

FRYE & CHESTERMAN, Lynchburg

# 70.
## PROJECT FOR FIRST NATIONAL BANK

*Interior Perspective*

925 Main St., Lynchburg
Presentation drawing, circa 1908
Signed lower left on mat: *Aubrey Chesterman, Architect*
Watercolor on board; 12 ¾ by 16 ¾ inches
Collection of Grady P. Gregory, Jr., A.I.A., Roanoke, Virginia, grandson of Edward G. Frye

FIGURE 1. *Vintage site photo, late 1920s–early 1930s,* **First National Bank,** *Lynchburg. (Photograph courtesy of Virginia State Library, Virginia Chamber of Commerce Collection.)*

Much of the exuberant character and high quality of architecture in Lynchburg and Roanoke during the late nineteenth and early twentieth centuries can be laid to the talents of Edward G. Frye and his various collaborators, such as Aubrey Chesterman. Frye was born in Bristol, Tennessee, and studied mathematics at Vanderbilt University before moving to Norfolk and apprenticing with an architect at an annual salary of $200 a year. He came to Lynchburg around 1890 and opened an office; by 1894–95 he was advertising himself with the "Best City References." Frye's style at this time was in the Picturesque veins of Queen Anne and Richardson Romanesque; he had a virtual stranglehold on local church designs, being responsible for three large new structures, two remodelings, and a campanile addition. His style shifted in 1902, the same year he took Aubrey Chesterman into partnership. Chesterman, a native of Richmond, had trained with the Richmond architect, Captain M. J. Dimmock, and then worked for Noland & Baskervill before coming to Lynchburg. How much Chesterman contributed to the new Beaux-Arts look that began to emerge in the firm's designs, and how much Frye would have changed on his own are open questions, but the firm began to design buildings very much in the American Renaissance mode. Clearly viewed as one of the Commonwealth's leading firms, Frye & Chesterman were associated with the Virginia Capitol addition ( SURVEY NO. 67 ) and dominated Lynchburg architecture until 1913, when the lure of larger work in Roanoke drew them to what has been nicknamed "The Star City." Chesterman stayed briefly, then opened a separate office in Danville before returning to Lynchburg in 1917, where he practiced until his death two decades later.[1]

The buildings of Frye & Chesterman in Lynchburg and Roanoke record the impact of McKim, Mead & White and others identified with the American Renaissance. The firm produced designs in the Georgian, American Colonial, Jeffersonian, Italian Renaissance, and Roman idioms, and in Lynchburg built the Academy of Music (1905, 1911), Jones Memorial Library (1905–08), Virginia Christian College (now Lynchburg College; 1908–09), several clubs, and scores of houses. For many of these works, Aubrey Chesterman created masterful renderings very much in the style of the leading New York architectural firms.

The renderings for the First National Bank of Lynchburg well illustrate the sophistication Chesterman brought to Lynchburg. He had obviously studied the renderings of Hughson Hawley and Francis L. V. Hoppin (both of whom worked for McKim, Mead & White) and used typical trademarks, such as women or girls in red dresses and plenty of white highlights. Perspective apparently gave him some problems, but he was able to communicate atmosphere successfully. The interior rendering captures the lush richness, the highly polished Greek, Italian, and French marbles, bronze grilles, and the ivory and gold-leaf ceiling.[2]

The full story of the First National Bank design is complicated, for the designer of record was Philip Thornton Marye (1872–1935), a native Virginian who had practiced in Newport News until 1904, when he moved to Atlanta and established an important practice.[3] Apparently Marye had won a small closed competition for the bank project, and the building that was erected in 1908–09 followed, on the exterior, his design.[4] Frye & Chesterman had submitted at least two drawings, a colored exterior, and the interior. The interior as constructed closely follows Frye & Chesterman's proposal. The exact story is unclear, but probably Chesterman's interior rendering so impressed the bank directors that they ordered it to be followed. Whether Frye & Chesterman oversaw the work is unknown. Unfortunately, this wonderful interior was obliterated during a 1950s remodeling.[5]       RGW

NOTES

1.   S. Allen Chambers, Jr., *Lynchburg: An Architectural History* (Charlottesville: University Press of Virginia, 1981), 315–17,357–359, 411, and elsewhere; interview with Grady P. Gregory, AIA [Frye's grandson] of Roanoke, December 21, 1989; "Aubrey Chesterman" entry in, *Encyclopedia of Virginia Biography* (New York: Lewis Historical Publishing Co, 1915), 5:581. Conflict exists in this last entry, which cites Chesterman's birth date as 1875; the date of the partnership's origin, given as 1902, is also unclear. Letter, Catherine Stovall [Chesterman's granddaughter] to author, October 30, 1990, confirms the 1874 birthdate. Chambers, *Lynchburg,* 357, notes that Frye and Chesterman apparently split up briefly in 1906.

2.   Chambers, *Lynchburg,* 381, quotes the *Lynchburg News,* June 2, 1909, on the interior.

3.   Henry F. and Elise Rathburn Withey, *Biographical Dictionary of American Architects (Deceased)* (Los Angeles: New Age, 1956), 395.

4.   Marye's design appears in *American Architect* 96 (November 1909): no. 1767.

5.   Chambers, *Lynchburg,* 379–81, which also reproduces the Frye and Chesterman drawings.

Attributed to AUBREY CHESTERMAN, 1874–1937

for

FRYE & CHESTERMAN, Lynchburg

# 71.
# CITY AUDITORIUM AND MARKET

*Elevation*

Main St. between Eleventh and Twelfth Sts., Lynchburg
Presentation drawing, circa 1908
Watercolor and ink on board; 14 ½ by 19 ½ inches
Collection of Grady P. Gregory, Roanoke, Virginia

FIGURE 1. **City Auditorium and Market,** *now Advance Auto Parts, Lynchburg.*

The City Auditorium and Market of Lynchburg is typical of the "civic art" or American Renaissance spirit that gripped many city fathers in the first three decades of the twentieth century. Emboldened by the World's Columbian Exposition of 1893, the writings of journalists such as Charles Mulford Robinson, and replanning schemes like the McMillan plan for Washington, D. C., of 1902, many cities undertook to beautify and rebuild along Classical lines. American cities, it was argued, could equal in charm and beauty those of the Old World, while at the same time avoid their decay. Conceived as a partnership between culture, politics, and commerce, buildings of both public and private character, along with parks, statues, and planning, would contribute to the overall harmonious character of a city. Frye & Chesterman were the principal architects of the American Renaissance in Lynchburg, Virginia. After his sojourn in Roanoke and Danville, Chesterman returned to Lynchburg and designed one of the greatest civic art projects in the state, Monument Terrace (1924–26).[1]

Frye & Chesterman's design for a new City Auditorium and Market replaced an 1873 market on the same site that was strictly utilitarian in appearance. The tradition of a city-owned market dates back to 1805, and Frye & Chesterman's building was the fourth in that lineage. While no specific buildings can be identified as the source for Frye & Chesterman's design, there were numerous prototypes, such as Italian Renaissance palazzi and eighteenth-century English and American market halls. Peter Harrison's Brick Market in Newport, Rhode Island (circa 1761) had the same tripartite division, as did Italian Renaissance palazzi, which originally had commercial space on the ground floor. More recently McKim, Mead & White had revived the palazzo formula for a variety of purposes, from the Boston Public Library (1887–95) to New York City clubhouses, and the Russell and Erwin Building, New Britain, Connecticut (1883–85). This last, while more vertical, has many of the same features and details as City Market, and used red brick on the upper floors.[2] In Lynchburg, Frye & Chesterman delineated the purposes clearly: the base was the market and the *piano nobile* contained the 2,023-seat auditorium. The market was reached through the double doors of the five arches in the base and the one-story extensions to either side, while access to the large auditorium was through the elaborately framed doors of the projecting pavilions at the ends of the main block. A cornice projecting vigorously above an elaborate frieze and a tile roof completed the composition.

This rendering, probably by Aubrey Chesterman, illustrates both the draftsman's talent and his weakness as an architectural presenter. The New York renderer Hughson Hawley is the most obvious influence; typically, the structure is shown as a part of street life, and Chesterman has applied the conventions of a girl in a red—here maroon—dress, a flight of birds in the sky, and clouds, although his technique is slightly more Impressionistic and fuzzy than Hawley's. Chesterman's vehicles are crudely drawn, and he never portrays a building in three dimensions or perspective; they are always flat facades.

Still, though, the drawing is a convincing rendition of what Frye & Chesterman saw as appropriate for civic and commercial life in Lynchburg at the turn of the century. While glimmers of this vision still remain in places, the auditorium and market were rendered obsolete by a new Armory and Market built in 1932, and the older building was sold. Subsequent owners have not appreciated its architectural value; the ground floor has been covered over and the warm red tapestry brick and details of the upper floors have been painted out. RGW

NOTES

1. S. Allen Chambers, *Lynchburg: An Architectural History* (Charlottesville: The University Press of Virginia, 1981), 432–435; Chambers covers the City Market and Auditorium, 361–65.

2. All are illustrated in *A Monograph of the Works of McKim, Mead & White* (5 vols., published 1915–20; reprint, New York: Dover, 1990).

FRANK RUSHMORE WATSON, 1859–1940

for

WATSON & HUCKEL, Philadelphia

# 72.
# CHRIST CHURCH (EPISCOPAL) NORFOLK

*Perspective*

Olney Road at Stockley Gardens, Norfolk
Presentation drawing, circa 1910
Signed on mat, along bottom: *Watson & Huckel*
Watercolor on board; 29 by 24 ½ inches
Collection of Christ & St. Luke's Church, Norfolk, Virginia

FIGURE 1. *Site photo,* **Christ Church,** *Norfolk.*

The first decades of the twentieth century saw the last great flowering of the Gothic Revival, due in large measure to the efforts of Ralph Adams Cram, the style's principal theoretician, promoter, and practitioner. In a copious outpouring of articles, books, and speeches, Cram advocated a more scholarly and archaeological approach to Gothic design, urging architects to emulate actual historical models and to repudiate the eclecticism of the late Victorian period. Cram's "new" Gothic emphasized the vertical possibilities of the style and avoided applied decoration, preferring the integral ornament of the original medieval. The resultant buildings had a cleaner, lighter aspect than their nineteenth-century predecessors.[1]

Christ Church, designed in 1910 by Frank Watson of the Philadelphia firm of Watson & Huckel, is clearly a child of Cram's crusade, and Cram himself published it (along with the work of other sympathetic architects) to illustrate his theories in 1915.[2] Watson chose as his model the Perpendicular Gothic of England's sixteenth century, recalling Christ Church's Anglican roots as Norfolk's oldest parish, formed in the 1630s. With its massive granite exterior, intricately carved sandstone interior, and richly colored German stained glass, the building also proclaimed the wealth and influence of its socially prominent parishioners.

This anonymous but well-executed presentation perspective is drawn on a generous scale, befitting its subject. The drawing shows the church substantially as it was built, with the exception of the parish hall to the right of the main body of the church, which was never constructed. The rendering is very specific to place and time, depicting neighboring buildings and landscape features with some accuracy, dressing its scale figures in the fashions of the day, and capturing a rather jaunty automobile, complete with trailing exhaust, as it proceeds before the church. The drawing is very much in the mainstream of architectural rendering, attempting to give the viewer as realistic an experience as possible of the proposed design. It is interesting to note that photographs of the building are almost invariably taken from the same vantage point as the rendering. The architects obviously believed their rendering to be of high quality, since they exhibited it in New York, Philadelphia, and other cities in 1910–1912.[3]

The building's architect, Frank R. Watson, was one of Philadelphia's most important ecclesiastical architects of the early twentieth century. He apprenticed in the office of Edwin F. Durang, a noted architect of Roman Catholic churches, and after five years opened his own office in 1882 or 1883. He may also have spent a year in France after his apprenticeship, an important element in a young architect's training in this period of strong influence from the Ecole des Beaux-Arts. In his practice, Watson continued to seek commissions for religious buildings, but broadened his scope to include work for other denominations. He entered into partnership with Samuel Huckel in 1902, and Watson & Huckel continued until Huckel's death in 1917. Watson practiced alone until 1922, when he associated with George Edkins and William Heyl

Thompson, and the partnership with Thompson lasted until Watson's death in 1940. Of interest among Watson's numerous works in the Philadelphia area is St. Mark's Church, Frankford (1907), which bears many similarities to Christ Church. Watson's other Virginia work is St. Stephen's Episcopal Church in Richmond (1928).[4]                           DAD III

NOTES

1.  Montgomery Schuyler, "The works of Cram, Goodhue,& Ferguson," *Architectural Record* 29 (January 1911): 1–87.

2.  Ralph Adams Cram, *American Churches* (New York: The American Architect, 1915), vol. 1, pls. 81–83. See also "Christ Church at Norfolk, Virginia," *Southern Architect and Building News* 34 (February 1915): 24–28.

3.  On the back of the mat is appended a tag with the following exhibition record: Philadelphia Chapter & T-Square Club, 1911; Architectural League of New York, 1910; AIA Exhibit-South Bend Architectural Club, June 1912; Louisville Chapter AIA, 1912; John Herron Art Institute, 1912.

4.  Sandra Tatman and Roger Moss, *Biographical Dictionary of Philadelphia Architects: 1700–1930* (Boston: G.K. Hall & Co., 1985), 832–39. Henry F. and Elaine Rathburn Withey, *Biographical Dictionary of American Architects(Deceased)* (Los Angeles: New Age Publishing Co., 1956), 306, 638.

WILLIAM CHURCHILL NOLAND, 1865–1951

HENRY BASKERVILL, 1867–1946

for

NOLAND & BASKERVILL, Richmond

# 73.

## SWANNANOA

*Residence for
Major James H. Dooley
Front Elevation*

Afton Mountain (Nelson County)
Presentation and working drawing, 1911
Signed upper right: *Noland & Baskervill*;
dated upper left: *June 1911*
Ink on linen; 27 ¾ by 43 inches
Collection of Baskervill & Son, Richmond, Virginia

FIGURE 1. *Site photo,* **Swannanoa.**

Swannanoa is one of the few Virginia houses that rivals the lavish "cottages" of Newport, or the vast country places of Long Island and the Berkshires. Largely constructed of Georgia marble, it exemplifies the American Renaissance and the pre-income-tax era. Thorstein Veblen identified a passion for "conspicuous consumption" that seemed to grip American millionaires as they vied with one another to construct giant houses that would only be occupied for small portions of the year. The architects of these palaces envisioned an American aristocracy and were consequently inspired by the palaces of European royalty as their prototypes.

The railroad magnate James H. Dooley, who commissioned Swannanoa, exemplifies the American Renaissance patron. Dooley (1841–1922) was born in Richmond and served in the Confederate Army. While he was later known as "Major," the rank seems to have been appropriated: his father was a major, but the younger Dooley only earned the rank of lieutenant. He read for the law, served briefly in the state legislature, and became involved in real estate and railroads, in time controlling both the Southern and the Seaboard Airline, along with other business interests. By 1890 he was a millionaire. In 1869 he married Sallie (Sarah) O. May (1846–1925) of Staunton.[1] Architecture was a necessity for a businessman like Dooley; it expressed power and status. Noland & Baskervill became his architects and made extensive additions for the Dooleys at their Richmond house, Maymont (originally designed in 1893 by Edgerton Rogers), and then designed Swannanoa, the Dooleys' summer residence in the Blue Ridge mountains of western Virginia. After Major Dooley's death, Henry Baskervill designed his mausoleum at Mrs. Dooley's request.

The Richmond firm of Noland & Baskervill was founded in 1897 and continued until 1917, when Noland left to practice on his own. Baskervill kept the firm, which became Baskervill & Lambert, then Baskervill & Son in 1932. William Noland had originally been the firm's main designer, while Henry Baskervill handled the engineering and business aspects.[2] Born in Hanover County, Virginia, Noland had attended local schools and Episcopal High School in Lynchburg. He learned architecture while working for firms in New York, Philadelphia, Roanoke, and Richmond, and during two years of travel in Europe. Exactly who Noland first worked for is unknown, except that he spent time in the office of a Philadelphia firm, Cope and Stewardson. Although their particular Gothic and Jacobean Revival had little apparent effect on Noland, he did adopt their method of a close and very accurate study of original forms and details. When Noland opened an office in Richmond in 1896, he invited Henry Baskervill to join him. Noland was the "dean" of Virginia architects, an honor attested by his election as the first president of the Richmond Architects' Association in 1911 and his award of the first license when state registration of architects was established in 1920.[3] Henry Baskervill was born in Richmond and, like Noland, he also attended Episcopal High School,

then studied at Cornell University, where he graduated with a degree in electrical engineering. He returned to Richmond as Assistant City Engineer and became involved in the construction of the new City Hall (SURVEY NO. 58). The firm of Noland & Baskervill quickly rose to the top, designing in Richmond the Virginia State Capitol additions (SURVEY NO. 67), St. James's Episcopal Church, St. Luke's Hospital, Beth Ahabah Temple, Second Baptist Church, The Berkeley apartments, and many houses. They also worked extensively around the state.

Swannanoa is located at the top of Afton Mountain in the Blue Ridge Mountains, with superb views of the Rockfish and Shenandoah valleys. Mrs. Dooley was interested in the location because it was close to her childhood home in Staunton. By the spring of 1911 Major Dooley had purchased the site and began negotiating with Noland & Baskervill on the design. The Dooleys had visited Italy in the summer of 1910 and had become infatuated with Italian culture. Swannanoa became a large project, with Noland & Baskervill designing not only the main house but an entire estate as well: gates, stables, manager's cottage, and terraced gardens. Construction of the house was completed in 1913, at an estimated cost of $300,000.[4]

The design for the main house was inspired by the twin-towered facade of the sixteenth-century Villa Medici in Rome. Traditionally attributed to Annibale Lippi, it was a building well known to Americans as the home of the French Academy. At the World's Columbian Exposition of 1893 McKim, Mead & White had adopted the Villa Medici's design for their New York State Building. However, Swannanoa is not a copy, for there are major differences in the fenestration and the Virginia mansion is far more horizontal than its Italian model. The broad expanse of the "front elevation" shown here was really designed not as a point of entry but as an impressive frontispiece for the approach drive and as a platform from which to view a panoramic landscape spreading to the east. The porte-cochère was on the opposite side. A large central hall with an impressive staircase lighted by a large Tiffany window dominated the interior. The house quickly became one of the showpieces of the Blue Ridge Mountains, and its fame and popularity have continued to the present day.[5]                    RGW

NOTES

1.   Information on the Dooleys comes from archives at the Maymont Foundation, Richmond, and, Lyon G. Tyler, *Men of Mark in Virginia* (Washington, D.C.: Men of Mark Publishing Co., 1906): 1, 187–89.

2.   L. Moody Simms, Jr., "William Churchill Noland: Richmond Architect," *The Richmond Quarterly* 3 (Spring 1981): 43–44; Betsy Updike, "Henry Eugene Baskerville & William Churchill Noland: Richmond's Response to the American Renaissance" (M. A. thesis, University of Virginia, 1987); and information from the Baskervill office. Baskervill added an "e" to his name in the 1920s, but a later generation removed it.

3.   "Architects Form an Association," *The Concrete Age* 15 (October 1911): 26.

4.   Information from archives at Maymont. Letters regarding Swannanoa are at the Virginia Historical Society. Other drawings exist for this project at Baskervill.

5.   In 1948 Walter and Lao Russell leased Swannanoa as the headquarters for their University of Science and Philosophy. Walter died in 1963; Lao in 1988. The house is still occupied by their University, and the building is open to the public. The future of Swannanoa, however, is uncertain.

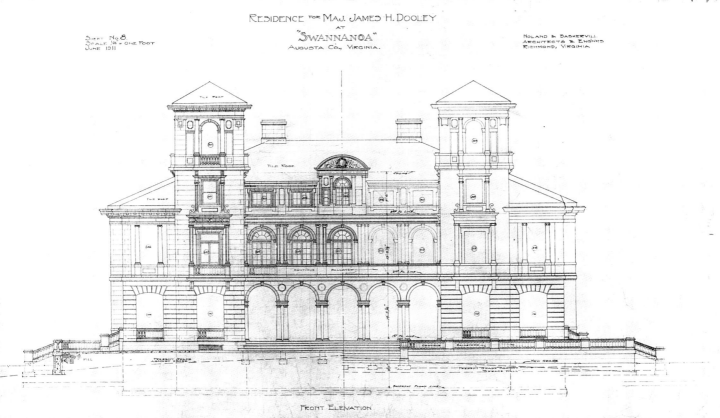

RESIDENCE FOR MAJ. JAMES H. DOOLEY
AT
"SWANNANOA"
AUGUSTA CO., VIRGINIA.

SHEET NO 8
SCALE 1/4" = ONE FOOT
JUNE 1911

NOLAND & BASKERVILL
ARCHITECTS & ENGINRS
RICHMOND, VIRGINIA.

FRONT ELEVATION

RALPH ADAMS CRAM, 1863–1942

for

CRAM, GOODHUE & FERGUSON, Boston

# 74.
# RICHMOND
# COLLEGE
# DORMITORY NO. 1
# FOR MEN

*(Jeter Hall,*
*University of Richmond)*
*Plan and Elevation*

Richmond
Preliminary presentation drawing, circa 1912
Signed lower right: *Cram, Goodhue & Ferguson*
Ink and watercolor on paper; 24 ½ by 35 inches
Collection of Avery Library, Columbia University, New York

FIGURE 1. *Site photo,* **Jeter Hall.**

Cram, Goodhue & Ferguson were the most important Gothic revivalists in America during the late nineteenth and early twentieth centuries. Originally founded by Ralph Adams Cram in 1889, the firm had evolved to include Bertram Goodhue (1869–1924) and Frank Ferguson (1861–1926), who first became known for their use of the Gothic Revival style in a series of Episcopal churches around Boston. The style was part of the American Arts and Crafts Movement in its attention to detail, its craftsmanship, and its rejection of machine-manufacturing processes in crafts and furniture-making. As the leader in the firm, Cram campaigned for the Gothic not only because he felt it was the one true form suitable for worship, but also because he saw it as the basis for American life. He wrote several hundred articles, edited several magazines, including *Christian Art,* and authored twenty books, among them *Church Building* (1901) and *The Gothic Quest* (1907). A high-church Episcopalian, Cram changed the face of American ecclesiastical architecture, putting Protestant denominations, from Unitarians to Baptists, in essentially Anglo-Catholic Gothic churches. The firm was also capable of designing in other styles, such as the Colonial (which can be seen at Sweet Briar College), Mediterranean, and Art Deco. In their work as campus architects, they designed buildings for West Point, Princeton, Bryn Mawr, Mount Holyoke, Virginia Military Institute, Wellesley, and Williams. In day-to-day operations, Cram was responsible for the overall plan, massing, and form, and then Goodhue or, after 1902, others—such as Frank Cleveland (1877–1950)—would develop the decoration and detail, while Ferguson oversaw the engineering and administrative business. Goodhue set up a New York branch in 1902 and left the firm in 1914.[1]

The work of Cram, Goodhue & Ferguson at the new (Westhampton) campus of Richmond College (now University of Richmond) was directed by Cram, and Ferguson acted as liaison. Founded in 1830 as an academy to teach Baptist ministers, Richmond College had outgrown its downtown location by the turn of the century. Under the dynamic leadership of Dr. Frederick William Boatwright, who served as president from 1894 to 1946, the College purchased a large tract of land at the western edge of Richmond in Henrico County and engaged Ralph Adams Cram and his firm to design the new college.[2] The firm did six buildings between 1910 and 1914. In the 1920s they did a few more, and then they were replaced by Richmond firms.[3] Cram's vision was spelled out in his dedication talk, in which he assailed recent changes in education as "heresy," and lauded the "sacred soil of Virginia," where "the Christian religion will never be driven forth as an enemy of mental development and that a vague intellectualism will never be held up as the end and aim of the school in place of that development of high Christian character, which is its eternal object." In terms of architecture, he explained, "We are trying . . . to abandon all that is ephemeral and time-saving in architecture and go back to the perfect style that was developed by our kin in the old home over-seas, to express just these high and eternal ideals of education."[4]

The plan was loosely based on English collegiate models (Cram specifically noted Oxford, Cambridge, Winchester, and Eton) with a series of quadrangles and towers, however somewhat loosened and not as compact nor as urban. Stylistically the buildings were a cross between Jacobean and Elizabethan, and while there are English models for the red brick, in this case the local Virginia tradition certainly played a role in the choice. The rendering of "Dormitory No. 1 for Men," now named Jeter Hall, illustrates well the Medieval Picturesque of Cram and partners. The rendering, while not by Goodhue (who in the early years set the office style), betrays some of his influence in the crisply handled details and in the brickwork. Although asymmetrically planned and massed, still the three-building complex is balanced by the dining hall and the extension to the right. The main wing is articulated by tower-like pavilions at either end which, though unequal in size and form, provide balance. Behind the various maneuvers of oriels, gables, and doors, one can see the highly rational plan and fenestration. The rendering presents a very compelling picture of the charms and mysteries of American collegiate life.

RGW

NOTES

1. Richard Guy Wilson, "Ralph Adams Cram: Dreamer of the Medieval," in *Medievalism in American Culture,* ed. B. Rosenthal and P. Szarmach (Binghamton: SUNY, Medieval and Renaissance Texts & Studies, 1989), 193–214; Douglas Shand Tucci, *Ralph Adams Cram, American Medievalist* (Boston: Boston Public Library, 1975); and Ann Miner Daniel, "The Early Architecture of Ralph Adams Cram, 1889–1902" (Ph.D. diss., University of North Carolina at Chapel Hill, 1978).

2. Woodford B. Hackley, *Faces on the Wall* (Richmond: Virginia Baptist Historical Society, [1972]), 4–5. See also Stuart L. Wheeler, "Building for the Centuries: The New Jerusalem," UR's Collegiate Gothic Architecture," *The University of Richmond Magazine* 52 (Winter 1990): 2–6.

3. Other drawings exist for this project.

4. Ralph Adams Cram, "Laying of the Corner Stone at Westhampton," *Religious Herald,* June 19, 1913: 6.

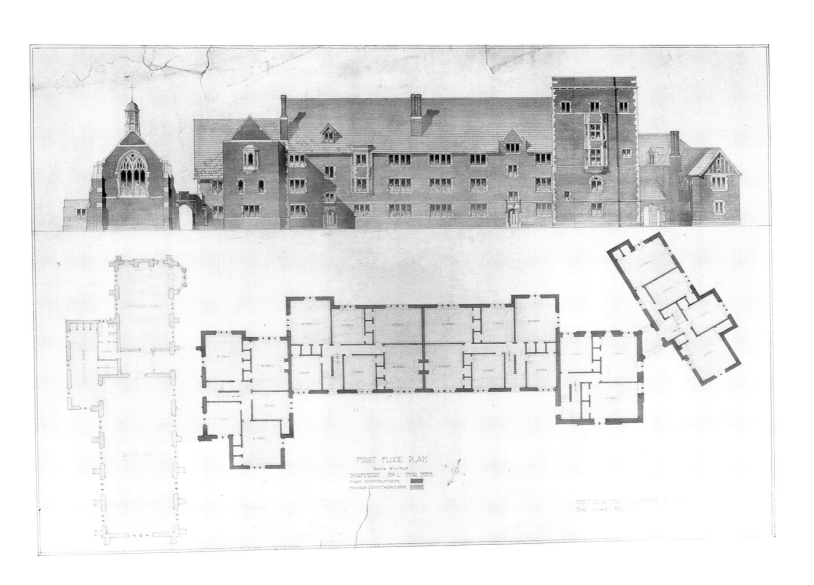

FIRST FLOOR PLAN
Scale ⅛" = 1 Foot
DORMITORY Nº 1 FOR MEN
FIRST CONSTRUCTION
FUTURE CONSTRUCTION

# 75.
# FIRST NATIONAL BANK

*(Chesapeake and Ohio Railway Building)*
*Perspective*

Ninth and East Main Sts., Richmond
Sketch, circa 1912–13
Black conté crayon with black ink on paper; 9 by 5 ½ inches
Collection of the Honorable Sir Clive Bossom, London, England

FIGURE 1. *Vintage photo, circa 1913,* **First National Bank,** *Richmond. (Photograph courtesy of the Cook Collection, The Valentine Museum.)*

The First National Bank Building in downtown Richmond was Alfred Charles Bossom's first venture into skyscraper construction.[1] Bossom, born and educated in England, had come to the United States in 1903 to practice architecture. His marriage to Emily Bayne in 1910 brought him into contact with banking and railroad interests through his father-in-law, Samuel Bayne. The First National Bank Building in Richmond was commissioned by the Chesapeake and Ohio Railway Company, with Bayne offering full restitution if the building by this young and untried architect was a failure.

With Bayne's help, and that of Francis Kimball, an established New York architect who served as a consultant, Bossom's first major commission was a success.[2] As he worked, he developed ideas, such as the nature of a bank, that would be fundamental to his later career: "The building externally should look like a BANK and should call attention to itself by its substantial and conservative appearance."[3] Another concern was that of "time and progress." Careful scheduling of the progress of the construction was necessary so that laborers and materials would be available when needed, and so that the client would be able to move in on the day specified.[4] The building was designed in 1910 and built in 1912–13.

During these early years Bossom remodeled some smaller banks—the Richmond Savings Bank, the interior of the Virginia Trust Company (then located in the Travelers Building), and perhaps the Union Bank. His second major skyscraper stands two blocks from the First National Bank Building—the Virginia Electric and Power Company. Constructed in 1915, it shows Bossom's ability to use imaginative decoration. A popular roof-garden was surrounded by standards that discharged high-pressure steam on which red lights played, giving the appearance of flaming braziers. Above the lower entablature, Bossom placed a row of tall, hooded electric lampposts. Ringed with lights, the building must have been a very dramatic sight in the Richmond of the early twentieth century.

In 1922 Bossom's temple-type Virginia Trust Company rose next to the First National Bank Building. Based on Italian Renaissance prototypes, the great triumphal arch, four stories high, is filled with fine metal decoration. We are fortunate to have these two structures side-by-side, for we see Bossom both as designer of skyscraper and of temple-type bank, and his progress toward greater simplification and boldness of forms.

Skyscraper construction by Bossom included two of the three apartments Bossom put up: in Richmond the 1922 Monroe Terrace Apartments (now Johnson Hall of Virginia Commonwealth University) and the nearby Prestwould Apartments of 1928. His non-skyscraper Parkmont Apartment building on Rivermont Avenue in Lynchburg (1915–16) has been altered. His People's Bank (Rockingham County Office Building) on Court Square in Harrisonburg is a six-story skyscraper that fits very well into the Richardsonian town square. Temple-type banks include the

1914 alterations to the First National Bank in Lexington, the 1915–16 Lynchburg National Bank, the 1918 Covington National Bank and a bank in Clifton Forge, and the 1919 Citizens National Bank in Covington.

Bossom's early work was largely in Virginia and North Carolina, but after World War I he received major commissions for banks such as the Seaboard Bank in New York (demolished), the First National Bank (Federal American National Bank) in Washington, D.C. (restored), and the Magnolia Building (Mobil Oil) in Dallas. Standing 450 feet, the Magnolia was reputed to be the tallest structure in the Southeast for many years. By the mid 1920s Bossom turned to pre-Columbian architecture for inspiration, with resulting early Art Deco-type skyscrapers—such as the Liberty Bank in Buffalo and the Petroleum Building in Houston.

Bossom and his family returned to England in 1926 where, within a few years, he was elected to Parliament. On his retirement in 1959 he was created a life peer, taking the title Lord Bossom of Maidstone.                                    MBC

NOTES

1.    The major publication on Bossom is by Dennis Sharp, with contributions from Peter Wylde and Martha B. Caldwell, *Alfred C. Bossom's American Architecture, 1903–1926* (London: Book Art, 1984).

2.    Alfred Charles Bossom, *Building to the Skies: the Romance of the Skyscraper* (London and New York: The Studio Ltd.,1934), 38.
"The first big sky-scraper I had the chance of designing was the twenty storey headquarters of the Chesapeake and Ohio Railway at Richmond, Virginia, the tallest building of its kind to be built in the Southern States. I was young, unknown and inexperienced and the owners who had like[d] my designs suggested that I should have an older man associated with me. I went accordingly to Mr. Francis H. Kimball, a king among architects of the day, and the man whose adaptation of caisson foundations did more than anything else to make skyscrapers possible. Although a stranger, he received me without delay, and I explained the situation.
"He replied unhesitatingly, 'Certainly, I will look over your drawings, check your specifications, examine your contracts, and visit the building to see you make no mistakes.'
"I naturally asked what remuneration he would expect for such services as these. 'Well,' he said, 'the fee on that building would be somewhere between $50,000 and $75,000, but if you will give me $1,000 I shall be quite satisfied.'
" 'You see,' he added, 'if you score a big success down there in Richmond, it will help to make tall buildings popular and in the natural course of events I shall get my full share.'
"It was large-mindedness such as this that made some of the architects of America seem not so much smaller than the skyscrapers they designed."

3.    Alfred Charles Bossom, "The Requirements of a Modern Bank Building," *The Bankers Magazine* 83 (November 1911): 658; see also Sharp, *Bossom's American Architecture,* 76ff.

4.    Bossom, *Building,* 119–120. The Richmond bank had to be completed in nine months: "It took a little over three months to put down the foundations which were dug by hand by open cut method nearly 80 feet into the ground. I can assure you that I almost got housemaid's knees praying that none of the shoring would give way in the holes while the men were digging. Less than six months after the foundations were finished, that 250 feet building was completed and the railway moved in on the appointed day. Such a performance would have been impossible had it not been known in advance where everything was coming from and on what date, and in what quantities, and where to put it and what to do with it on arrival."

WILLIAM LEIGH CARNEAL, 1881–1958

JAMES MARKHAM AMBLER JOHNSTON, 1885–1955

for

CARNEAL & JOHNSTON, Richmond

# 76.
# RICHMOND DAIRY
# COMPANY BUILDING

*Elevations*

401 West Marshall St., Richmond
Presentation drawings, 1913
Inscribed upper right: *Carneal & Johnston*; dated upper left:
*January 1913*
Colored ink on linen; two drawings, 28 by 15 inches each
Collection of Carneal & Johnston Architects, Richmond,
Virginia

FIGURE 1. *Site photo*, **Richmond Dairy Company Building** *after 1988 restorations.*

A building as an advertisement for the activity it houses has a long and ancient lineage, though in most cases this is a metaphorical relationship, especially when connected to commerce: banks are designed as temples, stores as palaces, and factories with church-like towers. And of course, buildings often have signs: giant teeth for dentists, shoes for cobblers, and three gold balls for pawn shops. But a building that is itself a virtual sign for its commercial purpose is more rare. At the Richmond Dairy Company building, giant milk-bottle-shaped forms are appended to the building's three street-fronting corners. This design and the resultant building express clearly that the activity on the inside had to do with bottling milk; no words or other signs were necessary.

Stylistically the building is vaguely Medieval with its crenellations and low jack arches. Covered in cream-colored terra cotta, the bottle forms provide a stark and unsettling contrast to the building's red brick walls. The inherent plastic qualities of milk bottles seem to have attracted other architects as well: similar structures with milk bottles or containers can be found in Memphis, Tennessee, and San Antonio, Texas.

For many years Carneal & Johnston has been one of Virginia's largest architectural firms. William Leigh Carneal was born in Richmond and trained in engineering at Virginia Military Institute, graduating in 1903. Back in Richmond he worked briefly with the architect C. K. Howell, then independently, before meeting Johnston in 1907 and forming a partnership in 1908.[1] James Markham Ambler Johnston was born in Rockbridge County, Virginia, and studied engineering at Virginia Polytechnic Institute, then Cornell, graduating with a master's degree in 1905. While Johnston did become registered as an architect, he was primarily the engineering half of the firm.[2] This combination of engineering and architecture, along with good business sense, gave the firm its well-deserved prominence. Both partners were very active in outside business and civic activities, which helped them obtain jobs. The firm worked on projects across the state, from Virginia Polytechnic Institute in Blacksburg to the University of Richmond, the State Office Building on Capitol Square, and the Department of Highways and Transportation Building. They also worked as local associates with out-of-state firms, such as John Eberson and Ralph Adams Cram (see Central National Bank and the Carillon Tower, SURVEY NOS. 89, 92).

The drawings for the Richmond Dairy Company building are examples of the professional quality one could expect from a firm like Carneal & Johnston. They accomplish two purposes: they give a sense of the overall form and appearance of the structure, and they include important structural information.[3] While it is tempting to see the Richmond Dairy building as an adventuristic design, indicating a celebration of American vernacular forms, perhaps avant-garde or even pre-Pop Art, there is no evidence to support such a conclusion. Rather, Carneal & Johnston probably saw the design in straightforward professional terms, as

another job to get done. To many architects at the time, the design would have been considered utterly tasteless and not even architecturally significant. Only a later generation, with different tastes and the lens of nostalgia, finds it attractive. After several decades in dereliction, the building was renovated to serve as artists' studios in 1988.                                    RGW

NOTES

1.    Obituary, *Richmond Times-Dispatch*, February 24, 1958: 1,6. See also Robert P. Winthrop, *Architecture in Downtown Richmond* (Richmond: Junior Board of Historic Richmond Foundation, 1982), 239.

2.    Entry in *American Architects Directory*, ed. George C. Koyl (New York: R. R. Bowker Co, 1955), 281.

3.    One of the drawings has been published with commentary in *The Art of Architecture in Downtown Richmond, 1798–1989*, exh. cat. (Richmond: Second Presbyterian Church, 1989), 21–22.

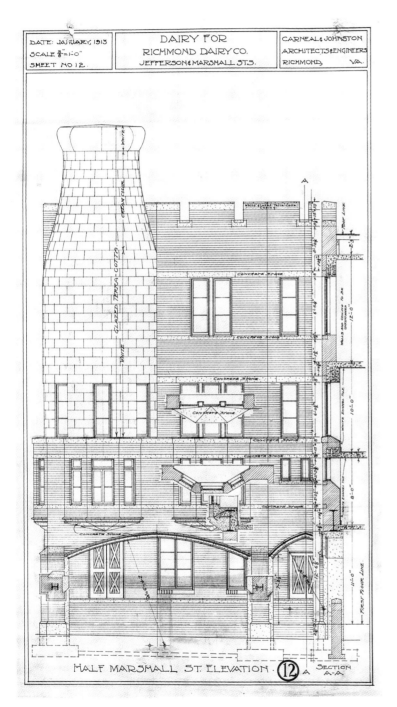

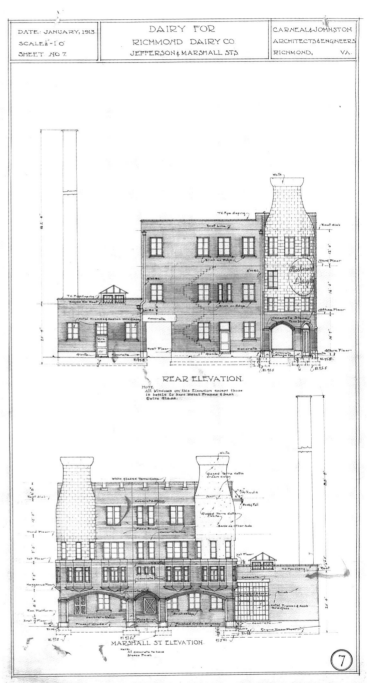

EDWARD GRAHAM FRYE, 1870–1944

FRANK STONE, 1886–1952

for

FRYE and STONE, Roanoke

Drawing by HUGHSON HAWLEY

# 77.
# BOXLEY
# BUILDING

*Perspective*

418 Jefferson St., Roanoke
Presentation drawing, 1921
Signed and dated lower right: *Hughson Hawley, 1921*
Watercolor and ink on paper; 26 ½ by 15 inches
Collection of W. W. Boxley Co., Roanoke, Virginia

FIGURE 1. *Site photo,* **Boxley Building.**

After the Roanoke-based firm of Frye & Chesterman was dissolved in 1917, Edward Frye took into partnership Frank Stone, a native of Bristol, Tennessee, whose five brothers also became architects. Stone had attended Tulane University, then worked in New York and Chicago, including a stint with D. H. Burnham and Company. He had worked for Frye & Chesterman on Roanoke's Municipal Building in 1913–15 and, after designing concrete ships in Philadelphia during World War I, he returned to Roanoke and went into partnership with Frye in 1920. Frye & Stone participated fully in the growth and development of Roanoke, a major city at the southern end of the Shenandoah Valley, designing such landmarks as the City Market (1922), the Colonial National Bank (1926–27), and scores of other prominent buildings.[1] Stone continued the practice when Frye retired in 1931, by which time he had succeeded in founding an architectural and building dynasty in Roanoke.

The Boxley Building was commissioned by William Wise ("W. W.") Boxley (1861–1940), a leading builder, developer, railroad contractor, and quarry owner, who was also mayor of Roanoke in the early 1920s when this building was constructed.[2] Intended as a symbol of Roanoke's progressive nature, as well as a commercial venture, the Boxley Building was Roanoke's entry into the tall-building sweepstakes of the early twentieth-century. At eight stories high it dominated downtown Roanoke until it was surpassed five years later by the twelve-story Colonial National Building, two blocks up the street. Boxley had apparently sponsored a limited competition among local firms, since a rendering by the architects Eubank & Caldwell of Roanoke also exists.[3] Both the Eubank & Caldwell and the Frye & Stone renderings are for a seven-story structure; before construction the height had been increased to eight stories. Frye & Stone followed the standard format of tall office-building at the time: a tripartite division, continuous vertical lines to emphasize height, and Classical detailing. This format owed a great deal to Chicago's tall buildings and the work of Burnham, for whom Stone had worked, among others.[4] The steel frame is covered on the Jefferson Avenue elevation with a limestone base, intermediate stories of beige-enameled brick with terra-cotta spandrel panels, a terra-cotta top floor, and a deep copper cornice. The side elevation is treated much more plainly: the limestone, terra cotta, and copper trim stop after one bay, and the remainder is in tan brick.

This rendering by Hughson Hawley (1850–1936), the dean of American presentation renderers, indicates the aspirations of both the client and the architects. This was by now a very standard format for Hawley, who estimated he made more than 11,000 renderings in his career. The drawing has plenty of street life, traffic, women in frilly dresses (including one in the requisite red), and a flight of birds, as well as a precise rendering of the building.[5] It obviously convinced Mr. Boxley, as ground was broken in September 1921 and the building was occupied by October 1922.                                  RGW

NOTES

1.   See Stone obituary, *Roanoke Times*, January 22, 1952; letter to author from Elizabeth Stone, daughter of the architect, September 13, 1990; and W. L. Whitwell and Lee W. Winborne, *The Architectural Heritage of the Roanoke Valley* (Charlottesville, University Press of Virginia, 1982). See also Calder Loth, ed., *The Virginia Landmarks Register* (Charlottesville: University Press of Virginia, 1986), 400.

2.   *A History of the W. W. Boxley Company* (Roanoke: Boxley Co., 1985).

3.   The rendering signed by Chas. Bachmann is in the possession of the Boxley Company.

4.   Carl W. Condit, *The Chicago School of Architecture: A History of Commercial and Public Building in the Chicago Area* (Chicago: The University of Chicago Press, 1964); and John Zukowsky, ed., *Chicago Architecture 1872–1922: Birth of a Metropolis* (Munich: Prestel-Verlag, 1987).

5.   "Hughson Hawley, Scenic Artist and Architectural Painter," *Pencil Points* 9 (December 1928): 761–74.

WILLIAM MITCHELL KENDALL, 1856–1941

for

McKIM, MEAD & WHITE, New York

# 78.
## ARLINGTON MEMORIAL BRIDGE

*Elevations*

Potomac River between Arlington, Virginia, and
Washington, D.C.
Presentation drawings, 1923–24
Inscribed lower right: *McKim, Mead & White*
Ink, pencil and watercolor on paper; 42 by 134 inches
Collection of the National Archives, Washington, D.C.

FIGURE 1. **Arlington Memorial Bridge,** *looking to the west. (Photograph courtesy of the Arlington Convention and Visitor's Service.)*

In size, composition, detail, and panoramic sweep, this drawing is unparalled in American architectural graphics; it argues persuasively for the construction of a great symbolic gateway to the nation's Capitol and a link between the North and the South. To the far right side the Lincoln Memorial is shown, and to the left the Custis-Lee Mansion and Arlington Cemetery, prime symbols of that deeply wrenching experience of the Civil War, and now finally reunited by a great memorial bridge.[1]

Ideas for a bridge across the Potomac that would also symbolize the joining of the North and the South had been advanced since the mid nineteenth century, and competitions were held in 1886 and again in 1899–1900. In 1901–02 the Senate Parks Commission, also known as the McMillan Commission— Daniel Burnham, Charles Follen McKim, Frederick Law Olmsted, Jr., and Augustus Saint-Gaudens—as part of their grand and formal redesign of The Mall, proposed the Lincoln Memorial and a low-lying linking bridge with Arlington Cemetery. It was Charles Follen McKim (1847–1909) of the New York firm of McKim, Mead & White who made the design that was essentially the one carried to execution some twenty-five years later. The recommendations of the McMillan Commission were controversial, and it took some time before a Commission of Fine Arts was established in 1910. The Lincoln Memorial was finally commissioned and erected between 1912 and 1922 following designs by a McKim protégé, Henry Bacon (1866–1924).

The Memorial Bridge project was still undecided when, on Armistice Day, November 11, 1921, during the dedication of the Tomb of the Unknown Soldier at Arlington Cemetery, a monstrous traffic jam on the two existing Washington bridges caused the presidential party to be one and a half hours late. The next day the Commission of Fine Arts met with President Harding concerning the Memorial Bridge. The Lincoln Memorial was dedicated in 1922 and shortly thereafter Congress voted funds for the bridge. There were some sentiments for a site further up the river, but strenuous arguments were advanced for the Lincoln Memorial-Arlington Cemetery site. Henry Bacon proclaimed that the bridge "will add to the meaning and solemnity of both places."[2] The Commission of Fine Arts emphasized that a bridge should be considered as part of the grand plan of Washington extending into Northern Virginia and Arlington Cemetery. The Memorial Bridge Commission agreed, comparing the entry into the city with the great avenues of approach to Rome and claiming that a great highway, the Lee Highway coming clear across the country, would enter the city by a Memorial Bridge inspiring "loyalty, patriotism, and devotion to country."[3]

Instead of a competition for the bridge's design, the Commission made a direct selection from three firms; it was a foregone conclusion that McKim, Mead & White would be chosen. The main designer, William Mitchell Kendall (1856–1941), had been McKim's right-hand man, entering the firm in 1882

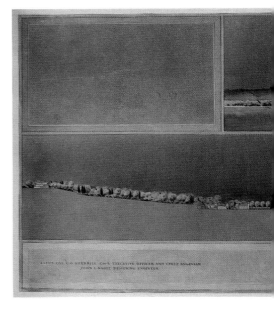

and becoming a partner in 1906. In an act of patriotism, the firm reduced their normal fee for the project. Thoroughly committed to McKim's American Renaissance Classicism, Kendall designed a low Roman-arched structure with a lift gate in the middle of the Potomac channel.[4] Columbia Island near the Virginia shore became a great plaza joining the Lee Highway from the North and the Mount Vernon Parkway from the South. Two 181-foot-high columns, representing North and South, were to mark the spot. From there the axis would continue with a smaller bridge and a tree-lined Avenue of the Heroes, terminating in a large exedra marking the entrance to Arlington Cemetery. As built between 1926 and 1932, the sculptural embellishments shown in the rendering were altered, and Columbia Island never received its colossal columns. Constructed of reinforced concrete and steel, the bridge is veneered in dressed North Carolina granite; the piers have bas-relief eagles in twelve-foot discs and the arch keystones have bison faces, all carved by C. Paul Jennewein.[5]            RGW

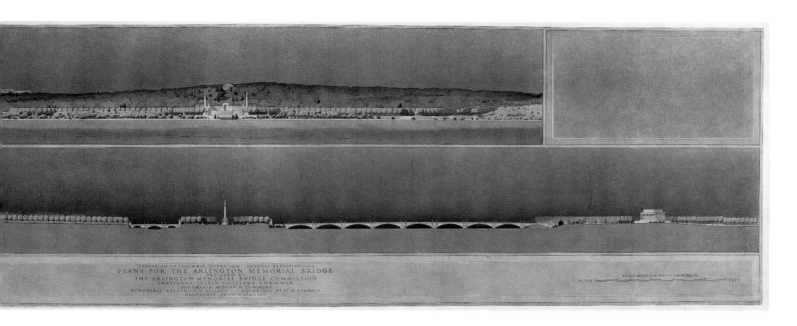

ELEVATION OF COLUMBIA ISLAND *upper* GENERAL ELEVATION *lower*
PLANS FOR THE ARLINGTON MEMORIAL BRIDGE
PREPARED BY
THE ARLINGTON MEMORIAL BRIDGE COMMISSION
PRESIDENT CALVIN COOLIDGE CHAIRMAN
HONORABLE ALBERT B. CUMMINS
HONORABLE FREDERICK H. GILLETT    HONORABLE BERT M. FERNALD
HONORABLE JOHN W. LANGLEY
SCALE                    MCKIM MEAD AND WHITE ARCHITECTS                    FEET

NOTES

1.    See Donald Beekman Myer, *Bridges and the City of Washington* (Washington, D.C.: U. S. Commission of Fine Arts, 1974):17–25; Frederick A. Emery, "Washington's Historic Bridges," *Records of the Columbia Historical Society*, XXXVIII (1957):49–70; Sue A. Kohler, *The Commission of Fine Arts: A Brief History 1910–1984* (Washington, D.C.: Commission of Fine Arts, 1984):16–26; Joanna S. Zangrando, "Monumental Bridge Design in Washington, D. C. as a Reflection of American Culture, 1886 to 1932," Ph. D. diss., George Washington University, 1974; and Kresscox Associates, "Historic Structures Report, Arlington Memorial Bridge, Washington, D.C." (unpublished, 1986), copy in National Capital Region, National Park Service, Washington, D.C. The National Archives also owns two versions of a Memorial Bridge design by Ernest Flagg probably executed in 1899–1900.

2.    Henry Bacon, "The Architecture of the Lincoln Memorial," *The Lincoln Memorial* (Washington, D.C.: Government Printing Office, 1927):42; see also Richard Guy Wilson, "High Noon on the Mall: Traditionalism versus Modernism, 1920–1970," *Mall in Washington, 1791–1991*, ed. R. Longstreth, in *Studies in the History of Art* (Washington, D.C.: National Gallery of Art, 1991): 143–167.

3.    U. S. Congress, *Report of the Arlington Memorial Bridge Commission*. 68th Congress, 1st Sess. Senate Doc. no. 95 (Washington, D.C.: Government Printing Office, 1924):5.

4.    Other presentation drawings for this project exist in the National Archives. This drawing was previously illustrated in Bates Lowery, *Building a National Image: Architectural Drawings for the American Democracy, 1789–1912*, exh. cat. (Washington, D.C.: National Building Museum, 1985): pl.107; and as a poster, "National Design Competition—Women In Military Service for America Memorial-Arlington National Cemetery," 1989.

5.    On the Lincoln Memorial end of the bridge, Leo Friedlander's *Valor* and *Sacrifice*, while commissioned in 1931, were not installed until September 1951.

HENRY BASKERVILL, 1867–1946

A[LFRED]. GAREY LAMBERT, active 1916–1938

for

BASKERVILL & LAMBERT, Richmond

# 79.
# STONY POINT

*Residence for Lewis G. Larus
East Elevation*

3400 Stony Point Rd., Richmond (Chesterfield County)
Presentation drawing, 1924
Signed and dated lower right: *Baskervill & Lambert,
October 1924*
Black and colored ink on linen; 24 ⅝ by 42 ½ inches
Collection of Baskervill & Son, Richmond, Virginia

In the annual "Country House" issue of *Architectural Record* for 1925, A. Lawrence Kocher wrote that while American Colonial was the current preferred style, a strong second was English Tudor, Elizabethan, and Jacobean.[1] The so-called Tudorbethan or Stockbroker Tudor was in many ways a pure fiction for Americans, a total import. True, some of the seventeenth-century colonial buildings could be considered Elizabethan or Jacobean, but that was not the source for the revival. An interest in this earlier English architecture had appeared sporadically in America during the mid and later nineteenth century, but it was not until the early years of the twentieth century that a real fad for large country and suburban places in this mock Tudorbethan began to appear.[2] By the 1920s, fueled by magazines like the English *Country Life* and books of architectural details, along with popular novels and Hollywood movies set in that era, the Tudor Revival was in full swing. Virginia, with its traditional and historical identification with England, became a natural setting for the style. In addition, 1926–28 saw the actual import of entire buildings, such as two Richmond houses: Virginia House ( FIGURE 3.39 ), built from portions of Warwick Priory and Wormleighton Tower, and Agecroft Hall ( FIGURE 3.40 ), a late fifteenth-century Lancashire manor house that was dismantled and re-erected on a site overlooking the James River.[3]

Richmond architects Henry Baskervill and William Noland had dissolved their partnership in 1917. Since Baskervill, who was primarily an engineer, needed a designer, he took into partnership A. Garey Lambert. Lambert's career is unclear. He had practiced in Richmond, was with Baskervill until 1932, and then worked at Colonial Williamsburg.[4] He returned to Richmond briefly in the late 1930s, after which his career cannot be traced. Apparently Lambert was the one primarily responsible for Stony Point.[5]

Stony Point is located at the edge of Bon Air, a community that was a summer retreat for wealthy Richmonders across the James River in Chesterfield County (now annexed to Richmond). Stony Point House was commissioned by the wealthy and urbane Lewis Griffin Larus (1887–1966), a vice-president of his family's successful tobacco firm, Larus Brothers and Company. Known locally as "Squire Larus," he had purchased forty-nine acres at Stony Point in 1915 and upgraded a Victorian house on the site. When the house burned in 1924 he turned to Baskervill & Lambert for a house in the most up-to-date "olde" style.[6]

The rendering for the front elevation of Stony Point shows how English Tudor motifs were grafted onto an American country house in the South. While certain elements such as the half-timbering, slate roof, and brick chimney stacks have English origins, the basic form is that of a large, well-appointed American house. The half-timbering is applied and is not structural. A pergola and an enclosed porch, both necessary to shield against the hot summer sunlight, are appended. The small-paned fenestration is far too ample and too regularized; each bank of windows is

form of the house is arranged around an axis at the front door and the wings balance one another. Contrived attempts to make the house appear as if it had grown over time are shown in the partial brick construction and the remains of a diaper pattern in the gable to the far right. Stony Point was intended to impress in size, style, and detail, and in its own way, the rendering achieves the same end: it indicates the very high quality of architectural drawing and attention to precise details. Every stone is rendered individually, and the addition of red and brown inks to what normally would have been a black-and-white drawing makes it even more impressive.

The interior was equally impressive: a large Great Hall is at the center, huge hand-hewn beams were supposedly imported from England, and a large fireplace and mantel dominate one wall, while on the opposite, the staircase rises up. Samuel Yelland of Philadelphia provided the wrought-iron fixtures. To the rear, Richmonder Charles F. Gillette laid out a formal garden enclosed by a brick wall. Although Stony Point never contained the land of an English manor house, still the appearance was given that here resided an English squire and his family.[7]                    RGW

NOTES

1.   A. Lawrence Kocher, "The American Country House," *Architectural Record* 58 (November 1925): 402–43.

2.   Gavin Townsend, "The Tudor House in America: 1890–1930" (Ph.D. diss., University of California at Santa Barbara, 1986).

3.   Helen Scott Townsend Reed, "Agecroft Hall, Richmond Virginia," *The Magazine Antiques* 123 (February 1983): 392–98.

4.   Information is scanty on Lambert, and the date of the partnership is disputed; Baskervill & Son records indicate 1918–32; as does information from John Wells, Virginia Department of Historic Resources.

5.   Per letter to author from Baskervill employee Bonnie McCormick, dated 18 July 1990.

6.   Interview with Michael Holland (faculty member, Stony Point School), September 5, 1990; interview with Robert Lee Traylor Larus, Jr., September 7, 1990; Calflin, Richardson, Hale, *Bon Air/A History* (Bon Air: Hale Publishing Co., 1977), 104–05; *Men of Mark in Virginia* (Richmond: Men of Mark Pub. Co., 1936), 79–80.

7.   In 1966 the property was rented to become the campus for the Stony Point School, and was purchased for that use in 1971.

FIGURE 1.  *Site photo,* **Stony Point.**

· SOUTH · ELEVATION · OF · PORCH ·

· EAST · ELEVATION ·
Scale ⅛" = 1'-0"

RESIDENCE FOR
LEWIS G. LARUS, ESQ.
STONY POINT
CHESTERFIELD CO, VIRGINIA

BASKERVILL & LAMBERT
ARCHITECTS
RICHMOND, VIRGINIA

OCTOBER 1924

STANHOPE S. JOHNSON, 1882–1973

RAYMOND O. BRANNAN, 1892–1974

for

JOHNSON & BRANNAN, Lynchburg

# 80.
# HOTEL
# MONTICELLO

*Interior Perspectives,*
*Lobby and Dining Room*

500 Court Square, Charlottesville
Presentation drawings, circa 1924
Watercolor and ink on paper, mounted on board;
Dining Room 12 ½ by 22 ⅝; Lobby 17 ⅛ by 19 ¾ inches
Collection of Jones Memorial Library, Lynchburg, Virginia

FIGURE 1. *Site photo,* **Hotel Monticello,** *now*
*500 Court Square commercial complex.*

Stanhope Johnson ran one of the most important and successful architectural firms in south central Virginia during the period 1920 to 1950.[1] Born and raised in Lynchburg, he apprenticed there with the firm of Frye and Chesterman beginning in 1899. By the age of twenty Johnson was listed as assistant designer to Frye. In 1909 he left to set up a brief partnership with Charles Pettit and James McLaughlin, with offices in Lynchburg and Danville, where they designed the Roanoke Female College in 1910. Pettit left in 1913 and McLaughlin in 1917 to set up their own separate practices. Between 1919 and 1933 Johnson entered into an extremely successful partnership with Raymond O. Brannan, in which Brannan handled the business and marketing and Johnson was in control of design.[2] Headquartered in Lynchburg, where much of his work was located, his firm designed all types of buildings, from houses to schools. He also became known for hotels, being responsible for more than twenty of them in Virginia, North and South Carolina, and Florida.

Stylistically, Johnson's career has an amazing consistency; his early work followed the American Renaissance Classicism, as interpreted for Virginia by his Lynchburg colleague Edward G. Frye: red brick, white trim, and full-columned porticoes. By the 1920s Johnson was extremely competent in various forms of the Colonial, Georgian, and Jefferson Revivals, which he adapted to various building types. There was some flirtation with Art Deco as in the Allied Arts Building (circa 1929; see SURVEY NO. 90) and the Lynchburg City Armory, 1931.

The Hotel Monticello was Charlottesville's entry into the high-rise building competition that erupted across America in the 1920s. Not even small towns like Charlottesville were exempt, as local businessmen attempted to prove that they were as up-to-date and modern as those of the big cities. At twelve stories the tallest structure in the city, the Monticello dominated its skyline. On its roof was placed what was reputed to be the world's largest searchlight, with a beam visible for more than three hundred miles.[3] Placed across the street from the Albemarle County Courthouse and two blocks off Main Street, the Monticello was intended to be a luxury hotel with first-class services. Several studies for the exterior show that Johnson experimented with different decorative treatments, though the tripartite division of a limestone base with high arches, red brick intermediate floors, and a limestone top floor and cornice remain constant. The hotel's name, the red and off-white colors, and certain features—like the semicircular windows at the base—indicate the building was considered an homage to Mr. Jefferson.

The public spaces on the ground floor were elaborate and much commented upon. Apparently Johnson designed these in conjunction with a decorating firm from New York, W. P. Nelson & Co., for their name appears on the reverse of the dining-room drawing.[4] As drawings they are marvelous period pieces showing the original colors and furniture. Architecturally they are an amalgamation of several different

styles and motifs, though generically their source is French eighteenth-century, which appealed to the glitzy hotel trade of the period. Both the renderings and the actual spaces—the latter covered in highly reflective tiles, plaster, and marble—display a cold, almost harsh, shine typical of 1920s public areas. To soften this anonymous quality the furnishings were obviously chosen to reflect local traditions: the lobby features a Colonial settle and a tallcase clock; shield-back chairs appoint the dining room. Both areas seem designed to prove that Charlottesville had style equal to any other American city in the 1920s.     RGW

NOTES

1.   The major treatment of Johnson's career is in Samuel Allen Chambers, *Lynchburg: An Architectural History* (Charlottesville: University Press of Virginia, 1981), 359.

2.   Born in Greenville, Tennessee, Brannan worked as a chemist at the Lynchburg Foundry until 1917. In that year, he joined Johnson's firm as the office manager and became his partner in 1919. See *Hill's Lynchburg City Directory* (1917–19); his obituary appears in *Lynchburg News,* 30 August 1974, B4: 1.

3.   K. Edward Lay, "Charlottesville's Architectural Legacy," *The Magazine of Albemarle County History* 46 (May 1988):94.

4.   Only the dining room drawing is so signed.

LOBBY
HOTEL MONTICELLO
CHARLOTTESVILLE VA.
STANHOPE S. JOHNSON & R. O. BRANNAN
ARCHITECTS
LYNCHBURG VA.

DINING ROOM
HOTEL MONTICELLO
CHARLOTTESVILLE — VA.
STANHOPE S. JOHNSON & R. O. BRANNAN
ARCHITECTS · LYNCHBURG VA.

Attributed to PAUL PHILIPPE CRET, 1876–1945

in association with

MARCELLUS E. WRIGHT, 1881–1962

# 81.
## VIRGINIA WAR MEMORIAL COMPETITION ENTRY

*Perspective*

Richmond (unbuilt)
Presentation drawing, circa 1925
Watercolor on board; 21 by 35 inches
Collection of Marcellus Wright Cox & Smith, Richmond,
Virginia

Following World War I, Virginia sought to memorialize her ninety thousand citizens who served in the war. In 1919 Governor Westmoreland Davis appointed the Virginia War History Commission to investigate setting up shrines to the "Great War." The 1920 Acts of Assembly provided that the state would build a memorial in Richmond. The types of memorials discussed included suggestions for a state library or auditorium, a triumphal arch or gateway to Capitol Square, and a carillon. The War Memorial Commission, created under Governor E. Lee Trinkle in 1924, established the Program of Competition for a site chosen in Byrd Park, on the Pump House Loop. It was decided that the state memorial should be a "monumental" or non-utilitarian type, budgeted at $250,000. Six teams competed, each employing an out-of-state architect in association with a Virginia architect and a sculptor.[1] In September 1925 the jury unanimously picked the design of Philadelphia architect Paul Cret with Marcellus E. Wright of Richmond and sculptor Berthold Nebel of New York. Wright had studied under Cret at the University of Pennsylvania, and Marcellus Wright, Jr., was enrolled there in 1925.

Cret had been trained in architecture at the Ecole des Beaux-Arts in his native Lyons and at the Ecole des Beaux-Arts in Paris. He learned the academic approach to design that instilled in his work a formality that was highly appropriate for public commissions. His attention to detail and fine craftsmanship in rendering gave his projects an appeal that was both artistic and thoroughly professional. Cret left the Ecole in 1903 to teach architecture at the University of Pennsylvania. He was a popular teacher and was widely respected in the architectural community. His Pan American Union Building (1907–10) in Washington, D.C., with Albert Kelsey, established for him a reputation in government architecture that would bring him many other public projects, including libraries, museums, post offices, and courthouses. His style of "stripped Classicism" culminated in his Federal Reserve Board Building (1935) in Washington, D.C. From 1926 to 1932 he served as an advisor to the American Battle Monuments Commission for cemeteries and memorials built in Europe after the war. Cret designed three monuments, a chapel, tablets, and the cemetery headstone for the A.B.M.C. He also designed war memorials for Pennsylvania, Providence, and Frankford (Philadelphia).[2]

Cret's winning design for the Virginia War Memorial was regarded as showing "a profound knowledge of architectural form [and] respecting the architectural tradition of Virginia, while adding to that tradition fresh and unusual but wholly consistent elements."[3] The memorial is a screen of granite columns at the end of a reflecting pool. The monumental screen separates the bronze brazier and public space in front from the grave of Virginia's unknown soldier in the solemn semicircular grove behind. The four square columns *in antis* are flanked by massive pylons standing 60 feet high. The monument is 130 feet long. The entablature is inscribed with "Virginia," the dates of American involvement in the war (1917–18), and the names of the battles in which Virginians fought: Château-Thierry, St. Mihill, and Argonne-Meuse. On the altar beneath the brazier are the words "Their Fighting Made Victory." Across the front of the platform, two bas-reliefs glorify the war efforts of Virginia's men and women. The majestic front symbolizes victory and is dedicated to those living who served. Through the columns, shrouded by high hedges and trees, lies a shrine to those who died in battle.[4]

The memorial becomes the visual and physical terminus of Blanton Avenue, creating a southern counterpoint to the East-West march of heroes down Monument Avenue. The austere Greek character of Cret's memorial is a symbolic and intentional departure from the figural Civil War statues of the turn-of-the-century, though the dedication ceremony for the cornerstone was in conjunction with birthday tributes to Confederate heroes Robert E. Lee and Thomas J. Jackson. The dedication day parade, on January 19, 1926, moved from the Capitol westward to Monument Avenue to honor the Civil War leaders before heading south to William Byrd Park.

Three months after the dedication ceremony, work was halted on the memorial. Public agitation to build a carillon in Richmond gained enough support in the Virginia Assembly for the state to re-commit the war memorial to one in the form of a bell-tower by Ralph Adams Cram (see SURVEY NO. 92). The state settled with Cret, Wright, and Nebel according to the terms of the Program, which provided for abandonment.                    SAK

NOTES
1.   See "Program of a Competition," Papers of Governor E. Lee Trinkle (Richmond: Virginia State Archives, 1925).

2.   For more background see Theophilus Bailou White, *Paul Philippe Cret: Architect and Teacher* (Philadelphia: Art Alliance, 1973); and Elizabeth G. Grossman, "Paul Philippe Cret: Rationalism and Imagery in American Architecture" (Ph.D. diss., Brown University, 1980).

3.   "Report of the War Memorial Commission," Senate Document 10 (Richmond: Archives of the General Assembly of Virginia, 1924), 9.

4.   Cret's competition entry was published in *American Architect* 130 (August 5, 1926): 99–100; and *The Architectural Record* 59 (January 1926): 90–91, as well as in many Virginia newspapers, especially September 25–28, 1925, and January 18–20, 1926, the respective dates of the award of the jury and the dedication of the grounds. See also Susan A. Kern, "Virginia's World War I Memorial: Government Versus Public Opinion" (M.A. thesis, University of Virginia, 1990).

Attributed to MARCELLUS E. WRIGHT, 1881–1962

with

CHARLES M. ROBINSON, 1867–1932

and

CHARLES CUSTER ROBINSON, died 1963

# 82.
## ACCA TEMPLE MOSQUE

*Perspective*

Monroe Park at Laurel and Main Sts., Richmond
Presentation drawing, 1925
Ink, pencil, and watercolor wash on paper; 26 by 36 inches
(by sight)
Collection of Marcellus Wright Cox & Smith, Architects,
Richmond, Virginia

FIGURE 1. *Site photo*, **Acca Temple Mosque.**

One of the best-known twentieth-century buildings by Richmond architects, the Mosque ranks with other exotic structures of the 1920s like Eberson's Loew's Theatre (SURVEY NO. 88). The use of exotic or atmospheric imagery for large entertainment structures was common in the 1920s, and the Shriners erected similar buildings for conventions and as profit-making ventures in other cities, as well. The Mosque in Richmond served an array of functions: it housed an auditorium seating approximately 4,600; as well as a ballroom, a forty-two room hotel, a restaurant, gymnasium, swimming pool, bowling alley, roof gardens, and offices.

Commissioned by the Masonic Order of Acca Temple, Ancient Arabic Order, Nobles of the Mystic Shrine, popularly known as the Shriners, the Mosque served as a money-making venture and also stood as a public-spirited gesture to provide a first-class auditorium for the City of Richmond. The brain-child of Clinton L. Williams, the Potentate of Acca Temple in 1918, the Shriners began selling stock in the venture in 1922. Design work began shortly thereafter, ground was broken in February 1926, and the opening performance was held on October 28, 1927, though the building was not fully completed until early 1928.[1] The Depression caused the Shriners to forfeit the building, and in 1940 the City of Richmond took it over and continues to operate it.[2]

This rendering, attributed to Marcellus E. Wright, captures well the essentially pictorial application of Islamic and Spanish decorative elements to what is essentially a very rational design. The architects developed three successive plans for the structure, each more elaborate and more expensive.[3] A steel framed structure, the exterior has a limestone base with tan brick and tile upper floors. Twin minarets flank the entrance arch and low, mosque-like domes cap the corner pavilions. The building sparkles with gold and silver leaf and glazed terra-cotta tile from Spain, Italy, and Tunisia, as well as America. The ornamental tile was done by J. R. Ray of the Richmond Tile and Mosaic Works. Similar detailing is found on some of the interior spaces; for instance, the original stage draperies allegedly represented a sultan's tent-hangings, studded with artificial emeralds, rubies, and diamonds. The interior decoration was carried out under the direction of J. Frank Jones of the Rambush Company of New York. The Islamic motifs certainly fit well with the Shriners, but the lavish movie sets of the 1920s must have also contributed to the style, not to mention other large entertainment pavilions, like McKim, Mead & White's Madison Square Garden (1887–91) in New York.

Marcellus E. Wright, Sr., founder of one of Virginia's largest and oldest architectural firms, was the lead designer on the temple. He associated with Charles M. Robinson for the production of the extensive working drawings required. Robinson in turn involved his son, Charles Custer Robinson, who was responsible for the Mosque's acoustical work. Acting as an architectural advisor on the project was the French-born Paul Philippe Cret, under whom Wright had studied at the University of Pennsylvania. Additionally, Cret had been involved with Wright on the Virginia War Memorial competition project in the 1920s (see SURVEY NO. 81).[4]

Born in Loudoun County, Virginia, Charles M. Robinson operated a large architectural firm in Richmond. His father, James T. Robinson, had also been an architect. Charles Robinson learned the trade through the apprentice system, studying with a Grand Rapids designer and then with John Kevan Peebles in Norfolk. After practicing in Altoona and Pittsburgh, Pennsylvania, Robinson opened an office in Richmond and eventually designed most of Richmond's public schools between 1910 and 1929, along with other buildings throughout the state.[5] His son Charles S. Robinson worked in the firm.

Marcellus E. Wright, born in Hanover County, Virginia, attended public school in Richmond and at age sixteen began work for Noland & Baskervill.[6] After five years Wright moved to Philadelphia to work for Cope & Stewardson, took courses at the School of Industrial and Applied Arts, and then studied architecture at the University of Pennsylvania, graduating in 1905. Upon graduation Wright traveled in Europe and worked in several cities before opening an office in Richmond. He designed many notable buildings around Virginia such as the Old Point Comfort Hotel in the Tidewater area and the Hotel John Marshall in Richmond, as well as buildings in Washington, D.C., and Baltimore. His son, Marcellus E. Wright, Jr. (born 1907), also became an architect, joining the firm in the 1930s. The senior Wright was very active in a number of organizations and was a member of the advisory board of architects for the Colonial Williamsburg Restoration. The fact that he was a thirty-second degree Scottish Rite Mason and a member of the Acca Temple surely assisted in his obtaining the Mosque commission.
                                                              RGW

NOTES

1.    David Robinson, "Build What, Mr. Williams? A Summary of the History and Architectural Greatness of Richmond's Mosque," June 1978, unpublished paper in the collection of the Valentine Museum, Richmond, Virginia. Also "Acca's Mosque Underway," "The Mosque Auditorium," and "Great Schumann-Heink Thrills 5,000 as Acca Temple Opened," *Richmond Times-Dispatch*, February, 7, 1926: 1, 8; "Exercises to Mark Opening of New Mosque Auditorium," and "South's Largest Theatre to Open," *Richmond News Leader*, October 28 and 29, 1927: 24, B–24.

2.    "The Mosque History," informational handout distributed by The Mosque.

3.    A photocopy of an undated and unidentified newspaper article for project No. 2 is at the Valentine Museum, Mosque File. This drawing is illustrated in Travis C. McDonald, Jr., *The Art of Architecture in Downtown Richmond, 1798–1989*, exh. cat. (Richmond: Second Presbyterian Church, 1989), 27–28; and William B. O'Neal, *Architectural Drawing in Virginia, 1819–1969*, exh. cat. (Charlottesville: School of Architecture, University of Virginia, 1969), 124–25. Other drawings exist for this project.

4.    Evidence of Cret's involvement can be found in the Paul Cret Archive, University of Pennsylvania, Philadelphia.

5.    Robert P. Winthrop, *Architecture in Downtown Richmond* (Richmond: Historic Richmond Foundation, 1982), 242.

6.    Obituary, *Richmond Times-Dispatch*, December 8, 1962: 4; *Encyclopedia of Virginia Biography* 6 (New York: Lewis Historical Pub. Co., 1915), 517; *History of Virginia*, 147.

WILLIAM GRAVES PERRY, 1883–1968

THOMAS MOTT SHAW, 1878–1964

ANDREW H. HEPBURN, 1880–1970

for

PERRY, SHAW & HEPBURN, Boston

# 83.
# COLONIAL
# WILLIAMSBURG
# RESTORATIONS

*Aerial Perspectives:*

*Restored House of Burgesses
with Its Surroundings*

*Restored Court & Palace Greens
with Their Surroundings*

Williamsburg
Presentation drawings, 1927–28
Colored pencil over photoprint; 10 ¾ by 23 ⅜ inches
Collection of the Colonial Williamsburg Foundation,
Williamsburg, Virginia

Colonial Williamsburg is Virginia's great architectural creation of the twentieth century and among her greatest contributions to American architecture. Although promoted and popularly viewed as an authentic re-creation of Virginia's colonial capital on the eve of the Revolution in the eighteenth century, in reality Colonial Williamsburg more accurately reflects the values held during its re-creation by the architects who restored it.[1]

These two renderings were produced early in the project and illustrate attitudes of the 1920s along with initial schemes for the restoration of the major buildings. They were probably made by Andrew Hepburn as part of a set to show the Reverend W. A. R. Goodwin and John D. Rockefeller II.[2] In November 1926, Goodwin persuaded Rockefeller to pay for an architect to prepare preliminary drawings for the restored town. Goodwin approached Thomas Tallmadge of Chicago, who declined, and then Charles A. Coolidge of Boston, who recommended the young firm of Perry, Shaw & Hepburn. Goodwin had met Perry in 1926 when Perry had supplied gratis drawings and later some door handles to help with the restoration of the Wythe house that Goodwin had purchased to serve as the rectory for Bruton Parish Church. Perry accepted immediately and was soon in Williamsburg measuring the town with Goodwin at night, to avoid warning the residents that soon their property would be avidly sought-after. The first purchase authorized by Rockefeller was on December 7, 1926, for the Ludwell-Paradise house. Acquisitions continued in 1927 and 1928 and in June 1928, Mr. and Mrs. Rockefeller were named as the project's sponsors.

The firm of Shaw & Hepburn had been established shortly after World War I. Perry joined in 1923; it was small—about five draftsmen in addition to the three principals—and had a modest practice of houses, churches, and academic buildings done in the tasteful Revival modes. The three partners had conventional academic backgrounds: Perry had attended Harvard, MIT, and the Ecole des Beaux-Arts; Shaw graduated from Harvard and the Ecole; and Hepburn trained at MIT. All three partners worked on Williamsburg, but Hepburn, in his capacity as coordinator of the Boston

and Williamsburg office, did all the "serious delineation before 1930."[3]

One of the conditions held by Rockefeller and advocated by Goodwin was a total town restoration, not just isolated buildings or areas. These drawings, though done very early in the project, are remarkably prescient of what would be attempted. The bird's-eye view was an older tradition for portraying cities—widely used in America—and had found recent favor in the American "City Beautiful" Movement that Perry and his partners knew well.[4] In these renderings by Hepburn, all of modern Williamsburg is cleaned away from the central core: a modern school that stood at the head of the Palace Green in front of the site of the Governor's Palace (burned in 1781) is gone, along with modern bank buildings, Chevrolet dealerships, iron watertowers, and the miscellany of modern commercial civilization. Hepburn depended upon the "Frenchman's Map" of 1782, which had recently been discovered in the William and Mary Library; he also studied documents of on-site observations and applied a liberal dose of imagination. Of particular interest is the conjectural appearance of the Governor's Palace and the Capitol, which would be significantly revised after the December 1929 discovery of the so-called Bodleian Plate, a copperplate engraving that showed accurate views of the Wren Building, the Capitol, and the Governor's Palace. Instead of reconstructing the Capitol to its appearance in 1775, it was backdated to a conjectural date of 1701–47.[5] Other notable features are the radiating street pattern in front of the Capitol, the fact that the southern vista for the Palace Green is closed, and the columns on the James City County Courthouse. As an image, the town has far too many trees (which would remain) and a neat, precise quality: the yards and gardens are well tended, the houses are painted and not ramshackle, and altogether it is a bucolic vision of a twentieth-century, upper-middle-class suburban town.          RGW

NOTES

1.    The literature on Colonial Williamsburg is voluminous, though there has been little scholarly consideration of its twentieth-century origins. Basic background can be found in: Thomas H. Taylor, Jr., "The Williamsburg Restoration and its Reception by the American Public: 1926–1942" (Ph.D. diss., George Washington University, 1989), and Charles B. Hosmer, Jr., *Preservation Comes of Age: From Williamsburg to the National Trust, 1926–1949* (Charlottesville: University Press of Virginia, 1981), vol.1: 11–73. Other considerations can be found in George Humphrey Yetter, *Williamsburg Before and After: The Rebirth of Virginia's Capital* (Williamsburg: Colonial Williamsburg Foundation, 1988), 49–71; Edward A. Chappell, "Architects of Colonial Williamsburg," in *Encyclopedia of Southern Culture,* ed. C. R. Wilson and W. Ferris (Chapel Hill: University of North Carolina Press, 1989), 59–61; Carl R. Lounsbury, "Beaux-Arts Ideals and Colonial Reality: The Reconstruction of Williamsburg's Capitol," *Journal of the Society of Architectural Historians* 49 (December 1990):373–89; and James D. Kornwulf, "So Good A Design," *The Colonial Campus of William and Mary: Its History, Background, and Legacy,* exh. cat. (Williamsburg: The College of William and Mary, Joseph and Margaret Muscarelle Museum of Art, 1989). One should also look at some of the early restoration accounts such as: "Restoration of Colonial Williamsburg," *Architectural Record* 78 (December 1935), entire issue.

2.    "Reminiscences of Andrews H. Hepburn," 1956: 12, Perry, Dean, Rogers & Partners files; letter from Robert C. Dean to George Yetter [Colonial Williamsburg Foundation], August 22, 1990. Dean, who joined Perry, Shaw & Hepburn in 1930 and became a partner in 1945, attributes the drawings to Hepburn.

3.    Letter, Dean to Yetter, August 22, 1990.

4.    John W. Reps, *Views and Viewmakers of Urban America* (Columbia: University of Missouri Press, 1984); on the aerial perspective and the City Beautiful movement see Richard Guy Wilson, "Renaissance in the Prairie," *Inland Architect* 24 (April 1980): 5–8.

5.    Lounsbury, "Reconstruction of Williamsburg's Capitol."

FIGURE 1. *Aerial photo,* **House of Burgesses.**

FIGURE 2. *Aerial photo,* **Governor's Palace and Greens.** *(Both photographs courtesy of the Colonial Williamsburg Foundation.)*

SKETCH OF RESTORED HOUSE OF BURGESSES WITH ITS SURROUNDINGS     WILLIAMSBURG     VIRGINIA
Perry Shaw and Hepburn, Architects     Boston, Massachusetts

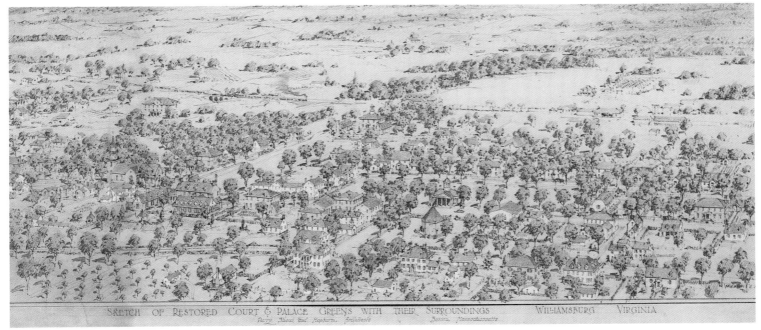

SKETCH OF RESTORED COURT & PALACE GREENS WITH THEIR SURROUNDINGS     WILLIAMSBURG     VIRGINIA
Perry Shaw and Hepburn, Architects     Boston, Massachusetts

Attributed to THOMAS TILESTON WATERMAN,
1900–1950

for

PERRY, SHAW & HEPBURN, Boston

# 84.
## COLONIAL WILLIAMSBURG RESTORATION

*Governor's Palace*
*Front Elevation*

Palace Green, Williamsburg
Working drawing, 1930
Inscribed: *Floor heights and window from Jefferson's data*
Graphite pencil on tracing paper, 23 ¼ by 38 ½ inches
Collection of Library of Congress, Washington, D.C.,
T. T. Waterman Collection

FIGURE 1. *Site photo, the restored* **Governor's Palace**, *Colonial Williamsburg.*

A centerpiece of the restoration of Williamsburg was the reconstruction of the Governor's Palace, which had burned nearly a century and a half earlier, in 1781. In actuality it was a totally new design based on historical sources.[1] Although many hands were involved in the reconstruction design, the principal force appears to have been Thomas Tileston Waterman. Born in New York City, Waterman attended private schools, and deciding against college and architecture school, he sought employment with Cram & Ferguson (see SURVEY NO. 92) in Boston. He became Ralph Adams Cram's personal assistant, and although his mentor's Gothic style never appealed to Waterman, he did admire Cram's methodology: his close and scientific study of original sources and details, with an eye toward new synthesis, not mere mimicry, would make a significant impact upon him. Waterman also worked for William Sumner Appleton of the Society for the Preservation of New England Antiquities and, together with Cram's influence, he developed an Arts and Crafts orientation toward the American past. As early as January 1926—well before Rockefeller's involvement—Waterman had been in Williamsburg photographing the Wren Building. In 1928 he was on the island of Majorca measuring the Cathedral of Palma for Cram when a letter arrived from Perry, Shaw & Hepburn asking him to join the team at Williamsburg. Waterman stayed at Williamsburg until December 1932, being involved with the Wren Building, the Capitol, Raleigh Tavern, and the Governor's Palace. Waterman went on to a substantial career as a restorationist in work at Winterthur, Delaware, and at Gadsby's Tavern in Alexandria, Virginia, among other projects. He also worked as an architect on buildings in Virginia, and as an architectural historian had numerous books to his credit. His important volumes on Virginia architecture came directly out of his Williamsburg experience, and his first one, *Domestic Colonial Architecture of Tidewater Virginia* (1932), was co-authored with John A. Barrows (1906–31), who had also worked at Williamsburg.[2]

This drawing of the projected front, or south, elevation of the Governor's Palace is attributed to Waterman; it has many features characteristic of his work, such as the figure for scale and the bold yet delicate outline.[3] It also illustrates the impact of the discovery of the Bodleian Plate in December 1929 (see Chapter 4, part 1) and actual archaeological investigations of the site. Measured floor plans by Thomas Jefferson—as noted along the bottom—helped to determine the dimensions of the rooms.[4] Additional extensive research had taken place on comparable buildings both in America and in England. Waterman became infatuated with nearby Rosewell, in Gloucester County, which he claimed was inspired by the Governor's Palace. In an article and later books, Waterman argued that many features of the Governor's Palace could be deduced from Rosewell. Rosewell, he claimed, was "the climax of Georgian architecture in the Colonies."[5] The major impact of Rosewell on the Palace restoration was the brick work of the ballroom

wing. Other drawings and accounts indicate that Walter Macomber, David Hayes, and John Barrows were involved in the development of the exterior elevations and the interiors.[6]

From the squat, three-bayed structure portrayed in Hepburn's earlier rendering (see SURVEY NO. 83), the Palace's design by 1930 had evolved to the tall, hipped-roof, elegant structure shown here. The front elevation is restored to approximately 1706, when construction originally began. An obsession with details is obvious; Waterman draws in portions of the rubbed brick discovered from archaeology. Other details are more creative, for in spite of the evidence of the Bodleian Plate, Waterman and compatriots decided upon a more aesthetically pleasing balustrade for the roof. Waterman has also made the cupola shorter and more in proportion with the building than the tall ungainly appendage shown in the plate. The pressures of getting work going is indicated by the notation, "Preliminary for Budget estimate only." As erected between 1932 and 1934, the Palace largely followed this drawing, though the window details, the balcony, and the end elevations of the flanking buildings were changed. The rear elevation was a reconstruction of the 1751–52 addition of a ballroom and supper room done under the administration of Lieutenant Governor Robert Dinwiddie.    RGW

NOTES
1.    Mark R. Wenger, "Reconstruction of the Governor's Palace in Williamsburg, Virginia," unpublished report, March 1980, is the most complete study.

2.    Fay Campbell, "Thomas Tileston Waterman: Student of American Colonial Architecture," *Winterthur Portfolio* 20 (Summer-Autumn 1985): 103–147; biographical entry in *National Cyclopedia of American Biography* (New York: James T. White, 1955), vol.40: 312; Fiske Kimball, "Thomas Tileston Waterman," *Journal of the AIA* 15 (May 1951): 240–241; Charles E. Peterson, "Thomas T. Waterman (1900–1951)," *Journal of the Society of Architectural Historians* 10, no. 2(1951): 25.

3.    Previously illustrated in Campbell, "Thomas Tileston Waterman," 115.

4.    Marcus Whiffen, *The Public Buildings of Williamsburg* (Williamsburg: The Colonial Williamsburg Foundation, 1958), gives background.

5.    Thomas Tileston Waterman and John A. Barrows, *Domestic Colonial Architecture of Tidewater Virginia* (New York: Charles Scribner's Sons, 1932), 87; Thomas T. Waterman, "Rosewell, Gloucester County, Virginia," *Architectural Forum* 52 (January 1930): 17–20.

6.    There are other elevations at the Library of Congress in the Waterman Collection. One drawing has a label that reads: "Original Layout Elevation Governor's Palace Williamsburg, Virginia Drawn by David Hayes From Designs by Thomas T. Waterman." Additional elevations are at Colonial Williamsburg and several are drawn by Barrows.

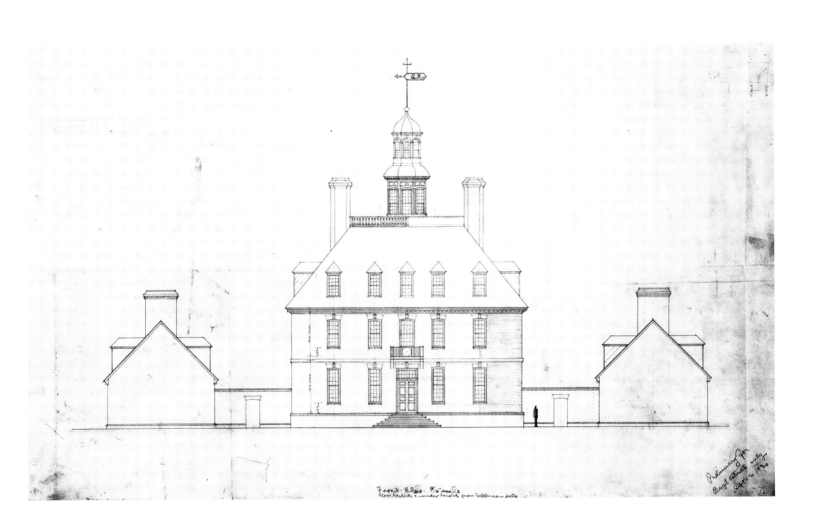

Attributed to ANDREW HEPBURN, 1880–1970

for

PERRY, SHAW & HEPBURN, Boston

# 85.
## COLONIAL WILLIAMSBURG RESTORATION

*Commercial Block XXIII (Merchant's Square) Perspective*

Williamsburg
Presentation drawing, circa 1929
Ink on drawing board; 16 ⅝ by 36 ⅛ inches
Collection of the Colonial Williamsburg Foundation, Williamsburg, Virginia

One of the major problems facing the restorationists at Williamsburg was where to place the commercial activities needed for twentieth-century living. The restoration of much of Duke of Gloucester Street meant the displacement of many businesses. The town was to be a living museum, and additionally there were many inhabitants living outside of the historical area who would continue to need commercial services. And then there would be the tourists, who would need a place to purchase their souvenirs—always a vital element—as well as to rest and eat. Typical of the freewheeling rationalization for some of the restoration was the explanation by William G. Perry: "It has been assumed that had the people of Williamsburg been faced with a similar problem in the eighteenth century, they might have solved it in this manner and with buildings similar in appearance to these."[1]

The solution was to group the commercial structures in a two-block area at the western end of the Duke of Gloucester Street. The site was chosen because it contained fewer original structures and already was a commercial area oriented to the College of William and Mary. A few of the existing structures were retained though heavily remodeled and incorporated into a pictorial assemblage of single and two-story buildings. Arthur Shurcliff did the initial planning for the area; the rendering shown is very much in the illustrative style common to historical novels of the period. Order is provided by the rhythmic grouping of the buildings and the trees. The precedents for the buildings' exteriors came from a number of places, including the towns of New Castle and Dover, Delaware, along with Annapolis, Maryland, and Alexandria, Virginia. Automobile parking was provided in lots behind the stores, and passageways led to the street which, during the day, was reserved for pedestrians.[2] While Merchant's Square as completed differs in some ways from the rendering, still the same ambiance and forms remain.[3]

Certainly the Colonial Revival style had been used for commercial buildings prior to Merchant's Square, but the coordinated complex would prove to be extremely significant. Indeed, it may have been the most influential aspect of the Williamsburg restoration, for in Merchant's Square concentrated planning, both in the division of traffic and pedestrians and in the style, can be seen as the seeds of shopping centers and malls since built across America.     RGW

*Commercial Group — Du[...]*

FIGURE 1. *Site photo,* **Merchant's Square** *as restored. (Photograph courtesy of the Colonial Williamsburg Foundation.)*

NOTES

1. William G. Perry, "Notes on the Architecture," in the "Restoration of Colonial Williamsburg" issue, *Architectural Record* 78 (December 1935): 373.

2. Thomas H. Taylor, "The Williamsburg Restoration and its Reception by the American Public: 1926–1942" (Ph.D. diss., George Washington University, 1989), 262–64.

3. A photograph of the second building from the right in the rendering appeared in "Restoration of Colonial Williamsburg," *Architectural Record* 78 (December 1935):445; on Market Square, see also George Humphrey Yetter, *Williamsburg Before and After* (Williamsburg: Colonial Williamsburg Foundation, 1988), 138–43.

*Street—Block XXIII—for—the Williamsburg Holding Corporation—Williamsburg, Virginia. — Perry Shaw and Hepburn Architects.*

ROBERT C. DEAN, born 1903

for

PERRY, SHAW & HEPBURN, Boston

# 86.
# COLONIAL
# WILLIAMSBURG
# RESTORATION

*Duke of Gloucester Street*
*Block X*
*Plan and Elevations*

Williamsburg
Presentation drawing, circa 1931
Inscribed: *Perry Shaw & Hepburn*
Watercolor and ink on heavy paper; 27 ¼ by 37 ⅜ inches
Collection of Colonial Williamsburg Foundation,
Williamsburg, Virginia

FIGURE 1. *Site photo,* **Duke of Gloucester Street.** *(Photograph courtesy of the Colonial Williamsburg Foundation.)*

With the announcement of the Rockefeller patronage for the restoration of Williamsburg to its eighteenth-century appearance, the scale and tenor of the architectural work increased significantly. An unparalleled research effort developed, archives and libraries across the United States and abroad were searched, and extensive field work was undertaken not only in Williamsburg and the surrounding area, but also throughout the eastern United States. Perry, Shaw & Hepburn would continue as supervising architects until 1934 but, given the size of the project and the fact that all three partners continued to reside in Boston, many decisions fell to their employees in Virginia. Additionally, an "Advisory Committee of Architects," with members such as Fiske Kimball and Ralph Adams Cram, and a committee from the Association for the Preservation of Virginia Antiquities, had to be satisfied as well as the local community, the New York construction firm of Todd and Brown, and of course Rockefeller and the Reverend Mr. Goodwin.

Among the architects sent south was Walter Macomber, who had come up through the apprentice system in various New England offices. Macomber, the project's first "resident architect," was known for his obsession with recording the details of traditional buildings, a custom that would have a lasting impact upon the work at Williamsburg. He was bolstered in late 1929 by A. Edwin Kendrew (born 1903), whom the firm sent down to organize and create order out of the chaos that had developed. A number of young, talented, and hard-drinking draftsmen were engaged as well. Among the most famous, because of his later publications on Virginia architecture, was Thomas Tileston Waterman. Another was David Hayes, a young draftsman already working for the firm in Boston, and John Barrows, who came from Norfolk. Back in Boston the firm hired Robert C. Dean (born 1903), who had trained at the Fontainebleau School in France and then at MIT. Dean would be responsible for turning the field notes and archaeological data into finished drawings.

The landscape designer for the project, Arthur A. Shurcliff (1870–1957), had university training in engineering and science and had worked for the firm of Frederick Law Olmsted in Boston, on the Biltmore House in Asheville, North Carolina, and the Boston "Emerald Necklace" of the Fenway and parks. Shurcliff had become known for his historical landscape creations. He had worked on Old Sturbridge Village in Massachusetts, and for the Archibald McCreas at nearby Carter's Grove on the James River, beginning in 1927. Shurcliff based his work at Williamsburg upon diligent research of some thirty-eight different colonial sites in Virginia, as well as other documents. He has been described as a "dramatic, Wildean character," whose independence of mind and enthusiasm of garden projects led him at times to go over the heads of his employers and directly to the Williamsburg executives or even to Rockefeller himself.[1]

Important in setting the tone for the restoration was not just the large buildings (the Capitol, the Gov-

ernor's Palace, and the College of William and Mary), but also the smaller scale housing and landscaping. Block surveys based on research of the historic district, were carried out; the results both showed extant eighteenth-century buildings that could be restored and projected new structures. These were a combination of many talents, though certainly Shurcliff dominated in the elaborate garden design. The rendering for Block X is but one of many done for Duke of Gloucester Street by Robert Dean. Showing both the streetscape and the site plans, these renderings were intended to impress graphically, as they do; indeed, as Dean has remembered, they were specifically for "Mr. Rockefeller."[2] Conjured up was a pictorial vision of a neat Colonial village, and while the buildings differ in size and materials, an overall order is imposed though the rhythmic placement of trees lining the street. The neat houses would become models for suburban developments across the United States.          RGW

NOTES
1.   Edward A. Chappell, "Architects of Colonial Williamsburg," in *Encyclopedia of Southern Culture*, C. R. Wilson and W. Ferris, eds. (Chapel Hill: University of North Carolina Press, 1989), 59–61.

2.   Letter, Robert C. Dean to author, January 4, 1991.

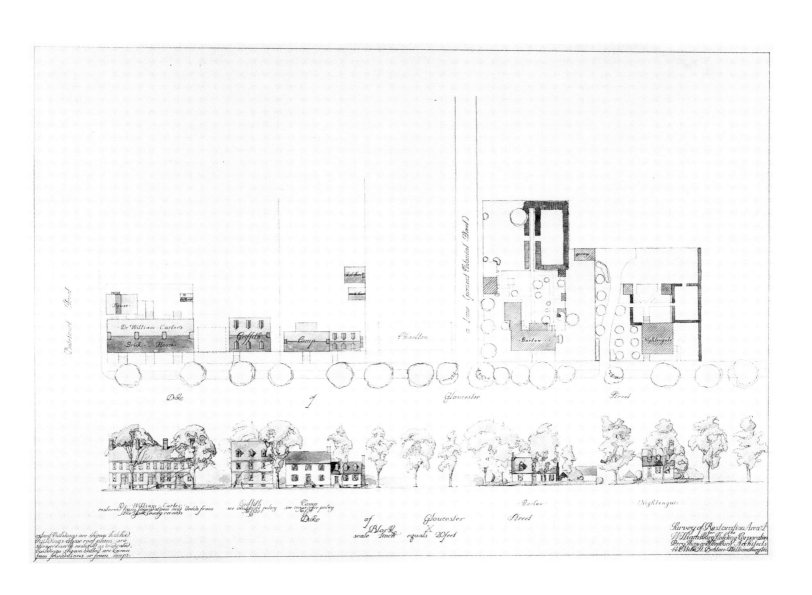

WILLIAM LAWRENCE BOTTOMLEY, 1883–1951

for

BOTTOMLEY, WAGNER & WHITE, ARCHITECTS

New York City

# 87.
# WAVERLEY HILL

*Residence for*
*Herbert McKelden Smith, Esq.*
*Perspective*

3001 North Augusta St., Staunton
Presentation drawing, 1928–30
Signed and dated lower left: *Bottomley, Wagner & White,*
*Architects, New York City, 1928–30*
Mechanical print of charcoal drawing on paper with colored
pencil added; 11 by 24 inches
Private Collection

FIGURE 1. *Site photo,* **Waverley Hill,** *Staunton.*

Of those who best managed to accommodate modern requirements within the older form of the Virginia plantation house, William Lawrence Bottomley is the acknowledged master. Bottomley's name is virtually synonymous with Colonial Revival architecture in Virginia. More than once he expressed his belief in the value of the plantation house. In a published interview in 1929, for example, he emphasized, "I believe we should do everything possible to preserve this old southern ideal of country house architecture because it is one of the finest things we have and it is still vital."[1] His commitment is amply shown in Waverley Hill, where he adopted the form of a Tidewater Georgian house and placed it on a hilltop in the Shenandoah Valley, an area of the state that had never experienced this form of architecture in the eighteenth century.

An irony exists with Bottomley's Virginia association, however, for he neither lived nor had an office in Virginia; he was simply the most successful in producing strongly evocative houses that recalled Virginia's past. William Lawrence Bottomley was born and raised in New York City; he attended Columbia's School of Architecture, the American Academy in Rome, and the Ecole des Beaux-Arts in Paris. His office was always in New York City, and he designed New York townhouses, clubs, hotels, and the palatial River House apartments on the East River, along with public buildings and many country houses throughout the East and the South. Today known for his Virginia Georgian Revival houses, Bottomley, like other creative revivalists of the period, worked in a variety of styles from Mediterranean to Art Déco. He had several partners throughout his career, but he was always the major designer. Additionally he wrote numerous articles for architectural periodicals; authored *Spanish Details* (New York: William Hellburn, 1924); and chaired the committee that produced *Great Georgian Houses of America* (1933–37), in which Virginia houses dominate.[2] Bottomley's first Virginia work came in 1915 with a large stucco-covered Neo-Georgian house west of Richmond, and the following year he received a commission on Monument Avenue. In the next quarter-century he received at least forty-seven more commissions in the state, primarily for houses, and saw about thirty-five of them completed.[3]

Waverley Hill, for Herbert McKelden Smith at Staunton, Virginia, represents Bottomley at the peak of his career. Smith ran a profitable coal and ice business in Staunton; he had never farmed in his life but in the mid 1920s he purchased 250 acres outside of town and began to raise registered Angus cattle. His new house was to be a manor house for the farm. The name "Waverley Hill" came from Mr. Smith's grandfather's house in Rockingham County, which had been named for a country house mentioned in novels by Sir Walter Scott. Bottomley received the commission in 1928, construction began in 1929, and while the house was largely completed that year, some alterations were made in 1930. The cost was approximately $75,000.[4]

The presentation rendering shows the south or entrance front of Waverley Hill as it was substantially

completed. Bottomley has taken the classic form of the James River plantation house, extended it into a five-part composition and modernized it with the glazed hyphens. The twin end-pavilions have blank niches, occupied in the rendering by urns, which Bottomley replaced with molded eagles in late 1929. The central block resembles the north elevation of Carter's Grove, with its tall hipped roof and chimneys that were extensively restored and altered in 1928. The north, or garden, elevation has molded brick door surrounds reminiscent of Carter's Grove, while the doorway in the south elevation seems instead to have been inspired by the Hammond-Harwood house in Annapolis. Waverley Hill was built of early-nineteenth-century brick from a recently demolished house; the central block was laid up in Flemish bond and the wings in common bond, clearly intending to suggest construction phased over a period of time. Not shown or even suggested in the rendering is the brilliant siting of the house on a hilltop and the dramatic perspective across the rear. On a cross axis to the entrance hall is an enfilade of over 130 feet that stretches through seven separate spaces, from the library on the west (right) pavilion to a garden room in the east (left) pavilion, which overlooks Mr. Smith's farm and provides a stunning view of the Shenandoah Valley.              RGW

NOTES
1.  John Taylor Boyd, Jr., "The Country House and the Developed Landscape: William Lawrence Bottomley Expresses His Point of View about the Relation of the Country House to Its Environment in an Interview," *Arts and Decoration* 31 (November 1929): 100.

2.  Architect's Emergency Committee, *Great Georgian Houses of America* 1 (New York: The Kalkhoff Press, 1933); Vol. 2 (New York: The Scribner Press, 1937). Eight of Bottomley's patrons are listed as subscribers.

3.  William B. O'Neal and Christopher Weeks, *The Work of William Lawrence Bottomley in Richmond* (Charlottesville: University Press of Virginia, 1984); Davyd Foard Hood, "William Lawrence Bottomley In Virginia: The 'Neo-Georgian' House in Richmond" (M. A. thesis, University of Virginia, 1975); and H. Stafford Bryant, Jr., "Two Twentieth-Century Domestic Architects in the South: Neel Reid and William L. Bottomley," *Classic America* 1, no. 2 (1972):30–36.

4.  Interviews with Dr. and Mrs. H. McKelden Smith, October 7, 1989, and January 12, 1990. In his thesis, Davyd Foard Hood, 90, notes that the original name was "The Ridgeway." Other drawings for this project are in the possession of the present owners.

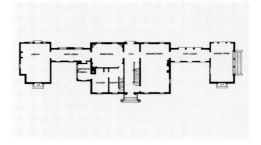

FIGURE 2. *Plan of* **Waverley Hill.**

Residence for
Herbert McK. Smith Esq
Staunton, Va

## 88.
# LOEW'S THEATRE
# AND OFFICE
# BUILDING

*Elevation*

Sixth and East Grace Sts., Richmond
Presentation and working drawing, 1927
Signed and dated lower right: *John Eberson, 6–20–27*
Ink on linen, 43 ⅛ by 48 ⅝ inches
Collection of The Mitchell Wolfson, Jr., Collection;
courtesy of The Wolfsonian Foundation, Miami, Florida

FIGURE 1. *Vintage photo,* **Loew's Theatre,**
*1928. (Photograph courtesy of the Cook Collection,
The Valentine Museum.)*

John Eberson was considered one of the nation's three leading theatre architects and was at the height of his Atmospheric Theatre period when he designed the Loew's Theatre in Richmond in 1927, marking still another link in his partnership with the Loew's Corporation, a prominent theatre chain. Eberson designed nine other theatres for Loew's in Virginia: in Hampton, Buena Vista, Harrisonburg, Alexandria, Suffolk, Staunton, Leesburg, and Lexington.

Eberson's background prepared him well for the architecture of entertainment. Born in Bukovina (Austro-Hungary, now Romania) in 1875, he attended the Technological College in Vienna, where he majored in engineering. During his stay in Vienna, he came to know and love the elaborate ornamentation of the buildings, the illusionary ceilings, the ultra-Baroque ornamentation, and the general air of excitement that permeated the city at the turn of the century. Leaving Vienna in 1901, Eberson came to America and settled in the St. Louis area, where he found a position with George H. Johnston, a theatre designer. He became actively involved in all phases of theatre architecture, from actual construction to set design. Traveling for Johnston Realty and Construction Company through the South and the Midwest, he supervised the construction of various Nickelodeon theatres. During the St. Louis Exposition of 1904, Eberson formed an alliance with Karl Hoblitzelle, theatre entrepreneur, for whom he would later develop the Atmospheric Theatre style.[1]

When Eberson formed his own firm in 1904, he moved to Hamilton, Ohio, where he continued to build theatres. In 1910 he followed the theatre-building boom to Chicago, where he began to diverge from the Beaux-Arts style that had been so popular with theatre-owners of the day, and as early as 1913 he built a modified stars-and-clouds theatre in San Antonio, Texas. Eberson remained in Chicago until 1926 when, at the request of the Loew's Corporation, he moved to New York.[2] It was in 1923, in Houston, however, that Eberson opened his first complete Atmospheric Theatre. Audiences were overwhelmed, as they would later be in Richmond, by the feeling of openness in the auditorium, of starlit, cloud-filled "skies," of lighting displays that could be changed to create dawns and sunsets, and of luxurious lobbies and corridors that put European palaces to shame. The auditorium dripped with ornamentation and statuary from Classical antiquity. *Putti* floated from an elaborately "carved" proscenium arch. Walls intended to simulate portions of building exteriors were punctuated by lighted window-openings, arches, and ornate balconies that framed even more decoration: artificial plants, trees, and statuary. Stuffed birds of every variety perched on balconies, hung in flight from the sky-blue ceilings, and nested in the foliage.[3]

When Loew's accepted Eberson's plans for their Richmond theatre—the only Atmospheric Theatre he built in Virginia—he was already designing several others for them. He had completed Loew's Akron in Ohio and the Century Theatre in Baltimore. The first design for the Richmond building was dated April 20,

1927, with the last recorded revision done on June 20, 1927.[4] The theatre opened on April 9, 1928, a little ahead of the thirteen-month time frame usually allotted for such buildings. The auditorium was a typically ornate example of Eberson's Atmospheric Style and was large by present standards, with seating planned for 2,217. The theatre's final cost was $1,250,000, which included a $5,000 bonus given voluntarily to the architect for his efficiency and good work.[5]

The building's corner entryway, jutting above the horizontal lines of the main building, is covered by face-brick punctuated by terra-cotta triangles that divide the surface into geometric shapes. The heavily ornamented quatrefoil of the upper facade is further accented by *putti* floating on the already ornamented surface. An ultra-Baroque pediment frames the upper facade against the sky. Two elegant, paired pilasters spaced equidistant from the entryway separate it visually from the rest of the building. The decorative cresting and frieze on the Grace Street side of the theatre are also richly ornamented with terra cotta, as was the top of the original marquee and ticket booth. Storefronts with two-story windowed bays line the wall of the building's left side. The window on the Grace Street side serves to ornament both the exterior and interior of the building. The paned cathedral-glass window serves as a focal point inside, where it is placed at the top of the grand staircase. This theatre is important historically not only because it was built by John Eberson, but also because it is the only example of an Atmospheric Theatre in Virginia and is still operating, a glorious playback of the fantasy-filled days when movies were most magical and the buildings that housed them kept pace with their dreams.        JP

NOTES
1.  "John Eberson," *National Cyclopedia of American Biography* (New York: James T. White, 1955), 40:362–63. Conversations with Drew Eberson, son of the architect and successor to the firm, during the period 1983 to 1990 were invaluable in piecing together the Eberson biographical material.

2.  Ibid. See also *Theatre Catalogue* (Philadelphia: Jay Emanuel Publications, 1948–49), 11; and *San Antonio Express*, June 9, 1929.

3.  See Jane Preddy, *Palaces of Dreams: The Movie Theatres of John Eberson,* exh. cat. (San Antonio: McNay Art Museum, 1990); Richard Stapleford and Jane Preddy, *Temples of Illusion: The Atmospheric Theaters of John Eberson,* exh. cat. (New York: Hunter College, Bertha and Karl Leubsdorf Art Gallery, 1988); and Jane Preddy, *Glamour, Glitz and Sparkle: The Deco Theatres of John Eberson* (Chicago: Theatre Historical Society of America, 1989)

4.  Working drawings from Eberson Archives, New York City; see also Elroy E. Quenroe, "John Eberson in Richmond, Virginia—Architect for the Twenties," (M. A. thesis, University of Virginia, 1975); and Quenroe, "Movie House Architecture, Twenties Style," *Arts in Virginia* 26 (Fall 1976): 22–31.

5.  "Loew's Theatre, Richmond, Virginia," Nomination Form, National Register of Historic Places, Washington, D.C. Letter, Loew's Incorporated to John Eberson, May 23, 1928, Eberson Archives, Wolfson Foundation of Decorative and Propaganda Arts, Miami, Florida.

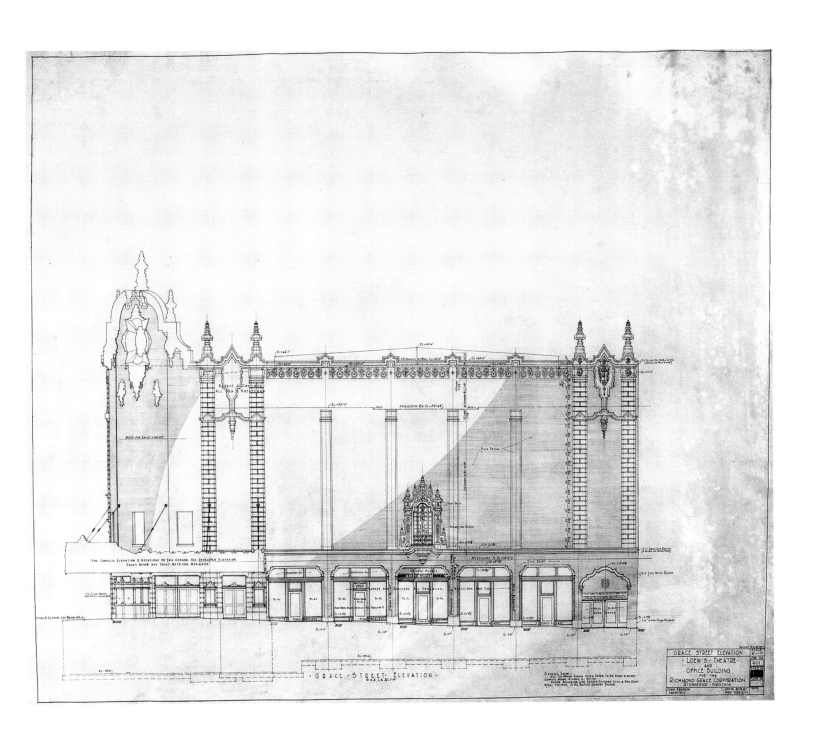

·GRACE·STREET·ELEVATION·

JOHN EBERSON, 1875–1954

in association with

CARNEAL, JOHNSTON & WRIGHT, Richmond

# 89.
## LIGHT FIXTURE FOR CENTRAL NATIONAL BANK

*Perspective*

219 E. Broad St., Richmond
Presentation drawing, circa 1929
Colored pencil and wash on tracing paper;
26 ¾ by 11 ¾ inches
Collection of Central Fidelity Bank, Richmond, Virginia

The attempt by American architects to create a new language reflecting current art movements, especially Cubism, along with the rise of industrialization and the Machine Age, is nowhere better shown than in this drawing for a light fixture. Composed of simple geometric forms telescoping downward on the wall and inlaid with flat patterns, the fixture recalls a setback skyscraper turned upside down. The interweaving of these simple forms into a complex pattern of decorative geometry is the essence of what is today called Art Déco, though in the 1920s and 1930s it would have been known as Art Moderne, or as a bank officer described it in 1930, "Modern American with vertical element of design."[1] Influenced by many sources—including the Paris *Exposition Internationale des Arts Décoratifs et Industriels Modernes* of 1925, the work of architects Bertram Goodhue and Eliel Saarinen, and the new perceptions of the machine as art—the Art Déco style became the embodiment of sophistication in the late 1920s.

Central National Bank was Richmond's major contender in the skyscraper race during the 1920s; at twenty-four stories and 278 feet (plus 46 feet for the flagpole), it was the tallest structure in the city and one of the highest in the South.[2] A competition existed between businessmen in several American cities (New York, Chicago, Los Angeles, Atlanta, Charlottesville, Lynchburg, and Roanoke) to erect eye-catching skyscrapers that would advertise the "go-getting" spirit of their respective cities in the Jazz Age. Richmond and Central National Bank were not to be left out. The bank had been chartered in 1911, and by the 1920s was one of the largest in the city. Originally located further east on Broad Street at 307, the bank's directors, under the leadership of president William Harry Schwarzschild, purchased a site on the corner of Third and Broad in August 1928. Surrounding the corner site was the Broad-Grace Arcade, still under construction, that had been designed by John Eberson in conjunction with Carneal, Johnston & Wright. Just having completed the Loew's Theatre ( SURVEY NO. 88 ), Eberson had already achieved a considerable reputation in Richmond, and the bank turned to him for the design of their new structure. Although better known as a movie-house architect, Eberson had designed numerous commercial buildings and one skyscraper, the Niels Esperson Building in Houston (1927). His initial design for Central National Bank was a ten-story Italian Renaissance *palazzo*. But the aspirations of the bank's officers were for more stories, so the height was increased to twelve stories, then fifteen, and by November 1928 to twenty-four stories.[3] It is unknown whether the new height or the directives of the bank's officers made Eberson change his design, but what finally emerged was a superb example of Art Déco.

Design work for the building was completed and construction began in March 1929; opening ceremonies were held in June 1930, by which time business conditions had changed drastically. While Eberson was responsible for the design, Carneal, Johnston &

Wright managed the project in Richmond.[4] The resultant design took the setback form, mainly at the upper floors at the corners. Verticality was emphasized by dark brick spandrels beneath each window in the tower and brick pilasters that narrow as they near the top. Heavily ornamented both at the top and the base, the entrance was a limestone-and-granite facade with a large round semi-Renaissance arch and brass doors. Inside the great banking hall, measuring 58 by 125 feet and nearly 40 feet tall, was one of the most spectacular spaces in the city. The interior was richly ornamented with a multicolored and patterned terrazzo floor and a ceiling of intricate plaster panels with floral and geometrical patterns. Much of the ornamentation came from French and Viennese design sources. Of the many glories of the interior, the lighting fixtures stand out. Given the attention Eberson directed to his theatre interiors, his firm probably designed them and then had them manufactured by a lighting house in New York—either Rambusch, or Cox, Nostrad & Gunnison. A number of different light fixtures were designed and made; this one was for the main hall.

RGW

NOTES
1.    Handwritten note on letter from E. D. Pearson to Ralph L. Dombrower, November 6, 1930, in building file, Central Fidelity Bank. For background on the terminology and sources see: Richard Guy Wilson, Dianne Pilgrim, and Dickran Tashjian, *The Machine Age in America, 1918–1941* (New York: Abrams, 1986), 351–52, note 7; and Richard Guy Wilson, "Introduction: Art Déco and John Eberson," *The 1989 Annual of the Theatre Historical Society of America* 16 (1989): 8–11.

2.    Actually, the building had only twenty-one floors of rentable space; the top three floors were given over to mechanical equipment.

3.    Elroy E. Quenroe, "John Eberson in Richmond, Virginia: Architect for the Twenties" (M. A. thesis, University of Virginia, 1975); and promotional brochure, *The Central National Bank Building* (Richmond: Central National Corporation and Morton G. Thalhimer, Inc., 1930).

4.    Plans in possession of Central Fidelity Bank are signed by both firms; most of the plans are dated March 1929, and then have revision dates of later in March, then June and September 1929.

FIGURE 1. *Interior view,* **Lobby, Central National Bank.**

FIGURE 2. *Exterior view,* **Central National Bank.**

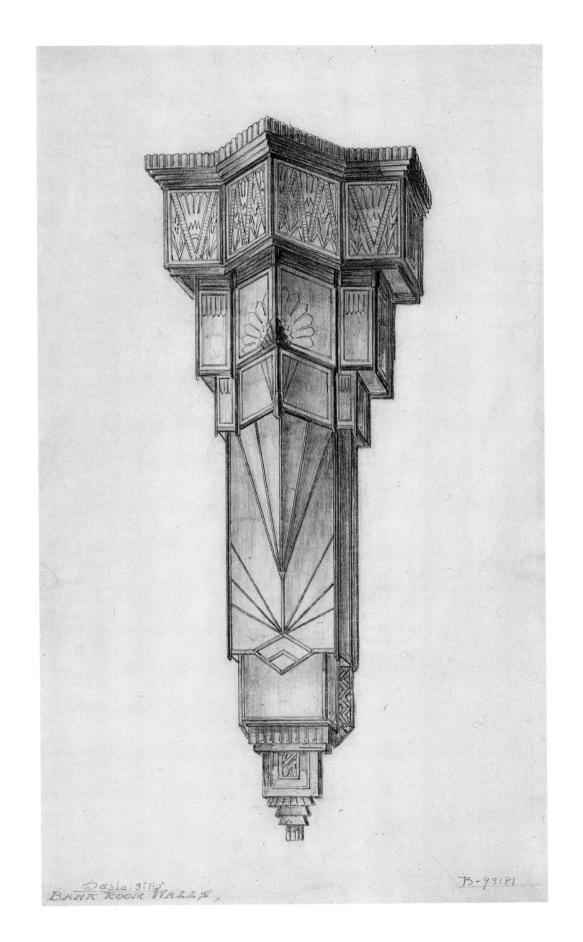

Scale: 3"=1'0"
BANK ROOM WALLS,

B-93181

STANHOPE S. JOHNSON, 1882–1973

RAY O. BRANNAN, 1892–1974

for

JOHNSON & BRANNAN, Lynchburg

# 90.
# ALLIED ARTS
# BUILDING

*North Elevation*

Eighth and Church Sts., Lynchburg
Presentation rendering, circa 1929
Watercolor on paper mounted on board; 28 ⅝ by 13 ⅝ inches
Collection of the Jones Memorial Library, Lynchburg, Virginia

FIGURE 1. *Site photo,* **Allied Arts Building,** *Lynchburg. (Photograph courtesy of Richard Cheek, Belmont, Massachusetts.)*

Conceived as the symbol of a progressive era in the history of Lynchburg, the Allied Arts Building (1928–1931) projected a modern image for the city and for the architectural firm of Johnson & Brannan.[1] As the city's tallest building, it dominated the skyline until 1973, when it was surpassed in height by the Fidelity Bank Building. Through its distinctive Art Déco style, the Allied Arts Building demonstrated the enterprising spirit of Lynchburg and the broad abilities of Johnson & Brannan.

By the time his firm received the commission in 1928, Stanhope S. Johnson had established a statewide reputation as a Colonial Revival architect. In 1919 he formed a partnership with Ray Brannan.[2] Together they designed a series of commercial structures, including the Hotel Monticello in Charlottesville (SURVEY NO. 80).[3] While both buildings are basically multi-story blocks, the architects abandoned the conservative brick-and-stone facades of the Hotel Monticello to create in the Allied Arts Building a thoroughly modern structure that proudly announced its place in twentieth-century architecture.[4] The success of the architects in creating a statement of the period is demonstrated by its rank as one of the best Art Déco buildings in Virginia.[5]

The preliminary drawings for the building indicate that the design went through radical changes before leaving the drawing board.[6] The rendering shown here, of the north elevation, illustrates an early scheme and places the building on the opposite side of Eighth Street from the actual construction site. It represents an intermediate stage in the design process and exhibits many of the ideas that were developed in the building as constructed.

This rendering presents the building as a rectangular block rising sixteen stories above Church Street. The facade has a slight horizontal division above the second story, which provides a base for the shaft. This break also separates the two commercial floors from the office space within the shaft. From this base, four dominant piers rise without interruption to the top of the structure. These piers encase the load-bearing steel girders and reveal the skeletal construction of the building. Between these piers, the windows and their spandrels are recessed to create a second plane on the face of the facade. They work with smaller piers which separate the coupled windows to develop strong secondary lines that reinforce the upward movement of the building. In addition to the vertical bands, the windows change from rectangular to segmental forms on the penultimate floor, to augment the appearance of upward thrust.

In a later rendering of the north facade, the architects enhance the verticality of the building by enlarging the secondary piers between the windows and extending them into the same plane as the four structural piers. With this drawing, the exterior of the building appears as a series of vertical stripes similar to the Daily News Building in New York.[7] This drawing also places the building on the west side of Eighth Street.

The problems of the base and the top are addressed in a third rendering of the same facade. Through a series of overlays, this rendering shows a number of proposed solutions that would define both the base and the top. The overlays introduce polychromy into the facade, which Johnson and Brannan adopt in the finished design. They use greenstone on the base to separate the first three stories from the shaft, and employ the same stone for the window spandrels to blend with the window voids and to create the darker vertical ribbons that contrast with the yellow brick of the piers. With the brick piers, these ribbons create an A-B-C-B-A rhythm that is carried across all four facades.

At the fifteenth floor, the main shaft of the building changes from a rectangular slab to an octagonal crown. The corner piers also terminate at this point. While the interior piers continue across the face of the octagon, they are transformed into a series of stepped-back buttresses that make the main block appear to disintegrate around the crown. To contrast with the buttresses, this octagonal crown is faced with the same greenstone employed on the base. Above the seventeenth floor, the attic and its buttresses are dressed totally in greenstone. These innovations are executed in the final design.

The third rendering also introduced a penthouse that the firm of Johnson & Brannan designed as their offices. Returning to the roots of their practice, the firm rejected the Art Déco style for the office interiors and decorated the major rooms with neo-Georgian paneling and woodwork. After the dissolution of the partnership in 1936, the offices atop the Allied Arts Building remained the home and symbol of Johnson's practice until his retirement in 1968.[8]          DDMcK

NOTES

1.  Johnson and Brannan received the commission for this building before the Wall Street crash of 1929. Despite the onset of the Depression, the building continued as scheduled; construction in Lynchburg did not slow until after the building's completion. In fact, in the summer of 1932, Lynchburg led the state and ranked seventeenth nationally for the month of June in new construction starts. See "Lynchburg First in Building," *Daily Advance,* August 18, 1932, p.3.

2.  Born in Greenville, Tennessee, Brannan worked as a chemist at the Lynchburg Foundry until 1917. In that year, he joined Johnson's firm as the office manager and became his partner in 1919. See *Hill's Lynchburg City Directory* (1917–1919), and his obituary in *Lynchburg News,* August 30, 1974, B4:1.

3.  S. Allen Chambers, Jr., *Lynchburg: An Architectural History* (Charlottesville: University Press of Virginia, 1981), p.432. Throughout his discussion of Johnson & Brannan, Chambers identifies Brannan incorrectly as R.J. Brannan.

4.  Author's interview in 1982 with Addison Staples, an associate of the firm during the period. According to Staples, the architects wanted to design the building in "the style of the day" and persuaded the Allied Arts Corporation that the tallest building in Lynchburg should also be the most modern.

5.  See William B. O'Neal, *Architecture in Virginia* (New York: Walker, 1968), p.179; and Joni Belah, "Sleek, But Overlooked," Associated Press article in *Lynchburg News,* May 31, 1987, B7:2.

6.  The complete drawings for the Allied Arts Building are in the collection of the Jones Memorial Library, Lynchburg.

7.  The similarity of the Allied Arts Building to the Daily News Building (which was under construction during the same period), as well as its departure from the firm's usual Colonial Revival genre has given rise to a tradition in Lynchburg that the firm hired a New York architect to design the facade. This legend cannot be substantiated, but its continuation among present-day architects of Lynchburg pays tribute to the building's superior design.

8.  Brannan established an independent practice in 1936, according to Hill's *Lynchburg City Directory* (1936).

STANHOPE S. JOHNSON, 1882–1973

RAYMOND O. BRANNAN, 1892–1974

WILLIAM ADDISON STAPLES, 1899–1983

for

JOHNSON & BRANNAN, Lynchburg

# 91.
## GALLISON HALL

*Residence for Mr. & Mrs.
Julio Suarez-Galban,
Elevation and Interior
Perspectives*

24 Farmington Dr., near Charlottesville (Albemarle County)
Presentation drawings, 1930
Inscribed: *WAS 30*
Colored pencil on tracing paper; Entrance Front 15 by 36
inches; Drawing Room 6 ¾ by 14 ½ inches; Living Room 5 ¼
by 13 ⅜
Collection of Jones Memorial Library, Lynchburg, Virginia

FIGURE 1. *Site photo,* **Gallison Hall.**

Gallison Hall is one of the great twentieth-century country places in Virginia and shows Stanhope Johnson's talents as a residential designer who could incorporate a variety of sources into a single design. Assisting Johnson in the design of Gallison Hall was William Addison Staples, a young man in the office who possessed great drawing talents. Staples was born in Lynchburg and studied architecture at Carnegie Institute of Technology (now Carnegie-Mellon University) in Pittsburgh. He worked for Johnson from 1923 to 1938, and then for Lynchburg architect Pendleton S. Clark.[1] Also a key figure in the design of the great house was Charles F. Gillette, a popular landscape designer of the day who created an English-style geometric garden for the grounds.

Mr. and Mrs. Julio Suarez-Galban commissioned Johnson in 1930 to design a country place for them on forty-four acres at Farmington Country Club near Charlottesville, Virginia. The original Farmington House has additions, designed by Jefferson, dating from 1802. The couple could afford to build such an elaborate house in 1931–33 despite the onset of the Depression. Both were wealthy; his money came from the sugar trade. The name of the house was derived from the two names G[alban] and Allison, the latter being the family name of Mrs. Galban's mother.

Inspired no doubt by the recent Colonial Revival mansions of William Lawrence Bottomley (see Waverley Hill, SURVEY NO. 87), Duncan Lee's work at Carter's Grove (FIGURES 1.37A, 3.42), and the restoration at Williamsburg (SURVEY NOS. 83–86), Johnson and Staples drew upon a number of sources. The mansion's entrance elevation drawing gives some impression of the drama of the approach to the house, on axis down a boxwood- and tree-lined drive. The focus is on the main block, and the wings to either side push forward to create an entrance court. Not visible are two wings for the garden on the left and the stables and garage on the right. The entrance front, with its tall hipped roof and outer chimneys, recalls Westover (FIGURE 1.32), though dormers have been added. The clustered chimney stacks in the wings draw upon Bacon's Castle (FIGURE 1.5). From Monticello came the idea of oversized bricks and tinted mortar. A similar Jefferson inspiration is the arcade, which comes from the ranges at the University of Virginia.

The interior followed the same process, a series of literal quotes: the library was modeled on the hall at Stratford, the Lee ancestral home; the staircase in the main hall is copied from Gadsby's Tavern in Alexandria; the living room's paneling, (lower right) recalls features at Shirley on the James; and the drawing room (far right), with its large arches, combines features drawn from Inigo Jones, William Buckland's work at Gunston Hall in Fairfax County (FIGURES 2.8, 2.9), and Woodlands in Philadelphia.[2]

Evident in Staples's highly detailed interior drawings is the impact of the New York decorator and architect Ogden Codman, Jr. Staples has given a new perspective to Codman's very popular interior eleva-

tion drawings of the 1890s, but the close attention to furniture and the drapery on the piano reflect Codman's impact. The rigorous detailing of "correct" sources is also from Codman, along with Edith Wharton's American Renaissance classic, *The Decoration of Houses* (1897), in which eighteenth-century taste is advanced as the touchstone for modern interiors.[3] While eighteenth-century sources were recalled at Gallison Hall, modernity appears in its pale pastel colors, its commodious rooms, the grouping of furniture, and

the mixture of styles. This design sighs with twentieth-century nostalgia for an imagined past, one of historical novels and celluloid images, a time that never existed, now made real with great conviction. RGW

NOTES
1. Obituary, *Lynchburg News*, November 14, 1983, Jones Memorial Library, Lynchburg, clipping file; and John Wells, *Virginia Architects*, Virginia Historic Landmarks Commission, unpublished ms.

2. Geoffrey Henry, National Register of Historic Places Nomination Form, January 1990.

3. See Pauline Metcalf, *Ogden Codman and the Decoration of Houses* (Boston: David R. Godine, 1988).

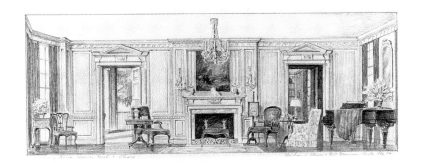

RALPH ADAMS CRAM, 1863–1942

for

CRAM & FERGUSON, Boston

in association with

CARNEAL, JOHNSTON & WRIGHT, Richmond

# 92.
# CARILLON TOWER

*Virginia War Memorial
Elevations*

William Byrd Park, Richmond
Working drawing, 1931
Stamped lower right: *Cram & Ferguson, Boston, Mass./
Carneal, Johnston & Wright, Richmond, Virginia/
Associated Architects;* Dated: *8-17-31*
Pencil on tracing paper; 41 ½ by 30 inches
Collection of Carneal & Johnston, Richmond, Virginia

FIGURE 1. *Site photo,* **The Carillon,** *Byrd Park,
Richmond.*

Richmond's Carillon is the result of two originally separate interests operating in Virginia during the 1920s. The first was the state's provision for building a memorial to those Virginians who served in World War I. The second was the desire of a citizens' group for a bell tower. When the state held a formal competition for a war memorial in 1925 a carillon, designed by Baskervill & Lambert in association with Pittsburgh architect E. D. Ellington and New York sculptor John Gregory, was entered and judged with the other entries but did not place. The winning entry by Paul Philippe Cret (see SURVEY NO. 81) was a noble granite arcade with a formal hierarchy of symbolic spaces. Three months after the ground-breaking for Cret's design, construction was halted to examine options for a memorial in the form of a carillon.[1]

As a fashionable public image the carillon gained note early in the twentieth century, and its popularity soared following the War. Between 1922 and 1925, eleven carillons were dedicated in the United States; only three had stood before the war. Not only did the form have many Old World precedents in campaniles and watchtowers, but the "singing tower" was the subject of celebration after American troops liberated many of the European towns where such poetic structures stood. In 1925 a *National Geographic* article by William Gorham Rice on "The Singing Towers of France and Belgium" was widely circulated across middle America and was no doubt a catalyst in the Virginia carillon campaign.[2]

The Virginia Citizens Carillon Committee, led by Granville G. Valentine, persuaded the General Assembly of Virginia to reassess a carillon as a memorial. The primary argument against the carillon design that had been entered in the 1925 competition was that it could only be inferior because of the $250,000 budget for construction. Either the tower would be too short or the set of bells incomplete. The Virginia Citizens Carillon Committee proposed to raise private funds to pay for a full set of bells if the state would use the entire budget to build the tower. In 1926 the War Memorial Commission chose, without competition, Richmond architects Carneal, Johnston & Wright, in association with Cram & Ferguson of Boston, to design the tower. Ralph Adams Cram was one of eleven architects to design overseas memorials for the American Battle Monuments Commission.[3]

Cram's carillon design provided the Virginia Citizens Carillon Committee with the romantic vehicle for their case. They popularized the "tower of melody" and its "Georgian feel," vying to make Virginia's carillon nationally celebrated. It would be the thirtieth carillon in the United States and fifth largest. They claimed it would be heard for 400 square miles, carrying music to those mothers and soldiers who were bedridden or who could not travel. They pleaded that the bells could play "the soldiers' old songs . . . the National Anthem . . . the hymn General Lee liked. . . . The dead would live in the music they loved."[4] Cram presented the style as imposed by the (*nature*) culture and history of Virginia, "the great Southern exponent

of that noble Colonial architecture which has such distinction and essential American quality."[5]

Virginia's carillon was dedicated on October 15, 1932, with a parade, dignitaries, and all the requisite fanfare. As intended, the plaza before the tower held the public gathering, and the deck around the base was the platform for speakers and guests. From the platform, the large bronze door opened to the main octagonal room in the structure. In other rooms in the base, the Virginia Carillon Commission established a museum of war relics. Five stories above, unseen hands played patriotic and traditional songs.[6] This large drawing of the Carillon is essentially as it was built.

RGW

NOTES

1.   Susan A. Kern, "Virginia's World War I Memorial: Government versus Public Opinion" (M.A. thesis, University of Virginia, 1990).

2.   William Gorham Rice, "The Singing Towers of Holland and Belgium," *National Geographic* 47 (March 1925): 359–76, and, by same author, *Carillon Music and Singing Towers of the Old World and the New* (New York: Dodd, Mead, 1925).

3.   Elizabeth G. Grossman, "Architecture for a Public Client: The Monuments and Chapels of the American Battle Mounuments Commission," *Journal of the Society of Architectural Historians* 43 (May 1984): 119–43.

4.   *Richmond News Leader,* October 14, 1932.

5.   Letter from Cram & Ferguson to Bolling H. Handy, 16 November 1927, papers of Granville G. Valentine, Valentine Museum, Richmond, Virginia.

6.   Today the Carillon is owned by the City of Richmond and is the focus of many memorial services; there have recently been fund-raising efforts to preserve the structure. Many pamphlets and clippings about the Carillon are in the collection of the Valentine Museum, Richmond.

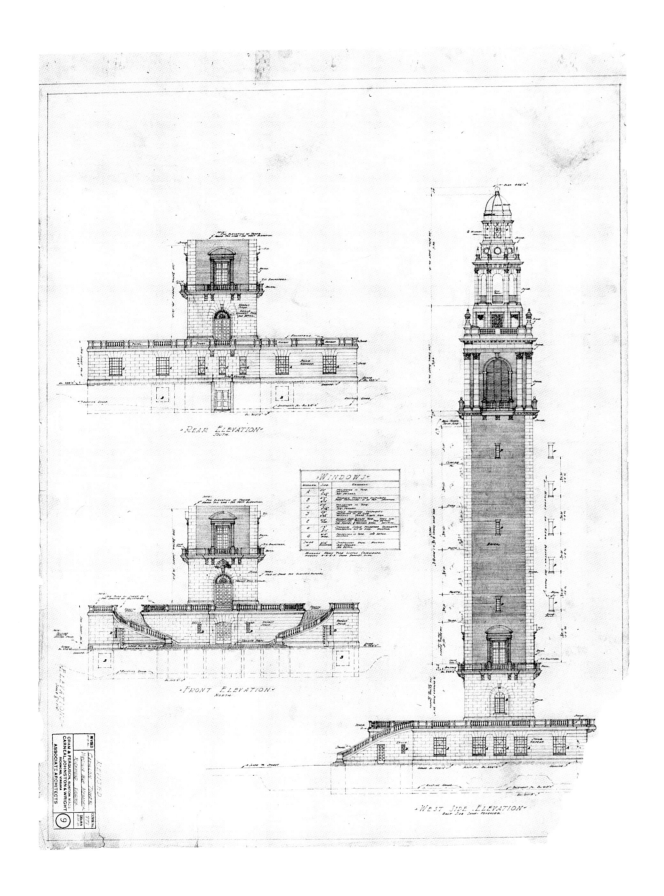

·REAR ELEVATION·
SOUTH

·WINDOWS·

·FRONT ELEVATION·
NORTH

·WEST SIDE ELEVATION·
EAST SIDE SIMILAR REVERSED

CRAM & FERGUSON, BOSTON, MASS.
CARNEAL, JOHNSTON & WRIGHT
RICHMOND, VIRGINIA
ASSOCIATE ARCHITECTS

9

JOHN KEVAN PEEBLES, 1866–1934

FINLEY FORBES FERGUSON, 1875–1936

for

PEEBLES & FERGUSON, Norfolk

# 93.
# VIRGINIA MUSEUM OF FINE ARTS

*Elevation*

The Boulevard at Grove Ave., Richmond
Presentation drawing, 1932
Signed lower right: *Peebles and Ferguson, Architects*
Pencil, ink, and red chalk on tracing paper, mounted on board;
14 ⅝ by 41 ½ inches
Collection of Virginia State Library, Richmond, Inventory No.
755.44, Z10, 1932

For more than forty years (1892–1934) John Kevan Peebles ran an important architectural practice from Norfolk that exerted a wide impact not only on architecture in Virginia but also throughout the South. Born in Petersburg, Virginia, Peebles earned a civil engineering degree at the University of Virginia (which had no school of architecture at that time), worked briefly in Tennessee, and then became associated with James E. R. Carpenter (1867–1932) in Norfolk, where he learned the craft of architecture.[1] Carpenter had studied architecture at the Massachusetts Institute of Technology, worked for H. H. Richardson in Boston, and had practiced in Nashville before coming to Norfolk.[2] Carpenter and Peebles went into partnership in 1892 and one of their first buildings was Fayerweather Gymnasium at the University of Virginia ( FIGURE 3.34 ). Peebles's connection with the University would continue for years: he urged the hiring of McKim, Mead & White in 1896, designed Minor Hall in 1910, and was associated with others in the design of Memorial Gymnasium, Monroe Hill Dormitories, Scott Stadium, McKim Hall, Thornton Hall, and Clark Hall. Peebles left Carpenter about 1898, formed a short-lived partnership with Thomas McKnight Sharpe until 1900, then pursued an independent career for several years. He was part of the design group for the expansion of the Virginia State Capitol, and served as chairman of architectural design for the Jamestown Tercentennial Exposition of 1907. In 1917 Peebles went into partnership with Finley Ferguson, who had also studied at MIT and practiced architecture in Norfolk. Peebles was the senior design partner and the firm was extremely successful. Peebles designed buildings across Virginia, including the Grace Covenant Methodist Church, Richmond (1923); the First National Bank Building, Roanoke (1910); and the Hotel Monticello, Norfolk (1898, 1918). Peebles's architectural preferences never strayed far from his earliest building, the temple-faced Fayerweather Hall, or his heroes, McKim, Mead & White. He was a perfect example of the American Renaissance architect in Virginia—committed to a Classical solution as commensurate with the state's heritage, except for churches, when a form of medievalism might be more appropriate.

Peebles's design for the Virginia Museum of Fine Arts illustrates his belief that architecture should be committed to the preservation of tradition, especially during such a period of turmoil as the 1930s. The Virginia Museum traces its origins back to a gift from Judge John Barton Payne, who donated fifty paintings to the Commonwealth in 1919. In 1932 Payne was persuaded by Governor John Garland Pollard to contribute $100,000 as a challenge grant toward the construction of an art museum to serve as a permanent home for the collection. A bill accepting the gift and authorizing the Governor and an Art Commission to raise funds for the museum was hurried through the General Assembly in February 1932.[3] The Commission engaged Erling H. Pederson of Philadelphia, who specialized in museum planning, as an advisor, and

Peebles & Ferguson as architects. The firm produced this drawing as part of the museum fund-raising campaign in 1932. After successfully rallying private support, along with a grant from the New Deal Public Works Administration with the help of Senator, and former governor, Harry Flood Byrd, the cornerstone was laid in December 1933, a contract was awarded for the building in May 1934, and the new Virginia Museum of Fine Arts opened its doors on January 16, 1936.[4] After Peebles's death in August 1934, the design and construction was overseen by Ferguson.

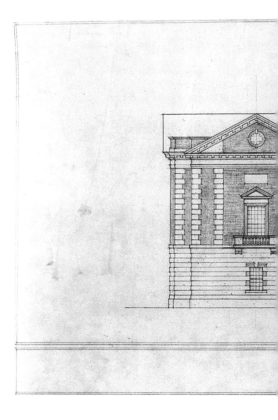

Peebles & Ferguson's design was very much in the Beaux-Arts mode with its central entrance, cross-axial halls, particulate spaces for exhibits, and extensive skylights, which would be hidden behind parapets and attics and not visible from the street. As the elevation drawing illustrates, a limestone base and red-brick *piano nobile* would have a central temple pavilion and reiterated end pavilions.[5] The initial phase of construction eliminated the end pavilions. A memorandum accompanying the drawing stated: "the design of the structure is that of the English Renaissance of the Wren period. . . . It is believed that this style is appropriate, that it is free from coldness and the reserve of the severely Classic and the somewhat startling character of much of the so-called Modern."[6]       RGW

NOTES

1.   Peebles's birth date has been inaccurately cited by many as 1876, see: Henry F. and Elsie R. Withey, *Biographical Dictionary of American Architects(Deceased)* (Los Angeles: New Age, 1956), 464–65. I have relied on an unpublished paper, "John Kevan Peebles, Virginia Architect," 1990, by David A. Dashiell III, who has kindly furnished me a copy.

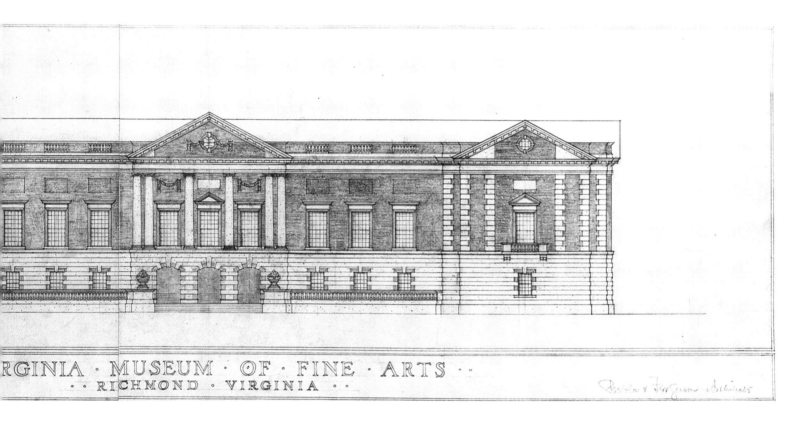

RGINIA · MUSEUM · OF · FINE · ARTS ··
·· RICHMOND · VIRGINIA ··

2.    Letter from Andrew Allison to author, April 20, 1989, Allison is preparing a thesis on Carpenter.

3.    State of Virginia, *Acts of Assembly* (1932), 61–62. Legislation authorizing the operation of the museum was *Acts of Assembly* (1934), 270–73.

4.    Background material can be found in articles in *The Four Arts* 2 (April 1935), which is devoted to the Virginia Museum. See also, "Creation of Virginia Museum came during an unlikely time," *Richmond Times-Dispatch*, January 12, 1986, K2: 22.

5.    This drawing was previously illustrated in William B. O'Neal, *Architectural Drawing in Virginia, 1819–1969* (Charlottesville: School of Architecture, University of Virginia, 1969), 128–29.

6.    Peebles & Ferguson, "Museum-Memoranda," June 11, 1932, Virginia Museum of Fine Arts, Virginia State Library and Archives, Richmond, Virginia. As Finley F. Ferguson explained in "Some Notes on the Planning and Design of the Museum, *The Four Arts* 2 (April 1935): 8–9, "The style used is, of course, that of the English Renaissance, of the period known as 'Georgian.' Many English examples were studied and the influence of Inigo Jones, probably the greatest architectural genius England ever had and of Wren may be traced in the details of the building."

MILTON GRIGG, 1905–1982

FLOYD E. JOHNSON, born 1909

for

GRIGG & JOHNSON, Charlottesville

# 94.
## HOLLYMEAD
## RENOVATIONS

*(now Silver Thatch
Bed & Breakfast)
Bird's-Eye Perspective*

Route 29 and Hollymead Dr. (Albemarle County)
Presentation drawing, 1935
Signed and dated: *Fl. Johnson, [19]35*
Colored pencil on tracing paper, mounted on board;
27 ¼ by 38 ½ inches
Collection of Browne, Eichman, Dalgliesh, Gilpin, & Paxton,
P.C., Architects, Charlottesville, Virginia

FIGURE 1. *Site photo,* **Hollymead.**

This drawing could only have been done after 1930. Although the subject, the renovation of an old house, is traditional, the rendering in aerial perspective could only have been done after the advent of European Modernism through *de Stijl*, the Bauhaus, and the work of Le Corbusier in the 1920s. Bird's-eye views had been used earlier for architectural renderings, but never in this manner. In their quest to create a new and radically modern architecture, the Modernists sought to show buildings in a new way: as abstract geometry.[1] Certainly the perspective now available from dirigibles and airplanes played a role, but the primary purpose of this aerial view was to show how buildings are composed of geometrical forms, not merely as exercises in historical styles. The bird's-eye vantage-point became a new design tool; the building could be seen as a volumetric form and the parts analyzed from a different perspective than the traditional elevation. In this drawing by Floyd Johnson, the layout of the sheet and the delineation of the house and the landscape become an abstract composition. Its character brings to mind the geometry of paintings by Piet Mondrian. Such a perspective is unsettling. It takes the viewer a minute or two to understand it, and it is a view that would seldom, if ever, be possible, except from an aerial vantage-point.

Although radically modern in presentation techniques, the project is also extremely traditional in that it illustrates the bifurcate nature of much of Virginia's twentieth-century architecture. It illuminates a staple of Virginia architectural practice, the renovation of old country houses. In this case Hollymead was a venerable house, dating from circa 1780, in northern Albemarle County. Milton Grigg and his associate Floyd Johnson were engaged to plan the renovations; only a portion of those shown were actually carried out.

Grigg and Johnson were two of the strongest personalities in mid-twentieth-century Virginia architecture. Both graduated from the University of Virginia's architecture program, Grigg in 1929 and Johnson in 1934. The School of Architecture at that time maintained a strong Beaux-Arts and traditionalist orientation, which lasted well into the 1940s, though students in the 1930s were already very much aware of the new Modernist currents. Milton Grigg's earliest employment, from 1929 to 1932, was as a draftsman for the Boston firm of Perry, Shaw & Hepburn, in their restorations at Colonial Williamsburg. Such experience further imbued him with both deeper knowledge of and closer commitment to traditional architecture.[2] Grigg set up practice in Charlottesville in 1932 and began to work closely with Fiske Kimball as restoration architect on Monticello. This Jefferson connection would continue for the rest of his life, both at Monticello and in other projects, such as the discovery and restoration of Edgemont, which is attributed to Jefferson. In 1935 Grigg hired Johnson, then a fresh new graduate from the University; they were partners from 1938 to 1940.[3] Johnson had considerable facility with pen and brush, and his paintings won many awards in these years. After World War II Johnson

established his own partnership in Charlottesville as Johnson, Craven & Gibson, which continues today. Grigg continued to practice alone for a while in Charlottesville and in 1964 established a partnership that continues today as Browne Eichman Dalgliesh Gilpin & Paxton. Johnson has also continued an association with Monticello.

As practicing architects in a small city in central Virginia, both Grigg and Johnson designed buildings in a variety of styles but both remained committed to historical imagery. Grigg's best-known later works include not only houses in the Charlottesville area, but also more than two hundred churches he designed or remodeled elsewhere, the United States Embassy in Canberra, Australia (1961), and a variety of historic preservation projects. Johnson is now best known for his many residences both in Virginia and the Southeast, as well as the Boar's Head Inn, Piedmont Community College, and work at the University of Virginia, all in Charlottesville. In 1989 Johnson received the Ross Award from the Classical America Society for his continuance of the Classical tradition.

RGW

NOTES

1. Reyner Banham, *Theory and Design in the First Machine Age* (New York: Praeger, 1967), Chap. 21.

2. Information about Milton Grigg comes from several personal interviews conducted with him in 1980, and interviews with Mrs. Ella Grigg in 1982, as well as information supplied by his partners Henry Browne and Douglas Gilpin. See also Grigg in *American Architects Directory*, ed. George S. Koyl (New York: R. R. Bowker Co., 1955): 281; Richard Guy Wilson, "Milton Grigg & Joseph Oddenino," *Charlottesville Daily Progress* (September 21, 1982), 41, reprinted in *Early Churches of Culpeper County, Virginia: Colonial and Ante-Bellum Congregations*, eds. Arthur Dicken Thomas, Jr., and Angus McDonald Green (Culpeper, Virginia: Culpeper Historical Society, 1987), 331–32.

3. Information on Johnson comes from an interview with the author, December 15, 1989. Transcripts of interviews with Durward Potter, an architectural historian, summer-fall, 1989, have also been furnished to the author. Additional information was supplied by the office of Johnson, Craven & Gibson, Charlottesville.

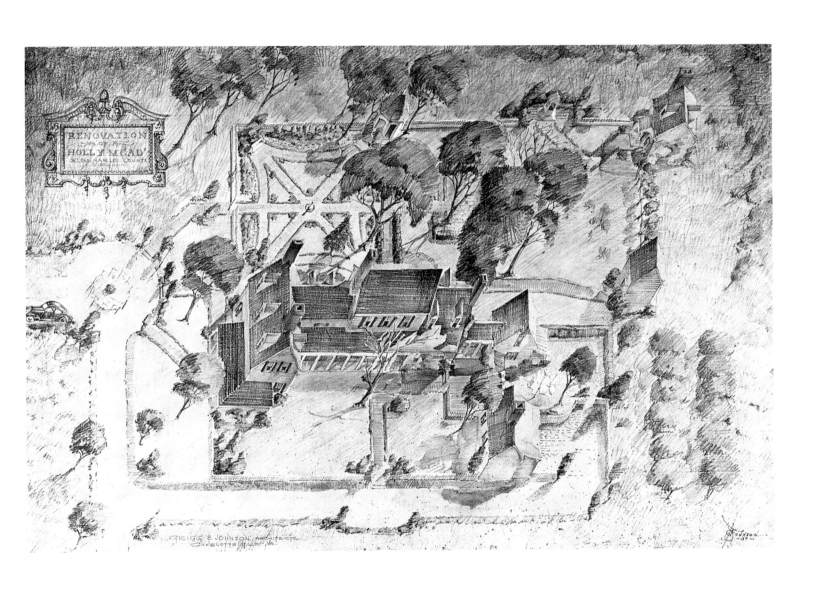

# 95.

## RESIDENCE FOR DR. HENRY WILSON WILLIAMS

### *North Elevation*

200 New St., Petersburg
Working drawing, 1939
Signed and dated, bottom right: *W. H. Moses Jr. Des./ Hampton Va/4-12-'39*
Pencil on tracing paper; 15 by 21 inches
Collection of the estate William Henry Moses, Jr., Hampton, Virginia

William Henry Moses, Jr., a leading architectural educator, established the Architecture Department at Hampton Institute in Hampton, Virginia in 1940. Born in Cumberland County, Virginia, Moses attended Philadelphia's Central High School and received his bachelor's degree in architecture at the Pennsylvania State University, where he studied under A. Lawrence Kocher. After working for several years in New York, Moses came to Hampton Institute in 1934 as an instructor in the Building Construction Program. In 1940 the president of the Hampton Institute, Malcom Shaw MacLean, asked him to set up a program in architecture, and Moses remained as head of that department until his retirement in 1971.

In 1938 Moses had won the competition for the design of the Virginia Pavilion for the 1939 New York World's Fair; the subsequent removal and replacement of his design, allegedly because of his race, but ostensibly for reasons of cost and thematic inappropriateness, caused considerable public outcry. His architectural practice was extensive in the Tidewater area. His numerous designs for residences and commercial buildings include the Colonial Inn and the People's Building and Loan Office, both in Hampton, and a motel at Buckroe Beach.[1]

Moses's design for a suburban house for his brother-in-law in Petersburg, Virginia, illustrates his design excellence and competence. Generically the house fits into the half-timbered Tudor style that had been popularized in the 1910s and 1920s as seen in Baskervill & Lambert's Stony Point ( SURVEY NO. 79 ). By the 1930s the idiom had become appropriate for smaller suburban lots and specific reference to historical models is absent. Here, for instance, the reference is generalized: the house is constructed of brick with small amounts of applied half-timber, gabled roofs, and an oriel window. The house is compactly organized; Dr. Williams had an office at home, which accounts for the lower front entry. The house caused astonishment in Petersburg, not only that a black resident could afford such a dwelling, but also that the architect himself was black.[2]        RGW

NOTES
1. Based on author interview of William H. Moses, Jr., 10 February 1990.

2. Interview with Moses.

FIGURE 1. *Site photo, the* **Williams House.**

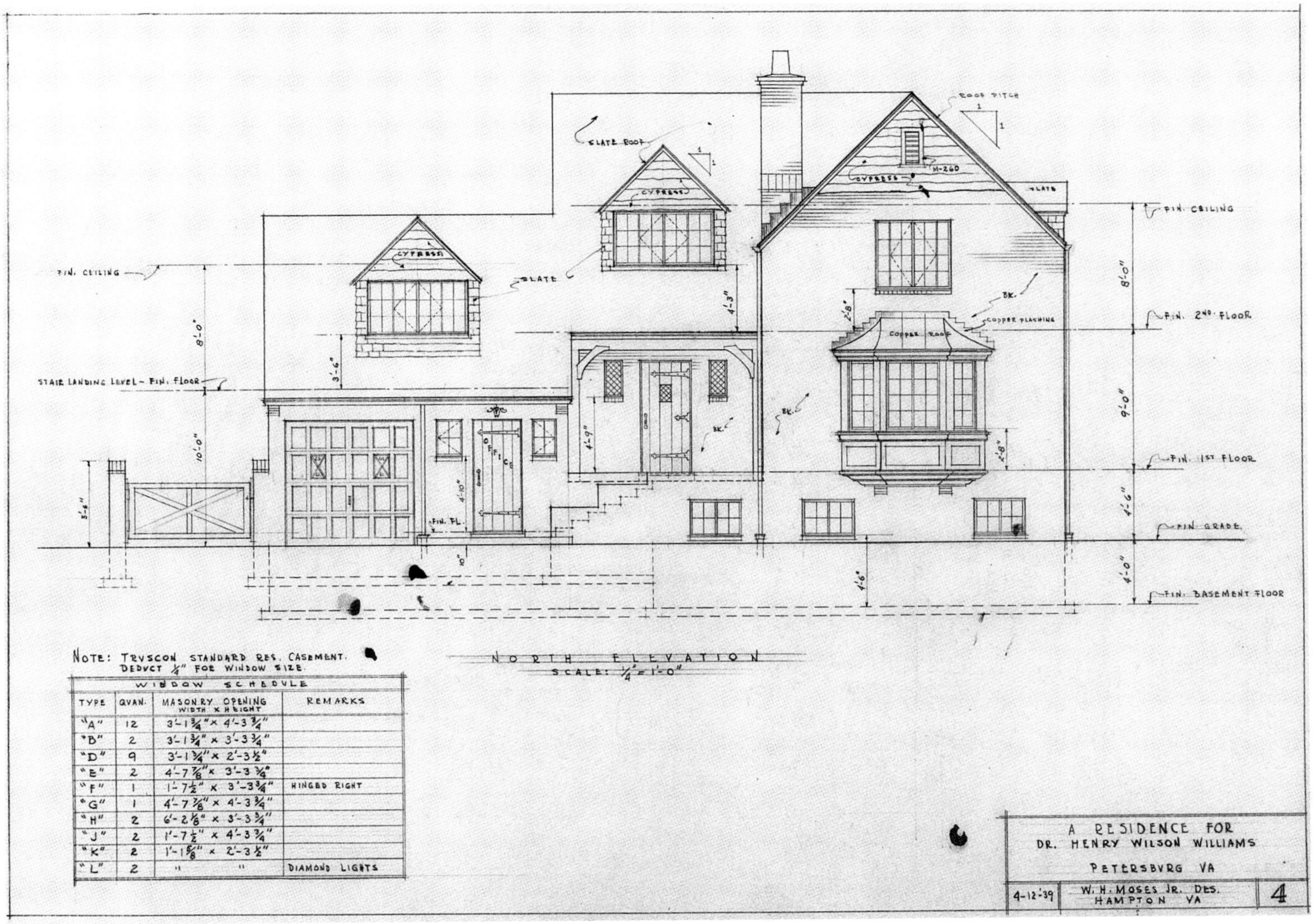

ROOF PITCH
SLATE ROOF
CYPRESS
SLATE
FIN. CEILING
FIN. 2ND FLOOR
COPPER ROOF
COPPER FLASHING
BK.
STAIR LANDING LEVEL – FIN. FLOOR
OFFICE
FIN. FL.
FIN. 1ST FLOOR
FIN. GRADE
FIN. BASEMENT FLOOR
NORTH ELEVATION
SCALE: 1/4" = 1'-0"
NOTE: TRUSCON STANDARD RES. CASEMENT.
DEDUCT 1/4" FOR WINDOW SIZE.
WINDOW SCHEDULE
TYPE | QUAN. | MASONRY OPENING WIDTH X HEIGHT | REMARKS
"A" | 12 | 3'-1 3/4" x 4'-3 3/4" |
"B" | 2 | 3'-1 3/4" x 3'-3 3/4" |
"D" | 9 | 3'-1 3/4" x 2'-3 1/2" |
"E" | 2 | 4'-7 7/8" x 3'-3 3/4" |
"F" | 1 | 1'-7 1/2" x 3'-3 3/4" | HINGED RIGHT
"G" | 1 | 4'-7 7/8" x 4'-3 3/4" |
"H" | 2 | 6'-2 1/8" x 3'-3 3/4" |
"J" | 2 | 1'-7 1/2" x 4'-3 3/4" |
"K" | 2 | 1'-1 5/8" x 2'-3 1/2" |
"L" | 2 | " " | DIAMOND LIGHTS
A RESIDENCE FOR
DR. HENRY WILSON WILLIAMS
PETERSBURG VA
4-12-39
W. H. MOSES JR. DES.
HAMPTON VA
4

# 96.
# HOUSE FOR
# LOREN B. POPE

*(Pope-Leighey House)*
*Perspective, Elevation, Plan*

East Falls Church (now relocated to Woodlawn Plantation, Fairfax County; maintained as a property of the National Trust for Historic Preservation)
Presentation drawing, 1939
Architect's stamp on middle right; dated at right: *1939*
Graphite and colored pencil on tracing paper; 30 by 38 inches
Collection of The Frank Lloyd Wright Foundation, Scottsdale, Arizona, inv. no. 4013.01.
Photograph of drawing © 1969 The Frank Lloyd Wright Foundation.

FIGURE 1. *Site photo,* **Pope-Leighey House.**

Of Frank Lloyd Wright's various designs for Virginia buildings, the house he did for Loren Pope in 1939 is easily the best known and the most important. Designed and built for a site in Falls Church in 1939–40, the Popes sold the house in 1947 to Robert and Marjorie Leighey. When the house was threatened with demolition because of the extension of Interstate 66 eastward into Washington, a massive preservation campaign was organized. As a result, the house was dismantled and reconstructed on the site of the National Trust's Woodlawn Plantation, Mt. Vernon, Virginia, where it has remained open to the public since 1965.[1]

Frank Lloyd Wright, America's most famous modern architect, created a distinctive version of modern architecture. Born in southern Wisconsin, Wright came to maturity in the Chicago area in the 1890s and 1900s. He was the leader, with Louis Sullivan, of a small group of like-minded Arts and Crafts architects concerned with creating an American architecture based on the midwestern landscape. Their low-rise houses became known as the Prairie Style, or Prairie School. Wright achieved tremendous success with 167 buildings completed by 1909, but then, partially due to personal problems, entered a fallow period that lasted until the mid 1930s. He re-emerged on the national scene at age sixty-nine with his stunning Fallingwater in Bear Run, Pennsylvania, and the Johnson Wax Building in Racine, Wisconsin (both 1936), and his innovative low-cost Usonian house. Always a flamboyant personality who dressed distinctively and understood intuitively the importance of publicity, Wright became a dominant figure, extensively praised and lauded though not necessarily followed, for the remainder of his life.[2]

The rendering for the Pope House well illustrates the features of Wright's Usonian house scheme or, as he described it, "The house of moderate cost is not only America's major architectural problem but the problem most difficult for her major architects."[3] To Wright the issue was simplicity and elimination: not to ape the large house on Main Street, but to create a distinctive house that could be built at moderate cost. The rendering is economical in giving an elevation with floor, site, furniture plan, and a perspective, so that the client, normally not accustomed to reading architectural drawings, can understand it at once. The garage is eliminated in place of a carport; the basement is replaced by a concrete slab that contains radiant heating; all unnecessary hardware and ornament (downspouts, etc.) have disappeared; the roof would be flat or low-pitched; prefabricated-wood wall paneling eliminated costly on-site labor; the wood inside and out would be left unfinished to eliminate costly painting; the interior, through floor-to-ceiling openings, flows effortlessly with the garden; the living and dining rooms are combined; and furniture, where practicable, is built-in.

Loren and Charlotte Pope were exactly the type of clients Wright was hoping to attract: they had become enthralled with Wright through his autobiography and became true believers. Pope wrote to Wright explaining he was a newspaperman with the Washington *Evening Star* and could only afford a $5,500 house. Wright replied tersely, "Of course I am ready to give you a house."[4] The drawing illustrated is a preliminary design that Wright did without ever visiting the site; later he would visit. Modifications were made to cut the costs and it was reoriented on the site by Pope, with the help of a Wright apprentice, Gordon Chadwick, who came to oversee construction. When the house was completed in 1941, Loren Pope eloquently described the experience of living there as "like living with a great and quiet soul."[5]     RGW

NOTES

1.   The site at Woodlawn, while similar to the original site at Falls Church in also being wooded, has some significant differences: the orientation is not North-South but East-West, and instead of approaching the house from below, one now approaches from above. Extensive background on the house and its rescue are in *The Pope-Leighey House*, ed. Terry B. Morton (Washington, D.C.: National Trust for Historic Preservation, 1969).

2.   The literature on Wright is overwhelming; the best is Robert C. Twombly, *Frank Lloyd Wright* (New York: Harper & Row, 1973); and Norris Kelley Smith, *Frank Lloyd Wright: A Study in Architectural Content* (Englewood Cliffs, N.J.: Prentice-Hall, 1966). Also important are Wright's own writings, especially *An Autobiography* (New York: Horizon Press, 1977).

3.   Frank Lloyd Wright, *The Living House* (New York: Horizon Press, 1954), 79. This book contains Wright's best description of the Usonian house.

4.   Letters from August 18 and September 2, 1939, reprinted in *The Pope-Leighey House*, 15.

5.   Loren Pope, "The Love Affair of a Man and his House," *House Beautiful* 90 (August 1948): 34. Loren Pope has been one of the most articulate of Wright's clients; in addition to Pope's reminiscences in *The Pope-Leighey House*, 53–58 see his "Five Decades Later," in *Frank Lloyd Wright Remembered*, ed. P. Meehan, (Washington, D.C.: Preservation Press, in production as of 1991); and the video recording: *A Conversation Between Richard Guy Wilson and Loren Pope, "The Pope-Leighey House" A Frank Lloyd Wright Design* by the National Trust for Historic Preservation and Woodlawn Plantation, 1990. After leaving the house, the Popes intended for Wright to design a house for them in Loudoun County, but it proved to be too expensive.

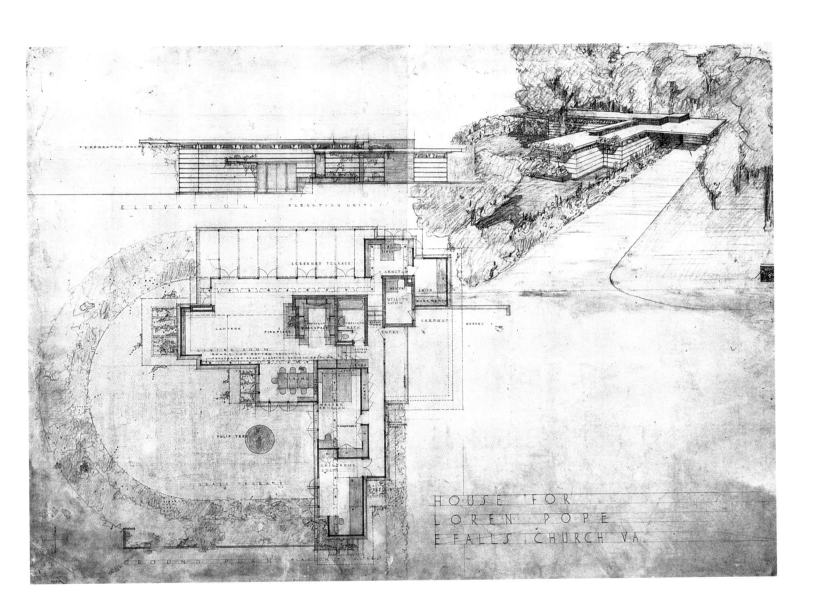

ELEVATION  ELEVATION UNITS

GROUND PLAN

HOUSE FOR
LOREN POPE
E FALLS CHURCH VA.

HOWARD L. CHENEY, 1889–1969

Drawing by HUGH FERRISS, 1889–1962

# 97.
# NATIONAL AIRPORT

*Perspective*

George Washington Memorial Parkway (Arlington County)
Preliminary presentation drawing, circa 1939–41 (?)
Inscribed upper right: *Gravelly Point, Washington, D. C.*
Charcoal on tracing paper, mounted on board;
11 ¼ by 17 ½ inches
Collection of the Avery Architectural and Fine Arts Library,
Columbia University, New York City

FIGURE 1. *Vintage photo,* **National Airport,** *circa 1950s. (Photograph courtesy of the Library of Congress.)*

This drawing by Hugh Ferriss captures the drama and energy of arrivals and departures at a busy air terminal as the new transportation machines of the twentieth century are made ready for flight. Drawn in his highly individualistic style—with dramatic contrasts of black charcoal on white paper with bold, simple, architectonic forms—this drawing synthesizes the magic of air travel at the new National Airport in Alexandria, Virginia: McDonnell-Douglas DC-3s are loaded, unloaded, and serviced by their handlers, while onlookers lean over the observation deck in front of the giant-columned portico.

Hugh Ferriss achieved success as an architectural renderer, not a designer, though he was trained as an architect at Washington University in St. Louis. He moved to New York and began to work as an independent renderer emerging in the early 1920s with a projected series of skyscrapers and speculative proposals for other architects. His bold, personal style of charcoal drawing made a major impact on architects and they began to manipulate their building masses accordingly.[1] The drawing for National Airport was done about 1939; the one shown is a preliminary study for a finished rendering, now lost, that appeared in Ferriss's *Power in Buildings.*[2]

The construction of National Airport was the culmination of a decade-long struggle to provide the Washington, D.C., area with an adequate terminal and field. The existing Washington-Hoover field, located across the Fourteenth Street Bridge in Virginia, had the dubious distinction of being known as the most dangerous in the United States; the noted airman Wiley Post claimed "that there were better landing grounds in the wilds of Siberia than in Washington."[3] Understanding the need for a modern airport, especially as war threatened, President Franklin D. Roosevelt pushed through Congress the Civil Aeronautics Act (later called the Federal Aviation Administration—FAA) in 1938. This legislation allowed the federal government to build and operate an airport. The site as inscribed on Ferriss's drawing would be "Gravelly Point," on the Potomac River, near Alexandria, where the Army Corps of Engineers had been depositing stand and gravel from a dredging operation. The airport was built on 729 acres, 500 of which were landfill and served as the runways. Because of a seventeenth-century agreement, the runways were considered part of Washington, D.C., while the terminal area was deemed part of Virginia.

Designed and built under the aegis of the Public Buildings Administration, Howard Lovewell Cheney was selected as consulting architect to design all of the airport's buildings.[4] Cheney had been educated at the University of Illinois and had a practice in Chicago until he came to Washington, D.C., to work for the Office of the Supervising Architect in the Public Buildings Administration. He in turn asked Charles M. Goodman to serve as the chief designer (see Powell House and Hollin Hills project, SURVEY NOS. 99 and 100). The exact design responsibilities are unclear; apparently Goodman designed a building

that was streamlined in appearance with extensive glass facades.[5] But when President Roosevelt reviewed the designs, however, as he did for many federal building projects, he preferred a more classical approach, suggesting that the main facades should reflect a national image, such as the portico of Mount Vernon, the other main Potomac River landmark (compare SURVEY NO. 98, FIGURE 1 and SURVEY NO. 5).[6] The design was consequently altered to eight square piers for the entrance portico and round cylindrical columns *in antis* on the runway side. The terminal, completed in June 1941, is an example of classic Art Déco, extremely simplified, even streamlined in appearance, with restrained but appropriate decorative details. Carefully planned with separate levels for different activities and dominated by a large central lobby and concourse, National Airport was ranked as the second largest in the world after Berlin's and "the first among all airports in the extensiveness of its ultramodern equipment and facilities."[7]    RGW

NOTES

1. Hugh Ferriss, *The Metropolis of Tomorrow* (New York: Ives Washburn, 1929); reprint edition, with Carol Willis, *Drawing Towards Metropolis* (Princeton, New Jersey: Princeton Architectural Press, 1986).

2. Hugh Ferriss, *Power in Buildings* (New York: Columbia University Press, 1953). See also, Jean Ferriss Leich, *Architectural Visions: The Drawings of Hugh Ferriss* (New York: Whitney Library of Design, 1980), 130–131, 137. The rendering shown also appeared in Richard Guy Wilson, Dianne Pilgrim, and Dickran Tashjian, *The Machine Age in America 1918–1941* (New York: Abrams, 1986), 182.

3. Quoted in John Walter Wood, *Airports: Some Elements of Design and Future Development* (New York: Coward-McCann, 1940), 141; an excellent account of the entire development is James M. Goode, "Flying High: The Origin and Design of National Airport," *Washington History* 1 (Fall 1989): 4–25.

4. See *Who Was Who in America* (Chicago: Marquis, 1985), 75; and Cheney file, archives of the American Institute of Architects, Washington, D.C.

5. None of these drawings have been located. There are additional presentation drawings of the classical Art Deco terminal and hangers in the National Archives, Washington, D.C.

6. William B. Rhodes, "Franklin D. Roosevelt and Washington Architecture," *Records of the Columbia Historical Society* 52 (1989): 139–43.

7. *Aero Digest* (June 1941): 21, quoted in Goode, "Flying High," 5. The complex was extensively published. See Joseph Hudnut, "Washington National Airport," *Architectural Forum* 75 (September 1941): 169–176; "Washington National Airport," *Architectural Record* 90 (October 1941): 48–57; "Washington National Airport," *Architect and Building News* 168 (November 28, 1941): 132–135.

HOWARD L. CHENEY, 1889–1969

# 98.
## GLASS PARTITION FOR NATIONAL AIRPORT

*Proposed Elevation*

Presentation drawing, circa 1940
Inscribed lower right: *Carved Glass Partition for/Airport Bldg, Washington, D.C./Harriton Carved Glass/404 East 49 Street, New York City*
Pastel on board, 9 ½ by 22 inches
Collection of the National Archives, Washington, D.C., inv. no. RG 121

This drawing is for an etched-glass partition of mural proportions. Designed for one of the passenger entrances to National Airport, it was apparently never produced for the site, though smaller panels of etched glass were installed there. Harriton Carved Glass of New York City was one of America's leading suppliers of decorative glass from the 1920s through the 1960s. Such glass went out of fashion after World War II and the Harriton works closed in the 1960s.[1]

The scene depicted is an excellent example of an Art Déco-ish Modernized Classicism that developed in the 1920s and 1930s and became the equivalent of an official style for federal architecture. Similar figures and scenes were portrayed in statues, murals, elevator doors, and window grills in many public buildings. A Grecian figure with decorous drapery is borne aloft by wings; the flow of drapery and the line of the wings echo each other. The figure is balanced by atmospheric effects and the new symbols of the Machine Age—airplanes and skyscraper cities. Symbolizing departure with the ascending airplane on the right and arrival with the descending airplane on the left, the designer—whether Cheney, a draftsman, or someone working for the Harriton Company—has taken liberties with the profile of Washington, D.C., which never attained such skyscraper proportions. The aircraft shown are also advanced for the date, since twin-engine DC-3s were the common carriers, and four-engine aircraft were still only in the experimental stage. Overall, the design is an excellent example of the decorative possibilities of the latest transport machines, shown in highly stylized settings.     RGW

NOTE
1.   Information derived from conversations with William Weber, Rambusch Incorporated, New York; and Sam Shefts, Carved Glass Company, Bronx, New York, September 11, 1990.

FIGURE   1.   **National Airport, Passenger Entrance Portico.** *(Photograph courtesy of the Library of Congress.)*

# 99.
# COUNTRY PLACE FOR MR. AND MRS. OSCAR M. POWELL

*Perspective*

Forestville, north of Great Falls (Fairfax County)
Preliminary sketch, 1940
Signed and dated lower right: *Charles Goodman, December 1940*
Pencil on tracing paper; 13 ⅜ by 21 ½ inches
Collection of Charles M. Goodman, Alexandria, Virginia

FIGURE 1. *Vintage photo of* **Powell House,** *circa 1940s. (Photograph courtesy of Charles M. Goodman.)*

More than any other individual, Charles M. Goodman brought modern architecture to mid-twentieth-century Virginia. A figure of international stature, Goodman's impact can scarcely be measured; known as the "Production House Architect," more than 100,000 of his designs were erected in the 1950s as a result of his involvement in the National Homes Corporation.[1] His designs formed the basis of the generic Modern American house and school, widely imitated in every part of the country. Goodman was a member of a socially committed generation who believed that modern technology and materials gave the architect a new responsibility. For him, good design could influence how people live and how they relate to Nature. Consequently Goodman focused as much effort on siting, landscaping, and interior plans as he did on designing prefabricated components. The result was a body of architecture of great distinction that captured Americans' imagination for many years.

Charles ("Chuck") Goodman was born in New York City and studied architecture at Chicago's Armour Institute (now Illinois Institute of Technology).[2] Although Mies van der Rohe would not arrive to transform Armour's architecture school until 1937, Modernist ideas were already in the air, and the legacy of both the earlier Chicago School and Wright were much discussed. Goodman would later be influenced by the elemental simplicity of Mies, but he could never accept the steel frame for housing. As a result, his houses always retained a Wrightian feel for the site and an affinity for contact with Nature. With his wife, Charlotte, who was very active in local Democratic politics, Goodman moved to Old Town Alexandria in 1934, and became a design architect with the Supervising Architect's Office in the U. S. Treasury Department in 1935. His work began in the modernized, decorated classicism (Art Déco) common in much public building of the 1930s and included the Federal Building in New Orleans, Washington's National Airport (see SURVEY NOS. 97–98), and the U. S. government group at the 1939 New York World's Fair, among others. As the Art Déco style diminished, Goodman always retained certain elements of an innate Classicism, as can be seen in his strong structural bay systems, hierarchical organization, and the relation of plan to form. He left the government and established his own architectural practice in 1939; in the next two years he designed a number of contemporary suburban houses that mark the beginning of nearly three decades of involvement in innovative domestic design. During World War II Goodman was head architect for the Air Transport Command and designed several airport installations. After the war he resumed private practice and became involved with the award-winning Hollin Hills development project. Interest in economical residential construction led him to a five-year contract with the largest industrial fabricator of housing, the National Homes Corporation, and involvement with a number of other firms, including ALCOA, for the "Alcoa House of 1957." Goodman also designed many commercial buildings, as well

portions of the new planned community at Reston. While his office was from time to time in Washington, D.C., Goodman always lived in Alexandria, in a nineteenth-century house that he extensively remodeled and added to, and that eventually became a mecca for architectural pilgrimages.

Goodman's design for the Powell residence in 1940 illustrates the changes that had occurred, both in American residential design and in architectural drawing itself. Instead of the elegant and fastidious color presentation drawings common to the Beaux-Arts system, which Goodman would have considered "unreal" and elitist, he relied on black-and-white pencil drawings. But while he labels his drawing a "sketch," its delicacy and detail indicate a designer of great precision and sophistication at work. Located on the hillside of a large site with a view of a waterfall, and surrounded by beech, sycamore, poplar, and other trees and shrubs, the design reflects some influence of Wright's contemporary Usonian houses. With siding in vertical redwood and masonry walls of a native brownstone from a nearby quarry, the approach and northern facade is closed with few openings and contains a carport, while the southern facade, with the view, is virtually a wall of glass. Conventional plans are inverted, enclosure is gone, all the principal rooms adjoin outdoor living spaces, and the bedrooms are placed beneath the main living quarters. A variety of natural woods are used on the interior. While completed in 1942, the house was not published until 1947, when it immediately earned for Goodman a national following.[3]                                   RGW

NOTES
1. "Here are the New Prefabs Whose Values Every Builder Must Meet," and "Biggest Prefabber, Jim Price of National, Builds the Biggest Prefab of them All," *House & Home* 4 (November 1953): 102–111; 7 (December 1956): 150–153; "Prefab Schools," *Architectural Forum* (April 1955): 133–137.

2. Information on Goodman comes from an interview with the architect, December 7, 1989, and from Gregory K. Hunt of Alexandria, who is preparing a book-length study of Goodman.

3. "Houses Built into a Hillside," *Architectural Forum* 86 (June 1947): 94–97.

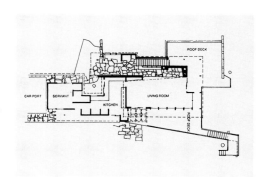

FIGURE 2. **Powell House,** *plan of upper level.*

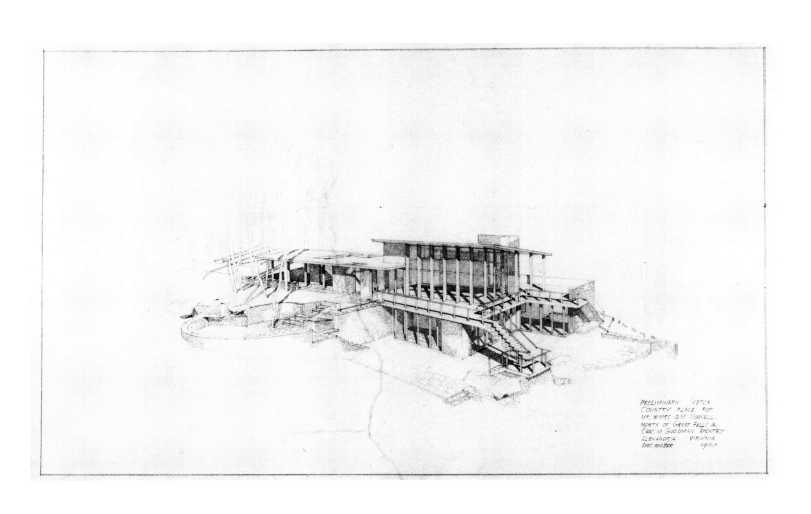

PRELIMINARY SKETCH
COUNTRY PLACE FOR
MR. & MRS. G.M. POWELL
NORTH OF GREAT FALLS VA.
CHAS. M. GOODMAN ARCHITECT
ALEXANDRIA VIRGINIA
DECEMBER 1940

Attributed to DAVID CONDON, born 1916

for

CHARLES M. GOODMAN, F.A.I.A., born 1906

# 100.
# HOLLIN HILLS
# UNIT HOUSE

*Type 7C, Perspective*

Alexandria (Fairfax County)
Study, circa 1955
Pencil on vellum; 13 ½ by 20 ¾ inches
Collection of Charles Goodman, Alexandria, Virginia

FIGURE 1. *Site photo of another* **Hollin Hills House type.**

Hollin Hills is Virginia's most noteworthy contribution to modern architecture in the twentieth century. A subdivision of 463 contemporary houses located on 300 acres of heavily wooded and uneven terrain, it has an international reputation as being a paradigm of modern design integrated with nature. Widely illustrated in architectural and housing periodicals when first developed in the 1950s, the houses received a variety of awards including citations from *Life* and *Parents'* magazines and a design award from the AIA. The development received international acclaim with its selection by the American Institute of Architects on the occasion of its centenary, in 1957, as one of the "Ten Buildings in America's Future." [1]

Hollin Hills was the product of a farsighted and innovative developer, Robert Davenport, and the architect Charles Goodman. Davenport had begun work as a developer before World War II, and in 1946, casting about for a new site, purchased a hilly site south of Alexandria. About the same time he met Charles Goodman, who convinced him, "You can't use a conventional house on that land." As Davenport later explained, "Chuck Goodman is a very competent architect, but he is also a good promoter." [2] Goodman laid out a plan in which site-clearance—bulldozing—was kept to a minimum, roads followed the contours of the hills, and the natural setting was preserved as much as possible. Common park lands and open spaces were set aside, and a landscape plan was included with each house. Lou Bernard Voight was the initial landscape architect, followed by Dan Kiley, then Eric Paepcke. Houses were sited to take advantage of southern exposures and views, hence they were placed at angles on the lots, and in contradiction to standard site planning of the day. Some were even placed below the roadway in order to fit the house plan to the land. Finally, fences were strongly discouraged.

Goodman explained that the houses were for "a community development designed to meet the general average living requirements of the middle-income group." [3] Wanting to avoid the replicated look of most subdivisions, a number of house plans in different sizes were designed; costs were to be kept down through prefabricated millwork, standardization, simplified carpentry, the avoidance of intricate details, and the use of modern technology and materials such as concrete slab floors, steel sash windows, and by grouping all utilities in central cores. Although the Federal Housing Administration looked questioningly at the project and refused full financial support in the project's early years, Davenport was able to obtain Veterans' Administration mortgages. In his quest to create a modern community, Davenport arranged financing so that the new residents could purchase contemporary furniture and housewares from Knoll, Kurt Versen, and other modern furnishings stores. [4]

House types in Hollin Hills were not known by the contemporary builder's jargon, such as "Jefferson" or "Malibu," but instead with figures, 2B4k4 and the like. The house shown in the delicate rendering by David Condon, who worked for Goodman in the 1950s, is a pitched-roof design originally done in the late 1940s and upgraded in the mid 1950s with a new fireplace and chimney design, and transom windows in the end elevation. The fireplace is pulled out from the wall and treated as though it were a piece of abstract modern sculpture. Enclosing walls are treated as panels of glass or siding in three-foot sections. As an image of a house, this design falls about midway in the spectrum of housing types Goodman developed for Hollin Hills. Some earlier designs were more conservative on the exterior, though open on the interior. Goodman did go on to develop flat-roofed boxy designs reminiscent of those by Mies van der Rohe, and houses with sail-like, butterfly roofs. All of the Hollin Hills houses were constructed by Davenport's builder, C. R.(Mac) McCalley, and the last Davenport-Goodman house was constructed in 1971.

Hollin Hills was a success from the beginning; houses sold immediately to a very special type of client. Many were government-employed professionals, and all were well educated. A typical claim was that the community had the highest per capita rate of post-baccalaureate degrees in the United States. One resident summed them up in 1987: "We were young, we were veterans, and we were liberal." As Goodman himself explained, "We designed it to appeal to the kinds of activists who joined conservation associations and so on." [5]                                               RGW

NOTES

1. "Best Houses Under $15,000: Eight Fine, Mass-produced Examples Show Buyers What They Can Get in Low-priced Homes," *Life* (September 10, 1951): 123–127; Richard Bennett, "Judges Report on *Parents' Magazine's* 1950–51 Builders' Competition," "A House That Fits Into a Friendly Community," and "It's A Perfect Family House," *Parents' Magazine* (February, 1952): 54–61; "Here are the Merchant Built Winners of the Homes for Better Living Awards: Sponsored by the A. I. A. in Cooperation with *House and Home, Better Homes and Gardens*, and N. B. C.," *House and Home* (June 1957): 104–115, 139–151; "Notable Modern Buildings" *Life* (June 3, 1957): 59–62ff.; "Good Builders Do a Fine Job" and "Nature Preserved in a Tract," *Life* (September 15, 1958): 72–73; Paul Rudolph, "Frank Adding Up of Assets, Debits of a Fine House," and "New Homes, Wacky and Staid: A Sensible Buy in the Suburbs," *Life* (November 24, 1961): 111–116; *Mid-Century Architecture in America: Honor Award of the American Institute of Architects*, ed. Wolf von Eckardt (Baltimore: Johns Hopkins Press, 1961), 210; Frederick Gutheim, *1857–1957 One Hundred Years of Architecture in America* (New York: Reinhold, 1957), 16.

2. Davenport quoted in *Hollin Hills: A History into the Fourth Decade*, comp. Marion Tiger (Alexandria: Civic Association of Hollin Hills, 1984), 13.

3. Quoted in Katherine Morrow Ford and Thomas H. Creighton, *The American House Today* (New York: Reinhold, 1951), 64.

4. "Builder's Project," *Architectural Forum* (December 1949): 80–83.

5. Quoted in Benjamin Forgey, "Built to Beat Time," *Washington Post,* May 21, 1983, D1: 6.

# 101.
## JOHNSON HOUSE PROJECT

*Elevation*

Charlottesville (unbuilt)
Presentation drawing, 1940
Signed and dated lower left: *Floyd Johnson, 1940*
Watercolor, colored pencil, and ink on paper;
13 by 24 ½ inches
Collection of Floyd E. Johnson, Charlottesville, Virginia

Although never built, this small house by Floyd Johnson for his wife and himself conveys many features of the new American suburban architecture of the 1930s and 1940s. The drawing itself is a masterpiece of presentation, evoking ease of lifestyle and contentment. The style of sketching, by which a few simple pencil strokes can convey different types of vegetation, textures, materials, and atmosphere, is eminently suited to the subject. Stylistically the house vaguely recalls features of nineteenth-century vernacular buildings in Virginia: the vertical board-and-batten-siding, the small-paned windows, the dovecote, the jerkin-head roof, the grillwork, and the large chimney. But fundamentally the house is Modern, for these historical images clothe a suburban ranch house with an attached garage, and all the major living spaces are placed on one floor.

While indebted to both the earlier bungalow phenomenon and the Period House of the 1920s, this new suburbanism drew upon more regional images. In the case of Virginia this meant Colonial and Federal prototypes and nineteenth-century vernacular styles. These houses were basically small (under 2,000 square feet) and frequently laid out with all rooms on one floor. The western ranch-house type was often cited as a source, though on the East Coast the open, U-shaped plan was seldom used. It was the informality of the ranch house, with its generous openings to the exterior, that was considered most significant. Johnson has taken the single-story format of the ranch house and adapted it to conditions in Virginia. RGW

G.[EORGE] EDWIN BERGSTROM, 1876–1955

DAVID JULIUS WITMER, 1888–1973

# 102.
# THE PENTAGON

*United States War Department (Department of Defense) Aerial Perspective*

Arlington County

Presentation drawing, 1941

Signed and dated lower right: *T. Stathes, 7-21-41*

Colored pencil on tracing paper, mounted on board;

18 ¼ by 24 inches

Collection of the National Archives, Washington, D.C.

FIGURE 1. *Aerial photo,* **The Pentagon.** *(Photograph courtesy of the Department of Defense, Media Depository, Washington, D.C.)*

A building, a place, and certainly a mind-set, the Pentagon evokes the Cold War and American military supremacy. The Pentagon is largely known as a vast, anonymous building-mass: a gray bulk one passes quickly on a nearby parkway, or sees across acres of asphalt parking lots, or remembers from aerial background shots on television news. To its designers in 1941 it was only from an aerial perspective that the concept and size of what was then the world's largest office building, some 6,240,000 square feet, could be presented. As such, it has generally become known as a large geometrical form existing almost beyond time or place, though it was constructed at Arlington, Virginia, in a remarkably short period of sixteen months during 1941 and 1942.

The idea of a single structure to house and centralize all the dispersed units of the War Department had been kicked around in Washington for years. In the 1930s one proposal was to build a large War Department structure south of the Mall, to balance the Federal Triangle then under construction on the Mall's north side. By 1941, with Europe and Asia at war and military preparations at home, Secretary of War Henry L. Stimson assigned top priority for a new structure to be built in Arlington, Virginia. The Chief Consulting Architect for the War Department, G. Edwin Bergstrom, along with David J. Witmer, became co-chief architects for the new building. They held a weekend *charette*, or design summit, in July and came up with the pentagon shape shown in Stathes's rendering. The shape fit the site they were given, although shortly thereafter the project was assigned to a new site, overlooking the Potomac and across from the Jefferson Memorial, site of the old Washington-Hoover Airport. Although the building was significantly redesigned and the inner configuration changed from the finger- or barracks-like arrangement shown in this drawing, the pentagon-shape remained. Such a shape, which bore a vague resemblance to traditional fortress forms, apparently appealed to the military mind. Efficiency called for any shape that approached a circle, to allow the greatest area with the shortest walking distances. The result was a series of concentric rings of office spaces in a few horizontal planes. Apparently a service core, with bus terminals and cafeterias, was considered, but again the restrictive construction schedule did not allow it to be developed. It was also suggested that in official Washington, "no building is a real Government building unless it has a court in the middle of it."[1] Basic designs were completed in two months and ground was broken in September 1941. Construction companies John McShain of Philadelphia (who did National Airport), Doyle & Russel, and Wise Contracting, working in three shifts around the clock, completed the building in December 1942.[2]

The exterior of the Pentagon was summed up by architectural critics as "the less said the better: in essence it is the official Washington front," and "far from, yet reminiscent of, the classic tradition."[3] Limestone was stretched to cover the 4,600-foot perimeter of the exterior, and 140-foot-long colonnades of squared columns articulated each of the five facades. Stylistically the building followed the modernized or "stripped" Classicism common in government buildings during the 1930s and favored by President Franklin D. Roosevelt, who had approval on the design.[4]

Both architects who worked with the Construction Division of the U. S. Army Corps of Engineers were from Southern California. G. Edwin Bergstrom was born in Wisconsin and graduated in architecture from M.I.T. in 1899. He was in practice with John Parkinson in Los Angeles from 1905 to 1915, when he set up his own office and designed many commercial and public buildings. In 1919 he organized the Allied Architects Association of Los Angeles, which concentrated on public works. He served as president of the American Institute of Architects between 1939 and 1941, and from this position he was asked to advise on the defense build-up and was appointed the co-architect of the Pentagon.[5] David J. Witmer, who was born in Los Angeles, received his architectural training at Harvard, then returned home to establish a successful practice that specialized in private and public housing. Bergstrom brought Witmer east to collaborate on one of the best known and most famous (or infamous) structures in the world. If credit need be assigned, apparently Bergstrom acted more as the manager and Witmer was the real designer of the team.[6]

RGW

NOTES

1. "Pentagon Building, Arlington, Va.," *Architectural Forum* 78 (January 1943):46; see also entire article, pp. 37–52.

2. Interview with General Frederick Clarke, Army Corps of Engineers, July 9, 1990; Clarke noted that a round-the-clock construction schedule for the Pentagon was unusual for the time and set the stage for many World War II building feats.

3. "Pentagon Building," 39; "The Army's Pentagon Building," *Architectural Record* 93 (January 1943):63.

4. William B. Rhoads, "Franklin D. Roosevelt and Washington Architecture," *Records of the Columbia Historical Society* 52 (1989):139–43.

5. Obituary, *New York Times* June 21, 1955, 31; *Who was Who in America* (Chicago: Marquis, 1973): 5: 56; *National Cyclopedia of American Biography* (New York: James T. White, 1918), 16: 368–69; and Bergstrom file, American Institute of Architects archives.

6. Witmer file, American Institute of Architects Archives, Washington, D.C.

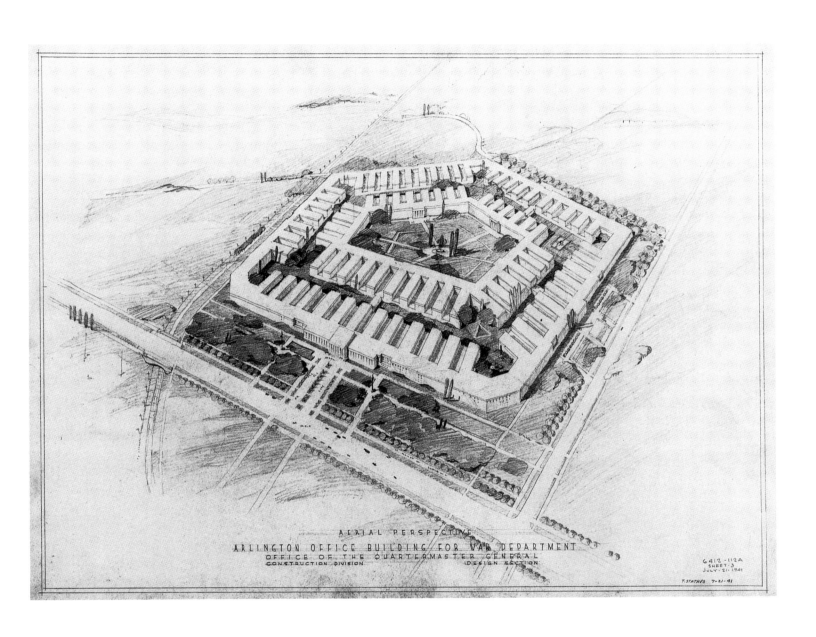

AERIAL PERSPECTIVE
ARLINGTON OFFICE BUILDING FOR WAR DEPARTMENT
OFFICE OF THE QUARTERMASTER GENERAL
CONSTRUCTION DIVISION                    DESIGN SECTION

6412-112A
SHEET-3
JULY-21-1941

T. STATHES  7-21-41

# 103.
## SHEFF STORE BUILDING

*(now Dan Kain Trophies, Inc.)*
*Perspective*

3100 N. Washington Blvd., Clarendon
Presentation drawing, 1945
Charcoal and graphite on tracing paper; 10 ¼ by 16 ¾ inches
Signed and dated lower right: *Donald H. Drayer, Arch't./1945*
Collection of the Library of Congress, Washington, D.C.,
Donald Drayer Archive

FIGURE 1. *Site photo of the* **Sheff Store Build-**
ing, *now Dan Kain Trophies, Inc.*

At first thought, on the purely functional level, the application of streamlining to buildings seems ludicrous: cars, planes, ships, and trains can move and their speed and efficiency might be increased by smooth, rounded shells, but buildings are stationary objects; they do not move, although air and wind do move across them. The concept of streamlining or contouring objects to decrease their drag through air or water was an old idea that, in the hands of industrial designers, found new favor in the 1930s. Norman Bel Geddes penned his *Horizons* (Boston: Little, Brown, 1932), a popular book that foretold a future of fast and efficient machines, all housed in smooth shells. As the concept of streamlining quickly caught on among architects, buildings with rounded corners and smooth, aerodynamically efficient surfaces, began to crop up across the country. In most cases they were only facade jobs, to symbolize what was hoped were efficient businesses that bustled inside. Streamlining became especially popular as a remodeling tool; a number of companies specialized in facade kits of porcelain enamel panels that could be applied to buildings along the main streets of small towns, the growing automobile strips.[1]

This rendering by Donald H. Drayer is a superb example of streamlining. The business exemplifies modernity; it was essentially a new type of store, only developed in the late 1920s, devoted to labor-saving machines for the up-to-date and efficient home. Stocked with sleekly contoured appliances, the building is itself the latest model. The design, a single-story structure on a street-corner with a cylindrical tower or marquee, bears a strong resemblance to designs by Robert Smith, Jr., for the Austin Company in the late 1930s. A large commercial design-build firm that advertised extensively in trade publications, the Austin Company was important in popularizing streamlining for retail applications.[2] Drayer's design uses a smooth, taut, limestone skin; the windows have aluminum frames and there is an aluminum band along the top.

Donald Hudson Drayer was born in Metropolis, Illinois, graduated from Washington University's School of Architecture in 1931, and came to Washington, D.C., to work in the Office of the Architect of the Public Buildings Administration. Drayer set up his own firm in 1941, and after the war he emerged as an important commercial architect in the capital area, designing motels, offices, shopping centers, and apartments. Among his notable works are the Arlington Towers Apartments (FIGURE 4.43), built in 1955.[3]

RGW

NOTES
1. Donald J. Bush, *The Streamlined Decade* (New York: George Braziller, 1975); Richard Guy Wilson, Dianne H. Pilgrim, and Dickran Tashjian, *The Machine Age in America, 1918–1941* (New York: Abrams, 1986).

2. Martin Greif, *The New Industrial Landscape: The Story of the Austin Company* (Clinton, New Jersey: Main Street Press, 1978). The Austin Company prototype is a drive-in laundry, designed in 1937, and reproduced in Wilson, et al., *The Machine Age*, 183.

3. *American Architects Directory* (New York; R. R. Bowker, 1955), 143.

APPLIANCES by Sheff

STORE BUILDING
CLARENDON, VIRGINIA.
DONALD H. DRAYER ARCHT.
1945

# 104.
## PROJECT
## FOR A HOUSE

*Perspective*

Unbuilt
Presentation drawing, circa 1948
Stamped lower right: *Milton L. Grigg*
Charcoal with white highlighting on green paper;
9 by 16 ¼ inches
Collection of Browne, Eichman, Dalgliesh, Gilpin, & Paxton, P.C.,
Architects, Charlottesville, Virginia

Milton Grigg became one of the masters of the medium-sized suburban house in Virginia during the 1930s, 1940s, and 1950s. While he did design some larger country-styled homes, much of his work was for houses of approximately 2,000 to 2,500 square feet. Designs such as this project, possibly for a house in Harrisonburg, illustrate his adaptation of traditional forms. In many cases Grigg borrowed employed elements from Virginia's past—columns and porticoes—but simplified and recombined them in a new way. This project has some relation to Jefferson's work and to Monticello, which Grigg worked on for many years. The central pavilion is brought forward in a gable, and the proportions of the second floor are shrunk, all mindful of features from Jefferson's early designs for Monticello, before 1776. Grigg only uses a single story porch, however, and not a double loggia.

Grigg's rendering style is reminiscent of Royal Barry Wills (1895–1962), a popular Colonial Revivalist from Boston. Wills specialized in small suburban houses and was extremely successful in publishing his designs in books and popular magazines. Several of his books, *Better Houses for Budgeteers* (New York: Architectural Book Publishing Co., 1941), and *Houses for Homemakers* (New York: Watts, 1945), show a rendering technique that Wills popularized. Grigg would certainly have known of Wills, since their work was published in the same magazine.[1] Around 1940 Wills developed a technique in which his house designs were shown in perspective in charcoal with white highlights on green paper. Grigg's rendering techniques were directly derived from Wills, though with a Virginia accent.

Houses similar to this project were erected in the Hessian Hills area of Charlottesville.　　　RGW

NOTE
1.　See *House & Garden* 76 (August 1939), section 2, 6, for a Grigg & Johnson house for Mr. James H. Burnley, Charlottesville; and pages 2–3, 17 for a Wills house for Mr. Maynard S. Renner, Lincoln, Massachusetts.

GORDON BUNSHAFT, 1909–1990

for

SKIDMORE, OWINGS & MERRILL, New York

# 105.
# REYNOLDS METALS COMPANY EXECUTIVE OFFICE BUILDING

*Presentation Section*

6601 West Broad St., Richmond
Photographic reproduction of preliminary study, circa 1956
Present location of original drawings is unknown

FIGURE 1. *The atrium of the Reynolds Metals building follows the Classical geometry of squares and rectangles, accented by the sound and motion of a splashing fountain and the natural beauty of a 40-foot-tall magnolia tree. (Photograph courtesy of Reynolds Metals Company.)*

High-style corporate modernism made its first, and in many ways most impressive, appearance in Virginia with the Reynolds Metals Building, designed and built between 1953 and 1958. A corporate Versailles, the building exemplifies a trend in post-World War II America for major corporations to build grand headquarters in the suburbs. In this case the location was five miles from downtown Richmond, a relatively flat and featureless site. Intended as a showcase for the firm's major product, aluminum—the "new" material of the twentieth century—the building is wrapped in shiny, weatherproof aluminum trim that offsets the extensive glazing. Aluminum is also used for the sun louvers on the southern, eastern, and western facades, appears on the interior as partitions, hardware, and special file cabinets, and is even used for the interior duct work.

With an entryway approach along a 245-foot-long reflecting pool (which doubles as a 205,000-gallon reservoir for the cooling and irrigation system), the building is rigidly symmetrical (see FIGURE 3.22). Sitting on a low podium of white concrete with quartz chips, the rectangular bulk of the building is carried at ground level by a peristyle of aluminum-faced piers. Designed around an open atrium, the classical allusion is reinforced by the facade elevation of a base, piano nobile, and cornice common to the Italian palazzo tradition.

To the architect of the building, Gordon Bunshaft, the design was not so much classical as formal, though he noted that, "this is how a temple should have been approached."[1] Known for his elegant designs and gruff personality, Bunshaft dismissed self-conscious historicism along with overly verbal interpretations. When asked to supply a written commentary on the design he replied: "I am an architect. I express what I believe through the buildings I have done over the past thirty years. They are the language I use—not the written word."[2]

The firm of Skidmore, Owings & Merrill had been founded in Chicago in 1936 by Louis Skidmore (1897–1962) and Nathaniel Owings (1903–1984). A New York office was opened shortly thereafter, and in time they had offices in many cities. John Merrill (1896–1975), an engineer, joined them in 1939. None of the founding partners were renowned as designers, rather they were skilled politicians and businessmen who provided the backup for talented designers such as Gordon Bunshaft. By the late 1940s the Skidmore firm (also known by its initials SOM) had become the architects of choice for corporate leaders. Uncompromisingly modern, SOM offered to their clients not just a corporate image but also many services; they designed the building, did the engineering and the landscaping, chose furnishings, and selected the art for the walls. (For Reynolds Bunshaft chose examples of Picasso, Albers, and other modern masters.) Bunshaft was the head designer in the New York office and the person most responsible for SOM's commanding position. Born in Buffalo, New York, Bunshaft received a conventional Beaux-Arts-oriented training at MIT before joining the firm in 1937. With buildings

such as Lever House, New York (1949–52), and the Connecticut General Life Insurance building in Bloomfield, Connecticut (1954–57), he reformed the look of corporate America. Bunshaft had an extensive career with many honors and in 1988 he received the Pritzker Architecture Prize. SOM designed a number of other buildings in Virginia and Bunshaft was responsible for the Philip Morris Cigarette Manufacturing Plant in Richmond (1968 to 1974).

For a project such as the Reynolds Building, SOM would produce a number of high-quality presentation aids, both to help the clients understand the design, and for future publication of the building. Unfortunately all of the materials, including a model, are now lost. The drawing illustrated was part of the presentation package and was used in post-occupancy publications even though it is technically inaccurate.[3] The porte-cochère or entrance pavilion at the far right was never constructed and instead the cantilever of the entrance canopy was extended. Also, the drawing shown here does not display the utilities core at the rear. Graphically severe in its black-and-white contrast, the drawing effectively conveys basic information on the shape, the clear-span floor levels, and the atrium, dominated by a forty-foot-high magnolia tree.

Upon its completion the Reynolds Metals Building was hailed as one of the finest works of recent architecture and appeared in numerous national and international publications and exhibitions.[4] At home in Virginia, the building was selected as one of *The Old Dominion's Twelve Best Buildings*, an exhibition sponsored by the Virginia Museum of Fine Arts.[5] Not everyone agreed; Frank Lloyd Wright, scheduled to speak at the University of Virginia, pronounced: "If anything less Virginian could be imagined, I could not."[6] Wright's petulant dismissal ignores that although the Reynolds building appears modern, with its bright perpetually new aluminum, its basic form is inspired by the same sources that Jefferson so admired.                                                          RGW

NOTES

1.   Quoted in Carol Herselle Krinsky, *Gordon Bunshaft of Skidmore, Owings & Merrill* (New York and Cambridge: Architectural History Foundation and MIT Press, 1988), p. 63.

2.   Quoted in *Contemporary Architects*, ed. A.L. Morgan and C. Naylor (Chicago: St. James Press, 1987), p. 136.

3.   An extensive search has failed to locate any original materials, except for a set of faded working drawings, in the possession of the Reynolds Metals Company. These drawings are signed by Louis Skidmore, who was the only firm member with a Virginia architect's license. They are dated between 1956 and 1958. The image reproduced comes from the files of the Virginia Museum of Fine Arts and was used in conjunction with the exhibition cited in note 5, below.

4.   Among the many publications see Ernst Danz, *Architecture of Skidmore, Owings & Merrill 1950–1962* (New York: Frederick A. Praeger, 1963), 82–89; *Form-Givers at Mid-Century*, exh. cat. (American Federation of Arts and *Time Magazine*, 1958), 50; "Reynolds wraps itself a package in aluminum," *Architectural Forum* 109 (September 1958), 90–97; Thomas K. Fitzpatrick, "A New Palace in the Piedmont," *Journal of the AIA* 30 (December 1958), 42–46; "Reynolds Metals General Office," *Mechanical Contractor*, 65 (October 1958), 42–48; and "Ole Virginny Modern," *Time* (October 14, 1958): 88.

5.   Frederick D. Nichols and William B. O'Neal, *Architecture in Virginia 1776–1958: The Old Dominion's Twelve Best Buildings* (Richmond: Virginia Museum of Fine Arts, 1958), n.p. Also it appears in William B. O'Neal, *Architecture in Virginia: An Official Guide to Four Centuries of Building in the Old Dominion* (New York: Walker & Co. for the Virginia Museum, 1968), 43.

6.   Quoted in *Lynchburg* News, October 3, 1958; clipping in scrapbook at the Reynolds Metals Building.

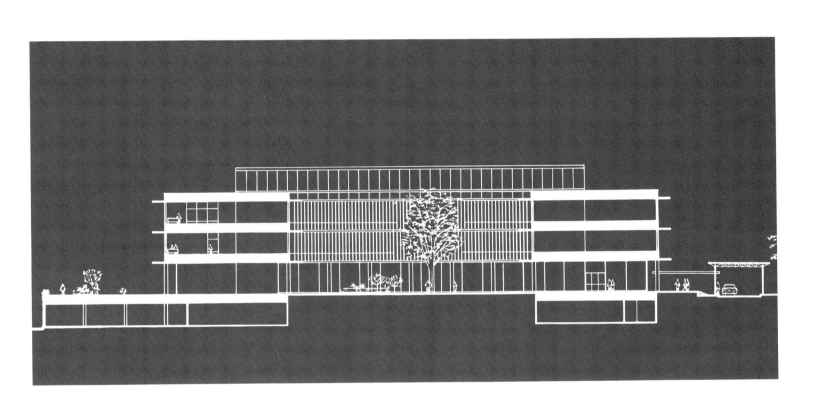

# 106.
## WOMEN'S DORMITORY BUILDING

*(Davidson Hall)*
*Hampton Institute*
*Perspective*

Hampton
Presentation drawing, circa 1956
Signed lower right: *Hilyard R. Robinson Architect*
Colored pencil on tracing paper, 13 ½ by 21 inches
Collection of Hampton University Archives, Hampton, Virginia

The architectural development of Hampton Institute (now Hampton University) after the work of Richard Morris Hunt in the 1860s–1880s (see SURVEY NO. 56) followed General Armstrong's guidelines: a well designed environment would serve as a catalyst in the education of students. J. C. Cady of New York added a Romanesque chapel and tower in 1882, and the Boston firm of Ludlow & Peabody designed several buildings in a red brick Classical mode that attracted attention in the early twentieth century.[1] After a hiatus from the 1920s to the 1940s, new buildings were called for and growth took place. But by then several changes had occurred: Modernism, especially the International Style, was the reigning idiom in American design. An architecture department had been established at Hampton under William Henry Moses, who took great interest in expanding the campus in a contemporary mode and in engaging black architects to carry out the work.

Of the leading black architects of the day, Hilyard Robinson of Washington, D.C., was among the best known. Emerging in the late 1920s with a series of winning designs, Robinson became a leading expert on housing and slum clearance in the 1930s. His Langston Terrace Public Housing Project (1937) in Washington, D.C., became a landmark in American housing with its Modernist style and its successful use of sculpture. Born in Washington, D.C., Robinson had received his education at the Philadelphia Museum and School of Industrial Arts, then the University of Pennsylvania, and received both the Bachelor and the Master of Architecture degrees from Columbia University in 1924 and 1931. Robinson then took up postgraduate studies in city planning at the University of Berlin in 1931 and 1932, when he visited the Bauhaus School and came into contact with the new ideas of the European Modernists. He served as head of the Department of Architecture at Howard University between 1926 and 1933, and he would later continue to be associated with the school. In 1934 he was appointed consulting architect for the National Capital Advisory Committee, to select sites for slum clearance, and then as senior architect for the United States Suburban Resettlement Administration. He designed many housing projects and other works throughout the 1940s and 1950s, and at times he worked with the Los Angeles-based architect Paul Williams and others. In addition to designing the Women's Dormitory at Hampton Institute, Robinson also collaborated with William Henry Moses on the design for Armstrong Hall in 1960.[2]

Robinson's dormitory for women is a classic example of the 1950s International style. The aerial perspective of the rendering was a common feature of the style, a view that became more frequent after the advent of the airplane. The aerial view also serves to emphasize certain architectural features identified with the International style: volume rather than mass, regularity rather than symmetry, and the avoidance of applied decoration.[3] The building is shown as a taut volume; roofs and walls are portrayed as thin membranes. Construction was steel frame and concrete slabs; the walls were thin brick curtains. The emphasis on the roof terrace and pipe railings was a particularly European feature of the 1920s and 1930s. The asymmetrical placement of the low commons room, and its opening to the exterior with large plate-glass walls, also recalled features of the International style. But although the building does owe debts to designs by Le Corbusier, Mies van der Rohe, and Walter Gropius, Robinson's building is not a mere copy, but an original creation. Sensitively sited, the commons and most of the student rooms have a view of Hampton Creek, which passes in front, while the red-brick exterior blends with the existing campus structures.    RGW

NOTES

1. John Taylor Boyd, Jr., "The Hampton Normal and Agricultural Institute, Hampton, Va.," *Architectural Record* 46 (August 1919):123–32.

2. For information on Robinson, I am indebted to Glen B. Lerner, Historic Preservation Division, Government of the District of Columbia, who has carried out extensive research. See also *American Architects Directory* (New York: R. R. Bowker, 1962), 593; *Historical Negro Biographies* (New York: Historical Negro Biographies, 1967), 243–244; *The Negro Almanac* (New York: John Wiley & Sons, 1983), 1063–64. Robinson's archives are at the Moorland-Spingarn Research Center, Howard University, Washington, D. C.

3. Henry-Russell Hitchcock and Philip Johnson, *The International Style: Architecture since 1922* (New York: Norton, 1932).

WOMENS DORMITORY BUILDING HAMPTON INSTITUTE VIRGINIA
HILYARD R. ROBINSON ARCHITECT

# 107.
## DULLES INTERNATIONAL AIRPORT

*Perspective*

Chantilly (Loudoun County)
Preliminary sketch, 1958
Pencil on tracing paper; 18 by 34 ½ inches
Collection of the Museum of Modern Art, New York, Gift of
Aline Saarinen, ASC. 125.66

FIGURE 1. *Site photo taken from outside terrace*, **Dulles Airport.**

While Washington International Airport (as the project was known in the office of Eero Saarinen and Associates) was conceived as a gateway to the capital city, its form owed as much to its location in Virginia's Piedmont Valley. Eero Saarinen, who died ten months before its completion, stated that he initially wanted to "place a strong form between earth and sky that seems both to rise from the plain and hover it."[1]

The airport's image is its suspended roof form, a compact structure 170 feet wide and 600 feet long. The design *parti*, esthetically potent as it is, was arrived at only after a rigorous analysis of all aspects of the problem. Originating as a commission to Ammann and Whitney Engineers, the project was a collaboration between consultants, yet in many ways Dulles Airport (named for former Secretary of State John Foster Dulles in the last days of the Eisenhower Administration) is the best representative of the Saarinen method. At the time of its inception, the project was to rewrite standards as the nation's first all-jet airport and was planned from the outset for expansion. Its 9600-acre site could fit over Washington's northwest area, and all of National Airport could fit into the space reserved for the terminal area alone. Central to the solution was Saarinen's wish to allow for indeterminate expansion with a concept that would limit disruption to operations, and to decrease distances for passenger travel. From this emerged the decision to dispense with the standard American "finger" terminal arrangement into a centralized, linear shed for passengers, with separate and remote servicing for planes, and a link between both functions. Saarinen was unique among his contemporaries in recognizing that "the valid approaches to modern architectural problems are vastly more varied than any single-minded approach would indicate," a search for form rooted in functionalism but also concerned with expanding modernism's formal language.[2] On one level, the concept of the Mobile Lounge, a vehicle to connect passengers from terminal to plane, not as a bus but as a direct extension of the departure lounge itself, was the conceptually correct innovation, "one which brought the passenger to the plane rather than the plane to the passenger."[3] To achieve Dulles Airport, the Lounge had to be invented. It was due to Saarinen's success as a practitioner that the concept was developed and adopted. However, his idea was not to celebrate technology, but rather to put it in service of a better definition of the issues within the problem. The architectural container ultimately became the connection between all elements of the airport, and the symbol of its synthesis of functions.

At Dulles Airport, Saarinen sought to retain the unchanging scale of pedestrian movement in the face of an enormous shift in technological and environmental scale. The concern for the passenger begins a scenographic experience that orchestrates movement from its start on a seventeen-mile access road, linked to Washington's Beltway system. In the approach, "as the perspective shifts, the road relaxes, and there, on its two extended, concave podia rises a temple to the friendly power of flight."[4] The passenger engages the terminal directly, since grade-separated vehicular arrival points locate all entries at ticket counters; the interior "great hall" concept is created by an unobstructed space in which support functions appear as furniture, and the distance from arrival to Mobile Lounge is only a few hundred feet.

The terminal's form "resembles a huge, continuous hammock suspended between concrete trees."[5] The hovering image is achieved by the projecting thrust of the main support piers, 65 feet high on the field side, and 43 feet on the approach side. Structurally, the sixteen pairs of supports are cantilever beams, braced against the thrust of the hanging suspension roof by large footings and a main floor serving as a strut between opposing supports. Technologically, the free-span interior was achieved by prefabricated planks spanning 10 feet between steel cables, which were slung across the span in a catenary curve, an innovative method of erection that did not require interior scaffolding. The monolithic integrity of the roof was achieved by poured concrete "ribs" between adjacent rows of planks. The autonomy of the roof structure is maintained by the design of the infill glass, which furthers and counterpoints its curved geometry and, while resistant to wind loading, remains a gossamer transparent membrane.

The dynamic geometry of Dulles Airport draws upon multiple allusions; its curvilinear forms recall the drawings of Erich Mendelsohn, thereby reinstating expressionist architecture as a source. It also recalls the great railway arrival sheds of the nineteenth century or, in its whiteness, Federal architecture. As critic Peter Carter summarized, "Saarinen was aware of today's technology in its widest sense . . . as a means of achieving a many-faceted architectural expression within the tradition of the modern masters. To advance the symbolic and environmental content of that tradition he explored special architectural vernaculars for each project . . . it precluded the possibility of a personal style, a fact which set him apart from any of his contemporaries."[6]                               PCP

NOTES
1.  Dulles International Airport," *Architectural Record* (July 1963): 103.

2.  Cranston Jones, *Architecture Today and Tomorrow*, (New York: McGraw-Hill, 1961), 137.

3.  Horace Sutton, "Booked for Travel: A Ground-to Air Missive," *Saturday Review* 46 (January 12, 1963): 59.

4.  Edgar J. Kaufmann, Jr., "Critique" in "Dulles International Airport," *Progressive Architecture* (August 1963): 94.

5.  Eero Saarinen quoted in "Dulles International Airport," *Architectural Record* (July 1963): 109.

6.  Peter Carter, "Eero Saarinen 1910–1961," *Architectural Design* (December 1961): 537.

# 108.
## CHEMISTRY BUILDING PROJECT

*University of Virginia*
*Model*

Charlottesville (unbuilt)
Presentation model, circa 1961
Cardboard and wood; 36 by 32 ¼ by 7 inches
Collection of the University of Virginia, Charlottesville, on permanent loan to the Louis I. Kahn Collection, Architectural Archives, University of Pennsylvania, and Pennsylvania Historical and Museum Commission, Philadelphia

In the early 1960s, the University of Virginia hired Louis I. Kahn to design a chemistry building. Kahn had recently risen to prominence with the celebrated Salk Institute for Biological Studies in La Jolla, California, and the Richards Medical Research Building at the University of Pennsylvania. The reputation Kahn established with these buildings was an artistry of space and light formed of heavy masonry or concrete. Kahn's division of a building's parts into the so-called servant and served space provided efficient solutions for the modern necessities of institutional structures. Kahn grew up in Philadelphia and studied architecture under the Beaux-Arts tutelage of Paul Philippe Cret at the University of Pennsylvania. Kahn's Classical training at Penn and at the American Academy in Rome, coupled with his own impressions of the ancient world, provided him with a different background than many of his Modernist contemporaries. Kahn strove to create an architecture that at once addressed the fundamentals of post-and-lintel structure and the formality of Classical design, while exploring the most modern technology. As a professor at Penn and at Yale, Kahn's power as a lecturer was legendary. His strong personal commitment to design also carried into the work of his own firm. The combination of Kahn's built works, his theory, and his teaching established him as one of this century's greatest architects.

Kahn's challenge at the University of Virginia was to design a distinctive modern research and classroom facility located near the newly completed Physics Building and a proposed Life Science Building. The university required a brick exterior, which Kahn recognized as a desire for a "red-and-white" building.[1] The complex program demanded offices, a library, an auditorium, and a minimum of six different types of research space for 200 faculty and graduate students, as well as classroom space for 1200 undergraduates. In addition to general safety measures, the different divisions of the building had to be insulated from the noise, potential leakage, or exhaust of the others and meet all current codes required for funding from the National Institutes of Health.[2]

This model presents the most developed of the three schemes discussed for the building. A second scheme used a series of pavilion-like towers to allow greater articulation of usage as well as greater flexibility on the severe topography of the site. A third was similar to the first, but with total enclosure of the auditorium by the building wings. In the design shown, Kahn monumentalized the auditorium as the central and visual anchor of the building, flanked by the two wings with offices and lab spaces. The U-shape forms a large "outdoor room" just off the site on McCormick Road and also allows many routes of access—both to the serious researcher and to the mass of classroom traffic. This arrangement of interior and exterior rooms and corridors responds to what Kahn called the "societal needs" of the users of a building.

The hiring of Kahn for the Chemistry Building reflected a trend on American campuses of "collecting" buildings by great architects. The Chemistry Building Committee spoke of the need for an "imaginative architect" when it chose Kahn. With deadlines nearing and the design over-budget, the Committee questioned the layman's ability to interpret the dollar value of the blank brick walls.[3] Such walls, it was feared, seemed "too fortress-like or cold in appearance," and the contract was cancelled in 1964.[4] As guardian of Jefferson's Neoclassic legacy, the University of Virginia could not accommodate the twentieth-century Modernism in the brickwork of Louis Kahn.

SAK

NOTES

1. Letter from Louis Kahn to Edgar Shannon, November 27, 1962, as reprinted in Heinz Ronner and Sharad Jhaveri, *Louis I. Kahn, Complete, Works 1935–1974* (Boulder, Colorado: Westview, 1977), 181.

2. "Chemistry Building, 2nd Revised Program," July 14, 1961, archives, University of Virginia, Charlottesville.

3. Minutes, Chemistry Building Committee Meeting, January 16, 1964, archives, University of Virginia.

4. Quoted in Minutes of Chemistry Building Committee Meeting, taken by Frederick D. Nichols, April 8, 1963, University of Virginia.

WILLIAM TURNBULL, JR., born 1935

for

MLTW/TURNBULL ASSOCIATES, San Francisco

# 109.
# WARREN
# ZIMMERMANN
# HOUSE

*Model*

Great Falls (Fairfax County)
Presentation model, 1974
Model-maker: Paul Lobush
Wood, foam-core, and fiberglass; 37 by 38 by 38 inches
Collection of William Turnbull, San Francisco

FIGURE 1. *Site photo,* **Zimmermann House.** *(Photograph by Cervin Robinson, courtesy of William Turnbull & Associates, San Francisco.)*

The Zimmermann house is one of Virginia's best known and most widely published houses of the past twenty years. Its design represents a special aspect of Postmodernism in that it is not so much a stylistic solution, but rather a response to the owner's particular desires and to the environmental nature of its site. The architect of this residence, William Turnbull, claims that a house should embody the occupants' dreams and desires, their aspirations and expectations. Mrs. Zimmermann, recalling a childhood spent at her grandparents' house on the coast of Maine, wanted lots of porches—all around the house. Her husband wanted a house that would be sun-drenched and light-filled, the exact opposite. The solution was house-as-porch, or porch-as-house, in which a free-standing redwood lattice facade covers an inner core. Located on a ridge overlooking the Potomac River flood plain, the house is lifted up, as if on stilts. Over-scaled openings in the lattice facade and a translucent plastic roof allow light to fill the house inside. The model shows in schematic form the contrast between the outer lattice and box-like form and the inner, much more articulated, house. The inner house plan recalls late-nineteenth-century dwellings with its several bays and its large stairhall.[1]

The house's overall boxy form, the random openings, and the shed roof all recall William Turnbull's earlier work in California. Born in New York City, Turnbull attended Princeton and studied in France, then worked briefly for Skidmore, Owings & Merrill in San Francisco. In 1961 he entered into a partnership with Charles Moore, Donlyn Lyndon, and Richard Whitaker, in the firm Moore Lyndon Turnbull Whitaker. Their work at Sea Ranch, California, beginning in 1964, was one of the first major challenges to the reigning orthodoxy of Modernism. The project became an instant landmark. Instead of creating an alien design, the partnership created buildings in sympathy with the environment and based upon the regional, wooden-house vernacular. Charles Moore (born 1925) became the acknowledged leader of the group, however several of his younger partners like Turnbull would, after Moore's departure for the East Coast, emerge as major talents in their own right. Over the years a loose association was kept up among the partners, who went by the initials MLTW, adding the actual designing partner's name on any given project credits. Turnbull remained in the Bay Area, working from time to time with Moore, and even providing graphics on occasion, as he did for the book *The Place of Houses* (New York: Holt, Rinehart and Winston, 1974). He has also taught, most notably at the University of California at Berkeley. The work of MLTW and of Turnbull, in particular, exhibits a preference for jarring contrasts, towers, and additive elements that break up the usual geometrical purity of most Modernist designs. They liked rough textures and blunt contrasts between materials: wood in a natural or semifinished state butts unceremoniously into gypsum walls in the Zimmermann house. Generally absent is the finicky and obsessive detailing of East Coast Post-

modernists; instead, as the model so well illustrates, their West Coast style reveals a more casual attitude to design.[2]                                                RGW

NOTES

1.    According to information provided in a letter to the author from William Turnbull, Jr., dated December 11, 1989, the house has been published more than twenty-five times since 1974. Among his citations: "MLTW/Turnbull Associates," *Progressive Architecture* 56 (January 1975):54–55; "Zimmermann House, Outside in," *Progressive Architecture* 57 (February 1976):72–75; "A House in a Box," *Architectural Review* 159 (June 1976): cover and 381; "William Turnbull, Jr.," *A + U* 73 (January 1977):132–133; "First Honor Award," *House and Home* 50 (October 1976):104–105; Paul Goldberger, "This whole house is a porch," *New York Times Sunday Magazine* August 29, 1976, 38–39; Douglas Davis, "Art," *Newsweek* October 6, 1976, 65–69. Additional drawings exist for this project in San Francisco, in the collection of the architect.

2.    Other work by Turnbull can be found in: "Special Issue, Charles Moore and Company,"*GA Global Architecture Houses* 7 (October 1980):42–61.

ROBERT VENTURI, born 1925

JOHN RAUCH, born 1930

DENISE SCOTT BROWN, born 1931

for

VENTURI & RAUCH, Philadelphia

with

VVKR (VOSBECK VOSBECK KENDRICK REDINGER)

Alexandria

# 110.
## CAROL M. NEWMAN LIBRARY RENOVATION AND ADDITION

*Virginia Polytechnic Institute and State University*

*Perspective*

Blacksburg
Presentation drawing, 1971 by W. G. Clark, born 1942
Dated: *August 5, 1971*
Ink on mylar, 20 by 32 inches
Collection of Venturi, Scott Brown & Associates, Inc.,
Philadelphia

FIGURE 1. *Site photo,* **Newman Library.** *(Photograph courtesy of the Photo Lab, Virginia Polytechnic Institute and State University, Blacksburg.)*

The Philadelphia architectural firm of Venturi & Rauch was a pioneer of what has come to be known as Postmodernism. Founded in 1964, the firm received national renown in 1966 with the publication of Robert Venturi's *Complexity and Contradiction in Architecture*.[1] Venturi called his book a "gentle manifesto" against the rigid rules and anti-historicism of orthodox Modernism, which he felt too often produced bland and inexpressive buildings. He called instead for a rich and complex architecture that could draw inspiration from both modern experience and historical tradition. Controversial for its challenge to the status quo, *Complexity and Contradiction* became something of a bible of Postmodernism.

Venturi and partner Denise Scott Brown have continued to explore theoretical aspects of contemporary architecture and culture in numerous articles and speeches, and in two further books, *Learning from Las Vegas* and *A View from the Campidogilio*.[2] The firm became Venturi, Rauch & Scott Brown in 1982 and, when managing partner John Rauch withdrew in 1989, Venturi, Scott Brown & Associates.

The addition to the Newman Library, the firm's only Virginia building, belongs to a rich body of work that gives realization to Venturi's theories. Among the best known of the partners' projects are the house Venturi designed for his mother in 1962 and the Guild House apartment building for the elderly in Philadelphia (1964). The firm's 1991 addition to the National Gallery, London, continues the dialogue between tradition and modern experience with a witty and unconventional use of Classical elements.

The Newman Library addition, while unmistakably a contemporary building, attempts to harmonize with the original library's "Collegiate Gothic" style through use of similar materials. Its curved shape, reminiscent of the firm's better known (but unbuilt) design for the Yale Mathematics Building (1969), allowed for a compact plan that reduced the amount of land needed to accommodate the extension. The 100,000 square feet of additional space nearly doubled the library's volume capacity.[3]

The perspective drawing of the addition illustrated here belongs to a group of drawings by architect W. G. Clark that represents a rare deviation from the firm's usual distinctive graphic style, developed by Venturi early in his career. The "Venturi style" is based on simplified, almost cartoon-like line drawings that, with the enhancement of relatively flat planes of color, are used even for the firm's most important presentation drawings. At least in part, this is intended to ensure that the viewer never forgets that he or she is looking at a drawing, in contrast to more illusionistic renderings that try to imitate photographs. Also the strong, unambiguous line allows for easier reproduction by a variety of means. In fact, the actual drawing was never seen by the client; photographic reproductions of it would have been used in presentations.

Clark's drawing style during his tenure with the firm is distinguished by a strong use of vertical lines of varying weight and separation to define planes, height-

ening the sense of abstraction in an already abstract style. The Newman addition drawing clearly defines the building outline in the Venturi way, but the most fully realized examples of this evocative style depend almost entirely on the vertical line, adding detail with various cross-hatchings.

Clark remained with the firm until 1975, when he left to follow a distinguished design career of his own; he joined the faculty of the School of Architecture at the University of Virginia in 1989. After Clark's departure, the firm of Venturi & Rauch returned to the more canonical Venturi drawing style and has remained with it almost exclusively ever since. DAD III

NOTES
1.   Robert Venturi, *Complexity and Contradiction in Architecture* (New York: The Museum of Modern Art, 1966).

2.   Robert Venturi, Denise Scott Brown, Steven Izenour, *Learning from Las Vegas* (Boston: M.I.T. Press, 1972).

3.   R. Venturi and D. Scott Brown, *A View from the Campidoglio* (New York: Harper & Row, 1984).

REFERENCES
Venturi, R., and Scott Brown, D. *A View from the Campidoglio.* New York: Harper & Row, 1984.

von Moos, Stanislaus. *Venturi, Rauch and Scott Brown. Buildings and Projects.* New York: Rizzoli, 1987.

JAMES WINES, born 1932

for

SITE INC., New York City

# 111.
## RICHMOND FOREST BUILDING

### *Best Products Company*

Parham and Quioccasin Rds., Richmond (Henrico County)

### *Perspective and Elevation*
Presentation drawing, 1978
Signed and dated: *SITE J. W.* [James Wines] *1978*
Ink on paper, 13 ¾ by 17 inches
Collection of Sydney and Frances Lewis, Richmond

### *Model*
Presentation model, 1978
Cardboard, wood, and metal; 6 by 24 by 27 inches
Collection of the Museum of Modern Art, New York.
Best Products Company, Inc., Architecture Fund

FIGURE 1. *Site photo,* **Best Products Co., Forest Building,** *Richmond.*

Best Products Company's patronage of avant-garde, controversial architecture is one of the most significant chapters in the recent history of American architecture. Founded by Sydney and Frances Lewis, Best is a catalogue showroom merchandise chain, one of the largest in the nation, with headquarters in Richmond, Virginia. Most of the showrooms are located in suburban shopping centers and are large, volumetric, rectangular, flat-roofed buildings. Their nominal architectural character, like most shopping-center buildings, is banal at best.

Best's founders, Sydney and Frances Lewis, are serious art collectors who have concentrated on decorative arts of the Art Nouveau and Art Déco periods, and contemporary art, from Pop to Neo-Realist and Expressionist. As an extension of their esthetic sensibilities, they commissioned James Wines of SITE to develop a special series of company showrooms. The first, Best's *Peeling Wall Project* in Richmond (1971–72), was followed by Best showrooms that feature other innovative effects in Houston, Sacramento, Miami, and elsewhere. Best Products also commissioned Venturi, Rauch & Scott Brown to redesign the company logo, and to design a showroom for a location in suburban Bucks County, Pennsylvania. The Lewises also sponsored a series of designs by leading Postmodernists, shown at the Museum of Modern Art; commissioned Hardy Holzman Pfeiffer to design the company headquarters building in Richmond; and were instrumental in obtaining the commission for the Hardy firm to design the 1985 wing of the Virginia Museum of Fine Arts (see SURVEY NO. 112).[1]

James Wines, principal partner of SITE, describes himself as an environmental artist, and his work as "de-architecture." Trained not as an architect but as a sculptor at Syracuse University, Wines first worked primarily as a sculptor. In 1969 he founded SITE (an acronym for Sculpture In The Environment) with partners Alison Sky, Emilio Sousa, and Michelle Stone. Wines has taught at Cooper Union in New York and the New Jersey School of Architecture in Newah, New Jersey, and SITE's work has been shown to international acclaim. "Our work comes from an attitude that anything is possible," Wines explains, "which is much more akin to the thinking of artists than of architects."[2] While Wines's earliest work appeared in conjunction with early Postmodernism and although, like Robert Venturi, he was also influenced by the Pop Art of the 1960s, he claims that a major difference is his avoidance of theoretical issues, instead concentrating upon the viewer's psychological response to the situation, such as a facade that appears to be peeling away, or a forest that is invading the walls of a structure. As he says, "We try to go beyond what is accepted."[3] SITE's work appeals to the mental rather than the formal aspects of architecture, and depends upon a humorous, intuitive response to the project rather than a somber intellectualization.

The site selected for Best's Forest Building (1978–80) was a heavily wooded suburban area, so Wines developed the concept that the building should appear as if the vegetation and showroom were one and the same: that the trees were growing up out of the interior space and perhaps even threatening to consume the structure. This drawing, which represents an early stage of the project, shows the structure surrounded not only by trees but also invading the showroom walls, or growing out of the top of the roof. As the model indicates, which is closer to the project as constructed, the trees appear to have penetrated the facade, within a long breach in the structure. Trees are also massed around the exterior to give the sense of invasion. Also the parking lot has trees scattered about, as if they had sprung up out of the asphalt. As actually experienced, the area where the trees penetrate the walls appears more as a vestibule, since the glass wall of the store is repeated beyond. And as is also common with SITE's work, while immediacy of the concept has a certain unsettling aspect, its overall impact is more that of a slightly miscued joke than a profound architectural experience. RGW

NOTES

1. *Buildings for Best Products, U. S. A.* (New York: Museum of Modern Art, 1979).

2. "Interview: James Wines, Joshua Weinstein, SITE," *Progressive Architecture* 71 (August 1990):116–17. Background can be found in: *SITE, Architecture as Art* (New York: St. Martin's Press, 1980); *SITE Buildings and Spaces,* exh. cat. (Richmond: Virginia Museum, 1980); and Olivier Boissiere, *Gehry, SITE, Tigerman, Trois Portraits de l'Artiste en Architecture* (Paris: Editions du Moniteur, 1981).

3. "Interview," *Progressive Architecture.*

RICHMOND FOREST BUILDING - BEST PRODUCTS CO.

EDWARD A. SMITH, JR., A.I.A., born 1940

FREDERIC H. COX, JR., F.A.I.A., born 1933

for

MARCELLUS WRIGHT COX & SMITH, ARCHITECTS

Richmond

# 112.
# E. CLAIBORNE ROBINS SCHOOL OF BUSINESS ADDITION

*University of Richmond*
*Isometric Projection*

Westhampton area, Richmond
Presentation axonometric, 1982
Drawn by Edward Taylor Davis (born 1957)
Dated: *February 1982*
Ink on mylar; 21½ by 22 inches
Collection of Marcellus Wright, Cox & Smith, Architects,
Richmond, Virginia

FIGURE 1. *Site photo*, **Robins School of Business Addition, University of Richmond.** *(Photograph copyright Whit Cox, courtesy of Marcellus Wright Cox & Smith, Architects, Richmond.)*

At first glance this building on the University of Richmond campus appears to be part of the original fabric designed by Ralph Adams Cram back in the 1910s and continued by other architects. Built of red brick with white limestone details, it fits very comfortably with the earlier architecture. Only when one approaches and observes the odd entrance arch with the spiral column on one side and then enters to discover a soaring space inside does it become apparent that this is a building designed and erected some seventy years later.

The Robins addition is a fine example of another side to contemporary Postmodernism.[1] In this case the chief designer, Ed Smith, explained it as a continuation of the campus's original architecture, really a "replication" but with the addition of "funky details," such as the entrance, downspout, "odd bird" sculptures, and then the interior, a "surprise."[2] This aspect of Postmodernism differs from the straight historicism practiced by some designers such as Robert A. M. Stern (SURVEY NO. 116), or the historical abstractions of Michael Graves (SURVEY NO. 115). Smith's Robins design is contextual—the building fits the environment—but it also contains a critique of the environment, a witty irreverence. Smith has recognized that the very accurate replication of historical forms that appear in Cram's original buildings is no longer relevant, and that the late twentieth century has its own self-deprecatory humor. The building is a modern steel-frame structure with brick veneer walls: the original structural and symbolic function of the details was lost long ago.

Another clue to the later date of the building is the rendering by Edward Taylor Davis, who was in the firm's office at the time. It is an axonometric drawing, a type of aerial projection first developed in the 1920s and used frequently by Modernists. Cram or the other firms would never have used such a view, which is an aerial that flattens out the form to reveal the relationships among parts. Emphasized is the volumetric quality of the building, not its elevations, which become thin partitions over the frame.

The University of Richmond has been fortunate in the additions to their campus after Cram's original designs. Cram was replaced in the early 1920s by Charles M. Robinson, who designed the chapel and the administrative quadrangle. From the mid 1920s until the mid 1950s Carneal & Johnston were the campus architects, completing most recently the landmark Boatwright Library with its large Gothic tower, in 1954. After employing several out-of-town architects, the University turned to the firm of Marcellus Wright Cox & Smith as campus architects.[3] The firm, founded by Marcellus Wright, has been responsible for many Richmond buildings, including the 1988 rehabilitation of the Loew's Theatre of the late 1920s (see SURVEY NO. 88) and the completion of the Best Products headquarters building. Edward Smith, the partner in charge of the design, studied architecture at the University of Virginia. In addition to numerous new buildings, Smith has been in charge of the rehabil-

itation of Cram's other Virginia campus at Sweet Briar College (see FIGURE 3.30). RGW

NOTES
1. Publications of the Robins include: Richard Guy Wilson, "Showbiz-Glamour: Architecture in the Eighties," *Inform* 1 (January-February 1990): 8–11.

2. Interview with Edward Smith, October 27, 1989.

3. Interview with Randolph L. Darnell, Physical Plant, University of Richmond, May 26, 1989.

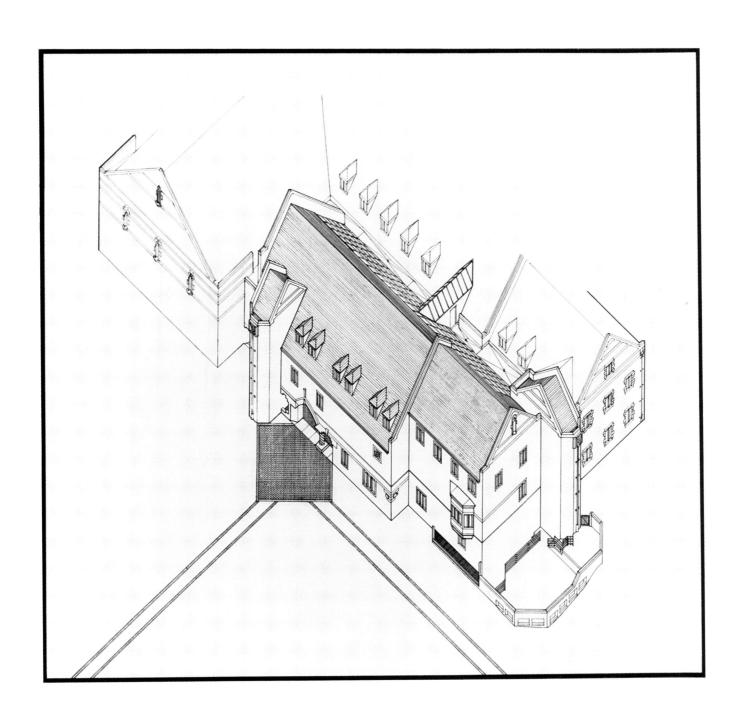

HUGH HARDY, born 1932

MALCOLM HOLZMAN, born 1940

NORMAN PFEIFFER, born 1940

for

HARDY HOLZMAN PFEIFFER ASSOCIATES,
New York

# 113.
## VIRGINIA MUSEUM OF FINE ARTS WEST WING ADDITION

*West Elevation*

The Boulevard at Grove Ave., Richmond
Presentation drawing, circa 1982
Watercolor and tape on paper; 23 ⅝ by 113 ⅜ inches
Collection of Virginia Museum of Fine Arts, Richmond,
Archives

FIGURE 1. *Site photo,* **Virginia Museum of Fine Arts, West Wing,** *view from southwest.*

Virginia's opposing orientations—past and future—are subtly inferred in this Postmodern addition to the Virginia Museum of Fine Arts by Hardy Holzman Pfeiffer Associates. Designed to house several very different collections—gifts of eighteenth- and nineteenth-century French and English paintings and sculpture from Mr. and Mrs. Paul Mellon, and from Sydney and Frances Lewis, Art Nouveau and Art Déco decorative arts with contemporary paintings and sculpture—the wing indicates these contrasts as well. As the rendering for the west elevation illustrates, the exterior of the wing is mounted on a massive rusticated limestone base with deep striations.[1] Above this rise nearly solid limestone walls, with projecting cornices and polished granite bands that line up with the original Peebles & Ferguson elevation. This homage to the earlier building carries with it a subversive quality, however, for the detailing of the cornice bands has different textures and projections that are handled in a casual, almost random, manner as they disappear and reemerge. This massive wall of stone provides a sense of security and recalls earlier Classical formats, yet it is visually far more weighty than the original red-brick facade (see SURVEY NO. 93). This stone wall also bears two totally alien features: glass-enclosed stair wells, radically modern and abstract in both shape and materials, that are disconcertingly abutted against the limestone; and their steel-webbed joists, painted a pale blue-green, fully visible against the terra-cotta bricks. This dialogue between history and radical modernism has a further subtlety: it recalls other donations by the Mellon family, specifically to the National Gallery of Art in Washington, D.C.: the West Building by John Russell Pope, 1936–41, and the East Building by I. M. Pei, 1968–78.[2]

The firm of Hardy Holzman Pfeiffer has specialized in creating designs that subtly comment upon and subvert accepted conventions.[3] Architects Hugh Hardy, Malcolm Holzman—who was the partner-in-charge for the Virginia Museum—and Norman Pfeiffer formed a partnership in 1967. Their backgrounds are diverse: Hardy was trained at Princeton, Holzman at Pratt Institute, and Pfeiffer at the University of Washington. When they emerged in the 1970s, they brought with them a series of unconventional designs that questioned, in a sometimes shocking manner, the reigning orthodoxy of Modernism. Their Orchestra Hall in Minneapolis (1974) had exposed, painted ductwork in the lobby and huge chunky cubical blocks in the concert hall ceiling. In retrospect their work predated what came to be labeled Postmodernism in the late 1970s. They increasingly used historical elements, though in an unconventional and at times unsettling manner. In 1981 they received the AIA Firm Award. Their previous Virginia work was the Richmond headquarters building (1981) for Best Products Company, founded by art patrons Sydney and Frances Lewis. For the Lewises Hardy Holzman Pfeiffer had a bold, unabashed quality that was well-suited to their collecting interests and complemented the architecture they had commissioned for their company's catalogue

merchandise showrooms. The Lewises greatly influenced the choice of Hardy Holzman Pfeiffer for this, the fourth addition to the Virginia Museum.[4]     RGW

NOTES

1. Presentation elevations for the south and north facades, as well as extensive working drawings, are in the Museum's archives.

2. For commentary on the addition see Darl Rastorfer, "Putting it All Together," *Architectural Record* (June 1986):154–163; Carlton Knight III, "Virtuoso Performance in Stone," *Architecture* 75 (January 1986):40–45; Robert P. Winthrop and Robert Merritt, "West Wing: tour de force for art," *Richmond Times-Dispatch* (December 1, 1985): G1; Jane Addams Allen, "Virginia Museum's Bold, New West Wing," *Washington Times Magazine* (November 29, 1985), M:4–6; Linda Walters, "The West Wing, A Grand Tradition Continues," *Arts in Virginia* 23 (1982–83): 40–43.

3. Information supplied by HHPA. For background see Michael Sorkin, *Hardy Holzman Pfeiffer* (New York: Watson-Guptill, 1981).

4. The Virginia Museum of Fine Arts expanded by three earlier additions: the Theater Wing in 1954, the South Wing in 1970, and the North wing in 1976.

WEST ELEVATION

GEORGE E. HARTMAN, born 1936

WARREN J. COX, born 1935

for

HARTMAN-COX ARCHITECTS, Washington, D.C.

# 114.
## CHRYSLER MUSEUM ADDITIONS AND RENOVATIONS

Olney Road and Mowbray Arch, Norfolk

### Model
Made by Gene Goehrung, Trojan Models, 1984
Paper, foam core, plexiglass; 35 by 35 by 8 inches
Collection of the Chrysler Museum, Norfolk

### Interior Courtyard Perspective
Presentation drawing, circa spring 1983, by James Stokoe
Watercolor on paper; 18 by 14 inches
Collection of Hartman-Cox Architects, Washington, D.C.

FIGURE 1. **The Chrysler Museum,** *as renovated. (Photograph by Peter Aaron/Esto.)*

Hartman-Cox's redesign of the Chrysler Museum ranks as one of the most important recent works of architecture in Virginia. The recipient of numerous awards, the building has been hailed by critics: "A muddled eyesore transformed into a handsome asset."[1] The firm's work at the Chrysler illustrates not just a return to historical models that many leading architects have espoused, but also a renewed sensitivity to the context and the intentions of the original architects, Peebles & Ferguson.

George E. Hartman attended Princeton University with an undergraduate degree in art history and a graduate degree in architecture. His partner, Warren E. Cox, pursued the same path at Yale University. They met in the early 1960s while working for the Washington, D.C., firm of Keyes, Lethbridge & Condon, which they left to set up a partnership of their own in 1965. Their work up to the late 1970s was in the Abstract Modernist vein, though never overly aggressive, and with a strong spirit of fitting to the site. More and more, however, they began to draw upon local and regionalist models as with their Immanuel Presbyterian Church in McLean, Virginia (1978–80; FIGURE 3.47), which recalled nineteenth-century board-and-batten churches of the Virginia countryside. They increasingly rejected what they have termed the "inflexible" and "self-expressive and artiness" of much modernism for "associational values and qualities specific to the building type."[2] They have specifically identified themselves with the earlier generation of creative eclectics, such as John Russell Pope and Paul Cret.[3] Their work, such as Monroe Hall near the center of the University of Virginia campus, recalls the Georgian Revival style of the 1920s and 1930s, which was used for much of the campus expansion.

George Hartman, the partner-in-charge of the commission, found a difficult situation at Norfolk. Originally founded as the Norfolk Museum of Arts and Sciences, the museum was renamed the Chrysler Museum in 1971, when Walter P. Chrysler, Jr., donated his art collection to the city. The initial building of 1932–33, designed by Finley Ferguson of Peebles and Ferguson in association with Carlow, Browne & Fitz-Gibbon, also of Norfolk, was an Italian *palazzo* facade surrounding an open, U-shaped courtyard. The entrance was oriented to the Hague Inlet of the Elizabeth River. Unfortunately, this design was never fully completed and the courtyard was bricked up. In the 1960s, New York architects William and Geoffrey Platt added a wing and tower and changed the entrance to the side. Further additions in the 1970s, including a brutalist concrete box designed by Williams and Tazewell & Associates of Norfolk, made it one of the most inhospitable museums in the country.

Hartman's solution, visible both in the model and in the drawing, was to restore the original entrance through the arcade overlooking the Hague Inlet. This brought the visitor directly on axis into the courtyard, now covered with Florentine wooden trusses and a glass canopy, and thus immediately provides orientation. The drawing, a quick sketch for the museum's

board of directors, indicates with its open arcades, the grand—and newly designed—staircase, and open windows at the second story, how the courtyard will serve as the centerpiece of the museum. As constructed, numerous details of the courtyard, such as the cornice, were altered. The 1960s wing and tower were duplicated on the other side, a library was added across the back, and all of the earlier, inhospitable additions were covered in limestone to loosely duplicate the original facade. The model reveals both the sprawl of the museum and the dominance of the original architectural intentions. Seen in perspective the facade, with its twin towers, gives the air of an Italian hill-town transplanted to the Tidewater of Virginia.

RGW

NOTES

1. Benjamin Forgey, "The Chrysler Museum, Suddenly Splendid" *Washington Post* (February 26, 1989), G1: 10–11. See also Paul Goldberger, "A Museum Exhibits a Splendid Lack of Glitz," *New York Times* (June 4, 1989), H33; Vernon Mays, "A Remarkable Transformation," *Inform* 1 (July-August 1990):18–19.

2. Quoted in Andrea Oppenheimer Dean, "Firm of the Year: Hartman-Cox Very Much of Washington, D.C.," *Architecture* 87 (February 1988):45.

3. Based on author interviews with Warren Cox and George Hartman, 1989, 1990.

FIGURE 2. **Interior courtyard, Chrysler Museum.** *(Photograph by Peter Aaron/Esto.)*

# 115.
## CENTER FOR INNOVATIVE TECHNOLOGY

*Perspective*

2214 Rock Hill Road, Herndon
Presentation drawing, circa 1986
Signed lower right: *Brackett Zimmermann Associates*
Photo collage and airbrush on paper; 18 by 27 ¼ inches
Collection of the Virginia Center for Innovative Technology, Herndon, Virginia

FIGURE 1. *Site photo,* **Center for Innovative Technology,** *Herndon. (Photograph courtesy of Timothy Hursley.)*

The Center for Innovative Technology (CIT) is the most radically modern building yet constructed in Virginia and certainly the most controversial. Commentators have called it "an overdone architectural soufflé," "a flying pyramid," and "the leaning tower of Virginia," while an architect associated with the project has termed it "a study in vertical motion."[1] CIT is Virginia's entry into the high-tech sweepstakes, an attempt by the state to promote new business and technological research. Founded in 1984, CIT's board of directors decided they needed a landmark building, as a symbol and headquarters. A site was secured near Dulles Airport and a national competition, backed by a grant from the National Endowment for the Arts, was held in 1985 under the sponsorship of the Architecture Department at Virginia Polytechnic Institute. In what was described as a "national ideas" competition rather than a building competition, one of the finalists, Jennifer Luce, was hired by Arquitectonica.[2] Luce encouraged the firm to pursue the commission, which they secured in late 1985 in a joint venture with Ward/Hall Associates of Fairfax. The design was developed by Arquitectonica while Ward/Hall handled the construction phase. Construction began in April 1987 and the building was completed in March 1989.

The Arquitectonica (Spanish for architectural) firm of Miami is known for its bold and abstract Modernist work. Headed by Bernardo Fort-Brescia and Laurinda Spear, Arquitectonica gained recognition in the early 1980s with a series of large and colorful high-rise buildings in Miami (which frequently served as backdrops for the television series *Miami Vice*). While claiming to be resolutely Modernist and not succumbing to the historicism of Postmodernism, still Arquitectonica enjoyed the new freedom of eccentric forms and theatrics. CIT as built owes a debt to Jennifer Luce's original scheme as well as to numerous redesigns by office personnel, including Fort-Brescia. The various stages of the design all reveal an interest in Russian Constructivism of the 1920s, which developed a great following among some architects in the 1980s.[3] Tied in closely with the fad of Deconstructivist architecture, buildings were composed of wedge-shaped planes and volumes that seemed to disobey the normal rules of gravitation and construction.[4] "De-con," as it is termed, can be seen as a late Modernism, or as some prefer, "The Second Modernism," a rediscovery of abstract form. Strictly speaking, CIT is not Deconstructivist; its designers do not claim that as their theoretical base for this project, but the unsettling forms do reflect its influence. At the same time CIT can be seen as an attempt to create a structure that embodies the forward-looking principles of CIT and to relate to the presence of Dulles Airport, which is visible nearby. The design as fully developed dropped some of its Russian-Constructivist mannerisms for a bolder interplay of abstract forms.

The rendering, by the commercial studio of Brackett, Zimmermann was commissioned by the CIT board to show to potential sponsors.[5] The structure is composed of a series of violently distorted forms arranged in a seemingly haphazard manner on top of a black podium, which contains the parking garage and some services. Arrayed on the top of the podium are four forms: an upside-down pyramid, a low rise parallelogram, a semicircular bridge, and a wedge-shaped protrusion. Gold, green, silver, blue, and black reflecting-glass cover the two large forms: the bridge is sheathed in clear glass; and the auditorium wedge is covered in panels of white marble. While the different forms can be claimed to relate to their different functions—that is, the pyramid as an office tower, the horizontal parallelogram for software production, the bridge as lobby, and the wedge as auditorium—still they are obviously intended to catch and surprise the eye, and in that they succeed.          RGW

NOTES

1.   Edward Gunts, "Architecture Reflecting Innovation and Technology," *Baltimore Sun*, August 14, 1988: 3N; F. Housely Carr and Michael May, "Flipped pyramid, parallelogram," *Engineering News-Record*, May 14, 1987, 14. Other commentary is in: Vernon Mays, "A Machine in the Forest," *Progressive Architecture* 60 (August 1989):92–97; Benjamin Forgey, "The Topsy-Turvy Tower of Power," *Washington Post*, April 8, 1989, C1,4.

2.   All the competition drawings have been lost, according to Greg Hunt, who oversaw the competition for Virginia Polytechnic, in conversation with author, December 7, 1989.

3.   Early studies are with Arquitectonica.

4.   Philip Johnson and Mark Wigley, *Deconstructivist Architecture* (New York: Museum of Modern Art, 1988).

5.   Arquitectonica commissioned an airbrush rendering from Terry Gilbeault of Miami, which was published in Thomas Fisher, "Presenting Ideas," *Progressive Architecture* 60 (June 1989): 85; this original rendering, however, has been lost.

# 116.
## BRYAN HALL

*Arts and Sciences Building*
*University of Virginia*

Charlottesville

### Study for South Elevation
Preliminary sketch, 1987
Signed and dated: *Graves/*[19]'*87*
Colored pencil on tracing paper; 15 ½ by 32 inches
Collection of Michael Graves Architect, Princeton,
New Jersey

### South Elevation
Preliminary sketch, 1987
Signed and dated: *Michael Graves* [19]*87*
Colored pencil on tracing paper; 15 ½ by 32 inches
Collection of Michael Graves Architect, Princeton,
New Jersey

Photographs by William Taylor.

Michael Graves's design for the Arts and Sciences Building at the University of Virginia represents a much more personalized and idiosyncratic approach to the problem of designing at the university than does the more literal historicism of Robert A. M. Stern (see SURVEY NO. 117). Graves depends on historical references but he is both more eclectic and wide-ranging in his choices, and more abstract in their handling.

Graves was born in Fort Wayne, Indiana; received his bachelor of architecture degree at the University of Cincinnati and his master of architecture degree at Harvard. A period of study at the American Academy in Rome greatly influenced him. His practice is located in Princeton, New Jersey, and he has taught at Princeton University since 1962. His early work, which came to national attention in 1972 through the book *Five Architects*[1] was highly abstract and theoretical, and heavily indebted to the 1920s work of Le Corbusier and Cubist composition. Of the "New York Five" (as the architects in that book came to be known), Graves appeared to be hermetic and academic, appealing only to a small intellectual coterie. However, there was a historical element—albeit Le Corbusier—and as Postmodernism developed in the later 1970s with its embrace of a wider historical vocabulary, Graves's interests broadened. His winning design and the successful completion of the Portland Public Building Competition (1980–1983) placed him at the forefront of the Postmodernist generation. He was also the first to build on a large scale. Subsequent large commissions and a highly successful line of furniture and accessories have made Graves one of the foremost architects in the United States.[2]

His approach as revealed in the University of Virginia design holds respect for the Classical tradition, but never in a specific stylistic sense. The site for the new building is across a gully, with the McIntire Amphitheater (1921 by Fiske Kimball and Warren H. Manning) on the north, visible as the lower colonnade in Graves's north elevation, and between Cocke Hall (1896–1899 by McKim, Mead & White) on the east, and Minor Hall (1911 by John Kevan Peebles). For materials Graves adopted the university's standard red brick, white trim, and copper roof. The bulk of his building also recalls Virginia forms; however, the central pavilion and the fenestration treatment is much more abstract, recalling Art Déco—or modernized—Classicism of the 1920s and 1930s, and Viennese Modernism of the 1900s. These have been a special interest of Graves's.[3] His exterior detailing lacks the complexity of the earlier buildings, though he retains moldings and rustication. On the interior a series of cylindrical and figural spaces mark the entry sequence on the different levels.

Earlier in his career Graves produced myriads of small, almost cartoon-like studies of each design, with many alternatives. As his practice has grown, however, the amount of time available to devote to each project has shortened. Graves knew well the University of Virginia campus, having visited it many times, and his studies for this building consisted of only four sketches, the preliminary carried out in late 1987, and the revisions made about six months later.[4] Groundbreaking took place in 1990, with completion expected in 1994.                    RGW

NOTES
1.   *Five Architects: Eisenman, Graves, Gwathmey, Hejduk, Meier* (New York: Wittenborn & Co., 1972).

2.   K. Wheeler, P. Arnell, and T. Bickford, *Michael Graves, 1966–1981* (New York: Rizzoli, 1982); K. V. Nichols, P. J. Burke, and C. Hancock, eds., *Michael Graves, Buildings and Projects, 1982–1989* (Princeton: Princeton Architectural Press, 1990), 240–241, contains drawings of the University of Virginia building. See also, Richard Guy Wilson, "Michael Graves at Mid-Career," 11 years after *Five Architects*," *Architecture* 72 (July 1983):78–80.

3.   Graves has been an advisor of the New York Art Déco Society for many years and many of his designs refer to Art Déco or Vienna Modern.

4.   In addition to the drawing shown, there are two preliminary south elevation studies by Graves, and then working and publication drawings.

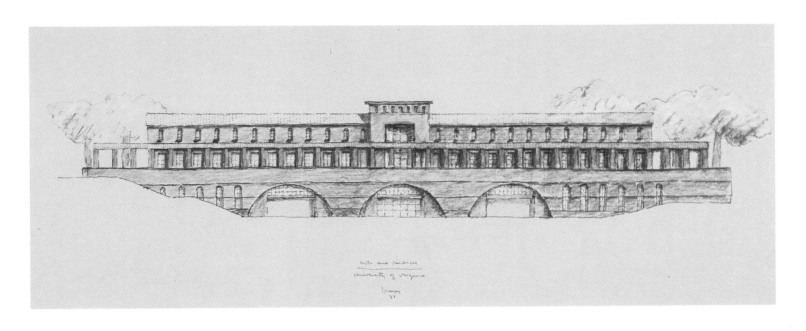

arts and sciences
University of Virginia
Graves
'93

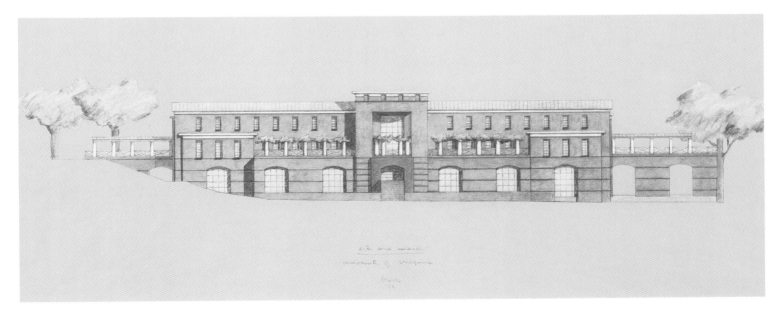

arts and sciences
University of Virginia
Graves
'93

ROBERT A. M. STERN, born 1939

in association with

MARCELLUS WRIGHT COX & SMITH, ARCHITECTS

Richmond

# 117.
## OBSERVATORY HILL DINING HALL ADDITIONS

*University of Virginia*
*South Elevation*

Charlottesville
Presentation drawing
Signed and dated: *Andrew Zega* (born 1961), *1989*
Watercolor on paper; 19 ½ by 34 inches
Collection of Robert A. M. Stern Architects, New York City

FIGURE 1. *Site photo,* **Dining Hall, University of Virginia.**

The effect of one aspect of the Postmodernist reorientation of the 1970s and 1980s towards a more historically contextual architecture is nowhere better shown than in this addition and alteration to an existing Modernist building. The architect, Robert A. M. Stern, has been one of the leaders of Postmodernism, both nationally and internationally; his many activities in addition to designing buildings—teaching, lecturing, writing architectural history and criticism, and organizing exhibits—have helped define Postmodernism. Born in New York, Stern studied architecture at Columbia University and earned a master's degree at Yale. His *New Directions in American Architecture* (1969; 2nd ed. 1977) helped to direct architectural debate and proclaimed a new "inclusive" sensibility in which buildings would fit their surroundings rather than stand apart from them. He worked for various architectural firms before opening his own office in 1965, sharing a partnership with John Hagmann from 1969 to 1977. The writing of architectural history has been intimately connected with his architectural practice. Among his many works are *George Howe: Toward a Modern American Architecture* (New Haven: Yale University Press, 1975) and *New York 1900* (New York: Rizzoli, 1983) and *New York 1930* (New York: Rizzoli, 1987). These writings have mirrored Stern's own evolution as he has moved from a witty transformation of historical details grafted onto Modernist buildings toward a more straight-laced historicism. In a sense, Stern has become an eclectic similar to those of this century's early decades, an architect capable of working in a variety of styles, from Colonial to Shingle, French Provincial, and others.[1] He currently espouses a revived Classicism, claiming to quote Oscar Wilde, "in matters of importance, style is everything."[2] In addition to the University's Dining Hall, Stern's other Virginia work includes the Sprigg Lane Dormitories for the University (1982–84) and several unbuilt projects for Richmond, all done in association with Marcellus Wright, Cox & Smith.

The original Observatory Hill Dining Hall, designed as part of a 1960s and 1970s expansion of the campus, was begun in 1972 by Williams and Tazewell. Located about a mile from the Jefferson Lawn, the new buildings were designed in several versions of abstract Modernism. The Dining Hall is a large, undistinguished structure with shed roofs. In 1982 Robert A. M. Stern was engaged to enlarge and remodel the Dining Hall. The budget was limited, to cover reorganization of the actual dining hall and serving facilities, and did not include alterations in the kitchen or the student lounge areas.

Taking his cue from the particulate and individualized scale of the Jefferson Lawn pavilions, Stern expanded the Dining Hall on the north and south with pavilion-like units that camouflage the old facility. These pavilions correspond to the Dining Hall's existing twenty-by-twenty-foot bays. Stern has acknowledged that Louis Kahn's ideas "about space made by four columns and light from above," were also a source.[3] On the north side four pavilions rest on a conventional brick podium while on the south—as shown in the rendering—the lower grade caused the pavilions to rest on an open loggia. The pavilion units, with their monitor- or cupola-like peaks, serve from the interior as enclosed porches. The interior dining space is ordered by square bay units that contrast to the food-serving area, which is curved. The space is open and luminous. Detailing is a mixture: the columns and entablature are relatively straightforward, inspired by Jefferson's use of the Tuscan order, though the exact source is William R. Ware's, *The American Vignola.*[4] The window mullions and small Chinese Chippendale balconies are crude metal reproductions.

The rendering by Andrew Zega, a Stern draftsman, was done five years after the commission was completed, to record the project. The drawing's precise detailing and the attempt at rendering cast shadows seems to be aimed at reviving the turn-of-the-century presentation drawings by Hughson Hawley and others, an architectural style much admired by Stern. However, the rendering lacks the figures and the freedom or ease of its predecessors; it is stilted and tight. The building itself has more of a casual air than the rendering. The contextualism, or its relationship to its surroundings, depends on the reference point, for the buildings next to the Dining Hall are all Modernist, while the Jefferson Academical Village is a good mile distant. Hence the additions by Stern can be seen as an attempt to revive and to reintroduce to the campus the Jeffersonian tradition itself.                    RGW

NOTES
1.   Peter Arnell and Ted Bickford, eds., *Robert A. M. Stern, 1965–1980* (New York: Rizzoli, 1981); and Luis R. Rueda, ed., *Robert A. M. Stern, Buildings and Projects, 1981–1985* (New York: Rizzoli, 1986).

2.   Quoted in "A Vision of The Prince," *Inform,* 1 (July/August 1990):10.

3.   Quoted in "A Classical Education," *Architectural Record* (November 1985):111–112.

4.   William R. Ware, *American Vignola* (Scranton, Pa.: International Text Book Co., part I, 1902; part II, 1906. Reprint. New York: W. W. Norton Co., 1977).

EDWARD A. CHAPPELL, born 1948

WILLIE GRAHAM, born 1957

VANESSA PATRICK, born 1953

for

COLONIAL WILLIAMSBURG FOUNDATION

DEPARTMENT OF ARCHITECTURAL RESEARCH

Williamsburg, Virginia

# 118.
## RECONSTRUCTED SLAVE QUARTER AT CARTER'S GROVE

*Colonial Williamsburg, Aerial Perspective*

Near Williamsburg (James City County)
Presentation drawing, 1990
Signed on bottom: *Jeffrey L. Bostetter, 11–15–90*
Pencil on rag tracing paper; 26 by 28 inches
Collection of the Colonial Williamsburg Foundation,
Department of Architectural Research, Williamsburg, Virginia

It is ironic, given the tilt of national politics, that the 1980s saw significant growth of pluralism among American history museums. Most prominent, perhaps, was the treatment of ethnic diversity and race relations. Colonial Williamsburg, for example, began to move away from a single-minded portrait of white middle-class history to one that encompassed subjects like insanity, industrial working conditions, and slavery. This new attention to diversity had a distinctly architectural focus, with the re-creation of the 1770 Public Hospital for the insane, portions of the James Anderson blacksmith complex, and the slave quarter at Carter's Grove—a nearby eighteenth-century plantation administered by Colonial Williamsburg.

The quarter at Carter's Grove offers visitors an opportunity to view eighteenth-century life from the perspective of the slaves rather than from that of their masters. The placement of the individual buildings there is based on their locations as revealed by archaeological excavations on the site in the early 1970s. Viewing this arrangement of structures, observers are asked to consider how it reflects the social relationships that once prevailed there—relationships between master and slave, between agricultural laborers and artisans, and between artisans and house servants.

The reconstruction is based on new fieldwork among surviving early Virginia and Maryland buildings, as well as on recent Chesapeake area archaeological excavations and documentary research. Because such buildings reflect a degree of pre-industrial cheapness and impermanence not directly paralleled by most surviving buildings, the Carter's Grove effort is as much an attempt to recapture a lost environment as are the earlier re-creations of seventeenth-century planters' houses and barns at St. Mary's City in Maryland.

This aerial perspective, by Jeffrey L. Bostetter (born 1960), shows the principal group of structures at the Carter's Grove quarter as completed: three houses, gardens, chicken pens, a corn crib—container of a staple food of the slaves—and outdoor spaces for work and social activities. Like the actual re-creation, this drawing is intended to suggest living conditions without romanticizing either the system of Chesapeake slavery or the slaves' struggle to survive it. Research began on the project in 1981, construction started in 1987, and the quarter was completed in 1990.[1]   EAC

NOTE
1.   Other presentation and design drawings by Edward Chappell, Willie Graham, William Macintire, and Vanessa Patrick exist in the Architectural Archive, Foundation Library, Colonial Williamsburg.

FIGURE 1. *Site photo,* **The Slave Quarters, Carter's Grove,** *as reconstructed in 1990. (Photograph courtesy of the Colonial Williamsburg Foundation.)*

# SELECTED BIBLIOGRAPHY

The following references are pertinent to discussion throughout this book. For additional references on a specific architect or building, see the Notes and References in the Survey entries.

Abbott, Carl. "Norfolk in the New Century: The Jamestown Exposition and Urban Boosterism." *Virginia Magazine of History and Biography* 85 (January 1977): 86–96.

Ackerman, James S. *The Villa: Form and Ideology of Country Houses*. The A. W. Mellon Lectures in the Fine Arts, The National Gallery of Art, 1985; Bollingen Series 35, 34. Princeton: Princeton University Press, 1990.

Adam, Robert, and James Adam. *The Works in Architecture of Robert and James Adam, Esquires*. 2 vols. London, 1773–79. New edition, with introduction by Henry Hope Reed. New York: Dover Publications, 1980.

*American Architects Directory*. ed. George S. Koyl. New York: R. R. Bowker Co., 1955, 1962.

American Institute of Architects Archives. "Bergstrom," "Cheney," and "Witmer" files. Washington, D.C.

Anderson, D. Wiley. *Short Reviews, A Few Recent Designs*. Circa 1904. (Photocopy on deposit at Virginia Department of Historic Resources).

——. *Specifications for Fireproofing and Additions to the Virginia State Capitol*. Richmond: no date.

Andrews, Wayne. *Pride of the South*. New York: Atheneum, 1979.

Archer, John. *The Literature of British Domestic Architecture, 1715–1842*. Cambridge, Massachusetts: The MIT Press, 1985.

Architect's Emergency Committee, *Great Georgian Houses of America* 1. New York: The Kalkhoff Press, 1933. Vol. 2. New York: The Scribner Press, 1937. Also reprint. New York: Dover, 1970.

"Architects Form an Association." *The Concrete Age* 15 (October 1911): 26.

*Architectural Drawing in Lexington, 1799/1926*. An exhibition presented by Washington and Lee University in cooperation with Virginia Military Institute and the Lexington and Rockbridge County Bicentennial Commission. Lexington: Washington and Lee University, 1978.

"The Army's Pentagon Building." *Architectural Record* 93 (January 1943): 63.

Arnell, Peter, and Ted Bickford, eds. *Robert A. M. Stern 1965–1980*. New York: Rizzoli, 1981.

*Art of Architecture in Downtown Richmond, 1798–1989*, exh. cat. Richmond: Second Presbyterian Church, 1989.

Axelrod, Alan, ed. *The Colonial Revival in America*. New York: W. W. Norton Co., 1985.

Baker, Paul. *Richard Morris Hunt*. Cambridge: MIT Press, 1980.

——. *Stanny: The Gilded Life of Stanford White*. New York: The Free Press, 1989.

Baldwin, Charles. *Stanford White*. New York: Dodd, Mead, 1931.

Banham, Reyner. *Theory and Design in the First Machine Age*. New York: Praeger, 1967.

Bannister, Turpin C., ed. *The Architect at Mid-Century: Evolution and Achievement*. vol. 1. New York: Reinhold Pub. Co., 1954: 357.

Barney, J. Stewart. "The Ecole des Beaux Arts, Its Influence on Our Architecture" and "Our National Architecture Will Be Established on Truth Not Tradition." *Architectural Record* 22 and 24 (November 1907 and November 1908): 333–42 and 381–86.

Beckerdite, Luke. "William Buckland and William Bernard Sears: The Designer and the Carver." *Journal of Early Southern Decorative Arts* 8 (November 1982): 6–41.

Benjamin, Asher, and Daniel Raynerd. *The American Builder's Companion: or, A New System of Architecture, particularly Adapted to the Present Style of Building in the United States of America*. 1806. Reprint. New York: Da Capo Press, 1972. Also 6th ed., 1827; reprint, intro. by William Morgan, New York: Dover Publications, 1969.

Berkeley, Ellen Perry, and Matilda McQuaid. *Architecture, A Place for Women*. Washington, D.C.: Smithsonian Institute Press, 1989.

Bibb, A. Burnley. "Old Colonial Work of Virginia and Maryland." *American Architect and Building News* 24 (15 June 1889): 279–281. Reprinted in *The Georgian Period*. New York: American Architect and Building News, 1898–1901.

Binney, Marcus. "An English Garden Suburb on the James." *Country Life* 177 (4 April 1985): 912–914.

Boissière, Olivier. *Gehry, SITE, Tigerman, Trois Portraits de l'Artiste en Architecture*. Paris: Editions du Moniteur, 1981.

Bossom, Alfred Charles. *Building to the Skies: the Romance of the Skyscraper*. London and New York: The Studio Ltd., 1934.

Bosworth, F. H., and Roy Childs Jones. *A Study of Architectural Schools*. New York: Charles Scribner's Sons, 1932.

Boyd, John Taylor, Jr. "The Country House and the Developed Landscape: William Lawrence Bottomley Expresses His Point of View about the Relation of the Country House to Its Environment in an Interview." *Arts and Decoration* 31 (November 1929): 100.

Boyd, Sterling M. "The Adam Style in America, 1770–1820." Ph.D. diss., Princeton University, 1966. Published in *Outstanding Dissertations in the Fine Arts*. New York: Garland Publishing, 1985.

Brown, Thelma Robins. "Memorial Chapel: The Culmination of the Development of the Campus of Hampton Institute, Hampton, Virginia, 1867–1887." M. A. thesis, University of Virginia, 1971.

Brown, Glenn. "Old Colonial Work in Virginia and Maryland." *American Architect and Building News* 22 (22 October; 19, 26 November 1887): 198–199, 242–243, 254. Reprinted in *The Georgian Period*. Parts 1–2. New York: American Architect and Building News, 1898–1901.

Brownell, Charles E. "The Italianate Villa and the Search for an American Style, 1840–1860." In Irma B. Jaffe, ed. *The Italian Presence in American Art, 1760–1860*. New York: Fordham University Press, 1989.

———, and Jeffrey A. Cohen. *The Architectural Drawings of Benjamin Henry Latrobe*. 2 vols. The Papers of Benjamin Henry Latrobe, Series 2, Architectural and Engineering Drawings. New Haven: Yale University Press, forthcoming.

Bruce, Philip Alexander. *History of the University of Virginia, 1819–1919: The Lengthened Shadow of One Man*. 5 vols. New York: The Macmillan Company, 1920–22.

Bryant, H. Stafford, Jr. "Two Twentieth-Century Domestic Architects in the South: Neel Reid and William L. Bottomley." *Classic America*. 1, no. 2 (1972): 30–36.

———. "Classical Ensemble." *Arts In Virginia* 11 (Winter 1971): 118–124.

Bush, Donald J. *The Streamlined Decade*. New York: George Braziller, 1975.

Campbell, Colen, et al. *Vitruvius Britannicus, or The British Architect*. 5 vols. 1715–1808. Reprint. New York: Benjamin Blom, 1972.

Campbell, Fay. "Thomas Tileston Waterman: Student of American Colonial Architecture." *Winterthur Portfolio* 20 (Summer-Autumn 1985): 103–147.

Campbell, Edward D. C., Jr., and Kym S. Rice, eds. *Before Freedom Came: African-American Life in the Antebellum South*. Richmond: The Museum of the Confederacy, 1991.

Caldwell, John Edwards. *A Tour through Part of Virginia, in the Summer of 1808 [with] an Account of . . . Monticello. . . .* New York: for the author, 1809.

Carrott, Richard G. *The Egyptian Revival: Its Sources, Monuments, and Meaning, 1808–1858*. Berkeley: University of California Press, 1978.

Carson, Cary, Norman F. Barka, William M. Kelso, Garry Wheeler Stone, and Dell Upton. "Impermanent Architecture in the Southern American Colonies." *Winterthur Portfolio* 17 (Summer/Autumn 1982): 95–119, and vol. 16 (Summer/Autumn 1981): 135–196.

Carter, Peter. "Eero Saarinen 1910–1961." *Architectural Design* 169 (December 1961): 537.

Chambers, S. Allen, Jr. *Lynchburg: An Architectural History*. Charlottesville: University Press of Virginia, 1981.

Chambers, Sir William. *A Treatise on the Decorative Part of Civil Architecture*. London, 1791. Reprint, with introduction by John Harris. New York: Benjamin Blom, 1968).

Chapin, J. R. "The Westover Estate." *Harper's* 42 (1871): 801–810.

Chappell, Edward A. "Architects of Colonial Williamsburg." *Encyclopedia of Southern Culture*. edited by C. R. Wilson and W. Ferris. Chapel Hill: University of North Carolina Press, 1989.

———. "Acculturation in the Shenandoah Valley: Rhenish House of the Massanutten Settlement." *Proceedings of the American Philosophical Society* 134 (1980): 55–89.

———. "Architectural Recording and the Open-Air Museum: A View from the Field."

———. *John A. Barrows and the Rediscovery of Early Virginia Architecture*. Exh. cat. Williamsburg: Colonial Williamsburg Foundation, 1991.

Christian, Frances Archer, and Susanne Williams Massie, eds. *Homes and Gardens in Old Virginia*. Richmond: Garrett and Massie, 1931.

Claflin, Mary Anne, and Richardson, Elizabeth Guy. *Bon Air: A History*. Richmond: Hale Publishing, [1977].

Clérisseau, Charles Louis. *Antiquités de la France*, Paris, 1778.

Coffin, Lewis A., Jr., and Arthur C. Holden. *Brick Architecture of the Colonial Period in Maryland and Virginia*. 1919. Reprint. New York: Dover, 1970.

Corrigan, Michael Patrick. "Puritans in Priestly Garb: The 'Gothic Taste' in Antebellum Virginia Church Architecture." Master of Arts thesis, Virginia Commonwealth University, 1988.

Cote, Richard Charles. "The Architectural Workmen of Thomas Jefferson in Virginia." 2 vols. Ph. D. dissertation, Boston University, 1986.

Cox, James A. D. "Frank Lloyd Wright and His Houses in Virginia." *Arts in Virginia* 13 (1972): 10–17.

Cram, Ralph Adams. *American Churches*. Vol. 1. New York: The American Architect, 1915.

———. *My Life in Architecture*. Boston; Little Brown & Co, 1936.

Curl, James Stevens. *The Egyptian Revival: An Introductory Study of a Recurring Theme in the History of Taste*. London: George Allen & Unwin, 1982.

Curran, Kathleen. "The German Rundbogenstil and Reflections on the American Round-Arched Style." *Journal of the Society of Architectural Historians* 47 (December 1988): 351–73.

Daniel, Ann Miner. "The Early Architecture of Ralph Adams Cram, 1889–1902." Ph.D. diss., University of North Carolina at Chapel Hill, 1978.

Davis, Vernon Perdue, and James Scott Rawlings. *Virginia's Ante-Bellum Churches: An Introduction with Particular Attention to Their Furnishings*. Richmond: Dietz Press, 1978.

Dixon, Roger, and Stefan Muthesius. *Victorian Architecture*. London: Thames and Hudson, 1978.

Dow, Joy Wheeler. *American Renaissance*. New York: William T. Comstock, 1904.

Downing, A. J. *The Architecture of Country Houses; Including . . . Cottages, Farm Houses, and Villas, . . . Interiors, Furniture, and . . . Warming and Ventilating*. 1850; reprint ed., New York: Da Capo Press, 1968.

———. *Cottage Residences: or, A Series of Designs for Rural Cottages and Cottage Villas, and Their . . . Grounds, Adapted to North America. . . .* New York: Wiley & Putnam, 1842. Also new ed., ed. George E. Harney, 1873; reprint as *Victorian Cottage Residences*, with preface by Adolf K. Placzek, New York: Dover Publications, 1981.

Downs, Arthur Channing. *Downing & The American House*. Newtown Square, PA: Downing & Vaux Society, 1988.

———. *Preliminary Report III: Brick & Architectural Terra Cotta (Part I), Brownstone (Downing and Upjohn), The Colonial Revival*. Newtown Square, PA: Downing & Vaux Society, 1990.

Dozier, Richard K. "The Black Architectural Experience in America." *AIA Journal* 65 (July 1976): 162–168.

Drexler, Arthur, ed. *The Architecture of the Ecole Des Beaux-Arts*. New York: Museum of Modern Art, 1977.

———. "The Early Works of Charles F. McKim, Country House Commissions." *Winterthur Portfolio* 14 (Fall 1979): 235–267.

Eggleston, Edward. "Social Conditions in the Colonies," *Century* 28 (October 1884): 848–871.

Fahlman, Betsy L., et al. *A Tricentennial Celebration: Norfolk, 1682–1982*, exh. cat. Norfolk: Chrysler Museum, 1982.

Ferriss, Hugh. *The Metropolis of Tomorrow*. New York: Ives Washburn, 1929.

———. *Power in Buildings*. New York: Columbia University Press, 1953.

——— with Carol Willis. *Drawing Towards Metropolis*. Reprint. Princeton, New Jersey: Princeton Architectural Press, 1986.

*Five Architects: Eisenman, Graves, Gwathmey, Hejduk, Meier*. New York: Wittenborn & Co., 1972.

Ford, Katherine Morrow, and Thomas H. Creighton. *The American House Today*. New York: Reinhold, 1951.

Foster, Gaines M. *Ghosts of the Confederacy: Defeat, The Lost Cause, and the Emergence of the New South, 1865 to 1913*. New York: Oxford University Press, 1987.

Francis, Dennis Steadman. *Architects in Practice, New York City, 1840–1900*. [New York]: Committee for the Preservation of Architectural Records, [1980?].

Frazier, William T. "T. J. Collins: A Local Virginia Architect and His Practice at the Turn of the Century." Master of Architectural History thesis, University of Virginia, 1976.

Fréart, Roland, Sieur de Chambray. *A Parallel of the Antient Architecture with the Modern, In a Collection of Ten Principal Authors who have written upon the Five Orders. . . . [With] an Account of Architects and Architecture, in an . . . Explanation of certain Tearms. . . . With Leon Baptista Alberti's Treatise of Statues*. Comp. and trans. by John Evelyn. 1664; reprint, Farnborough, England: Gregg International Publishers, 1970.

Futagawa, Yukio, ed. *Frank Lloyd Wright Monograph*. Tokyo: A.D.A., 1987.

Garrett, Elisabeth Donaghy. *At Home: The American Family, 1750–1870*. New York: Harry N. Abrams, Inc., 1990.

Germann, Georg. *Gothic Revival in Europe and Britain: Sources, Influences and Ideas*. Translated by Gerald Onn. Cambridge, Massachusetts: MIT Press, 1973.

Gibbs, James. *A Book of Architecture Containing Designs Of Buildings And Ornaments*. London, 1728. Reprint, New York: Benjamin Blom, 1968.

Glassie, Henry. *Pattern in the Material Folk Culture of the Eastern United States*. Philadelphia: 1968.

———. *Folk Housing in Middle Virginia*. Knoxville: University of Tennessee Press, 1975.

Goeldner, Paul. "Elijah E.Myers, Politics, Patronage and Professionalism." 1976.

———. "New Introduction & Commentary." in *Bicknell's Village Builder*. Watkins Glen: American Life Foundation & Study Institute, 1976 [1872].

Grady, Henry. *The New South, Writings and Speeches of Henry Grady*. Savannah: Beehive Press, 1971.

Gravell, Thomas L., and George Miller. *A Catalogue of American Watermarks, 1690–1835*. New York and London: Garland Publishing, Inc., 1979.

Green, Bryan Clark. "The Market House .in Virginia, 1736—ca.1860." Master of Architectural History thesis, University of Virginia, 1991.

Greif, Martin. *The New Industrial Landscape: The Story of the Austin Company*. Clinton, New Jersey: Main Street Press, 1978.

Greiff, Constance M. *Lost America: From the Atlantic to the Mississippi*. Princeton: Pyne Press, 1971.

Gutheim, Frederick. *1857–1957 One Hundred Years of Architecture in America*. New York: Reinhold, 1957.

Hall, Virginius Cornick. "The Virginia Historical Society: An Anniversary Narrative of Its First Century and a Half." *Virginia Magazine of History and Biography* 90 (January 1982): 100–105.

Hamlin, Talbot. *Benjamin Henry Latrobe*. New York: Oxford University Press, 1955.

———. *Greek Revival Architecture in America: Being an Account of Important Trends in . . . Architecture and . . . Life Prior to the War between the States*. 1944. Reprint. New York: Dover Publications, 1964.

Handlin, David P. *American Architecture*. New York: Thames & Hudson, 1985.

Harnsberger, Douglas James. " 'In Delorme's Manner . . . ': A Study of the Applications of Philibert Delorme's Dome Construction Method in Early 19th Century American Architecture." Master of Architectural History thesis, University of Virginia, 1981.

Harris, Eileen, assisted by Nicholas Savage. *British Architectural Books and Writers, 1556–1785*. Cambridge: Cambridge University Press, 1990.

Heck, Marlene Elizabeth. "Palladian Architecture and Social Change in Post-Revolutionary Virginia." Ph.D. dissertation, University of Pennsylvania, 1988.

———. "The Politics of Architecture in the Gilded Age: The Practice of Elijah E. Myers." University of Virginia, M.A. thesis, 1977.

Hewitt, Mark Alan. *The Architect & the American Country House*. New Haven: Yale University Press, 1990.

*Historical Negro Biographies*. New York: Historical Negro Biographies, 1967.

Hitchcock, Henry-Russell. *American Architectural Books: A List of Books, Portfolios, and Pamphlets on Architecture and Related Subjects Published in America before 1895*. New expanded ed., with contributions by divers hands. New York: Da Capo Press, 1976.

——— and William Seale. *Temples of Democracy: The State Capitols of the U. S. A.* New York: Harcourt Brace Jovanovich, 1976.

——— and Philip Johnson. *The International Style: Architecture Since 1922*. New York: W. W. Norton Co., 1932.

Holly, Henry Hudson. *Modern Dwellings in Town and Country*. New York: Harper & Brothers, 1878.

Hood, Davyd Foard. "William Lawrence Bottomley In Virginia: The 'Neo-Georgian' House in Richmond." M. A. thesis, University of Virginia, 1975.

———. "Georgian Revival Architecture." *Encyclopedia of Southern Culture*. ed. C. R. Wilson and W. Ferris. Chapel Hill: University of North Carolina Press, 1989.

Hosmer, Charles B., Jr. *Preservation Comes of Age: From Williamsburg to the National Trust, 1926–1949*. Vol. 1 Charlottesville: University Press of Virginia, 1981.

———. *Presence of the Past*. New York: G.P. Putnam's Sons, 1965.

Hotchkiss, J., ed. "Virginia: New Ways in the Old Dominion," *Scribner's* 5 (December 1872): 137–160.

Howell, Herbert H. "Washington International Airport—a model for the Jet Age." *Civil Engineering* 29 (May 1959): 42–45.

Hudnut, Joseph. "Washington National Airport." *Architectural Forum* 75 (September 1941): 169–176.

Isaac, Rhys. *The Transformation of Virginia, 1740–1790*. Chapel Hill: Published for the Institute of Early American History and Culture by the University of North Carolina Press, 1982.

Jackson, Giles and D. Webster Davis. *The Industrial History of the Negro Race of the United States*. Richmond: privately published, 1908.

Jacobus, John. *Twentieth-Century Architecture: The Middle Years 1940–65*. New York: Frederick A. Praeger, 1966.

*Jamestown Exposition Illustrated*. Norfolk: Jamestown Official Photographic Corp., 1907.

Jefferson, Thomas. *The Papers of Thomas Jefferson*. Edited by Julian P. Boyd, et al. 23 vols. to date. Princeton: Princeton University Press, 1950–.

———. *The Writings of Thomas Jefferson*. Compiled and edited by Paul Leicester Ford. 10 vols. New York: G. P. Putnam's Sons, 1892–99.

———. *The Writings of Thomas Jefferson*. Edited by Andrew A. Lipscomb and Albert Ellery Bergh. 20 vols. Washington, D. C.: issued under the auspices of The Thomas Jefferson Memorial Association, 1903–04.

Johnson, Philip, and Mark Wigley. *Deconstructivist Architecture*. New York: Museum of Modern Art, 1988.

Jolley, Harley E. *Painting with a Comet's Tail*. Boone, N. C.: Appalachian Consortium, 1987.

———. *The Blue Ridge Parkway*. Knoxville: The University of Tennessee Press, 1969.

Jones, Cranston. *Architecture Today and Tomorrow*. New York: McGraw-Hill, 1961.

Kalbian, Maral S. "The Ionic Order and the Progression of the Orders in American Palladianism before 1812." Master of Architectural History thesis, University of Virginia, 1988.

Kaplan, Wendy, ed. *"The Art that is Life": The Arts & Crafts Movement in America*, exh. cat. Boston: Museum of Fine Arts, 1987.

Kent, William, ed. *The Designs of Inigo Jones, Consisting of Plans and Elevations for Publick and Private Buildings . . . With some Additional Designs*. 2 vols. in 1. [London]: 1727. Also reprint, Farnborough, England: Gregg International Publishers, 1966.

Kimball, Fiske. *Thomas Jefferson, Architect: Original Designs in the Collection of Thomas Jefferson Coolidge, Junior*. 1916. Reprint, with introduction by Frederick Doveton Nichols. New York: Da Capo Press, 1968.

———. "Thomas Tileston Waterman." *Journal of the AIA* 15 (May 1951).

King, Edward. "The Great South: A Ramble in Scribner's Virginia." *Scribner's* 7 (April 1874): 645–674.

Kocher, A. Lawrence. "The American Country House." *Architectural Record* 58 (November 1925): 402–43.

Kohler, Sue A. *The Commission of Fine Arts: A Brief History 1910–1984*. Washington, D.C.: Commission of Fine Arts, 1984.

Kornwolf, James D. *"So Good A Design," The Colonial Campus of William and Mary: Its History, Background, and Legacy*, exh. cat. Williamsburg: The College of William and Mary, Joseph and Margaret Muscarelle Museum of Art, 1989.

Koyl, George S., comp. and ed., with Moira B. Mathieson. *American Architectural Drawings: A Catalog of Original and Measured Drawings of Buildings of the United States of America to December 31, 1917*. 5 vols. Philadelphia: Philadelphia Chapter, American Institute of Architects, 1969.

Krinsky, Carol Herselle. *Gordon Bunshaft of Skidmore, Owings & Merrill*. New York and Cambridge: The Architectural History Foundation and MIT Press, 1988.

Lahendro, Joseph Dye. "Fiske Kimball: American Renaissance Historian." Master's thesis, University of Virginia, 1982.

Lamb, Mrs. Martha J. *The Homes of America*. New York: D. Appleton & Co., 1879.

Lancaster, Clay. "Oriental Forms in American Architecture, 1800–1870." *Art Bulletin* 29 (September 1947):183–93.

Lane, Mills. *Architecture of the Old South: Virginia*. With editorial assistance by Calder Loth. Savannah: Beehive Press, 1987.

Lanford, Sarah Drummond. "Ralph Adams Cram as College Architect." Master's thesis, University of Virginia, 1981.

Langhorne, Elizabeth, K. Edward Lay, and William D. Rieley. *A Virginia Family and Its Plantation Houses*. Charlottesville: University Press of Virginia, 1987.

Langley, Batty. *The City and Country Builder's and Workman's Treasury of Designs: Or the Art of Drawing and Working the Ornamental Parts of Architecture. Illustrated by upwards of Four Hundred grand Designs . . . on One Hundred and Eighty-six Copper-Plates, . . .* New ed. 1750; reprint New York: Benjamin Blom, 1967.

Latrobe, B. Henry. *The Correspondence and Miscellaneous Papers of Benjamin Henry Latrobe*. Edited by John C. Van Horne at al. 3 vols. *The Papers of Benjamin Henry Latrobe*, Series 4. New Haven: Yale University Press, 1984–88.

———. *The Virginia Journals of Benjamin Henry Latrobe, 1795–1798*. Edited by Edward C. Carter II, et al. 2 vols. *The Papers of Benjamin Henry Latrobe*, Series 1. New Haven: Yale University Press, 1977.

———. *The Papers of Benjamin Henry Latrobe*. Microfiche edition. Edited by Thomas E. Jeffrey. Clifton, New Jersey: James T. White & Company, 1976.

———. *Latrobe's View of America, 1795—1820*. Edited by Edward C. Carter II, et al. *The Papers of Benjamin Henry Latrobe*, Series 3. New Haven: Yale University Press, 1985.

Lay, K. Edward. "Charlottesville's Architectural Legacy." *The Magazine of Albemarle County History*. 46 (I988): 29–95, 38–39, 94.

Leacroft, Richard. *The Development of the English Playhouse: An Illustrated Survey of Theatre Building in England from Medieval to Modern Times*. New ed. New York: Methuen, 1988.

—— and Helen Leacroft. *Theatre and Playhouse: An Illustrated Survey of Theatre Building from Ancient Greece to the Present Day*. London: Methuen, 1984.

Lee, W. Duncan. "The Renascence of Carter's Grove." *Architecture* 67 (April 1933): 185–95.

Leich, Jean Ferriss. *Architectural Visions: The Drawings of Hugh Ferriss*. New York: Whitney Library of Design, 1980.

Lerner, Max. "Thomas Fortune Ryan." *Dictionary of American Biography*. Vol. 8. New York: Scribner's, 1963.

Little, Lewis Peyton. *History of the First Baptist Church of Newport News Virginia from 1883 to 1933*. Newport News: Franklin Printing Company, 1936.

Longstreth, R., ed. *Studies in the History of Art*. Washington, D.C.: National Gallery of Art, 1991: 143–167.

Lossing, Benson J. *Mount Vernon*. New York: 1859.

Loth, Calder. "Notes on the Evolution of Virginia Brickwork from the Seventeenth Century to the Late Nineteenth Century." *Association for Preservation Technology Bulletin* 6, no. 2 (1974):82–120.

——, ed. *The Virginia Landmarks Register*. 3rd ed. Charlottesville: University Press of Virginia, for the Virginia Historic Landmarks Board, 1986.

—— and Julius Trousdale Sadler. *The Only Proper Style: Gothic Architecture in America*. Boston: New York Graphic Society, 1975.

Lounsbury, Carl R. " 'An Elegant and Commodious Building': William Buckland and the Design of the Prince William County Courthouse." *Journal of the Society of Architectural Historians* 46 (September 1987):228–40.

——. "Beaux-Arts Ideals and Colonial Reality: The Reconstruction of Williamsburg's Capitol." *Journal of the Society of Architectural Historians*. 49 (December 1990): 373–89.

——. "The Structure of Justice: The Courthouses of Colonial Virginia." In *Perspectives in Vernacular Architecture*. Vol. 3. Ed. Thomas Carter and Bernard L. Herman. Columbia, Missouri: University of Missouri Press, 1989.

Lowry, Bates. *Building a National Image: Architectural Drawings for the American Democracy, 1789–1912*, exh. cat. Washington, D.C.: National Building Museum, 1985.

Lyle, Royster, Jr., and Pamela Hemenway Simpson. *The Architecture of Historic Lexington*. Charlottesville: University Press of Virginia, 1977.

Lyne, Cassie Moncure. "Historic Homes in Virginia Owned by the duPonts . . ." *Richmond Magazine* 14 (November 1927): 19–22,46.

Maccubbin, Robert P., and Peter Martin, eds. *British and American Gardens in the Eighteenth Century*. Williamsburg: Colonial Williamsburg Foundation, 1984.

*Macmillan Encyclopedia of Architects*. Ed. Adolph K. Placzek. 4 vols. New York: Free Press, 1982.

Manning, Warren H. "Jamestown Exposition." *Transactions of the American Society of Landscape Architects, 1899–1908*. vol. 1 (1910): 83–88.

Massie, Mrs. William R., and Mrs. Andrew H. Christian, comp. *Descriptive Guide Book of Virginia's Old Gardens*. Richmond: Garden Club of Virginia, 1929.

McCausland, Elizabeth. *The Life and Work of Edward Lamson Henry, N.A., 1841–1919*. Albany: New York State Museum, 1945.

McCue, Elizabeth Bray. *Staunton, Virginia: A Pictorial History*. Staunton: Historic Staunton Foundation, 1985.

McDonald, Travis C., Jr. *The Art of Architecture in Downtown Richmond, 1798–1989*, exh. cat. Richmond: Second Presbyterian Church, 1989.

McGehee, Carden C., Jr. "The Planning, Sculpture, and Architecture of Monument Avenue, Richmond, Virginia." Master's thesis, University of Virginia, 1980.

McKee, Harley J. *Introduction to Early American Masonry: Stone, Brick, Mortar and Plaster*. National Trust/Columbia University Series on the Technology of Early American Building, 1. Washington, D.C., 1973.

McVarish, Douglas, with K. Edward Lay and Boyd Coons. "Architectural Education at the University of Virginia." *Colonnade* 3 (Summer 1988), 4 (Winter 1989), 4 (Summer-Autumn 1989): 27–36.

Meade, Bishop William. *Old Churches, Ministers, and Families of Virginia*. 2 vols. Philadelphia: J. B. Lippincott & Co., 1857.

Meeks, Carroll L.V. *The Railroad Station: An Architectural History*. New Haven: Yale University Press, 1956.

*Men of Mark in Virginia*. Richmond: Men of Mark Pub. Co., 1936.

Mencken, H. L. "The Sahara of the Bozart." in *Prejudices: Second Series*. New York: Alfred A. Knopf, 1920.

Michels, Eileen. "Late Nineteenth-Century Published American Perspective Drawings." *Journal of the Society of Architectural Historians* 31 (December 1972): 302.

Mitchell, Mary H. *Hollywood Cemetery: The History of a Southern Shrine*. Richmond: Virginia State Library, 1985.

*Modern American Homes*. Knoxville: Gaut-Ogden Co., 1903–1907.

*Modern Dwellings*. Knoxville: S. F. Newman and Co., 1898–1907.

*A Monograph of the Works of McKim, Mead & White 1879–1915*. New York: Architectural Book Pub. Co, 1915–20. Reprinted as *The Architecture of McKim, Mead & White*. R. G. Wilson, ed. New York: Dover, 1990.

Mordecai, Samuel. *Virginia, Especially Richmond, in By-Gone Days; with a Glance at the Present: Being Reminiscences and Last Words of an Old Citizen*. 2nd ed. Richmond: West and Johnston, 1860.

Morrill, Penny. *Who Built Alexandria?: Architects in Alexandria, 1750–1900*, exh. cat. Alexandria: Carlyle House Historic Park, 1979.

Morris, Robert. *Select Architecture, Being Regular Designs of Plans and Elevations Well Suited to both Town and Country*, 2nd ed. 1757; reprint, with foreword by Adolf K. Placzek, New York: Da Capo Press, 1973.

Myer, Donald Beekman. *Bridges and the City of Washington*. Washington, D.C.: U. S. Commission of Fine Arts, 1974.

*The Negro Almanac*. New York: John Wiley & Sons, 1983.

Nichols, Frederick Doveton. *Thomas Jefferson's Architectural Drawings . . . with Commentary and a Check List*. 5th ed. Boston: Massachusetts Historical Society, 1984.

Nichols, K. V.; P. J. Burke; and C. Hancock, eds. *Michael Graves: Buildings and Projects, 1982–1989*. Princeton: Princeton Architectural Press, 1990.

Nicholson, Peter. *The New Practical Builder, and Workman's Companion: Containing . . . the Most Recent . . . Methods . . . in . . . Carpentry, Joinery, . . . &c . . . Also, . . . Geometry, . . . Perspective, [etc.]; . . . an Extensive Glossary . . . and the Theory and Practice of the Five Orders, . . .* London: Printed for Thomas Kelly, 1823 [–25?].

"Observations in Several Voyages and Travels in America in the Year 1736." *The London Magazine*. July 1746.

*The Official Blue Book of the Jamestown TerCentennial Exposition*. Norfolk: Colonial Pub. Co, 1907.

"The Old State-House at Richmond, Virginia." *Architectural Record* 88 (December 1940): 16–18.

O'Neal, William Bainter. *Architectural Drawing in Virginia, 1819–1969*, exh. cat. Charlottesville: University of Virginia, School of Architecture, and Richmond: Virginia Museum of Fine Arts, 1969.

——. *Architecture in Virginia: An Official Guide to Four Centuries of Building in the Old Dominion*. New York: Walker & Company, for the Virginia Museum, 1968.

——. *Jefferson's Fine Arts Library: His Selections for the University of Virginia, together with His Own Architectural Books*. Charlottesville: University Press of Virginia, 1976.

—— and Christopher Weeks. *The Work of William Lawrence Bottomley in Richmond*. Charlottesville: University Press of Virginia, 1985.

Packer, Nancy Elizabeth. *White Gloves & Red Bricks: APVA 1889–1989*, exh. cat. Richmond: Association for the Preservation of Virginia Antiquities, 1989.

Page, Thomas Nelson. "Old Yorktown," *Century* 22 (October 1881): 801–186.

——. *The Old South*. New York: Scribner's, 1893.

——. *In Ole Virginia*. New York: Scribner's, 1897.

——. *The Old Dominion*. New York: Scribner's, 1908.

Palladio, Andrea. *The Architecture of A. Palladio; in Four Books*. Trans. Nicholas Dubois; ed. Giacomo Leoni. 2nd ed. 2 vols. London, 1721.

——. *I Quattro Libri dell'Architettura di Andrea Palladio*. 1570. Reprint with Ottavio Cabiati, "Nota al Palladio," 1945. Milan: Ulrico Hoepli, 1968.

——. *The Four Books of Andrea Palladio's Architecture*. Trans. Isaac Ware and Richard Boyle, Third Earl of Burlington. 1738; reprint, with introduction by Adolf K. Placzek, New York: Dover Publications, 1965.

*Palliser's Model Homes*, Bridgeport, Conn.: Palliser & Palliser, 1878. 2nd ed., rev., 1878.

*Palliser's New Cottage Homes and Details*. orig. 1887; reprint, New York: Da Capo, 1975.

Paulson, Darryl. "Masters of it all, Black Builders in this Century." *Southern Exposure* 8 (Spring 1980): 3–13.

Peebles, John Kevan. "Thos. Jefferson, Architect." *Alumni Bulletin [University of Virginia]* 1 (November 1894): 68–74.

Perry, William G. "Notes on the Architecture" and "Restoration of Colonial Williamsburg." *Architectural Record* 78 (December 1935): 373.

Peterson, Charles E. "Thomas T. Waterman (1900–1951)." *Journal of the Society of Architectural Historians*. 10.2 (1951): 25.

Pevsner, Nikolaus. *A History of Building Types*. The A. W. Mellon Lectures in the Fine Arts, The National Gallery of Art, 1970; Bollingen Series 35, 19. Princeton: Princeton University Press, 1976.

Poesch, Jessie. "Architecture." *Encyclopedia of Southern Culture.* C. R. Wilson and W. Ferris, eds. Chapel Hill: University of North Carolina Press, 1989.

Pope, Loren. "The Love Affair of a Man and his House." *House Beautiful* 90 (August 1948): 34.

———. "Five Decades Later." *Frank Lloyd Wright Remembered,* ed. P. Meehan. Washington, D.C.: Preservation Press, 1991.

Preddy, Jane. *Palaces of Dreams: The Movie Theatres of John Eberson,* exh. cat. San Antonio: McNay Art Museum, 1990.

———. *Glamour, Glitz and Sparkle: The Deco Theatres of John Eberson.* Chicago: Theatre Historical Society of America, 1989.

Quenroe, Elroy E. "John Eberson in Richmond, Virginia—Architect for the Twenties." M. A. thesis, University of Virginia, 1975.

———. "Movie House Architecture, Twenties Style." *Arts in Virginia* 26 (Fall 1976): 22–31.

Rasmussen, William M. S. "Designers, Builders, and Architectural Traditions in Colonial Virginia." *Virginia Magazine of History and Biography* 90 (April 1982):198–212.

———. "For Profit and Pleasure: The Art of Gardening in Colonial Virginia—Landon Carter's Sabine Hall" *Arts in Virginia* 21 (Fall 1980): 18–27.

———."Palladio in Tidewater Virginia: Mount Airy and Blandfield." *Building by the Book.* Charlottesville: University Press of Virginia, 1984.

———. "Sabine Hall, A Classical Villa in Virginia." *Journal of the Society of Architectural Historians* 39 (December 1980): 286–96.

Reed, Helen Scott Townsend. "Agecroft Hall, Richmond Virginia." *The Magazine Antiques* 123 (February 1983): 392–98.

Reid, Robert A., ed. *The Jamestown Exposition Beautifully Illustrated.* New York; Jamestown Official Photograph Corp., 1907.

Reiff, Daniel D. *Small Georgian Houses in England and Virginia: Origins and Development through the 1750s.* Newark, Delaware: University of Delaware Press, 1986.

Reps, John W. *Views and Viewmakers of Urban America.* Columbia: University of Missouri Press, 1984.

———. *Tidewater Towns, City Planning in Colonial Virginia and Maryland.* Williamsburg: Colonial Willliamsburg Foundation, 1972.

"Restoration of Colonial Williamsburg." *Architectural Record* 78 (December 1935).

Rhoads, William B. *The Colonial Revival.* New York: Garland Pub. Co, 1977, 2 vols.

Roth, Leland. *A Concise History of American Architecture.* New York: Harper & Row, 1979.

———. *McKim, Mead & White, Architects.* New York: Harper & Row, 1983.

Royall, Anne. *Sketches of History, Life, and Manners, in the United States.* 1826. Reprint. New York: Johnson Reprint Corporation, 1970.

Rueda, Luis R., ed. *Robert A. M. Stern, Buildings and Projects, 1981–1985.* New York: Rizzoli, 1986.

Saarinen, Eero. "Dulles International Airport." *Architectural Record* 134 (July 1963): 109.

Saylor, Henry H. "James River Colonial-Historic American style." *House & Garden* 67 (January 1935): 46–47, 58,60.

Schimmelman, Janice G. "Architectural Treatises and Building Handbooks Available in American Libraries and Bookstores through 1800." *Proceedings of the American Antiquarian Society,* vol. 95, pt. 2 (October 1985):317–500.

Schuyler, Montgomery. "The works of Cram, Goodhue,& Ferguson." *Architectural Record* 29 (January 1911): 1–87.

———. "The Works of the Late Richard M. Hunt." *American Architecture and Other Writings.* Vol. 2. W. Jordy and R. Coe, eds. Cambridge: Harvard University Press, 1961.

———. "The Work of Messrs. Barney and Chapman." *Architectural Record* 14 (September, 1904): 203–96.

Scott, Mary Wingfield. *Houses of Old Richmond.* 1941. Reprint. New York: Bonanza Books, n.d.

———. *Old Richmond Neighborhoods.* 1950. Reprint. Richmond: Valentine Museum, 1984.

Scully, Vincent, Jr. *The Shingle Style.* New Haven, Yale University Press, 1955.

Severens, Kenneth. *Southern Architecture.* New York: E. P. Dutton, 1981.

Sexton, Randolph Williams. *American Commercial Buildings of Today.* New York: Architectural Book Pub. Co., 1928.

Sharp, Dennis, with Peter Wylde and Martha B. Caldwell. *Alfred C. Bossom's American Architecture, 1903–1926.* London: Book Art, 1984.

Sheldon, George William. *Artistic Country-Seats* vol. 2. New York: D. Appleton & Co., 1886–87.

Shoppell, R. W., et al., *Turn-of-the-Century Houses, Cottages and Villas.* New York: Dover, 1983.

*Shoppell's Modern Houses.* Rockville Centre, N.Y.: Antiquity Reprints, 1983.

*SITE, Architecture as Art.* New York: St. Martin's Press, 1980.

*SITE Buildings and Spaces,* exh. cat. Richmond: Virginia Museum, 1980.

Smith, Darrell Hevenor. *The Office of the Supervising Architect of the Treasury: Its History, Activities, and Organization.* Baltimore: Johns Hopkins Press, 1923.

Smith, Norris Kelley. *Frank Lloyd Wright: A Study in Architectural Content.* Englewood Cliffs, N.J: Prentice-Hall, 1966.

Sobel, Mechal. *The World They Made Together: Black and White Values in Eighteenth-Century Virginia.* Princeton: Princeton University Press, 1987.

Sorkin, Michael. *Hardy Holzman Pfeiffer.* New York: Watson-Guptill, 1981.

*Southern Architecture Illustrated.* Atlanta: Harman Publishing Company, 1931.

Sprague, Stuart S. "Investing in Appalachia: The Virginia Valley Boom of 1889–1893." *Virginia Cavalcade* 241 (Winter 1975): 134–143.

Stanton, Phoebe B. *The Gothic Revival and American Church Architecture: An Episode in Taste, 1840–1856.* The Johns Hopkins Studies in Nineteenth-Century Architecture. Baltimore, 1968.

Stapleford, Richard, and Jane Preddy. *Temples of Illusion: The Atmospheric Theaters of John Eberson,* exh. cat. New York: Hunter College, Bertha and Karl Leubsdorf Art Gallery, 1988.

"The State Capitol of Virginia." *American Architect and Building News* 22 (12 November 1887): 235.

Stein, Susan, ed. *The Architecture of Richard Morris Hunt.* Chicago: The University of Chicago Press, 1986.

Stephenson, Mary A. *Carter's Grove Plantation: A History.* City unknown: Sealantic Fund, 1964.

Stiverson, Cynthia Zignego. *Architecture and the Decorative Arts: The A. Lawrence Kocher Collection of Books at the Colonial Williamsburg Foundation.* With an introduction by Lawrence Wodehouse and a foreword by Albert Frey. West Cornwall, CT: Locust Hill Press, 1989.

Stockton, Frank B. "The Later Years of Monticello," *Century.* vol. 34 (September 1887): 642–653, 654–658.

Stuart, James, with Nicholas Revett, et al. *The Antiquities of Athens.* 3 vols. 1763–95. Reprint. New York: Arno Press, 1980.

Swan, Abraham. *The British Architect: or, The Builder's Treasury of Stair-Cases.* New ed. 1758; reprint Da Capo Press, Series in Architecture and Decorative Art, vol. 3, New York, 1967.

Tatman, Sandra L., and Roger W. Moss. *Biographical Dictionary of Philadelphia Architects: 1700–1930.* Boston: G.K. Hall & Co., 1985.

Tatum, George B., and Elisabeth Blair MacDougall, eds. *Prophet with Honor: The Career of Andrew Jackson Downing, 1815–1852.* Dumbarton Oaks Colloquium on the History of Landscape Architecture XI. Washington, D.C., 1989.

Taylor, Thomas H., Jr. "The Williamsburg Restoration and its Reception by the American Public: 1926–1942." Ph.D. diss., George Washington University, 1989.

Taylor, Robert T. "The Jamestown TerCentennial Exposition of 1907" vol. 65 (1957): 169–208.

Templeman, Eleanor Lee, and Nan Netherton. *Northern Virginia Heritage.* privately published, 1966.

Thayer, R. H., compiler. *History, Organization, and Functions of the Office of the Supervising Architect of the Treasury Department.* Washington, D.C.: Government Printing Office, 1886.

Tidworth, Simon. *Theatres: An Architectural and Cultural History.* New York: Praeger Publishers, 1973.

Torre, Susana. *Women in American Architecture: a Historic and Contemporary Perspective.* New York: Whitney Library of Design, 1977.

Townsend, Gavin. "The Tudor House in America: 1890–1930." Ph.D. diss., University of California at Santa Barbara, 1986.

Tucci, Douglas Shand. *Ralph Adams Cram, American Medievalist.* Boston: Boston Public Library, 1975.

Tunnell, Spencer, II. "Stylistic Progression Versus Site Planning Methodology: An Analysis of the Residential Architecture of Philip Trammell Shutze." Master's thesis, University of Virginia, 1989.

Turner, Paul Venable. "Frank Lloyd Wright's Other Larkin Building." *Journal of the Society of Architectural Historians* 39(1980): 304–306.

———. *Campus: An American Planning Tradition.* The Architectural History Foundation/MIT Press Series, 7. New York, 1984.

Twombly, Robert C. *Frank Lloyd Wright.* New York: Harper & Row, 1973.

Tyler, Lyon G. *Men of Mark in Virginia.* Vol. 1. Washington, D.C.: Men of Mark Publishing Co., 1906.

U. S. Congress. Senate. *Report of the Arlington Memorial Bridge Commission.* 68th Congress, 1st sess., 1924. Doc. 95. Washington, D.C.: Government Printing Office.

Updike, Betsy. "Henry Eugene Baskerville & William Churchill Noland: Richmond's Response to the American Renaissance." M. A. Thesis, University of Virginia, 1987.

Upton, Dell. *Holy Things and Profane: Anglican Parish Churches in Colonial Virginia*. Architectural History Foundation Books, 10. New York, 1986.

———. "Pattern Books and Professionalism: Aspects of the Transformation of Domestic Architecture in America, 1800—1860." *Winterthur Portfolio* 19 (Summer/Autumn 1984):107–50.

———. "Traditional Timber Framing." *Material Culture of the Wooden Age*. Ed. Brooke Hindle. Tarrytown, New York: Sleepy Hollow Press, 1981.

———. "Vernacular Domestic Architecture in Eighteenth-Century Virginia." *Winterthur Portfolio* 17 (Summer-Autumn 1982):95–119. Reprinted in *Common Places: Readings in American Vernacular Architecture*. Edited by Dell Upton and John Michael Vlach. Athens: University of Georgia Press, 1986.

———. "New Views of the Virginia Landscape." *Virginia Magazine of History and Biography* 96 (October 1988):403–470.

Valmarana, Mario di, ed. *Building by the Book*. 3 vols. to date. Charlottesville: University Press of Virginia for the Center for Palladian Studies in America, 1984–.

Van Brunt, Henry. *Architect and Society, Selected Essays of Henry Van Brunt*. W. Coles, ed. Cambridge: Harvard University Press, 1969.

Venturi, Robert. *Complexity and Contradiction in Architecture*. New York: The Museum of Modern Art, 1966.

———, Denise Scott Brown, Steven Izenour. *Learning from Las Vegas*. Boston: M.I.T. Press, 1972.

——— and Denise Scott Brown. *A View from the Campidoglio*. New York: Harper & Row, 1984.

"The Virginia Chapter, AIA, A History." *Virginia Architect's Handbook*. Richmond: Virginia AIA, 1968.

Vitruvius. *The Ten Books on Architecture*. Trans. Morris Hicky Morgan. 1914; reprint New York: Dover Publications, 1960.

von Eckardt, Wolf, ed. *Mid-Century Architecture in America: Honor Award of the American Insitute of Architects*. Baltimore: Johns Hopkins Press, 1961.

von Moos, Stanislaus. *Venturi, Rauch and Scott Brown. Buildings and Projects*. New York: Rizzoli, 1987.

Ware, Isaac. *A Complete Body of Architecture. Adorned with Plans and Elevations, from Original Designs. In which are interspersed Some Designs of Inigo Jones, never before published*. 2nd ed. 2 vols. [1767–]1768; reprint Farnborough, England: Gregg International Publishers, 1971.

Ware, William R. *American Vignola*. Scranton, Pa.: International Text Book Co., part I, 1902; part II, 1906. Reprint. New York: W. W. Norton Co., 1977.

Ware, William Rotch, and Charles S. Keefe, eds. *The Georgian Period: Being Photographs and Measured Drawings of Colonial Work with Text*. Rev. ed. 3 vols. New York: U.P.C. Book Company, 1923.

Waterman, Thomas Tileston. *The Mansions of Virginia, 1706–1776*. 1946. Reprint. New York: Bonanza Books, 1965.

——— and John A. Barrows. *Domestic Colonial Architecture of Tidewater Virginia*. 1932. Reprint. New York: Dover Publications, 1969.

Wenger, Mark R. "Reconstruction of the Governor's Palace in Williamsburg, Virginia." Colonial Williamsburg Foundation Library Research Report Series. Williamsburg: Colonial Williamsburg Foundation Library, March 1980.

———. "The Colonial Revival in Virginia." Paper delivered at the Williamsburg Antiques Forum, sponsored by Colonial Williamsburg Foundation, 3 February 1987.

———. "Westover: William Byrd's Mansion Reconsidered." Master's thesis, University of Virginia, 1981.

———. "The Central Passage in Virginia: Evolution of an Eighteenth-Century Living Space." in C. Wells, ed. *Perspectives in Vernacular Architecture* 2. Columbia: University of Missouri Press,1986: 24–36 ,137–149.

———. "The Dining Room in Early Virginia." *Perspectives in Vernacular Architecture*. Vol. 3. Edited by Thomas Carter and Bernard L. Herman. Columbia, Missouri: University of Missouri Press, 1989.

Wheeler, K., P. Arnell, and T. Bickford. *Michael Graves 1966–1981*. New York: Rizzoli, 1982.

Whiffen, Marcus. "The Early County Courthouses of Virginia." *Journal of the Society of Architectural Historians* 18 (March 1959): 2–10.

———. *The Eighteenth-Century Houses of Williamsburg, A Study of Architecture and Building in the Colonial Capital of Virginia*. Williamsburg: Colonial Williamsburg Foundation, 1960. Williamsburg Architectural Studies. Revised. Williamsburg: Colonial Williamsburg Foundation, 1984.

———. *The Public Buildings of Williamsburg, Colonial Capital of Virginia: An Architectural History*. Williamsburg Architectural Studies, Vol. 1. Williamsburg: Colonial Williamsburg Foundation, 1958.

——— and Frederick Koeper. *American Architecture, 1607–1976*. Cambridge: MIT, 1981.

White, Theophilus Bailou. *Paul Philippe Cret: Architect and Teacher*. Philadelphia: Art Alliance, 1973.

*The White Pine Series of Architectural Monographs*. 26 vols. in 21. New York, 1915–40.

Whitwell, W. L., and Lee W. Winborne. *The Architectural Heritage of the Roanoke Valley*. Charlottesville: University Press of Virginia,1982.

Wilson, Richard Guy, ed. *Victorian Resorts and Hotels*. Philadelphia: The Victorian Society, 1982.

———. "American Architecture and the Search for a National Style in the 1870s." *Nineteenth Century* 3 (Autumn 1977): 74–80.

———. "Architecture and The Reinterpretation of the Past in the American Renaissance." *Winterthur Portfolio* 18 (Spring 1983): 69–87.

———. "Monument Avenue, Richmond." *Great American Avenues*. Washington, D.C.: AIA Press, forthcoming.

———. "Ralph Adams Cram: Dreamer of the Medieval" *Medievalism in American Culture*. ed. B. Rosenthal and P. Szarmach. Binghamton: SUNY, Medieval and Renaissance Texts & Studies, 1989.

———. "Showbiz-Glamour: Architecture in the Eighties." *Inform* 1 (January–February 1990).

———. "Michael Graves at Mid-Career, 11 years after *Five Architects*." *Architecture* 72 (July 1983): 78–80.

———. *McKim, Mead & White, Architects*. New York: Rizzoli, 1983.

——— and Hugh Ferriss. *Encyclopedia of Southern Culture*.

———, Dianne H. Pilgrim, and Dickran Tashjian. *The Machine Age in America, 1918–1941*. New York: Abrams, 1986.

———, Dianne Pilgrim, and Richard Murray. *The American Renaissance, 1876–1917*. Brooklyn and New York: The Brooklyn Museum and Pantheon, 1979.

Winthrop, Robert P. *Architecture in Downtown Richmond*. Edited by Virginius Dabney. Richmond: Junior Board of Historic Richmond Foundation, 1982.

Wittkofski, J. Mark. *Theses and Dissertations Relevant to Virginia Archaeology, Architecture, and Material Culture*. Bibliography Series, No. 3 (Revised). Richmond: Virginia Department of Historic Resources, 1991.

Wittkower, Rudolf. *Palladio and Palladianism*. New York: George Braziller, 1974.

Withey, Henry F., and Elsie Rathburn Withey. *Biographical Dictionary of American Architects (Deceased)*. Los Angeles: Hennessey & Ingalls, Inc., 1970.

Wood, John Walter. *Airports: Some Elements of Design and Future Development*. New York: Coward-McCann, 1940.

Wood, Peter H. "Whetting, Setting and Laying Timbers, Black Builders in the Early South." *Southern Exposure* 8 (Spring 1980):3–13.

Woods, Mary. "The First American Architectural Journals: The Profession's Voice." *Journal of the Society of Architectural Historians* 48 (June 1989):117–38.

Woodward, C. Vann. *Origins of the New South*. Baton Rouge: Louisiana State University, 1951.

"The Works of Carrère & Hastings." *Architectural Record* 27, (January 1910): 1–120.

Wright, Frank Lloyd. *An Autobiography*. New York: Horizon Press, 1977.

———. *The Living House*. New York: Horizon Press, 1954.

Wyatt, Edward A., IV, and James G. Scott. *Petersburg's Story: A History*. Petersburg: privately printed, 1960.

Yetter, George Humphrey. *Williamsburg Before and After: The Rebirth of Virginia's Capital*. Williamsburg: Colonial Williamsburg Foundation, 1988.

———. "Stanford White at the University of Virginia: The New Buildings on the South Lawn and the Reconstruction of the Rotunda in 1896." M. A. thesis, University of Virginia, 1980.

———. "Stanford White at the University of Virginia: Some New Light on an Old Question." *Journal of the Society of Architectural Historians* 40 (December 1981): 320–25.

# GLOSSARY

**Aedicule**    An adaptation of the Orders to frame an element such as a door, a window, or a hearth (see  F I G U R E   4.8 A / B , and  4.9 A / B , Abraham Swan's *chimneypieces* and those at *Mount Vernon*, copied from Swan). From a Latin word that means "little edifice"; an aedicule does look like a miniature building (see  F I G U R E   2.5 A , Inigo Jones, *Designs for Rustick Doors*).

**Architrave**    The lowest of the three major horizontal units that make up the main horizontal element (entablature) of a Classical Order (see  F I G U R E   2.5 , Palladio's *Five Orders of Architecture*). The word "architrave" comes from a French word that means "main beam," and an architrave can symbolize a building's principal set of beams, resting directly on the columns.

**Axonometric**    A modern form of drawing that combines a plan and elevations (and, sometimes, a section) to create an effect like perspective (see  S U R V E Y   N O .   112 , *Robins School of Business Auditorium*). A true perspective drawing shows certain parallel lines as converging ( S U R V E Y   N O .  70 , *First National Bank*, Lynchburg, and  S U R V E Y   N O .  100 , *Hollin Hills House Type* 7C), but in an axonometric these lines remain parallel and their regularity allows measurement of many of the elements in the drawing. Because the plan of an axonometric is laid out on right angles it is easier to draw than an an isometric, but what it adds in ease of drawing it lacks in distortion.

**Base**    A set of decorative moldings used at the bottom of a column or pilaster in most Classical Orders.

**Bow**    A curved or angled projection containing windows (see  S U R V E Y   N O S .  12 and 20 , *Monticello, Second House* and *Clifton*).

**Capital**    A shaped, often carved, element used at the top of a column or pilaster in the Classical Orders ( F I G U R E   2.5 , Palladio, *Five Orders of Architecture*). The word "capital" comes from the Latin word for "head," and a capital has much the same relation to a column shaft as a human head has to its body.

**Cornice**    The topmost of the three major horizontal units that run along the main horizontal element (entablature) of a Classical Order ( F I G U R E   2.5 , Palladio, *Five Orders of Architecture*). Also, the set of moldings at the top of a pedestal or a wall.

**Distyle in Antis**    A category for Classical temples ( F I G U R E   2.21 , *St. Paul's Covent Garden*). "Distyle in antis" means "with two columns between antas, or square pillars," and a distyle-in-antis temple has a portico of this pattern. The term comes from antiquity.

**Distyle in Muris**    A category of eighteenth-, nineteenth-, and twentieth-century buildings meant to look like Classical temples but lacking a full row of free-standing pillars across the front ( F I G - U R E   2.43 , Nicholson, *Design for a Chapel*, and F I G U R E   2.44 , T. U. Walter, *Old First Baptist Church*, Richmond). "Distyle in muris" means "with two columns between the walls," and a distyle-in-muris building has a pair of columns between two projecting sections of wall. The term appears in print for the first time in this book.

**Double-Pile**    A building (pile) that is two rooms deep. (See F I G U R E   1.32 , *Westover*).

**Earthfast**    A form of construction using wooden posts set directly into holes the earth. These posts form the vertical structural components of a building (see F I G U R E   1.2 , *Clifts Plantation*; see also post-hole.)

**Elevation**    A kind of geometrical drawing, or orthogonal projection. An elevation is a "vertical map" or diagram of an exterior wall, without perspective distortion (see F I G U R E   4.19 , Latrobe, *Richmond Theatre*).

**Entablature**    In a Classical Order, the horizontal beam that runs from column to column or pilaster to pilaster. An entablature usually has three parts: architrave, frieze, and cornice (see F I G - U R E   2.5 , Palladio, *Five Orders of Architecture*).

**Exedra**    A row of raised seats set against a wall and usually arranged in a curve. The word "exedra," from the Greek for "outside seating," is also applied loosely to a variety of similar elements.

**Frieze**    The middle of three major horizontal units that run along the main horizontal element (entablature) of a Classical Order (see F I G U R E   2.5 , Palladio, *Five Orders of Architecture*). Also, a decorative band, used independently of the Orders. A frieze often carries rich ornamentation (see F I G U R E   2.10 , *Ionic of Portunus*).

**Hyphen**    The one-story wing that connects taller units in buildings that have a five-part or seven-part layout (see illustrations, S U R V E Y   N O .   2 , *Skipwith House*).

**Isometric**    A modern form of drawing that combines a plan and elevations (and sometimes a section) to create an effect like perspective. A true perspective drawing shows certain parallel lines as converging ( S U R V E Y   N O .   70 , *First National Bank*, Lynchburg, and S U R V E Y   N O . 100 , *Hollin Hills House Type 7C*), but these lines remain parallel in an isometric (see S U R V E Y N O .   118 , reconstructed *Slave Quarters, Carter's Grove*), and this regularity permits an architect to measure many of the elements in the drawing with ease. An isometric is more difficult to draw than an axonometric because its plan is laid out on acute angles, but it looks less distorted.

**Metope**    The space between two triglyphs on a Doric frieze, from the Greek words for "between the openings (or eyes)." A metope can either have decoration ( F I G U R E   2.19 , Fréart's *Doric of the Baths of Diocletian*) or be plain ( F I G U R E   2.28 , *Doric Portico at Athens*).

**Mullion**    A vertical element, usually non-structural, between sets of windows or doors. (See F I G U R E   1.19 , *Nelson-Galt House*; compare with **muntin**.)

**Muntin**    The strip that separates one pane of glass from another in a window or door.

**Order**    The name for a combination of post and beam that is usually the principal decorative element in Classical architecture and sometimes the principal structure alone (see F I G U R E   2.5 , Palladio, *Five Orders of Architecture*). An Order normally consists of a column or pilaster and its entablature. It may also have pedestals below and pediments above. Many varieties of treatment exist, but five Orders are most commonly recognized.

**Pargetry**    Ornamental relief-work in plaster or stucco. See F I G U R E   1.8 , *pargetry fragment* from Sherwood House, Jamestown.

**Pedestal**    An extra support, sometimes placed under a column or pilaster ( F I G U R E   2.5 , Palladio's *Five Orders of Architecture*). Like an entablature and, more particularly, a column, a pedestal customarily has three parts: a molded base, a body called a dado or die, and a molded cornice.

**Pediment**    The name for a gable in Classical architecture. A pediment may have a triangular shape ( F I G U R E   2.15 , *Maison Carrée*) or a curved shape, or it may take an even more complicated form (see F I G U R E   4.9 A , Plate from Abraham Swan's *British Architect*).

**Perforated,**    as in "perforated dome." Punched through with holes (see Leoni, *Villa Rotonda*, F I G U R E   2.11 ) .

**Perspective**    In architecture, the term used to describe a drawing that illustrates a structure as though it were three-dimensional (see S U R V E Y   N O .   70 , *First National Bank, Lynchburg*, and S U R V E Y   N O .   100 , *Hollin Hills House Type 7C*).

**Piano Nobile**    In many buildings from the Renaissance onward, the principal floor level, raised one story above the ground ( F I G U R E   2.50 , *Palazzo Thiene*). From the Italian, *piano*, "plane" or "level," and *nobile*, "noble." The expression originally referred to the placement of the more dignified rooms above a dirty, dangerous, ignoble street.

**Pilaster**    An element of an Order in the form of a vertical strip that projects only slightly from a wall (see F I G U R E   2.50 , *Palazzo Thiene*).

**Plan**    A kind of geometrical drawing, or orthogonal projection. A plan ( F I G U R E   4.18 , Latrobe, *Richmond Theatre*) is essentially a map of one floor of a building.

**Post-Hole**    Earthfast construction using wooden posts actually set into holes in the earth, in the manner of fence-post construction (see F I G U R E   1.2 , *Clifts Plantation*).

**Pricking**    Tiny holes poked into a drawing, as a nearly invisible means of laying out the principal elements of the drawing, or of duplicating a drawing from one sheet of paper to another (see F I G U R E   4.21 , *Menokin* detail). Tracing and blue-printing largely eliminated the laborious practice of pricking in the late nineteenth century.

**Projection**    The method of casting the image of a three-dimensional object onto a surface. A perspective drawing ( S U R V E Y   N O .   17 , Latrobe, *Penitentiary*) is one kind of projection (conical projection), while a geometric drawing, such as an elevation ( S U R V E Y   N O .   16 , Latrobe, *Penitentiary*), is another (orthogonal projection).

**Scoring**    Lines pressed into a piece of paper with a sharp instrument as an almost invisible means of laying out drawings ( F I G U R E   4.22 , *five-part house*).

**Section**    One kind of geometrical drawing, or orthogonal projection. A section ( S U R V E Y   N O .   18 , *Richmond Theatre*) is a diagram of what the interior of a building would look like, without perspective distortion.

**Shaft**    The principal portion of a column or pilaster in most Classical Orders (see F I G U R E   2.5 ) . The shaft runs between the base and the capital.

**Triglyph**    An oblong plaque alternating with metopes along the frieze of the Doric order (see F I G U R E   2.19 , Fréart's *Doric of the Baths of Diocletian*, or F I G U R E   2.28 , *Doric Portico at Athens*). From the Greek words meaning "three-grooved," having two glyphs or channels near its center-line, with two half-channels at the edges, that add up to the third glyph.

# INDEX

# OF BUILDINGS, NAMES,

# PLACES

Page numbers are given for citations in text; where illustrations appear, figure numbers are also listed.

Drayer, Donald H., *Arlington Towers Apartments*, p. 178; fig. 4.43; *Sheff Store*, Clarendon, survey no. 103.

*Dulany House*, Warrenton, by George H. Frederick, p. 152; survey no. 55.

*Dulles Airport Terminal*, Fairfax County, by Eero Saarinen, pp. 83, 88, 107, 174, 175, 426; survey no. 107; sketch by Saarinen, figs. 4.45, 4.46; presentation drawing by Jay Barr, p. 177; fig. 4.51.

Dulles, John Foster, Secretary of State, airport named for, p. 410.

Durang, Edwin F., p. 340.

Eastern Shore, p. 5.

Eberson, John, pp. 89, 348; *Central National Bank (Central Fidelity Bank)*, Richmond, p. 102; survey no. 89; *Loew's Theatre*, Richmond, pp. 360, 384; survey no. 88.

*Edgemont*, attributed to Jefferson, p. 384.

Edkins, George, p. 340.

*Ednam*, Albemarle County, by D. Wiley Anderson, p. 113.

*Egyptian Building, Medical College of Virginia*, Richmond, by Thomas Stewart, pp. 68, 69; survey no. 37.

*Elk Hill (Archer Mansion)*, by Alexander J. Davis, survey no. 40.

Ellington, C. D., Pittsburgh architect, p. 380.

Ellis, Harvey, pp. 326, 330.

Esperson, Neils, Building, Houston, p. 374.

Essex County, *Blandfield*, pp. 26, 140; fig. 1.41.

Eubank & Caldwell, Roanoke architects, p. 350.

*Evergreen House*, see *Reid-White House*, survey no. 30.

Exall, Henry, pp. 166, 280, 286, 292.

Eyre, Wilson, pp. 90, 314.

Fairfax County, *Dulles Airport*, by Eero Saarinen, pp. 83, 88, 107; survey no. 107; presentation drawing, fig. 4.51; sketch by Saarinen, figs. 4.45, 4.46; *Falls Church*, p. 27; fig. 1.44; *Gunston Hall*, pp. 43, 55, 87, 120; figs. 2.8, 2.9; *Mount Vernon*, pp. 45, 46, 63, 87, 97, 109, 112; survey no. 5; *Large Dining Room*, p. 42; measured drawings of, p. 110; fig. 3.26; *Small Dining Room chimney piece*, fig. 4.8b; *West Parlor chimney piece*, fig. 4.8a; *Pohick Church*, p. 27; fig. 4.10. *Pope-Leighey House*, by Frank Lloyd Wright, pp. 83, 100; survey no. 96; *Powell House*, by Charles M. Goodman, survey no. 99; Reston, p. 98; *Zimmermann Residence*, by William Turnbull, survey no. 109.

*Fairfield*, Gloucester County, p. 8; fig. 1.12.

*Falls Church*, Fairfax County, pp. 27, 142; fig. 1.44.

Fauber, Everette, p. 123.

Fauquier County, *Melrose*, by Edmund G. Lind, survey no. 47; *Upperville*, p. 87.

Ferguson, Frank, see *Men's Dorm (Jeter Hall), University of Richmond*, survey no. 74.

Ferguson, Finley Forbes, see *Virginia Museum of Fine Arts*, survey no. 93.

Ferriss, Hugh, architectural renderer, p. 179; survey no. 97.

*First Baptist Church*, Alexandria, by T. A. Tefft, pp. 163, 286; fig. 4.34.

*First Baptist Church*, Lynchburg, p. 74.

*First Baptist Church*, Richmond, p. 68; fig. 2.44.

*First Baptist Church (Newport News Baptist Church)*, Newport News, by Reuben H. Hunt, survey no. 65.

*First National Bank*, Lynchburg, by Frye & Chesterman, p. 179; survey no. 70.

*First National Bank*, Richmond, by Alfred Bossom, survey no. 75.

Fishburn, Junius Blair, owner of *Mountain View*, p. 334.

*Fishburn Residence (Mountain View)*, Roanoke, p. 112; survey no. 69.

Fitzhugh, William, pp. 4, 9; portrait, copy of, by John Hesselius, fig. 1.4.

*Five-Part Palladian Country House*, survey no. 2.

Flagler, Henry M., p. 320.

Flaxman, John, p. 244.

Fletcher, Elijah, p. 284.

*Floyd Johnson House (project)*, by Floyd E. Johnson, pp. 86, 126; survey no. 101.

Fluvanna County, *Bremo*, by John Neilson, p. 73; survey no. 29; *Bremo Recess*, pp. 73, 110; survey no. 31.

Ford, Christopher, *Amelia County Courthouse*, survey no. 4.

*Forest Building, Best Products Co.*, Richmond, by James Wines, SITE, survey no. 111.

Fort-Brescia, Bernardo, Arquitectonica principal, p. 426.

*"Fort" Stover*, Page County, p. 28; fig. 1.46.

Fouquet, Jean-Pierre, model maker, *Virginia Capitol*, p. 155; survey no. 10.

*Fourth Baptist Church*, Richmond, p. 68.

Francisco & Jacobus, p. 105.

*Frascati*, Orange County, p. 87

Fréart de Chambray, Roland, pp. 39, 47, 51, 210, 220, 250, 252; *Parallèle de l'architecture*, pp. 47, 50, 51, 52; fig. 2.19.

Frederick, George H., p. 151; *H. Grafton Dulany House*, Warrenton, p. 152; survey no. 55.

Fredericksburg, home of Mary Washington, p. 109.

*Freemason Street Baptist Church*, Norfolk, by T. U. Walter, survey no. 36, fig. 1.

French, Daniel, undertaker at Pohick Church, p. 200.

Frohman, Philip, *St. Stephen's Episcopal Church*, Richmond, p. 192.

Frey, Albert, p. 124.

Frye, Edward Graham, pp. 91, 356.

Frye, Edward Graham, and Chesterman, Aubrey, p. 330; *City Auditorium and Market*, Lynchburg, p. 178; survey no. 71; *First National Bank*, Lynchburg, survey no. 70.

Frye, Edward Graham, and Stone, Frank, *Boxley Building*, Roanoke, survey no. 77.

*Gadsby's Tavern*, Alexandria, p. 378.

Gaines, Major Harry, builder, King William County, p. 134.

*Gallison Hall (Suarez-Galban Residence)*, Charlottesville, by Johnson & Brannon with William Staples, survey no. 91.

Galt, Mary Jeffery, p. 97.

Garden Club of Virginia, p. 97.

*Gatekeepers' Lodges, Mount Vernon*, Alexandria, survey no. 53.

Gay, Charles, house for, by A. J. Davis, p. 164; fig. 4.36.

Gaynor, John P., p. 280.

Gibbs, James, pp. 36, 41–42, 47; *Book of Architecture*, pp. 52, 140, 144, 210, 242, 266, 282; plate 58 from, p. 25; fig. 1.40; plate 63, pp. 26, 45; fig. 1.42; plate 1, p. 41; fig. 2.6; plate 17, survey no. 7, fig. 1.

Gibson, John, carpenter-architect, p. 298.

Giles, Thomas Tabb, Virginia-born architect, *Winterham*, p. 193.

Gill, George, stucco-worker, p. 278.

Gillette, Charles F., landscape designer, survey nos. 79, 91.

Glassie, Henry, p. 125.

Glave Newman Anderson, p. 107.

Gloucester County, *Belle Farm*, survey no. 6; chimney piece, fig. 4.2; *Poplar Spring Church*, p. 9; *Rosewell*, pp. 16, 17, 20; figs. 1.23, 3.43; staircase detail, fig. 4.5.

Godefroy, Maximilian, pp. 150, 155, 162, 312; *Washington Monument*, Richmond, p. 62; survey no. 22.

Goehrung, Gene, model-maker, survey no. 114.

Goforth, William Davenport, and Yarnell, Albert Ellis, *Hotel Altemonte*, Staunton, survey no. 59.

Goochland County, *Tuckahoe*, p. 22; fig. 1.35.

Goodhue, Bertram G., p. 274; see *Men's Dorm (Jeter Hall), University of Richmond*, survey no. 74.

Goodman, Charles M., p. 390; *Hollin Hills house, type 2*, Alexandria, pp. 107, 396–97; survey no. 100; *Oscar M. Powell House*, Fairfax County, survey no. 99.